The
ENCYCLOPEDIA
of the
SAYINGS
of the
JEWISH PEOPLE

The
ENCYCLOPEDIA
of the
SAYINGS
of the
JEWISH PEOPLE

MACY NULMAN

JASON ARONSON INC.
Northvale, New Jersey
Jerusalem

103

This book was set in 10 pt. Berkeley Book by Alabama Book Composition of Deatsville, Alabama.

Copyright © 1997 by Macy Nulman.

10 9 8 7 6 5 4 3 2 1

Library of Congress Cataloging-in-Publication Data

The encyclopedia of the sayings of the Jewish people / [compiled] by
  Macy Nulman.
        p.   cm.
    "The expressions are given in transliteration, along with the
original Hebrew, Aramaic, or Yiddish"—Introduction.
    Includes bibliographical references and index.
    ISBN 0–7657–5980–2 (alk. paper)
    1. Proverbs, Jewish.   2. Judaism—Quotations, maxims, etc.
3. Aphorisms and apothegms.   4. Jewish parables.   I. Nulman, Macy.
PN6414.E97   1997
398.9′089924—DC21   96–51944

Manufactured in the United States of America. Jason Aronson Inc. offers books and cassettes. For information and catalog write to Jason Aronson Inc., 230 Livingston Street, Northvale, New Jersey 07647.

Dedicated with love and pride
to our children and their spouses,
Judy and David Koenigsberg
and Rochelle and Efrem Nulman;
and to our beautiful grandchildren;
Binyamin Yehoshua, Tova Miriam,
and Rachel Tzipora Koenigsberg;
and Joshua David and
Jonathan Samuel Nulman.

May we deserve to see children and grandchildren
engaging in Torah and precepts.

And
In loving memory to our brothers and sister,
Seymour Rosenberg, Reuben Rosenberg,
Ruth Aboff, and Shlomo Nulman,
whose lives were marked by a love for *Yiddishkeit*.

CONTENTS

Introduction   xi
Acknowledgments   xiii
Biblical, Scriptural, and Talmudic Abbreviations   xv
Guide to Transliteration   xvii

BIBLE   1

THE PENTATEUCH   5

  The Book of Genesis   7
  Bereishit   9
  Noah   11
  Lekh Lekha   13
  Vayayra   15
  Hayay Sarah   16
  Toldot   16
  Vayaytzay   18
  Vayishlah   19
  Vayayshev   20
  Mikaytz   21
  Vayigash   21
  Vayehi   21

  The Book of Exodus   23
  Shemot   25
  Va'ayra   26
  Bo   27
  Beshalah   28
  Yitro   29
  Mishpatim   31
  Terumah   32
  Tetzaveh   33
  Ki Tisa   33
  Vayakhayl   36
  Pekuday   37

The Book of Leviticus   39
   Vayikra   41
   Tzav   41
   Shemini   41
   Tazri'a   43
   Metzora   43
   Aharay Mot   44
   Kedoshim   45
   Emor   48
   Behar   50
   Behukotai   52

The Book of Numbers   55
   Bemidbar   57
   Naso   58
   Beha'alotekha   58
   Shelah Lekha   60
   Korah   60
   Hukat   61
   Balak   61
   Pinhas   63
   Matot   64
   Masay   65

The Book of Deuteronomy   67
   Devarim   69
   Va'ethanan   70
   Aykev   72
   Re'ayh   73
   Shoftim   74
   Ki Taytzay   75
   Ki Tavo   76
   Nitzavim   77
   Vayaylekh   78
   Ha'azinu   78
   Vezot Haberakhah   79

PROPHETS AND HAGIOGRAPHA   81

TALMUD   111

LITURGY   203
   Liturgy   207
      Weekday Service   209
      Grace After Meals   219
      Minhah and *Ma'ariv*   220

Friday Evening Service   221
Zemirot   223
Shaharit and *Musaf* for *Shabbat*   224
Blessing of the New Month   225
Sabbath *Minhah* and *Motza'ay Shabbat*   226
Torah and *Haftarah*   229
Shalosh Regalim   231
Haggadah   234
Elul and *Selihot*   237
Rosh Hashanah   238
Yom Kippur   243
Hanukkah   248
Purim   249
Fasts   252

RABBINIC AND FOLK SAYINGS   253

Bibliography   291
Glossary   293
Index of Transliterations   299
Index of Hebrew, Yiddish, and Aramaic   319
Index of Biblical, Talmudic, and Rabbinic Passages   339

INTRODUCTION

My goal in writing this book has been to present a variety of adages, proverbs, axioms, and parables in three languages—Hebrew, Aramaic, and Yiddish. These were the three dialects the Jew used daily: Hebrew when praying, Aramaic when studying the Talmud, and Yiddish when conversing.

It is not by chance, then, that I have entitled this book *The Encyclopedia of the Sayings of the Jewish People* rather than *The Encyclopedia of Jewish Sayings*. The latter would perhaps have suggested solely Yiddish utterances and would therefore have given the reader a false impression of the intent of this work.

The nearly two thousand colorful sayings touch the entire core of human existence: the home, the family, the synagogue, and the community. Biblical and nonbiblical persons, happenings and circumstances, manners and customs, as well as various cities and countries, are the subjects of these popular sayings. Divided into four sections—Bible, Talmud, Liturgy, and Rabbinic and Folk Sayings—the expressions are arranged alphabetically, with cross references that are printed in small capital letters. Also included are sayings spoken on Sabbath and festivals, Hanukkah and Purim, Pesah, and Fast Days. The expressions are given in transliteration, along with the original Hebrew, Aramaic, or Yiddish.

This book explores the origin of each expression and its history, meaning, and usage. Many of these hard-to-find sayings

are explained for the first time. They are the wisdom and wit and the language and thought of the Jewish people passed down through the ages—a picturesque shorthand that simplifies conversation and telescopes entire concepts that might otherwise require several sentences to explain clearly.

The high regard with which these expressions were held is evident in the statement "Let not the parable be light in your eyes, for through it a man may gain a firm hold upon the Law" (*Shir Hashirim Rabbah* 1:8). Concerning popular sayings, Raba asked Rabbah b. Mari fifteen times about different expressions: "Whence can be derived the proverbial saying . . . ?" (*Baba Kamma* 92 a,b). Some of the expressions may appear to be jocular, promoting a certain merriment or cheerfulness. The Talmud (*Shabbat* 30b) relates that before Rabbah commenced his discourse for his students, he used to say something humorous (*milta debedihuta*) and the scholars were cheered; then he sat in awe and began his discourse.

The subject of this book is relevant to many disciplines and diverse groups of people. Writers, teachers, students, lecturers, folklorists, sociologists, linguists, and just plain folk can delight in what we say and why we say it and how these expressions have come to mean what they do. This book should sit on the shelf side-by-side with the Hebrew, Aramaic, and Yiddish dictionaries or the thesaurus, as an essential, easily accessible reference tool.

ACKNOWLEDGMENTS

ויהי נעם ה' . . . ומעשה ידינו כוננהו

"May the graciousness of the Lord God be upon us;
Establish Thou also upon us the work of our hands;
Yea, the work of our hands, establish Thou it."
—Psalms 90:17

This book might not have seen the light of day without the help of my beloved wife Sarah, who has contributed her insights concerning the inspiration behind and the meaning of many of the sayings; she has also performed the onerous tasks of brilliantly editing the work, collating many random items, typing and retyping the manuscript, and assiduously indexing the expressions.

My task would not be complete were I not to express my gratitude to Mr. Arthur Kurzweil, Vice President of Jason Aronson Inc., who encouraged me from the beginning in my work on this book. His enthusiastic interest in the proposed volume and his faith in my ability to see it through were highly encouraging. I am also indebted to my brother Dr. Louis Nulman, who helped me to clarify a number of expressions. In concluding this book, I am grateful to the Almighty for sustaining me and enabling me to study His Torah.

Macy Nulman
June 1996

Biblical, Scriptural, and Talmudic Abbreviations

A.Z.—*Abodah Zarah* (Talmud)
abbr.—abbreviated
ad loc.—at the place
Ar.—*Arakin* (Talmud)
Aram.—Aramaic
arr.—arranged
b.—*ben, bar* (son of)
B.B.—*Baba Batra* (Talmud)
B.C.E.—Before the Common Era
B.K.—*Baba Kamma* (Talmud)
B.M.—*Baba Metzi'a* (Talmud)
Bab. Tal.—Babylonian Talmud
Bek.—*Bekhorot* (Talmud)
Ber.—*Berakhot* (Talmud)
Bez.—*Bezah* (Talmud)
c.—circa (about)
C.E.—Common Era
cf.—confer (compare to, refer to)
chap.—chapter
Chron.—Chronicles, Book of
Dan.—Daniel, Book of
Deut.—Deuteronomy, Book of
Dr.—Doctor
e.g.—*exempli gratia* (for example)
Eccl.—Ecclesiastes, Book of
ed.—edited, editor, edition
Eduy.—*Eduyyot* (Talmud)
Erub.—*Erubin* (Talmud)
Esth.—Esther, Book of
et al.—et alia (and others)
etc.—et cetera (and others, and so forth)
Ex.—Exodus, Book of
Ez.—Ezra, Book of
Ezek.—Ezekiel, Book of
fem.—feminine
ff.—and the following pages
Fr.—French
Gen.—Genesis, Book of
Git.—*Gittin* (Talmud)

Hab.—Habakkuk, Book of
Hag.—Haggai, Book of; *Hagigah* (Talmud)
Heb.—Hebrew
Hor.—*Horayot* (Talmud)
Hos.—Hosea, Book of
Hul.—*Hullin* (Talmud)
i.e.—id est (that is)
ibid.—ibidem (in the same place)
Isa.—Isaiah, Book of
Jer.—Jeremiah, Book of
Jer. Tal.—Jerusalem Talmud
Josh.—Joshua, Book of
Judg.—Judges, Book of
Ket.—*Ketubot* (Talmud)
Kidd.—*Kiddushin* (Talmud)
Kel.—*Kelim* (Talmud)
Kil.—*Kil'ayim* (Talmud)
Lam.—Lamentations, Book of
Lat.—Latin
Lev.—Leviticus, Book of
Lit.—literally
Macc.—Maccabees
M.K.—*Mo'ed Katan* (Talmud)
Mak.—*Makkot* (Talmud)
Mal.—Malachi, Book of
masc.—masculine
Mat. Eph.—*Matteh Ephraim*
Meg.—*Megillah* (Talmud)
Me'il.—*Me'ilah* (Talmud)
Men.—*Menahot* (Talmud)
Mic.—Micah, Book of
Mish.—*Mishnah*
Ned.—*Nedarim* (Talmud)
Neg.—*Nega'im* (Talmud)
Neh.—Nehemiah, Book of
Nid.—*Niddah* (Talmud)
no., nos.—number, numbers
Numb.—Numbers, Book of

Obad.—Obadiah, Book of
Ohol.—*Oholot* (Talmud)
p., pp.—page, pages
par.—paragraph
Pes.—*Pesahim* (Talmud)
pl.—plural
Prov.—Proverbs, Book of
Ps., Pss.—Psalm, Psalms, Book of
pt.—part
R.—Rav, Rabban, Rabbaynu, Reb, Rabbi,
    Rebbe
R.H.—*Rosh Hashanah* (Talmud)
S.O.S.—Song of Songs, Book of
s.v.—*sub verbo* (under the entry)
Sam.—Samuel, Book of
San.—*Sanhedrin* (Talmud)
sec.—section
Shab.—*Shabbat* (Talmud)

Sheb.—*Shebi'it* (Talmud)
Shebu.—*Shebu'ot* (Talmud)
sing.—singular
Sof.—*Soferim* (Talmud)
Sot.—*Sotah* (Talmud)
Sukk.—*Sukkah* (Talmud)
Ta'an.—*Ta'anit* (Talmud)
Tam.—*Tamid* (Talmud)
Tem.—*Temurah* (Talmud)
Tos.—*Tosafot* or *Tosefta*
viz.—videlicet (namely)
vol.—volume, volumes
Yeb.—*Yebamot* (Talmud)
Yidd.—Yiddish
Zeb.—*Zebahim* (Talmud)
Zech.—Zechariah, Book of
Zep.—Zephania, Book of

Guide to Transliteration

The Hebrew and Aramaic words throughout the book use the following system for transliteration:

ay as in pay

ai as in by

e as in bed

i as in me

u as in moon

a as in drama

o as in saw or go

h instead of *ch* for the softer guttural sound of the Hebrew letter *het*, as in *hesed*

The Yiddish words use the following system for transliteration:

a as in ma

ay as in bye

ey as in hey

e as in bet

i as in bit or be

oy as in toy

tch as in cheap

tz as in cats

u as in full

uh as in but

kh is used in the Hebrew, Aramaic, and Yiddish instead of the guttural sound of the letter *kaf*—for example, *barukh* (Heb.), *demalkhuta* (Aram.) *knaydlakh* (Yidd.)

The accepted spellings for certain words, such as *Gott, Amen, Hallel, Sefer, Kol Nidre,* and so forth, have been retained in the Hebrew, Aramaic, and Yiddish.

BIBLE
תורה

מן התנ״ך ידך אל תנח

"Let not your hand forsake Torah, Nevi'im, and Ketuvim."

The word *TaNaKH*, from the initial letters of Torah (Pentateuch), *Nevi'im* (Prophets), and *Ketuvim* (Hagiographa) comprise, according to the *Masorah*, the twenty-four books by which the three parts of the Bible are known. The Talmud (Shab. 48a) tells of a Galilean who said before Rav Hisda, "Blessed be the Merciful One who gave a three-fold Torah [Pentateuch, Prophets, and Hagiographa] to a three-fold people [Priests, Levites, and Israelites], through a third-born [Moses was the third child born after Miriam and Aaron], on the third day [the third day after the Israelites had been told to sanctify themselves], in the third month [the month of *Sivan*, in which the Torah was given]."

The *Midrash* comments that the Bible was given publicly in the wilderness, in an ownerless place, so that the nations of the world should not say that they have no portion in it. Each word that came forth from the Almighty split into seventy languages so that it would address each nation in its own vernacular.

The expressions that follow represent the wise and witty maxims and phrases that were adopted into the Jew's daily speech. They cover the whole of human drama, including spiritual instruction and the depiction of fascinating epochs. A number of expressions are derived from *Rashi*, who wrote a phrase-by-phrase commentary on the Bible. His commentary is so popular that *Humash* (referring to the Five Books of Moses) and *Rashi* are almost synonymous. So inseparable are the two that when discussing the study of the Pentateuch, the expression in Yiddish is *lernen Humash mit Rashi* ("to study the *Humash* with the *Rashi*"). Many sayings are also in Yiddish since the Yiddish language served a wide range of communication needs. By translating the text into Yiddish, the *heder* (school house), the yeshivah, and the home disseminated knowledge and understanding of the Bible, the Talmud, and rabbinic literature. The Yiddish language flourished side-by-side with the Hebrew-Aramaic. Sayings that appear in the Book of Proverbs (*Mishle*) and Ecclesiastes (*Kohelet*) were not included, since they are readily accessible to the reader in many other translated editions.

THE PENTATEUCH
(According to Sidrah*)*

ספר חמשה חומשי תורה

The Book of Genesis
ספר בראשית

Bereishit / בראשית	9
Noah / נח	11
Lekh Lekha / לך לך	13
Vayayra / וירא	15
Hayay Sarah / חיי שרה	16
Toldot / תולדת	16
Vayaytzay / ויצא	18
Vayishlah / וישלח	19
Vayayshev / וישב	20
Mikaytz / מקץ	21
Vayigash / ויגש	21
Vayehi / ויחי	21

BEREISHIT (בראשית)

ANSHAY BEREISHIT (אנשי בראשית).
The word *Bereishit*, meaning "In the beginning," is the first word in the Bible. In the Hebrew and Yiddish languages, it took on the meaning of a time element, as in MISHAYSHET YEMAY BEREISHIT or LUHMIR UH-NFANGEN (UHNHAYBN) FUN BEREISHIT. As another example, the phrase *Anshay bereishit* refers to "first pioneers."

AYZER KENEGDO (עזר כנגדו). Concerning the creation of woman, Scripture states, "And the Lord God said [it is] not good [that] the man should be alone, I will make him a helpmeet for him" (*ayzer kenegdo*) (Gen. 2:18). The word *kenegdo* may imply either "at his side" (fit to associate with) or "over against him" (corresponding to him). *Rashi* (ad loc.) comments: *Zakhah-ayzer*, if he is worthy (she will be an *ayzer*), a help; *lo zakhah-kenegdo*, if he is not worthy (she will be *kenegdo*) against him, for strife.

BA SHABBAT BA'AH MENUHAH (בא שבת באה מנוחה). "[When] *Shabbat* came, rest came." It is written in Scripture, "And God finished on the seventh day His work which He had made" (Gen. 2:2). *Rashi* (ad loc.) asks: What did the world lack? Rest! *Ba'at Shabbat ba'at menuhah* ("There came the Sabbath, there came the rest"); thus was ended and completed the work of the creation. (Cf. also *Tos.* to San. 38a, s.v. *Hatzvah*.)

BEREISHIT BARI (בראשית בריא).
The first two words in Scripture are *Bereishit bara* (Gen. 1:1), meaning "In the beginning [God] created." The words *bara* ("created") and *bari* ("healthy" or "strong") have a similar sound. *Bereishit bari* thus implies that first and foremost one must be healthy.

BEZAYAT APEKHA TOKHAL LEHEM (בזעת אפיך תאכל לחם). "In the

sweat of thy face shalt thou eat bread" (Gen. 3:19). This is the sentence Adam received for eating from the tree of life against God's commandment.

This biblical expression became associated with man's toiling to eke out a livelihood.

BISHAT HEDVATA HEDVATA, BISHAT EVLA EVLA (בשעת חדוותא חדוותא, בשעת אבלא אבלא). "At the time of joy, let there be joy, at the time of mourning, mourning" (*Rashi*, Gen. 6:6). The *Midrash* states: One gentile asked R. Joshua b. Karha, saying to him: "Do you not admit that the Holy One, blessed be He, foresees the future?" Rabbi Joshua said to him, "Yes." The heretic said to him, "But it is written: 'It grieved Him at His heart' (that He had made the man)?" R. Joshua said to him, "Was there ever a son born to you?" The heretic said to him, "Yes." R. Joshua said to him, "And what did you do?" The heretic said to him, "I was happy and made everyone joyous." R. Joshua said to him, "And did you not know that his end would be to die?" The heretic said to him, "At the time of joy, let there be joy, at the time of mourning, mourning." R. Joshua said to him, "So are the works of the Holy One, blessed be He. Even though it is revealed before Him that their end would be to sin and to be destroyed, He did not refrain from creating them, for the sake of the righteous who are destined to arise from them" (cf. also *Bereishit Rabbah* 27:27 and 27:7).

GAN EDEN (גן עדן). Scripture states, "And the Lord God planted a garden eastward in Eden [*Gan be-Eden*] and He put there the man [*Adam*] whom He had formed" (Gen. 2:8). Both Adam and Eve were to live a life of ease, contentment, and peace in the Garden of Eden. Succumbing to temptation, they were driven out.

The Septuagint uses the Greek word *paradeisos* ("park") in translating *Gan Eden*, and thus Paradise and *Gan Eden* have become synonymous as designating the abode of sanctified souls after death. The Talmud (Ber. 28b) tells of Rabban Johanan b. Zakkai, who fell ill and his disciples went to visit him. When he saw them, he began to weep. When asked why he wept, he said, "When there are two ways [after death] before me, one leading to *Gan Eden* and the other to *Gehinnom*, and I do not know by which I shall be taken, shall I not weep?" According to Jewish lore, there is a celestial, as well as a terrestrial, *Gan Eden*, the earthly one being only a duplicate of the sublime heavenly one (*Rambam, Mish., San.* 86). *Gan Eden* became the name for a delightful beautiful place, as the verse in Joel 2:3 reads *ke-Gan Eden ha'aretz lefanav* ("the land is like the Garden of Eden before them").

The *Kitzur Shulkhan Arukh* writes, "It is meritorious to fast every year on the death anniversary of one's father and mother, in order to arouse repentence and self-examination, which, in turn, will help the departed parent to reach a higher sphere in *Gan Eden* (Solomon Ganzfried, 221:1). In the prayer *Ayl malay rahamim* ("Oh God, full of mercy") recited at the grave-side, at *Yizkor*, and at the YAHRTZEIT, the plea is made "May (his/her) resting place be in the Garden of Eden." When a person is deceased, the Yiddish expression uttered is *Zuhl (er/zi) huhbn a likhtikn Gan Eden*, inferring "May (he/she) rest in peace."

HASHOMAYR AHI ANOKHI? (השמר אחי אנכי?). A phrase in Genesis 4:9, meaning "Am I my brother's keeper?" This is Cain's response to God, when asked, "Where is Abel thy brother?" The question elicits a confession of guilt from Cain, after he slew Abel his brother because of jealousy (*Rashi*).

The retort "Am I my brother's keeper?" is sometimes asked sarcastically when one is questioned concerning another person's whereabouts.

KOL ADAM SHE'AYN LO ISHAH SHARUI BELO SIMHAH, BELO BE-RAKHAH, BELO TOVAH (כל אדם שאין לו אישה שרוי בלא שמחה, בלא ברכה, בלא טובה). R. Tanhum stated, in the name of R. Hanilai: "Any man who has no wife lives without joy, without blessing, and without goodness" (Yeb. 62b). "Without joy," for it is written, "And thou shalt rejoice, thou and thy house" (Deut. 14:26). By "house" (*bayit*) is meant one's wife (cf. Yom. 2a). "Without blessing," for it is written, "To cause a blessing to rest on thy house" (Ezek. 44:30). "Without goodness," for it is written, LO TOV HEYOT HA'ADAM LEVADO ("It is not good that the man should be alone") (Gen. 2:18).

LO TOV HEYOT HA'ADAM LE-VADO (לא טוב היות האדם לבדו). See KOL ADAM SHE'AYN LO ISHAH, and so forth.

LUHMIR UHNFANGEN (UHN-HEYBN) FUN BEREISHIT (לאמיר אנפאנגען (אנהייבן) פון בראשית). Literally, "Let's begin from *Bereishit*" ("The beginning"), signifying "Let's start from scratch." When desiring to review a matter comprehensively, especially summarizing its details, this Yiddish expression is used. See UHNHEYBN FUN UHNHEYB (FUN ALEF-BET, FUN BEREISHIT, FUN MAH-TOVU, FUN BARUKH SHE'AMAR).

MESUSHELAH'S YUHRN (TZAYTN) (מתושלח'ס יארן (צייטן)). Methuselah, son of Enoch, grandfather of Noah and the oldest of antediluvians, lived 969 years (Gen. 5:26). This Yiddish expression is applied to one who lives a long life (*yuhrn*—"years"), or designates antiquity (*tzaytn*—"times").

MIDAT HADIN, MIDAT HARAHA-MIM (מדת הדין, מדת הרחמים). "The qualities of justice and mercy"; two distinctive traits of God's dealing with man. *Rashi*, commenting on the phrase, "God created" (Gen. 1:1), writes, "Originally, it

entered His mind to create it [the world] in the attribute of justice only [bemidat hadin]. He perceived, however, that the world could not exist [if based on justice alone]. He therefore gave precedence to the attribute of mercy [midat rahamim] and united it with the attribute of justice [MIDAT RAHAMIM SHITAF HAKADOSH BARUKH HU LEMIDAT HADIN]. That is why it is written (Gen. 2:4) Beyom asot Hashem Elohim eretz veshamayim ('In the day that the Lord [Hashem, of mercy] God [Elohim, of justice] made the earth and heaven')." The Midrash (Bereishit Rabbah 12) states that the name YKVK is rahamim ("mercy") and the name Elohim is din ("justice"). According to the Talmud (Shab. 151b), anyone who shows no mercy to his fellow man can expect none from God.

In Eastern European countries, where poverty was rampant and food was scarce, one would humorously say (in Yiddish), regarding the slicing of any foodstuff, Er shnayt din darf men esn mit rahamim ("He slices sparingly and so one should exercise mercy"). In other words, eat less!

MIDAT RAHAMIM SHITAF HAKA-DOSH BARUKH HU LEMIDAT HA-DIN (מדת רחמים שיתף הקב"ה למדת הדין). See MIDAT HADIN, MIDAT HARAHAMIM.

MISHAYSHET YEMAY BEREISHIT (משׁשׁת ימי בראשׁית). Genesis 1:1–31 gives the details of the successive acts that took place in the first six days of creation. When indicating a certain age or length of time belonging to the distant past (long, long ago), the phrase mishayshet yemay Bereishit ("from the six days of creation") may be used.

The phrase occurs in the Talmud (Ket. 8b). Resh Lakish said to Judah, the son of Nahmani, "Rise [and] say something with regard to the mourners. He spoke and said: Our brethren, who are worn out, who are crushed by this bereavement [by this mourning], set your heart to consider this: This it is [that] stands forever, it is a path from the six days of creation [netiv hu

mishayshet yemay Bereishit]." That is, all die and you should not weep too much (Rashi).

OY LI MIYOTZRI OY LI MIYITZRI (אוי לי מיוצרי אוי לי מיצרי). Scripture states, "Then the Lord God formed [vay-itzar] man of the dust of the ground" (Gen. 2:7). The Talmud (Ber. 61a) comments that the word vayitzar is written with two yuds (whereas, in Gen. 2:19, when relating the creation of animals it has only one yud). The two yuds gave rise to the expression "Woe to me from my responsibilities to my Creator [yotzri]; woe to me from my struggle with evil inclinations [yitzri]," since man, as opposed to animals, is endowed with both a yaytzer tov ("a good inclination") and a yaytzer hara ("an evil inclination"). Equivalent expressions in English are: "between the devil and the deep blue sea," or "between a rock and a hard place."

TOHU VAVOHU (תוהו ובהו). Two words appearing in Genesis 1:2, referring to the earth that was "unformed and void." The expression tohu vavohu is often used, either in the Hebrew or Yiddish language, to describe "utter confusion," "chaos," and/or "worthlessness," "waste."

NOAH (נח)

ALTER TERAH (אלטער תרח). Literally, "old Terah." Terah was the father of Abram (Abraham) who, in his old age, went with his son Abram, his grandson Lot, and his daughter-in-law Sarai into the land of Canaan "and they came into Haran and dwelt there" (Gen. 11:31).

Terah was an idolator (Josh. 24:2), a maker of images, who had complained to Nimrod that Abram had broken his images. In turn, Abram was cast into a furnace of fire from which he was saved.

The appellation alter Terah is sometimes hurled at an elderly person who is not God-fearing.

AYVER MIN HAHAI (אבר מן החי). Literally, "a limb [cut off] from a living animal." Scripture states, "Only flesh with life thereof, which is the blood thereof, shall ye not eat" (Gen. 9:4). *Rashi* (ad loc.) comments that the restriction is twofold: cutting a limb from a live animal (*Ayver min hahai*) and eating the blood. The Talmud (Hul. 102a) likewise states, "As to the limb of a living creature, a descendent of Noah [see SHEVA MITZVOT BENAY NOAH] is warned against [eating] it."

BEN NOAH (בן נח). Noah, the ninth in descent from Adam (Gen. 5:28–32), was chosen to build the ark (Gen. 6:8–22). He was saved from the flood, together with his three sons, Shem, Ham, and Japheth (Gen. 7:8); "And of these the whole earth overspread" (Gen. 9:19).

The appellation *Ben Noah* designates a non-Jew. See SHEVA MITZVOT BENAY NOAH; see also ARAYL.

DOR HAFLAGAH (דור הפלגה). This appellation refers to the "generation of the division [of mankind]." After the flood of Noah, all the world spoke one universal language—*leshon ha-kodesh* (Hebrew). The people, fearing another cataclysm, attempted to build the Tower of Babel in order to wage war against the Diety. God confounded their plans and confused their language so that they could not understand one another, and, as a result, they ceased building. Scripture concludes, "Therefore was the name called Babel, because there did the Lord confound the language of all the earth and from thence did the Lord scatter them abroad upon the face of the earth" (Gen. 11:9). See DOR HAMABUL, DOR HAMIDBAR.

DOR HAMABUL (דור המבול). The word *mabul* ("flood") designates the flood of Noah. *Dor Hamabul* ("Generation of the Flood") is an appellation applied to those who were corrupt before God and, in turn, the earth was filled with violence

(Gen. 6:11); thus they brought upon themselves a flood that destroyed the world.

The word *mabul* also occurs in Psalms 29:10 and Isaiah 54:9, and the flood is referred to as *may Noah* ("the waters of Noah"). See DOR HAFLAGAH, DOR HAMIDBAR.

ER SHRAYBT NOAH MIT ZIBN GRAYZN (ער שרייבט נח מיט זיבן גרייזן). In Hebrew the name *Noah* is spelled with two letters, a *nun* and a *het.* To indicate a person's illiteracy and incompetence in spelling even a two-letter name, the Yiddish expression is "He writes [the name] Noah with seven mistakes." How is this possible? He begins with a *nun sofit* (the form used for the ending of a word); he aims for the *oy* sound, thus he writes *alpeh, vav, yud;* and then concludes with *aleph, khaf, hay.* Another way of arriving at seven mistakes is that he spells the name *Noah*—*nun, vav, aleph, het.* The additional letters *vav* (numerical value—six) and *aleph* (numerical value—one) add up to seven.

NOAH HAYAH TZADIK BEDORO-TAV (נח היה צדיק בדורותיו). Literally, "Noah was righteous in his generation" (after Gen. 6:9). *Rashi* (ad loc.) gives different interpretations for the word *bedorotav.* See YAYSH DORSHIN LESHEVAH VE-YAYSH DORSHIN LIGNAI.

Satirically, the phrase is used for the purpose of exposing and discrediting a person by intimating that what *was* yesterday *is* no longer today.

PESHUTO KEMASHMA'O (פשוטו כמשמעו). It is written in Scripture, "And he [Noah] sent forth a raven, and it went forth to and fro, until the waters were dried up from the earth" (Gen. 8:7). *Rashi* (ad loc.) gives two interpretations of the phrase "until the waters were dried up"; the first one is *peshuto kemashma'o* ("the plain meaning [of the text], in its usual sense") and the second is an *aggadic* interpretation.

The phrase *peshuto kemashma'o* is used in conversation when wishing to convey the idea that "I am telling you as it is," without any commentary.

SHEVA MITZVOT BENAY NOAH
(שבע מצות בני נח). Literally, the "seven laws" or "seven commandments" (given to the) descendents of Noah (see BEN NOAH). They are the establishment of courts of justice and the prohibition of blasphemy, idolatry, incest, bloodshed, robbery, and eating flesh cut from a living animal. The Talmud (San. 56b) gives a full account of these seven precepts that are vital to the existence of mankind.

YAYSH DORSHIN LESHEVAH VEYAYSH DORSHIN LIGNAI (יש דורשין לשבח ויש דורשין לגנאי). "Some explain it to his credit and others explain it to his discredit" (cf. *Rashi*, Gen. 6:9, s.v. *Bedorotav*). Scripture states, "Noah was a man righteous and wholehearted in his generations" (*bedorotav*). *Rashi* comments that there are some among the rabbis who explain *bedorotav* to his credit: All the more so had he lived in a generation of righteous people, he would have been even more righteous. But there are some who explain *bedorotav* to his discredit: In comparison with his own generation, he was considered righteous; but had he lived in the generation of Abraham, he would not have been considered of any importance.

Similarly, in the *Megillah* it is written, "And it came to pass in the days of Ahasuerus—the Ahasuerus who reigned [*hamolaykh*] from Hodu to Cush" (Esth. 1:1). It is written in the Talmud (Meg. 11a), Rab said: This indicates that he raised himself to the throne (because it does not mention who was king). AMRI LAH LESHEVAH VE'AMRI LAH LIGNAI ("Some interpret this to his credit, and some to his discredit"). Some interpret it to his credit, believing that there was no one else equally qualified for the throne. Others interpret it to his discredit, saying that he

was not deserving of the throne, but that he was very wealthy, and by means of lavish distribution of money, he rose to this royal position.

The adage *Yaysh dorshin leshevah veyaysh dorshin lignai* is used in many instances to evaluate a situation.

YAYTZER LAYV HA'ADAM RA MINE'URAV (יצר לב האדם רע מנעריו). After Noah and his family and all living creatures went forth out of the ark, Noah built an altar on which was offered burnt offerings. It was at this time that God promised that He would never curse the ground because of man *ki yaytzer layv ha'adam ra mine'urav* ("for the impulse of man's heart is evil from his youth" Gen. 8:21).

This biblical phrase is used when describing the wrestling of the *yaytzer hara* ("evil impulse") with the *yaytzer tov* ("good impulse"), the perpetual conflict within the heart of man.

LEKH LEKHA (לך לך)

ANSHAY SEDOM (אנשי סדום). Literally, "Men of Sodom." The name is applied to a community or group of Jews who are characterized as being wicked. Scripture records, "Now the men of Sodom were wicked and sinners against the Lord exceedingly" (Gen. 13:13). The biblical commentator *Rashi* comments, They were "wicked" with their bodies (immoral) and "sinners" with their money (uncharitable). For example, they did not permit giving poor wayfarers a piece of bread. Their unfair and selfish manner is referred to as MIDAT SEDOM. The Talmud (San. 109a, b) relates other instances of the wickedness of the men of Sodom. The *Midrash* describes how their judges were deceptive (*Bereishit Rabbah* 3).

Eventually, ". . . the Lord caused to rain upon Sodom and upon Gomorrah brimstone and fire from the Lord out of heaven; and He overthrew those cities, and all the plain, and all the inhabitants of the cities, and that which grew upon the ground" (Gen. 19:24–25). Thus, to reverse the order or arrangement, such as in the expression to "turn things topsy-turvy," the comparable Yiddish expression would be IBERKERN VI SEDOM VE'AMORAH.

BIVRITO SHEL AVRAHAM AVINU

(בבריתו של אברהם אבינו). A mode of speech associated with the circumcision of a Jewish child, meaning "With the covenant of Abraham, our father." Abraham was the first to be circumcised. God commanded him to circumcise all male children on the eighth day after birth. Scripture states, "This is My covenant, which you shall keep, between Me and [between] thy seed after thee; every male among you shall be circumcised" (Gen. 17:10).

The *Mishnah* (Avot 3:15) states that one who nullifies the covenant of our forefather Abraham (*Brito shel Avraham Avinu*)—he has no share in the World to Come.

IBERKERN VI SEDOM VE'AMORAH

(איבערקערען ווי סדם ועמרה). See AN-SHAY SEDOM.

LEKH LEKHA IZ BESER VI SHELAH LEKHA

(לך לך איז בעסער ווי שלך לך). *Lekh lekha* (lit., "Go for thyself"), the third portion of the Book of Genesis, and *Shelah lekha* (lit., "Send for thyself"), the fourth portion in the Book of Numbers, both stress a particular act or manner of moving. In the former the Lord said to Abram, "Get thee out of thy country, and from thy birthplace and from thy father's house unto the land which I will show thee" (Gen. 12:1). In the latter the Lord said to Moses, "Send thou men, that they may spy out the land of Canaan . . ." (Numb. 13:2). The Yiddish expression uses the biblical phrases to emphasize the fact that it is better to go yourself (*Lekh lekha*) rather than to send someone (*Shelah lekha*).

It often happens that a matter can be accomplished much more efficiently when one does it oneself, rather than delegating it to another person to do. In Yiddish one would say, *Beser geyn aleyn eyder shikn yenem.*

MIDAT SEDOM

(מדת סדום). See AN-SHAY SEDOM.

MIHUT VE'AD SEROKH-NA'AL

(מחוט ועד שרוך-נעל). After the battle that Abram (Abraham) fought against the four kings, the king of Sodom said to Abram, "Give me the persons [the captives that were mine], and take the goods to thyself" (Gen. 14:21). Abram said, "I will not take a thread nor a shoe-latchet [*mihut ve'ad serokh-na'al*] nor aught that is thine, lest thou shouldst say: I made Abram rich" (Gen. 14:23).

This biblical expression is used by a person who is insultingly offered something and who retorts in a similar fashion, "Don't make me rich!"—"Don't do me any favors!"

PERE ADAM

(פרא אדם). A derogatory appellation for one who is wild, reckless in spirit, savage, or unmannerly. This descriptive name Scripture applies to Ishmael, the son of Abram (Abraham) by Hagar, his concubine, born when Abram was fourscore-and-six years old (Gen. 16:16). The angel of the Lord said of Ishmael, "And he shall be a wild ass of a man: his hand shall be against every man, and every man's hand against him; and he shall dwell in the face of all his brethren" (Gen. 16:12). See YADO VAKOL VEYAD KOL BO.

YADO VAKOL VEYAD KOL BO

(ידו בכל ויד כל בו). Regarding Ishmael, son of Hagar, Sarai's handmaid, Scripture notes, "his hand [will be] against everyone and the hand of everyone against him" (Gen. 16:12). *Rashi* (ad loc.) comments, "'His hand [will be] against everyone,' denotes robbery. 'And the hand of everyone against him' means everyone will hate him and attack him." See PERE ADAM.

VAYAYRA (וירא)

AKAYDAT YITZHAK (AKAYDAH) (עקדת יצחק (עקדה)). *Akaydat Yitzhak* ("The Binding of Isaac") tells of Isaac (Gen. 22:1–19), the son of Abraham (Gen. 17:17–22), the second of the patriarchs, and father of Jacob and Esau (Gen. 21–35), who is offered up by Abraham as an offering unto God. The purpose was to apply a supreme test to Abraham's faith and to the faith and obedience of Isaac.

Remembering the merits of our forefathers by reciting this passage daily and by reading it as the Torah portion on the High Holy Days serves the Lord in the same manner as the martyrdom portrayed by Isaac.

The moving story of the *Akaydah* forms the subject of numerous *Selihot* recited during the Penitential period. In the fourteenth century the Maharil referred to the melody to which these *Selihot* were sung as the *Akaydah*-tune.

In the late 1800s the father of the Yiddish theater, Abraham Goldfaden, composed a biblical operetta called *Akaydat Yitzhak*.

HAS VEHALILAH (חס וחלילה). Two words used as an expression that means "God forbid!" or "Heaven forbid!" The two words have similar implications; *has* means "sparing" or "forbearance," and *halilah* means "far be it from." Scripture, in describing Abraham's intercession for Sodom, states, "That be far from Thee [*Halilah Lekha*] to do in this manner, to slay the righteous with the wicked" (Gen. 18:25); that is, it is foreign to Thy nature (cf. *Rashi*, ad loc.). Another scriptural verse using the term *halilah* is in Job 34:10: "Far be it [*halilah*] from God, that He should do wickedness, and from the Almighty, that He should commit iniq-

uity." The word *halilah* is sometimes used by itself. See HAS VESHALOM.

IM LO AKHSHAV AYMATAI? (אם לא עכשיו אימתי?). Lot's daughters thought that the world had been destroyed as it was in the generation of the flood and that it would be completely depopulated. "The firstborn daughter said to the younger, 'Our father is old'" (Gen. 19:31). *Rashi* comments, *Ve'im lo akhshav aymatai* ("And if not now, when?"). Perhaps he will die or cease to be able to beget. Therefore, they intoxicated him and slept with him and bore sons.

Hillel is reputed to have utilized this same expression: "He used to say: If I am not for myself, who will be for me? And if I am for myself, what am I? And if not now, when?" (Avot 1:14).

SHIKROTO SHEL LOT (שכרותו של לוט). See SHIKOR VI LOT.

SHIKOR VI LOT (שכור ווי לוט). Literally, "drunk like Lot"; a saying directed at someone who becomes intoxicated by excessive drinking.

Lot was a nephew of Abraham (Gen. 11:27–31). Verses in Genesis 19:32–33 read, "Come, let us make our father drink wine, and we will lie with him, that we may preserve seed of our father. And they made their father drink wine that night." From the incestuous intercourse between him and his two daughters, who believed that but for them the world could be completely depopulated, he became the progenitor of Moabites and Ammonites.

The Talmud (Erub. 65a) discusses the responsibilities of an intoxicated person. The ruling is, with the exception of the duty of prayer, an intoxicated man is held as responsible in all respects as a sober man. This ruling, however, applies only to one who does not reach the stage of Lot's drunkenness; however, one who does reach such a stage (of complete unconsciousness) is exempt from all responsibilities.

ZERIZIN MAKDIMIN LEMITZVOT

(זריזין מקדימין למצוות). *Vayashkaym Avraham baboker* ("And Abraham rose early in the morning") (Gen. 22:3) teaches that the whole day is valid for circumcision, but *zerizin makdimin lemitzvot*, "the zealous are early, [to perform] their religious duties" (Pes. 4a). The expression became part of the vocabulary of the Jew and is used whenever a *mitzvah* is performed.

ZEROK HUTRA LE'AVIRAH A'IKA-RAYH KA'AY

(זרוק חוטרא לאוירא אעיקריה קאי). "Cast a stick into the air, [and] it will stand upon its roots" (*Rashi*, Gen. 21:21)—that is, the earth from where it was cut.

In regard to the story of Hagar and Ishmael, Scripture states, "And he [Ishmael] dwelt in the wilderness of Paran, and his mother took him a wife out of the land of Egypt" (Gen., ibid.). Egypt was her native land, where she was reared; thus *Rashi's* quote.

HAYAY SARAH (חיי שרה)

AM-HA'ARETZ (עם-הארץ).

In Scripture the expression *am-ha'aretz* is used as a collective noun signifying "the people of the land" (Gen. 23:12). Since the time of the Second Temple, the appellation *am-ha'aretz* became descriptive of Jews who were ignorant of the traditional laws, who did not observe the rules of *tumah* ("uncleanliness") and *taharah* ("cleanliness") and did not adhere to the strict regulations of *ma'asayr* (tithe-separation) (cf. Mish., *Demai* 1:3; ibid., 2:3). The Talmud (Ber. 47b) adds: Anyone who does not recite the *Shema* evening and morning, or does not put on *tefillin* (phylacteries), or who has not a fringe on his garment, or a *Mezuzah* on his door, and does not bring up his sons to study Torah is considered an *am-ha'aretz*. Others say he is also an *am-ha'aretz* if he has not learned Talmud,

which explains the *Mishnah* (see also Sot. 22a). There are those who are of the opinion that the two words *amay ha'aratzot* in Ezra 9:11 and *amay aretz* in Nehemiah 10:31 refer to those who did not adhere to the strictness of the law.

In contradistinction to the *am-ha'aretz* there was the *Talmid Haham*, known as *havayr* ("an associate"). He was a member of an association of scrupulous observers of the law, especially in matters of tithes and purity (cf. *Demai* 2:3; Ber. 47b).

The expressions *am-ha'aretz* (designating an ignorant, boorish, unlettered person), *am-aratzut* (an act of doing something ignorantly), and *am-ha'aretz mide'oraita* (a complete ignoramus) eventually crept into the vocabulary of the Jew and are currently used.

The rabbis of Yavneh had a favorite saying concerning the uneducated *am-ha'aretz*: "I am God's creature and my fellow [i.e., the *am-ha'aretz*] is God's creature. My work is in the town and his work is in the country. I rise early for my work and he rises early for his work. Just as he does not presume to do my work, so do I not presume to do his work. Will you say, I do much [in the way of Torah] and he does little? We have learned: One may do much or one may do little; it is all one, provided he direct his heart to Heaven" (Ber. 17a; Men. 110a). See STAM MAKSHAN AM-HA'ARETZ.

TOLDOT (תולדות)

A KOL FUN AN AYSAV (א קול פון אן עשו).

Esau, the elder son of Isaac and Rebekah, twin brother of Jacob, was known as an *ish tzayid, ish sadeh* (a cunning hunter, a man of the field) (Gen. 25:27). His robust strength and rough aspect were typical of a wild and daring nature and he lived by the sword (Gen. 27:40).

Among Jews, Esau became the symbol of wickedness. Thus, when a harsh decree or statement was uttered, the phrase *A kol fun an Aysav* ("a voice of an Esau") was spoken.

ADASHIM MA'AKHAL TZARAH VE'AYVEL HAYN (עדשים מאכל צרה ואבל הן). "Lentils are a sorrowful and mournful food" (*Pirkay de-Rabbi Eliezer* 35). *Rashi* (Gen. 25:30) comments that Abraham died earlier than his time so as not to see Esau, his grandson, going forth to a wicked life. On that day Jacob cooked lentils to provide the first meal (*Se'udat Havra'ah*) for Isaac, the mourner.

And why lentils? One reason is that lentils resemble a sphere, "for mourning is a sphere making a circuit in the world." Another reason is that, just as lentils have no mouth, so the mourner has no mouth, for he is forbidden to speak. Thus, it is customary to provide eggs for the mourner's first meal, for they are round and have no mouth; so the mourner, throughout the first three days, does not answer the greeting of anyone and certainly does not greet anyone first. (See B.B. 16b.)

AYN DOMAH TEFILLAT TZADIK BEN TZADIK LITEFILLAT TZADIK BEN RASHA (אין דומה תפלת צדיק בן צדיק לתפלת צדיק בן רשע). Scripture states, "And Isaac entreated the Lord for his wife [Rebekah], because she was barren; and the Lord let Himself be entreated of him . . ." (Gen. 25:21). *Rashi* comments on "And the Lord let Himself be entreated of him," saying, "for the prayer of a righteous person who is the son of a righteous person is not equal (he is superior) to the prayer of a righteous person who is the son of a wicked person; therefore, He let Himself be entreated of him, and not of her" (cf. Yeb. 64a). God listened to Isaac because he was the son of a *tzadik* (Abraham) and thus it is rightfully said, "Abraham begat Isaac" (Gen. 25:19). (Cf. *Keli Yakar*, s.v. *Avraham holid et Yitzhak*.)

HAKOL KOL YA'AKOV VEHAYA-DAYIM YEDAY AYSAV (הקל קול יעקב והידים ידי עשו). A phrase in Gen. 27:22, meaning "The voice is the voice of Jacob, and the hands are the hands of Esau." When Isaac grew old and his eyes dim, he called Esau and asked him to prepare savory food for him, and he would then bestow the Lord's blessing upon him. Rebekah overheard this and, instead of giving prepared food to Esau, she gave it to Jacob. Isaac, thinking that Esau was before him, said, "The voice is the voice of Jacob, and the hands are the hands of Esau," and he blessed him.

This phrase describes the continuous struggle that exists between the descendants of Jacob, who represent Torah study, and the descendants of Esau, whose heritage was "by the sword shalt thou live" (Gen. 27:40). The Talmud (Git. 57b) interprets the phrase as follows: "'The voice' here refers to [the cry caused by] the Emperor Hadrian, who killed in Alexandria of Egypt sixty myriads on sixty myriads, twice as many as went forth from Egypt. 'The voice of Jacob': this is the cry caused by the Emperor Vespasian [Hadrian], who killed in the city of Bethar four hundred thousand myriads, or, as some say, four thousand myriads. 'The hands are the hands of Esau': this is the Government of Rome, which has destroyed our House and burnt our Temple and driven us out of our land." Another explanation is: "'The voice is the voice of Jacob': no prayer is effective unless the seed of Jacob has a part in it. 'The hands are the hands of Esau': no war is successful unless the seed of Esau has a share in it."

The phrase is sometimes used to describe the following: What you are saying (with your voice) is plausible (it is *kol Ya'akov*), but what you are doing by your actions (with your hands) is wrong (it is *yeday Aysav*).

MI SHE'AYNO NOTAYN LEYA'-AKOV NOTAYN LE'AYSAV (מי שאינו נותן ליעקב נותן לעשו). Literally, "if one doesn't give to Jacob, he will give to Esau" (*Vayikra Rabbah* 36:13). Jacob represents righteousness, while Esau depicts evil. For example, if a person does not give to charity, he may, God forbid, have to give to something unfavorable.

TORAH SHEBE'AL PEH HALA-KHAH LEMOSHE MISINAI (תורה שבעל פה הלכה למשה מסיני). It is written in Scripture (Gen. 26:5), "Because that Abraham harkened to My voice and kept My charge, My commandments, My statutes, and My laws [*vetoratai*], God promises to multiply thy seed and give unto thy seed all these lands." *Rashi* (ad loc.), quoting *Bereishit Rabbah*, comments on "And My laws": "This includes the Oral Law, the laws revealed to Moses on Sinai."

YOSHAYV OHEL (יושב אהל). An expression applied to a person who prefers to "stay-at-home." Usually, it is a person who indulges in Torah or similar studies, as the verse in Scripture states, "and Jacob was a quiet man, dwelling in tents" (Gen. 25:27). "Tents," according to the *Midrash* means "schools of religious study."

VAYAYTZAY (ויצא)

BERAHAYL BITKHA HAKETANAH (ברחל בתך הקטנה). A phrase in Genesis 29:18, meaning "for Rachel thy younger daughter." The verse reads, "And Jacob loved Rachel; and he said [to Laban]: I will serve thee seven years for Rachel thy younger daughter." The biblical commentator *Rashi* asks, "Why all these signs?" ("your daughter," "the young one") and answers, "For he recognized him [Laban] that he is a deceiver. [Therefore Jacob] said to him, I shall serve you for Rachel. But lest you say another Rachel from the market, the text states 'your daughter.' And lest you say, I shall change Leah's

name and call her name 'Rachel,' the text states 'the younger.'"

The phrase *be-Rahayl bitkha haketanah* may be appended when striking up a deal with a person and intimating specification or explicity. The buyer adds the phrase, indicating that the deal is clearly stipulated, declaring "Let's call a spade a spade."

ER HUHT GEHAT KEFITZAT HA-DEREKH (ער האט געהאט קפיצת הדרך). See KEFITZAT HADEREKH.

KAL SHEBEKALIM (קל שבקלים). "Light-minded." It is written in Scripture (Gen. 29:21), "And Jacob said unto Laban: Give me my wife for my days are fulfilled" (Jacob served for Rachel seven years). *Rashi* comments on "my days are fulfilled": "for I am eighty-four years old and when shall I establish the twelve tribes? And that is why he said 'and I will come unto her.' But even the most light-minded does not speak thus [*vehalo kal shebekalim ayno omayr kayn*]. However, [it was] in order to beget offspring that he spoke thus."

The Talmud (R.H. 35b) states that the Scripture places three of the most questionable characters (Jerubaal, Bedan, and Jepthah) on the same level as three of the most estimable characters (Moses, Aaron, and Samuel). This is to teach that the most worthless person (*Kal shebekalim*; lit., "the light ones of the lightest"), once he has been appointed as leader of the community, is to be accounted as the mightiest of the mighty.

Colloquially, the phrase *kal shebekalim* became associated with one who does not observe the precepts to the letter of the law, sometimes to the extent of being reckless or promiscuous.

KEFITZAT HADEREKH (קפיצת הדרך). An expression referring to a miracle happening to *tzadikim* ("pious ones") who, although they have to travel a long distance, manage to cross or decrease the distance and arrive at their destination in a shorter period of time than usual. When Jacob went out from Beer-Sheba and went to Haran (Gen. 28:10), *Rashi* comments (Gen. 28:17) that there was a contraction of the earth or that the earth shrank (*kaftzah lo ha'aretz*). The Talmud records, "Our Rabbis taught: For three did the earth shrink—Eliezer, Abraham's servant, for our father Jacob, and for Abishai, the son of Zerui'ah" (San. 95a, b; cf. also Hul. 91b).

Various legends known as *Kefitzat Haderekh Ma'asiyot* (*Kefitzat Haderekh* stories) evolved, which told of miracles regarding *tzadikim* jumping over an expanse of land.

In modern times, whenever a person arrives sooner than expected, the expression used is ER HUHT GEHAT KEFITZAT HADEREKH ("The distance was made shorter for him").

KOL DEVAR MA'AKHAL KARUI LEHEM (כל דבר מאכל קרוי לחם).

"Every type of food is called *lehem* [lit. bread]," (*Rashi*, Gen. 31:54). Scripture states, "And Jacob offered a sacrifice in the mountain and called his brethren to eat bread" (op. cit.). *Rashi* comments that this was a feast, as the word *lehem* appears in Daniel 5:1, *Avad lehem rav* ("He made a great feast") and in Jeremiah 11:19, *Nashhitah aytz belahmo* ("Let us destroy the tree with its fruit").

LEHEM LE'EKHOL UVEGED LILBOSH (לחם לאכל ובגד ללבש). A bib-

lical phrase meaning "bread to eat and raiment to put on" (Gen. 28:20). Jacob dreamt that he heard the voice of God to fulfill the covenant made with Abraham and Isaac. In the morning he set up an altar and made a promise; "And Jacob vowed a vow, saying [*laymor*]: 'If God will be with me and will keep me in this way that I go, and will give me bread to eat and raiment to put on, so that I can come back to my father's house in peace, then shall the Lord be my God.'" That is, I will

dedicate my life to Him. *Tosafot* comments that the word *laymor* in the verse signifies that future generations should thus vow when they encounter trouble (Hul. 2b, s.v. *Aval Amar*).

This request of bread to eat and raiment to put on was on the lips of every Jew throughout the ages.

RA'AH GAYHINOM PETUHAH MI-TAHTAV (ראה גיהנם פתוחה מתחתיו).

When Isaac grew old and his eyes were dim, he called Esau and asked him to prepare some savory food for him. For this, he would bestow the Lord's blessing upon him. Rebekah overheard this and she had Jacob fulfill this request. Isaac, thinking that Esau was before him, blessed him. When Esau came with the food he had prepared, Isaac said unto him, "Who are you?" and he said: "I am thy son, the firstborn, Esau." Scripture records that Isaac trembled exceedingly (Gen. 27:33). *Rashi*, commenting on "he trembled," gives the midrashic interpretation: "He saw *Gehinnom* [hell] opened beneath him" (*Ra'ah gayhinom petuhah mitahtav*).

VAYISHLAH (וישלח)

AHARON AHARON HAVIV (אחרון אחרון חביב).

When Jacob feared that Esau would wreak vengeance upon his wives or children "[And] he divided the children unto Leah, and unto Rachel, and unto the two handmaids. And he put the handmaids and their children foremost, and Leah and her children after, and Rachel and Joseph hindermost" (Gen. 33:1–2). *Rashi* (ad loc.) comments that placing Leah and her children last is because *aharon aharon haviv* ("the ones mentioned last of all are the ones most beloved").

In Jewish life, the saying *aharon aharon haviv* means that esteem is paid to those who come last. Actually, however, it is evident that the first one is *haviv* ("beloved"). For example, the *Tanna* of the *Mishnah* prefers (*haviv layh*) to begin with the case of a father who is heir to his son, rather than a son who is heir to his father (B.B. 108b). In another instance, the *Tanna* mentions first a tithe prescribed by the Rabbis and then those prescribed by the Torah. The Talmud (R.H. 12a) asks why aren't those mentioned first who are prescribed by the Torah? And answers, since the *Tanna* was especially pleased, because they were of rabbinic innovation, he mentions them first (*Aidi dehaviv layh akdamah*). It is thus possible that the phrase *aharon aharon haviv* does not necessarily apply in all instances (cf. Dov Yarden, *Midrash Lashon* [Jerusalem: Kiryat Sefer, 1956], pp. 87, 88).

AL RISHON RISHON VE'AL AHA-RON AHARON (על ראשון ראשון ועל אחרון אחרון). "To answer the first point first and the last point last" (*Rashi, Vayishlah* 32:19). Jacob had messengers precede him bearing gifts to placate Esau because he feared that Esau would wreak vengeance upon his wives or children. Scripture states, "You shall say: they belong to your servant Jacob; they are a present sent to my lord Esau." *Rashi* (ad loc.) comments, "The first [question he should answer] first, and the last [question he should answer] last." *Rashi* connects the first part of the sentence, "You shall say: they belong to your servant Jacob," to the preceeding sentence that asks, "Whose art thou?" ("to whom do you belong?"), and the second half, "they are a present sent to my lord Esau," as an answer to the second question in the previous sentence, "And to whose are these before thee?" ("to whom are these [gifts] being sent?").

BEMAKLI AVARTI ET HAYAR-DAYN (במקלי עברתי את הירדן). When Jacob approached his homeland, the fear of his brother Esau revived in him. Jacob pleaded for God's mercy and included in his plea, "For with my staff I passed over

the Jordan" (Gen. 32:11). *Rashi* (ad loc.) comments that he had neither silver nor gold, nor cattle—only a staff. Uttering the phrase is as if to say, "I myself have experienced all this."

HATZILAYNI NA MIYAD AHI MIYAD AYSAV (הצילני נא מיד אחי מיד עשו). The literal translation of this phrase is "Deliver me, I pray Thee, from the hand of my brother, from the hand of Esau" (Gen. 32:12). *Rashi* comments (ad loc.) on the repetition of "From the hand of my brother, from the hand of Esau," saying that it means "from the hand of my brother who does not conduct himself toward me like a brother, but like the wicked Esau."

Euphemistically, the phrase means "Please rescue me from this cruel man who is supposed to be my friend but instead is my enemy."

IM LAVAN GARTI (עם לבן גרתי). "I have sojourned [*garti*] with Laban" (Gen. 32:5). Laban, the Aramean, is synonymous with "deceiver." The word *garti* corresponds to the numerals denoting six hundred and thirteen (*gimmel* = 3 + *raysh* = 200 + *tav* = 400 + *yud* = 10), the number of biblical commandments (TARYAG MITZVOT). The *Midrash* comments that even though Jacob lived with Laban in a non-Jewish environment, he remained faithful to the Torah.

The phrase *im Lavan garti*, in daily parlance, signifies that "I have had enough experience with scoundrels"; "I had my fill of swindlers."

VAYAYSHEV (וישב)

HAYELED AYNENU (הילד איננו). Because Jacob loved his son Joseph more than his other sons, the brothers conspired to kill him, but Reuben prevented them from committing the murder. Instead, they cast him into an empty pit. When Reuben returned to the pit, he

found that Joseph was not there. He rent his clothes and said to his brothers, *Hayeled aynenu* ("The child is not there") (Gen. 37:30).

This expression is sometimes said in jest when someone flees from a situation in which he was involved. In other words, he does a disappearing act.

MAH PARATZTA ALEKHA PA-RETZ? (מה פרצת עליך פרץ). Tamar bore twins who were called Peretz and Zerah. The circumstances of their birth is detailed, in that Peretz kept the right of primogeniture over his brother. Scripture records that the midwife said, "Wherefore hast thou made a breech [breaking forth] for thyself?" (Gen. 38:29). The phrase came to symbolize "speed" or "swiftness."

MIKAYTZ (מקץ)

HALOM HALAMTI (חלום חלמתי). Pharaoh sent for Joseph to interpret his dream. He said, "*Halom halamti* ('I have dreamed a dream') and there is none that can interpret it" (Gen. 41:15).

This Hebrew phrase is often used when one's undertaking does not materialize.

HATA'AI ANI MAZKIR HAYOM (חטאי אני מזכיר היום). Pharaoh had two dreams that troubled him greatly. He told his dreams to all the magicians of Egypt, as well as to the wise men, but no one could interpret them (Gen. 41). "Then spoke the chief butler unto Pharaoh, saying: *Et hata'ai ani mazkir hayom* ("My sins I mention this day") (Gen. 41:9)—that is, not only his offense against the king, but also his sin against Joseph in forgetting him.

The phrase is sometimes used by a person admitting his wrongdoings.

SHALOM (שלום). See MIPNAY DARKAY SHALOM.

TZAYDAH LADEREKH (צדה לדרך). "Provision for the way" (Gen. 42:25, 45:21). Scripture tells of Joseph meeting his brothers in Egypt, who came, on the advice of their father Jacob, to purchase corn. After Joseph recognized them, he held Simeon as a hostage so that they would have to bring their youngest brother back with them on their next journey. Joseph commands, "to fill their vessels with corn, and to restore every man's money into his sack, and to give them provisions for the way." *Targum Onkelos* translates the word *tzaydah* as *zevadim*, meaning "outfit for traveling."

The phrase *tzaydah laderekh* is often used when preparing for a trip or a journey in life's venture.

VAYIGASH (ויגש)

BEN (YELED) ZEKUNIM (בן (ילד) זקונים). A child born to a person in his old age, as in *yesh lanu av zakayn veyeled zekunim katan* ("We have a father, an old man, and a child of his old age, a little one") (Gen. 44:20). Judah, who had assumed full responsibility for Benjamin, pleaded with Joseph. He told Joseph that the loss of Benjamin would, in all probability, kill his father.

The expression *Ben (yeled) zekunim* is currently used for a child born of parents far advanced in years.

VAYEHI (ויחי)

BAYN PORAT YOSAYF (בן פרת יוסף). A phrase said by the Patriarch Jacob, meaning "Joseph is a fruitful vine" (Gen. 49:22) and uttered by *Sephardim* to ward off an evil eye. The verse continues with *bayn porat alay ayin* ("a fruitful vine above the eye"). It is written in the Talmud, "R. Abbahu said with regard to this, Do not read *alay ayin*, but *olay ayin* ('rising above the [power of the] eye')"—

that is, superior to the evil eye. Thus it is derived that the evil eye will have no power over the offspring of Joseph. The phrase *Bayn Porat Yosayf* is currently found engraved on several buildings in Istanbul, Turkey. See BELI AYIN HARA (RA'AH).

KI VE'APAM HARGU ISH (כי באפם הרגו איש). A phrase in Genesis 49:6, meaning "for in their anger they slew men." This is part of Jacob's blessing on his deathbed to Simeon and Levi when he makes reference to their dealings with Hamor and the men of Shechem (Gen. 34:25–26).

The word *af* can mean "anger" or "nose." The biblical phrase is sometimes used as a witticism—that by the twist of the nose, men can be destroyed. By turning up one's nose, a person can be doomed.

MAH HABERIYOT OMROT? (מה הבריות אומרות?). "What would people say?" (*Rashi*, Gen. 50:21). Joseph said to his brothers ". . . fear ye not, I will sustain you and your little ones; and he comforted them, and spoke unto their heart" (ibid.). *Rashi* comments, "Through you, it became known that I am a free man. Now, if I were to kill you, what would the people say?"

The Talmud (Yom. 86a) states: "If a person studies Torah and *Mishnah*, and serves a TALMID HAKHAM, is honest in business, and is courteous to people, what do people say concerning him [*Mah haberiyot omrot*]? Happy is the father who taught him Torah, happy is the teacher who taught him Torah; . . . look how fine his ways are, how righteous his deeds!"

MEGALEH ZAYN DEM KAYTZ (מגלה זיין דעם קץ). "To reveal or divulge the end"—that is, the time when the Messiah will come. *Rashi* (Gen. 47:28), commenting on the phrase *Veyehi Ya'akov* ("and Jacob lived"), asks: Why isn't a space of nine letters left open (in the Torah) between the end of the preceding section (*Vayigash*) and the beginning of *Vayehi* (That is, why is this section completely closed [*stumah*]). And answers: Jacob desired to reveal the end (*legalot et hakaytz*) to his sons, but it was closed (*nistam*) from him. This same thought appears in Daniel 12:6, *Ad matai kaytz hapela'ot* ("How long shall it be to the end of the wonders?"). In talmudic times, too, there were those who tried to figure out when the Messiah will come. They were called *Mehashvay Kitzim* (San. 97b).

TA'ALA VE'IDANAYH SEGID LAYH (תעלא בעידניה סגיד ליה). When Jacob realized that his death was imminent, he made Joseph promise that he would bury him in the land of Canaan and not in Egypt. Joseph "swore unto him and Israel [Jacob] bowed down upon the head of the bed" (Gen. 47:31); that is, he worshipped God on the pillow of the bed. *Rashi*, commenting on "And Israel bowed down," says: "The fox, in his time, bows down to him (*Ta'ala ve'idanayh segid layh*]"; that is, when the fox (Joseph, the son) happens to be king, then even the lion, Israel, the father, must bow down to him.

This expression is often spoken when one must condescend to his elected officer or superior even if that person is younger or is disliked. See YIFTAH BEDORO KISHMUEL BEDORO.

The Book of Exodus
ספר שמות

Shemot / שמות	25
Va'ayra / וארא	26
Bo / בא	27
Beshalah / בשלח	28
Yitro / ותרו	29
Mishpatim / משפטים	31
Terumah / תרומה	32
Tetzaveh / תצוה	33
Ki Tisa / כי תשא	33
Vayakhayl / ויקהל	36
Pekuday / פקודי	37

SHEMOT(שמות)

ASAH ATZMO KE'ILU LO YADA

(עשה עצמו כאלו לא ידע).It is written in Scripture: "Now there arose a new king over Egypt, who knew not Joseph" (Ex. 1:8). Rashi comments, "He made himself [feigned] as though he did not know him" (cf. Sot. 11a).

In everyday speech the phrase ke'ilu lo yada has been contracted to kelo yada, meaning "as if one doesn't know." In Yiddish one would say, makhn zikh kelo yada ("pretend ignorance," or "play the fool").

AVODAT PEREKH (עבודת פרך).

"Extremely difficult labor." It is written in Scripture, "And the Egyptians made the children of Israel to serve with rigor" (befarekh) (Ex. 1:13). Rashi (ad loc.) comments on the word befarekh, "With hard labor, that crushes [mefarekhet] the body and breaks it."

This particular expression is uttered by one who is undergoing much physical or mental toil in order to eke out a livelihood.

DAYAH LETZARAH BESHATAH

(דיה לצרה בשעתה). "Sufficient is the evil in the time thereof" (Ber. 9b). On the phrase in Scripture "I Am That I Am" (Ex. 3:14) the Talmud states, "The Holy One, Blessed be He, said to Moses: Go and say to Israel, I was with you in your servitude, and I shall be with you in the servitude of the other kingdoms [Babylonian and Roman]. He said to Him: Lord of the Universe, sufficient is the evil in the time thereof. Thereupon the Holy One, Blessed be He, said to him: Go and tell them, 'I Am has sent me unto you'"—that is, it would suffice the Israelites to learn that "Eheyeh, I Will Be [with you], hath sent me unto you" (cf. also Rashi, Ex. 3:14).

The expression is used in conversation to indicate that there is no need to worry

ER BOYT PITHOM VE-RAAMSES

(ער בויט פתם ורעמסס). Scripture relates that in order to afflict the Israelites, the Egyptians set taskmasters over them. "And they built store-cities [aray miskenot] for Pharaoh, Pithom, and Raamses" (Ex. 1:11). Rashi comments that they made those cities "strong and fortified for a treasury."

In Yiddish, there is an expression, Er boyt Pithom Ve-Raamses ("He is building Pithom and Raamses"), intimating that he is accomplishing something out of ordinary, unusual.

ERETZ ZAVAT HALAV UDEVASH

(ארץ זבת חלב ודבש). A proverbial expression, meaning "a land flowing with milk and honey" (Ex. 3:8, 13:5; Numb. 13:27). This is a description of the Promised Land that God will give to the Israelites when they leave Egypt. From this verse, we learn that milk is permitted from a living animal; for if milk were not permitted, Scripture would not commend the country to us with something that was not fit to be eaten (Bek. 6b).

The Talmud (Ket. 111b) relates that "Rami b. Ezekiel once paid a visit to Bene-Brak where he saw goats grazing under fig trees, while honey was flowing from the figs, and milk ran from them, and these mingled with each other. 'This is indeed,' he remarked, '[a land] flowing with milk and honey.'"

HAMAGBI'AH YADO AL HAVAYRO AF AL PI SHELO HIKAHU NIKRA RASHA (המגביה ידו על חבירו אע״פ שלא הכהו נקרא רשע). "[Resh Lakish said:] He who lifts his hand against his neighbor, even if he did not smite him, is called a wicked man" (San. 58b), as it was written, "And he said unto the wicked man, Wherefore wouldst thou smite thy fellow" (RASHA, LAMAH TAKEH RAYEKHA) (Ex. 2:13). "Wherefore hast thou smitten" is

not said, but "wherefore wouldst thou smite," showing that although he had not yet smitten him, he was termed a wicked man.

RASHA LAMAH TAKEH RAYEKHA

(רשע למה תכה רעך). see HAMAGBI'AH YADO AL HAVAYRO, and so forth.

VAYAKAM MELEKH HADASH (ויקם

מלך חדש). A verse in Exodus 1:8 reads, "Now there arose a new king [Vayakam melekh hadash] over Egypt, who knew not Joseph." Rashi (ad loc.) quotes the Talmud (Sot. 11a), "Rab and Samuel [differ in their interpretation]; one said that he was really new, while the other said that his decrees were made new. He who said that he was really new did so because it is written "new"; and he who said that his decrees were made new did so because it is not stated that [the former king] died and he reigned [in his stead]."

The phrase Vayakam melekh hadash is a proverbial expression that is used when a person assumes a new office and either feigns to know nothing that took place prior to his election or sets up new rules.

VA'AYRA (וארא)

HAVAL AL DE'AVDIN VELO MISH-TAKHIN (חבל על דאבדין ולא

משתכחין). A common expression, meaning "Alas for those who are gone and no more to be found," often spoken when mourning the dead.

The saying appears in the Talmud (San. 111a) and in Rashi (Ex. 6:9, s.v. Mikotzer Ru'ah). Moshe is told by God that He will deliver the Israelites from the yoke of Pharaoh, bringing them to the land promised to Abraham, Isaac, and Jacob. Moshe gives God's message to Israel, but they do not listen to him because of their anguish. Moshe says to God, "For since I came to Pharaoh to speak in Thy Name, he hath done evil to this people; neither hast Thou delivered Thy people at all" (Ex. 5:23).

God answers Moshe, "Haval al de'avdin velo mishtakhin, I must mourn over the death of the patriarchs, Abraham, Isaac, and Jacob, who did not question My ways nor My promise and you [Moshe] say, lamah harayota ('Wherefore hast Thou dealt ill')." The patriarchs displayed complete confidence in God, but Moshe showed lack of confidence.

The Talmud (ibid.) tells of R. Eleazar, son of R. Jose, who once visited Alexandria, Egypt, and found an old man there who said to him, "Come, and I will show you what my ancestors did to your ancestors: Some of them they drowned at sea, some they slew by the sword, and some they crushed in the buildings." Thereupon, the Holy One, blessed be He, said, "Alas for those who are gone and no more to be found."

PILAY FELA'OT (PILAY FELA'IM)

(פלאי פלאות (פלאי פלאים)). "Remarkable wonders" ("Great miraculous events"). And the Lord said unto Moses: "Stretch forth thy hand toward heaven, that there may be hail [barad] in all the land of Egypt upon [the] man and upon [the] beast, and upon every herb of the field throughout the land of Egypt" (Ex. 9:22). It is written in Scripture, "But the wheat and the spelt were not smitten; for they ripen late" (ki afilot haynah). Rashi (ad loc.), quoting Midrash Tanhuma, interprets ki afilot as "remarkable wonders" (pilay fela'ot), which were wrought for them that they were not smitten.

The Talmud (Ber. 56b) utilizes the expression pilay fela'ot in conjunction with the following: "If one sees Phineas in a dream, a miracle [pele] will be wrought for him. If one sees an elephant in a dream, wonders [pela'ot] will be wrought for him; if several elephants, wonder of wonders [pilay fela'ot] will be wrought for him."

The expression for "amazing," "remarkable," or "marvelous" is haflay vafele. An expression that has been used from the Medieval period is kaytz hapela'ot ("the end of the marvels," "the end of the world").

BO (בא)

ARAYL (ערל). An *arayl* is an uncircumcised person. A verse in Exodus 12:48 reads, *Vekhol arayl lo yokhal bo* ("but no uncircumcised person shall eat thereof")—that is, partake of the *Paschal* meal (see BEN NOAH).

AYREV RAV (ערב רב). When the Jews left Egypt, the Torah states, *Vegam ayrev rav alah itam* ("And a mixed multitude went up also with them" [Ex. 12:38]). These were non-Jews or Jews from mixed marriages. It is believed that all the sins the Jews committed in the desert (such as that of the Golden Calf) were influenced by the *ayrev rav*.

The appellation *ayrev rav* is sometimes spoken in jest when a group of persons of diversified levels of education and religion come together.

BINARAYNU UVIZKAYNAYNU NAYLAYKH (בנערינו ובזקנינו נלך). "We will go with our young and with our old" (Ex. 10:9). Moses insisted that all the Israelites were to be set free. This phrase is used when implying that the entire Jewish people will participate and serve the Lord.

LO AYT ATAH LEHA'ARIKH BITE-FILLAH SHEYISRAEL NETUNIN BETZARAH (לא עת עתה להאריך בתפלה שישראל נתונין בצרה). Concerning the redemption of the Israelites from Egypt, God said to Moshe, "Wherefore criest unto Me" (Ex. 14:15). *Rashi* comments (ad loc.) that this teaches us that Moses was standing and praying. The Holy One, blessed be He, said to him, "Now is not the time to prolong in prayer, when Israel is placed in distress." The moment of anguish called not for prayer but for action. The verse (ibid.) con-

cludes, "Speak unto the children of Israel, that they go forward."

LO YEHERATZ KELEV LESHONO (לא יחרץ כלב לשונו). When Pharaoh is warned about the last plague, *Makat Bekhorot* ("Slaying of the firstborn"), Moshe says to Pharaoh, "But against any of the children of Israel *Lo yeheratz kelev leshono* ('shall not a dog whet his tongue')" (Ex. 11:7). This became a proverbial expression indicating safety and peace.

Concerning this expression, the humorous tale is told of a *Maggid* (a preacher) who wanted to preach a sermon in a hasidic *shtiebel* (hasidic house of worship). The worshipers, however, were not interested in hearing any sermons. The *Maggid* asked the *shamash* (beadle) to tell them that he wasn't really interested in preaching but only wanted to relate an incident that took place with a merchant. They finally consented to listen. This is the tale he told them:

> A Jewish merchant was once walking along the street and seemed very melancholy. A friend met him and asked, "Why are you so sad?" He answered, "I have an opportunity to make a good deal with a farmer and everytime I come to the farmer's house, the dogs begin barking; they want to tear me apart and from fear I run for dear life." His friend advised him, "The next time you approach the farmer's home, say the verse 'But against any of the children of Israel shall not a dog whet his tongue.'" The Jew again approached the farmer's home and this time, before he had a chance to say the verse, the dogs almost devoured him. Later, he met his friend and was asked how he made out. The Jewish merchant answered, "Perhaps the verse would have helped, but the dogs didn't even give me a chance to begin to utter it."

MI VAMI HAHOLKHIM (מי ומי ההלכים). Prior to the Israelites' departure from Egypt, Pharaoh said to Moses and Aaron, "Go serve the Lord your God; but who are they that shall go?" (*Mi vami haholkhim*) (Ex. 10:8).

The phrase is sometimes used when questioning, who, of all the people, is willing to go? or, who can be counted on?

MITZVAH SHEBA'AH LEYADEKHA AL TAHAMITZENA (מצוה שבאה לידך אל תחמיצנה). An expression meaning "a religious act in hand should not become sour by postponement." In other words, don't procrastinate when you are able to perform a *mitzvah*.

Rashi, in the name of the *Mekhilta*, comments (ad loc.) on the phrase *Ushemartem et hamatzot* ("And you shall observe the unleavened bread") (Ex. 12:17) so that it shall not reach a state of leavening. Rabbi Yoshiyah says, "Do not read *hamatzot* ('the unleavened bread') but *hamitzvot* ('the commandments')." The letters in the word *matzot* (*mem, tzadi, vav, tav*) are the same as in *mitzvot*. Just as one may not leaven unleavened bread, so one may not cause leavening [procrastinate] in reference to a commandment. If it comes to your hand, perform it immediately" (cf. also Meg. 6b, s.v. *Ayn Ma'avirin*).

SHELUHO SHEL ADAM KEMOTO (שלוחו של אדם כמותו). "The agent of a man is as he himself" (*Rashi*, Ex. 12:6; cf. also Ber. 34b). Scripture states that when preparing for Passover, every man shall take a lamb, "and ye shall keep it until the fourteenth day of the same month; and the whole assembly of the congregation of Israel shall slaughter it at dusk" (ibid.). *Rashi* asks: "And did all of them slaughter?" But from here (we learn) that the agent of a man is as he himself (Kidd. 41b).

BESHALAH (בשלח)

KERI'AT YAM SUF (קריעת ים סוף).
Exodus, chapter 14, describes the redemption of the children of Israel from Egypt and their passage across the Red Sea. Pharaoh and his armies pursued the emancipated people, and when they approached the sea, God caused the waters to part (*Keri'at Yam Suf*). The Israelites crossed over and the Egyptians followed them. God caused the waters to collapse and the Egyptians drowned. Moses and the people sang a paeon of praise (*Az Yashir*) to the Almighty, known as the *Shirah* or *Shirat Hayam* ("The Song of the Red Sea"). Miriam and all the women danced and sang the same song of victory.

Accomplishing matters that are herculean tasks is compared to *Keri'at Yam Suf*, as the following expressions reveal. The Talmud (Pes. 118a) states, KASHIN MEZONOTAV SHEL ADAM KE-KERI'AT YAM SUF ("A man's sustenance is as difficult [to provide] as the dividing of the Red Sea"), for it is written, "Who giveth food to all flesh" (Ps. 136:25) and near it, "To Him Who divided the Red Sea in sunder" (ibid. 13). Another expression is: KASHEH (KASHIN) LEZVOGAM KE-KERI'AT YAM SUF ("To effect a union between man and woman is as difficult as the dividing of the Red Sea") (San. 22a; Sot. 2b). It has been said that the reason for using *Keri'at Yam Suf* to describe this herculean task is that when the preliminaries to betrothal take place, either side may not be in agreement to the match or proposed marriage, making it difficult for a match-maker to finalize the matter. Thus, the two sides represent the waters that are parted; but once both parties agree, they come together as the waters did at *Keri'at Yam Suf*.

A Yiddish expression in the same vein would be UHNKUMEN VI KERI'AT YAM SUF ("to come by very hard"). See HAKADOSH BARUKH HU MEZAVAYG ZEVUGIM.

KETZAPIHIT BIDVASH (כצפיחת בדבש). "Like wafers made with honey" (Ex. 16:31). This is the description Scripture gives of the Manna that came down in the wilderness of Sinai within the area of the Israelites' encampment every morning except on Sabbaths. The Israelites ate the Manna for forty consecutive years,

"until they came to the land of Canaan" (Ex. 16:26–36). "The taste of it was the taste of a cake baked with oil" (Numb. 11:18). The Talmud (Yom. 75a) states that it contained the flavor of every conceivable dish. One had only to desire a specific food, and the Manna assumed its taste.

The expression *Ketzapihit bidvash* colloquially became associated with a food having a luscious taste. The Yiddish expression is *A ta'am vi ketzapihit bidvash* ("A taste like wafers made with honey").

OD ME'AT USEKALUNI (עוד מעט וסקלני).

When the Israelites journeyed from the wilderness of Sin and encamped in Rephidim, there was no water for them to drink. The people murmured against Moses, "Wherefore hast thou brought us up out of Egypt to kill us and our children and our cattle with thirst?" (Ex. 17:3). Moses cried out to God, "What shall I do unto this people, they are almost ready to stone me" (*Od me'at usekaluni*) (Ex. 17:4).

UHNKUMEN VI KERI'AT YAM SUF (אנקומען ווי קריעת ים סוף). See KERI'AT YAM SUF.

YITRO (יתרו)

AL HARISHONIM ANU MITZTA'ARIM VE'ATTAH BA LEHOSIF ALAYHEM (על הראשונים אנו מצטערים ואתה בא להוסיף עליהם).

When the Holy One, blessed be He, said to Moses in Midian, "Go return into Egypt," Moses took his wife and his two sons and Aaron went forth to meet him in the mountain of God (Ex. 4:19, 20, 27). Aaron asked him, "Who are these people?" and Moses answered, "My wife that I married in Midian and my sons." Aaron asked, "Where are you taking them?" to which Moses answered, "To Egypt." Aaron then said to Moses, "For the first [who are already in Egypt] we are grieved, and you come to

add to them!" (*Rashi, Yitro* 18:2, quoting the *Mekhilta*).

The Hebrew phrase is often spoken to convey the following: We are distressed about the past troubles or mistakes and you want to add new ones!

ER HUHT AVEKGEGANVET DEM HUMASH MITN LO TIGNOV (ער האט אוועקגעגנבעט דעם חומש מיטן מיטן לא תגנב). See LO TIGNOV.

ER IZ TZUM BARG SINAI NIT DERGANGEN (ער איז צום באַרג סיני ניט דערגאַנגען).

Chapter 19 in the Book of Exodus describes the preparations made for the Covenant at the foot of Sinai, where Israel's spiritual history began. God said to Moshe: "And be ready against the third day; for the third day the Lord will come down in the sight of all the people upon Mount Sinai" (Ex. 19:11).

The expression *Er iz tzum barg Sinai nit dergangen* ("He never made it to Mount Sinai") is hurled at a person who does not believe in the tenets of the Torah. It can also apply to one who does not adhere to certain *halakhic* principles or traditional *minhagim* (customs).

HEFRAYSH BAYN MAH SHE'-ADAM RO'EH LEMAH SHE'AHAYRIM MESIHIN LO (הפרש בין מה שאדם רואה למה שאחרים משיחין לו).

"'There is a difference between that which man sees and that about which others tell him'; for about that which others tell him, at times his heart [mind] is doubtful about believing" (*Rashi,* quoting the *Mehilta,* Ex. 20:19). "Ye yourselves have seen that I have talked with you from Heaven" (Ex. 20:19). God says to Moshe that the Israelites have been eye witnesses, and know the reality of "My revelation."

The expression LO DOMEH SHOMAYA LERO'EH ("You cannot compare hearing [from others] to seeing [yourself]," is similar (*Mekhilta* 19:9).

KAFA HAKADOSH BARUKH HU ALAYHEM ET HAHAR KEGIGIT

(כפה הקב״ה עליהם את ההר כגיגית). See
SHAM TEHAY KEVURATKHEM.

KOL HATHALOT KASHOT (כל
התחלות קשות). A proverbial saying that
means "all beginnings are difficult." It has
been on the lips of the Jew whenever
embarking on a new undertaking.

It originated in the time when preparations were made for the Covenant at Sinai.
God told Moses to say to the Israelites,
"Now, therefore, if ye will hearken unto
My voice indeed, and keep My covenant,
then ye shall be Mine own treasure from
among all peoples" (Ex. 19:5). *Rashi* (ad
loc.) comments in the name of the
Mekhilta, "it will be good [sweet] for you
for all beginnings are difficult" (cf. also
Tos. to Ta'an. 10b, s.v. *Pesi'ah*).

LO DOMEH SHOMAYA LERO'EH

(לא דומה שומע לרואה). See HEFRAYSH
BAYN　MAH　SHE'ADAM　RO'EH　LEMAH
SHE'AHAYRIM MESIHIN LO.

LO TIGNOV (לא תגנב). "Thou shalt
not steal" (Ex. 20:13; Deut. 5:17). This is
the eighth commandment in the Deca-
logue. *Rashi* (ad loc.), quoting the Talmud
(San. 86a), comments that "regarding the
stealing of persons does Scripture speak
here; 'Ye shall not steal' [*Lo tignovu* in Lev.
19:11] refers to stealing of money."

The Yiddish language has numerous
colorful expressions depicting a thief: *Ga-
NaV makht: gey, nem, bahalt* ("The meaning of the word *Ganav* is: go, take, and
hide"). Another is ER HUHT AVEKGEGANVET
DEM HUMASH MITN LO TIGNOV ("He robbed
the *Humash* [the Five Books of Moses],
together with 'Thou shalt not steal'"). A
thief was once reprimanded with *Es shteyt
duhkh lo tignov!* ("It is written 'Thou shalt
not steal!'"). And he answered: *Vuhs es
shteyt zuhl shteyn un vuhs es ligt leyg ikh in
keshene* ("That which stands, let it stand

and that which lies, I put into my
pocket").

Scripture states that when Moses came
down from the mount and saw the calf
and the dancing, his anger waxed hot
"and he cast the tables out of his hands
and broke them beneath the mount" (Ex.
32:19). Humorously, it is said that the
tablets broke into pieces and the *Lo*
("Thou shalt not") became separated from
the *tignov* ("steal"). The poor picked up
the *Lo* and the rich took up the *tignov*. See
SOF GANAV LITLIYAH; ROV GANVAY YISRAEL
GANVAY NINHU.

MINYAN OTIYOT SHEL ASERET HADIBROT HAYM TaRYaG (מנין
אותיות של עשרת הדברות הם תרי״ג).
"The number of letters in the Ten Commandments are *TaRYaG*" or six hundred
and thirteen (*Pesikta Zutorti, Yitro* 20:14).
TaRYaG, in turn, is the total number of
biblical precepts (*mitzvot*), consisting of
248 affirmative precepts and 365 negative
precepts. See TARYAG MITZVOT.

NASHIM TOMAR LAHEN BELA-SHON RAKAH (נשים תאמר להן בלשון
רכה). In preparation for the Covenant at
Sinai, Moshe is instructed by God, saying:
"Thus shalt thou say to the house of Jacob,
and tell the children of Israel" (Ex. 19:3).
Rashi, in the name of the *Mekhilta*, comments: "'To the house of Jacob,' these are
the women; you shall speak to them with
soft words." They are spoken to first
because it is they who rear the children in
the ways of God. It was the children who
were offered as guarantors to keep the
Covenant.

SHAM TEHAY KEVURATKHEM

(שם תהא קבורתכם) It is written in
Scripture: "And they stood under the
mount" (Ex. 19:17). This teaches that
"The Holy One, blessed be He, over-
turned the mountain upon them like an
inverted cask [*kafah alayhem hahar kegigit*]
and said to them, 'If ye accept the Torah,
'tis well; if not, there shall you be buried'

[*sham tehay kevuratkhem*]" (Shab. 88a; A.Z. 2b; *Rashi*, ad loc.). It is uncertain why God said *sham* ("there") instead of *po* ("here"). It seems logical that the word *po* be used since they were standing there. A homoletical interpretation is that *sham* refers to wherever Jews will be, in any country of the world, and if they do not accept the tenets of the Torah they will, Heaven forbid, perish.

Although the Israelites accepted the Torah at Mount Sinai by force, they re-accepted it, according to Raba, in the days of Ahasuerus; for it is written, "[the Jews] confirmed what they had already accepted long before" (Shab., ibid.).

The expression *kafa alayhem hahar ke-gigit* is sometimes used to signify "putting very strong pressure on," or "to force a decision."

YISRO'S NEMEN (יתרוס נעמען). The *Midrash* (*Shemot Rabbah* 1) states that Jethro, Moses' father-in-law, had seven different names: Re'uel, Jether, Jethro, Hobab, Heber, Keni, and Putiel (cf. also *Rashi*, Ex. 18:1). It was common then to have more than one name.

The Yiddish expression, *Yisro's nemen* ("Jethro's names"), is used when a person is called each time by another name or is constantly changing his or her name.

MISHPATIM (משפטים)

AHARAY RABIM LEHATOT (אחרי רבים להטת). Literally, "to turn aside after a multitude to pervert justice" (Ex. 23:2). From this, the Rabbis adopted the principle to "follow the majority" ("majority rules") when there is a controversy between an individual and the many (cf. Hul. 11a; Ber. 9a; B.M. 59a), except when it would be "to do evil."

AYIN TAHAT AYIN (עין תחת עין). Literally, "an eye for an eye" (Ex. 21:24); a law of retaliation signifying "measure for measure," practiced only in the case of

murder. If, however, a person blinded the eye of his fellow, he pays the value of his own eye; it does not mean taking the actual eye.

BEGAPO YAVO BEGAPO YAYTZAY (בגפו יבא בגפו יצא). Scripture states: "If you buy a Hebrew servant, six years shall he serve; and in the seventh he shall go free. If he came in by himself [*Im begapo yavo*], he shall go out by himself [*begapo yaytzay*]" (Ex. 21:2–3). *Rashi* (ad loc.) comments that the term "*begapo* ('is like') *bikhnafo* ('with his garments'); that is, he came in just as he was by himself" (not married).

The phrase is sometimes used in remorse upon the death of a person; that is, he came into the world by himself and is leaving the world in the same manner. It can also be used for a student who completes his studies and retains nothing. Likewise, it can pertain to a person who worked all his life and has nothing to show for it.

HAMOTZI MAYHAVAYRO ALAV HARAYAH (המוציא מחבירו עליו הראיה). If a person instituted an action against another, it rests on the plaintiff to produce the evidence. The Talmud (B.K. 46b) deduces this principle from the phrase in the verse "whosoever hath a cause [a legal problem], let him come near unto them" (Ex. 24:14).

HASHOHAD YE'AVAYR PIKHIM VISALAYF DIVRAY TZADIKIM (השחד יעור פקחים ויסלף דברי צדיקים). It is written in Scripture that a judge must not accept a gift, for "a gift blindeth them that have sight, and perverteth the words of the righteous" (Ex. 23:8). The Talmud (Ket. 105a) adds that a gift blinds the eyes of the wise, "and much more so those of the foolish."

LAKELEV TASHLIKHUN OTO (לכלב תשליכון אותו). "Ye shalt cast it to the dogs" (Ex. 22:30), referring to any meat that is not fit for consumption by Jews (not kosher).

The phrase may be used facetiously when inferring that a person should be cast aside, or "thrown to the dogs."

LO TEVASHAYL GEDI BAHALAYV IMO (לא תבשל גדי בחלב אמו). *Onkelos* renders this phrase in Exodus 23:19, *Lo taykhlun besar bahalav* ("Ye shalt not eat flesh and milk"), a prohibition that distinguishes the Jew from people of all other nations. The phrase, appearing three times in Scripture (Ex. 23:19; ibid., 34:26; Deut. 14:21), forbids meat and milk to be eaten together, to derive any benefit from it, or to be cooked together (Hul. 115b; *Mekhilta, Rashi*).

MIDVAR SHEKER TIRHAK (מדבר שקר תרחק). A warning in Scripture (Ex. 27:7), "From a false matter thou shalt keep thee far."

Although this warning is given to the judge, the litigants, and the witnesses, it was adopted as a rule for all.

NA'ASEH VENISHMA (נעשה ונשמע). An instinctive response by the Israelites, meaning "We will do and obey," and given when Moshe "took the book of the covenant and read in the ears of the people" (Ex. 24:7). By giving precedence to "we will do" over "we will obey," they promised to obey God's commands even before hearing them.

SEMIKHUT-HAPARASHAH (סמיכות-הפרשה). A phrase indicating "connection" or "relationship." *Rashi* (Ex. 21:1, s.v. *Ve'ayleh Hamishpatim*) asks, "And why was the section of [civil] laws placed next to the section [dealing with] the altar (*velamah nismekhah parashat dinin leparshat mizbayah*)?"

When a discussion takes place and someone speaks of irrelevant matters, a remark in Yiddish is sometimes made to that person: VUH FAR A SEMIKHUT HAPARASHAH

HUHT DUHS TZUTUHN MIT _____ ? ("What connection has this to do with _____ ?").

VUHS FAR A SEMIKHUT HAPARA-SHAH HUHT DUHS TZUTUHN MIT _____ ? (וואס פאר א סמיכות). (הפרשה האט דאס צוטאן מיט _____ ?).
See SEMIKHUT HAPARASHAH.

TERUMAH (תרומה)

KAFTOR VAFERAH (כפתור ופרח). The six branches of the *Menorah* (Candelabra) in the Temple had "three cups made like almond-blossoms in one branch, a knop and a flower [*kaftor vaferah*]; and three cups made of almond-blossoms in the other branch, a knop and a flower" (Ex. 25:33).

The word *kaftor* is described as "an ornament in the shape of a pomegranate." The expression *kaftor vaferah*, denoting pomegranate and blossom, became associated with excellence. When something innovative was uttered by someone, Rabbi Tarfon would say, *kaftor vaferah* (*Bereishit Rabbah* 91:12). Introducing a novel thought is a manifestation of the power that is hinted at in *kaftor vaferah* of the *Menorah* (Naftali Tzvi Yehudah Berlin, *Ha'aymek Davar*, s.v. *Ve'attah Tetzaveh*; Ex. 27:20).

KOL HAMOSIF GORAYA (כל המוסיף גורע). "He who adds [to the word of God] subtracts from it." This is deduced, according to R. Mesharshia in the Talmud, (San. 29a) from the phrase in *Parashat Terumah*, "two cubits [*amatayim*] and a half shall be the length thereof" (Ex. 25:10). That is, if the word *amatayim* were to be beheaded, it would read *matayim* ("two hundred"). Thus, by adding the aleph (*amatayim*), the number is reduced to two. R. Ashi said, "We derive the principle from *ashtay-esrayh* [eleven] curtains" (Ex. 26:7). That is, by removing the letter *ayin* from *ashtay-esrayh*, it reads *shetay-esrayh* ("twelve").

The same prohibition appears in Deuteronomy 4:2 and 13:1. From the phrase *Lo tosifu al hadavar* ("Ye shall not add unto the word") (Deut. 4:2), R. Shaman b. Abba learned that a *Kohen* who ascends to *dukhan* should not say, "Because the Torah has given me permission to bless Israel, I will add a blessing of my own, as for instance, 'The Lord, the God of your fathers, make you a thousand times so many more as ye are, and so forth'" (Deut. 11:1; R.H. 28b) Another verse forbidding this action is "Thou shalt not add thereto, nor diminish from it" (Deut. 13:1). *Rashi*, quoting the *Sifri*, gives the following examples: "five inscriptions in phylacteries" (instead of four), "five kinds in the *lulav*" (instead of four), and "four blessings for the Priestly Blessing" (instead of three).

Kol Hamosif Goraya became a proverbial expression denoting "The more you say, the worse you make it."

TOKHO KEVARO (תוכו כברו). Literally, "his inside is as his outside," signifying that a person's character should correspond to his exterior. Man must be as pure in his mind and heart as he appears in outward manner. This is inferred from a phrase in *Parashat Terumah* (Ex. 25:11), *mibayit umihutz tetzapenu* ("within and without shalt thou overlay it"), referring to the Ark that was overlaid with gold inside, where it was not visible to the eye, as well as outside where it was visible. "Raba said: Any scholar whose inside is not like his outside [*she'ayn tokho kevaro*], is no scholar" (Yom. 72b). Both inside and outside, there should be the same golden character.

The Talmud also records, "A *tanna* taught: On that day the doorkeeper was removed and permission was given to the disciples to enter. For Rabban Gamaliel had issued a proclamation [saying], no disciple whose character does not correspond to his exterior may enter the *Bet ha-Midrash*" (Ber. 28a; see also Shab. 16b).

TETZAVEH (תצוה)

AYN OSIN SHERAROT AL HATZIBUR PAHOT MISHNAYIM (אין עושין שררות על הצבור פחות משנים). "Any office conferring authority over the community must be filled by at least two persons" (B.B. 8b). From whence is this rule derived? R. Nachman said: Scripture says, "And they shall take the gold" (Ex. 28:5). The emphasis is on "they," denoting a minimum of two.

ES IZ NIT MA'ALAH UN NIT MORID (עס איז ניט מעלה און ניט מוריד). A Yiddish expression meaning "it is neither raising [*ma'alah*] nor lowering [*morid*]"; signifying sameness, tedious monotony, or want of variety. It is generally a criticism or reproach of an ironical or sarcastic nature.

Scripture (Ex. 29:27) states, "And thou shalt sanctify the breast of the wave-offering, and the thigh of the heave-offering, which is waved [*asher hunaf*] and which is heaved up [*va'asher huram*]." *Rashi* (ad loc.) comments that the word *huram* ("heaved up") denotes "moving up and down" (*leshon ma'aleh umorid*). The Hebrew words in the Yiddish expression were undoubtedly influenced by this wording (cf. also Men. 61a).

HARO'EH SHEMEN ZAYIT BAHALOM YETZAPEH LEMA'OR TORAH (הרואה שמן זית בחלום יצפה למאור תורה). "If one sees olive oil in a dream, he may hope for the light of the Torah" (Ber. 57a). This is based on the verse in Scripture "That they bring unto Thee pure olive oil beaten for the light" (Ex. 27:20).

KI TISA (כי תשא)

AL YESHANEH ADAM MIN HAMINHAG (אל ישנה אדם מן המנהג). "One should never break away from custom" (B.M. 86b); that is, "When in Rome, do as the Romans do." This is derived from the time when Moses was in Heaven for forty days and forty nights, "he did neither eat bread nor drink water" (Ex. 34:28). Moses ate no bread, whereas the Ministering Angels descended below and ate bread. See *Maharsha*; see also MINHAG MEVATAYL HALAKHAH.

AYGEL HAZAHAV (עגל הזהב). "The Golden Calf" described in Exodus 32, which was made by the Israelites when they became impatient about Moses' delay in returning after he ascended Mount Sinai to receive the Tablets. Aaron, complying with the Israelites' demand to provide a god to lead them, collected golden earings from the people and fashioned the gold into the shape of a calf, which they adopted as their god. Moses later descended and found the people dancing and singing before the golden calf, and he angrily shattered the tablets.

DINEN TZUM AYGEL HAZAHAV (TZUM GU-HLDENEM KALB)—"to worship the *Aygel Hazahav*" (the Golden Calf) became a Yiddish expression for idol-worshiping.

AYN KETORET BELI HELBENAH (אין קטורת בלי חלבנה). Scripture (Ex. 30:34) numbers *helbenah* (galbanum) among the spices of incense (*ketoret*). The expression means "There is no *ketoret* without *helbenah*." *Rashi* (ad loc.) comments that the odor of *helbenah* is bad. Its mixture with the other spices is "to teach us that it should not be unimportant in our sight to include among us in the assemblies of our fasts and our prayers the sinners of Israel that they should be numbered with us."

AYN MERATZIN LO LE'ADAM BESHA'AT KA'ASO (אין מרצין לו לאדם בשעת כעסו). "We must not try to placate a man in the time of his anger," R. Yohanan said, in the name of R. Jose, for it is written: "My presence shall go with thee and I will give thee rest" (Ex. 33:14). The

Talmud writes that the "Holy One, blessed be He, said to Moses: Wait until My countenance of wrath shall have passed away and then I shall give thee rest" (Ber. 7a; *Avot* 4:23).

DINEN TZUM AYGEL HAZAHAV (TZUM GUHLDENEM KALB) (דינען צום עגל הזהב (צום גאלדענעם קאלב). See AYGEL HAZAHAV.

KOL HAMEKABAYL PENAY RABO, KE'ILU MEKABAYL PENAY SHEKHI-NAH (כל המקבל פני רבו, כאילו מקבל פני שכינה). The verse in Scripture (Ex. 33:7) reads, "And it came to pass, [that] everyone that sought the Lord went out into the tent of meeting, which was without the camp." From this is derived that "he who pays his respect to his teacher is considered as one waiting on the Divine Presence" (Jer. Talmud, Erub. 5:1). *Rashi*, quoting the *Tanhuma*, comments "that he who visits an elder is like one who welcomes the Divine Presence" (s.v. *Kol Hamevakaysh Hashem*).

MAHATZIT HASHEKEL (מחצית השקל). A levy of a "half-*shekel*" imposed after the Exodus from Egypt upon all men, twenty years of age and upward, rich or poor alike (Ex. 30:14–15).

The payment had to be made by the first of *Nisan*. It was customary to remind the people of this fact by a special proclamation issued on the first of *Adar*. A special Torah portion that deals with the half *shekel* contribution was read (Ex. 30:11–16). The Sabbath on which it is read received a special name, *Shabbat Shekalim* or *Shabbat Parashat Shekalim* (Mish., Meg. 3:4).

It is customary to contribute *Mahatzit Hashekel* prior to reading the *Megillah* on Purim. A hint of the reason for this practice is found in the Talmud (Meg. 13b): God knew that Haman would one day pay *shekels* for the destruction of Israel. Therefore, the Israelites anticipated his *shekels* by contributing the *Mahatzit Hashekel* (cf. *Torah Temimah, Parashat Ki Tisa* 23).

MI LA-SHEM AYLAI (מי לה׳ אלי).

After Moses broke the Tablets upon seeing the golden calf and the idolatry of the people, he said: "Whoso is on the Lord's side let him come unto me" (Ex. 32:26). It was the sons of Levi who came forth to him.

This expression is used by a person who is arguing for a worthy cause and is seeking support. He would readily say, *Mi la-Shem aylai*.

MIKHLAL LAV ATTAH SHOMAYA HAYN (מכלל לאו אתה שומע הן).

Scripture (Ex. 30:17–21) specifies the laws for the *Kohanim* washing their hands and feet in a special laver before entering the *ohel mo'ayd* ("the tent of meeting"). Verse 21 reads "so that they shall wash their hands and their feet that they die not." *Rashi* comments on "that they die not": "But if they will not wash, they shall die; for in the Torah there are stated general statements, and from the negative you can derive the positive [*Mikhlal lav attah shomaya hayn*]."

The section concludes with "It shall be a statute forever to them, even to him and to his seed throughout their generations." Thus, it has become a practice to wash one's hands before beginning any of the statutory services, which are the equivalent of the sacrifices. Worshipers usually wash in lavers in the entrance to the synagogue.

The statement *Mikhlal lav attah shomaya hayn* has taken on a jocular meaning: "His 'no' sounds like 'yes.'"

NESHAMAH YETAYRAH NOTAYN HAKADOSH BARUKH HU BE'ADAM EREV SHABBAT, ULEMOTZA'AY SHABBAT KODESH NOTLIN OTAH MIMENU (נשמה יתרה נותן הקב"ה באדם ערב שבת, ולמוצאי שבת קודש נוטלין אותה ממנו).

"On the eve of the Sabbath the Holy One, blessed be He, gives to man an enlarged soul [*neshamah yetayrah*] and at the close of the Sabbath He withdraws it from him," for it says: "He ceased from work and rested" (Ex. 31:17).

Once it (the Sabbath) has ceased, woe that the (additional) soul is lost! (Bez. 16a). It is a play on the word *vayinafash*, which is taken to stand for *vai avdah nefesh*. Or, as others suggest, *vai aynah nefesh*—"the soul is no longer" (Bez., ibid.).

PIKU'AH NEFESH DOHEH SHABBAT (פקוח נפש דוחה שבת).

"Saving of life supersedes the Sabbath" (Yom. 85b). This is learned from a verse in Scripture (Ex. 31:13), "Only ye shall keep My Sabbaths." One might assume this means under all circumstances. Therefore, the text reads: "Only," namely, allowing for exceptions. Another verse alluding to this is "For it is holy unto you" (Ex. 31:14). That is, "it [the Sabbath] is committed to your hands, not you to its hands." The Talmud comments also, "If circumcision, which is [performed on but] one of the limbs of man, supersedes the Sabbath, the saving of a life, *a minori*, must supersede the Sabbath (Shab. 132a). See VAHAI BAHEM VELO SHEYAMUT BAHEM.

SHELOSH ESRAY MIDOT (שלש עשרה מדות).

The "Thirteen Attributes of Divine Mercy"; also referred to as *Yud Gimmel Midot* (*yud* = 10 and *gimmel* = 3, adding up to Thirteen Attributes). These verses from Scripture (Ex. 34:6–7) are read on fast days and during *Selihot*, at *Ne'ilah*, when removing the Torah scrolls from the Ark on festivals and, in some rites, when reciting *Tahanun*. For further details regarding this passage, see Macy Nulman, *The Encyclopedia of Jewish Prayer* (Northvale, New Jersey and London: Jason Aronson Inc., 1993), pp. 159, 160.

TAYN AYNEKHA VELIBKHA AL DEVAREKHA (תן עיניך ולבך על דבריך).

Moses said to the Lord: "See, Thou sayest unto me: Bring up this people" (Ex. 33:12). Moses felt that this was far too difficult a task to undertake and pleaded for Divine assistance. Commenting on the phrase "See [re'ay], Thou sayest unto me," *Rashi* comments that the word *re'ay* infers "direct Thine eyes and Thine heart upon Thy words" (*Tayn aynekha velibkha al devarekha*).

This biblical expression may be transferred to everyday life; that is, the Hebrew saying may substitute for "heed or concentrate on what you are saying or doing."

YISHAR KO'AH (YISHAR KO-HEKHA) (יישר כח (יישר כחך). Literally, "may your strength be firm"; also implying "thanks" or "congratulations." It is generally said to a *Kohen* after he completes the *Duchenen* or to a speaker after he delivers a speech. It may also be said to a person who has completed any task.

Its source is the Talmud (Shab. 87a; Men. 99b). God said to Moses, "Hew thee two tablets of stone like unto the first; and I will write upon the tablets the words which were on the first tablets, which thou didst break" (*asher shibarta*) (Ex. 34:1). The Talmud asks, "And how do we know that the Holy One, blessed be He, gave His approval?" And answers, "because it is said 'which thou didst break,' and Resh Lakish interpreted this: *Yishar ko'ah asher shibarta* ("all strength to thee that thou didst break")." God expressed His approval of Moses' action.

The words *yishar* and *asher* are regarded as coming from the same root as *ishayr*, meaning "to confirm," "strengthen"— thus, a play upon the words *asher shibarta* and *yishar (kohekha) sheshavarta* (cf. The Babylonian Talmud; *Seder Nashim*, Rabbi Dr. I Epstein, ed. [London: The Soncino Press, 1936], pp. 412ff).

YUD GIMMEL MIDOT (י"ג מדות).
See SHELOSH ESRAY MIDOT.

VAYAKHAYL (ויקהל)

AYN MA'AMIDIN PARNAYS AL HATZIBBUR ELA IM KAYN NAM-LIKHIN BETZIBBUR (אין מעמידין פרנס על הצבור אלא א"כ נמלכין בצבור). "We must not appoint a leader of

the community without first consulting it" (Ber. 55a). This is derived from the verse "See, the Lord hath called by name Bezalel, the son of Uri" (Ex. 35:30). "The Holy One, blessed be He, said to Moses: Do you consider Bezalel suitable? He replied: Sovereign of the Universe, if Thou thinkest him suitable, surely I must also! Said God to him: All the same, go and consult them. He went and asked Israel: Do you consider Bezalel suitable? They replied: If the Holy One, blessed be He, and you consider him suitable, surely we must!" (Ber., ibid.).

AZ VAYAKHAYL IZ A KNISH IZ PEKUDAY A VARENIK (אז ויקהל איז א קניש איז פקודי א וארעניק). Literally, "If [the word] *Vayakhayl* is a *knish*, *Pekuday* is a curd-dumpling." This humorous expression evolved when an illiterate person took *Targum Onkelos'* translation for *Vayakhayl* (which is *ve'akhnaysh*, meaning "to gather") and translated it as the food known as a *knish*. Since the *Sidrah Pekuday* is often read together with *Vayakhayl*, he linked them both and translated *Pekuday a varenik*. See VAYAKHAYL MOSHE—UKHENASH MOSHE.

VAYAKHAYL MOSHE—UKHENASH MOSHE (ויקהל משה—וכנש משה). It is said about the ADMOR (*Adoni, Mori Verebi*—my master, teacher, and rabbi) of Sochaczew (Abraham ben Ze'ev Nahum Bornstein, 1839–1910), the author of *Eglay Tal* and *Avnay Nayzer*, that when he was a child of about three or four years, he saw a pot of delicacies on a chest. He climbed up to attain this *nash* ("sweets" or "goodies"). His father caught him and scolded him, saying, "What are you doing on so high a chest?" Instead of answering *Ikh nash* ("I am tasting dainties"), he said, "Father, father, I am doing here what the *Targum* says on the verse in *Vayakhayl*; the *Targum* translates the words *Vayakhayl Moshe* by *ukhenash Moshe*" (actually, the word *ukhenash* means "to gather") (cf.

Tzvi Yehudah Mamelok, *Sefer Avir Haro'im*, vol. 1 [Poland, 1935], pp. 12, 13). See AZ VAYAKHAYL IZ A KNISH IZ PEKUDAY A VARENIK.

PEKUDAY (פְּקוּדֵי)

MA'ALIN BAKODESH VE'AYN MORIDIN (מעלין בקודש ואין מורידין). (We have a rule that) "We may raise an object to a higher grade of sanctity but must not degrade it to a lower" (Ber. 28a). The Talmud (Men. 99a) asks, "Whence is it inferred that we may not bring down [what is holy]? Rabbi says, From the verse 'And Moses reared up the Tabernacle, and laid its sockets, and set up the boards thereof, and put in the bars thereof, and

reared up its pillars'" (Ex. 40:18). The verse opens with the expression "reared up" and concludes with the same expression, thus signifying that what is holy must be "reared up" and kept exalted and not be brought down. The verse also teaches that since Moses himself had begun the erection of the Tabernacle, it would have been a degradation had he allowed others to complete it.

From the ruling that one should enhance, not lessen, the importance of holy matters, the law is that we do not sell a *Sefer Torah* in order to buy books or use the parchment designated for a *Sefer Torah* to write divorce documents (*gittin*) (cf. *Torah Temimah*; R. Baruch Halevi Epstein, *Sefer Shemot* 40:18, note 6).

The Book of Leviticus
ספר ויקרא

Vayikra / ויקרא   41

Tzav / צו   41

Shemini / שמיני   41

Tazri'a / תזריע   43

Metzora / מצרע   43

Aharay Mot / אחרי מות   44

Kedoshim / קדושים   45

Emor / אמר   48

Behar / בהר   50

Behukotai / בחקתי   52

VAYIKRA (וַיִּקְרָא)

LO YOMAR ADAM DAVAR LEHA-VAYRO ELA IM KAYN KORAHU

(לא יאמר אדם דבר לחבירו אלא אם כן קורהו). It is written in Scripture: "And the Lord called unto Moses, and spoke to him" (Lev. 1:1). The Talmud (Yom. 4b) asks, "Why does Scripture mention the call before the speech?" And answers, "The Torah teaches us good manners: a man should not address his neighbor without having first called him"; that is, one should not abruptly begin to speak. The reason for this is so that the one hearing may prepare himself to listen.

MEKABLIN KORBANOT MIPOSHAY YISRAEL KEDAY SHEYAHZERU BAHEN BITESHUVAH (מקבלין קרבנות מפושעי ישראל כדי שיחזרו בהן בתשובה). "One should accept sacrifices from the transgressors in Israel, so that they may be inclined to repent" (Hul. 5a; Erub. 69b). The Talmud continues, "but not from an Israelite apostate, or from one who offers a wine libation [to idols], or from one who profanes the Sabbath publicly." This is deduced from the phrase "of the cattle" (Lev. 1:2), which includes persons who are (devoid of merit) like animals.

PISHON PEH (פתחון פה). Literally, "Opening of the mouth"—that is, "to speak"—as in Ezekiel, "I will open thy mouth in the midst of them" (29:21) or "and never open thy mouth any more because of thy shame" (ibid., 16:63).

The Talmud (Men. 110a) states, concerning the phrase rayah niho'ah la-Shem ("of a sweet savor to the Lord")(Lev. 1:9), that neither ayl nor elohim (two names meaning God, and used according to the Maharsha, in connection with idols) is employed, but only the Lord (YKVK), so as not to give sectarians any occasion to rebel (pishon peh) by finding support in the Scripture for the heretical belief in the pluralities of the deities.

In colloquial usage, the expression pishon peh means "Don't give one an opportunity to 'open his mouth' and speak ill."

TZAV (צַו)

AYN GEDULAH BEFALTIN (BE-FALTAYRIN) SHEL MELEKH (אין גדולה בפלטין (בפלטרין) של מלך). "In the king's palace no rank is recognized" (Jer. Tal., Shab. 10:3). This is deduced from the phrase in Leviticus 6:3 vehayrim et hadeshen ("And carry forth the ashes"), signifying that even the Kohen, in his priestly garments, removed the ashes from the altar. This teaches that although a task may be unbefitting to a person, he should not approach the Holy One, blessed be He, with a haughty attitude; all are alike!

KOL HA'OSAYK BATORAH AYNO TZARIKH LO OLAH VELO MIN-HAH VELO HATAT VELO ASHAM (כל העוסק בתורה אינו צריך לא עולה ולא מנחה ולא חטאת ולא אשם). "Whosoever occupies himself with the study of the Torah needs neither burnt-offering, nor meal-offering, nor sin-offering, nor guilt-offering" (Men. 110a). The study of the Torah is an atonement like the offering of sacrifices. This is derived from the verse in Leviticus 7:37 "This is the law for the burnt-offering, [et cetera]."

SHEMINI (שְׁמִינִי)

ADAM MEKADAYSH ATZMO ME'AT MEKADSHIN OTO HARBAYH, MILMATAH—MEKADSHIN OTO MILMALAH, BA'OLAM HAZEH—MEKADSHIN OTO L'OLAM HABAH (אדם מקדש עצמו מעט מקדשין אותו הרבה. מלמטה—מקדשין אותו מלמעלה. בעוה"ז—מקדשין אותו לעוה"ב). "If a man sanctify himself a little, he becomes much sanctified. [If he sanctify himself] below, he becomes sanctified from above,

[if he sanctify himself] in this world, he becomes sanctified in the World to Come" (Yom. 39a). This is derived from the verse "Sanctify yourselves therefore, and be ye holy" (Lev. 11:44). *Rashi* (in the Talmud, ad loc.) gives the reason BA LETAHAYR MESAI'IN OTO ("If he comes to purify himself, he is helped" (cf. Yom 38b; Shab. 104a)).

BIGEDULAH MATHILIN MIN HAGADOL, UVIKLALAH MATHILIN MIN HAKATAN (בגדולה מתחילין מן הגדול. ובכללה מתחילין מן הקטן).

"In conferring honor we commence at the most distinguished; in cursing we commence with the least important" (cf. Taan. 15b; Ber. 61a). The former we learn from a scriptural verse, "And Moses said unto Aaron and unto Eleazar and unto Ithamar" (Lev. 10:6; Lev. 10:12); the latter from Genesis 3:14–20, where first the serpent was cursed—then Eve, and then Adam.

HAYAV ADAM LETAHAYR ET ATZMO BAREGEL (חייב אדם לטהר את עצמו ברגל).

The Talmud (R. H. 16b) states, "[R. Isaac said:] A man should purify himself for the festival, as it says, 'and their carcasses ye shall not touch'" (Lev. 11:8). Every male Israelite should be in a state of cleanliness in order to appear in the Sanctuary (cf. *Rashi*, ad loc.).

KOL ORAYV LEMINO (כל עורב למינו).

"Every raven after its kind" (Lev. 11:15). The Torah enumerates birds that are prohibited and that belong to a class categorized as birds of prey.

The expression jocularly refers to persons, all of one kind, who find each other. See MATZA MIN ET MINO; KOL OF LEMINO YISHKON.

MA'ALAY GAYRAH (מעלה גרה).

"Chew the cud" (Lev. 11:3–4). In order to consider the animal kosher to be eaten, three characteristics are requisite: (1) it must have a divided hoof; (2) it must be wholly cloven-footed; and (3) it must chew the cud. These three characteristics are probably necessary in order to differentiate the animal from one that is not suitable for human consumption and from those that are beasts of prey.

The phrase *ma'alay gayrah* is humorously applied to a "person who repeats himself" or who is "boringly repetitive."

PATUR BELO KELUM I EFSHAR (פטור בלא כלום אי אפשר).

"[To be] exempt completely is not likely." The verse "This is the law of cattle and of birds and of every living creature that moveth in the waters" (Lev. 11:46) has interposed birds between cattle and fish. Now, one cannot say that (in the case of birds) both organs of the throat must be cut, for they are, on the one hand, grouped with fish and one cannot say that none of the organs are to be cut (*lepotro belo kelum*), for they are, on the other hand, grouped with cattle. How is this to be explained? They are rendered fit by cutting one organ (Hul. 27b). This is a compromise between the requirements of cattle and of fish.

The expression *Patur belo kelum i efshar* is sometimes spoken in a situation in which certain demands are made of a person and he or she refuses.

SHEMINI SHEMONAH SHANAH SHEMAYNAH (שמיני שמונה שנה שמנה).

"If *Parashat Shemini* (in part or in full) is read eight times (in the same period), then the year will be full of good things." How is it possible to read *Parashat Shemini* eight times?

- At *Minhah* (of *Parashat Tzav*), up to *Shayni* 1
- Within that same week (on Monday and Thursday), up to *Shayni* 2
- At *Minhah* of *Shabbat Pesah*, up to *Shayni* 1
- *Minhah* of *Shabbat-Shemini Shel Pesah*, up to *Shayni* 1
- On Monday and Thursday within that week, up to *Shayni* 2
- *Shabbat Parashat Shemini* (complete *Sidrah*) 1

  ———
  8

TAZRI'A (תזריע)

KESHAYM SHEYETZIRATO SHEL ADAM AHAR BEHAYMAH HAYAH VE'OF, KAKH TORATO AHAR BE-HAYMAH HAYAH VE'OF (כשם שיצירתו של אדם אחר בהמה חיה ועוף, כך תורתו אחר בהמה חיה ועוף). "Just as the creation of man [took place] after [that of] every animal, beast and fowl, so are his [man's] laws specified after the laws of the animal, beast, and fowl" (Vayikra Rabbah 14:1).

The Sidrah Shemini, which precedes the Sidrah of Tazri'a, gives the laws of the animals, beasts, and fowl that are tamay ("impure") and those that are tahor ("pure"). From the Sidrah of Tazri'a that follows, we learn of those persons who are impure and those who are pure (cf. Rashi, Lev. 12:2).

TAZRI'A-METZORA RAYST KERI'AH DER BA'AL KERI'AH (KORAY) (תזריע-מצורע רייסט קריעה דער בעל-) קריאה (קורא). "The Ba'al Keri'ah tears [his garments] when he reads Tazri'a-Metzora." The two Sidrot Tazri'a-Metzora are usually read together on the Sabbath. Raysn keri'ah is "to tear one's clothes in mourning"; Ba'al Keri'ah is "the officiant who reads the Torah."

The two Sidrot Tazri'a-Metzora, among the other Sidrot that are read together in the year cycle, are reputed to be the most laborious to read; especially difficult is differentiating between the words hu (masculine) and hi (feminine), which appear numerous times in the text. Moreover, the text, which is rare, makes the manner of pronouncing the words seem troublesome. This Yiddish expression does not mean that the Ba'al Keri'ah actually tears his clothing, but it intimates that his plight is one in which he is uneasy and somewhat strained when reading these two Sidrot. The word keri'ah has two meanings: spelled with an ayin next to the last letter, it means "to tear"; spelled with

an aleph, it means "to read." It is possible, then, that since they sound similar, this wording was used in the Yiddish expression.

UVAYOM HASHMINI YIMOL (וביום השמיני ימול). See ZERIZIN MAKDIMIN LEMITZVOT.

METZORA (מצורע)

AMRAH TORAH: TEHAY TEMAYAH SHIVAT YAMIM KEDAY SHETEHAY HAVIVAH AL BA'ALAH KESHE'AT KENISATAH LEHUPAH (אמרה תורה: תהא טמאה שבעת ימים כדי שתהיה חביבה על בעלה כשעת כניסתה לחופה). "The Torah ordained: Let her be unclean for seven days in order that she shall be beloved by her husband as at the time of her first entry into the bridal chamber" (Nid. 31b). This is based on the verse "And if a woman have an issue and blood be her issue in her flesh, seven days shall she be in her impurity" (Lev. 15:19).

LE'OLAM YESAPAYR ADAM BELA-SHON NEKIYAH (לעולם יספר אדם בלשון נקיה). "One should always discourse in decent language" (Pes. 3a; see also Lev. 15:9, 20). See NIBUL PEH.

METZORA-MOTZI SHEM RA (מצורע-מוציא שם רע). "Resh Lakish said: What is the meaning of 'This shall be the law of the leper'? (Lev. 14:2). It means: This shall be the law for him who brings up an evil name; a play on the word metzora [a leper]—motzi-shem-ra, a slanderer. That is, the law for a slanderer is that he becomes a leper" (Ar. 15b).

It is written in Scripture, "Death and life are in the hand of the tongue" (Prov. 18:21). The word "hand" is used to say that just as the hand can kill, so can the tongue. The Talmud further elucidates, Deba'i hayyim belishnayh, deba'i mita bel-ishnayh ("He who wants to live can find life through the tongue [by studying Torah]; he who wants to die can find death through the tongue") (Ar., ibid.).

TEHAY TEMAYAH SHIVAT YAMIM

(תהא טמאה שבעת ימים). See AMRAH TORAH: TEHAY TEMAYAH SHIVAT YAMIM.

AHARAY MOT (אחרי מות)

AHARAY MOT-KEDOSHIM-EMOR

(אחרי מות-קדושים-אמר). These three successive portions appear in the Book of Leviticus. They mean, respectively, "after the death," (ye shall be) "holy," and speak." Often, the first two Sidrot, Aharay Mot and Kedoshim, are read on the same Sabbath, and linking all three Sidrot has given rise to the thought that after the death of a person, people will praise or glorify him. They will even go so far as to label him one of the kedoshim ("holy people"). It may also imply "Of the dead say naught but good!"

ARAYOT (עריות).

Leviticus 18:6–18 lists all of the forbidden sexual relationships that lead to Arayot (incest), such as blood-relations, wives of blood-relations, and the wife's blood-relations. The sages added secondary prohibited marriages (Sheniyot; see Yeb. 21a, b).

This portion, dealing with Arayot, is also read on Yom Kippur at Minhah (cf. Tos. to Meg. 29a, s.v. Lekhol Mafsikin; to Meg. 31a, s.v. Beminhah Korin Be'arayot).

Among the "Seven Commandments" given to the descendants of Noah, incest is the fourth (San. 56a).

BEHUKOTAYHEM LO TAYLAYKHU

(בחקתיהם לא תלכו). "In their statutes ye shall not walk" (Lev. 18:3). Commenting on this dictum, Rashi (ad loc.) states that this refers to the practices of the Amorites, namely, "things which are statutes for them, such as theater and stadiums."

Responsa literature is replete with the use of the argument "in their statutes ye shall not walk." For example, in the 1800s there arose the question of playing an organ at the weddings or birthdays of a king. On Shabbat it is surely forbidden. On weekdays, however, there were those authorities who permitted it and others who forbade it on the principle of huko-tayhem ("their statutes") (cf. Rabbi David Tzvi Hoffman, Sefer Melamed Leho'il [New York: A.L. Frankel, 1954], pp. 11–19). See HUKAT HAGOY.

DIBRAH TORAH KELASHON BENAY ADAM

(דברה תורה כלשון בני אדם). "Scripture employs human idiom" (Zeb. 108b); that is, the Torah uses an ordinary form of expression (see Lev. 17:3; Ber. 31b).

HUKAT HAGOY (חקת הגוי).

"Law or custom of the non-Jew." Scripture forbids Jews to emulate heathen customs of idolatrous (or superstitious) origins, based on the biblical commandment Uvehukotay-hem lo taylaykhu ("Ye shall not walk in their statutes") (Lev. 18:3) and Velo taylkhu behukat hagoy ("And ye shall not walk in the customs of the nation") (Lev. 20:23). Rashi (Lev. 18:3) comments, "These are the customs [namely], things which are statutes for them, such as their theaters and stadiums." Jews were not permitted to visit the theaters (arenas) of the gentiles because, according to R. Meir, blood was spilled and idols were worshiped there (Tosefta, A. Z. 2:5; A. Z. 18b; Jer. Tal., San. 40a). According to R. Meir (Sifra 85b) the darkhay ha-Emori ("the customs of the Amorites") were also forbidden. These customs included all heathen, supersti-tious, and idolatrous practices of the gen-tiles of that time (cf. Shab. 67a).

Other scriptural verses denouncing the law and customs of the gentiles are Ezek-iel 5:7 and 11:12. In modern times, the organ in the synagogue and worshiping without head-covering were halakhically forbidden, according to the dictum hukat hagoy (D.Z. Hoffmann, Sefer Melamed Leho'il no. 16 [1926], pp. 15ff). For further study of *hukat hagoy*, see *Rambam, Yad, Akum* 11:1–3; 12:1; *Shulkhan Arukh, Yoreh Dayah* 178. See BEHUKOTAYHEM LO TAYLAYKHU.

LA'AZAZAYL (לעזאזל). Scripture (Lev. 16:7–8) states, "And he shall take the two goats, and set them before the Lord at the door of the tent of meeting. And Aaron shall cast lots [*goralot*] upon the two goats; one lot for the Lord and the other lot for *Azazayl*."

The word *Azazayl* has been translated as: (1) "scapegoat"—that is, the goat escaping into the wilderness (Authorized version following the Vulgate); (2) "a strong and hard mountain"—from *az* meaning "strong," and *ayl*, "mighty" (*Rashi*, ad loc.); (3) "a name of a demon in the wilderness" (Ibn Ezra; Nachmanides); (4) "a mountain peak" from which the he-goat was hurled (Yom. 67b); and (5) "fallen angels" known as Aza and Azael (Yom., ibid.).

In the parlance of the Jew, it has become a form of speech thrown in without any grammatical connection, meaning "to hell," "to hell with it," or "Damn!" In Yiddish, one would say, *Geyn zuhl er tzum tayvel-la'azazayl*. Or, in Hebrew, *Laykh le'azah!* ("Go to hell!"), an abbreviation of *Azazayl*.

VAHAI BAHEM VELO SHEYAMUT BAHEM (וחי בהם ולא שימות בהם). "He shall live by them (Lev. 18:5), but he shall not die because of them." This is the reply to the question in the Talmud (Yom. 85a, b): "Whence do we know that in the case of danger to human life, the laws of Sabbath are suspended?" See PIKU'AH NEFESH DOHEH SHABBAT.

KEDOSHIM (קדושים)

ASUR LE'ADAM SHEYITOM KELUM KODEM SHEYEVARAYKH

(אסור לאדם שיטעום כלום קודם שיברך).
"One is forbidden to taste anything before

saying a blessing over it" (Ber. 35a). The verse in Scripture reads, "The fruit thereof shall be holy, for giving praise [*hillulim*] to the Lord" (Lev. 19:24). The fact that the word *hillulim* is in the plural indicates that there must be two praises—a blessing both before and after partaking of any food (Ber., ibid.). A similar expression is *Lo yitom adam kelum ad sheyevaraykh* ("One should not taste anything until he makes a blessing") (Jer. Tal., Ber. 6:1).

DAN ET HAVAYRKHA LEKHAF ZEKHUT (דן את חברך לכף זכות).

"Judge thy neighbor in the scale of merit." When seeing a person doing something that appears to be wrong, take a favorable view of his action (Shebu. 30a). This is derived from the verse in Leviticus 19:15, "In righteousness shalt thou judge thy neighbor." A similar statement appears in *Avot* 1:30, "Judge everyone favorably."

DE'ALAKH SANI LEHAVERKHA LO TA'AVID (דעלך סני לחברך לא תעביד).

See VE'AHAVTA LERAYAKHA KAMOKHA.

HAYN SHELKHA TZEDEK, VELAV SHELKHA TZEDEK (הן שלך צדק ולאו שלך צדק).

"Your 'yes' should be just and your 'no' should be just" (B.M. 49a). This is derived from Leviticus 19:35–36. The Torah states, "Ye shall do no unrighteousness in judgment, in meteyard, in weight, or in measure. Just balances, just weights, a just *ayfat* [somewhat larger than a bushel] and a just *hin* [a measure for liquids] shall ye have." The Talmud queries why it was necessary to mention *hin tzedek* when it is included in the preceding phrase, *ayfat tzedek*? And answers, "to teach you that your *hayn* ['yes,' a play on the word *hin*] should be just and your 'no' should be just." Even a verbal transaction should not be violated. Abaye added: "One must not speak one thing with the mouth and another with the heart." This gave rise to the variant expression *Yehay hayn shelkha hayn, velav shelkha lav* ("Let your 'yea' be 'yea' and your 'nay' be 'nay'").

Of one who is "limping between two opinions" (POSAYAH AL SHTAY HASE'IPIM) (1 Kings 18:21) and cannot make up his mind whether to give confirmation or rejection in answer to a question, the expression used is HAYN VELAV VERAFYA BEYADAYH (Lit., "yes and no, it was weak in his hand"); that is, he was uncertain about it (cf. Shab 113a). See MIKHLAL LAV ATTAH SHOMAYA HAYN.

HOKHAYAH TOKHI'AH ET AMITEKHA—AFILU MAYAH PE'AMIM—TALMID LERAV (הוכח תוכיח את עמיתך—אפילו מאה פעמים—תלמיד לרב). "Thou shall surely rebuke thy neighbor (Lev. 9:17)—even a hundred times—a disciple [must rebuke] his master." One of the Rabbis said to Raba: "Perhaps hokhayah means once, tokhi'ah twice?" He answered, "Hokhayah implies even a hundred times. As for tokhi'ah, I know only that the master [must rebuke] the disciple. How do we know that the disciple [must rebuke] his master? From the phrase hokhayah tokhi'ah, implying under all circumstances" (B.M. 31a). Reproof must, of course, be done gently and privately. One must not use insulting names or say anything embarrassing (Yad, Hilkhot Dayot 6:6–8). "Do not reprove a scorner, lest he hate you; reprove a wise man and he will love you" (Prov. 9:8).

KILAYIM (כלאים). Literally, "diverse kinds." Scripture prohibits the mingling of heterogeneous seeds, the crossing and yoking together of diverse animals, and covering oneself with SHA'ATNEZ (a composite of wool and linen) (Lev. 19:19; Deut. 22:9–11).

Kilayim is also the name of the nine chapters dealing with the above prohibitions and is part of Zera'im ("Seeds"), the first of the six divisions of the Mishnah.

LIFNAY IVAYR LO TITAYN MIKHSHOL (לפני עור לא תתן מכשול). "Thou shalt not put a stumbling-block before the blind" (Lev. 19:14). Rashi (ad loc.) explains, "Before one who is blind in a [certain] matter, do not place counsel which is not suitable for him. Do not say, 'Sell your field and purchase for yourself an ass,' while you seek an opportunity to take it from him [by this counsel]." The Talmud (M.K. 17a) gives as an example the verse, "put not a stumbling-block before the blind," and applies it to one who beats his grown-up son; this might cause him to rebel.

LO KATAYF VELO NATEF (לא כתף ולא נטף). Scripture states, "And thy vineyard thou shalt not glean [lo te'olayl]," that is, you shall not take the small separate branches that are on it . . . "for the poor and for the stranger thou shalt leave them" (Lev. 19:10). Rashi (ad loc.) asks, "What constitutes small separate branches?" And answers: kol she'ayn lo lo katayf velo natef, that is, ["the grapes hanging on a stalk] which has no arm or shoulder [its grapes hang loose and do not rest on other stalks as if on a shoulder as is usual with fully ripe grapes] and no trunk" (lit., "have no pendant") (cf. also Mishnah, Pe'ah 7:4).

Colloquially, lo katayf velo natef is applied to someone or something that is neither good nor bad, large or small, desirable or undesirable.

LO TA'AMOD AL DAM RAYEKHA (לא תעמוד על דם רעך). "Thou shalt not stand idly by the blood of thy neighbor" (Lev. 19:16). Rashi (ad loc.), quoting the Talmud (San. 63a), comments, "Thou shalt not stand idly by to behold his death while you are able to save him; for example, one drowning in a river, or when a wild beast or robbers come upon him." Furthermore, you are not at liberty to remain silent if a person is accused of a crime and your evidence would clear him (Torat Kohanim, Sifra).

LO TAYLAYKH RAKHIL BE'AMEKHA (לא תלך רכיל בעמיך). "Thou shalt not go up and down as a

tale-bearer among thy people" (Lev. 19:16). *Rashi* comments, "It is my opinion [that] it is because all inciters of quarrels and those that relate evil talk go into the houses of their friends to spy out what they can see of evil, or what they can hear of evil, in order to tell it in the marketplace; [consequently] they are called *holkhay rakhil*—that is, those that go about spying."

This verse gave rise to the Hebrew expression *ish rakhil* ("tale-bearer" or "slanderer"). In Yiddish the expression is *rekhilut trayberay* ("evil gossip") and the person doing it is labeled *rekhilut trayber* ("tale-bearer"), a person of evil tongue (*lashon hara*) (Jer. Tal., *Pe'ah* 1:1). See AVAK LESHON HARA; LASHON TELITAI KATIL TELITAI.

LO TIKOM VELO TITOR (לא תקם ולא תטר). A prohibition in the Bible, meaning, "Thou shalt not take vengeance, nor bear a grudge" (Lev. 19:18). *Rashi* (ad loc.), quoting the *Sifra* and Talmud, explains both instances: By vengeance is meant, "If one man says to another 'lend me your sickle' [and the latter] says to him, 'no' [and] on the morrow [the second man] says to him [to the first], 'Lend me your axe,' [and] [the first man] says to him, 'I will not lend it to you; just as you did not lend it to me'—this is taking vengeance." Be bearing a grudge is meant, "[If one] says to another, 'Lend me your axe,' [and] [the latter] says to him, 'no' [and] on the morrow [the latter] says to him, [to the first], 'Lend me your sickle,' [and] [the first man] says to him, 'Here it is. I am not like you who did not lend [it] to me'—this is bearing a grudge, for he guards the hatred in his heart even though he does not take vengeance."

LO TOKHLU KODEM SHETIT-PALELU AL DIMKHEM (לא תאכלו קודם שתתפללו על דמכם). R. Jose, son of R. Hanna, also said, in the name of R. Eliezer b. Jacob: "Do not eat before ye have prayed for your blood" (i.e., "life")

(Ber. 10b). This is derived from the verse, "Ye shall not eat with the blood" (Lev. 19:26). R. Isaac said, in the name of R. Johanan, who had it from R. Jose, son of R. Hanina, in the name of R. Eliezer b. Jacob: If one eats and drinks and then says the prayers, of him Scripture (1 Kings 14:9) says, "And hast cast Me behind thy back [*gavekha*]." Read not *gavekha* (thy back), but *gayekha* (thy pride). Says the Holy One, blessed be He: After this one has exalted himself, he comes and accepts the Kingdom of Heaven. That is, he reads the *Shema* (Ber., ibid.).

MIPNAY SAYVAH TAKUM VEHA-DARTA PENAY ZAKAYN (מפני שיבה תקום והדרת פני זקן). "Thou shalt rise up before the hoary head, and honor the face of the old man" (Lev. 19:32). The Talmud (Kidd. 32b) comments, "Would you stand up even before a wicked old man? Thus, the verse continues, 'honor the face of the *zakayn*' [the old man]; a *zakayn* is only one who has acquired wisdom [*zakayn, zeh shekanah hokhmah*]." Each of the letters in the word *ZaKayN* are an abbreviation for *Zeh Kanah Hokhmah* ("This one has acquired wisdom").

Rashi (ad loc.) comments regarding honoring an old man: "What is honoring? He must not sit in his place, nor contradict his words. The Talmud (ibid.) asks, in the name of R. Simeon b. Eleazar: How do we know that a Sage must not trouble [the people]? That is, that he should not intentionally pass the people if he has an alternate route. The Talmud answers: From the verse (ibid.) '. . . old man and thou shall fear.' Reading the phrase in this manner, disregarding the accent marks, it becomes a prohibition to the Sage."

ONA'AT DEVARIM (אונאת דברים). "Wounding one's feeling by words," "annoyance," "mortification." By *ona'ah* is meant "deception" or "fraudulent representation." Scripture states, "And if a stranger sojourn with thee in your land, you shall not do him wrong" (*lo tonu oto*)

(Lev. 19:33). The Rabbis went one step further and took the word to mean "offend" or "insulting speech" (cf. B.M. 58b).

SHA'ATNEZ (שעטנז). It is written in the Mishnah (Kilayim 9:1), "No [clothing material] is forbidden on account of KILAYIM except [a mixture of] wool and linen [Sha'atnez]." This is explicitly stated in Scripture, Leviticus 19:19, and Deuteronomy 22:11.

According to the Mishnah (Kilayim 9:8), the word Sha'atnez is a compound standing for shu'a (smoothed out by a process of "carding"), tawui ("spun"), and nuz ("twisted").

Various explanations have been given for this prohibition against mixing wool and linen: (1) It was worn by non-Jews during idol-worship (Maimonides, Moreh Nevukhim 3, chap. 37); (2) Because Cain brought linen seeds as an offering and Abel brought the firstborn of his sheep as an offering, God said it would not be proper for the offering of a sinner to be mixed with that of an innocent man's offering (Midrash Tanhuma, Gen. 9; Midrash Aggadah 5); and (3) Because weaving wool and linen together is like suggesting that the Almighty did not complete every item He made, and it would be denying the perfection of Creation (Ramban).

SINAT HINAM (שנאת חנם). "Causeless hatred." Scripture states, "Thou shalt not hate thy brother in thy heart" (Lev. 19:17). The Talmud (Ar. 16b) expounds upon this and says, "One might have believed one may only not smite him, slap him, curse him, therefore the text states: 'In thy heart.'"

Scripture speaks of "hatred in the heart." R. Nehemiah said: As a punishment for causeless hate, strife multiplies in a man's house, his wife miscarries, and his sons and daughters die young" (Shab. 32b). The Jerusalem Talmud states that "causeless hatred ranks with the three

cardinal sins: idolatry, immorality, and murder" (Yom. 1:1).

A prayer in the liturgy of Yom Kippur that asks God to forgive us for Sinat hinam is Al Hayt: "For the sin that we have sinned before You through baseless hatred."

VE'AHAVTA LERAYAKHA KAMOKHA (ואהבת לרעך כמוך). "Thou shalt love thy neighbor as thyself" (Lev. 19:18). R. Akiba said: This is a fundamental principle in the Torah (Rashi, ad loc., quoting Sifra). The Talmud (Shab. 31a) relates the story about a heathen who asked Hillel to teach him the whole Torah while standing on one foot (the briefest possible form). Hillel said to him: "'What is hateful to you, do not do to your neighbor' [DE'ALAKH SANI LEHAVAYRKHA LO TA'AVID]; that is the whole Torah, while the rest is the commentary thereof. Go and learn it." This became the "Golden Rule" in Judaism, underscoring Ahavat Yisrael: the love for one's fellow man and love for humanity in general.

EMOR (אמר)

AF AL PI SHEKOL HAMO'ADIM MITZVAH LISMO'AH BAHEM, AVAL BEHAG HASUKKOT HAYETAH BAMIKDASH SIMHAH YETAYRAH

אף על פי שכל המועדים מצוה לשמוח בהם. אבל בחג הסכות היתה במקדש שמחה יתירה). "Although on all festivals it is a mitzvah to rejoice, on Sukkot there was additional rejoicing in the Temple," as was written, "and ye shall rejoice before the Lord your God seven days" (Lev. 23:40) (cf. Rambam Lulab 18:2). This gave rise to the joyous processions in the Temple where the lulav (palm branch) and etrog (citron) were held in hand while singing psalms of praise to God.

ATZERET (עצרת). See KASHAH ALAI PERIDATKHEM.

AYN HAYAHID OMAYR KEDU-SHAH (אין היחיד אומר קדושה). "A man praying by himself does not say Kedushah." This is derived from the word "among" occurring in two verses in Scripture (Ber. 21b). One verse reads, "I will be hallowed among the children in Israel" (Lev. 22:32) and another verse reads, "Separate yourselves from among this congregation" (Numb. 16:21). As in the latter verse ten are implied, so in the former verse are ten implied (cf. Meg. 23b). The Jerusalem Talmud (Ber. 7:3) gives a different derivation. The verse in Leviticus 22:32 reads, "I will be hallowed among the children in Israel" and another verse in Genesis 42:5 reads, "And the sons of Israel came to buy among those that came." Just as in the latter verse ten are implied, so in the former verse ten are implied; from here it is learned that a davar shebikedushah ("a matter of sanctification") needs no less than ten.

HARO'EH ETROG BAHALOM, HADAR HU LIFNAY KONO (הרואה אתרוג בחלום, הדר הוא לפני קונו). It is written in the Talmud (Ber. 57a): "If one sees citron [hadar] in his dream, he is honored [hadar] in the sight of his Maker, since it says: 'The fruit of citrons [the etrog], branches of palm trees'" (Lev. 23:40).

HILLUL HASHEM (חלול השם). Literally, "profanation of the Divine Name." It is written in Scripture, "And ye shall not profane My Holy Name" (Lev. 22:32). The Mishnah states: "Wild beasts come upon the world for vain oaths and for desecration of God's Name" (Avot 5:11). That is, causeless hatred and prejudice are brought upon Israel. The Talmud warns, "If he has been guilty of the profanation of the Name, then penitence has no power to suspend punishment . . . only death finishes it" (Yom. 86a). See KIDDUSH HASHEM.

KASHAH ALAI PERIDATKHEM (קשה עלי פרידתחם). "It is difficult for

me to part with you" (Rashi, Lev. 23:36; Numb. 29:36; Sukk. 55a). God tells Moshe, "Seven days ye shall bring an offering made by fire to the Lord: on the eighth day a holy convocation shall be unto you; and ye shall bring an offering made by fire unto the Lord; it is [a day] of detention [Atzeret]." Rashi comments: "I have detained you with me like a king who invited his children to a feast for a certain number of days, [and] then came their time to depart, he said, 'My children, I request you, tarry with me one more day, it is difficult for me to part with you.'" Thus the name Shemini Atzeret a festival on its own account, distinct from Sukkot.

The word Atzeret is also used to convey "a general assembly" (Amos 5:21) or a "concluding celebration" (2 Chron. 7:9). The Torah also refers to the final day of Pesah as Atzeret (Deut. 16:8). In the Second Temple period, however, Atzeret was used exclusively to designate the festival of Shavu'ot since Shavu'ot is related to Passover (Lev. 23:15ff.) and is thus a "concluding celebration."

KIDDUSH HASHEM (קידוש השם). Literally, "to hallow the Name of God." Scripture states, "but I will be hallowed among the children of Israel" (Lev. 22:32), a positive injunction to every Israelite. An illustration of Kiddush Hashem is manifested in the following incident: Simeon ben Shetah (first century B.C.E.) once purchased an ass from an Arab. His pupils found a costly jewel on the neck of the animal, whereupon they joyously told their master that he could ease up in his work since the proceeds from the jewel would bring him a fortune. Simeon, however, replied that the Arab had sold him the ass only, and not the jewel; and he returned it to the Arab. The Arab exclaimed, "Praised be the God of Simeon ben Shetah!" (Deuteronomy Rabbah 3:3; Jer. Tal., B.M. 2:8c). Through his honesty and integrity he "sanctified the Name of God in public."

The Talmud (Sot. 10b) records that both Joseph and Judah merited that their names contain a letter or letters from the Name of the Holy One, blessed be He, because of their sanctifying the Heavenly Name. The letter *hay*, one of the letters of the Tetragrammaton, was added to Joseph's name (Yehosef) (cf. Ps. 81:6) and the four letters of the Tetragrammaton occur in Judah's name (YeHUdaH). As for Noachides (BENAY NOAH) "sanctifying the Name of God," the Talmud (San. 74b) relates that by observing their seven precepts, they are already sanctifying the Divine Name.

The highest form of *Kiddush Hashem*, according to Jewish law, is martyrdom. Jewish law demands that a Jew surrender his life rather than desecrate the Name of God by public apostasy (*Shulhan Arukh, Yoreh Dayah* 157). See HILLUL HASHEM.

KOL HAMEHALAYL ET HAMO'-ADOT, MA'ALIN ALAV KE'ILU HILAYL ET HASHABBATOT (כל המחלל את המועדות. מעלין עליו כאילו חלל את השבתות). "Whosoever desecrates the festivals is charged as though he had desecrated the Sabbath" (*Rashi*, quoting the *Sifra* in Lev. 23:3). This is a response to the question "What reference has the Sabbath to the festivals?" In the previous verse, Lev. 23:2, God tells Moses to "Speak unto the children of Israel" that they fix the festivals, and in the following sentence (Lev. 23:3) the Sabbath is ordered.

KOL SHE'AYNO BEMISHNAH AYNO BEMA'ASEH (כל שאינו במשנה אינו במעשה). Literally, "One who does not study cannot practice." Scripture (Lev. 22:31) states, "And ye shall keep My commandments [*Ushemartem mitzvotai*] and do them [*va'asitem otam*]." The *Sifra* (quoted in *Rashi*) comments, "And ye shall keep" denotes study; "And do them" denotes practice. Thus, in order to practice (properly) one must study.

PARASHAT EMOR SHERT MEN DI LEMER (פרשת אמר שערט מען די לעמער). A jocose expression, meaning "*Parashat Emor* shearing of the lambs [takes place]." The portion of *Emor* describes the lamb as a sacrificial animal-offering. Leviticus 22:23 and 22:28 give the quality and direction of the lamb-offering. Verse 23:12 gives the lamb-offering in connection with the bringing of the *Omer* on Passover. Verse 23:18 describes the offering of lambs on *Shavu'ot*. Although verses 23:25 (Rosh Hashanah), 23:27 (Yom Kippur), and 23:36 (Sukkot) make general mention of bringing offerings, specifications of the lamb-offerings are described in Numbers 29:2–7, 29:7–13.

BEHAR (בהר)

EVEN MASKIT LO TITNU BE'-ARTZEKHEM LEHISHTAHAVOT ALEHA (אבן משכית לא תתנו בארצכם להשתחות עליה). "Ye shall not place any figured [mosaic] stone in your land, to bow down unto it" (Lev. 26:1). Kneeling or prostration upon a stone floor in a place other than the Temple of Jerusalem is forbidden. It thus became the custom, when bowing at *Alaynu* and in the *Avodah* on Yom Kippur, to spread out some green leaves or a cloth on the place where one will kneel (*Orah Hayyim* 131:8).

EYN MUHL IN A YOVEL (איין מאל אין א יובל). See YOVEL.

KERATEM DEROR BA'ARETZ LE-KHOL YOSHVEHA (קראתם דרור בארץ לכל ישביה). "Proclaim liberty throughout the land unto all the inhabitants" (Lev. 25:10); a verse in Scripture describing the Jubilee Year, when the emancipation of slaves and release of landed property from mortgage takes place. R. Yehudah said (R.H. 9b; cf. *Rashi*, ad loc.): The etymology of the word *deror* is "freedom," as one who dwells (*kim-*

dayayr) in a dwelling; that is, one who dwells in any place that he desires and is not under the authority of others. In Ezekiel 46:17 the phrase *shenat hadror* ("the year of liberty") is used.

This biblical phrase is inscribed on the Liberty Bell, a historic relic in Independence Hall in Philadelphia, U.S.A. It was first hung in 1753 and rung in July, 1776, to proclaim the Declaration of Independence. Although it was taken to Allentown and hidden (1777–78) during the British occupation of Philadelphia, it was later returned. In 1781 it was moved from the steeple to the brick tower. It became cracked in 1835, and today it is exhibited resting on its original timbers.

LE'OLAM YIDOR ADAM BE'ERETZ YISRAEL VE'AFILU BA'IR SHERU-BAH NOKHRIM (לעולם ידור אדם בארץ ישראל ואפילו בעיר שרובה נכרים). "One should always live in the Land of Israel, even in a town most of whose inhabitants are idolators" (Ket. 110b); for it is said in Scripture, "To give you the Land of Canaan, to be your God" (Lev. 25:38). This implies that only in the Land of Canaan would He be their God. *Rashi*, quoting the *Sifra*, comments: "For whosoever dwells in the Land of Israel, I am his God; and whosoever goes out from it, is as one who practices idolatry." The Talmud (ibid.) asks, but may one serve God anywhere? And answers that "living outside the land of Israel may be regarded as worshiping idols," as can be learned from King David, who was told, "Go serve other gods" (1 Sam. 26:19) and was driven out and was compelled to seek shelter from Saul in the country of Moab and the land of the Philistines. His banishment was equivalent to his being told to go and serve foreign gods. (Cf. *Maharsha* finds this answer somewhat difficult.)

LO YAKNIT ISH HAVAYRO (לא יקניט איש חבירו). "One should not provoke his fellowman" (*Rashi*, *Behar* 25:17). This is *Rashi's* commentary on the scriptural command "And ye shall not wrong one another." The Talmud (B.M. 58b) states that this refers to verbal wrongs. For example, if a man is penitent (*ba'al teshuvah*), one must not say to him, "Remember your former deeds." If he is the son of proselytes (*ben gayrim*), he must not be taunted with "Remember the deeds of your ancestors." If he is a proselyte (*gayr*) and comes to study the Torah, one must not say to him, "Shall the mouth that ate unclean and forbidden food, abominable and creeping things, come to study the Torah, which was uttered by the mouth of Omnipotence?" If he is visited by suffering, afflicted by disease, or has buried his children, one must not speak to him as his companions spoke to Job.

According to R. Johanan (who said, on the authority of R. Simeon b. Yohai) verbal wrong is more heinous than monetary wrong, because of verbal wrong, it is written, "and thou shalt fear thy God," but this is not said of monetary wrong. R. Eleazar said that verbal wrong affects the victim's person, the other only his money. R. Samuel b. Nahmani said that with monetary wrong, restoration is possible, but it is not with verbal wrong.

MAH INYAN SHEMITAH AYTZEL HAR SINAI (מה ענין שמיטב אצל הר סיני). "What connection has the Sabbatical year with Mount Sinai?" *Rashi* (ad loc.) asks this question in regard to the verse (Lev. 25:1) "And the Lord spoke unto Moses on Mount Sinai, saying . . ." *Rashi* elaborated, "Were not all the commandments stated from Sinai?" And answers: "Just as [regarding] the Sabbatical year there were stated its generalizations, and its details, and its minutiae from Sinai, so were all [laws] stated, that is, their generalizations, details, and minutiae from Sinai."

This popular expression is often used during any conversation when an irrelevant or irregular statement is made, meaning "What does one thing have to do with the other?"

NESHEKH: DEKA NAKHIT LAYH, DEKA SHAKIL MINAYH MIDI DELO YAHIV (נשך: דקא נכית ליה, דקא שקיל מיניה מידי דלא יהיב). "[There is] *Neshekh*, for he 'bites' him [the debtor] by taking from him something which he [the creditor] did not give" (B.M. 60b). This refers to taking interest, which is forbidden according to the Torah (Lev. 25:36). See also NESHEKH RIBIT SHEHI KIN-SHIKHAT NAHASH, and so forth.

NESHEKH: RIBIT SHEHI KINESHI-KHAT NAHASH-VE'AYNO MAR-GISH, UFITOM HU MEVATBAYT VENOFAYAH AD KADKADO (נשך: ריבית שהיא כנשיכת נחש-ואינו מרגיש ופתאום הוא מבטבט ונופח עד קדקדו). "*Neshekh* means interest [*ribit*], since it is like the bite of a snake which is not felt, but suddenly it swells and blows up as far as his head." So with interest, one does not feel it and it is not noticeable until the interest increases and causes one to lose much money (*Rashi*, Ex. 22:24; see also *Rashi*, Lev. 25:36). See also NESHEKH: DEKA NAKHIT LAYH, and so on.

RIBIT (ריבית). See NESHEKH: RIBIT, and so on.

VEHAY AHIKHA IMAKH (וחי אחיך עמך). "That thy brother may live with thee" (Lev. 25:36). R. Eleazar gave the reason for claiming direct interest in court because Scripture states, "Take thou no usury of him, or increase: but fear thy God that thy brother may live with thee" (ibid.). This implies return it to him, that he may be able to "live with thee" (B.M. 61b, 62a). R. Akiba interprets "that thy brother may live with thee" as follows: "If two are traveling on a journey [far from civilization], and one has a pitcher of water, if both drink, they will [both] die, but if only one drinks, he can reach civilization; thy life takes precedence over his life. 'With thee' implies that thy life

takes first place and he has a right to life after yours is assured" (B.M., ibid.).

YOVEL (יובל). "A jubilee"; or "a year of jubilee." The year is so named from the blast (Heb. *Yovel*; lit., "a ram's horn") by which it was announced (cf. *Rashi*, Lev. 25:10). Leviticus 25:13 calls it *Shenat Hayovel* ("The year of the jubilee")—that is, the fiftieth year after seven *Shemitot* ("seven Sabbatical years"), when all debts were canceled and every man returned to his possession.

The expression HAG HAYOVEL is used when a person or an institution celebrates its fiftieth year. A person whose anniversary is being celebrated is called *ba'al-yovel* (Heb.), or *der yovilar* (Yidd.). When something seldom happens, the Yiddish expression is EYN MUHL IN A YOVEL, signifying, "Once in a lifetime."

BEHUKOTAI (בחקתי)

AYN HANAVI RESHA'I LEHADAYSH DAVAR MAYATAH (אין הנביא רשאי לחדש דבר מעתה). "A prophet may henceforth [i.e., after Moses] make no innovations" (Shabu. 104a). This is derived from the verse "These are the commandments" (Lev. 37:34).

BET-HAKENESET SHEHARAV . . . KEDUSHATAN AF KESHEHAYN SHOMEMIN (. . . בית הכנסת שחרב קדושתן אף כשהן שוממין). "If a synagogue has fallen into ruins . . . their holiness remains even when they are desolate" (Meg. 28a); implied from the verse "I will bring your sanctuaries into desolation" (Lev. 26:31).

HEVU AMAYLIM BATORAH (הוו עמלים בתורה). *Rashi*, commenting on the verse "And My commandments ye keep," writes (Lev. 26:3), "Study the Torah laboriously" for the purpose of observing and fulfilling (the commandments), as it is stated, "that ye learn them and observe to do them" (Deut. 5:1).

IM AYN SHALOM AYN KLUM

(אם אין שלום אין כלום). "If there is no peace, there is nothing" (Rashi, Lev. 26:6). Scripture enumerates various blessings in the wake of obedience. Among these blessings is "And I will give peace in the land" (ibid. 26:6). Rashi elucidates by commenting, "Perhaps you will say: Behold, there is food, and there is drink; [but] if there is no peace, there is nothing"; peace is balanced against everything.

Scripture uses the word venatati ("and I will give") three times: once as a blessing for food and drink (Lev. 26:4–5), the second time regarding peace (Lev. 26:6–10), and a third time regarding the Bet Hamikdash, "and My soul shall not abhor you" (Lev. 11–12). Since the blessing of peace is enumerated separately, this shows that it is on the same level as the other blessings. See MIPNAY DARKAY SHALOM.

SHTAY TOROT NITNU LEYISRAEL, AHAT BIKTAV VE'AHAT BE'AL PEH

(שתי תורות ניתנו לישראל אחת בכתב ואחת בע"פ). The plural form vehatorot, used in Lev. 26:46, denotes that "Two Torot were given to the Israelites, one written and one oral." The phrase, in the same verse, "in Mount Sinai by the hand of Moses" teaches that the entire Torah— its laws, its grammar, and its meaning— were given to Moses at Sinai (cf. Rashi, ad loc.; Torat Kohanim).

TOKHAHAH (תוכחה).

A word meaning "warning" or "admonition," referring to two Pentateuchal sections: Leviticus 26:14–45 and Deuteronomy 28:15–68. These sections contain enumerations of evils for disobedience, sickness and defeat, exile, fruitless labor, invasion and siege, and plagues. The Mishnah (Meg. 3:6) labels them "Kellalot" ("Curses"). Because of the fearful rebukes enumerated in these sections, they are read in an undertone and different customs arose regarding calling up a person for this Aliyah. Generally, the Ba'al Keri'ah or the shamash is called.

A Yiddish expression utilizing the idea of evil befalling a person is Di gantze tokhahah huht zikh oysgeguhsn oyf im ("All calamities befell him"). A similar expression is Oysluhzen di (gantze) tokhahah oyf _____ ("heap curses on _____ ").

A stubborn or wicked person is referred to as ish tokhahot, as in the verse Ish tokhahot maksheh oref ("He, that being often reproved, hardens his neck") (Prov. 29:1).

The Book of Numbers
ספר במדבר

Bemidbar / במדבר   57

Naso / נשא   58

Beha'alotekha / בהעלתך   58

Shelah / שלח   60

Korah / קרח   60

Hukat / חקת   61

Balak / בלק   61

Pinhas / פנחס   63

Matot / מטות   64

Masay / מסעי   65

BEMIDBAR (במדבר)

DOR HAMIDBAR (דור המדבר). "The generation of the wilderness"; a name applied to the Israelites who sojourned forty years in the desert (Ex. 16:35) in complete desolation (*midbar*) (Numb. 20:4–5).

The generation of the wilderness is called Darda (from *dar*, meaning "generation," and *da*, "knowledge") (1 Kings 5:11). The *Midrash* (Prov. to 1:1) comments that this name was given them "because they were extremely knowledgeable" (*benay dayah*). Israel's virtues in Torah, prophesy, and kingship date from the time in the wilderness (*Shir Hashirim Rabbah* 3:6). This is derived from Canticles 3:6, "Who is this that cometh up out of the wilderness?"

The *Mishnah* (San. 10:3; cf. also San. 110b) evaluates the *Dor Hamidbar* as follows: "The generation of the wilderness have no share in the future world and will not stand at the [last] judgment, as it is written, 'in this wilderness they shall be consumed, and there they shall die' (Numb. 14:35); this is R. Akiba's view. R. Eliezer said: Concerning them it is said, 'Gather My saints together unto Me, those that have made a covenant with Me by sacrifice'" (Ps. 50:5). See DOR HAMABUL, DOR HAFLAGAH.

KOL HAMELAMAYD ET BEN HAVAYRO TORAH, MA'ALAH ALAV HAKATUV KE'ILU YOLDO (כל המלמד את בן חבירו תורה, מעלה עליו הכתוב כאלו ילדו). R. Samuel b. Nahmani said, in R. Jonathan's name: "He who teaches the son of his neighbor the Torah, Scripture ascribes it to him as if he had begotten him, as it says, 'Now, these are the generations of Aaron and Moses' (Numb. 3:1). Further on, it is written, 'These are the names of the sons of Aaron' (Numb. 3:2): thus teaching thee that Aaron begot and Moses taught them; hence they are called by his name" (San. 19b).

An extended version with the same idea is: Resh Lakish said: "He who teaches Torah to his neighbor's son is regarded by Scripture as though he had fashioned him—as though he himself had created the words of the Torah (R. Eleazar)—as though he had made himself (Raba)" (San. 99b).

As for teaching one's own son Torah, "R. Joshua b. Levi said: If any man teaches his son Torah, Scripture accounts it to him as if he had received it from Mount Horeb, as it says (Deut. 4:9–10), 'And thou shalt make them known unto thy children's children,' and immediately afterwards it is written, 'The day that thou stoodest before the Lord thy God in Horeb'" (cf. Ber. 21b).

MIDBAR (MIDBARDIK) (מדבר (מדברדיק)). The word *midbar* ("wilderness") appears in various biblical passages (Numb. 20:4–5; Deut. 8:15; Jer. 2:2; 22:6; Ps. 107:4; 33–36). *Midbar* (Heb.) or *midbardik* (Yiddish) is used when experiencing an "arid," "uninhabited," or "uncultured" area.

TALMID SHELO RA'AH SIMAN YAFEH BEMISHNATO HAMAYSH SHANIM, SHUV AYNO RO'EH (תלמיד שלא ראה סימן יפה במשנתו חמש שנים, שוב אינו רואה). "If a student does not see a sign of blessing [progress] in his studies after five years, he never will." This is derived from two scriptural verses: One verse says, "From twenty and five years old and upward" (Numb. 8:24); and another verse says, "From thirty years old and upward" (Numb. 4:3; 4:23). How are these verses to be reconciled? Thus, at the age of twenty-five (the Levite enters the service) for training, and at the age of thirty he performs service (Hul. 24a).

TOV LATZADIK VETOV LISHKHAYNO (טוב לצדיק וטוב לשכנו). Scripture, in describing the Levites and their duties, states, "And those that were to pitch before the Tabernacle eastward, before the tent of meeting toward the sunrising, were Moses and Aaron and his sons" (Numb. 3:38). *Rashi* (ad loc.) comments on the phrase "Moses and Aaron and his sons," that next to them was the standard of the camp of Judah, and those that pitched by him, Issachar and Zebulun. *Tov latzadik, tov lishkhayno* ("It is well with the righteous, and well with his neighbor"). Since they were neighbors of Moses, who engaged in the study of the Torah, they also became great in Torah.

NASO (נשא)

IKAR SHIRAH MIN HATORAH
(עיקר שירה מן התורה). Belvati, in the name of R. Johanan, inferred that we derive the biblical basis for song (*shirah*) in the Sanctuary from the verse, "To do the work of service" (Numb. 4:47). The Talmud (Ar. 11a) asks: "Which work needs [depends on] service? Say: That is song."

LO MEKOMO SHEL ADAM MEKHABDO ELA ADAM MEKHABAYD ET MEKOMO (לא מקומו של אדם מכבדו אלא אדם מכבד את מקומו).
"[R. Jose says:] It is not the place that honors the man but it is the man who honors the place" (Ta'an. 21b). The same is found in connection with the Tent of Meeting in the wilderness: so long as it remained pitched, the Torah commanded, "That they put out of the camp every leper" (Numb. 5:2), but once the curtains were rolled up (and they continued their journeying) both those with a running issue (sores) and the lepers were permitted to enter therein.

NESI'AT KAPAYIM (נשיאת כפים). Literally, "raising the hands"; the name given to the Priestly Blessing, taken from Numbers 6:24–26. Other appellations are: *Birkat Kohanim* ("Priestly Blessing") and DUKHENEN (from *dukhan*, "platform"). It is called *Birkat Kohanim* (Heb.) only when the *Sheli'ah Tzibbur* recites it in the *Amidah* as a prayer (rather than as a blessing) for remembrance of the *Kohen* who lifted his

hands (*Nesi'at Kapayim*) daily in the Temple to bless the people. But when the *Kohanim* themselves lift their hands, the term *Nesi'at Kapayim* (Heb.) is used. *Dukhenen* (Yidd.) is derived from the place where the *Kohanim* stood while performing the blessing.

BEHA'ALOTEKHA (בהעלתך)

ASHRAYKHEM SHETIZKU LIHYOT SHAMASHIM LAMAKOM (אשריכם שתזכו להיות שמשים למקום). It is written in Scripture, "Take the Levites from among the children of Israel, and cleanse them" (Numb. 8:6). *Rashi* (ad loc.) comments on "Take the Levites": that is, take them with kind words, saying: *Ashraykhem shetizku*—"Fortunate are you that you have merited to be servants to the Omnipresent."

AYL NA REFA NA LAH (אל נא רפא נא לה). "O God, I beseech Thee, heal her [now], I beseech Thee" (Numb. 12:13). The five-word plea made by Moses on behalf of Miriam is a model of brevity.
The Talmud tells of a time when "it happened that a certain disciple went down before the Ark in the presence of R. Eliezer, and he cut the prayer very short. His disciples said to him, 'How concise this fellow is!' He replied to them, 'Is he any more concise than our Master Moses, who prayed, as it is written: O God, I beseech Thee, heal her [now], I beseech Thee'" (Ber. 34a)? Prior to this, the Talmud makes mention of one who prolonged the prayer to great length. After the disciples complained, the response forthcoming was "Is he drawing it out any more than our Master Moses, of whom it is written, 'The forty days and the forty nights [that I fell down]'" (Deut. 9:25). The *Sifri* gives the rationale for both incidents—that is, there is a time to be brief and time to be lengthy, and here Moses was brief so that it should not be said that his sister was in trouble and he was standing and praying.

From this phrase, we learn that if one prays on behalf of his fellow, one need not mention his name, since Moses did not mention the name of Miriam (Ber., ibid). *Rashi* (ad loc.) comments that Scripture teaches one proper conduct and that a person who asks something of his fellow-man should say two or three words of supplication and then make his requests.

AYN MUKDAM UME'UHAR BATO-RAH (אין מוקדם ומאוחר בתורה). Literally, "there is no 'before' or 'after' in the Torah" (*Rashi*, Numb. 9:1); that is, there is no strict chronological sequence in the Torah. Scripture states, "And the Lord spoke unto Moses in the wilderness of Sinai, in the first month of the second year after they were come out of the land of Egypt, saying . . ." (Numb. 9:1). *Rashi*, commenting on "In the first month," writes that the section at the beginning of the Book of Numbers was not stated until the month of *Iyyar* and this *parashah* was said prior to that, in *Rosh Hodesh Nisan*. From this, we learn that there is no strict chronological sequence in the Torah. *Rashi* asks, "And why did it not begin with this section? Because it is a disgrace for Israel that all forty years that the Israelites were in the wilderness, they did not offer save this *paschal*—offering alone" (cf. Pes. 6b).

AYN ZAKAYN ELA HAKHAM (MI SHEKANAH HOKHMAH) (אין זקן (אלא חכם (מי שקנה חכמה). "A *Zakayn* can only refer to a Sage (he who has acquired wisdom)" (Kidd. 32b), for it is said, "Gather unto Me seventy men of the elders of Israel" (Numb. 11:16). From this phrase, we also learn that God has bestowed honor upon elders (*Sifri*). See MIPNAY SAYVAH TAKUM VEHADARTA PENAY ZAKAYN.

MOSHE ANAV ME'OD MIKOL HA'ADAM, AF MAYAVOT (משה עניו מאד מכל האדם, אף מאבות). "Moses was

very meek above all the men, even the Patriarchs" (*Sifri*, Beha'alotekha 12:3). *Rashi* (ad loc.) comments that he was humble and tolerant. The Talmud (Ned. 38a) records: "R. Johanan said: The Holy One, blessed be He, causes His Divine Presence to rest only upon him who is strong, wealthy, wise, and meek. . . . Meek, for it is written, 'Now the man Moses was very meek.'"

NUN HAFUKHAH (נון הפוכה). Literally, "an inverted [letter] *nun*." At the beginning (*Vayehi binso'a ha'aron*, "And it came to pass when the Ark set forward") and at the end (*rivavot alfay Yisrael*, "unto the ten thousands of the families of Israel"), two verses (*Bemidbar* 10:35–36) are preceded and followed by a reversed *nun*, which distinguishes and divorces the adjoining passages. The Talmud (Shab. 116a) states that this is to teach that this is not its place. Rabbi said because it ranks as a separate Book. "R. Simeon b. Gamliel said: This section is destined to be removed from here and written in its [right place]"—that is, in Numbers 2, which deals with the disposition of the Israelites according to their banners and their traveling arrangements. The Talmud asks, "And why is it written here?" And answers: In order to provide a break between the first [account of] punishment ("And they moved away from the mount of the Lord") (Numb. 10:33) and the second [account of] punishment ("And the people were as murderers") (Numb. 11:1)." These two verses serve as a relief from the gloomy effect that would otherwise be produced. In the future it will be inserted in its rightful place in the chapter on the banners.

SHO'ALIN VEDORSHIN BEHILKHOT HAPESAH KODEM HAPESAH SHELOSHIM YOM (שואלין ודורשין בהלכות הפסח קודם הפסח שלשים יום). "Questions are asked and lectures are given on the laws of Passover for thirty days before Passover" (Pes. 6a). The rea-

son for this is that Moses was standing on the First Passover and giving instructions about the Second Passover (for those who were unable to celebrate it at the proper time), as it is written, "Let the children of Israel keep the Passover at its appointed season" (Numb. 9:2) and it is written, "And there were certain men, who were unclean by the dead body of a man" (Numb. 9:6). The latter verse concerns Moses giving instructions about the Second Passover.

SHELAH (שלח)

HALOMAYD TORAH VE'AYNAH MELAMDAH ZEHU DEVAR HA-SHEM BAZAH (הלומד תורה ואינה מלמדה זהו דבר ה' בזה). The Talmud (San. 99a) states, "[R. Meir used to say:] He who studies the Torah but does not teach it, is alluded to in 'he hath despised the word of the Lord'" (Numb. 15:31). R. Johanan said: "One who studies the Torah but does not teach it is like the myrtle in the desert" (R.H. 23a), because no one enjoys its fragrance.

KOL DEVAR SHEKER SHE'AYN OMRIM BO KETZAT EMET BITHI-LATO AYN MITKAYAYM BESOFO (כל דבר שקר שאין אומרים בו קצת אמת בתחלתו אין מתקים בסופו). After forty days the spies returned from their mission of scouting the land of Canaan and reported, "and surely it floweth with milk and honey" (Numb. 13:27). Rashi comments in the name of Midrash Rabbah, "[They stated this because] every false thing regarding which there is not said some truth at first, it will not be established in the end." That is, any lie that does not begin with some truth will not endure. Therefore, the spies opened their malicious account with the undeniable truth that it is, indeed, "a land flowing with milk and honey" (cf. Sot. 35a).

RE'IYAH MAYVI'AH LIDAY ZEKHI-RAH (ראיה מביאה לידי זכירה). In Parashat Tziztit (Numb. 15:37–41) we say, "That ye may look upon it and remember . . . and do them." Looking (upon it) leads to remembering (the commandments); and remembering leads to doing them (Men. 43b).

ZEKHIRAH MAYVI'AH LIDAY MA'ASEH (זכירה מביאה לידי מעשה). See RE'IYAH MAYVI'AH LIDAY ZEKHIRAH.

KORAH (קרח)

ASHIRUT SHEL KORAH (עשירות של קרח). See RAYKH VI KORAH.

AYN MAHZIKIN BEMAHLOKET (אין מחזיקין במחלוקת). "One must not be unyielding [hardhearted] in a quarrel" (San. 110a). This is derived from the scriptural verse "And Moses rose up and went unto Dathan and Abiram" (Numb. 16:25). Moses disregarded his own pride and dignity and went to the rebels in an attempt to end the dispute.

AZ S'GEYT DI SEDRAH KORAH KUMEN OYF: KARSHN, RETEKH, KHREYN (אז ס'גייט די סדרה קרח קומען אויף: קארשן, רעטעך, כריין (חריין)). "When the portion of Korah is read, cherries, radish, and horseradish are fully grown." This whimsical expression possibly came into existence because the initial letters in KoRaH spell out karshn, retekh, and khreyn (the spelling of khreyn with a kaf was changed to a het). It is also probable that in this season of the year, when Korah is read, these edibles are fully grown and are harvested.

KINDER MEGADAYL TZU ZAYN MUZ MEN HUHBN KORAH'S ASHI-RUT UN SHIMSHON HAGIBOR'S GEVURAH (קינדער מגדל צו זיין מוז מען האבן קורח'ס עשירות און שמשון הגיבור'ס גבורה). "To raise children one

must possess Korah's wealth and Samson's heroic strength." Korah is reputed to be a possessor of extraordinary wealth, having discovered one of the treasures that Joseph had hidden in Egypt (Pes. 119a; San. 110a), and Samson is known for his strength, as the Talmud (Sot. 9b) states that he could uplift two mountains and rub them together like two clods of earth. See RAYKH VI KORAH.

RAYKH VI KORAH (ריֵיךְ ווי קרח). "Rich like Korah," an expression used when speaking of a wealthy person who is miserly.

Korah, who staged a revolt against the authority and status of Moses at the time of the wandering in the desert (Numb. 16), possessed extraordinary wealth. He is known to have discovered treasures that Joseph had hidden in Egypt. The keys of Korah's treasures (Korah's *Otzrot*, comments the Talmud) formed a load for three hundred mules (Pes. 119a; San. 110a). Korah's wealth (*Ashirut shel* Korah) was not the gift of Heaven and he perished on account of his greediness (*Numb. Rabbah* 22:7).

HUKAT (חֻקַּת)

AYN DIVRAY TORAH MITKAIMIN ELA BEMI SHEMAYMIT ATZMO ALEHAH (אֵין דברי תורה מתקיימין אלא במי שמֵמית עצמו עליה). Resh Lakish said, "The words of the Torah can endure only with him who sacrifices [kills] himself for it" (Ber. 63b; Shab. 83b), as it is said, "This is the Torah; when a man dieth in a tent" (Numb. 19:14). The word "tent" (*ohel*) is taken to mean, according to the *Midrash*, a place of learning, as is written, "and Jacob was a quiet man, dwelling in schools of religious study" (*yoshayv ohalim*). Concerning the same verse, R. Jonathan said: "One should never abstain from the *Bet Hamidrash* and from Torah, even in the hour of death" (Shab., ibid.).

MI SHEMEVAKSHIM MIMENU MEHILAH LO YEHAY AKHZARI MILIMHOL (מי שמבקשים ממנו מחילה לא יהא אכזרי מלמחול). "One from whom forgiveness is asked should not be so cruel as not to forgive" (*Rashi*, quoting *Tanhuma*, Numb. 21:7). This is derived from the incident in which the Israelites spoke against God and against Moses, saying, "Wherefore have ye brought us out of Egypt to die in the wilderness for [there is] no bread and [there is] no water and our soul loatheth this light bread" (Numb. 21:5). As a result, they were punished and many people died. Later the people came to Moses and said they had sinned because they had spoken against the Lord and Moses and asked him to pray to God. Moses readily forgave them and prayed for their deliverance. We learn, therefore, that when a man is asked to forgive, he must not cruelly refuse to do so.

SHIMU NA HAMORIM (שמעו נא המורים). "Hear now, ye rebels" (Numb. 20:10). The Lord instructed Moses to take the rod and speak to it before the Israelites, "so thou shalt bring forth to them water." Instead, Moses struck the rock and, because of this, God said to Moses and Aaron, "therefore ye shall not bring this assembly into the land which I have given them." Before Moses smote the rock, he and Aaron "gathered together the assembly before the rock and he said unto them, 'Hear now, ye rebels [hamorim], are we to bring you forth water out of this rock?" *Rashi* comments that the word used is *hamorim*, (which denotes) "ye rebels"; in the Greek language (it denotes) "fools"; they (presumed to) teach their teachers, or imagined themselves to be wiser than their leaders.

BALAK (בלק)

HUTZPA, AFILU KELAPAY SHEMAYA MAHANAY (חוצפא, אפילו כלפי שמיא מהניא). R. Nahman said:

"Impudence [hutzpa], even against Heaven, is of avail"; at first, it is written, "Thou shalt not go with them" (Numb. 22:12). Subsequently, it is said, "Rise up, and go with them" (Numb. 22:20) (San. 105a). God said to Balaam, "If thou art bound to go to thy destruction, do so." Balaam's insistence forced from God His consent for him to go. Thus, we learn that boldness will carry its point even against Heaven. See BE'IKVOT MESHIHA HUTZPA YISGAY VEYOKER YA'AMIR. See also HUTZPA.

IKH VEL MIT IM LERNEN BALAK

(איך וועל מיט אים לערנען בלק). Literally, "I will learn Balak with him," a remark meaning, "I will teach him a lesson." Balak, King of Moab, after learning that Israel had conquered the Amorites, feared an invasion. He invited Balaam to come and curse the Israelites, believing that they would be defeated. Instead, the Lord made Balaam bless Israel. Balak was taught the lesson that it is the Lord Who decides everything. When the expression *Ikh vel mit im lernen Balak* is used, it means that someone's actions are faulty or unfit, he cannot get away with it. He will be taught a lesson. It is God Who makes final decisions.

Another version of the saying is *Er lernt mit im Balak* ("He learns Balak with him"). Balak happens to be a difficult *Sidra*. Children were often hit by their *melamed* when they were unable to comprehend the text and, therefore, the expression was uttered whenever there was the capacity to understand any text.

LO MIDUVSHAYKH VELO MAYUKTZAYKH

(לא מדובשך ולא מעוקצך). "Neither your honey nor your sting" (*Rashi*, Numb. 22:12). *Rashi* quotes the *Midrash* on the phrase "Thou shalt not go with them" (Numb. 22:12): "[Balaam] said to Him: If so, let me curse them in the place where I stand; [the Lord] said to him: 'Thou shalt not curse the people.' [Balaam] said to Him: 'If so, I will bless

them.' [The Lord] said to him: 'They are not in need of your blessing; for they are blessed.' The proverb [states]: They say to the bee, '[We desire] neither your honey nor your sting.'"

MAH TOVU OHALEKHA YA'AKOV MISHKENOTEKHA YISRAEL (מה

טבו אהליך יעקב משכנתיך ישראל). "How goodly are thy tents, O Jacob; thy dwelling-places, O Israel!" (Numb. 24:5); a verse spoken by the wicked Balaam, an enemy of the Jews who was employed by the Moabite king Balak to curse Israel and who, instead, blessed them. Tradition explains the word "tents" (*ohalekha*) as an allusion to the Jews' synagogues and "dwellings" (*mishkenotekha*) to schools for religious instruction (San. 105b). In all other instances, his intentions (curses) were eventually fulfilled except those concerning the synagogues and schoolhouses, as these were destined never to disappear from Israel. As for its inclusion into the prayer service upon entering the synagogue prior to the morning service, see Macy Nulman, *Encyclopedia of Jewish Prayer* (Northvale, New Jersey/London: Jason Aronson Inc., 1993), pp. 233, 234.

MITOKH SHELO LISHMAH BA LISHMAH (מתוך שלא לשמה בא

לשמה). "For doing good with an ulterior motive, there comes doing good for its own sake." The Talmud (Pes. 50b; Sot. 22b) states that "a man should always occupy himself with Torah and good deeds." Despite his impure intentions and initial lack of interest, he will eventually do them with sincere motives. For example, as a reward for the forty-two sacrifices that Balak, king of Moab, offered (though he did not offer them for their own sake) (Numb. 23:1, 14, 29), he merited that Ruth should issue from him, and from her issued Solomon, of whom it is written (1 Kings 3:4) "A thousand burnt-offerings did Solomon offer" (Sot. 47a).

This expression is often used regarding anything a person does when his sincerity is questionable. See TORAH LISHMAH.

PINHAS (פנחס)

AVAR ZEMANO (YOMO) BATAYL KORBANO (עבר זמנו (יומו) בטל קרבנו). "If its time [day] passed, its offering is canceled" (cf. Rashi, Numb. 28:10, in the name of Sifre). The scriptural verse reads "[This is] the burnt-offering of Sabbath, of [every] Sabbath [beshabbato]." Rashi comments, "But not the burnt-offering of one Sabbath on another Sabbath. That is, in the event that he did not offer it on this Sabbath, I might think that he should offer two on the following Sabbath; [therefore] Scripture states, 'on its Sabbath,' informing us that if its day passed, its offering is canceled."

The colloquial expression is used every time a person does not do what he or she should do in its proper time.

AYN ADAM MITKANA BIVNO VETALMIDO (אין אדם מתקנא בבנו ותלמידו). See BEKHOL ADAM MITKANA HUTZ MIBNO VETALMIDO.

BEKHOL ADAM MITKANA HUTZ MIBNO VETALMIDO (בכל אדם מתקנא חוץ מבנו ותלמידו). "[R. Jose b. Honi said:] Of everyone a man is jealous, except his son and his disciple (San. 105b). His son—this is deduced from Solomon [David's servants were not fearful to wish Solomon a greater name than his own, since they knew he would not be jealous of his own son]. "His disciple"— [is deduced] if you like, say 'Let a double quantity of thy spirit be upon me' (2 Kings 11:9); or if you like, say from, 'And he laid his hands upon him and gave him a charge'" (Numb. 27:23). The latter alludes to Moses giving his spirit to Joshua.

Another variant of this expression is AYN ADAM MITKANA BIVNO VETALMIDO ("A person is not jealous of his son and his disciple").

BENAY KORAH LO MAYTU (בני קרח לא מתו). A proverbial folk saying, inferring that "rabble-rousers are always at work." Scripture states, "Notwithstanding, the sons of Korah died not" (Numb. 26:11). The Talmud comments, "A tanna taught: It has been said on the authority of Moses our master: A place was set apart for them in the Gehenna, where they sat and sang praises [to God]." Rashi (Numb., ibid.) comments that at first they were in the evil council but at the time of dispute they had thoughts in their hearts of repentence and thus there was set apart for them a high place in Gehenna.

To the sons of Korah are ascribed eleven psalms (42, 44–49, 84, 85, 87, and 88). According to Rashi, the sons of Korah are responsible for their composition. Another opinion is that they were composed by David to be performed by Korah's descendants, who were Levite singers in his time (Radak).

HETZYO LASHEM VEHETZYO LA-KHEM (חציו לה' וחציו לכם). ["R. Joshua said:] Divide it: [devote] half to God and to yourselves" (Pes. 68b). One verse says, "A solemn assembly to the Lord thy God" (Deut. 16:8), whereas another verse says, "There shall be a solemn assembly unto you" (Numb. 29:35). R. Joshua took this to mean "Divide it: [devote] half of it to eating and drinking, and half of it to the Bet Hamidrash." Thus, on the festival, rejoicing is not merely permitted but is a religious duty.

KATZON ASHER AYN LAHEM RO'EH (כצאן אשר אין להם רעה). "As sheep which have no shepherd" (Numb. 27:17). God instructs Moses to appoint a man (Joshua) over the congregation, "Who may go out before them, and who may lead them out, and who may bring

them in; that the congregation of the Lord be not as sheep which have no shepherd" (ibid.). See also 1 Kings 22:17; 2 Chron. 18:16.

The expression may be applied to any group of people who have no leadership and are therefore scattered and helpless, without direction or goals.

KAYN BENOT TZELAFHAD DOVROT (כן בנות צלפחד דברת). The daughters of Tzelafhad had argued: "Why should the name of our father be done away from among his family because he had no son? Give us a possession among the brethren of our father." God said to Moses, "The daughters of Tzelafhad speak right" (Numb. 27:7).

In a jocular manner, this may infer, "Don't argue with women, but do what they say!"

KOL HAHOLAYK AL RABO KE- HOLAYK AL HASHEKHINAH (כל החולק על רבו כחולק על השכינה). ["R. Hisda said:] Whoever contends against [the ruling of] his teacher [it] is as though he contended against the *Shekhinah*" (San. 110a), as it says, "when they strove against the Lord" (Numb. 26:9).

MATOT (מטות)

BELI NEDER (בלי נדר). "Without vow." The sacred and binding character of a vow is given in Scripture, Numbers 30:3: "When a man voweth a vow unto the Lord . . . he shall not break his word." Again, in Deuteronomy 23:24, Scripture states, "That which is gone out of thy lips thou shalt observe and do."

It is customary to recite a formula known as *Hatarat Nedarim* ("Annulment of Vows") before Rosh Hashanah and/or Yom Kippur. This formula is for vows that were made in the heart, either while awake or dreaming, which were then

forgotten and not kept (cf. Jacob Emden, *Bet Ya'akov*, p. 316).

The pious are careful, when obligating themselves to do something, to utter *Beli neder*. This is as if to say that they do not take it upon themselves as a vow but rather as a mere thought expressed in words.

KOL ADAM SHEKO'AYS, IM HA- KHAM HU HOKHAMATO MIS- TAKELET MIMENU (כל אדם שכועס, אם חכם הוא חכמתו מסתלקת ממנו). ["Resh Lakish said:] As to every man who becomes angry, if he is a Sage, his wisdom departs from him" (Pes. 66b). We learn this from Moses, for it is written, "And Moses was wroth with the officers of the host . . ." (Numb. 31:14). And it is written, "And Eleazar the priest said unto the men of war that went to the battle: This is the statute of the law which the Lord hath commanded Moses . . ." (Numb. 31:21). From this, it is deduced that since Moses became angry and his judgment was flawed, the law regarding the cleansing of vessels that had belonged to heathens became concealed from him (cf. *Rashi*, ad loc.).

LE'OLAM YASHLIM ADAM PARA- SHIYOTAV IM HATZIBBUR SHE- NAYIM MIKRA VE'EHAD TARGUM (לעולם ישלים אדם פרשיותיו עם הצבור שנים מקרא ואחד תרגום). "R. Huna b. Judah says, in the name of R. Ammi: A man should always complete his *parashot* together with the congregation, [reading] twice the Hebrew text and once the [Aramaic] *Targum*" (Ber. 8a, b). The Talmud continues, Even such verses as *Atarot* and *Dibon*, which are names that are not translated in the *Targum* (Numb. 32:3), for if one completes his *parashot* together with the congregation, his days and years are prolonged. This practice is known as MA'AVIR SIDRAH ZAYN ("reviewing the weekly portion"). The individual does this by cantillating with the *Te'amim* and then chanting the *Targum* in a similar cantillatory style. For a further study of this practice, see Macy Nulman, *Concise Encyclopedia of Jewish Music* (McGraw-Hill Book Company, 1975), p. 157.

MASAY (מסעי)

ARAY MIKLAT (ערי מקלט). Literally, "cities of refuge." Scripture (Numb. 35:9–15) tells of six cities that served as places to shelter anyone who might accidentally commit manslaughter. By fleeing into one of those cities, the person who committed the murder was protected against "life for a life" and was granted a fair trial (See also Josh. 20:1–9; Mak. 9bff.). The Torah states that the principle roads leading to the *aray miklat* should be kept open so that every fugitive would be able to find a refuge (Deut. 19:3). The unintentional manslayer remained in the city of refuge until the death of the *Kohen Gadol* (cf. Mak. 11a).

The expression *aray miklat* is used as a general term, meaning "a place to run away."

KOL TAYVAH SHETZERIKHAH LAMED BITHILATAH HITIL LAH HAKATUV HAY BESOFAH (כל תיבה שצריכה למ"ד בתחילתה הטיל לה הכתוב ה' בסופה). ["R. Nehemiah said:] In the case of every word which requires a *lamed* at the beginning, Scripture has placed a *hay* at the end" (Yeb. 13b). For example, "to Divlatayim" appears as "Divelataimah" (Numb. 33:47) instead of "Ledivlatayim." (Cf. the Talmud [ibid.] for other examples.)

MASA'OT (מסעות). Literally, "journeys" or "stages" (see Numb. 33); referring to the itinerary of forty-two stages by which the Israelites journeyed from Egypt to the Plains of Moab. The sentences are short and begin with *Vayisu* ("And they journeyed") and end with *vayahanu* ("and pitched"). They are read with the *shirah* melody, making it possible to read two sentences in succession. Each resting place in the forty-year journey serves not only as a memorial of historical interest, but is of deep religious significance.

The Book of Deuteronomy
ספר דברים

Devarim / דברים	69
Va'ethanan / ואתחנן	70
Aykev / עקב	72
Re'ayh / ראה	73
Shoftim / שפטים	74
Ki Taytzay / כי תצא	75
Ki Tavo / כי תבוא	76
Nitzavim / נצבים	77
Vayaylekh / וילך	78
Ha'azinu / האזינו	78
Vezot Haberakhah / וזאת הברכה	79

DEVARIM (דברים)

KERAV LEGABAY DEHINA VE'-IDAHAYN (קרב לגבי דהינא ואידהן).

The Lord's command toward the conquest of the Holy Land starts at Horeb. Scripture states, "Turn you and take your journey . . . as far as the great river, the river Euphrates" (Deut. 1:7). The river Euphrates is not really greater, but smaller, than the others (cf. Gen. 2:14), but its greatness is due to the fact that it is mentioned in connection with the Holy Land and anything connected with the Holy Land is great (cf. *Rashi* and *Maharsha*). Thus says Simeon b. Tarfon, *Kerav legabay dehina ve'idahayn* ("Go near a fat man, and be fat") (Shebu. 47b). *Rashi* (Deut., ibid.) compares this situation with touching a person smeared with oil; if you touch him, you, too, will become smeared with oil.

A similar expression in Yiddish is *Arum a fetn tuhp iz zikh gut tzu raybn* (lit., "It is good to rub against a greasy pot"), meaning, it is good to hang out with one who is wealthy, or one who has power or influence.

MAH BAYN HAKHAM LENAVON? NAVON DOMEH LESHULHANI TAGAR (מה בין חכם לנבון? נבון דומה לשלחני תגר).

Moses, no longer able to manage the large number of Israelites in moving ahead toward the conquest of the Holy Land, said to the Israelites, "Get you, from each of your tribes, wise men, and understanding, and full of knowledge, and I will make them heads over you" (Deut. 1:13). *Rashi* (ad loc.) asks: What is the difference between wise men [*hakhamim*, pl.] and understanding men [*nevonim*, pl.]? A wise man [*hakham*] resembles a wealthy money-changer; when people bring him *denars* to consider [that is, to exchange], he considers [and earns], and when they do not bring [them] to him, he [merely] sits and gazes. A *hakham* is the same; if he is told a wise thing, he

listens and understands, but if he is not told a wise thing, he doesn't seek out to know wisdom. An understanding man resembles a merchant money-changer [*navon domeh leshulhani tagar*]. When people bring him money to consider [to exchange], he considers, and when they do not bring it to him, he seeks about and brings [money] of his own. A *navon*, too, does likewise; if he is told a wise thing, he listens; if, however, he is not told a wise thing, he struggles in his own mind and comes up with something wise. In other words, the *hakham* is one who, when told a wise thing, understands what is told to him. A *navon* is one who understands how to innovate a wise thing himself.

The Talmud (Hag. 14a) expounds and states: NAVON ZEH HAMAYVIN DAVAR MITOKH DAVAR ("*Navon* [means] one who understands one thing from another"); that is, he is able to draw conclusions on the basis of the knowledge imparted to him.

The word *hakham* (lit., "wise" or "sage") is found in such statements as: AYZEHU TALMID HAKHAM? KOL SHESHO'ALIN OTO HALAKHAH BEKHOL MAKOM VE'OMERAH or AYZEHU HAKHAM? HARO'EH ET HANOLAD. The reason that the word *hakham* is always preceded by *talmid* (thus, TALMID HAKHAM (pl.), TALMIDAY HAKHAMIM) is because as long as he considers himself a student (*talmid*) in his own eyes, in that he still needs to study because the Torah is bottomless, he is a *hakham* ("a wise person"), but if he considers himself a *hakham* and no longer needs to study, he is neither a *hakham* nor a *talmid* (Rabbi Abraham Isaac Sperling, *Ta'amay Haminhagim*, in the name of *Yismah Moshe, Parashat Toldot*, sec. *Likutim* 84).

Spanish-Portuguese Jews use the title HAKHAM for the local rabbi. In responsa literature written c. 1235–c. 1310, the title *le-hakham Rabbi _____ (RaSHBa*, nos. 79, 395) is utilized. Turkish Jewry designated its chief rabbi as HAKHAM BASHI (*hakham*, meaning "sage" or "wise man," and *bashi*, "head" or "chief"). The expression was first used at the end of 1836 or the beginning of 1837. In Israel the title RISHON LE-ZION ("first of Zion") was given to the head of the Sephardic rabbis, a seat he holds in Jerusalem.

MISHNEH TORAH (משנה תורה). The oldest name of the fifth book of the Pentateuch, popularly known as *Devarim* ("Words"), after the initial phrase in the book. The name *Mishneh Torah* means "Repetition of the Law," of which *Deuteronomion* is the approximate Greek translation.

SHALOSH SHEL PURANUT (שלש של פרענות). Literally, "Three [*Haftarot*] of chastisement." During the three Sabbaths that intervene between the Fast of the Seventeenth of *Tammuz* and the Ninth of *Ab*, the prophetic portions that are read contain prophecies of rebuke. They are: Jer. 1:1–2:3; Jer. 2:4–28, 3:4, 4:1–2; and Isaiah 1:1–27. See SHEVA DENEHEMTA.

SHEVA DENEHEMTA (שבע דנחמתא). "Seven [*Haftarot*] of consolation." On the seven Sabbaths following *Tishah b'Ab*, seven prophetic readings of consolation and comfort are read from the Book of Isaiah. They are chapters 40, 49, 51, 54, 60, and 61.

A total of one hundred and forty-four verses are read in all Seven Consolation *Haftarot*, corresponding to the one hundred and forty-three verses of admonition that are contained in all the verses of admonition in the Torah. The verses of consolation exceed these of admonition by one.

The first Sabbath after the Ninth of *Ab* is called *Shabbat Nahamu* ("Sabbath of Consolation"). Its name is derived from the opening words in the prophetic portion for *Haftarah Va'ethanan, Nahamu, Nahamu Ami* ("Console, console My people") (Isa. 40). See SHALOSH SHEL PURANUT.

TEHIYAT HAMAYTIM MIN HATO-RAH (תחיית המתים מן התורה). "Resurrection of the dead is derived from the Torah" (San. 90b, 91b). A verse in Scripture reads, "Behold, I have set the land before you: go in and possess the land which the Lord swore unto your fathers, to Abraham, to Isaac, and to Jacob, to give unto them [*latayt lahem*] and to their seed after them" (Deut. 1:8). The verse does not read, "to give unto you" [*latayt lakhem*], but "to give unto them." From this, it is deduced that the concept of resurrection is derived from the Torah.

The thought of resurrection is expressed in the second benediction of the *Amidah*: "Blessed are You, Hashem, Who resurrects the dead [*mehayayh hamaytim*]. "The same idea appears in the Preliminary section of the *Shaharit* service: "Blessed art Thou, O Lord, Who restorest the soul of the dead."

VA'ETHANAN (ואתחנן)

GADOL HA'OSEH MAYAHAVAH YOTAYR MIN HA'OSEH MAYIRAH (גדול העושה מאהבה יותר מן העושה מיראה). R. Simeon b. Eleazar says: "Greater is he who acts from love than who acts from fear" (Sot. 31a). On the phrase *le'elef dor* ("to a thousand generations") (Deut. 7:9) *Rashi*, interpreting the Talmud, comments: But below (Deut. 5:10) it states *la'alafim* ("unto thousands of generations")? And answers: Here, where it is adjacent to "those that keep His commandments," it states "to a thousand," but where it is adjacent to "those that love Me," that is, those who act out of love, whose reward is greater, it states "to thousands."

GEDOLAH TEFILLAH YOTAYR MIMA'ASIM TOVIM (גדולה תפלה יותר ממעשים טובים). (R. Eleazar said:) "Prayer is more efficacious even than good deeds" (Ber. 32b). The Talmud continues, "for there was no one greater in good deeds than Moses our Master, and yet he was answered only after prayer, as it says,

'Speak no more unto Me' (Deut. 3:26), and immediately afterwards, 'Get thee up into the top of Pisgah'" (Deut. 3:27). Thus, we learn that although his good deeds did not avail to procure him permission to enter the land, prayer accomplished for him the vision of Pisgah.

HA'OMAYR AYN LO ELA TORAH AFILU TORAH AYN LO (האומר אין לו אלא תורה אפילו תורה אין לו). "Whosoever says that he has only [an interest in the study of the] Torah [that is, not in its observance], he has no [reward] even [for the study of the] Torah" (Yeb. 109b). Scripture said, "That ye may learn them and observe them" (Deut. 5:1), implying that whosoever is engaged in observance of the laws of the Torah is also regarded as being engaged in study, but whosoever is not engaged in observance is not regarded as being engaged in study.

HAVIVIN YISRAEL LIFNAY HAKADOSH BARUKH HU YOTAYR MIMALAKHAY HASHARAYT (חביבין ישראל לפני הקב"ה יותר ממלאכי השרת). "Israel is dearer to the Holy One, blessed be He, than the ministering angels." Whereas Israel sings praises to the Lord every hour, the ministering angels sing praises but once a day (or, according to others, periodically). And whereas Israel mentions the Name of God after every two words, as it is said, "Hear, O Israel, the Lord . . ." (Deut. 6:4), the ministering angels only mention the Name of God after every three words, as it is written, "Holy, Holy, Holy, the Lord of Hosts" (Isa. 6:3).

KOL HAMELAMAYD (BEN) BENO TORAH MA'ALAH ALAV HAKATUV KE'ILU KIBLAH MAYHAR HOREB (כל המלמד את (בן) בנו תורה מעלה עליו הכתוב כאילו קבלה מהר חורב). See KOL HAMELAMAYD ET BEN HAVAYRO TORAH, and so on.

LE'OLAM YESADAYR ADAM SHEVAKHO SHEL MAKOM VE'AHAR KAKH YITPALAYL (לעולם יסדר אדם שבחו של מקום ואח"כ יתפלל). (R. Simlai expounded:) "A man should always first recount the praise of the Holy One, blessed be He, and then pray" (Ber. 32a). This is derived from Moses, for it is written, "And I besought the Lord at that time" (Deut. 3:23ff.), and it continues, "O Lord God, Thou hast begun to show Thy servant Thy greatness and Thy strong hand; for what god is there in heaven and earth . . ." And then Moses says, "Let me go over, I pray Thee, and see the good land . . ." (Deut. 3:25).

Because of this, the Men of the Great Assembly instituted that the first three blessings of the *Amidah* (*Avot, Gevurot, Kedushat Hashaym*) should be blessings of praise and those that follow should be blessings of *tefillah*.

LE'OLAM YESHALAYSH ADAM SHENOTAV: SHLISH BEMIKRA, SHLISH BEMISHNAH, SHLISH BIGEMARA (לעולם ישלש אדם שנותיו: שליש במקרא, שליש במשנה, שליש בגמרא). (R. Safra said, on the authority of R. Hanania:) "One should always divide his years into three: [devoting] a third to *Mikra*, a third to *Mishnah*, and a third to Talmud" (Kidd. 30a). This is derived from the word *veshinantam*, in the verse "and thou shall teach them diligently [*veshinantam*] unto thy children" (Deut. 6:7); read not *veshinantam* but *veshilashtam* ["you shall divide into three"]. *Rashi* (ad loc.), quoting the *Sifre*, comments on the word *levanekha* ("unto thy children") that TALMIDIM KERUYIM BANIM, VEHARAV KARUI AV ("Disciples are termed children and the teacher is termed father"). The former is derived from "Ye are the children of the Lord your God" (Deut. 14:1); also from "The children [disciples] of the prophets that were at Beth-el" (2 Kings 2:3); and similarly with Hezekiah, who taught the Torah to all of Israel, and he called them

children, as it is stated, "My children, be not now negligent" (2 Chron. 29:11). A teacher is termed "father," as it is stated, "My father, my father, the chariots of Israel . . ." (2 Kings 2:12).

LO TOSIFU (לא תוסיפו). See KOL HA-MOSIF GORAYA.

SEKHAR MITZVAH BEHAI ALMA LEKA (שכר מצוה בהאי עלמא ליכא). (R. Jacob said): "There is no reward for precepts in this world" (Kidd. 39b). The Talmud cites R. Jacob's teaching that there is not a single precept in the Torah whose reward is stated at its side, which is not dependent on the resurrection of the dead (i.e., the next world). Thus, in connection with honoring parents, it is written, "that thy days be prolonged, and that it may go well with thee" (Deut. 5:16).

TALMIDIM KERUYIM BANIM, VEHARAV KARUI AV (תלמידים קרויים בנים, והרב קרוי אב). See LE'OLAM YESHALAYSH ADAM SHENOTAV, and so on.

YIRAT SHAMAYIM (יראת שמים). "The fear of God." It is written in Scripture, "Thou shalt fear the Lord thy God" (Deut. 6:13). Similarly, it is written, "Thou shalt not curse the deaf, nor put a stumbling block before the blind, but thou shalt fear thy God; I am the Lord" (Lev. 19:14). Job stated that God said to man, HAYN YIRAT HASHEM HI HOKHMAH, VESUR MAYRA BINAH ("Behold, the fear of the Lord, that is wisdom; and to depart from evil is understanding") (Job 28:28).

Great emphasis is placed on the fear of God, which depends on a person's own choice, as the Talmud cites R. Hanina's saying HAKOL BIDAY SHAMAYIM HUTZ MIYIRAT SHAMAYIM ("Everything is in the hands of Heaven except the fear of Heaven") (Ber. 33b). R. Akiba broadened the concept of fear of God to include scholars. The verse states, *Et Hashem Elohekha tira* ("Thou shalt fear the Lord, thy God"); the addi-

tional word *et* in the sentence instructs us to include scholars, since they are repositories of God's word (Pes. 22b). Likewise, the *Mishnah* (*Avot* 4:15) cites Rabbi Elazar, who preached that the "reverence for your teacher [should be] as the reverence of Heaven."

The request to fear God in daily living was incorporated into the Babylonian scholar Rav's supplication *Yehi Ratzon* ("May it be Thy will"), which he uttered daily upon the completion of the *Amidah* (Ber. 16b). It was adapted in the first half of the eighteenth century in the Polish rite, with variations, to be recited at *Birkat Hahodesh*. Here, *Yirat shamayim* appears twice: "a life in which there is fear of sin" and "a life in which we will have love of Torah and fear of Heaven."

AYKEV (עקב)

AMKHA (עמך). When referring to Jews, the word *amkha* ("Your people") is used, as in the phrase "destroy not Thy people [amkha], Thine inheritance" (Deut. 9:26). The term also took on the meaning "the common folk," "the masses," or "the ordinary people."

BIRKAT HAMAZON DE'ORAITA (ברכת המזון דאורייתא). See VE'AKHALTA VESAVATA UVAYRAKHTA.

HAKOL BIDAY SHAMAYIM HUTZ MIYIRAT SHAMAYIM (הכל בידי שמים חוץ מיראת שמים). (R. Hanina said): "Everything is in the hands of Heaven except the fear of Heaven" (Ber. 33b), as it says, "And now, Israel, what doth the Lord require of thee, but to fear the Lord, thy God" (Deut. 10:12). Man's moral character depends on his own choice; all his qualities are fixed by nature. See YIRAT SHAMAYIM.

HAYAV ADAM LEVARAYKH MAYAH BERAKHOT BEKHOL YOM (חייב אדם לברך מאה ברכות בכל יום). (It was taught: R. Meir used to say), "A man is bound to say one hundred blessings daily" (Men. 43b), as it is written, "And now, Israel, what doth the Lord thy God require of thee?" (Deut. 10:12). The word *mah* ("what") is interpreted as though it were written *mayah* ("one hundred") (cf. Tos., s.v. *Sho'ayl May'imakh*).

KESHAYH OREF (קשה ערף). A phrase meaning "obstinate" or "stubborn," as in *ki am keshay oref attah* ("for thou art a stiffnecked people") (Deut. 9:6). The expression "stiffnecked," implying "unbending" or "rigorous," stems from the idea of a stubborn ox that refuses to submit to the yoke. See also Ex. 32:9.

KOL ADAM SHEYASH BO GASOS HARU'AH KE'ILU KOFER BA'IKAR (כל אדם שיש בו גסוס הרוח כאלו כפר בעיקר). "Every man in whom is haughtiness of spirit is as though he had denied the fundamental principle [the existence of God]" (Sot. 4b), as it is said, "Thine heart be lifted up and thou forget the Lord, thy God" (Deut. 8:14).

LO AL HALEHEM LEVADO YIHYEH HA'ADAM (לא על הלחם לבדו יחיה האדם). "Man does not live by bread only" (Deut. 8:3). Scripture teaches that there is more to man's existence than food alone. Spiritual life is equally necessary to sustain man.

SHAKAYTZ TESHAKTZENU VETA'-AYV TETA'AVENU KI HAYREM HU (שקץ תשקצנו ותעב תתעבנו כי חרם הוא). Scripture states that you shall not bring an abomination (*to'ayvah*) into your house; "thou shalt utterly detest it, and thou shalt utterly abhor it, for it is banned" (Deut. 7:26). *To'ayvah* is a contemptuous term for an idolatrous image.

It was customary that whenever a Jew noticed anything in the nature of idolatry, he would utter the words *shakaytz teshaktzenu*, rejecting it as abominable and abhorrent. See A.Z. 46a, 47b.

RE'AYH (ראה)

KOL HAMERAHAYM AL HABERI-YOT MERAHAMIN ALAV MIN HASHAMAYIM (כל המרחם על הבריות מרחמין עליו מן השמים). "He who is merciful to others, mercy is shown to him by Heaven" (Shab. 151a). This is derived from the phrase "And He shall give [show] thee mercy and have compassion upon thee" (Deut. 13:18).

Another expression derived from the same phrase is *Kol hamerahaym al haberiyot beyadu'a shehu mizaro shel Avraham Avinu* ("Whoever is merciful to his fellow-man is certainly of the children of our father Abraham") (Bez. 32b). The verse (Deut. 13:18) ends with "unto thy fathers"—namely, the Patriarchs. Thus, if one lacks mercy, "unto thy fathers" cannot be applied to him.

LE'OLAM YEHAY KASPO SHEL ADAM MATZUI BEYADO (לעולם יהא כספו של אדם מצוי בידו). (R. Isaac said:) "One's money should always be ready to hand" (B.M. 42a), for it is written, "and thou shalt bind up the money in thy hand" (Deut. 14:25). The reasoning behind this is so that advantage can immediately be taken of a trading bargain that is available.

LO TITGODEDU, LO TA'ASU AGU-DOT AGUDOT (לא תתגודדו, לא תעשו אגודות אגודות). Scripture states, "Ye shall not cut yourselves" (Deut. 14:1)—that is, the Israelites were forbidden to gash themselves in their grief. Since the sentence begins with "Ye are children of the Lord your God," they were to regard bereavement as His decree and thus accept His decree.

The root of the word *titgodedu* is taken as *agad*, meaning "to bind," implying the homiletic interpretation that the Israelites should not form factions or separate groups or sects; a holy people must be a united people (cf. Yeb. 14a; *Sifri*).

LO TOSAYF ALAV VELO TIGRA MIMENU (לא תוסף עליו ולא תגרע ממנו). See KOL HAMOSIF GORAYA.

TEHAY HAVIVAH ALEKHA MITZVAH KALAH KEMITZVAH HAMURAH (תהא חביבה עליך מצוה קלה כמצוה חמורה). Regarding the warning against the eating of blood, Scripture states, "Observe and hear all these words which I command thee" (Deut. 12:28). *Rashi* (ad loc.), quoting in the name of *Sifre* concerning "all these words," said that a "light commandment should be cherished by you just as a difficult commandment."

SHOFTIM (שפטים)

BAL TASHHIT (בל תשחית). "Not to destroy, ruin, or spoil"; a prohibition of wasteful destruction of any sort. Scripture states, "When thou shalt besiege a city a long time, in making war against it to take it, thou shalt not destroy [lo tashhit] the trees thereof by wielding an axe against them" (Deut. 20:19). The Rabbis deduce from this verse the prohibition of destruction of natural resources, or of anything useful to man. "R. Simeon b. Eleazar said, in the name of Halfa b. Agra, in R. Johanan b. Nuri's name: He who rends his garments in his anger, he who breaks his vessels in his anger, and he who scatters his money in his anger, regard him as an idolator" (Shab. 105b; cf. ibid. 140b and 129a).

HASAGAT GEVUL (הסגת גבול). Literally, "removal of landmarks." Stones or heaps of stones were used in ancient days to define the boundary of a man's field. Their removal, in order to enlarge one's own estate, was considered theft. In Deuteronomy 19:14 it is said, "Thou shalt not remove thy neighbor's landmark, which they of old time have set." Moreover, Scripture declares: "Cursed be he that removes his neighbor's landmark; and all

the people shall say *Amen*" (Deut. 27:17). *Hasagat gevul* took on new dimensions in later times. It was extended to include unfair encroachment upon another man's honor, livelihood, or activity. R. Yehudah he-Hassid wrote that the declaration "Thou shalt not remove thy neighbor's landmark" even applies to the fixed melodies for scriptural readings. One should not read the Torah with the cantillation of *Nevi'im* or *Ketuvim*, or read *Nevi'im* with the cantillation of Torah or *Ketuvim*, or read *Ketuvim* with Torah or *Nevi'im* cantillation, based on each being Sinaitic in origin (*Sefer Hasidim*, par. 302).

LO TASIG GEVUL RAYAKHA (לא תסיג גבול רעך). See HASAGAT GEVUL.

TALMUD MAYVI LIDAY YIRAH, VEYIRAH- LIDAY SHEMIRAH, USHEMIRAH - LIDAY MA'ASEH (תלמוד מביא לידי יראה ויראה-לידי שמירה, ושמירה-לידי מעשה). Scripture defines the selection, the qualifications, and the duties of the king in governing the people. Among other attributes, he himself was to study and obey the laws. "And it shall be with him, and he shall read therein all the days of his life; that he may learn to fear the Lord his God, to keep all the words of this law and their statutes, to do them" (Deut. 17:19). The *Sifri* (ibid.) comments on this and says, "Study brings one to fear, fear leads to observance, and observance results in action."

TZEDEK TZEDEK TIRDOF (צדק צדק תרדף). It is written in Scripture, "Justice, justice shall you pursue" (Deut. 16:20). The repetition of the word "justice" indicates the necessity of stricter investigation than is implied by the single use of the word (cf. San. 32b).

When a case results in an unjustified decision, the meaning of the statement is distorted and a sarcastic remark is sometimes made: "You should chase out [drive away] justice." The word *tirdof*, as it is used here, is derived from *radaf*, meaning "to chase."

UVI'ARTA HARA MIKIRBEKHA (ובערת הרע מקרבך). Scripture (Deut. 17:2–7) prescribes punishment when idolatry is detected and concludes, "and thou shalt put away the evil from the midst of thee" (Deut. 17:7).

This biblical expression is often uttered when detecting some foreign influence that is contrary to Torah-true Judaism.

YIFTAH BEDORO KISHMUEL BE-DORO (יפתח בדורו כשמואל בדורו). "Jephthah in his generation [was to be regarded] as Samuel in his generation" (*Rashi*, Deut. 19:17). Commenting on the scriptural phrase "That shall be in those days" (ibid.), the Talmud (R.H. 25b) states that Jephthah in his generation is like Samuel in his generation, in order to teach you that the most worthless person, once he has been appointed as a leader of the community, is to be accounted as the mightiest of the mighty. Jephthah was a judge in his time, as Samuel was a judge in his time, even though Samuel was greater than Jephthah. This teaches that we must accept the authority of office, be its holder great or small. See TA'ALA VE'IDANAYH SEGID LAYH.

KI TAYTZAY (כי תצא)

ANI VE'EVYON (עני ואביון). Two Hebrew words meaning "poor and needy," as in "Thou shalt not oppress a hired servant that is poor [*ani*] and needy [*evyon*]" (Deut. 24:14).

Of the two Hebrew words, the *evyon* is more desperate than the *ani*. A verse in *Ayshet Hayil* (Prov. 31:20) reads *Kapah parsah le'ani, veyadeha shilhah la'evyon* ("She stretches out her palm to the poor; she reaches forth her hands to the needy"). To the *ani* she uses one hand, but to the *evyon*, two hands; thus she recognizes that the *evyon* needs more than a

helping hand (cf. Rabbi Shelomoh Wertheimer, *Bayur Shaymot Hanirdafim Shebe-TaNaKH* [New York], 1953). In spite of this, the Talmud (B.M. 111b) states that since *ani* precedes *evyon* in the verse, the *ani* is paid his day's wages prior to the *evyon*. The rationale for this is that the *evyon* is a desirous person who, in his utter destitution—which is greater than that of an *ani*—longs for everything. In his longing, he is not ashamed to ask, which an *ani* is too proud to do.

In Yiddish, one usually uses the expression *Er iz an ani ve'evyon* ("He is poor and needy"). See ANI HASHUV KEMAYT.

BAYN SORAYR UMOREH (בן סורר ומורה). "A stubborn and rebellious son" (Deut. 21:18). Scripture states that this disobedient son can be brought by his parents to the elders of the city and they can stone him to death. The *Mishnah* (San. 8) lays down the age limit within which the term "son" is applicable and the conditions that must be fulfilled before he can be stoned.

The Talmud (San. 71a) comments that in the biblical sense, regarding execution, "There never has been a 'stubborn and rebellious son' and never will be." Why, then, was the law written, asks the Talmud? And answers, "That you may study it and receive reward."

In Jewish community life, when a person is disobedient and does not listen to authority, the appellation *Bayn sorayr umoreh* is sometimes applied to him.

DARKO SHEL ISH LAHZOR AL ISHAH VE'AYN DARKAH SHEL ISHAH LAHZOR AL ISH (דרכו של איש לחזר על אשה ואין דרכה של אשה לחזר על איש). "It is the way of a man to go in search of a woman, but it is not the way of a woman to go in search of a man" (Kidd. 2b). This is inferred from the biblical verse "When a man taketh a wife" (Deut. 22:13, 24:1). The Talmud compares this to a person who loses an article; it is the loser who goes in search of the

article—meaning that man, having lost his rib, seeks to recover it.

LE'OLAM YEVAKAYSH ADAM RAHAMIM SHELO YEHALEH (לעולם יבקש אדם רחמים שלא יחלה).

(R. Isaac the son of Reb Judah said:) "Let one always pray for mercy not to fall sick" (Shab. 32a). If he falls sick, he is told, Show thy merits and be quit. This is derived, according to Mar Ukba, from the verse, "If any man fall from *mimenu*" (Deut. 22:8). It is "from him" (*mimenu*) that proof of merit must be brought so that he be entitled to recover.

MOTZA SEFATEKHA TISHMOR (מוצא שפתיך תשמר).

"That which is gone out of thy lips thou shalt observe" (Deut. 23:24). This precept warns one to keep the word or promise one has made.

The Talmud (R.H. 6a) comments, concerning "That which is gone out of thy lips," that it is an affirmative precept and that "Thou shalt observe" is a negative precept. *Rashi* explains negativism as, Do not be late in fulfilling your own words, according to the rule laid down by R. Abin, in the name of Ila'a, who said: "Whenever there occur in Holy Writ the expressions 'take heed' ('observe' or 'keep'), 'lest,' or 'do not,' they are negative precepts" (Men. 99b).

TZA'AR BA'ALAY HAYYIM (צער בעלי חיים).

Literally, "the suffering or cruelty to animals." The Torah stresses the needs and feelings of animals, as is written, "Thou shalt not muzzle the ox when he treadeth out the corn" (Deut. 25:4). It is cruelty to excite the animal's desire for food and to prevent its satisfaction. This prohibition applies to all animals employed in labor, and not to the ox alone. According to the Talmud (Shab. 128b; B.M. 32b), "[The avoidance of] suffering of dumb animals is a biblical law." For other laws concerning protection of animals, see Exodus 20:10; Leviticus 22:28; and Deuteronomy 5:14 and 22:10.

VEYATAYD TIHYEH LEKHA AL AZAYNEKHA (ויתד תהיה לך על אזנך).

Concerning the holiness of the camp, Scripture states, "And thou shalt have a peg among thy implements" (Deut. 23:14) and concludes that you shall dig with it "and cover that which cometh from thee." Bar Kappara expounded on this phrase: *al tikray azaynekha* ("do not read thy implements") *ela al oznekha* (but "upon thy ear"); this means to say that if a man hears an unworthy thing, he shall plug his ears with his finger. This is similar to what R. Eleazar said concerning the fingers of man; they resemble pegs and each one has been made for its own purpose. And why are the fingers pointed like pegs? The reason is that if a man hears an unworthy thing, he shall plug his fingers into his ears. According to the school of R. Ishmael, the whole ear is hard and the earlobe soft, so that if something unworthy is heard, one should bend one's earlobe into it. Thus, the ear will become closed (Ket. 5a, b).

KI TAVO (כי תבוא)

AYN HATORAH NIKNIT ELA BEHAVURAH (אין התורה נקנית אלא בחבורה).

"The knowledge of the Torah can be acquired only in association with others" (Ber. 63b). This, according to the Talmud, is derived from the rare word *haskayt* (Deut. 27:9), implying: Make yourselves into groups (*kitot*) to study the Torah.

This same word, according to the Talmud (ibid.), teaches LE'OLAM YILMOD ADAM TORAH VE'AHAR KAKH YEHGEH ("A man should always first learn Torah and then scrutinize it"). One should listen first to the teacher, and then discuss what he has said. This meaning is also understood in *Haskayt ushema Yisrael* ("Keep silence, and hear, O Israel") (Deut. 27:9): Be silent (*has*) and then discuss (*katayt*).

From the letters in the same two words, *HaSKayT USheMA*, it is deduced that one is not permitted to interrupt in the following prayer recitals: *Hallel, keri'at Sefer Torah, bebirkat Kohanim, behanahat Tefillin, be'amirat Vidui, beteki'at Shofar bikri'at Megillah*, and *sefirat Omer* (cf. Abraham of Przemayl [Premsla], *Matteh Moshe*, par. 810, in the name of Saadia Gaon).

KOL HA'OSAYK BATORAH NEKHA-SAV MATZLIHIN LO (כל העוסק בתורה נכסיו מצליחין לו). "Whosoever occupies himself with the Torah, his possessions shall prosper" (A.Z. 19b), as is written, "Observe therefore the words of this covenant, and do them, that ye may make all that ye do to prosper" (Deut. 29:8). This same thought is repeated in the Prophets (Josh. 1:8) and a third time in Hagiographa (Ps. 1:2–3).

KOL RAM: BEKOLO SHEL RAM (קול רם: בקולו של רם). The ceremony of the solemn blessing and doom was antiphonal in character; the Levites speaking and the people responding with an *Amen*. Scripture (Deut. 27:14) states, "And the Levites shall speak, and say unto all the men of Israel with a loud voice [*kol ram*]." The Jerusalem Talmud (Sot. 7:2) interprets the phrase *kol ram* to mean *bekolo shel ram* ("With the voice that sits on high"), signifying that God is in agreement.

LE'OLAM YILMOD ADAM TORAH VE'AHAR KAKH YEHGEH (לעולם ילמוד אדם תורה ואחר כך יהגה). See AYN HATORAH NIKNIT ELA BEHAVURAH.

MAKAH ASHER LO KATUV (מכה אשר לא כתוב). "A plague which is not written" (Deut. 28:61). In the section of Scripture called "The Warnings," there are the curses declaring what God would bring upon Israel in the event of complete apostasy. Scripture states, "Also every sickness, and every plague, which is not written in the book of the law, them will

the Lord bring upon thee, until thou be destroyed" (ibid.).

Colloquially, the phrase is sometimes used to describe a horrible situation that engulfs a person or persons.

TEHAY YETZI'ATKHA MIN HA'OLAM KEVI'ATKHA LE'OLAM— BELO HAYT (תהא יציאתך מן העולם—כביאתך לעולם—בלא חטא). "Your exit from the world shall be as your entry therein; just as you entered it without sin, so may you leave it" (B.M. 107a). This interpretation is given for the verse in Scripture "Blessed shall thou be when thou cometh in, and blessed shalt thou be when thou goest out" (Deut. 28:6).

NITZAVIM (נצבים)

HAYAV ADAM LILMOD ET BENO LASHUT AL HAMAYIM, VE'IM LO LAMDO HAYAV LILMOD ET ATZMO (חייב אדם ללמד את בנו לשוט על המים. ואם לא למדו חייב ללמד את עצמו). "It is compulsory for a man to teach his son to swim [float] in water, and if he does not teach him, it is obligatory for him to learn himself" (Jer. Tal., Kidd. 1:7). This is derived from "that thou mayest live, thou and thy seed" (Deut. 30:19). Moreover, his life may depend on it (See Bab. Tal., Kidd. 30b).

HAYAV ADAM LILMOD ET BENO UMANUT, VE'IM LAV HAYAV LILMOD ET ATZMO (חייב אדם ללמד את בנו אומנות. ואם לאו חייב ללמד את עצמו). "It is compulsory for a man to teach his son a craft, and if he wasn't taught, it is obligatory for him to teach himself" (Jer. Tal., Kidd. 1:7). This is derived from the scriptural verse "that thou mayest live, thou and thy seed" (Deut. 30:19).

The Babylonian Talmud (Kidd. 30b) specifies that a means of livelihood may include business as well.

VAYAYLEKH (וילך)

AF AL PI SHEHAYNIHO LO AVOTAV LE'ADAM SEFER TORAH, MITZVAH LIKHTOV MISHELO

(אף על פי שהניחו לו אבותיו לאדם ס"ת, מצוה לכתוב משלו). (Rabbah said:) "Even if one's parents have left him a *Sefer* Torah, yet it is proper that he write one of his own" (San. 21b), as it is written, "Now therefore write ye this song [*Ha'azinu*] (Deut. 32:1–43) for you" (Deut. 31:19). In order to fulfill this *mitzvah*, it has become customary for the *Sofer* who completes the writing of the Torah to leave the final sentences of the Torah in outline. At the *Siyum*, the letters in those sentences are filled in by different individuals, who thereby symbolically take part in writing a *Sefer* Torah.

HAKHAYL (הקהל). Literally, "Assemble"; the opening word in Deuteronomy 31:12, signifying an assembly of men, women, children, and the "stranger that is within your gates." The purpose is "that they may hear, and that they learn, and fear the Lord your God, and to observe to do all the words of this teaching." *Rashi*, quoting the Talmud (Hag. 3a), comments that the men were assembled "to learn," the women "to hear," and the children "to cause recompense to those who bring them."

The event took place "At the end of every seven years, in the set time of the year of release, at the Feast of Tabernacles" (Deut. 31:10). The reading was done, according to the *Mishnah*, by the King (Sot. 7:6). The ceremony of *Hakhayl* has recently been revived symbolically in Israel.

HAZAK VE'EMATZ (חזק ואמץ). "Be strong and of good courage" (Deut. 31:7; 1 Chron. 22:13). Moses gave this instruction to Joshua in the presence of all Israel, saying, "for thou shalt go with this people

into the land which the Lord hath sworn unto their fathers to give to them."

The Talmud (Ber. 32b) states, "Our Rabbis taught: Four things require to be done with energy [vigor], namely, [study of] the Torah, good deeds, praying, and one's worldly occupation. Whence do we know this of Torah and good deeds? Because it says, 'Only be strong [*rak hazak*] and very courageous [*ve'ematz me'od*] to observe, to do according to all the law' (Josh. 1:7); 'be strong' in Torah, and 'be courageous' in good deeds" (cf. also Josh. 1:18).

The phrase *hazak ve'ematz* became a wish to be given to a person for welfare or good fortune, and so on. *Payyetanim* ("poets") of the Middle Ages would often append *hazak ve'ematz* after their names, which appeared in an acrostic form. For example, Gershom b. Judah (960–1028) of France and Germany, known as *Me'or Hagolah* ("Light of the Exile"), appends the phrase after his name in the supplication recited in the *Selihot* on the Fast of Gedalia, *Geroni Nihar Zo'ayk* (cf. Macy Nulman, *The Encyclopedia of Jewish Prayer* [Northvale, New Jersey: Jason Aronson Inc., 1993], p. 141). See HAZAK HAZAK VENITHAZAK: HAZAK UVARUKH.

KOHEN KORAY RISHON VE'AHARAV LEVI (כהן קורא ראשון ואחריו לוי). "A priest [*Kohen*] is called up first to read the Torah and after him a Levite [*Levi*]" (Git. 59a). This, according to R. Mattenah, is because Scripture says, "And Moses wrote this law, and delivered it unto the priests, the sons of Levi" (Deut. 31:9).

HA'AZINU (האזינו)

AD SHE'OL TAHTIT (עד שאול תחתית). "Unto the depths of the nether-world" (Deut. 32:22). The word *She'ol*, according to the belief of ancient peoples, was a resting place for the dead and it is sometimes translated as "grave."

The phrase appears in the four-stanza *Pizmon, Ezkerah Elohim*, recited in the Ashkenazic rite at *Ne'ilah*, at the *Selihot* for the fifth penitential day, and on *Ta'anit BeHaB*. A line in the poem reads, *ve'ir ha-Elohim mushpelet ad she'ol tahtiyah* ("while the city of God is degraded to the nethermost depth").

When reaching bottom, a person will sometimes utter the phrase with a sigh.

SHELOSHAH SHE'AKHLU KE'E-HAD HAYAVIN LEZAMAYN (שלשה שאכלו כאחד חייבין לזמן). "Three who eat together should invite one another to say grace" (Ber. 45a). This is derived from the verse "For I will proclaim the name of the Lord; ascribe ye greatness unto our God" (Deut. 32:3).

VAYISHMAN YESHURUN VAYIVAT (וישמן ישורון ויבעט). "But Yeshurun [from *yashar*, 'to be righteous'] waxed fat and kicked" (Deut. 32:15). The statement is used ironically as a rebuke to Israel's ingratitude and faithlessness. The Talmud states, "This bears out the popular saying *Melay keraysayh zenay bishay* ('A full stomach is a bad sort')."

The expression *Vayishman yeshurun vayivat* is generally applied to a person who becomes ungrateful after acquiring riches and importance.

VEZOT HABERAKHAH (וזאת הברכה)

AD MAYAH VE'ESRIM SHANAH (עד מאה ועשרים שנה). "Until a hundred and twenty years." Scripture states, "And Moses was a hundred and twenty years old when he died; his eye was not dim, nor his natural force abated" (Deut. 34:7). When wishing someone long life, the phrase *ad mayah ve'esrim shanah*, the traditional Jewish wish, is used.

Although generations earlier the average life span was much longer, by Moses'

generation it was reduced and 120 years became the norm (cf. R. Shmuel Yerushalmi, *The Torah Anthology-Me Am Lo'ez*, trans. by R.E. Touger, [New York/Jerusalem: Moznaim Publishing Corporation]).

Other luminaries who lived 120 years were R. Johanan b. Zakai (R.H. 31b), Hillel, and R. Akiba (*Sifri*). See TIZKEH LESHANIM RABOT.

AYN HA'OLAM MITKAYAYM ELA BISHVIL MI SHEMAYSIM ATZMO KEMI SHE'AYNO (אין העולם מתקיים אלא בשביל מי שמשים עצמו כמי שאינו). "The world exists only on account of [the merit of] him who makes himself as if he were nonexistent" (Hul. 89a); for it is written, "And underneath are the everlasting arms" (Deut. 33:27)—that is, those who are underneath (the humble) are the arms (support) of the world.

KOL HAME'ANAYG ET HASHAB-BAT NITZUL MISHIBUD MAL-KHUYOT (כל המענג את השבת נצול משעבוד מלכיות). "He who delights in the Sabbath is saved from the servitude of the Diaspora" (Shab. 118b). This is derived from the following biblical verses: Isaiah 58:13–14, where it is written, "and call the Sabbath a delight . . . and I will cause thee to ride upon the high places," and Deuteronomy 33:29, where it is written, "And thou shalt tread upon their high places."

LO KAM NAVI OD BEYISRAEL KE-MOSHE (לא קם נביא עוד בישראל כמשה). "There hath not risen a prophet since in Israel like unto Moses" (Deut. 34:10). This is reiterated in the "Thirteen Principles of Faith," based upon the formulation of *Rambam* (Maimonides) in his *Commentary to Mishnah* (*Sanhedrin* 10), "I believe with complete faith that the prophecy of Moses our teacher, peace upon him, was true, and that he was the father of the prophets—both those who preceded him and those who followed

him" (principle 7). It appears again paraphrased in the medieval hymn *Yigdal*, composed by the *Dayyan* ("Judge"), Daniel b. Yehudah, in fourteenth-century Rome: "In Israel none like Moses arose again—a prophet who perceived His vision clearly. God gave His people a Torah of truth, by means of His prophet, the most trusted of His household."

About the *Rambam* (Moses Maimonides), a similar expression was uttered, MI-MOSHE VE'AD MOSHE LO KAM KEMOSHE ("There had not risen from Moshe to Moshe another like Moshe"). The *Rambam* was held in such esteem that he was referred to as the "second Moses." Another expression used in the same manner is that of the Hebrew poet Yisrael (ben Moshe of Najara, 1555–1628), of whom it was said, *Lo kam be-Yisrael ke-Yisrael* ("There will not rise another Yisrael like Yisrael"). He is known for composing some 450 *Zemirot*, among them the popular *Ka ribbon alam ve'almaya* ("O Creator, Master of this world and all worlds").

PROPHETS
AND HAGIOGRAPHA
(In Alphabetical Order)

נביאים וכתובים

A'ALEH ET YERUSHALAYIM AL ROSH SIMHATI (אעלה את ירושלים על ראש שמחתי). "I will elevate Jerusalem above my chiefest joy" (Ps. 137:6). Jerusalem is foremost, no matter what the occasion of personal happiness (Ibn Ezra, ad loc.). The first part of the sentence reads, "Let my tongue cleave to the roof of my mouth if I remember thee not." The destruction of Jerusalem must be remembered on any joyful occasion.

This idea gave rise to the custom of a bridegroom placing ashes on his head prior to the marriage ceremony, as well as breaking a glass at the conclusion of the ceremony.

AD MATAI? (עד מתי?). "Until when?", as in ad matai lo yukhlu nikayon ("How long will it be before they attain innocence?") (Hos. 8:5).

AD MATAI ELOHIM YEHAREF TZAR, YENA'AYTZ OYAYV SHIMKHA LANETZAH (עד מתי אלהים יחרף צר, ינאץ אויב שמך לנצח). "How long, O God, shall the adversary reproach? Shall the enemy blaspheme Thy Name forever?" (Ps. 74:10).

ADAM LAHEVEL DAMAH, YAMAV KETZAYL OVAYR (אדם להבל דמה, ימיו כצל עובר). "Man is like a breath; his days are like a passing shadow" (Ps. 144:4).

ADAM LE'AMAL YULAD (אדם לעמל יולד). "Man was born to labor" ("toil") (Job 5:7), as in Eccl. 2:11, uve'amal she'amalti ("and on the labor that I labored").

R. Eleazar concluded that by the phrase Adam le'amal yulad is meant le'amal ba-Torah ("One was created to labor in the Torah") (San. 99b). The Maharsha offers a homiletical etymology that the word LeAMaL is composed of the initial letters Lilmod Al Menat Lelamayd ("to learn for the purpose of teaching").

AHOR VAKEDEM TZARTANI (אחור וקדם צרתני). "Thou hast hemmed me in behind and before" (Ps. 139:5), meaning, I am always in Your Hand and cannot escape without Your consent.

AHOZ BEKARNOT HAMIZBAYAH (אחוז בקרנות המזבח). "And it was told to Solomon, saying, behold, Adoniyahu fears King Solomon: for, lo, he has caught hold on the horns of the altar" (ahoz bekarnot hamizbayah) (1 Kings 1:51).

The expression suggests a person who is holding onto something dear and expensive in order to save his life by it.

AKHOL VESHATO KI MAHAR NAMUT (אכול ושתו כי מחר נמות). "Let us eat and drink for tomorrow we shall die" (Isa. 22:13). This phrase conveys the sentiment: Let us enjoy the present and trust as little as possible to the future.

AL TAGIDU VEGAT (אל תגידו בגת). "Tell it not in Gat" (2 Sam. 1:20). When the news of the defeat of Mount Gilboa reached David and he eulogized over Saul and Jonathan, he said not to speak of this happening in Gat (a city of Philistia) nor publish it in the streets of Ashkelon, lest the daughters of the Philistines rejoice and triumph.

The expression Al tagidu vegat took on the meaning "Don't spread the news in the street." (The word gas in Yiddish means "street".)

AL TASHLIKHAYNI LE'AYT ZIKNAH (אל תשליכני לעת זקנה). "Cast me not off in the time of old age" (Ps. 71:9). This request is the prayer of an old man (David or Jeremiah) who, in declining health and strength, which made him more exposed to the attacks of the wicked, pleaded for God's protection.

The verse appears in the plural (tashlikhaynu) in the Selihot of the Ashkenazic rite. This verse, as well as the adjacent ones in the prayer, are recited with much intensity and fervor. See AL TASHLIKHAYNU LE'AYT ZIKNAH.

AL TIVTEHU VINDIVIM, BEVEN ADAM SHE'AYN LO TESHU'AH

אל תבטחו בנדיבים. בבן אדם שאין לו) (תשועה. "Put not your trust in princes, nor in the son of man, in whom there is no help" (Ps. 146:3). The psalmist indicates that human aid often proves to be a broken reed.

AL YITHALAYL HAGIBOR BIGVU-RATO

(אל יתהלל הגבור בגבורתו). "Let not the mighty man glory in his might" (Jer. 9:22).

AL YITHALAYL HOGAYR KIMFA-TAYAH

(אל יתהלל חגר כמפתח). "Let not him that girds his harness boast himself as he that takes it off" (1 Kings 20:11). This is the message that the king of Israel, Ahav, sent to Ben-Hadad, the king of Amram, when he threatened to send his servants to take Ahav's choicest possessions.

The statement he made was that the person who girds his harness and is going to war should not boast, because he does not know if he will return victorious; but the person who is removing his gird may boast, because he came from battle and was victorious.

The English equivalent is "Don't count your chickens before they are hatched."

ALAI YAHSHEVU RA'AH LI

(עלי יחשבו רעה לי). "Against me do they devise my harm" (Ps. 41:8). This psalm has been labeled "A sufferer's prayer"; that is, at a time of sickness the person's suffering is heightened by the plotting of enemies.

ANI LEDODI VEDODI LI

(אני לדודי ודודי לי). "I am my beloved's and my beloved is mine" (S.O.S. 6:3). The initial letters of each word read ELUL, the month prior to Rosh Hashanah. It is incumbent upon all to prepare themselves with teshu-vah (repentance), prayer, and charity thirty days before Rosh Hashanah, the day when one stands in judgment before God. If Israel will long to turn in a complete teshuvah to their Father Who is in Heaven, then His longing will go out to them, and He will accept them in teshuvah (R. Moses b. Abraham of Przemsyl [Premsla], Matteh Moshe, sec. 5; Inyan Rosh Hodesh Elul ve-Rosh Hashanah, p. 247; see also Abudraham, who attributes this interpretation to various preachers).

ANI VE'AFSI OD

(אני ואפסי עוד). "I am, and none else beside me" (Isa. 47:8; ibid., 47:10). Isaiah bitterly attacks pagan practices, and prophesied the destruction of Babylon. The text reads: "For thou hast trusted in thy wickedness: thou has said, none sees me. Thy wisdom and thy knowledge, it has perverted thee, and thou hast said in thy heart, I am, and none else beside me. Therefore shall evil come upon thee . . . and ruin shall come upon thee suddenly" (Isa. 47:10–11).

The consequences are ill-fated when one says Ani ve'afsi od.

ARAYLAH OZNAM VELO YUKHLU LEHAKSHIV

ערלה אזנם ולא יוכלו) (להקשיב. Thus says the Lord of Hosts . . . "Their ear is uncircumcised, and they cannot hear" (Jer. 6:10); that is, their ear is clogged. "The word of the Lord is unto them [the Israelites] a reproach; they have no delight in it."

ARZAY HALEVANON

(ארזי הלבנון). "The Cedars of Lebanon" (Isa. 2:13, 14:8); an appellation for the Torah scholars. Just as this tree is very tall, so are the Torah scholars above the people. They stand as the lofty of the world and are described by the psalmist ke'erez balevanon yisgeh ("like a cedar in Lebanon he will grow tall") (Ps. 92:13).

Arzay Halevanon are the initial words of a Kinah recited in the Ashkenazic tradition on Tishah b'Ab morning (see Macy Nulman, The Encyclopedia of Jewish Prayer

[Northvale, N.J.: Jason Aronson Inc., 1993], p. 37).

ASAYH IMI OT LETOVAH (עשה עמי אות לטובה). "Display for me a sign for good" (Ps. 86:17). In this verse, the person asks God to work on his behalf and provide a visible manifestation of Divine favor.

ASHRAY HAGOY ASHER HASHEM ELOHAV (אשרי הגוי אשר ה' אלהיו). "Happy is the nation whose God is the Lord" (Ps. 33:12).

ASHRAY KOL HOSAY VO (אשרי כל חוסי בו). "Happy are all they that take refuge in Him" (Ps. 2:12).

ASHRAY NESUI PESHA KESUI HATA'AH (אשרי נשוי פשע כסוי חטאה). "Happy is he whose transgression is forgiven, whose sin is pardoned" (Ps. 32:1).

ATTAH BA AYLAI BEHEREV UVAHANIT UVKHIDON VE'ANOKHI VA AYLEKHA BESHAYM HASHEM TZEVA'OT (אתה בא אלי בחרב ובחנית ובכידון ואנכי בא אליך בשם ה' צבאות). David said to the Philistine: "Thou comest to me with a sword and with a spear, and with a javelin; but I come to thee in the name of the Lord of Hosts" (1 Sam. 17:45).

AVAD HASID MIN HA'ARETZ (אבד חסיד מן הארץ). "The good man is perished out of the earth" (Mic. 7:2). Micah bemoans the situation, "There is no upright one among men: they all lie in wait for blood; each man hunts his brother with a net." He concludes, "Who is a God like Thee, Who pardons iniquity and forgives the transgressions of the remnant of his heritage? . . . And, Thou wilt cast all their sins into the depths of the sea" (Mic. 7:18–19).

AVANIM SHAHAKU MAYIM (אבנים שחקו מים). "The waters wear the stones"

(Job 14:19). Even stone is worn away by water. The Talmud (Kidd. 30b) tells us that the School of R. Ishmael taught: "My son, if this repulsive wretch [the *yaytzar hara*] assail thee, lead him to the schoolhouse. If he is of stone, he will dissolve, for it is written, 'Ho, everyone that thirsts, come to the water' (Isa. 55:1) [that is, the Torah]; and it is said, 'The waters wear away the stones'" (ibid.).

AVOT AKHLU VOSER VESHINAY BANIM TIKHENAH (אבות אכלו בסר ושני בנים תקהינה). "The fathers have eaten sour grapes, and the children's teeth are set on edge" (Jer. 31:28; Ezek. 18:2). The children will not be punished for the fathers' sins. "As I live, says the Lord God, you shall not have occasion any more to use this proverb in Israel. Behold, all souls are Mine; . . . the soul that sins, it shall die" (Ezek., ibid.; cf. San. 39a).

AYIN LO RA'ATAH (עין לא ראתה). Isaiah describes God's greatness, such as when the mountains melted away at God's Presence on Mount Sinai. "For since the beginning of the world men have not heard, nor perceived by ear, neither has the eye seen [*ayin lo ra'atah*] that a god beside Thee, should do such a thing for him that waits for Him" (Isa. 64:3).

AYMAT MAVET (אימת מות). "A great fright"; as Scripture states, *Ve'aymat mavet naflu alai* ("And the terrors of death are fallen upon me") (Ps. 55:5). In the English language one says, "I was scared to death."

AYN ADAM ASHER LO YEHETA (אין אדם אשר לא יחטא). "There is no man who does not sin" (1 Kings 8:46).

AYN OMER VE'AYN DEVARIM (אין אומר ואין דברים). "There is no speech and there are no words" (Ps. 19:4).

AYNAI VELIBI SHAM KOL HAYAMIM (עיני ולבי שם כל הימים). "My eyes and My heart shall be there perpetually"

(1 Kings 9:3; 2 Chron. 7:16). This is what the Lord tells Solomon when He hallowed the house that Solomon had built.

AYNAY KOL YISRAEL ALEKHA

(עיני כל ישראל עליך). "The eyes of all Israel are upon thee" (1 Kings 1:20). Bathsheba was concerned that King David had not appointed Solomon, his son, to reign after him. He was not aware that Adonijah was reigning. Bathsheba says, "And thou, my lord, O King, the eyes of all Israel are upon thee, and thou shouldst tell them who shall sit on the throne of my lord, the king, after him" (ibid.).

BA'EREV YALIN BEKHI VELABOKER RINAH

(בערב ילין בכי ולבוקר רנה). "In the evening one retires weeping, but in the morning there is a cry of joy!" (Ps. 30:6). Weeping comes at night when it is dark; the time of salvation and goodness arrives in the morning when it is light and joyful (cf. Radak, ad loc.).

BAMEH KOHAKHA GADOL

(במה כחך גדול). "In what lies your great strength?" (Judg. 16:6). This is what Delila wanted to know about Samson. The phrase can be applied to any situation in which the quality or state of being strong is evident.

BANIM GIDALTI VEROMAMTI VEHAYM PASHU VI

(בנים גדלתי ורוממתי והם פשעו בי). "I have reared and brought up children [the Israelites], and they have rebelled [sinned] against Me" (Isa. 1:2).

BARUKH HAGEVER ASHER YIVTAH BA-SHEM

(ברוך הגבר אשר יבטח בה'). "Blessed is the man who trusts in the Lord, and whose hope the Lord is" (Jer. 17:7).

BARUKH HASHEM YOM YOM

(ברוך ה' יום יום). "Blessed be the Lord, day by day" (Ps. 68:20). This is an expression used to thank God every day. The Talmud (Bez. 16a) relates this verse in reference to a trait Hillel the Elder had. It is said that Shammai the Elder ate his meals his entire life in honor of the Sabbath. Thus, if he found a well-favored animal, he said, Let this be for the Sabbath. If, afterwards, he found one better-favored, he put aside the second for the Sabbath and ate the first. Hillel, on the other hand, had a different trait, because all of his works were for the sake of Heaven. He trusted in God that he would obtain something worthy for the Sabbath. He said, "Blessed be the Lord, day by day"— that is, thank God every day, do not worry about tomorrow.

BA'U MAYIM AD NAFESH

(באו מים עד נפש). A verse in Psalms 69:2, beginning with the words "Save me, O God," and continuing with "for the waters are come in even unto my soul." The latter part of the verse intimates drowning in a sea of troubles. The phrase ba'u mayim ad nafesh is uttered whenever a situation is critical or unbearable; in other words, "My troubles have reached their climax."

BAYT HAKEVAROT (KEVAROT)

(בית הקברות (קברות)). Literally, "house of graves," that is, a cemetery. The name occurs in the Bible (Neh. 2:3) and the Talmud (San. 46a). Euphemistic names are Bayt ha-Hayyim ("House of Life") and Bayt Olam or Bayt Almin ("House of Eternity").

BEFIV SHALOM ET RAYAYHU YEDABYR, UVEKIRBO YASIM ARBO

(בפיו שלום את רעהו ידבר, ובקרבו ישים ארבו). "One speaks peaceably to his neighbor with his mouth, but in his heart he lies in wait for him" (Jer. 9:7). God describes the falsehood of the people of Israel. Through deceit they refuse to know Me, says the Lord.

BEFIV UVISFATAV KIBDUNI VE-LIBO RIHAK MIMENI (בפיו ובשפתיו כבדוני ולבו רחק ממני). God said: (this people) . . . "with their mouth and with their lips do honor Me, but have removed their heart far from Me" (Isa. 29:13). Thus the Lord concludes that the only hope is Israel's sanctification of God's Name and acceptance of His religious and moral values.

BEFIV YEVARAYKHU UVEKIR-BAM YEKALELU (בפיו יברכו ובקרבם יקללו). "With the mouth does each one of them bless, but inwardly they curse" (Ps. 62:5). These are the words of David, who trusts in God alone, and nobody else, in the hour of need.

BELAYV SHALAYM (בלב שלם). "With a perfect heart," as in *belayv shalaym hitnadvu la-Shem* ("with a perfect heart they offered willingly to the Lord") (1 Chron. 29:9).

BELAYV VALAYV YEDABAYRU (בלב ולב ידברו). "With a double heart do they speak" (Ps. 12:3). People think one thing but express the opposite; however, God's assurances are genuine and permanent.

BETAH BA-SHEM VA'ASAYH TOV (בטח בה' ועשה טוב). "Trust in the Lord, and do good" (Ps. 37:2). *Rashi* comments (ad loc.): Do not say if I will not steal or if I will give to charity, what will I have for my own sustenance? Instead, trust in God and do good and you will merit to dwell in your land.

BEYAD HAZAKAH UVIZRO'A NETUYAH-EMLOKH ALAYKHEM (ביד חזקה ובזרוע נטויה-אמלוך עליכם). God says to the Israelites, through Ezekiel, "With a mighty hand, and with a stretched out arm . . . will I be King over you" (Ezek. 20:33).

BILA HAMAVET LANETZAH, UMAHAH HASHEM DIMAH (בלע המות לנצח, ומחה ה' דמעה). "He will swallow up [destroy] death forever; and the Lord God will wipe away tears from off all faces" (Isa. 25:8). This verse is usually used as an ending for a funeral oration, or the first half may be written as part of an obituary.

BOR KARAH VAYAHPERAYHYU, VAYIPOL BESHAHAT YIFAL (בור כרה ויחפרהו, ויפל בשחת יפעל). "He has dug a pit and dug it deep, only to fall into his own trap" (Ps. 7:16). The Yiddish equivalent is *Ver es gruhbt a grub far yenem falt aleyn arayn* ("Whoever digs a pit for someone else, falls into it himself").

DABAYR, KI SHOMAYA AVDEKHA (דבר, כי שמע עבדך). "Speak, for thy servant heareth" (1 Sam. 3:10). Although Eli, Samuel's predecessor, told Samuel to lie down, and if he were to be called, he should say, "Speak, Lord; for Thy servant heareth" (ibid., 3:9), Samuel omitted God's Name, since he was not certain that He could have revealed Himself to him (cf. *Rashi, Kimhi,* ad loc.).

The phrase is generally used as a retort when someone demands the listener's undivided attention.

DEREKH RESHA'IM TOVAYD (דרך רשעים תאבד). "The way of the wicked will perish" (Ps. 1:6).

DEVASH VEHALAV TAHAT LE-SHONAYKH (דבש וחלב תחת לשונך). "Honey and milk are under thy tongue" (S.O.S. 4:11). According to Rabbi Levi, the phrase is said of "Whoever reads the Bible with its delightful tone and tune" (*Song of Songs Rabbah* 4:11).

EMET MAYERETZ TITZMAH (אמת מארץ תצמח). "Truth springeth out of the earth" (Ps. 85:12). In other words, the truth will eventually appear; as the Yiddish expression states: *Emet kumt aroys vi boyml oyfn vaser* ("Truth comes up like oil upon water").

The remainder of this verse is *vetzedek mishamayim nishkab* ("And righteousness hath looked down from heaven"). The earth is mentioned before Heaven because moral reformation must begin with man; once begun on earth, it receives impetus from the help that comes from above.

ESA AYNAI EL HEHARIM, MAYAYIN YAVO EZRI? (אשא עיני אל ההרים, מאין יבא עזרי?). A verse in Psalms 121:1, meaning "I raise my eyes to the mountains; whence shall my help come?"

GAM ALAYIKH TA'AVAR KOS (גם עליך תעבר כוס). "The cup shall pass over unto thee also" (Lam. 4:21). The "cup," according to *Rashi*, refers to the cup of punishment and the destruction that will eventually fall upon Romans (identified as the biblical Edom), who Jeremiah foresaw would destroy the Second Temple.

The expression denotes, "Your time, too, will come."

GAM ANI HAKHAM KAMOKHA (גם אני חכם כמוך). The false prophet said to the true prophet of Yehudah, "I am a prophet also as thou art" (1 Kings 13:18).

GAM BOSH LO YAYVOSHU VEHIKALAYM LO YADA'U (גם בוש לא יבשו והכלם לא ידעו). See LO YODAYA AVAL BOSHET.

GAM ET HATOV NEKABAYL-VE'ET HARA LO NEKABAYL? (גם את הטוב נקבל-ואת הרע לא נקבל?). "Shall we receive good [at the hand of God], and shall we not receive evil?" (Job 2:10). This is what Job said to his wife when he was smitten with vile sores from the sole of his foot to his crown. Job remained steadfast and did not sin with his lips as his wife wished he [would] do.

GAM NAVI GAM KOHEN HANAYFU (גם נביא גם כהן חנפו). "For both prophet and priest are hypocrites" (Jer. 23:11). God says that even those from whom all learn are false pretenders to virtue or piety.

HOK NATAN VELO YA'AVOR (חק נתן ולא יעבור). "He issued a decree that will not change" (Ps. 148:6). God instituted the laws to which the sun and the moon must conform: the sun shines by day and the moon by night (cf. *Rashi*, ad loc.).

HOK VELO YA'AVOR (*Tosafot Yom Tov*, introduction to the *Mishnah*), meaning "a strong decree from which [one cannot] turn aside," became a colloquial expression based upon this verse.

HAKOT BALASHON (הכות בלשון). "To speak evil or slander," as in the phrase *venakayhu valashon* ("and let us smite him [Jeremiah] with the tongue") (Jer. 18:18).

HAKSHIVAH BEKOL TAHANUNOTAI (הקשיבה בקול תחנונותי). See HAKSHIVAH TEFILATI.

HAKSHIVAH TEFILATI (הקשיבה תפלתי). "Listen to my prayer" (Ps. 61:2). A similar expression is HAKSHIVAH BEKOL TAHANUNOTAI ("Heed the sound of my supplication") (Ps. 86:6).

HARHEV PIKHA VA'AMALAYHU (הרחב פיך ואמלאהו). "Open thy mouth wide, and I will fill it" (Ps. 81:11). *Rashi* (ad loc.) comments, "Request of Me all your heart's desires and I will fulfill them." The Jerusalem Talmud (Ta'an. 3:6) remarks that when a person requests all his needs, he displays his trust in God's strength and generosity, which know no bounds. The Babylonian Talmud (Ber. 50a) states, "That [the verse] was written with reference to words of the Torah."

HASAR LEHEM (חסר לחם). A poor person who lacks even bread for his soul, as in 2 Samuel 3:29, venofayl baherev vahasar lehem ("and fall by the sword, or lack bread").

HASAYKH ET RAGLAV (הסך את רגליו). Saul took three thousand chosen men out of all Israel and went to seek David and his men. He came to the sheepcotes by the way [probably caves] and Saul went in "to cover his feet" (Hasaykh et raglav), a euphemism for "to relieve himself" (cf. Judg. 3:24, cf. also Rashi and Redak, ad loc.).

HASHEM LI LO IRA, MAH YA-ASEH LI ADAM (ה' לי לא אירא, מה יעשה לי אדם). "Hashem is with me, I have no fear; how can man affect me?" (Ps. 118:6).

HASHEM MORISH UMA'ASHIR (ה' מוריש ומעשיר). "The Lord makes poor, and makes rich" (1 Sam. 2:7).

HASHEM NATAN VASHEM LA-KAH (ה' נתן וה' לקח). "The Lord gave, and the Lord has taken away" (Job 1:21). This is the expression of the proverbial Job—righteous, wise, God-fearing, wealthy—who is put to the most difficult of tests at the behest of Satan. After Satan tells him of all his material losses, as well as of the death of his sons, he rends his coat, shaves his head, prostrates himself, and says, "Naked I came out of my mother's womb, and naked I shall return there: the Lord gave, and the Lord has taken away; blessed be the Name of the Lord."

HASHMI'INI ET KOLAYKH (השמיעני את קולך). "Let me hear your voice" (S.O.S. 2:14). This part of the verse, the Yalkut Shir Hashirim states, refers to Hallel, which should be recited with song and with a sweet voice. The continuation of the verse, "for your voice is sweet," alludes to Hodu ("Give thanks"),

"and your countenance comely" refers to Ana Hashem hoshi'a na ("We beseech Thee, O Lord, send now prosperity").

Hashmi'ini et kolaykh may be directed at one who is asked to sing and/or who has previously refused.

HAVAH LI VERAKHAH (הבה לי ברכה). "Give me a blessing" (Judg. 1:15). This is the plea made by Akhsa to her father, Kaleb. Her request was that she be given a field whereby she would be able to have sustenance.

HAYAH HAKINOR LE'AYVEL (היה הכנור לאבל). Joy and happiness have passed and have turned to sorrow and pain, as in vayehi le'ayvel kinori ("Therefore my lyre is turned to mourning") (Job 30:31).

HAYITPA'AYR HAGARZEN AL HAHOTZAYV BO? (היתפאר הגרזן על החוצב בו?). "Shall the ax boast itself against him that hews with it?" (Isa. 10:15). God says to Assyria, You are a mere tool in My hand. Just as the hammer cannot say to the hacker that he is not activating the hammer and the hammer is acting on its own, so the tool (Assyria) is in the hand of the Almighty, who is using the implement with full command and power.

HAZORE'IM BEDIMAH BERINAH YIKTZORU (הזורעים בדמעה ברנה יקצורו). "They that sow in tears shall reap in joy" (Ps. 126:5). Just as the farmer sows his field with tears and anxiety, doing good deeds and mitzvot, which entails a certain immediate sacrifice of time and effort, eventually brings joy.

The Yiddish equivalent is Az men zeyt in laydn, shnayt men in freydn.

HIKAVAYD VESHAYV BEVAY-TEKHA (הכבד ושב בביתך). "Keep thy glory and stay at home" (2 Kings 14:10). After making war on the Edomites and defeating them, Joash said to Amaziah,

"Thou hast indeed smitten Edom, and thy heart has lifted thee up: keep thy glory and stay at home, for why shouldst thou meddle with evil that thou shouldst fall, thou and Judah with thee?" (ibid.).

This expression may be used to warn a person to stay away from trouble. It alludes to the Yiddish expression *Krikh nit vu men darf nisht* ("Don't go where you don't belong").

HIKON LIKRAT ELOHEKHA YISRAEL (הכון לקראת אלהיך ישראל).
"Prepare to meet thy God, O Israel" (Amos 4:12). The Book of Amos rebukes the sins of Israel and warns that in spite of punishment, they should be prepared to serve God.

A Sephardic *Mahzor* utilizes this verse to express the idea that, if possible, one should attire oneself in beautiful clothing when reciting *Selihot*, in order to fulfill the words "Prepare to meet thy God, O Israel" (*Mahzor Zekhor Le'avraham Lerosh Hashanah, Dinim, Levorna* [reprinted in Jerusalem, 1977], p. 3b). See GARTL.

HOSHI'AH HASHEM KI GAMAR HASID (הושיעה ה' כי גמר חסיד).
"Help [Save], Lord; for the devout man ceaseth" (Ps. 12:2). In a degenerate society, those who hold fast to the truth are in danger of their lives.

HOY HA'OMRIM LARA TOV VELATOV RA (הוי האומרים לרע טוב ולטוב רע).
"Woe to them that call evil good, and good evil" (Isa. 5:20).

IKHLU MASHMANIM USHETU MAMTAKIM (אכלו משמנים ושתו ממתקים).
"Eat [dainties] sumptuously and drink sweet beverages" (Neh. 8:10). This is what Nehemiah, Ezra, and the Levites told the people to do after they taught them the Torah and declared this day to be a holy day to the Lord.

Ekhol mashmanim shetay mamtakim are the opening words of the third stanza of the Sabbath table-hymn *Yom Zeh Mekhu-*

bad ("This day is most honored"), which is attributed to an unidentified author by the name of "Yisrael."

IM ESHKAHAYKH YERUSHALAYIM TISHKAH YEMINI (אם אשכחך ירושלים תשכח ימיני).
"If I forget thee, O Jerusalem, let my right hand forget its cunning" (Ps. 137:5). After returning from Babylon and viewing with horror the havoc wrought in the city he dearly loved, the psalmist was motivated to write this verse.

This verse has remained on the lips of the Jew throughout his exiles.

IM LO TA'AMINU KI LO TAYAMAYNU (אם לא תאמינו כי לא תאמנו).
"If you have no faith, you shall not be believed" (Isa. 7:9). God says that the capital of Ephraim is Shomron and the head of Shomron is Pekah b. Remaliah (who will not be in a similar position in Jerusalem). "You, Ahaz, and your nation will not believe in my vision because I know you do not have faith in the Lord; you are wicked."

A similar Yiddish expression is *Der vuhs gleybt nit dem tzveytn, iz a bavayz az meken im zelbst nisht gleybn* ("One who does not believe another is himself not believed").

ISH DAMIM (איש דמים).
"A bloodthirsty man," as in *ish damim umirmah* ("a bloodthirsty and deceitful man") (Ps. 5:7).

ISH HAYASHAR BE'AYNAV YA'ASEH (איש הישר בעיניו יעשה).
"Every man did that which was right in his eyes" (Judg. 17:6). Colloquially, the phrase can be translated as, Man shall do what is right in his own eyes, thus leading to anarchy.

ISH SEFATAYIM (איש שפתים).
"Excessive talk," as in *ve'im ish sefatayim yitzdak* ("and should a man full of talk be accounted in the right?") (Job 11:2).

ISH TAHAT GAFNO VETAHAT TE'AYNATO (איש תחת גפנו ותחת תאנתו). "Every man under his vine and under his fig tree" (Mic. 4:4). This is the prophesy Micah has about the rescue of Jerusalem and "the end of days." See YASHVU ISH TAHAT GAFNO VETAHAT TE'AYNATO.

JEROBO'AM BEN NEBAT (ירבעם בן נבט). The first king of the divided kingdom of Israel. He was known as a plotter for Solomon's throne (1 Kings 11:26–40), for setting up a kingdom of tribes, and for establishing idolatry (1 Kings 13:1).

Rabbinic literature is violently hostile to Jerobo'am, who "sinned and caused Israel to sin" (1 Kings 15:30). Jerobo'am was so named because he fomented strife (*merivah*) amongst the nation (*am*) by introducing calf-worship, and he caused strife (*merivah*) between Israel and their Father in Heaven (cf. San. 101b).

It became customary to use the name "Jerobo'am ben Nebat" for one who sins and causes others to sin.

KA'ANAVIM BAMIDBAR (כענבים במדבר). Like finding something very important or rare in a place where one has no hope of finding it, as in "I found the Isarelites like grapes in the wilderness" (*ka'anavim bamidbar*) (Hos. 9:10).

KA'ASHER ASETAH ASU LAH (כאשר עשתה עשו לה). "As she has done, do to her!" (Jer. 50:15). Jeremiah said to the Israelites, in the name of God, take vengeance upon her (Babel); what she did to Jerusalem, do to her.

KA'ASHER ASITA YAYASEH LAKH (כאשר עשית יעשה לך). In the only chapter that has come down from the Prophet Obadiah, verse 1:15 reads, "as thou has done, it shall be done to thee." This entire chapter is devoted to an account of the destruction of Edom. The Edomites are the type of people who ought to be friends but are not; they ought to be helpers but, in the day of calamity, are found "standing on the other side." The prophet denounces their "violence against their brother Jacob" and stresses the fact that Zion shall be saved from its predicament; its savior will bring punishment down upon Edom.

The phrase *Ka'asher asita yayaseh lakh* came to mean that "you will be repaid for what you have done."

KA'ASHER ASITI KAYN SHILAM LI ELOHIM (כאשר עשיתי כן שלם לי אלהים). "As I have done, so has God requited me" (Judg. 1:7). After Judah smote ten thousand men in Bezek, Adonibezek fled and was caught, and his thumbs and great toes were cut off. He said, "I ordered that seventy kings' thumbs and great toes should be cut off for gathering the food that fell down. Just as I did, God repaid me." Thus he merited being brought to Jerusalem and he was buried there, because he confessed that God had repaid him MIDAH KENEGED MIDAH ("measure for measure").

KA'ASHER ASU LI KAYN ASITI LAHEM (כאשר עשו לי כן עשיתי להם). "As they did to me, so have I done to them" (Judg. 15:11). This is the reply Samson gave to the three thousand men of Judah when they confronted him with "Knowst thou not that the Philistines are rulers over us? Why did you slaughter them?"

KA'ASHER DIMITI KAYN HAYATAH, VEKHA'ASHER YA'ATZTI HI TAKUM (כאשר דמיתי כן היתה, וכאשר יעצתי היא תקום). The Lord of Hosts has sworn, saying, surely "as I have thought [concerning Ashur], so has to come to pass [you Nebuchadnezzar saw the prophecy of the prophets of Israel that became reality with Sennacherib]; and as I have purposed, so it shall stand" (Isa. 14:24).

KA'ASHER E'ESEH KAYN TA'ASUN (כאשר אעשה כן תעשון). "Whatever I do, so shall you do" (Judg. 7:17). This is the instruction given by Gideon, the fifth judge of Israel, to his three hundred men when he broke into the enemy's camp and, with the help of the rest of Israel, crushed Midian, killing all their officers (ibid., 8:25).

KA'ASHER YAHALOM HARA'AYV VEHINAYH OKHAYL, VEHAYKITZ VERAYKAH NAFSHO (כאשר יחלום הרעב והנה אוכל, והקיץ ורקה נפשו). "As when a hungry man dreams, and behold, he eats [that is, he dreams that he is eating]; but he awakes and his soul is empty" (Isa. 29:8), so shall the multitude of all the nations be, that fight against Mount Zion.

KA'ASHER YATEH HARO'EH ET BIGDO (כאשר יעטה הרעה את בגדו). God instructed Jeremiah to tell the men of Yehudah that He would smite the land of Egypt through the hands of Nebuchadnezzar. "He shall fold up the land of Mitzrayim, as a shepherd folds up his garment" (*Ka'asher yateh haro'eh et bigdo*) (Jer. 43:12)—that is, like a shepherd who throws his clothing over his shoulder as he leads his flock before him (cf. *Rashi*, ad loc.).

KA'EVED KADONAV (כעבד כאדניו). Isaiah tells the people of Israel that God will empty out the land of *Eretz Yisrael* and all classes will be alike. "As with the servant, so with his master" (Isa. 24:2).

KAROV HASHEM LENISHBERAY LAYV (קרוב ה' לנשברי לב). "The Lord is close to those of broken heart" (Ps. 34:19).

KASHAH KHISHOL KINAH (קשה כשאול קנאה). "Jealousy is cruel as the grave" (S.O.S. 8:6).

KASPAM UZEHAVAM LO YUKHAL LEHATZILAM (כספם וזהבם לא יוכל להצילם). "Their silver and gold shall not be able to deliver them" (Ezek. 7:19; Zep. 1:18). This is the word of God that came to Ezekiel, regarding the Israelites' transgressions. Zephaniah also foresaw the dreadful fate that lay in store for the wicked nations.

KATON VEGADOL SHAM HU (קטן וגדול שם הוא). "The small and great are there" (Job 3:18), meaning that in the World to Come, it will be evident who is important and who is not.

KEDABAYR AHAT HANEVALOT TEDABAYRI (כדבר אחת הנבלות תדברי). After Job was smitten with vile sores, his wife said to him, Curse God and die. He said to her, "Thou speakest as one of the foolish women speak" (Job 2:10). He argued, Shall we receive good at the hand of God, and shall we not receive evil?

KEFATISH YEFOTZAYTZ SELA (כפטיש יפצץ סלע). God says that His word is "like a hammer that breaks the rock in pieces" (Jer. 23:29). The prophet should speak His word faithfully and tell his own dream as it is.

KELI AYN HAYFETZ BO (כלי אין חפץ בו). "An object that no one cares for" (Jer. 22:28; 48:38). With this description, God refers to Konyahu, son of Yehoyakim. Also, the Lord says, I have broken Moab like an unwanted vessel.

KERAHAYM AV AL BANIM (כרחם אב על בנים). "As a father has compassion upon his children, so has God shown mercy to those who fear Him" (Ps. 103:13). God demonstrates one of His attributes, "The Lord is full of compassion" (ibid., 8).

KERAV AYLEKHA (קרב אליך). A phrase meaning "depart from me," "distance yourself from me," "stand back," or "flee or remove yourself," as in *kerav aylekha al tigash bi* ("stand by thyself, come not near to me") (Isa. 65:5).

KEREM HASHEM TZEVA'OT BAYT YISRAEL (כרם ה׳ צבאות בית ישראל). "The vineyard of the Lord of Hosts is the house of Israel" (Isa. 5:7). Israel is compared to a vineyard; everything that is done to a vineyard, God did to Israel.

KESHOSHANAH BAYN HAHOHIM (כשושנה בין החוחים). "As a lily among the thorns" (S.O.S. 2:2). Just as Solomon makes a comparison between his beloved (the shepherdess) and the women of Jerusalem, so the phrase is applied to one who personifies value or excellence, in contrast to those who are inferior (like thorns).

KETZUTZAY PAYAH (קצוצי פאה). Literally, "the corners of hair cut off." A nickname for those who shave their heads all around and leave a clump of hair in the middle (Jer. 9:25).

KEVAD OZEN (כבד אזן). "Hard of hearing." A verse in Isaiah (59:1) reads, "Behold, the Lord's hand is not shortened, that it cannot save; neither is His ear heavy, that it cannot hear" (*velo khavdah ozno mishmo'a*).

KIRHOK MIZRAH MIMA'ARAV (כרחק מזרח ממערב). A phrase in Psalms 103:12, meaning "As far as the east is from the west." The verse continues, "has He distanced our transgressions from us." God's infinite kindness is recounted in this psalm.

The phrase is often used to indicate a diametrically opposite or entirely different thought or opinion—in other words, poles apart.

KISHMO KAYN HU, NABAL SHEMO UNEBALAH IMO (כשמו כן הוא, נבל שמו ונבלה עמו). "For as his name is, so is he; Nabal is his name, and folly is with him" (1 Sam. 25:25). Nabal, a man of great wealth, refused payment to David's men in return for protecting his sheep while grazing. In addition, he implied that David was a rebellious slave (1 Sam. 25:5–11). The name "Nabal" (lit., "fool") thus suits him.

KOL ASHER BILVAVEKHA AGID LAKH (כל אשר בלבבך אגיד לך). "All that is in thy heart I will tell you" (1 Sam. 9:19). Samuel makes this statement to Saul, inferring, "Everything you want to know I will tell you" (cf. *Metzudot David*, ad loc.).

KOL ASHER YA'ASEH YATZLI'AH (כל אשר יעשה יצליח). "And in whatsoever he doeth he shall prosper" (Ps. 1:3). This refers to one who has not walked in the counsel of the wicked, nor stood in the way of sinners, nor sat in the seat of the scornful. Because he trusts in God and perseveres, he reaches his goal.

KOL ASHER YEDABAYR BO YAVO (כל אשר ידבר בוא יבוא). "All that he saith cometh surely to pass" (1 Sam. 9:6); a phrase, concerning Samuel, that the servant said to Saul. He (Samuel) is great in prophesying, and whatever he says becomes reality!

KOL ATZMOTAI TOMARNAH (כל עצמתי תאמרנה). "All my bones shall say: Hashem, who is like unto Thee" (Ps. 35:10). The authors of the books *Hamanhig, Shibbolei Haleket,* and *Sefer Hasidim* expressed the view that the custom of swaying during prayer is a precept derived from this verse.

KOL DEMAMAH DAKAH (קול דממה דקה). A phrase appearing in 1 Kings 19:12 and in the High Holy Day prayer *Unetaneh Tokef,* meaning "a still, thin voice" or a "gentle whisper." *Rashi* (ad loc.) comments that it is a sound that comes from the stillness, but the actual voice is not heard; it is hushed sound. Others say it is the voice of God, and when He speaks, all are quiet.

KOL KORAY BAMIDBAR (קול קורא
(במדבר). "A voice cries: [prepare] in the wilderness [the way of the Lord]" (Isa. 40:3). The verse is saying that a Heavenly voice cries to make a road through the desert for the return of exiled Israel.

The word *bamidbar* has been linked to the first two words, thus reading, "A voice crying in the wilderness." It has become a maxim for an unheeded call or a vain appeal.

KOL ME'AHAVAYIKH SHEKHAY-HUKH (כל מאהביך שכחוך). "All thy lovers have forgotten thee" (Jer. 30:14), says the Lord to the people of Israel. But, "I will restore health to thee . . . because they called thee an outcast, saying, this is Zion; for whom no one cares" (ibid., 30:17).

KOL ROZ LA ANAYS LAKH (כל רז
(לא אנס לך). "No secret is too difficult for you" (Dan. 4:6). This is what Nebuchadnezzar said to Daniel when he asked him to interpret the dream he had seen. The Talmud (Hul. 59a) states that Rab applied the same phrase to Samuel, who stopped Rab from eating a young deer whose hind legs were broken.

LABOKER MISHPAT (לבוקר משפט).
"[O house of David, thus says the Lord]; execute judgment in the morning" (Jer. 21:12). It is much better to judge or concern oneself with judgment in the morning. In other words, "sleep on it."

LAILAH LAKHEM MAYHAZON
(לילה לכם מחזון). Concerning the prophets who make the people of Israel err, the Lord says: "It shall be night for

you, that you shall not have a vision" (Mic. 3:6).

LAMAH KAKHAH RIMITINI (למה
(ככה רמיתני). "Why has thou deceived me so?" (1 Sam. 19:17). This question was asked by Saul to Michal, as to why he let his enemy (David) go and escape.

LAMAH TIHEYEH KE'ISH NID-HAM (למה תהיה כאיש נדהם). Jeremiah asks God to save the people of Israel. "Why shouldst Thou be as a man surprised, [as a mighty man that cannot save]") (Jer. 14:9).

LAMAH YOMRU HAGOYIM (למה
(יאמרו הגוים). "Why should the nations say" ("where is their [the Israelites] God" (Ps. 79:10). The next phrase is a call for retribution: "Let the avenging of Thy servants' blood that is shed be made known among the nations in our sight" (ibid.).

The phrase *Lamah yomru hagoyim* was borrowed and used when a Jew did something unbefitting. He was reprimanded and queried as to "Wherefore should the non-Jew say?"—meaning, a Jew's behavior should be beyond reproach.

LASHAV HIRBAYT REFU'OT TE'A-LAH AYN LAKH (לשוא הרביתי
(רפאות, תעלה אין לך. "In vain shalt thou use many medicines; for thou shalt not be cured" (Jer. 46:11). This is what the Lord said to Pharaoh, the king of Egypt, who was defeated at the hands of Nebuchadnezzar, king of Babylonia.

LASHAV TITYAPI (לשוא תתיפי). "In
vain shalt thou make thyself fair" (Jer. 4:30). God tells the Israelites: Making yourself comely will not help because thy lovers will despise you and they will seek your life.

LASHON MEDABERET GEDOLOT
(לשון מדברת גדולות). "The tongue that speaketh proud things" (Ps. 12:3), an

expression intimating a person who speaks with haughtiness.

LASHON REMIYAH (לשון רמיה). King David said, I cried out to God and He answered me. "O Lord, deliver my soul from lying lips, from a deceitful tongue" (*lashon remiyah*) (Ps. 120:3). You, tongue, how can you be restrained if you are between the lips and the teeth, and if this does not help to restrain you, what will? (*Metzudat David*).

LAYKH BEKHOHAKHA ZEH (לך בכחך זה). Gideon, the fifth judge of Israel, complained that the Lord had forsaken us, and delivered us unto the hands of Midian. An angel declared, "Go in this thy might and save" (Judg. 6:14). The angel gave him a sign and the spirit of the Lord came upon Gideon. He then set out to wage war against Midian. At Gideon's request, God demonstrated His intention of saving Israel by performing the miracle of the dew and the woolen fleece (ibid., 6:36–40).

LE'EVIL YAHARAG KA'AS, UFOTEH TAMIT KINAH (לאויל יהרג כעש, ופתה תמית קנאה). Eliphaz, Job's friend from Teman, reprimands him for crying to God because of his suffering. He tells Job to call and see if anyone will answer. Praying to the holy angels will also not be heeded, "For anger kills the foolish man, and envy slays the simpleton" (Job 5:2).

LEHAVDIL BAYN HAKODESH LE-HOL (להבדיל בין הקדש לחל). A phrase in Ezekiel 42:20, meaning "to make a separation between the holy and the common"—that is, to distinguish or differentiate between the sacred and the profane.

LEHEM TZAR UMAYIM LAHATZ (לחם צר ומים לחץ). An expression used to describe the scarcity or lack of food and drink, as in *lehem tzar umayim lahatz* ("the bread of adversity, and the water of affliction") (Isa. 30:20).

LEKHA DUMIYAH TEHILAH (לך דמיה תהלה). "To You, silence is praise" (Ps. 65:2). The Talmud (Meg. 18a) gives the following homily, based on this phrase: "The best medicine of all is silence." *Rashi* (ad loc.) comments that elaboration of God merely detracts because of what is left unsaid, and thus silence is His most expressive praise. See MILAH BESALA UMASHTOKA BITRIN.

LEKHU VENAKAYHU BALASHON (לכו ונכהו בלשון). "Come, let us smite him with the tongue" (Jer. 18:18). This is what the people of Anathot said one to another concerning Jeremiah. They wanted to do away with him by bearing false witness so that they would not have to pay heed to any of his words.

LEMA'AN TZIYON LO EHESHEH ULEMA'AN YERUSHALAYIM LO ESHKOT (למען ציון לא אחשה ולמען ירושלים לא אשקוט). "For the sake of Zion, I will not remain silent; and for the sake of Jerusalem, I will not rest" (Isa. 62:1).

LEMI ATTAH VE'AY MIZEH AT-TAH? (למי אתה, ואי מזה אתה?). "To whom dost thou belong and from where dost thou come?" (1 Sam. 30:13). David asked this question of the young Egyptian, a sick slave who was abandoned.

LERIK YAGATI LETOHU VE-HEVEL KOHI KHILAYTI (לריק יגעתי לתהו והבל כחי כליתי). "I have labored in vain, I have spent my strength for naught, and in vain" (Isa. 49:4). These are the words of Isaiah, who concludes, "yet surely my judgment is with the Lord, and my reward with my God."

LESHAYM VELITHILAH ULETI-FARET (לשם ולתהלה ולתפארת). The Lord says that He caused the house of Israel and the whole house of Judah to cleave to Him so that they might be "unto

[Him] for a people, and for a name and for a praise, and for a glory" (Jer. 13:11).

LESHONAM HEREV HADAH
(לשונם חרב חדה). When David fled from Saul and hid in the cave, he cried out to God that he was among such a people "whose tongue is a sharp sword" (Ps. 57:5).

LI HAKESEF VELI HAZAHAV NE'UM HASHEM TZEVA'OT (לי הכסף ולי הזהב נאום ה' צבאות). Haggai urged Zerubbabel, Joshua, the son of Jehozadak, and the rest of the people to rebuild the Temple, which lay in ruins. His words were effective, and the Temple was completed in the sixth year of Darius' reign. "The silver is mine and the gold is mine, says the Lord of Hosts" (Hag. 2:8). Thus, I can give it to whomever I wish. He also says: "The glory of this latter house shall be greater than that of the former . . . and in this place I will give peace. . . ." (ibid., 2:9).

LIBI UVESARI YERANENU EL AYL HAI (לבי ובשרי ירננו אל אל חי). "My heart and my flesh [that is, my mind and body] sing for joy unto the living God" (Ps. 84:3).

LIMDU LESHONAM DABER SHEKER (למדו לשונם דבר שקר). "They have taught their tongue to speak lies" (Jer. 9:4). Jeremiah reprimands the people of Israel, who proceed from evil to evil and who, through deceit, refuse to know God.

LISHMO'A EL HARINAH VE'EL HATEFILLAH (לשמע אל הרנה ואל התפלה). "To hearken unto the song and unto the prayer" (1 Kings 8:28). The Sages comment on this verse, "Where there is song [rinah], there shall be prayer [tefillah]" (Ber. 6a).

The phrase is the refrain in the Pizmon Bemotza'ay Menuhah, recited at the first Selihot. Occasionally, it was printed on the

ticket that a Jew purchased for a seat in the synagogue for the High Holy Days. The phrase is found in the introduction to a contract made in 1861 between the officers of the Great Synagogue of the old city of Berdichev and the Sheli'ah Tzibbur, R. Chaim Yeruchom Blindman (known as Yeruchom Hakatan).

LO ALAYKHEM (LO ALAYNU) (לא עלינו) (עליכם) (אליכם). "Let it [trouble] not come unto you" ("upon you," when spelled with the letter ayin) (Lam. 1:12, cf. also San. 104b).

Lo alaynu means "let it not come upon us" or "Heaven save us." In Yiddish, the term nebich is used instead of these two Hebrew expressions. For example, Er iz nebich shvakh ("The poor thing, he is weak"). The Yiddish term is a contraction from the German Nie bei euch or the Yiddish Nisht bay aykh, gedackht ("May it never come upon you").

LO ALMAN YISRAEL (לא אלמן ישראל). The Lord says, "Behold, I will raise up against Babel, and against them that dwell in Levqamay (Kasdim, Jer. 51:1) . . . for Israel has not been widowed" (ibid., 51:5). That is to say, "the situation is not hopeless; Israel still has reserves."

LO DIBARTI VELO ALTAH AL LIBI (לא דברתי ולא עלתה על לבי). "Neither did I speak it, nor has it come into my mind" (Jer. 19:5). God tells Jeremiah to go out and proclaim his words to the kings of Yehudah and the inhabitants of Jerusalem. "They have foresaken Me by building high places of the Ba'al, to burn their sons with fire for burnt offerings to the Ba'al, which I command not, nor spoke it, neither came it into My mind."

LO EL HINAM DIBARTI (לא אל חנם דברתי). "Not in vain did I speak" (Ezek. 6:10). God said, I will pay back the house of Israel for their evil abominations and

not in vain did I say that I would do this evil to them.

LO EMNA MIKEM DAVAR (לא אמנע מכם דבר). "I will keep nothing back from you" (Jer. 42:4). This is what Jeremiah answered the captains of the forces, Johanan the son of Kareah and Yazania the son of Hoshaya, when they asked him to pray to God for them and to show them the proper way to walk and the things they may do.

LO ISH BESORAH ATTAH HAYOM (לא איש בשרה אתה היום). "Thou shalt not be the bearer of tidings this day" (2 Sam. 18:20). This is what Joab said to Ahimaz concerning the reporting of Absalom's death. This report would weigh more heavily on the king than the news of victory.

LO KAM KAMOHU (לא קם כמהו). The Book of Kings records the righteousness of Josiah, the king of Judah (640–609 B.C.E.), whose reign was marked by a great national revival. In evaluating Josiah, it is written: "Before him there was no king like him . . . nor did any like him arise after him" (*lo kam kamohu*) (2 Kings 23:25; ibid., 18:5).

The phrase is applied when speaking of a truly great person.

LO KAYAMIM HARISHONIM (לא כימים הראשונים). "Not as in the former days" (Zech. 8:11). In former days, before the building of the *Bet Hamikdash*, there was no blessing in the work of man or animal. Now that you have begun to build the *Bet Hamikdash*, God said, "there shall be the seed of peace, the vine shall give her fruit, the ground shall yield its increase, and the heavens shall give their dew . . . and you shall be a blessing; fear not, but let your hands be strong" (ibid., 8:9–13).

LO LE'AYZER VELO LEHO'IL (לא לעזר ילא להועיל). "Not for help nor

for profit" (Isa. 30:5). All of Israel were ashamed of a people (the Egyptians) who could not profit them, and whom they could neither help nor profit; it was a shame and also a reproach that they encountered in Egypt.

LO LEFANAV HANAYF (לא לפניו חנף). "A hypocrite shall not come" (Job 13:16). Job tells his friends: "Hold your peace, let me alone, that I may speak and let come on me what will. . . . This also shall be my salvation: for a hypocrite shall not come before Him" (Job 13:12–16).

LO LEMA'ANKHEM ANI OSEH (לא למענכם אני עשה). "I do not do this for your sakes" (Ezek. 36:22). God tells Ezekiel to tell the people, "I do not do this for your sakes, O house of Israel, but for My Holy Name's sake, which you have profaned among the nations . . ." (ibid.).

LO MAHSHEVOTAI MAHSHEVO-TAYKHEM VELO DARKAYKHEM DERAKHAI (לא מחשבותי מחשבותיכם ולא דרכיכם דרכי). The Lord says: "My thoughts are not your thoughts, neither are your ways My ways" (Isa. 55:8). Thus, seek the Lord while He may be found.

LO NAVI ANOKHI VELO BEN-NAVI ANOKHI (לא נביא אנכי ולא בן-נביא אנכי). "I am no prophet, neither am I a prophet's son" (Amos 7:14). Amaziah, the idolatrous priest of Beth-el, said to Amos, "Do not prophesy again at Beth-el; for it is the king's sanctuary, and it is a royal house." Amos answered Amaziah, "I am no prophet, neither am I a prophet's son; but I was a herdsman, and a dresser of sycamore trees, and the Lord took me as I followed the flock and the Lord said to me: Go prophesy to my people Israel" (ibid., 7:14, 15).

This saying is used by someone when referring to a future situation.

LO NOFAYL ANOKHI MIKEM (לא נופל אנכי מכם). "I am not inferior to you"

(Job 12:3, 13:2). Job engaged in lengthy philosophical disputations with four friends: Eliphaz the Temanite, Bildad the Shuhite, Zophar the Naamathite, and Elihu, the son of Barachel the Buzite. Job directed this question mainly to Zophar, as the verse reads, "I am as one who is become a laughing stock to his friend" (Job 12:4).

LO SHALAVTI VELO SHAKATETI VELO NAHTI VAYAVO ROGEZ (לא שלותי ולא שקטתי ולא נחתי ויבא רגז). "I had no repose, nor had I rest, nor was I quiet; yet trouble came" (Job 3:25).

LO TA'AMINU KI YESUPAR (לא תאמינו כי יספר). "You will not believe, though it be told you" (Hab. 1:5). Habakkuk saw, through prophetic inspiration, that Nebuchadnezzar would dominate the entire world and would do harm to the Israelites. Because the Israelites see Nebuchadnezzar's success, Torah observance is slackened and justice does not go out triumphantly. Habakkuk tells the Israelites, "Look among the nations, and behold, and be struck with amazement; for a deed will be performed in your days, which you will not believe, though it be told you" (ibid.).

LO TAKUM PA'AMAYIM TZARAH (לא תקום פעמים צרה). Nahum prophesied the destruction of Nineveh. He depicted the progress of the siege and the capture of the city and the joy of Israelites at its destruction. He said to the people of Nineveh, "What do you contrive against the Lord? [Do you think you will be rescued from His hand?] He will make an utter end; affliction shall not rise up a second time [lo takum pa'amayim tzarah]" (Nahum 1:9). Affliction will not come to you twice; you will perish once only.

LO TAKUM VELO TIHEYEH (לא תקום ולא תהיה). "It shall not stand; neither shall it come to pass" (Isa. 7:7). God says to Isaiah that the evil counsel of Aram, Ephraim, and the son of Remal-

yahu shall not stand or come to pass. Do not fear them.

LO TE'UNEH AYLEKHA RA'AH (לא תאונה אליך רעה). "No evil shall befall you" (Ps. 91:10). The Talmud (Ber. 55b) records: R. Hisda said, in the name of R. Jeremiah: This means that you will not be disturbed either by bad dreams or by evil thoughts.

LO VEHAYIL VELO VEKO'AH KI IM BERUHI (לא בחיל ולא בכח כי אם ברוחי). "Not by might, nor by power, but by My spirit, saith the Lord of Hosts" (Zech. 4:6). The message, that the spirit of God remains with those who are saintly in character, is the word of the Lord to Zerubbabel.

LO VEMOTO YIKAH HAKOL, LO YAYRAYD AHARAV KEVODO (לא במותו יקח הכל, לא ירד אחריו כבודו). "For when he dieth, he shall carry nothing away; his wealth shall not descend after him" (Ps. 49:18). The English equivalent is "You can't take it with you."

LO YADA BAYN YEMINO LISMOLO (לא ידע בין ימינו לשמאלו). "[Persons] that cannot discern between their right and their left hand" (Jonah 4:11). The Lord sent Jonah to Nineveh to urge the people of that corrupt city to repent. Not wishing to help Israel's enemies repent and thereby make Israel more culpable in God's sight, Jonah refused to obey the Divine command. In the end, however, Jonah was forced to come to Nineveh and rouse its inhabitants to repentance. Vexed, Jonah went outside the city to see what would become of it. God prepared a gourd to come up over him, that it might be a shade over his head. Overnight, the plant withered. When Jonah, faint with heat, asked that he might die, God said to him: "Thou art concerned about a gourd for which thou hast not labored, neither made it grow, which came up in the night, and perished in a

night; and should I not be concerned for Nineveh, that great city, in which are more than one hundred and twenty thousand persons that cannot discern between their right hand and their left hand, and also much cattle?" (Jonah 4:10–11).

This expression, not being able "to discern between the right and left hand," is applied to one who is not cognizant or informed of a situation.

LO YASHAVTI VESOD MESAHAKIM (לא ישבתי בסוד משחקים). Jeremiah said to God, "I sat not in the assembly of the merrymakers" (Jer. 16:17). "I sat not alone because of Thy hand," meaning, Your prophecy.

LO YIGRA MITZADIK AYNAV (לא יגרע מצדיק עיניו). "He [God] withdraws not His eyes from the righteous" (Job 36:7). This statement was made by Elihu, the youngest of Job's four friends, who declared this when a Divine revelation came upon him while he slept.

LO YIPALAY MIMEKHA KOL DAVAR (לא יפלא ממך כל דבר). "Nothing is hidden from You" (Jer. 32:17). This is what Jeremiah said to God after he had bought a piece of land in the city of Anathot. He complained: "Why did You tell me to buy this land when You well know that we will be driven out."

LO YIRAVU VELO YITZMA'U VELO YAKAYM SHARAV VASHAMESH (לא ירעבו ולא יצמאו ולא יכם שרב ושמש). "They shall not hunger nor thirst; neither shall the heat nor sun smite them" (Isa. 49:10). These are the words of God comforting His people.

LO YODAYA AVAL BOSHET (לא יודע עול בשת). "The unjust knows no shame" (Zep. 3:5). A verse with a similar thought is GAM BOSH LO YAYVOSHU VEHIKALAYM LO YADA'U ("But they were not at all ashamed, neither could they blush") (Jer. 8:12; cf. also ibid., 6:15).

A comparable Yiddish expression is *Shpay a besti'e in panim zuhgt er a regn geyt* ("Spit a brute in the face and he says, 'It is raining'").

LO YOSIFU LEDA'AVAH OD (לא יוסיפו לדאבה עוד). "They shall not languish in sorrow anymore" (Jer. 31:11). This is what God tells Jeremiah to tell the people of Israel, "for I will turn their mourning to joy, and will comfort them and make them rejoice from their sorrow" (ibid., 31:12).

LO YITAYN LE'OLAM MOT LATZADIK (לא יתן לעולם מוט לצדיק). The Holy Spirit answers David, "Cast thy burden upon the Lord, and He will sustain you; He will never allow the faltering of the righteous [*Lo yitayn le'olam mot latzadik*]" (Ps. 55:23). If it happens that the righteous person slips, it is not forever; God helps him again.

LO YITZLAH LAKOL (לא יצלח לכל). "It was not fit for anything," or "it was profitable for nothing" (Jer. 13:7). This refers to the girdle that Jeremiah was commanded to hide in Perat.

Colloquially, the phrase *lo yutzlah* refers to one who lacks good fortune and is a ne'er-do-well, a failure.

LO ZEH HADEREKH (לא זה הדרך). "This is not the way" (2 Kings 6:19). After the Syrian warriors were struck blind, Elisha said, "This is not the way" and offered to lead them to the person and the place that they sought. He led them to Samaria.

Colloquially, the expression took on the meaning "This is not the means to a particular end or method of life or action."

LOVEH RASHA VELO YESHALAYM VETZADIK HONAYN VENOTAYN (לוה רשע ולא ישלם וצדיק חונן ונותן). "The wicked borroweth, and payeth not; but the righteous dealeth graciously, and giveth" (Ps. 37:21).

MADU'A DEREKH RESHA'IM TZA-LAYHAH (מדוע דרך רשעים צלחה). "Why does the way of the wicked prosper?" (Jer. 12:1).

MEH KOL HEHAMON HAZEH? (מה קול ההמון הזה?). Israel was beaten by the Philistines, the Ark of God was taken, and Hofni and Phineas (Eli's two sons) were slain. Eli, who judged the people for forty years, and was ninety-eight years old, heard a crying noise and said: *Meh kol hahamon hazeh* ("What is the noise of this multitude?"; 1 Sam. 4:14).

MAH MATOK MIDVASH UMEH AZ MAYARI? (מה מתוק מדבש ומה עז מארי?). "What is sweeter than honey and what is stronger than a lion?" (Judg. 14:18). This is the answer to the riddle that Samson asked the Philistines.

The phrase *matok midvash* is applied to any unusual taste of a food or of a spoken word.

MAH TOV UMAH NA'IM SHEVET AHIM GAM YAHAD (מה טוב ומה נעים שבת אחים גם יחד). "How good and how pleasant it is for brethren to dwell together in unity!" (Ps. 133:1)—that is, when the Israelites, who are called brothers, will sit together in the land of Israel.

MAH YADATA VELO NAYDA (מה ידעת ולא נדע). Eliphaz, Job's friend, says to him, "What knowst thou, that we know not?" (Job 15:9). Eliphaz argues with Job for turning his spirit against God: What kind of wisdom do you (Job) have that we have not?

MAR NEFESH (מר נפש). "Embittered of soul" or "discontented" (1 Samuel 22:2). A description of about four hundred men who followed David to the cave of Adullam as a precaution, in case Saul might wreak his vengeance upon them.

The phrase *mar nefesh* is also used in Judges 18:25, where it infers "angry fellows," or perhaps "men of nasty temper."

MASHGI'AH MIN HAHALONOT (משגיח מן החלונות). A phrase in Song of Songs 2:9, meaning "He looketh in through the windows."

The Book of Songs of Songs is understood by the *Midrash* and *Targum*, as well as by medieval commentators, as depicting the spiritual marriage between God and Israel after the Revelation at Sinai. Peering through the lattice-window is interpreted by the *Midrash* to mean that the *Shekhinah* is looking through the outstretched hand of the priest when he blesses the people.

In Jewish life a *mashgi'ah* (from *shagayah*, "to look," "gaze at") is appointed to supervise the observance of *kashrut* regulations. When he does not fulfill this requirement, the phrase *Mashgi'ah min hahalonot* is humorously applied to him, for instead of being in the kitchen, he is looking through the windows.

MAYAZ YATZA MATOK (מעז יצא מתוק). See AYN RA SHE'AYN BO TOV.

MAYEMINIM UMASMILIM (מימינים ומשמאלים). "Both the right [hand] and the left" (1 Chron. 12:2)—that is, ambidextrous. This describes the mighty men who came to David at Ziklag while he was outlawed because of Saul. They were armed with bows and could use both the right hand and the left with equal ease in slinging stones and shooting arrows.

MAYHAYIL EL HAYIL (מחיל אל חיל). "[They advance] from strength to strength" (Ps. 84:8). R. Levi b. Hiyya said that this refers to "One who, on leaving the synagogue, goes into the house of study and studies the Torah; he is deemed worthy to welcome the Divine Presence" (Ber. 64a). R. Hiyya b. Ashi, in the name of Rab, remarked on this verse: "The

disciples of the wise have no rest either in this world or in the World to Come" (ibid.) because they are always progressing in their spiritual strivings.

When wishing a person who is about to advance in any endeavor the capacity for excellence or vigor, the expression used is "May you go *mayhayil el hayil.*"

MAYRESHA'IM YAYTZAY RESHA

(מרשעים יצא רשע). "Out of the wicked cometh forth wickedness" (1 Sam. 24:13); that is, wicked and vengeful deeds spring only from wicked men.

MEKHABDAI AKHABAYD UVOZAI YAYKALU (מכבדי אכבד ובזי יקלו).

The Lord saith: "For them that honor Me [i.e., the children of Phinehas] I will honor, and they that despise Me [i.e., the children of Eli] shall be lightly esteemed" (1 Sam. 2:30).

MENAY MENAY TEKAYL UFARSIN

(מנא מנא תקל ופרסין). In the days of Belshazzar, king of Babylon, the gold and silver vessels taken from the Temple at Jerusalem were brought out "and the king and his lords, his wives and his concubines drank from them" (Dan. 5:3). At the instant of this sacrilege, a disembodied hand appeared and wrote on the palace wall *Menay Menay Tekayl Ufarsin* (ibid., 5:25), which no one could decipher until Daniel was summoned. Daniel read and interpreted these four words as follows: *Menay*—God has numbered thy kingdom, and brought it to an end. *Tekayl*—Thou are weighed in the balances, and art found wanting. *Ufarsin*—Thy kingdom is divided, and given to Medes and Persians. "In that night Belshazzar . . . was slain; And Darius the Mede received the kingdom" (ibid., 5:30, 6:1).

Menay Menay Tekayl Ufarsin has become associated with the expression "See the handwriting on the wall"—in other words, "a dire forewarning."

MI SHAMA KAZOT, MI RA'AH KA'AYLEH? (מי שמע כזאת, מי ראה כאלה?). "Who has heard of such a thing; who has seen such a thing?" (Isa. 66:8). Isaiah continues: "Shall the earth be made to bring forth in one day; or shall a nation be born in one moment," as it happened? Traces of the envisioned end of days were already seen at this time. Israel will emerge from spiritual darkness to the light that will shine for them in Zion.

MIKAF RAGLO VE'AD KADKADO LO HAYAH VO MUM (מכף רגלו ועד קדקדו לא היה בו מום). See MIKAF REGEL VE'AD ROSH AYN BO METOM.

MIKAF REGEL VE'AD ROSH AYN BO METOM (מכף רגל ועד ראש אין בו מתם). "From the sole of the foot even to the head there is no soundness in it" (Isa. 1:6). Using the same descriptive language, a verse in 2 Samuel 14:25 states, MIKAF RAGLO VE'AD KADKADO LO HAYAH VO MUM ("From the sole of his foot to the crown of his head there was no blemish in him"—that is, Absalom).

The phrase *Mikaf regel ve'ad rosh* has been colloquially taken to mean "from top to bottom."

MIKOL MELAMDAI HISKALTI (מכל מלמדי השכלתי). "From all my teachers I grew wise" (Ps. 119:99); that is, I learn from every teacher. They taught me that Your testimonies are my conversation (cf. Radak, ad loc.). Ibn Ezra (ad loc.) interprets the phrase to mean, "I have become wiser than all my teachers"; that is, he maintains that all his conversations are God's testimonies which have given him the truest discernment of Torah and thus he has learned more than from his teachers. The *Mishnah* (*Avot* 4:1) teaches, "Ben Zoma says: Who is wise? He who learns from every person, as it is said: 'From all my teachers I grew wise.'"

MILAYDAH UMIBETEN UMAY-HAYRAYON (מלדה ומבטן ומהריון).

Their honor will depart from them (that is, the Ten Tribes) "from birth, pregnancy, and conception" (Hos. 9:11).

Colloquially, the expression infers "from the beginning" or "from the start."

MIN HAPAHAT EL HAPAH (מן הפחת אל הפח).

Literally, "from the pit to the trap"; a saying based on Isaiah 24:18, which states, "And it shall come to pass, that he who flees from the noise of the fear shall fall into the pit [*pahat*]; and he that comes up out of the midst of the pit shall be taken in the trap" (*bapah*).

The English equivalent is "from the frying pan into the fire."

MIN HAYOM HAHU VAHALAH (מן היום ההוא והלאה).

"From that day onwards" (Ezek. 39:22). If Israel would not repent of their own accord, Ezekiel taught, the Almighty would redeem them and make them repent against their will for His Name's sake. "So the house of Israel shall know that I am the Lord their God from that day onwards" (ibid.).

MIPI OLELIM VEYONKIM YISA-DETA OZ (מפי עוללים וינקים יסדת עז).

"Out of the mouths of babes and sucklings You have established strength" (Ps. 8:3). The psalmist emphasized the spiritual power that comes from the mouth of infants.

MISHIKHMO VAMALAH GAVO'AH MIKOL HA'AM (משכמו ומעלה גבה מכל העם).

Describing Saul's stature, Scripture states, "from his shoulders and upward he was higher than any of the people" (1 Sam. 9:2). The description is applied to any distinguished person who excels in talent and understanding.

MOSHAYL BA'ADAM TZADIK MOSHAYL YIRAT ELOHIM (מושל באדם צדיק מושל יראת אלהים).

Among David's last words are a description of an ideal ruler: "He that rules over men must be just, ruling in the fear of God" (2 Sam. 23:3).

NA'ALAMIM (נעלמים).

Literally, "they who hide themselves," as in *ve'im na'alamim lo avo* ("nor with hypocrites will I go") (Ps. 26:4). These are persons who conceal their evil intentions behind an outward semblance of friendship.

NAFLAH ATERET ROSHAYNU (נפלה עטרת ראשנו).

"The crown of our head is fallen" (Lam. 5:16). This verse refers to the destruction of the First and Second Holy Temples.

The phrase is often said or printed on an announcement when the head of the family or a great person dies.

NAYTZAH YISRAEL LO YE-SHAKAYR (נצח ישראל לא ישקר).

"The glory [a title of God] of Israel will not lie" (1 Sam. 15:29), inferring that there is hope for Israel.

NEHBA EL HAKAYLIM (נחבא אל הכלים).

Literally, "hidden among the baggage" (1 Sam. 10:22). Samuel gathered up all the Israelites and selected Saul to be king. Scripture states, "When they sought him, he could not be found. Therefore, they inquired again of the Lord, 'Did the man come here?' And the Lord answered, 'Behold, he is hidden among the baggage.'"

The expression is applied to one who is shy, "timid," "unassuming," or "keeps in the background."

NETZOR LESHONKHA MAYRA (נצר לשונך מרע).

"Keep thy tongue from evil" (Ps. 34:14). A similar verse appears in Proverbs 18:21, "Death and life are in the power of the tongue."

The verse, prefixed with "My Lord," appears in the closing meditation, composed by Mar, the son of Ravina (fourth century), of every *Amidah* prayer (see

Macy Nulman, *The Encyclopedia of Jewish Prayer* [Northvale, New Jersey and London: Jason Aronson Inc., 1993], p. 125).

NILAYTI HINAHAYM (נלאיתי הנחם). "I am weary of relenting" (Jer. 15:6). The Lord says to the people of Israel, "Thou hast forsaken Me . . . I will stretch out My hand against you and destroy you; I am weary of relenting" (ibid.).

NILAYTI KHALKAYL VELO UKHAL (נלאיתי כלכל ולא אוכל). Jeremiah said to God that he speaks to the people of violence and ruin and they deride him. He no longer wishes to speak in His Name. But God's word is like a burning fire infusing his bones. "I am weary with containing myself, and I cannot" (Jer. 20:9).

NILAYTI NESO (נלאיתי נשא). "I am weary of enduring them" (Isa. 1:14). Isaiah, speaking in the Name of God, tells the Israelites that their sacrifices on New Moons and feasts are vain offerings and are troublesome.

NIMSHAL KABEHAYMOT NIDMU (נמשל כבהמות נדמו). "He [man] is like the beasts that perish" (Ps. 49:13). He prides himself on his wealth and possessions, achieving utter insignificance. Bodily, he achieves the same end as an animal.

NISHARNU ME'AT MAYHARBEH (נשארנו מעט מהרבה). "We are left but a few of many" (Jer. 42:2). These are the words said to Jeremiah by all of the captains of the forces, including the son of Kareah, a captain of the scattered remnants of the army of Judah. They requested that Jeremiah accept their supplication and pray to God for them, so that God will show them the way to walk and the things they should do.

ODKHA MAHAZIK BETUMA-TEKHA (עדך מחזיק בתמתך). After Satan smote Job with vile sores from the sole of his foot to his crown, his wife said to him, "Dost thou still retain thy integrity?" (Job 2:9). She wished that he would curse God and die.

ONEG SHABBAT (ענג שבת). Isaiah (57:13) writes, among other duties *Vekarata la-Shabbat oneg* ("and call the Sabbath a delight"), "then shalt thou delight thyself in the Lord . . ." The Talmud (Shab. 118b) states, "Rab Judah said, in Rab's name: He who delights in the Sabbath is granted his heart's desires, for it is said, 'Delight thyself also in the Lord; and He shall give thee the desires of thine heart' (Ps. 37:3). Now, I do not know what this 'delight' refers to; but when it is said, 'and thou shalt call the Sabbath a delight' (Isa., ibid.), *hevay omayr zeh oneg Shabbat* ['you must say that it refers to the delight of the Sabbath']."

The *Oneg Shabbat* movement became popular in Tel-Aviv, Israel, when the Hebrew poet Hayyim Nahman Bialik (1873–1934) introduced Sabbath afternoon gatherings in the form of Torah study and *zemirot*. In the United States and elsewhere, such gatherings were instituted on Friday nights or Sabbath afternoons.

OY (אוי). A word expressing "pain," "grief," or "sorrow," as in *Oy lanu ki lo hayetah kazot* ("Woe to us, for there has not been such a thing") (1 Sam. 4:7). Other words expressing sorrow are: *Ah*, as in *Ah el kol to'avot ra'ot* ("Alas for all the evil abominations") (Ezek. 6:11), *Voy*, as in *Voy ledin kad yakum din* ("Woe to the one [Esau] when that one [Jacob] shall rise") (A.Z. 11b); *Alelai* as in *Alelai lo ki hayiti ke'aspay kayitz* ("Woe is to me for I am like the last of the summer fruits") (Mic. 7:1), *Avoy* as in *Lemi oy lemi avoy* ("Who cries, Woe? Who cries, Alas?") (Prov. 23:29), and *Oyah* as in *Oyah li* ("Woe unto me") (Ps. 120:5). Sometimes the two expressions *oy* and *avoy* are uttered in one breath producing *oy vavoy*, signifying great stress or anguish.

PANIM SHEL EKHAH (פנים של אֵיכה). "A gloomy face," an expression used among Spanish Jews. The third of the Five Scrolls in the Bible is known as *Ekhah*. It laments the fall of the Jews and Jerusalem after the destruction of the First Temple. The *Midrash* interprets the word as *tokhahah* ("admonition"). R. Nehemia says: *Ayn ekhah ela kinah*, the word *ekhah* must mean "lamentation" (*Ekhah Rabbah* 1:1).

PEH EHAD (פה אחד). Literally, "one mouth," that is, "with one accord" (Josh. 9:2). All the kings who were on the same side of the Jordan as the Israelites decided, with one accord, to war with Joshua and the Israelites (cf. also 1 Kings 22:13).

PI KEHEREV HADAH (פי כחרב חדה). ["He has made my] mouth like a sharp sword" (Isa. 49:2).

PI TZADIK YEHEGEH HOKHMAH (פי צדיק יהגה חכמה). "The mouth of the righteous man utters wisdom" (Ps. 37:30).

POSAYAH AL SHTAY HASE'IPIM (פוסח על שתי הסעיפים). The question asked in 1 Kings 18:21 is, *Ad matai atem poshim al shtay hase'ipim?* ("How long will you go limping between two opinions?"). The phrase has come to mean "to waver," "to vacillate," "to be indecisive." See HAYN SHELKHA TZEDEK, VELAV SHELKHA TZEDEK.

RABU MISA'AROT ROSHI SONAI HINAM (רבו משערות ראשי שנאי חנם). "They that hate me without a cause are more than the hairs of my head" (Ps. 69:5).

RAHAYL MEVAKAH AL BANEHAH (רחל מבכה על בניה). "Rachel weeping for her children" (Jer. 31:14). Rachel, the matriarch of Israel, was the wife of Jacob and the mother of Joseph and Benjamin. She appears as the central character, often in connection with the theme of Jeremiah

31:14–15. Jeremiah visualizes her weeping in Ramah for her children who are in exile. See also *Rashi* to Genesis 48:7.

RAYSHIT HOKHMAH YIRAT HA-SHEM (ראשית חכמה יראת ה'). "The beginning of wisdom is the fear of God" (Ps. 111:10).

Colloquially, the first two words, *Rayshit hokhmah*, came to stand for "the first condition is to begin with *hokhmah*" (wisdom).

ROFAY ELIL KULKHEM (רפאי אלל כלכם). "You are all physicians of no value" (Job 13:4). Job, in his lengthy philosophical disputation with his four friends, makes this statement. *Rashi* (ad loc.) comments that the word *alal* is the name of a vein in the neck. When it is severed, there is no cure. Job says: "You, my friends, are like those who want to cure this vein. Just as there is no remedy for it, so your talk does not help me."

Colloquially, the expression *Rofay elil* refers to a doctor who does not know his work and does not cure.

ROMEMOT AYL BIGRONAM, VEHEREV PIFIYOT BEYADAM (רוממות אל בגרונם, וחרב פיפיות בידם). "The lofty praises of God are in their throats, and a double-edged sword is in their hand" (Ps. 149:6). The sentence is explained in the following manner: While Israel praised God, they remained armed for further battle. The Maccabean warriors are described as fighting with their hands and praying to God with their hearts (2 Macc. 15:27), thus keeping this verse in their minds and hearts.

The verse became an enigmatic saying for a person who has a honeyed tongue, but a heart of gall—or, a hypocrite.

SEH FEZURAH YISRAEL (שה פזורה ישראל). "Israel is a scattered sheep" (Jer. 50:17). Just as scattered sheep are separated from their herd, so is Israel separated from its land. "And I will bring Israel back again to his habitation" (ibid., 19), says the Lord.

SHAMOR MAHSOM LEFEH (שמור מחסום לפה). "Guard your mouth with a muzzle," as in eshmerah lefi mahsom ("I will guard my mouth with a muzzle") (Ps. 39:2).

SHIVITI HASHEM LENEGDI TAMID (שויתי ה' לנגדי תמיד). "I have set the Lord always before me" (Ps. 16:8). The Shulhan Arukh, Orah Hayyim 1:1, quotes this verse with the comment, "This is the leading principle in religion [Hu klal gadol batorah], and in the upward strivings of the righteous who walk ever in the presence of God." The word shiviti became a cliché for Jewish devotion and common language.

A plaque called SHIVITI is sometimes put up in synagogues in front of the worshipers. It contains the above verse, as well as other verses concerning the Torah and Jewish law, and is usually decorated with various shapes and colors. The decoration includes the seven-branched Menorah of the Temple. It is also printed in Siddurim and, when reciting Psalms 67, it is appropriate to have a mental picture of the Menorah (cf. Macy Nulman, The Encyclopedia of Jewish Prayer [Northvale, New Jersey: Jason Aronson, Inc., 1993], pp. 207, 208). See MIZRAH.

SHOKHAYN (YORAYD) AFAR (שוכן (יורד) עפר). An expression meaning "dead." It is written in Isaiah 26:19, "Awake and sing, you that dwell in dust [shokhayn afar]: for thy dew is as the dew on herds, and the earth shall cast out the shades of the dead."

SHOLAYF HEREV (שולף חרב). A nickname for "a warrior," as in mayah ve'esrim elef ish sholayf herev ("a hundred and twenty thousand men that drew sword") (Judg. 8:10).

SHOMAYR PETAYIM HASHEM (שומר פתאים ה'). "The Lord preserveth the simple" (Ps. 116:6). The Book of Proverbs states, Peti ya'amin lekhol davar ("A simple man believes everything") (14:15), denoting that he is naive and thus can be influenced both for good and bad. He therefore needs instruction and discipline (cf. also Yeb. 12b; Shab. 129b).

The phrase, in daily parlance, is used regarding a person who is lacking in sense or is simply foolish.

SIMU YAD AL PEH (שימו יד על פה). "Lay your hand upon your mouth" (Job 21:5). Job is saying to his four friends, Hear my speech and then you will mock. "Turn to me and be astonished and lay your hand upon your mouth" (ibid.), because you will not know what to answer me.

SOMAYKH HASHEM LEKHOL HANOFLIM (סומך ה' לכל הנפלים). A verse appearing in Psalms 145:14 and recited three times daily in Ashray, meaning "The Lord upholds all that fall." (See Macy Nulman, The Encyclopedia of Jewish Prayer [Northvale, New Jersey: Jason Aronson, Inc., 1993], p. 43.

TAHAT AHAVATI YISTENUNI (תחת אהבתי ישטנוני). "In return for my love they are my adversaries" (Ps. 109:4). This is David's personal cry and a cry to those who will oppress Israel in exile.

TAMOT NAFSHI IM PELISHTIM (תמת נפשי עם פלשתים). Samson said, "Let me die with the Philistines" (Judg. 16:30). The Philistines gathered in their temple for a religious festival and Samson joined them. Uttering a final prayer to the Lord for vengeance for the Philistines' cruelty in putting out his eyes, he seized the temple pillars and brought the building toppling down, killing himself and the three thousand worshipers.

The expression *tamot nafshi im Pelishtim* has become closely associated with the spirit of vengeance. A person will even inflict harm upon himself as he takes revenge on someone who caused him injury or offense.

TEMOTAYT RASHA RA'AH (תמותת רשע רעה). "Evil shall kill the wicked" (Ps. 34:22). The very evil that they set in motion will destroy them (*Rashi, Radak*, ad loc.). Ibn Ezra comments that the singular Hebrew form of evil is a sufficient stroke to put an end to the wicked; the righteous, however, are able to survive many such blows.

TORAT HASHEM TEMIMAH (תורת ה' תמימה). "The law of the Lord is perfect" (Ps. 19:8).

TZARAH KORAH LEHAVERTAH (צרה קוראה לחברתה). "One misfortune follows another" (*Rashi*; Ps. 42:8). *Rashi* makes this comment on the phrase *Tehom el tehom koray* ("Deep calleth unto the deep"—that is, as roaring water descending upon Israel in exile).

The English equivalent is "Misfortunes never come singly."

UGAH BELI HAFUKHAH (עגה בלי הפוכה). "[Ephraim is] a cake not turned" (Hos. 7:8). Ephraim is like a cookie that is baked on coals and, before it is turned over to the other side, it is burned; thus the cookie is not baked well. This expression is applied to a person who is half-baked.

VA'ANI VA'AR VELO AYDA (ואני בער ולא אדע). "I was brutish and ignorant" (Ps. 73:22). These are the words spoken by Asaph. He was perturbed by the sight of wicked men triumphing and flourishing (*Metzudat David*, ad loc.), and yet never wavered. This is a fitting phrase to utter when realizing that an error has been made.

VEHAGITA BO YOMAM VALAILAH (והגית בו יומם ולילה). After Moshe died, God tells Joshua that the Torah shall not depart from his mouth; "but thou shalt meditate therein day and night" (Josh. 1:8). By doing this, his ways will prosper and he will be successful.

VELAMAH TITGAREH BERA'AH (ולמה תתגרה ברעה). "Why shouldst thou meddle with evil?" (2 Kings 14:10). "Thou [Amaziah] hast indeed smitten Edom, and thy heart has lifted thee up: keep thy glory and stay at home: for why shouldst thou meddle with evil, that thou shouldst fall, thou, and Judah with thee?" (ibid.).

VEROSHO LA'AV YAGI'A (וראשו לעב יגיע). "His head reaches the clouds" (Job 20:6); an expression signifying "he is exceedingly arrogant." It may also signify "of highest rank."

YAGDIL TORAH VEYADIR (יגדיל תורה ויאדיר). "That the Torah be made great and glorious" (Isa. 42:21). Isaiah says, God wishes to open your ears for [Israel's] righteousness sake, thus He magnifies the Torah (cf. *Rashi*, ad loc.). The *Tanna* R. Hananiah b. Akashyah augmented this with the excerpt RATZAH HAKADOSH BARUKH HU LEZAKOT ET YISRAEL LEFIKHAKH HIRBAH LAHEM TORAH UMITZVOT ("The Holy One, blessed be He, desired to enlarge Israel's merits, therefore He multiplied for them Torah and commandments"), as it is said (ibid.), "The Lord desired for the sake of its [Israel's] righteousness that the Torah be made great and glorious" (Mak. 3:16). This *Mishnah* is usually appended after every study session, since the *Kaddish Derabbanan* can only be recited after public study of *Aggadah*. Although *Pirkay Avot* is *Aggadah*, it is also recited after each chapter to uphold the custom of reciting this passage after every study session.

YAGI'AH YARDAYN EL PIHU (יגיח יברדן אל פיהו). "He drinks up a river" (Job 40:23). This refers to the SHOR HABAR. The phrase became an enigmatic saying for "a drunkard."

YAHAYV HOKHMETA (HOKHMAH) LEHAKIMIN (יהב חכמתא (חכמה) לחכימין). Nebuchadnezzar, king of the Babylonian Empire, (B.C.E. 605–561) had a dream. Neither the magician nor the conjurer nor the Kasdian were able to interpret it for him. After he had slain them, he called upon Daniel. Daniel apprised his companions, Hananiah, Mishael, and Azariah, to beg mercy from God concerning this secret. The secret was revealed to Daniel in a night vision and Daniel blessed God. Among God's attributes, he mentions "He gives wisdom to the wise" (*Yahayv hokhmeta lehakimin*) (Dan. 2:21).

YAMIM YEDABAYRU (ימים ידברו). "Days should speak" (Job 32:7). Job argues that there is no justice in the world but nevertheless he cleaves to God and seeks justification of His ways. One of his younger friends, Elihu, the son of Barachel the Buzite, leads a discussion with three older friends and says *Amarti yamim rabim* ("I thought of talking these days") and assumes the duty of replying to Job.

This saying can generally be used when one contemplates expressing a view as a speaker, interpreter, or questioner.

YARSHI'AKHA FIKHA VELO ANI, USEFATEKHA YA'ANU VAKH (ירשיעך פיך ולא אני. ושפתיך יענו בך). "Thy own mouth condemns thee, and not I: yea, thy own lips testify against thee" (Job 15:6). Eliphaz, from Teman, was Job's friend, and, in a philosophical disputation, Eliphaz confronts Job with the above remark.

YASHVU ISH TAHAT GAFNO VETAHAT TE'AYNATO (ישבו איש תחת גפנו ותחת תאנתו). "They shall sit every man under his vine and under his fig tree" (Mic. 4:4), an expression denoting complete rest and total tranquility. See ISH TAHAT GAFNO VETAHAT TE'AYNATO.

YAYIN NESEKH (יין נסך). See YAYIN YESAMAH LEVAV ENOSH.

YAYIN YESAMAH LEVAV ENOSH (יין ישמח לבב אנוש). "Wine gladdens man's heart" (Ps. 104:15). Similar expressions are "wine which cheers God and men" (Judg. 9:13) and "wine makes life joyful" (Eccl. 10:19). *Radak* (Ps. 104:15) comments that moderation, not abstinence, is advocated in wine consumption. Drinking wine drives out melancholy, heightens the intellect, and prepares the mind for prophecy. An allusion to using wine when making *Kiddush* are the seventy words (without *yom hashishi* and *ki vanu vaharta*, which some rites exclude), which are equivalent to that of the word *yayin* ("wine") (cf. *Zohar* 3, *Emor* 95a; *Tikkunay Zohar, Tikkun* 23). Wine is also used at *Havdalah* and for the four cups at the Passover *Seder*.

Scripture considers drinking too much wine to be contemptuous, as is written, "Wine is treacherous" (Hab. 2:5) or "He who loves wine and oil shall not be rich" (Prov. 21:17). Scripture also cites the law of the Nazirite who must abstain from intoxication: "he shall abstain from wine and strong drink" (Numb. 6:3).

When the Second Temple was destroyed, large numbers of Israelites became ascetics and did not drink wine. R. Joshua, after lengthy conversation, persuaded them by saying, "My sons, come and listen to me; not to mourn at all is impossible . . . to mourn overmuch is also impossible, because we do not impose on the community a hardship which the majority cannot endure" (B.B. 60b).

A wine forbidden to the Jew, called YAYIN NESEKH (wine from which a libation has been poured on the altar), is wine known or suspected to have been handled by an idolator. The supposition was that the idolator may have dedicated the wine as an offering to his deity. The expression is derived from *yayn nesikham* ("wine of their drink-offering") in Deuteronomy 32:38. Thus, any wine that comes in contact with a non-Jew (*stam yaynam*) is forbidden, as we are told that Daniel "resolved that he would not defile himself with the king's food, nor with the wine which he drank" (Dan. 1:8).

A wine reserved for the feast of the righteous in the future world is the YAYIN HAMESHUMAR. This, according to R. Joshua b. Levi, is "the wine which has been preserved [*Yayin Meshumar*] in its grapes from the six days of creation" (Ber. 34b). See LEHAYYIM; SHOR HABAR.

YEFAYH-FIYAH (יפה-פיה). A word meaning "pretty" or "very beautiful." It is written in Jeremiah 46:20, *Eglah yefayh-fiyah mitzrayim* ("Egypt is a very fair heifer"); that is, Egypt is a very beautiful calf.

Colloquially, the expression *eglah yefayh-fiyah* became associated with "a pretty but foolish woman" or "dainty but dumb."

YEGI'A KAPEKHA KI TOKHAYL, ASHREKHA VETOV LAKH (יגיע כפיך כי תאכל, אשריך וטוב לך). "When you eat the labor of your hands, you are praiseworthy, and it shall be well with you" (Ps. 128:2). This teaches the dignity of honest work. God sends His blessing when man toils with his own two hands; he is praiseworthy in this world and it is good for the World to Come. (See *Rashi* and *Radak*, ad loc.)

YEHERAD LIBI VEYITAR MIME-KOMO (יחרד לבי ויתר ממקומו). "My heart trembles and is moved out of its place" (Job 37:1). These are the words of Elihu, the youngest friend of Job, who is astonished at God's actions in this world.

YEHI MAKIRAYKH BARUKH (יהי מכירך ברוך). "Blessed be he that did take knowledge of thee" (Ruth 2:19). Naomi, Ruth's mother-in-law, guessed from the abundance of corn she brought home and the joy on her face that gleaning had been done in the field of a particularly friendly owner. Thus, she asked, "Where hast thou gleaned today?" and continued with, "blessed be he [Boaz] that did take knowledge of thee."

YESHARIM DARKHAY HASHEM, TZADIKIM YAYLKHU VAM UFO-SHIM YIKASHLU VAM (ישרים דרכי ה'. צדיקים ילכו בם ופושעים יכשלו בם). "The ways of the Lord are right, and the just do walk in them; but the transgressors shall stumble in them" (Hos. 14:10).

It is told that a person approached a hasidic rebbe in a derisive manner and said to him, "You are always singing wordless tunes, using such syllables as *bim-bim*, *bi-ri-bam* and so forth." "True," answered the rebbe, "it depends on who sings the *bam*, *tzadikim yaylkhu bam*, *ufoshim yikashlu bam*."

YIRAT HASHEM HI HOKHMAH, VESUR MAYRA BINAH (יראת ה' היא חכמה, וסור מרע בינה). See YIRAT SHAMAYIM.

YODAYA SEFER (יודע ספר). "A learned person," as in *asher yitnu oto el yodaya sefer* ("which is given to one that is learned") (Isa. 29:11).

YOM BESORAH HU VA'ANAHNU MAHSHIM (יום בשרה הוא ואנחנו מחשים). The prophet Elisha said, "Hear the word of the Lord," that in Shomron fine flour and barley will be sold. Four afflicted men went to the camp of Aram and ate and drank. They then said to each other that they were not behaving correctly, "the day is a day of good tidings, and we hold our peace" (*Yom besorah hu va'anahnu mahshim*) (2 Kings 7:9), meaning, we have something good to tell the Israelites and we are keeping quiet.

YOSIF AL HATATO FESHA (יסיף על חטאתו פשע).

Elihu, the youngest of Job's four friends, said to God that Job should be punished, for he "adds rebellion to his sin" (*Yosif al hatato fesha*) (Job 34:37) with his talk against God.

ZAKHARTI LAKH HESED NE'URAYIKH AHAVAT KELULOTAYIKH (זכרתי לך חסד נעוריך אהבת כלולתיך).

"I remember in thy favor, the devotion of thy youth, thy love as a bride" (Jer. 2:2). God said to the People of Israel, I remember the kindness that I did with you in your youth, when I chose you. "Thy love as a bride" is reminiscent of the canopy under which you stood at Mount Sinai to accept the Torah (cf. *Metzudat David*, ad loc.).

ZEH BEKHOH VEZEH BEKHOH (זה בכה וזה בכה).

"One [said] in this manner, and another [said] in that manner" (1 Kings 22:20); two different ways of saying something.

ZOKHEH TZU ZAYN TZU ZEN BENEHAMAT TZIYON VIRUSHALAYIM (זוכה צו זיין צו זען בנחמת ציון וירושלים).

"To merit to see the restoration of Zion and Jerusalem"; a wish based on the consolation of the prophets regarding the redemption of the Jewish people, as appears in Isaiah 40:1: *Nahamu nahamu ami* ("Comfort ye, comfort ye, My people").

When making an oath, one may say *Koh ereh benehamah* ("May I live to see the restoration of Israel").

TALMUD
תלמוד

גמרא (תלמוד) אין לך מדה גדולה מזו

Our rabbis taught: They who occupy themselves with "Talmud—There can be nothing more meritorious."
(B.M. 33a)

Next to the Bible, no book plays so important a role in Judaism as the Talmud. Alternatives to the title "Talmud" ("study") are *Gemara* ("learning") or the abbreviation *SHaS* (*Shishah Sedarim*), alluding to the *shishah sidray Mishnah*, the six main orders or sections of the *Mishnah*. Originally, the name "Talmud" was applied only to the *Gemara*, but it now includes the *Mishnah*. The *Gemara* is contained in sixty-three tractates (Babylonian Talmud).

In both the *Mishnah* and the Talmud, the names of the orders and tractates reflect their contents rather than their authorship. Section one (eleven tractates) is called *Zera'im* ("Seeds"), section two (twelve tractates) is called *Mo'ed* ("Season"), section three (seven tractates) is called *Nashim* ("Women"), section four (ten tractates) is called *Nezikin* ("Damages"), section five (eleven tractates) is called *Kodashim* ("Holy things"), and section six (twelve tractates) is called *Taharot* ("Cleanliness" or "Purities").

When the name "Talmud" is used, it refers to the Babylonian Talmud (Talmud *Bavli*), which was concluded by the academies of Babylonia at the beginning of the sixth century. There is another Talmud, known as the Jerusalem Talmud (Talmud *Yerushalmi*), which was completed during the fifth century; only thirty-nine tractates remain. Because of the vastness of the subject matter covered by the Talmud, the expression YAM HATALMUD is used.

The maxims that follow in Aramaic are culled from Talmud *Bavli* and Talmud *Yerushalmi*. Those that are in Hebrew are from the *Mishnah*, since Judah ha-Nasi (c. 135–c. 220 C.E.), the redactor of the *Mishnah*, hoped to revive Hebrew among Jews of Palestine who spoke Aramaic. Some sayings are in Yiddish and they are based on the Talmud. The rich variety of subjects dealt with by the maxims are taken from human life (*milay de'alma*) and from regulations for the practice of religious life. *Halakhic* rulings or lengthy religious discussions often end with the quotation of a popular saying. These maxims, scattered among the discussions, played an extraordinary part in shaping Jewish character.

The sayings in *Pirkay Avot* ("Ethics of the Fathers"), one of the sixty-three tractates of the *Mishnah*, are not given here since they appear in most prayerbooks and are read and studied during the year on Sabbath afternoons.

A YUHR MIT A MITVUHKH (יאר א
מיטוואך א מיט). "A year and a Wednesday
[day]"; signifying an extended period of
time. The *Mishnah* (Ket. 2a) states: A
maiden is married on the fourth day of the
week (Wednesday) so that if the husband
had a claim as to her virginity he could go
early on the morning of the fifth day of the
week (Thursday) to the court of justice
when it sits in the town. Another *Mishnah*
(Ket. 57a) states: "A virgin is allowed
twelve months from the [time her in-
tended] husband claimed her [after their
betrothal], [in which] to prepare her marriage outfit. And, as [such a period] is
allowed for the woman, so is it allowed for
the man for his outfit. Waiting the twelve
months and getting married on Wednesday constitutes *A yuhr mit a mitvuhkh*,
thus making it a considerable extent of
time.

ADAM KAROV AYTZEL ATZMO
(עצמו אצל קרוב אדם). "Every man is
considered a relative to himself" (San.
9b). A person always loves himself and
considers his actions righteous. In a sarcastic sense, the expression is sometimes
applied to another person who is close to
him or who agrees with him. See AYN
ADAM MAYSIM ATZMO RASHA.

ADAM MU'AD LE'OLAM (אדם
לעולם מועד). "[Damage done] by a human being must, under all circumstances,
be restored in full" (B.K. 3b). Ignorance of
the law is no excuse and he is a *mu'ad*
(liable in full) whether the damage was
done intentionally or unintentionally, or
whether he was awake or asleep.

**ADAM SHE'AYN BO DAYAH ASUR
LERAHAYM ALAV** (דעה) בו שאין אדם
עליו לרחם אסור). "[R. Eleazar said:]
Whosoever lacks knowledge, one may
have no mercy upon him" (San. 92a), as it
is written, "For it is a people of no
understanding: therefore He that made
them will not have mercy upon them, and

He that formed them will show them no
favor" (Isa. 27:11).

The MaHaRSHA (Morenu Ha-Rav
SHmuel Adels [Edels]) explains this saying as follows: Surely one must have
mercy on all God's works so that their
form, as created, should not cease to exist.
But since this man was created with the
ability for knowledge and good sense, but
now lacks them, he therefore loses his
form and is not in the category of "all His
works." Thus, he should not be pitied,
because God originally made him upright
with mind and reason.

**ADAYIN LO HIGI'AH LAHATZI
YOFYAH SHEL SARAH** (לא עדיין
שרה של יופיה לחצי הגיעה). Scripture
states, with reference to Abishag the
Shunamite, of the tribe of Issachar, whom
David, in his old age, introduced into his
harem: "And the damsel was fair, until
[she was] exceedingly [so]" (1 Kings 1:4).
R. Hanina b. Papa said, "Yet she never
attained to half of Sarah's beauty, for it is
written 'until [ad] . . . exceedingly
[me'od]; 'exceedingly' itself not being included" (San. 39b); that is, she reached
only the point of medium beauty. (With
regard to Sarah's beauty, see *Rashi*, Gen.
23:1.)

This expression points out that the
woman described is not as beautiful as she
was thought to be.

ADERABA(H) (אדרבה)אדרבא). See
IPKHA MISTABRA.

AF AL PI KHAYN (כן פי על אף). An
expression meaning "nevertheless," "all
the same," or "after all" (Ber. 63b).

**AF AL PI SHEHAKHAM GADOL
ATTAH, AYNO DOMEH LOMAYD
MAYATZMO LELOMAYD MAY-
RABO** (.אתה גדול שחכם פי על אף
מרבו ללומד מעצמו לומד דומה אינו).
"Although you are a great scholar, one
who studies on his own is not on a par

with one who learns from his master" (Ket. 111a).

AF AL PI SHEHATA, YISRAEL HU (אַף עַל פִּי שֶׁחָטָא, יִשְׂרָאֵל הוּא). "Even though [the people] have sinned, they are still [called] Israel" (San. 44a). Rashi (ad loc.) comments that since it does not specify that the nation (ha'am) sinned, the holy name (Israel) is still applied to them.

AF ATTAH OSEH OZNEKHA KE'AFARKESET (אַף אַתָּה עֲשֵׂה אָזְנְךָ כָּאַפַּרְכֶּסֶת). "Also do thou make thine ear like the hopper" (Hag. 3b). The Talmud asks: Should a man say, How, in these circumstances (in view of the contradictory opinions held by the scholars), shall I learn Torah? Therefore, the text says: All of them are given from one Shepherd; One God gave them; one leader uttered them from the mouth of the Lord of all creation, blessed be He, for it is written: "And God spoke all these words" (Ex. 20:1).

The ear is compared to a hopper (afarkeset). The hopper is described as being funnel-shaped: more enters it than issues from it—that is, one should hear all views and then sift them and accept only the true.

AFILU HEREV HADAH MUNAHAT LO AL TZAVARO SHEL ADAM, AL YIMNA ATZMO MIN HARA-HAMIM (אֲפִילוּ חֶרֶב חַדָּה מוּנַחַת לוֹ עַל צַוָּארוֹ שֶׁל אָדָם, אַל יִמְנַע עַצְמוֹ מִן הָרַחֲמִים). "Even if a sharp sword rests on man's neck, he should not desist from prayer" (Ber. 10a), as it says, "Though He slay me, yet will I trust in Him" (Job 13:15). This teaches that a person should never despair.

AGAV URHA (אַגַּב אוּרְחָא). Literally, "in passing" or "incidentally" (DEREKH AGAV). For example, the Mishnah states, "Ten genealogical classes went up from Babylon" (Kidd. 4:1). The Talmud (Kidd. 69a) asks, "Why is it particularly taught

'went up from Babylon'; let him state, migrated to Eretz Yisrael?" The Talmud answers, "He [the Tanna] thereby tells us something en passant [agav urhayh] that Eretz Yisrael is higher than all [other] countries." Although the Tanna was speaking of one thought ("going up"), he incidentally lets us hear another thought. (See also Agav urhakh in San. 95b.)

AGMAT NEFESH (עַגְמַת נֶפֶשׁ). Literally, "grief of the soul" (Shab. 115a), that is, a "state of displeasure and irritation." The Talmud states, "It was taught, in accordance with R. Johanan: If Yom Kippur falls on the Sabbath, the trimming of vegetables is permitted. Nuts may be cracked and pomegranates scraped from the [time of] Minhah and onwards, on account of one's agmat nefesh." The reason is that if breaking the fast had to be delayed while these are being prepared, it would cause much annoyance and irritation (cf. R. Zerahyah ha-Levi, Ba'al Hama'or, c. 1160, Marginal Gloss).

Colloquially, the phrase is associated with any "aggravation," "heartache," or "sorrow."

AHAVAH MEVATELET (MEKALKE-LET) ET HASHURAH, VESINAH MEVATELET (MEKALKELET) ET HASHURAH (אַהֲבָה מְבַטֶּלֶת (מְקַלְקֶלֶת) אֶת הַשּׁוּרָה, וְשִׂנְאָה מְבַטֶּלֶת (מְקַלְקֶלֶת) אֶת הַשּׁוּרָה). "Either through love or hate a person can go off the right path." The Talmud (San. 105b) states that a tanna taught, on the authority of R. Simeon b. Eleazar, that love disregards the rule of dignified conduct and this is deduced from Abraham, for it is written, "And Abraham rose up early in the morning, and saddled his ass" (Gen. 22:3). (Even though saddling an ass is unbecoming for a great man, in his love for God and eagerness to carry out His commands, Abraham did it.) Hate, likewise, disregards the rule of dignified conduct. This is deduced from Balaam, for it is written, "And Balaam rose up in the morning, and

saddled his ass" (Numb. 22:21). ("Balaam the wicked" hated the Israelites and he disregarded the rule of dignified conduct and saddled the ass himself.)

AHAYNU BENAY YISRAEL (אחינו בני ישראל). Literally, "Our Jewish brethren." The expression, slightly changed to "Our brethren, the house [bayt] of Israel," was uttered twice: once by R. Akiba (M. K. 21b) and again by R. Zadok (Yom. 23a). The phrase *Ahaynu kol bayt Yisrael* ("Our brethren, the whole house of Israel") is said in the prayer service proper, on Mondays and Thursdays after the Torah is read. Nehemiah 5:8 uses the term *Ahaynu Hayehudim* ("our brethren, the Jews.").

AL AHAT KAMAH VEKHAMAH (על אחת כמה וכמה). "All the more so" or "so much the more." The Talmud (Ber. 5a) cites the case, "tooth and eye are only one limb of the man, and still [if they are hurt], the slave thereby obtains his freedom. How much more so with painful sufferings which torment the whole body of man!" This law is derived from an inference drawn from a minor premise to a major one, known in Hebrew as KAL VAHOMER (*a fortiori*). (See also Ber. 63b.)

AL DE'ATAYFT ATEFUKH, VESOF METAYEFAYIKH YETUFUN (על דאטפת אטפוך. וסוף מטיפיך יטופון). Hillel once saw a skull floating on the water. As an expression of the idea of Divine retribution, he said to it: "Because you drowned others, they drowned you; and those who drowned you will be drowned, too" (Sukk. 53a; Avot 2:6).

AL HA'AYTZIM VE'AL HA'AVANIM (על העצים ועל האבנים). "Among the trees or among the stones" (Yeb. 64a). Scripture states, "To be a God unto thee and to thy seed after thee" (Gen. 17:7). The Talmud (ibid.) comments, "Where there exists 'seed after thee' dwells the Divine Presence [among them]; but where

no 'seed after thee' exists, among whom should it dwell, among the trees or among the stones?" See DABAYR EL HA'AYTZIM VE'EL HA'AVANIM.

AL REGEL AHAT (על רגל אחת). Literally, "[to] stand on one foot"; actually, it means "in a hurry" or "in brief." The Talmud (Shab. 31a) tells the well-known story: "A certain heathen came before Shammai and said to him, 'Make me a proselyte on condition that you teach me the whole Torah while I stand on one foot.' Thereupon he repulsed him with the builder's cubit which was in his hand. When he went before Hillel, he said to him, 'What is hateful to you, do not do to your neighbor (cf. Lev. 19:18): that is the whole Torah, while the rest is the commentary thereof; go and learn it.'"

AL TATZAR TZARAT MAHAR KI LO TAYDA MAH YULAD YOM (אל תצר צרת מחר כי לא תדע מה ילד יום). The Talmud (Yeb. 63b) states, "Do not worry about tomorrow's trouble for thou knowest not what the day may beget." Tomorrow may come and you may be no more and so you have worried about a world that is not yours. See DAYAH LETZARAH BESHATAH.

AL TEHI BIRKAT (KILLELAT) HEDYOT KALAH BE'AYNEKHA (אל תהי ברכת (קללת) הדיוט קלה בעיניך). "Let not the blessing [curse] of an ordinary man be lightly esteemed in your eyes" (Meg. 15a; Ber. 7a). Two great men in their generation received blessings from ordinary men, which were fulfilled: David from Araunah and Daniel from Darius. Abimelech cursed Sarah.

AL TIFROSH MIN HATZIBBUR (אל תפרוש מן הציבור). See AL YOTZI ADAM ET ATZMO MIN HAKLALL.

AL TISHAL ET HAROFAYH, SHE'AL ET HAHOLEH (אל תשאל את הרופה. שאל את החולה). "Do not ask

the doctor, ask the patient" (based on Yom. 83a). The Talmud states, R. Jannai said: If the patient says, I need food, and the physician says, He does not need it, we listen to the patient because of the verse, "The heart knoweth its own bitterness" (Prov. 14:10). If, however, the physician says he needs it, while the patient says that he does not need it, we listen to the physician because a stupor has seized the patient and he does not feel the lack of food.

AL YA'AMOD ADAM BEMAKOM SAKANAH LOMAR SHE'OSIN LI NAYS (אל יעמוד אדם במקום סכנה לומר שעושין לי נס). R. Jannai said: "A man should never stand in a place of danger and say that a miracle will be wrought for him" (Shab. 32a).

AL YALBIN PENAY HAVAYRO BE-RABIM (אל ילבין פני חבירו ברבים). "One should not publicly put his neighbor to shame" (B.M. 59a) for he will have no portion in the World to Come. The Talmud (Ber. 43b) also states: "It is better for a man that he should cast himself into a fiery furnace rather than that he should put his fellow to shame in public. Whence do we know this? From Tamar, of whom it says, 'When she was brought forth . . .'" (Gen. 38:25). Tamar did not mention Judah's name, even to save herself from the stake.

AL YATIL ADAM AYMAH YETAY-RAH BETOKH BAYTO (אל יטיל אדם אימה יתרה בתוך ביתו). Both R. Hisda and R. Abbahu said: "A man should never terrorize his household" (Git. 6b, 7a). The Talmud enumerates various sins that this man will commit as a result of coercing his household by intimidation.

AL YESHANEH ADAM BENO BAYN HABANIM (אל ישנה אדם בנו בין הבנים). Raba b. Mehasia said, in the name of R. Hama b. Goria, in Rab's name: "A man should never single out [favor]

one son among his other sons" (Shab. 10b). The Talmud continues, "for on account of the two *sela's* weight of silk, which Jacob gave Joseph in excess of his other sons, his brothers became jealous of him and the matter resulted in our forefathers' descent into Egypt."

AL YESHANEH ADAM MIMINHAG HA'IR AFILU BENIGGUNIM (אל ישנה אדם ממנהג העיר אפילו בניגונים). See MINHAG MEVATAYL HALAKHAH.

AL YIFTAH (TIFTAH) ADAM PIV (PEH) LASATAN (אל יפתח (תפתח) אדם פיו (פה) לשטן). "A man should never speak in such a way as to give an opening to Satan." A similar expression in the English language is "Speak of the devil and he's sure to appear."

R. Joseph of the Talmud (Ber. 19a) said: What text proves this? Because it says: "We were almost like Sodom" (Isa. 1:9). What did the prophet reply to them? "Hear the word of the Lord, ye rulers of Sodom" (ibid., 1:10). Because Isaiah compared the people to Sodom and Gomorrah, they were addressed as "rulers of Sodom," "people of Gomorrah." This is to illustrate the way in which ominous words can have an evil effect (cf. also Ket. 8b).

AL YOTZI ADAM ET ATZMO MIN HAKLAL (אל יוציא אדם את עצמו מן הכלל). "[Samuel said:] A man should never exclude himself from the general body" (Ber. 49b). This principle is stated in conjunction with reciting the formula for *zimmun*. He should always say, "Let us bless."

The expression *Al yotzi adam et atzmo min haklal* also took on the same meaning as AL TIFROSH MIN HATZIBBUR ("Do not separate yourself from the community") (*Avot* 2:5; cf. also Ta'an. 11a), meaning that when the people of Israel are in distress you, too, should share in whatever befalls them.

ALAI VE'AL TZAVARI (עלי ועל צוארי). Literally, "upon me and upon my neck," that is, on "my responsibility" (Pes. 8b; A.Z. 30a). The Talmud (Pes., ibid.) states that Rab was asked: "Do scholars who reside out of town run a risk in passing through fields in the early morning or after nightfall when going to the academy?" His reply was, "Let them come; the risk is upon myself and my neck" (my responsibility). Then he was asked about returning after nightfall. He answered, "I do not know." It was stated that R. Eleazar said: Those sent to perform a religious duty will not suffer hurt, neither in their going nor in their returning.

AMDU SA'AROTAV (עמדו שערותיו). See MAKHOR SA'AR HAROSH.

AMOD AL DEVARAV (עמוד על דבריו). "Persist in his opinion" (Eduy. 1:4)—that is, not to change one's mind and be stubborn in his opinion and not agree with others. The *Mishnah* (ibid.) asks: And why do they record the opinions of Shammai and Hillel [in the previous *Mishnah*]? "To teach the following generations that a man should not [always] persist in his opinion, for behold, the fathers of the world [namely, Hillel and Shammai] did not persist in their opinions"; and they, too, agreed with the Sages, although originally they had different views.

ANI HASHUV KEMAYT (עני חשוב כמת). "A poor man is accounted as dead" (Ned. 64b). The Talmud cites four who are regarded as dead: a poor man, a leper, a blind person, and one who is childless. The poor man's life is compared to a dead person in the sense that he has no possessions (cf. Ned. 64b; ibid. 7b).

When referring to a community that can afford a proper salary or charity, the expression is AYN TZIBBUR ANI ("No community is poor"). When describing a person who portrays himself as impoverished

and wanting, the saying is *Ke'ani bapetah* ("like a beggar at the door"). See ANIYUT KEMITA.

ANI MAYVI LAKHEM RE'AYAH MIN HATORAH VE'ATEM MEVI'IN LI RE'AYAH MIN HASHOTIM! (אני מביא לכם ראיה מן התורה, ואתם מביאין לי ראיה מן השוטים). R. Ishmael replied to the rabbis at the schoolhouse: "I bring you proof from the Torah and you bring me proof from fools!" (Nid. 30b). See AYN MEVI'IN RE'AYAH MIN HASHOTIM.

ANI OMAYR LEKHA DEVARIM SHEL TA'AM VE'ATTAH OMAYR LI MIN HASHAMAYIM YERAHAMU (אני אומר לך דברים של טעם ואתה אומר לי מן השמים ירחמו). "I am telling you plain facts, and you say Heaven will show mercy!" (A.Z. 18a). This is the reply of R. Hanina to R. Jose b. Kisma, when he said to him, You are occupied with Torah, publicly gathering assemblies, contrary to the Roman decree. Don't you know that it is God Who ordained the Roman nation to reign and, in spite of this, you reply that Heaven will show mercy!

ANI SHELOMOH (אני שלמה). "I am Solomon!" I am clever and important. There is a legend (Git. 68b) that the demon Asmodeus (Ashmedai, Ashmadai; see Pes. 110a) once occupied the throne of Solomon and went about assuming Solomon's identity. He was finally recognized as not being the king because his legs were like those of a cock, and he was dethroned.

When one constantly boasts or brags and portrays himself as having knowledge, the expression *Ani Shelomoh* is jocularly applied.

ANIYAY IRKHA KODMIM (עניי עירך קודמים). "The poor of thy city get preference" (B.M. 71a). Scripture relates, "If thou lend money to any of my people that is poor by thee" (Ex. 22:24), if the choice lies between thy poor (thy relatives) and the general poor of thy town, thy poor come first; if between the poor of thy city and the poor of another town, the poor of thine own town have prior rights.

The English equivalent is "Charity begins at home."

ANIYUT KEMITAH (עניות כמיתה). "Poverty leads to death" (Ned. 7b). Unnecessary utterance of the Divine Name always leads to poverty, and poverty leads to death. See ANI HASHUV KEMAYT.

ANUS RAHAMANA PETARAYH (אנוס רחמנא פטריה). "[He was] unavoidably prevented, and the Divine Law exempts such" (Ned. 27a). The Talmud gives an instance wherein a man declared that if he did not appear within thirty days, these rights would be void. Subsequently, he was unavoidably prevented from appearing, and Rabbah ruled that it was unavoidable and that Divine Law exempted him; for it is written, "But unto the damsel shalt thou do nothing" (Deut. 22:26); this refers to a betrothed maiden who was violated against her will.

APIKOROS (EPIKUROS, EPIKIROS) (אפיקורוס). A word used to signify a heretic, or one who is lax in Jewish religious observances. The word has its origin in those who follow the Greek philosopher Epicurus (342/1–270 B.C.E.). The Epicurean philosophy was interpreted in terms of a life that was free from fear, a life of luxury and sensuous enjoyment.

Specifically, the Apikoros (apikorsim, pl.) is one who does not believe in the Divine origin of the Torah and in prophecy (Yoreh Dayah 158:2). According to the Mishnah, he has no share in the future world (San. 90a). Since he denies the authority of Torah, the Talmud (San. 99a) states, HAMEVAZEH TALMID HAKHAM, APIKOROS HAVAY ("He who insults a student of the Torah is an apikoros"). The rabbis extended this and said, "An apikoros is also one who despises a rabbi or who insults

his neighbor in the presence of a rabbi" (cf. Shabbetai b. Meir ha-Kohen, Siftay Kohen to Yoreh Dayah 158:6). According to the Orah Hayyim, if an apikoros utters a blessing, it is not permissible to respond with amen (215:2), and a person suspected of being an apikoros is not permitted to serve as a Sheli'ah Tzibbur (5:18). (See also San. 99a.)

ARBA (DALET) AMOT (ארבע (דלת) אמות). Both in the Mishnah and the Talmud (Erub. 48a), the measurement of "four cubits" has definite implications in halakhah. The Talmud (Ber. 8a) states, "Since the day the Temple was destroyed, God has nothing in His world except the four cubits of halakhah; that is, the Lord loves the gates [of the synagogue] that are distinguished through halakhah." Thus, Abaye prayed only in the place where he studied.

Concerning arba amot, the Talmud and Mishnah discuss various rulings governing the measurements of a sukkah (Sukk. 3a, b), building a wall next to a neighbor (B.B. 2:4), praying in a clean place (Ber. 3:5), thinking of Torah learning while walking (Yom. 86a), and walking after a meal (Shab. 41a). The prohibition of removing or taking something out of one domain to another on Shabbat takes into account arba amot (cf. Shulhan Arukh, Orah Hayyim 349).

The Talmud (Ber. 18a) states, "A dead body affects four cubits in respect to the recital of the Shema"; that is, a dead person affects the area of four cubits around him. This resulted in the Yiddish expression Az mer blaybt nisht dem mentch vi di dalet amot, intimating that after a person dies, all that he has left is his four cubits.

ARBA'IM YOM KODEM YETZIRAT HAVLAD BAT KOL YOTZAYT VE'OMERET: BAT PLONI LIPLONI (ארבעים יום קודם יצירת הולד בת קול) (יוצאת ואומרת: בת פלוני לפלוני). "[Rab Judah has said, in the name of Rab]: Forty days before the creation of a child, a BAT KOL issues forth and proclaims, The daughter of A is for B" (Sot. 2a).

ARBAKH ARBA TZARIKH (ערבך ערבא צריך). "Your guarantor needs a guarantor" (Sukk. 26a). The *Mishnah* states that when one is engaged on a religious errand, casual eating is permitted outside the *sukkah*, but sleeping is not permitted because the person may fall into a deep sleep. Abaye said: "With reference to that which has been taught, 'A man may indulge in casual sleep while wearing his *tefillin*, but not in regular sleep'; why do we not [in the case of the *sukkah*] fear lest he falls into a deep slumber? R. Joseph, the son of R. Ila'i, said, [The latter refers to when] the person entrusts others with the task of waking him from his sleep. R. Mesharsheya hesitated: Does not 'Your guarantor need a guarantor?'" That is, the person asked to wake him might fall asleep?

The expression may be used generally as follows: The guarantor you bring is not trustworthy; he himself needs someone to be a guarantor.

ASARAH BATLANIM (עשרה בטלנים). Literally, "ten men of leisure"; the ten unoccupied men who attend synagogue (Meg. 5a). The *Mishnah* (Meg. 1:3) states that a town was regarded as large if it had ten *batlanim* who frequented the synagogue. The ten *batlanim* of the synagogue are included among the population of 120 who make a town eligible for a *Sanhedrin* (San. 1:6). The Talmud (B.K. 82a) also states that the ten verses of the Torah that are read on Mondays and Thursdays correspond to the ten *batlanim*. *Rashi* (ibid., ad loc.) comments that "these ten *batlanim* abstain from every other work and are supported by the community for the purpose of attending to all congregational work, but especially to be in time for the regular service." Maimonides (*Yad*, Meg. 1:8) also regards them as "assigned to the synagogue for communal needs."

In the late twelfth century, Benjamin of Tudela met in Baghdad with the institution of the ten *batlanim*. Their sole occupation consisted of discharging communal affairs. They rendered decisions on legal and religious questions for all the Jewish inhabitants of the country.

The word *batlan* (sing.) in hasidic circles became associated with those who sit in the Rebbe's court or in a *shtieble* and occupy themselves with *hasidut*. In the Yiddish usage, the term became pejorative and meant one who is "impractical," an "idler," "unemployed," and "inefficient." The term *batlanut* implies "idleness," "triviality," or "absurdity."

ASHIRIM MEKAMTZIN (עשירים מקמצין). "The rich are sparing or frugal" (Men. 86a). Regarding the oil recommended for the meal-offerings, the *Mishnah* (ibid., 85b) states, "One may not bring it from a manured field" because the olives grown there are of inferior quality. Also, "one may not bring *anfakinon* [sap of the olives]." The Talmud states, "R. Hiyya used to throw it away, while R. Simeon, son of Rabbi, used to dip his food in it [*ashirim mekamtzin*]." It was R. Simeon, the son of the *Nasi*, a wealthy man, who used it with his food (cf. Hul. 46a).

ASMAKHTA BE'ALMA (אסמכתא בעלמא). "Merely a support" (Men. 92b); that is, a scriptural text used as a support for a rabbinical enactment. See KULAY ALMA LO PELIGI; ALMA DEKUSHTA; INSHAY DE'ALMA; MILAY DE'ALMA.

ASYA DEMAGAN BEMAGAN, MAGAN SHAVYAH (אסיא דמגן במגן, מגן שויה). "A physician who heals for nothing is worth nothing" (B.K. 85a); that is, an unpaid physician is likely to be careless. Similarly, ASYA REHIKA AYNA AVIRA ("If the physician is a long way off, the eye will be blind") (ibid.); that is, a physician from afar has a blind eye. He is little concerned about the fate of the person. Or, the eye

will be blind before he arrives. See TOV SHEBAROFIM LEGAYHINOM.

ASYA REHIKA AYNA AVIRA (אסיא רחיקא עינא עיירא). See ASYA DEMAGAN BEMAGAN, MAGAN SHAVYAH.

ATARTI TELAT GANVAY LO MIK-TAL (אתרתי תלת גנבי לא מיקטל). See SOF GANAV LITLIYAH.

ATIK YOMIN (עתיק יומין). "Ancient of Days" (Pes. 119a). A verse in Isaiah 23:18 has the phrase velimkhaseh atik ("and for stately clothing"). The Talmud (ibid.) asks, "What does 'and for stately clothing' mean? This refers to him who 'conceals' [mekhaseh] the things which the ancient [atik] of days concealed. And what is that? The secrets of the Torah." Others explain that it "refers to him who reveals the things that the ancient of days concealed [kisah]. And what is it? The reasons of the Torah." Daniel 7:13 describes a vision that came to the atik yomaya ("Ancient of Days"), referring to God. In Daniel 7:9 Atik Yomin ("Ancient of Days") refers to God, who is conceived to be the timeless dispenser of time.

AVAK LESHON HARA (אבק לשון הרע). "The fine shades of slander" (B.B. 164b, 165a); one of the three transgressions that no man escapes every day. The Talmud asks that surely it is possible to avoid slander. And answers: "but the fine shades of slander [lit, "dust"]; not actual, but hinted, or implied slander" (were meant). See LASHON TELITAI KATIL TELITAI; LO TAYLAYKH RAKHIL BE'AMEKHA.

AVINU SHEBASHAMAYIM (אבינו שבשמים). "Father Who is in Heaven" (Mish., Sot. 9:15). R. Eliezer the Great says: From the day the Temple was destroyed, the Sages began to be like school teachers, school teachers like synagogue attendants, synagogue attendants like common people, and the common people became more and more debased. . . .

Upon whom is it for us to rely? Upon "our Father Who is in Heaven" (Avinu Shebashamayim).

With the establishment of the State of Israel in 1948, Avinu Shebashamayim became the initial words of a prayer recited for its welfare. The prayer was composed and approved by the Chief Rabbinate of Israel.

The Yiddish equivalent is Fuhter in Himl ("Father in Heaven"). This phrase, as well as Hartziger Fuhter ("Merciful Father") and Derbarimdiker ("The Merciful One"), are Yiddish phrases that R. Levi Yitzhak of Berdichev and other hasidic masters interjected into their prayers. A surname known today for R. Levi Yitzhak of Berdichev is Derbarimdiker (S.A. Horodetzky, Hasidism and the Hasidim 2:80, note 8).

AVIRA DE'ERETZ YISRAEL MAH-KIM (אוירא דארץ ישראל מחכים). "The atmosphere [climate] of the land of Israel makes one wise" (B.B. 158b), since it is conducive to the study of Torah. Moreover, the land of Israel, the vicinity in which the word of God was made known to man, gives the land a special spiritual atmosphere.

AVODAH ZU TEFILLAH (עבודה זו תפלה). A verse in Scripture reads, "To love the Lord your God and serve Him with all your heart" (Deut. 11:13). The Talmud (Ta'an. 2a) asks: "What is Service of the Heart [Avodah]? You must say, Prayer [Tefillah]."

AYIN HARA (עין הרע). See BELI AYIN HARA (RA'AH).

AYLU VE'AYLU DIVRAY ELOHIM HAYYIM HAYN (אלו ואלו דברי אלהים חיים הן). The Talmud (Erub. 13b) writes of R. Abba, who stated, in the name of Samuel, that for three years there was a dispute between Bet Shammai and Bet Hillel; the former asserting, "The halakhah is in agreement with our views" and the latter contending, "The halakhah is in agreement with our views." A BAT KOL announced that "the utterances of both are the words of the living God" (Aylu ve'aylu divray Elohim hayyim hayn), but the halakhah is in agreement with the ruling of Bet Hillel. The Talmud continues, stating that the reason Bet Hillel was entitled to have the halakhah fixed in agreement with their rulings is because they were kindly and modest, they studied their own rulings and those of Bet Shammai (cf. Ber. 10b), and were even so humble as to mention the actions of Bet Shammai before theirs.

AYN ADAM MAKNEH DAVAR SHELO BA LE'OLAM (אין אדם מקנה דבר שלא בא לעולם). "One cannot transfer that which has not come into the world" (B.M. 33b); that is, it is nonexistent.

AYN ADAM MAYSIM ATZMO RASHA (אין אדם משים עצמו רשע). "No man may declare himself wicked" (Yeb. 25b; Ket. 18b; San. 9b). Raba said: "Every man is considered a relative to himself, and no one can incriminate himself."

AYN ADAM NITPAS BISHAT TZA'ARO (אין אדם נתפס בשעת צערו). Raba said: "A man is not held responsible for what he says when in distress" (B.B. 16b). This is derived from the verse "Job speaketh without knowledge, and his words are without wisdom" (Job 34:35). Rashi comments that since it says "without knowledge" but not "with wickedness," this indicates that he is not responsible for his words when under severe physical or mental strain or oppression.

AYN ADAM RO'EH HOVAH LE'ATZMO (אין אדם רואה חובה לעצמו). Raba said that when a disciple came before him in a lawsuit, he would not lay his head upon his pillow before seeking some points in his favor. The Maharsha comments that Raba was certainly not partial, but he believed that if

a scholar would engage in a lawsuit, he knew that right was on his side. Mar, son of R. Ashi, would not judge in a scholar's lawsuit, giving the reason that although the scholar is as dear to him as himself, "a man cannot see [anything] to his own disadvantage" (Shab. 119a).

AYN ADAM RO'EH NEGA'AY ATZMO. R. MEIR OMAYR: AF LO NEGA'AY KEROVAV (אין אדם רואה נגעי עצמו. ר' מאיר אומר: אף לא נגעי קרוביו). The Mishnah (Neg. 2:5) states: "A man may examine all signs of leprosy except his own. R. Meir ruled: Not even the leprosy signs of his relatives."

The words may simply infer that "A person does not see what plagues him." R. Meir adds: "He does not even see nega'im of his relatives"; he has no self-judgment.

AYN ADAM YODAYA MAH BELIBO SHEL HAVAYRO (אין אדם יודע מה בלבו של חברו). The Rabbis taught that seven things are hidden from man. Among them is one that is often heard from the lips of people: "A man does not know what is in his neighbor's heart" (Pes. 54b).

AYN ANI ELA BEDAYAH (אין עני אלא בדעה). Abaye said that we have it on tradition that "no one is poor unless he lacks knowledge" (Ned. 41a). See ADAM SHE'AYN BO DAYAH ASUR LERAHAYM ALAV.

AYN BERAYRAH (אין ברירה). "No retrospective selection" (Git. 24b); that is, the legal effect resulting from an actual selection previously undefined as to purpose. For example, a person had two wives with the same name and he ordered the scribe to write a letter of divorce for one of the wives whom he may choose to divorce in the future. Neither of them can be divorced (ayn berayrah) because, at the time the divorce was drafted, it was not written with special intention (lishmah) for the specific wife he had intended to divorce.

AYN BERAKHAH METZUYAH BE-TOKH BAYTO SHEL ADAM ELA BISHVIL ISHTO (אין ברכה מצויה בתוך ביתו של אדם אלא בשביל אשתו).

"Blessings rest on a man's home only on account of his wife" (B.M. 59a), for it is written, "and he treated Abram well for her sake" (Gen. 12:16). And thus did Raba say to the townspeople of Mahuza, "Honor your wives, that ye may be enriched" (ibid.). See LE'OLAM YEHAY ADAM ZAHIR BIKHVOD ISHTO.

AYN DOHIM EVEN AHARAY HA-NOFAYL (אין דוחים אבן אחרי הנופל).

"You do not cast a stone after the fallen" (Kidd. 20b); in other words, "Don't hit a man when he's down" (Yiddish: *An umgefalenem shluhgt men nit*). The Talmud states, "The school of R. Ishmael taught: Since this man became an acolyte in the service of idolatry, I might have said, Let us cast a stone after the fallen. Therefore it is said, 'After that he is sold he may be redeemed, one of his brethren shall redeem him.'" (Lev. 25:48). This teaches a lesson in tolerance.

AYN HABOR MITMALAY MAY-HULYATO (אין הבור מתמלא מחוליתו).

See AYN HAKOMETZ MASBI'A ET HA'ARI.

AYN HAKADOSH BARUKH HU MEKAPAYAH SEKHAR KOL BERI-YAH, AFILU SEKHAR SIHAH NA'AH (אין הקב"ה מקפח שכר כל בריה, אפילו שכר שיחה נאה).

R. Hiyya b. Abba said that R. Johanan had stated: "The Holy One, blessed be He, does not deprive any creature of any reward due to it, even if only for a becoming expression" (B.K. 38b).

AYN HAKADOSH BARUKH HU NOTAYN HOKHMAH ELA LEMI SHEYAYSH BO HOKHMAH (אין הקדוש ברוך הוא נותן חכמה אלא למי שיש בו חכמה).

["R. Johanan said]: The Holy One, blessed be He, gives wisdom only to one who already has wisdom" (Ber. 55a). This is derived from the verse "He giveth wisdom unto the wise, and knowledge to them that know understanding" (Dan. 2:21). Tahlifa from the West heard and repeated it before R. Abbahu. He said to him: "You learn it from there (Dan., ibid.), but we learn it from this text, namely, 'In the hearts of all that are wise-hearted I have put wisdom'" (Ex. 31:6).

AYN HAKHI NAMI (אין הכי נמי).

When the Talmud questions a ruling or asks with respect to which law it is likened, it answers *ayn hakhi nami* ("That indeed is [quite] so") (Kidd. 6a).

AYN HAKOMETZ MASBI'A ET HA'ARI (אין הקומץ משביע את הארי).

"A handful cannot satisfy a lion" (Ber. 3b). After David studied the Torah until dawn, the wise men of Israel came to him and said, "Your people require sustenance!" He said to them, "Let them go out and make a living one from the other" (Let the rich support the poor). They said to him: "A handful cannot satisfy a lion," nor AYN HABOR MITMALAY MAYHULYATO ("nor can a pit be filled up with its own clods").

AYN HASHKHINAH SHORAH MI-TOKH ATZVUT (אין השכינה שורה מתוך עצבות).

"The Divine Presence does not rest [upon man] through gloom" (Shab. 31a). Judaism does not encourage the doctrine espousing that, through self-torture or self-denial, one can discipline oneself to reach a high state, spiritually or intellectually (cf. Ned. 10a).

AYN HAVUSH MATIR ATZMO MIBAYT HA'ASURIM (אין חבוש מתיר עצמו מבית האסורים).

"The person cannot free himself from jail" (Ber. 5b). R. Johanan once fell ill and R. Hanina went to visit him. R. Hanina extended his hand to him and raised him. The Talmud asks why could not R. Johanan raise himself? That is, if he cured R. Hiyya b. Abba, why couldn't he cure himself? And the answer was: The prisoner cannot free himself from jail; meaning, a depressed or sick person cannot cure himself if others do not help him.

AYN KAROV RO'EH ET HANE-GA'IM (אין קרוב רואה את הנגעים). "A relation cannot inspect [leprous] plagues" (Zeb. 101b, 102a). The Talmud ponders as to who confined Miriam as a leper. It couldn't be Moses, because he was a zar (non-priest) (cf. Lev. 13:2). Aaron, too, could not shut her away because he was a relative, and a relative cannot inspect (leprous) plagues. The Talmud concludes that it was the Holy One, blessed be He, Who bestowed great honor upon Miriam in that moment, and declared, I am a priest. I will shut her away, I will declare her a definite (leper), and I will free her.

The expression Ayn karov ro'eh et hanega'im took on an enigmatic meaning, "a person from within does not see the troubles."

AYN KATAYGOR NA'ASEH SANAY-GOR (אין קטיגור נעשה סניגור). "The accuser may not act as defender" (R.H. 26a). The Talmud asks, Why doesn't the High Priest enter the inner precincts (the Holy of Holies, on Yom Kippur) in garments of gold to perform the service? (he wore garments of linen only) (cf. Lev. 16:4,23). The answer the Talmud gives is because the accuser may not act as defender; gold is called the accuser in reference to the Golden Calf (cf. also Ber. 59a; Kidd. 5a).

AYN KIDDUSH ELA BEMAKOM SE'UDAH (אין קידוש אלא במקום סעודה). "[Samuel said:] Kiddush is valid only where the meal is eaten" (Pes. 101a). This is based on the verse Vekarata leshabbat oneg ("And ye shall call the Sabbath a delight")(Isa. 58:13), that is, where there is delight as in a festive meal, there shall you recite Kiddush (Rashbam, Pes. 101a; cf. Tosafot, s.v. Al Yeday).

AYN LO MO'AH BEKADKEDO (אין לו מוח בקדקדו). "[This man] has no brains in his skull" (Men. 80b).

AYN LO RA'INU RA'AYAH (אין לא ראינו ראיה). See LO RA'INU AYNAH RA'AYAH.

AYN MAZAL LEYISRAEL (אין מזל לישראל). "There is no mazal [planetary influence] to Israel" (Shab. 156a). Israel's fate depends on no planet but rather on Divine Providence.

In the Middle Ages, however, there were those who considered astrology an authentic science. Among them were Ibn Gabirol, Saadia Gaon, Ibn Ezra, and others who believed that astrologers could foretell certain events by the position and the movement of the stars. This gave rise to the expressions MAZAL-TOV ("good luck") and, conversely, mazal-ra ("bad luck") (cf. HAKOL TALUI BEMAZAL, etc; cf. also Tos. to M.K. 28a, s.v. Ela Bemazla).

AYN ME'ARVIN SIMHAH BESIM-HAH (אין מערבין שמחה בשמחה). "One rejoicing may not be merged in another rejoicing" (M.K. 8b). This is the reason the Mishnah rules that one may not take a wife during the festival week because the festival will lose its significance in the midst of the marriage festivities.

Colloquially, the expression has been applied to the idea that you do not unite two separate, unshared things into one.

AYN MESIHIN BISE'UDAH (אין מסיחין בסעודה). The Talmud (Ta'an. 5b) relates that R. Nahman and R. Isaac were sitting at a meal and R. Nahman asked R. Isaac to expound on something. He replied, in the name of R. Johanan, "One should not converse at meals" (lest the windpipe acts before the gullet, thereby endangering one's life).

AYN MESHIVIN ET HA'ARI LE'A-HAR MITAH (אין משיבין את הארי לאחר מיתה). "You do not refute the lion

[i.e., the words of a great person] after he is dead" (Git. 83a). If he were alive, he would be able to justify his words and find answers to the objections.

AYN MEVI'IN RE'AYAH MIN HA-SHOTIM (אין מביאין ראיה מן השוטים).
The Sages said to R. Eliezer: "Proof cannot be brought from fools" (Shab. 104b). See ANI MAYVI LAKHEM RE'AYAH MIN HATORAH, VEATEM MAYVI'IN LI RE'AYAH MIN HASHOTIM.

AYN MIDRASH BELO HIDUSH (אין מדרש בלא חידוש). "There is no exposition [of learning] without renewal," or "Every school has its novelty." Similarly, the Jerusalem Talmud (Sot. 3:4) states: *I efshar lebayt hamidrash shelo yehay bo davar hadash bekhol yom* ("It is impossible that something new should not be studied everyday in an institute of learning"). (See Hag. 3a.)

AYN MIKRA YOTZAY MIDAY PE-SHUTO (אין מקרא יוצא מידי פשוטו).
See PARDAYS.

AYN NIKHNASIM LEHURVAH MIP-NAY HAHASHAD (אין נכנסים לחורבה מפני החשד). See HASHAD.

AYN ONSHIN ELA IM KAYN MAZHIRIN (אין עונשין אלא אם כן מזהירין). "[The Almighty] does not punish without previous warning" (cf. San. 56b; Jer. Talmud, Yom. 1:5).

AYN ORAYAH MAKHNIS ORAYAH (אין ארח מכניס ארח). "A guest cannot bring another guest with him" (cf. B.B. 98b). "Although hospitality to guests [wayfarers] is greater than welcoming the presence of the *Shekhinah* ('Divine Presence')" (Shab. 127a), this applies only to one's own home or even one's own food. The Talmud (Hul. 94a) tells of an incident in which guests took the food set before them and gave it to the host's child, and this eventually led to a great tragedy. The rule is that "The guests may not give from

what is set before them to the son or daughter of the host, unless they have the host's permission to do so." Hence, a guest cannot bring his friends with him or even behave like a host.

In the following expression, guests have been compared to fish: YOM ALEPH -ORAYAH; YOM BET-TORAYAH; YOM GIMMEL-SORAYAH ("The first day a guest; the second day a burden; the third day a stench" (actually, a "pest")).

AYN RIBUI AHAR RIBUI ELA LEMA'AYT (אין רבוי אחר רבוי אלא למעט). "An extension after an extension has no [other significance] save to limit" (Pes. 23a). That is to say, an amplification following an amplification intimates restriction. This is the same inverse principle as a rule in the English language, "a double negative is a positive."

A jocular implication is "The more you say, the worse you make it."

AYN SHENAY KOLOT NIKH-NASIM BE'OZEN AHAT (אין שני קולות נכנסים באזן אחת). Literally, "two voices cannot go into one ear" (Jer. Tal. Meg. 4:1), meaning, it is impossible to hear two thoughts at the same time. See TARTAY KALAY MAYHAD GAVRA LO MISHTAMA'AY; TRAY KALAY LO MISHTAMA'AY.

AYN SHOTEH NIFGA (MARGISH) (אין שוטה נפגע (מרגיש)). "A fool is not stricken" (does not feel) (Shab. 13b). The Talmud (ibid.) inquired as to who wrote *Megillat Ta'anit* (the scroll of fasting). It was Hananiah b. Hezekiah and his companions, who cherished their troubles. We, too, cherished our troubles, observed R. Simeon b. Gamliel, but we are inadequate to write them down. Another reason he gave was "a fool is not assailed." *Rashi* (ad loc.) comments, A fool does not perceive the troubles that surround him. So we, too, do not perceive our miraculous escapes. See SHOTEH AYN LO TAKANAH.

AYN SOMKHIN AL HANAYS (אין סומכין על הנס). "We do not rely on a miracle" (Pes. 64b). The Mishnah (Pes. 64a) states, "The Passover offering was slaughtered in three divisions ('assembly,' 'congregation,' and 'Israel')". After each division entered the Temple court, the doors were closed. Abaye said: "They [the doors] locked themselves." Raba said: "We learned 'they locked.'" The Talmud asks: "Wherein do they differ?" They differ with respect to relying on a miracle. Abaye said, "'They locked themselves'; as many as entered, entered, and we rely on a miracle [that the doors should shut themselves when sufficient had entered]." Raba said, "'They locked,' and we do not rely on a miracle." Another situation in which we do not rely on a miracle is when the Talmud (Pes. 50b) states that the monies that come from overseas never contain a sign of blessing, because a miracle does not occur every day (Lav bekhol yoma mitrahaysh nisa). That is, considerable danger is involved with the transport of freight at sea, and one might very easily suffer loss.

Colloquially, the expression Ayn somkhin al hanays is said to any person who relies on an event or an effect in the physical world that deviates from the known laws of nature.

AYN TZIBBUR ANI (LAYT TZIBBUR KULAYH MEYA'ANI) (אין צבור (עני) (לית צבור כוליה מיעני). "There is no poor congregation [community]" (Jer. Tal., Git. 45:1). A congregation can carry (support) everything if it so desires. See ANI HASHUV KEMAYT.

AYNI YODAYA MAH ATTAH SAH (איני יודע מה אתה שח). "I do not know what you say" (Shebu. 49b); that is, it never happened. The Mishnah (ibid.) discusses the case in which an owner said: "Where is my ox?" and the reply to him was, "I do not know what you say" (I do not understand you and this never occurred).

AYNO DOMEH LOMAYD MAYATZMO LELOMAYD MAYRABO (אינו דומה לומד מעצמו ללומד מרבו). "Studying on your own is not on a par with studying with a master" (Ket. 111a).

AYNO DOMEH MI SHEYAYSH LO PAT BESALO LEMI SHE'AYN LO PAT BESALO (אינו דומה מי שיש לו פת בסלו למי שאין לו פת בסלו). "You cannot compare one who has bread in his basket with one who has no bread in his basket" (Yom. 18b). The Yiddish equivalent is Der zater gleybt nit dem hungerikn ("The satiated person does not believe the one who is hungry").

AYNO DOMEH SHONAH PIRKO MAYAH PE'AMIM LESHONAH PIRKO MAYAH VE'AHAT (אינו דומה שונה פרקו מאה פעמים לשונה פרקו מאה ואחת). A proverbial saying by Hillel, meaning "reviewing a lesson a hundred times cannot be compared with reviewing it a hundred and one times" (Hag. 9b). Since books were unavailable, frequent verbal repetition engraved the subject in one's mind.

This idea of repetition was transmitted at yeshivot throughout the ages. When a student came to an examination before the Suvalker Rav, Rosh Yeshiva at Rabbi Isaac Elchanan Theological Seminary, Rabbi David Lifshitz, of blessed memory, he would ask, "How many times did you review?" The student answered, "four or five times." He then said, "Review it a sixth time."

AYNO MA'ALEH VE'AYNO MORID (אינו מעלה ואינו מוריד). See LO MA'ALEH VELO MORID.

AYTZAH TOVAH KA MASHMA LAN (עצה טובה קא משמע לן). "It wants to teach us good advice" (Ket. 96b). This expression appears in talmudic discourse and it infers that it is not the halakhah that is being taught but only giving recom-

mendation regarding a decision or course of conduct.

AYZEHU ASHIR? KOL SHEYAYSH LO NAHAT RU'AH BE'OSHRO (איזהו עשיר? כל שיש לו נחת רוח בעשרו). "[Our Rabbis taught]: Who is wealthy? He who has pleasure in his wealth" (Shab. 25b; cf. also *Avot* 4:1).

AYZEHU HAKHAM? HARO'EH ET HANOLAD (איזהו חכם? הרואה את הנולד). Alexander of Macedon put ten questions to the elders of the south country. Among the questions was, "Who is wise?" The answer: He who discerns what is about to come to pass (Tam. 32a). See also *Avot* 4:1.

AYZEHU TALMID HAKHAM? KOL SHESHO'ALIN OTO HALAKHAH BEKHOL MAKOM VE'OMERAH (איזהו תלמיד חכם? כל ששואלין אותו הלכה בכל מקום ואומרה). "Who is a scholar? He who is asked a *halakhah* in any place and can state it" (Shab. 114a). That is, he can interpret questions of law anytime and anyplace. The significance of this statement has to do with a scholar being appointed to a position in his own town or as the head of an academy. Another tractate (Ta'an. 10b) asks a similar question and answers, "A disciple is one who is asked any question of *halakhah* in connection with his studies and can answer it—even though it is on a subject dealt with in the Tractate *Kallah*" (a tractate not usually studied, according to *Rashi*).

AZ DI VELT ZUHGT ZUHL MEN GLEYBN (אז די וועלט זאגט זאל מען גלייבן). See HAVERKHA KERAYIKH HAMRA UKAFA LEGABAYKH MOSH.

AZUT PANIM (עזות פנים). "An insolent person" or "one who has HUTZPA [HUTZPAH]" (Ta'an. 7b). R. Salla said, in the name of R. Hamnuna: "Any person who is insolent stumbles in the end into sin."

Rabbah, the son of R. Huna, said: "It is permissible to call 'wicked' anyone who is insolent." R. Nahman, the son of R. Isaac, said: "One may even hate him" (ibid.).

"Rab Judah said, in Samuel's name: Pashur, son of Immer, had four hundred slaves—others say, four thousand slaves—and all became mixed up in the priesthood, and every priest who displays impudence is [descended] from none but them" (Kidd. 70b).

BA LETAHAYR MESAI'IN OTO (בא לטהר מסייעין אותו). See ADAM MEKADAYSH ATZMO ME'AT MEKADSHIN OTO HARBAYH, and so on.

BA'AL DAVAR (בעל דבר). Literally, "the party concerned" or the "principal in the matter" (Git. 3a). According to the kabbalists, it is also a nickname for Satan. It has become another name for the *malakh hamavet* ("Angel of Death"). It may also refer to the "person in question" or "culprit."

BA'AL HANAYS AYNO MAKIR BE-NISO (בעל הנס אינו מכיר בנסו). "The person for whom a miracle is performed is unaware of the miracle" (Nid. 31a). This is implied from the verses, "Who doeth wondrous things alone" (Only God alone knows it) (Ps. 72:18) "and blessed be His glorious Name forever" (ibid., 19).

BA'AL TESHUVAH (בעל תשובה). "A repentant sinner"; one who regrets that he has sinned and corrects his conduct and ways. The Talmud (Yom. 86b) asks: "How is one proved a repentant sinner? Rab Judah said: If the object which caused his original transgression comes before him on two occasions, and he keeps away from it." Scripture is replete with verses based on *teshuvah* ("return"): "And shalt return unto the Lord thy God" (Deut. 30:2); "Let the wicked forsake his way, and the unrighteous man his thoughts: and let him return to the Lord, and He will have mercy upon him; and to our

God, for He will abundantly pardon" (Isa. 55:7). It is written in the Talmud (Sukk. 53a), "Our Rabbis taught: Some of them used to say, 'Happy our youth that has not disgraced our old age.' These were the men of piety and good deeds. Others used to say, 'Happy our old age which has atoned for our youth.' These were the penitents (*ba'alay teshuvah*). Both, however, said, 'Happy he who hath not sinned, but let him who hath sinned return and He will pardon him.'" The Talmud ascribes higher rank to the *ba'al teshuvah* than to the *tzadik* ("completely righteous") (see MAKOM SHEBA'ALAY TESHUVAH OMDIN TZADIKIM GEMURIM AYNAM OMDIN). "R. Samuel b. Nahmani said, in the name of R. Jonathan: Great is repentance, because it prolongs the days and years of man (Yom., ibid.), as it is said, 'And when the wicked turneth from his wickedness . . . he shall live thereby'" (Ezek. 33:19).

BAHADAY HUTZA LEKI KARBA

(בהדי הוצא לקי כרבא). "Together with the shrub, the cabbage is smitten" (B.K. 92a); that is, the good suffer with the bad.

A Yiddish expression spoken in a similar vein is *Az mehakt holtz faln shpener* ("When you chop wood, splinters fall").

BAHADAY KIVSHAY DERAHAMANA LAMAH LAKH? בהדי כבשי

(דרחמנא למה לך?). "What have you to do with the secrets of the All-Merciful?" (Ber. 10b). This is what Isaiah said to Hezekiah when he went to visit him upon the suggestion of the Holy One, blessed be He. Hezekiah believed that if he had children, they would not be virtuous. Thus, Isaiah said to him, "You should have done what you were commanded, and let the Holy One, blessed be He, do that which pleases Him."

This expression can be applied to any situation in which a person is obligated by Heaven to do something and does not do it.

BAKDAYRAH SHEBISHAYL BAH NITBASHAYL (בקדרה שבשל בה

נתבשל). "In the pot in which they cooked were they cooked" (Sot. 11a). Pharaoh wanted to outwit the Israelites and pondered with what to afflict them. Fire and the sword were ruled out. The only thing that would be effective would be water because the Holy One, blessed be He, had already sworn that He would not bring a flood upon the world. Pharaoh was, however, unaware that although He would not bring a flood upon the whole world, He would bring it upon one people. This, R. Eleazar said, is what is meant by "Yea in the thing wherein they dealt proudly [*zadu*] against them" (Ex. 18:11)—that in the pot in which they cooked were they cooked (the verb "they dealt proudly" resembles in form another with the meaning "they cooked" [*zadu*]).

A parallel Yiddish expression is *Ver es gruhbt a grub farn andern, der falt alayn arayn* ("He who digs a hole for another, falls in himself").

BAKI BEHADRAY TORAH (בקי

בחדרי תורה). "Well-acquainted with the chambers [intricacies] of the Law" (Kidd. 10b); a remark made by one talmudic scholar to another, concerning his process of reasoning in a question of law. The expression is currently used when speaking of a learned Torah scholar.

Other such expressions are: BAKI LIDROSH BATORAH ("One who possesses a thorough knowledge of the Torah, as well as the Prophets and the Hagiographa, the *Midrash, halakhot,* and *aggadot,* and all the benedictions") (Ta'an. 16a). This is a prerequisite for a *Sheli'ah Tzibbur*; BAKI BEHESHBONOT HAYAH (a good arithmetician) (Bek. 5a). The latter refers to Moshe; BAKI BEREFU'UT ("familiar with medicine") (Yom. 49a) refers to R. Hanina; and BAKI BESITRAY TORAH ("Well-acquainted with the secrets of the Law") (Jer. Tal., Ket. 5:4).

The word *baki* (lit., "expert," "skilled," "erudite," or "learned") may be used in conjunction with any study or craft. For example, one may say he is a *baki be-SHaS* (one who is learned in the *Shishah Sedarim* [six orders], alluding to the *Shishah Sidray Mishnah*). Or, he has *beki'ut* ("erudition") in a particular subject matter.

BAKI BEHESHBONOT HAYAH (בקי בחשבונות היה). See BAKI BEHADRAY TORAH.

BAKI BEREFU'OT (בקי ברפואות). See BAKI BEHADRAY TORAH.

BAKI BESITRAY TORAH (בקי בסתרי תורה). See BAKI BEHADRAY TORAH.

BAKI LIDROSH BATORAH (בקי לדרוש בתורה). See BAKI BEHADRAY TORAH.

BAR-BAY RAV DEHAD YOMA (בר-בי רב דחד יומא). R. Idi, the father of R. Jacob b. Idi, used to spend three months on his journey and one day at school, and the rabbis called him "One day scholar" (Hag. 5b).

BAR DA'AT (בר דעת). "An intelligent being" (B.M. 80b). The Talmud discusses a case in which a person is engaged to carry a certain burden, which was increased by a *kab* (a certain measure of capacity). He broke down, making his employer liable. Is he not an intelligent being (*bar da'at*), queries the Talmud, to throw it down if it is too heavy for him? Abaye answered that as soon as he picked it up, and before realizing that it was too heavy for him, he fell under it.

The appellation *bar da'at* is generally used for any person who has common sense.

BAR SAMKHA (בר סמכא). "A person to be relied upon" or "an authority" (Yeb. 64b; Git. 6b; Kidd. 44a). For example, the Amora Abin was a *Bar samkha* because he repeated and revised what he heard.

BAR URYAN (בר אוריין). "A learned person" (Git. 31b). R. Huna and R. Hisda were once sitting together when Geniba

passed by them. Said one of them: Let us rise before him for he is a learned man (*nikum mikamayh devar uryan hu*). Rashi translates *bar uryan* as *ben Torah*, "a learned person" (cf. Git. 62a; s.v. *Bar Uryan*).

The word *bar* means "possessing a certain quality," as in BAR DA'AT, BAR SAMKHA, *bar hakhi* ("old enough" or "competent"), *bar bay rav* ("a young student"), *bar mazal* ("lucky person"), and *bar mitzvah* ("one who has to observe the Law").

BARI VESHEMA BARI ADIF (ברי ושמא ברי עדיף). In the case of "sure and perhaps, sure is better [preferable]" (Ket. 12b; B.K. 118a). The Talmud gives as an example the case of a person who asserts a certainty and says to another person, "You owe me money," and the person from whom the money is claimed neither denies nor admits the claim; judgment is given for the one who asserts a certainty. An equivalent in the English language is "A bird in the hand is worth two in the bush."

BARUKH DAYAN HA'EMET (ברוך דין האמת). After someone's death, those persons who are not obligated to observe mourning utter, *Barukh dayan ha'emet* ("Blessed be the Judge of truth"), not including the Divine Name and His Kingship. The mourners recite the complete blessing when they rend their garments (*Mishnah Berurah* 223:8; see also ad loc. Be'ayr Haytayv 223:6).

The Talmud (Ber. 54a, 59b; Pes. 50a) cites the phrase *Barukh dayan ha'emet* upon hearing evil tidings.

BAT KOL (בת קול). A term appearing numerous times in the Talmud, as well as throughout Hebrew literature, referring to a reverberating sound or voice descending from Heaven to offer guidance in human affairs (cf. Dan. 4:28). It is not actually a Heavenly voice that is heard, but the reverberation caused by the voice from Heaven (a secondary voice), similar to the reverberation caused by the striking of an object. Thus, the term *Bat Kol* (lit., "daughter of a voice" or "daughter of a sound") is used to designate a small voice and distinguish it from the normal voice (*Tos.* to San. 11a, s.v. *Bat Kol*). It is recorded that the *Tanna* Rabbi Yosi heard a *Bat Kol* cooing like a dove in the ruins of Jerusalem (Ber. 3a).

BAT TEHILAH SIMAN YAFEH LE-BANIM (בת תחלה סימן יפה לבנים).
(R. Hisda said:) "If a daughter [is born] first, it is a good omen for the sons" (B.B. 141a). Some say it is because she rears her brothers, and others say it is because the evil eye has no influence over them—that is, a male child born first may cause the envy of other mothers. To R. Hisda, daughters were dearer than sons because his daughters married husbands who were among the greatest of their generation— namely, Raba, Rami b. Hama, and Mar Ukba b. Hama.

BATAR ANYA AZLA ANYUTA (בתר עניא אזלא עניותא).
"Poverty follows the poor" (B.K. 92a). The comparable Yiddish expression is *Der dalut shlept zikh nuhkhn uhreman*. Raba asked Rabbah b. Mari, From where is this popular saying derived? He replied, We have learned: The rich used to bring the firstfruits (Exod. 34:26) in baskets of gold and silver (and took back the baskets), but the poor brought them in wicker baskets made out of the bark of willow, and thus gave the baskets, as well as the firstfruits, to the priest.

BATAY KENAYSIYOT AYN NOHA-GIN BAHEN KALUT ROSH (בתי כנסיות אין נוהגין בהן קלות ראש).
"Synagogues must not be treated with light-mindedness or disrespect" (Meg. 28a). It is not proper to eat or drink in them, nor to dress up in them, nor to stroll about in them, nor to go into them in summer to escape the heat and in the rainy season to escape the rain, nor to deliver a private

funeral address in them. It is proper to read Scriptures in them and to repeat the *Mishnah* and to deliver public funeral addresses.

BATAYL BESHISHIM (בטל בששים).
In everyday parlance, the expression came to mean "of no significance," "lost in a larger quantity," or "diluted beyond recognition."

The expression is derived from the talmudic ruling *Kol isurin shebatorah be-shishim* ("All prohibited substances of the Torah are [neutralized] in sixty-fold") (Hul. 98a; A.Z. 69a), provided that the taste of the forbidden substance can no longer be felt in the mixture.

BAYN KAKH UVAYN KAKH (בין כך ובין כך).
The *Mishnah* (Ohol. 11:7) discusses the case of a dog that had eaten the flesh of a corpse, and it died and was lying over the threshhold of a house. Does the house become unclean? Various conditions were outlined. R. Judah b. Bathyra said, "Whether the one condition or the other applies, the house becomes unclean" (*Bayn kakh uvayn kakh habayit tamay*). In another tractate (Shab. 125b), another case is discussed and the Talmud asks, MAI BAYN KAKH UVAYN KAKH ("What does 'in both cases' mean?").

BAYRA DESHATIT MINAYH LO TISHDAY BAYH KELA (בירא דשתית מיניה לא תשדי ביה קלא).
The Talmud (B.K. 92b) states that Raba said to Rabbah b. Mari: Whence can be derived the popular saying, "Into the well from which you once drank water, do not throw clods?" He replied: As is written, "Thou shalt not abhor an Edomite, for he is thy brother; thou shalt not abhor an Egyptian because thou wast a stranger in his land" (Deut. 23:8). Thus, never despise that from which you once derived good. *Bemidbar Rabbah* (22:4) has a similar proverb, *Bor sheshatita mimenu al tizrok bo even* ("Cast no stones into the well that hath given you water").

In Yiddish one says *Varf nisht keyn shteyn in dem brunen fun velkhen du trinkst* ("Do not throw a stone into the well from which you drink").

BE'AL KORHO (KORHAH) (בעל (כרחו (כרחה). "Against his [her] will"; "by force" (Sot. 20a). When agreeing against one's will or agreeing perforce under compulsion, the expression *anah amen be'al korho* would be uttered.

BEDEREKH SHE'ADAM ROTZEH LAYLAYKH, BAH MOLIKHIN OTO (בדרך שאדם רוצה לילך, בה מוליכין אותו). In accordance with the doctrine of free will, "One is allowed to follow the road he wishes to pursue" (Mak. 10b). A scriptural verse that echoes the same thought is *vehabotayah ba-Shem hesed yesovevenu* ("But he that trusteth in the Lord, mercy compasseth him about") (Ps. 32:10). A Yiddish saying expressing the same idea is *Az menempt zikh fir, helft der Aybershter* ("God helps those who bring themselves out from under"). See HABA LETAHAYR MESAI'IN OTO.

BEHADRAY HADARIM (בחדרי חדרים). See MARIT AYIN.

BE'IKVOT MESHIHA HUTZPA YISGAY VEYOKER YA'AMIR (בעקבות משיחא חוצפא יסגא ויוקר יאמיר). "In the footsteps of the Messiah [just before his advent] impudence will prevail [increase] and honor dwindle" (Sot. 49b). R. Nehemiah said: In the generation of Messiah's coming, impudence will increase [*ha'azut tarbeh*], esteem be perverted" (San. 97a). R. Shesheth said: "Impudence is sovereignty without a crown" (San. 105a); that is, it wields great power and lacks nothing but a crown (see also B.B. 155b). See HUTZPA, AFILU KELAPAY SHEMAYA MAHANAY.

BELASHON SAGI NAHOR (בלשון סגי נהור). *Sagi nahor* (lit., "abundance of light") is a euphemism for a blind person.

The expression is purposely uttered so as not to use a disparaging word. The euphemism is used in the Hebrew and Yiddish languages in every instance, since the Sages stressed that "man should at all times express himself in fitting terms" (Pes. 3a).

The Talmud (Ber. 58a) relates that R. Shesheth was blind (*sagi nahor*) and was ridiculed by a certain Sadducee. Some say that the Sadducee's eyes were put out and others say that R. Shesheth cast his eyes upon him and he became a heap of bones.

BELI AYIN HARA (RA'AH) (בלי עין (הרע (רעה). The term denotes "May there be no evil eye." The Yiddish equivalent is *Kayn-ayin-huhre,* often contracted as *Kaynehuhra.* Sometimes the name "evil eye" is euphemistically called *gut oyg* ("good eye"). In German, it is *Unbeschrieen* or *Unberufen.* It became a widespread belief that AYIN HARA ("the eye of the evil") of an envious or begrudging glance or through excessive admiration or astonishment could work evil upon the person at whom it was directed. The Talmud (Sot. 36b) also refers to it in the Aramaic *ayin bisha* and states that ninety-nine people out of a hundred die through an evil eye (B.M. 107b). According to *Avot* 2:13–14, *ayin hara* is the worst quality that a man should shun.

Post-talmudic literature gives two explanations for *ayin hara:* (1) it contains an element of fire that spreads destruction (cf. Judah Loew b. Bezalel [*Maharal*], *Netivot Olam* 107d); and (2) the glance of an angry man's eye calls forth an evil angel who takes vengeance on the cause of his wrath (Manasseh b. Israel, *Nishmat Hayyim* 3:27).

Because of caution regarding an evil eye, members of a family (two brothers, a father, and a son, and some authorities are stringent regarding a grandfather and his grandson) do not follow each other when called up to the Torah (*Orah Hayyim* 146:6).

Various folk beliefs and folk customs are practiced to avert an evil eye. The above expressions are uttered, followed by spitting several times. If one gets sick because of an *ayin hara*, it is the custom to exorcise (Yidd. *Uhptzushprekhen*) the evil eye. Some eighty anti-evil practices of East European Jewry are mentioned by R. Lilienthal (cf. *Yiddishe Filologye* 1 [Warsaw, 1924]). See BAYN PORAT YOSAYF.

BEMAYZID (במזיד). "Willfully" or "wantonly." The opposite would be BE-SHOGAYG ("unintentionally" or "inadvertantly") (Yeb. 53b).

BEMIDAH SHE'ADAM MODAYD BAH MODEDIN LO (במדה שאדם מודד בה מודדין לו). See MIDAH KENEGED MIDAH.

BERA KARAYAH DE'ABUHA (ברא כרעיה דאבוה). "Like father like son." The Talmud (Erub. 70b) uses the phrase *yoraysh karayah de'abuha hu* ("an heir steps into his father's place") and is consequently entitled to all his rights. See REHAYLA BATAR REHAYLA AZLA, KE'UVDAY IMAH KAKH UVDAY BERATA.

BERIKH RAHAMANA DIHAVAKH NIHALAN VELA YEHAVAKH LE'AFRA (בריך רחמנא דיהבך ניהלן ולא יהבך לעפרא). A blessing usually said to a person who has recovered from a serious illness. Its meaning is "Blessed be the All-Merciful Who has given you back to us and has not given you back to the dust" (Ber. 54b). This blessing was first said by R. Hanna of Baghdad and other rabbis to Rab Yehudah, when they visited him after his recovery from an illness.

BESHA'AT HADHAK (בשעת הדחק). "In case of emergency" (Nid. 9b). The phrase may also mean "in case of need or pressure," as in *besha'at dohko* ("just when he needs it") (Hag. 5a).

BESHOGAYG (בשוגג). See BEMAYZID.

BIRKAT HABAYIT BERUBAH (ברכת הבית ברובה). "The blessing of a house [is proportionate] to its size" (Ket. 103a). The more members there are in a household, the cheaper the cost of living. According to *Rashi* (ad loc.), they help each other and are recompensed; thus, the luck of the multitude is better. According to *Tosafot* (ad loc.) NAYR LE'EHAD NAYR LEMAYAH ("A lamp for one is a lamp for a hundred") (Shab. 122a).

BISHIVAH SHEL MALAH (בישיבה של מעלה). "In the Heavenly Academy" (Pes. 53b). The scholars asked: Was Thaddeus, the man of Rome, a great man or a powerful man? R. Jose b. Abin said: "He cast merchandise into the pockets of scholars [that is, he gave them opportunities for trading]" and R. Johanan said: Whoever casts merchandise into the pockets of scholars will be privileged to sit in the Heavenly Academy, as it is said, "For wisdom is a defense even as money is a defense" (Eccl. 7:12).

Bishiva shel malah are the opening words of a short paragraph recited by the *Sheli'ah Tzibbur* or the rabbi prior to *Kol Nidre* on Yom Kippur eve (cf. Macy Nulman, *The Encyclopedia of Jewish Prayer* [Northvale, New Jersey: Jason Aronson Inc., 1993], p. 119).

BISHLOSHAH DEVARIM ADAM MISHTANEH MAYHAVAYRO: BEKOL, BEMAREH UVEDA'AT (בשלשה דברים אדם משתנה מחברו: בקול, במראה ובדעת). "[R. Meir used to say:] In three things man differs from his fellow: in voice, appearance, and mind [that is, his thoughts]" (San. 38a).

BISHLOSHAH DEVARIM ADAM NIKAR: BEKOSO, BEKISO UVEKA'ASO, VEYAYSH OMRIM AF BESAHAKO (בשלשה דברים אדם ניכר: בכוסו, בכיסו ובכעסו, ויש אומרים אף בשחקו). "R. Ila'i said: By three things may a person's character be determined: by his cup [the effect and amount of his drink], by his purse [his dealing in money matters and charity giving], and by his anger; and some say by his laughter also" (Erub. 65b).

BIZKHUT NASHIM TZIDKANI-YOT SHEHAYU BE'OTO HADOR NIGALU YISRAEL MIMITZRAYIM (בזכות נשים צדקניות שהיו באותו הדור נגאלו ישראל ממצרים). "[R. Avira expounded:] As reward for the righteous women who lived in that generation, the Israelites were delivered from Egypt" (Sot. 11a). The Talmud relates that these women drew up pitchers half-full of water and half-full of fish. They carried the water and fish to their husbands in the field and took care of all their needs.

BIZMAN SHEYISRAEL OSIN RE-TZONO SHEL MAKOM AYN KOL UMAH VELASHON SHOLTOT BA-HEN (בזמן שישראל עושין רצונו של מקום אין כל אומה ולשון שולטות בהן). "When Israel does the will of the Omnipresent, no nation nor any language-speaking group has any power over them" (Ket. 66b). These were the words of R. Johanan b. Zakkai upon meeting Nakdimon b. Gorion's daughter, an unfortunate woman, whose father's and father-in-law's wealth had disappeared. Although Nakdimon b. Gorion gave charity, it was for his own glorification and he did not give in accordance with his means.

DA LIFNAY MI ATTAH OMAYD (דע לפני מי אתה עומד). "Know before Whom you are standing." The Talmud (Ber. 28b) states that when R. Eliezer fell ill, his disciples went to visit him. They asked him to teach them the paths of life so that through them they might attain the life of the future world. Among other things, he said, Keshe'atem mitpallelim de'u lifnay mi attem omdim ("When you pray, know before Whom you are standing") and in this way you will attain the future world.

This motto often appears in synagogues above the reader's desk.

DAMIM TARTAY MASHMA (דמים תרתי משמע). The word damim has two meanings, "blood" and "money," signifying that sometimes they are one. For example, one may say this is "blood-money."

The phrase Damim tartay mashma appears in the Talmud (Meg. 14b). The Talmud states, "The word damim [blood-guilt] is plural, to indicate two kinds of blood." Abigayil came to David and David said, "Blessed be thy discretion and blessed be thou, that has kept me this day from blood-guilt" (1 Sam. 25:33), that is, the blood of uncleanness and capital punishment.

DARDAKAY MELAMAYD (דרדקי מלמד). "A teacher of small children," as in MAKRI DARDAKAY ("a reading teacher for beginning children") (B. B. 21a). The word dardakay also appears in tractate Sabbath (89b): Lo besavay ta'amah velo bedardakay aytzah ("There is no reason in old men, and no council in children")—that is, old men have no rationale and small children cannot advise (see Maharsha, ad loc.).

DAVAR AHAYR (דבר אחר). Literally, "another matter." An expression for an ugly object or occurrence. When discussing it, the person does not wish to mention the specific name. For example, the Talmud (Men. 109a) states, The priests who ministered in the Temple of Onias may not minister in the Temple in Jerusalem. And, needless to say, (this is so of priests who ministered to) another matter (ledavar ahayr), a euphemism for idolatry. (See also Ber. 8b; Shab. 119b).

The term may also mean "another explanation" or "another remark" and/or "a knave," or a "miser and hardhearted."

DAVAR EHAD LEDOR VE'AYN SHENAY DEVARIN LEDOR (דבר אחד לדור ואין שני דברין לדור). "There is only one leader to a generation, not two" (San. 8a). Scripture states, "For thou [Joshua] must go with this people" (Deut. 31:7). Moses places Joshua on the same level as the people. Another text reads, "For thou shalt bring the Children of Israel" (Deut. 31:23). Here, Joshua is declared their leader. The Almighty said to Joshua, You must show your authority. "Take a rod and strike them upon the head; there is only one leader to a generation, not two" (cf. also *Rashi* to Deut. 31:7, s.v. *Ki Attah Tavo*).

This is the source of the Yiddish expression *Bistu, bistu* ("If you are the person of commanding leadership, then be it!").

DAVAR SHE'AFILU TINOKOT SHEL BAYT RABAN YODIN OTO (דבר שאפילו תינוקות של בית רבן יודין אותו). "A matter which even school children know" (Sot. 35a). This is what the Holy One, blessed be He, said to David, who called words of the Torah "songs." He told him he will stumble in a matter that even school children know; that is, the Ark had to be carried upon the shoulders of the Levites and yet David brought it in a wagon.

Colloquially, the expression is said to a person concerning anything that is well-known.

DAVAR SHELO BA LE'OLAM (דבר שלא בא לעולם). Literally, "something which has not come into the world"; nonexistent.

The Talmud contains statements such as, "A man cannot consecrate anything that is not yet in existence" (Ket. 58b), or, "A man cannot transfer that which is nonexistent" (B.M. 33b; B.B. 63a). See LO HAYAH VELO NIVRA and LO DUBIM VELO YA'AR.

DAVAR VELO HATZI DAVAR (דבר ולא חצי דבר). Scripture states, "A matter

shall be established by two witnesses" (Deut. 19:15). It is written in the Talmud (B.K. 70b), "R. Akiba used to say 'A matter' [*davar*] but not half a matter [*hatzi davar*]. The appearance of two hairs are the sign of puberty in a girl. A 'half matter' is when two witnesses testify that there was one hair on her back and two other witnesses state that there was one hair in front, as in this case the first two testified that she was still a minor and the others also testified that she was still a minor."

Colloquially, the phrase *davar velo hatzi davar* took on a general meaning: If you begin something, finish it! Don't do half of the task that you undertook (*hithalta gemor*). The *Tanhuma* (*Aykev* 6) states, *Hamathil bemitzvah yehay gomayr et kulah* ("If you begin a *mitzvah*, finish it completely").

DER IN HIML ZUHL UNZ (MIR) HELFN (דער אין הימל זאל אונז (מיר) העלפן). "The One in Heaven should help us [me]." The substitution of the Yiddish word *Himl* ("Heaven") for God is a common usage. Scripture contains the expression, "It is Heaven that rules us!" (Dan. 4:23). Antigonous of Sokho said, "Let the fear of Heaven (*Mora Shamayim*) be upon you" (Avot 1:3).

According to Resh Lakish, there are seven Heavens; the King, the Living God, high and exalted, dwells over them in *Aravot* (the Seventh Heaven) (Hag. 12b). Rabbi Johanan (Levi) said, "*Teshuvah* ["repentence"] is so great that it reaches the Throne of Glory [*Kisay Hakavod*]," that is, the Seventh Heaven (*Sefer Orhot Tzadikim*, Eshkol Jerusalem, 1967, 26:177). When one is extremely happy, the Yiddish expression is *In zibetn himl* ("In Seventh Heaven"). This may be derived from the fact that the Throne of Glory abides in the Seventh Heaven.

DER KOHEN HUHT ZIKH IN IM TZESHPILT (דער כהן האט זיך אין אים צעשפילט). "The *Kohen* in him was activated." It is an accepted fact that a

Kohen is, by temperament, prone to anger (*ka'ason*). This opinion appears in the Talmud (Kidd. 70b), which bases this belief on the biblical phrase *ve'amekha kimerivay kohen* ("for Thy people are as the quarrelsome among priests") (Hos. 4:4).

Yiddish expressions emphasizing that the *Kohen* is an irascible person who is provoked to anger are: *A Kohen tzvishn Kohanim* ("[He is] a *Kohen* among *Kohanim*)—that is, his anger has no bounds; *Ayleh toldot Kohen* ("These are the generations of the *Kohen*"), signifying that the characteristic of the *Kohen* to flare up is very old.

DEREKH AGAV (דרך אגב). See AGAV URHAH.

DEREKH ARUKHAH UKETZARAH, DEREKH KETZARAH VA'ARU-KHAH (דרך ארכה וקצרה, דרך קצרה וארכה). "This road is long but short and that one is short but long" (Erub. 53b). R. Joshua b. Hananiah remarked that no one has ever had the better of him except a woman, a little boy, and a little girl. The incident with the little boy happened when he was on a journey and noticed a little boy sitting at a crossroads. He asked the boy which road to take to get to the town. The boy replied, "This one is short but long, and that one is long but short." He proceeded along the short but long road. When he approached the town, he discovered that it was hedged by gardens and orchards. R. Joshua b. Hananiah said to him, "My son, did you not tell me that this road was short?" He replied, "Did I not tell you that it was also long?" R. Joshua kissed him upon his head and said to him, "Happy are you, O Israel, all of you are wise, both young and old."

This incident teaches that when setting out on a journey or a venture, the road may seem long but, in reality, it is short—or vice versa.

DEVARIM BETAYLIM (דברים בטלים). "[Our rabbis taught:] One should not stand up to say *tefillah* while immersed in sorrow, or idleness, or laughter, or chatter, or frivolity, or idle talk [*devarim betaylim*], but only while still rejoicing in the performance of some religious act" (Ber. 31a); for example, reciting a verse such as Psalms 144 (cf. also A.Z. 16b).

The expression *devarim betaylim* generally applies to a person or persons involved in frivolous or trashy talk.

DEVARIM SHEL TA'AM (דברים של טעם). "Words that are spoken according to reasoning and insight" (A.Z. 18a).

DEVAYKUT (דבקות). Literally, "clinging unto" or "cleaving"; that is, a cleaving to God, such as in the phrase in Deuteronomy 13:5 that reads, *uvo tidbakun*, "and unto Him shall ye cleave." The Talmud (Sot. 14a) states that this can be fulfilled by imitating God and emulating His attributes. Different ideas of *devaykut* appear in kabbalistic literature.

In Jewish music the *devaykut* style, which is characteristically mystical, meditative, couched in nonmetrical free-form, and sung in a slow tempo, is stressed by *hasidim*. Its adherents refer to these tunes as *devaykele*, using the endearing diminutive *le*.

DIN PERUTAH KEDIN MAYAH (דין פרוטה כדין מאה). "A lawsuit involving a mere *perutah* [the smallest of coins] must be regarded as of the same importance as one involving a hundred" (San. 8a). That is, if a lawsuit comes before the judge involving a *perutah* and after that a lawsuit comes that involves a greater amount, priority should not be given to the lawsuit involving the greater amount, but the order should be as they came before the judge. In the eyes of the judge, the small amount should be the same as the large amount. This applies to all matters in justice pertaining to priority.

DINA DEMALKHUTA DINA (דינא דמלכותא דינא). Samuel (c. 177–257

C.E.), head of the Nehardea Academy and an authority on civil law, laid down the principle that "The law of the land [where Jews live] is binding [in civil cases]" (Ned. 28a).

DIRAH NA'AH VE'ISHAH NA'AH VEKHAYLIM NA'IM MARHIVIN DATO SHEL ADAM (דירה נאה ואשה נאה וכלים נאים מרחיבין דעתו של אדם).
"[Three things] increase a man's self-esteem: a beautiful dwelling, a beautiful wife, and beautiful clothes" (Ber. 57b).

DIVRAY KHIBUSHIM (דברי כבושים).
"Words of admonition" (Ta'an. 16a). In giving the order of the service for fast days (to ask for rain), the *Mishnah* (Ta'an. 15a) states, "The elder among them addresses them with words of admonition [to repentance]," words that influence the hearts of the listeners.

DOK BEKHAKAY VETISHKAH BE-NIGRAY (דוק בככי ותשכח בניגרי).
It was taught, in R. Meir's name: "Chew well with your teeth and you will find it in your steps" (Shab. 152a). *Rashi* (ad loc.) comments: "Eat much and you will find the food in your walk; it will fortify your vigor."

DOR YATOM (דור יתום).
"An orphan generation" (Hag. 3b); inferring a generation that has no leadership.

EFRO'AH SHELO NITPATHU AYNAV (אפרח שלא נתפתחו עיניו).
"A chicken whose eyes are not yet opened" (Bez. 6b). The Talmud discusses using a chicken that was hatched on a festival. According to the Rabbis, it is forbidden, and according to R. Eliezer b. Jacob, it is even forbidden on weekdays.

Colloquially, the expression became associated with a person who does not see (observe) and does not know and recognize the world.

EHAD BEPEH VE'EHAD BELAYV (אחד בפה ואחד בלב).
Literally, "he who speaks one thing with his mouth and another thing in his heart" (Pes. 113b). In other words, an insincere or hypocritical person. According to the Talmud (ibid.), the Holy One, blessed be He, hates such a person.

EHAD HAMARBEH VE'EHAD HA-MAMIT UVILVAD SHEYEKHA-VAYN LIBO LASHAMAYIM (אחד המרבה ואחד הממעיט ובלבד שיכוין לבו לשמים).
"One may do much or one may do little; it is all one, provided he directs his heart to Heaven" (Ber. 17a; Men. 110a). See AM-HA'ARETZ.

ELA MAI (אלא מאי).
"What then" (is the interpretation) (Pes. 42b). In conversation the expression may mean, "so what?" or "but what happens?"

The Hebrew word *ela* means "but," as in the Yiddish *Er zuhgt er ken duhs, ela-vuh-den er vil nit* ("He says he can do it, but [what else?] he does not want to").

GADOL HADOR (גדול הדור).
"The great man of the generation" (M.K. 22b). The Talmud (ibid.) refers to Rabbi and R. Jacob b. Aha as the great men of the generation.

In every period of Jewish history, one or two persons have been referred to as *gadol* (*gedolim*, pl.) *hador* (cf. Ber. 63a). See GAVRA RABBAH.

GADOL HAME'ASEH (HAMA'ASEH) YOTAYR MIN HA'OSEH (גדול המעשה יותר מן העושה).
"[R. Eleazar said:] He who causes others to do good is greater than the doer" (B.B. 9a), as it says, "And the work of righteousness [*tzedakah*] shall be peace, and the effect of righteousness quiet and confidence forever" (Isa. 32:17).

GALGAL HU SHEHOZAYR BA'-OLAM (גלגל הוא שחוזר בעולם).
"It is a wheel [*galgal*] that revolves in the world"

(Shab. 151b; cf. also *Rashi*, Gen. 25:30). Scripture states, "Thou shalt surely give him [the poor], and thy heart shall not be grieved when thou givest unto him; because that for this thing [*biglal*] the Lord thy God will bless thee in all thy work. . . ." (Deut. 15:10). R. Eleazar ha-Kappar said: Let one always pray to be spared this fate (poverty), for if he does not descend (to poverty), his son will, and if not his son, his grandson. The word *biglal* is similar to *galgal*. Thus the school of R. Ishmael taught: It is a wheel (*galgal*) that revolves in the world.

The *galgal* revolving has been interpreted to mean the planets (*mazalot*) that move in the world. Only through mercy can one's *mazal* change for the good. It is written in the Talmud that R. Hiyya said to his wife: "When a poor man comes, be quick to offer him bread, so that others may be quick to offer it to your children" (ibid.) (cf. *Torah Temimah*, Deut. 15:37).

GAM ZU LETOVAH (גם זו לטובה). "This also is for the best" (Ta'an. 21a; San. 28b). Tales are told about the *Tanna* Nahum Ish Gamzu (late first and early second century C.E.), who was so called because whatever misfortune befell him, he would declare, *Gam zu letovah*.

Pious Jews also utter *Gam zu letovah* upon every happening, whether for good or bad. See KOL MAH DE'AVID RAHAMANA, LETAV AVID.

GAMAL HAPORAYAH BA'AVIR (גמל הפורח באויר). See MIGDAL HAPORAYAH BA'AVIR.

GANOV DA'AT HABERIYOT (גונב דעת הבריות). "He who steals the mind of people" (Shab. 39a); that is, he deceives.

GAVO'AH LO YISA GEVOHIT, SHEMA YAYTZAY MAYHEN TOREN (גבוה לא ישא גבוהית, שמא יצא מהן תורן). "An abnormally tall man should not marry an abnormally tall woman, lest

their children be tall and thin" (Bek. 45b).

GAVRA RABBAH (גברא רבה). "A great man" (B.K. 59a). Eliezer (Eleazar) Ze'era was once charged for putting on a pair of black shoes and standing in the marketplace of Nehardea. He claimed he was mourning over Jerusalem. He was put into prison because they considered this arrogance. He argued, "I am a great man" (*Gavrah rabbah*) and, to prove it, he was given permission to ask a question on a legal point. His answer to the question turned out to be in keeping with Samuel, whose court flourished in the town. They then released him. See GADOL HADOR.

GEDOLAH SINAH SHESONIM AMAY HA'ARETZ LETALMIDAY HAKHAMIM (גדולה שנאה ששונאים עמי הארץ לתלמידי חכמים). "Great is the hatred of the ignorant [unlettered] for the learned [scholarly]" (Pes. 49b). See AMHA'ARETZ.

GEDOLIM TZADIKIM BEMITATAM YOTAYR MIBEHAYAYHEM (גדולים צדיקים במיתתם יותר מבחייהם). "The righteous are greater after death than in life" (Hul. 7b), for it is written, "And it came to pass, as they were burying a man that, behold, they spied a raiding party; and they cast the man into the tomb of Elisha: and as the man came there, he touched the bones of Elisha, he revived, and stood up on his feet" (2 Kings 13:21). In order to revive the dead in his lifetime, Elisha had to exert himself both in action and prayer (2 Kings 4:33–35), but, after his death, his mere touch revived a man; thus, it tends to prove that the righteous are more powerful after death than when alive.

GEMARA GEMIRAY LAH (גמרא גמירי לה). See GEMARA GEMIRNA SEVARA LA YEDANA.

GEMARA GEMIRNA SEVARA LA YEDANA (גמרא גמירנא סברא לא ידענא). Concerning the removal of the ashes from the inner altar preceding the trimming of the five lamps, Abaye said: "I know it [i.e., the order] by tradition, but I do not know the reason" (Yom. 33a). A similar talmudic statement is GEMARA GEMIRAY LAH ("I learned it through the *mesorah*") (Ber. 54b). There are laws whose source is not revealed in the Torah; they were transmitted from generation to generation.

GENAYVAT DA'AT (גנבת דעת). Literally, "to steal one's mind" by any manner of misrepresentation. Scripture (2 Sam. 15:6) states, "So Absalom stole the hearts of the men of Israel; that is, he deceived or duped the men of Israel. It is written in the Talmud (Hul. 94a), "It is forbidden to deceive people, even gentiles"; it is forbidden to create a false impression (cf. also Jer. Tal., San 24:1).

GIRSA DEYANKUTA (LA MISHTAKHA) (גרסא דינקותא (לא) משתכחא). "Studies of one's youth" (are not forgotten) (cf. Shab. 21b). What we first learn, we best know and well remember.

HA BEHA TALYA (הא בהא תליא). An Aramaic phrase, meaning "one is dependent on the other" (cf. Shab. 135b). The phrase is used in conversation when relying on, or being subject to, something else for support.

HABA LETAHAYR MESAI'IN OTO (הבא לטהר מסייעין אותו). See ADAM MEKADAYSH ATZMO ME'AT MEKADSHIN OTO HARBAYH, and so on.

HABATALAH MEVI'AH LIDAY SHI'AMUM (הבטלה מביאה לידי שעמום). "Idleness leads to idiocy" (*Mishnah*, Ket. 59b).

HAD BEDARA (חד בדרא). "One in a generation" (Ket. 17a). When R. Samuel, the son of R. Isaac, died, a pillar of fire came between him and the world. And the tradition is that a pillar of fire makes such a separation either for one in a generation (*had bedara*) or for two in a generation. This phenomenon occurred only for very great and pious men.

The expression *had bedara* is currently used for an exceptional, world-pious Torah scholar.

HADELET HANINELET LO BIMHAYRAH TIPATAYAH (הדלת הננעלת לא במהרה תפתח). "The door [to prosperity] has been shut [and] will not speedily be opened" (B.K. 80b). The Talmud asks, What is meant by this statement? Mar Zutra said it means that once a person fails in his attempt to secure ordination, he cannot obtain it so easily again. R. Ashi said it means that one who is in disfavor is not readily taken back into favor. Proverbially, the saying expresses the idea that if good luck departs from a person, it does not readily return to him, and if a tragedy befalls him, it will not depart hastily.

HADRAT PANIM ZAKAN (הדרת פנים זקן). "The glory of the face is its beard" (Shab. 152a). This is one of the three things R. Joshua b. Karhah enumerated to a certain eunuch (*gavza'ah*) who was demeaning him. The other two advantageous characteristics he mentioned were that the rejoicing of one's heart is a wife and the heritage of the Lord is children (Ps. 127:3).

Generally, when one's looks are impressive, usually by mark of distinction of having a beard, he is said to have a *hadrat panim*.

HAFOKH HAKE'ARAH AL PIHAH (הפוך הקערה על פיה). "To turn the dish upside down" (B.B. 16a). The expression denotes challenging Providence and declaring God's works worthless. Differences of opinion between Raba and Abaye and R. Eliezer and R. Joshua concerning Job's beliefs are mentioned in the Talmud: Did he sin with his lips or his heart, or did Job refer only to Satan?

HAHOSHAYD BIKSHAYRIM LOKAH BEGUFO (החושד בכשרים לוקה בגופו). "[Resh Lakish said:] He who entertains a suspicion against innocent [worthy] men is bodily afflicted" (Shab. 97a), for it is written, (And Moses . . . said) "But behold, they will not believe me" (Numb. 20:12); but it was revealed to the Holy One, blessed be He, that Israel would believe. God said to Moses: (HAYM) MA'AMINIM BENAY MA'AMINIM ("They are believers, [and] descendents of believers")— "They are believers," as it is written, "and the people believed" (Ex. 4:31) and "the descendents of believers," as is written, and he [Abraham] believed in the Lord" (Gen. 15:6; Shab., ibid.). God said that Moses and Aaron did not believe (Numb. 20:12) and Moses was smitten (Ex. 4:6). See MARIT AYIN; AYN NIKHNASIM LEHURVAH MIPNAY HAHASHAD; HASHAD.

HAI ALMA (KEVAY) HILULA DAMYA (האי עלמא (כבי) הלולא דמיא). "The world [from which we must depart] is like a wedding feast" (Erub. 54a). Just as the wedding feast ends all too soon, the expression implies, Do not postpone enjoyment or pleasures. A similar English proverb is, "Make hay while the sun shines."

HAYAY SHA'AH (חיי שעה). Literally, "temporal life"; either pertaining to "short duration," "present life," "transitory pleasure," or to the secular as distinguished from the sacred or eternal. Psalms 45:3 reads, "You are beautiful beyond other men." *Rashi* (ad loc.) comments, You are distinguished from those men who are engaged in transitory drudgery (*ha'oskim*

bimlekhet hai sha'ah). The Talmud (Shab. 10a) relates that Raba saw R. Hamnuna prolonging his prayers and he said, "They forsake eternal life [*hayay olam*] and occupy themselves with temporal life [*hayay sha'ah*]." It seems that he considered study of Torah (eternal life) a religious observance in itself.

When inquiring as to the health of a person, he or she may answer sarcastically, in Yiddish, *Hai sha'ah iz oykh gelebt* ("Existing for a limited time is also living").

HAITA DEKATRI SAVART VEKIBALT (חייתא דקטרי סברת וקבלת). "You have agreed to a bag sealed with knots (*Rashi* Ket. 93a, B.M. 14b) or wind" (*Rashi*, B.K. 9a). That is, you bought it at your own risk and it is your fault that you did not examine the purchase.

HAKADOSH BARUKH HU LIBA BA'AY (הק״בה לבא בעי). See RAHAMANA LIBA BA'AY.

HAKADOSH BARUKH HU MAKDIM REFU'AH LEMAKAH (הקב״ה מקדים רפואה למכה). "God brings the healing before the blow." The Yiddish equivalent is *Gott shikt (tzu) di refu'ah far der makah*. This saying is derived from the Talmud (Meg. 13b), concerning the opening words of the chapter in *Megillah* (3:1): "After these things." After what? queries the Talmud. "Raba said: After God had created a healing for the blow [which was eventually going to fall upon Haman]. For Resh Lakish has said: The Holy One, blessed be He, does not smite Israel unless He has created for them a healing beforehand, as it says, 'When I have healed Israel, then is the iniquity of Ephraim uncovered'" (Hos. 7:1). The opposite is true of other nations. "He smites them first, and then creates for them a healing, as it says: 'The Lord will smite Egypt, smiting and healing'" (Isa. 19:22).

HAKADOSH BARUKH HU MEDAK-DAYK IM SEVIVAV KEHUT HASA'-ARAH (הקב"ה מדקדק עם סביבין כחוט השערה). "The Holy One, blessed be He, deals strictly with those around Him even to a hair's breadth" (Yeb. 121b). See KEHUT HASA'ARAH.

HAKADOSH BARUKH HU NATAN BE'ISHAH BINAH YOTAYR MIBA'-ISH (הקב"ה נתן באשה בינה יותר מבאיש). "The Holy One, blessed be He, endowed the woman with more under-standing [binah] than the man" (Nid. 45b). This is derived from the scriptural passage, "And the Lord built [vayiven] the rib" (Gen. 2:22). The word binah is analo-gous to that of vayiven.

HAKHAM, ZEH TALMID HAMAH-KIM ET RABOTAV (חכם, זה תלמיד המחכים את רבותיו). "A wise [man] is a disciple who makes his teachers wise" (Hag. 14a). Opposed to the wise man is the fool. Expressions describing this char-acteristic are HAKHAM BALAILAH (lit., "wise when asleep") or Hakham mide'oraita, ("a perfect fool"), a euphemism for Bur Mide'oraito ("a blockhead"). See A HAKHAM FUN MAH NISHTANAH.

HAKOL BIDAY SHAMAYIM HUTZ MITZINIM PAHIM (הכל בידי שמים חוץ מצינים פחים). "Everything is by the hand of Heaven, except cold and heat" (Ket. 30a). It is said that "cold [tzinim] and heat [pahim] are in the way of the crooked man; he that guards his soul shall be far from them" (Prov. 22:5). The words tzinim and pahim are translated in the verse as "thorns" and "snares," but they may also be rendered as "cold" and "heat." With care and prudence, man can avoid many evils, without being a fatalist and blaming Providence (cf. A.Z. 3b).

HAKOL KEMINHAG HAMEDINAH (הכל כמנהג המדינה). Regarding the prac-tice of repeating or not repeating certain

verses in Hallel, or pronouncing a blessing after it, the Talmud (Pes. 119b) states, "It all depends on local custom." The equiva-lent English expression is "When in Rome, do as the Romans do!" See MINHAG MEVATAYL HALAKHAH.

HALAKHAH LEMA'ASEH (הלכה למעשה). "The halakhah in actual prac-tice"; that is, the practical lesson (Ber. 24a). The Talmud (ibid.) discusses the rule of placing one's tefillin in different places: under the pillow, under the place of one's feet, and between the coverlet and the pillow (not opposite to one's head). The Talmud relates that "R. Hamnuna, the son of R. Joseph, said: Once when I was standing before Raba, he said to me: Go and bring me my tefillin, and I found them between the coverlet and the pillow, not opposite his head, and I knew that it was a day of ablution [for his wife], and I perceived that he had sent me in order to impress upon me a practical lesson [hala-khah lema'aseh]."

In daily discussion concerning any matter, one may ask, What is the halakhah lema'aseh? How should I act? or, what is the rule or actual practice?

HALAKHAH LEMOSHE MISINAI (הלכה למשה מסיני). "A law transmitted from Moses on Mount Sinai" (Pe'ah 2:6). "Nahum the scribe said, 'I have a tradition from R. Me'asha, who received it from Abba, who received it from the Zugot (two chiefs of the Sanhedrin), who received it from the prophets as a halakhah of Moses from Sinai.'" These laws are part of the Oral Law, possessing biblical authority.

Maimonides (Yad, Tefillin 1:6–8) writes, concerning three kinds of parchment de-signed for the writing of a Torah scroll, tefillin and Mezuzot, that they are Hala-khah Lemoshe Misinai. The Sefer Torah should be written on gevil (whole parch-ment), the tefillin on kelaf (the exterior part of a split hide), and Mezuzah on *dukhsustus* (the inner part of the split hide).

The phrase *Halakhah Lemoshe Misinai* is popularly translated as an "ancient tradition" or "as if they were handed down to Moses from Sinai." An example is the prayer-modes transmitted by the *Maharil*, called *Niggunay Sinai*, that are used in the synagogue (cf. Rabbi G. Felder, *Sefer Yesoday Yeshurun*, Toronto, Canada, 1954, p. 40).

HALAKHAH VE'AYN MORIM KAYN (הלכה ואין מורים כן). "This is the *halakhah*, but one does not teach it [publicly]" (Bez. 28b). The Talmud records that R. Judah permitted even the preliminaries for preparing the food on a festival. This included sharpening a knife, which is a preliminary. However, even if the *halakhah* is according to R. Judah and is permitted, we do not teach it publicly, in order that people not treat festivals lightly.

HALOMAYD VE'AYNO HOZAYR DOMEH LEZORAYA VE'AYNO KOTZAYR (הלומד ואינו חוזר דומה לזורע ואינו קוצר). R. Joshua b. Karha said: "Whosoever studies Torah and does not review, it is likened unto one who sows without reaping" (San. 99a).

HAMA'AKHAL MAYVI ET HASHAYNAH (המאכל מביא את השינה). The *Mishnah* (Yom. 1:4) states that the Elders of the Court would not let the High Priest eat much on the eve of the Day of Atonement, near nightfall, because "food brings about sleep." Ibn Ezra (*Kohelet* 12:4) uses the expression HAMA'AKHAL YOLID HASHAYNAH ("Food gives rise to sleep").

HAMA'AKHAL YOLID HASHAYNAH (המאכל יוליד השנה). See HAMA'AKHAL MAYVI ET HASHAYNAH.

HAMAKOM YERAHAYM ALEKHA BETOKH SHE'AR HOLAY YISRAEL (המקום ירחם עליך בתוך שאר חולי ישראל). The Talmud (Shab. 12a, b) dis-

cusses various expressions used on the Sabbath when visiting a sick person. R. Jose would say, "May the Omnipresent have compassion upon you in the midst of the sick of Israel."

HAMALBIN PENAY HAVAYRO BARABIM KE'ILU SHOFAYKH DAMIM (המלבין פני חבירו ברבים כאלו שופך דמים). "He who publicly shames (i.e., 'makes pale') his neighbor is as though he shed blood" (B.M. 58b). Since the blood of the victim's face is drained when shamed, it is as though he had shed his neighbor's blood.

HAMATHIL BEMITZVAH OMRIM LO GEMOR (המתחיל במצוה אומרים לו גמור). "One who begins a *mitzvah* is told to complete it" (after Jer. Tal., R.H. 1:8). In English the expression is "Once you pledge, don't hedge," or in Yiddish, *Ver es zuhgt alef, muz zuhgn bet* ("Whoever says *alef* must say *bet*"). See MAY-ALEF VE'AD TAV.

HAMEKABAYL TZEDAKAH VE'AYNO TZARIKH LEKAKH, SOFO AYNO NIFTAR MIN HA'OLAM AD SHEYAVO LIDAY KAKH (המקבל צדקה ואינו צריך לכך, סופו אינו נפטר מן העולם עד שיבא לידי כך). "If a man accepts charity and is not in need of it, his end [will be that] he will not pass out of the world before he reaches such a condition" (Ket. 68a).

HAMESAHAYK BEKUVYA (המשחק בקוביא). See PASUL LE'AYDIM.

HAMEVAKAYR HOLEH NOTAYL EHAD MISHISHIM BETZA'ARO (המבקר חולה נוטל אחד מששים בצערו). "[R. Abba son of R. Hanina said:] He who visits a sick person takes away a sixtieth of his pain" (Ned. 39b); that is, he alleviates

his pain somewhat (see *Maharsha* for further elucidation).

HAMEVAZEH TALMID HAKHAM, APIKOROS HAVAY (המבזה תלמיד חכם. אפיקורות הוי). See APIKOROS (EPIKUROS, EPIKOROS).

HANA'ASEH AYN LEHASHIV (הנעשה אין להשיב). "What's done cannot be undone"; this is based on the Talmud (R.H. 29b), whose text reads *ve'ayn meshivin le'ahar ma'aseh* ("and what has been done is no longer open to discussion").

The *Mishnah* (ibid.) states, "If the festive day of the New Year fell on a Saturday, they used to blow the *shofar* in the Temple, but not in the country. After the destruction of the Temple, Rabban Johanan b. Zakai ordained that it should be blown [on Sabbath] in every place where there was a *Bet Din*. R. Eliezer said that Rabban Johanan b. Zakai laid down this rule for Yavneh only." It once happened that New Year fell on a Sabbath and Rabban Johanan said to Benay Bathyra, "Let us blow the *shofar*." They said to him, "Let us discuss the matter." He said to them, "Let us blow and discuss it afterwards." Then they blew the *shofar* and said to him, "Let us now discuss the question." He replied: "The *shofar* has already been heard in Yavneh, and what has been done is no longer open to discussion."

In Yiddish, one says, *Uhpgetuhn iz farfaln!* ("What's done is done!").

HANIFTAR MIN HAMAYT AL YOMAR LO LAYKH LESHALOM ELA LAYKH BESHALOM (הנפטר מן המת אל יאמר לו לך לשלום אלא לך בשלום). "[R. Abin the Levite also said]: One who takes leave of the dead [on leaving the funeral procession] should not say to him 'Go to peace,' but 'Go in peace' (Ber. 64a), as it says, 'But thou [Abram] shalt go to thy fathers in peace'" (Gen. 15:15).

HANOSAY ISHAH TZARIKH SHE-YIVDOK BE'AHEHAH (הנושא אשה צריך שיבדוק באחיה). "[Raba said]: He who [wishes] to take a wife should inquire about [the character of] her brothers" (B.B. 110a). For it is said, "And Aaron took Elisheva of Amminadab, the sister of Nahshon" (Ex. 6:23). Why, then, should it be expressly stated, "the sister of Nahshon"? From this, it is to be inferred that he who takes a wife should inquire about (the character of) her brothers. It was taught that most children resemble the brothers of the mother (Soph. 15:10).

HA'OKHAYL BASHUK DOMEH LE-KELEV (האוכל בשוק דומה לכלב). "[Our Rabbis taught]: He who eats in the marketplace is like a dog" (Kidd. 40b). The Talmud (ibid.) continues: "and some say he is unfit to testify. R. Idi b. Abin said: The *halakhah* agrees with the latter."

The *Kallah Rabbati* (10) writes that "He who eats in the marketplace is in the company of a dog."

HARBAYH LAMADETI MAYRABO-TAI, UMAYHAVAYRAI YOTAYR MAYRABOTAI UMITALMIDAI YO-TAYR MIKULAM (הרבה למדתי מרבותי. ומחברי יותר מרבותי ומתלמדי יותר מכלם). R. Hanina said: "I have learnt much from my teachers, and from my colleagues more than from my teachers, but from my disciples more than from all" (Ta'an. 7a). This was said in conjunction with the idea that words of the Torah are likened to a tree; just as a small tree may set on fire a bigger tree, so, too, it is with scholars—the younger sharpen the minds of the older.

HARARIM HATELUYIM BESA'ARAH (VE'AYN LAHEM AL MAH SHEYIS-MOKHU) (הררים התלים בשערה (ואין להם על מה שיסמכו)). "Mountains hanging by a hair [and they have nothing to support them]" (*Mishnah*, Hag. 1:8). This refers to things that seem great and

important and, in reality, have no basis. Or, it refers to a spiritual or moral subject that is built on a tottering foundation.

HARAY SHULHAN, HARAY BASAR, VAHARAY SAKIN VE'AYN LANU (PEH) LE'EKHOL (הרי שלחן. הרי בשר. והרי סכין ואין לנו (פה) לאכל). R. Johanan said: "Behold a table, meat, and knife, yet we have no mouth to eat" (Kidd. 46a), inferring that the *Mishnah* stands before us, but it is inexplicable.

Often a situation seems clear, yet it cannot be explained, interpreted, or accounted for.

HAS VESHALOM (חס ושלום). An expression spoken in the same manner as HAS VEHALILA, meaning "God forbid!" or "Heaven forbid!" The expression is used throughout the Talmud. For example, "It was taught, R. Simeon b. Yohai said: Heaven forbid [*has veshalom*] that the Torah be forgotten in Israel (Shab. 138b), for it is said, 'for it shall not be forgotten out of the mouths of their seed'" (Deut. 31:21). Other talmudic references are: Pes. 74b, 83b; Hag. 4b, 16a; Ned. 22a; Ket. 103b; Meg. 31b; San. 11a.

HASH BEROSHO YA'ASOK BA-TORAH (חש בראשו יעסוק בתורה). "[R. Joshua b. Levi said:] If he feels pain in his head, let him engage in the study of the Torah" (Erub. 54a), since it is said, "For they [both the Written and Oral law] shall be a chaplet of grace unto thy head" (Prov. 1:90).

HASHAD (חשד). A Hebrew word meaning "suspicion." A person should not do anything, even though it is suitable, since it may lead to suspicion that the person is doing a transgression. For example, the Talmud (Ber. 3a) states, AYN NIKHNASIM LEHURVAH MIPNAY HAHASHAD ("One must not go into a ruin because of suspicion"). On the other hand, we should not suspect a person of doing something wrong unless

there is evidence of it. See HAHOSHAYD BIKSHAYRIM LOKAH BEGUFO; MARIT AYIN.

HASHAKH HA'OLAM BA'ADO (חשך העולם בעדו). An expression inferring that "a catastrophe befell him," as in the talmudic statement of R. Alexandri: "The world is darkened for him whose wife has died in his days" (San. 22a).

HASHEM YERAHAYM (השם ירחם). An expression meaning "God will have mercy"; He will help and rescue. R. Jose b. Kisma said to R. Hananiah (Hanina) b. Teradion, "I have heard about you that you sit and occupy yourself with Torah, and publicly gather assemblies, and keep a scroll [of the Law] in your bosom. This is contrary to the Roman decree." He replied, MIN HASHAMAYIM YERAHAMU ("Heaven will show mercy") (A.Z. 18a). See OTIYOT PORHOT.

HASHMAYA LE'OZNEKHA MAH SHE'ATTAH MOTZI MIPIKHA (השמע לאזניך מה שאתה מוציא מפיך). "Let your ear hear what your mouth utters" (Ber. 13a). The Talmud (ibid.) discusses the dispute between Rebbi and the Rabbis: Rebbi says that the *Shema* must be recited in the original language because Scripture says, "and they shall be" (*vehayu*) (Deut. 6:6), implying, As they are, they shall remain. The Rabbis, however, say that it may be recited in any language because Scripture says "hear" (ibid., 6:4), implying, In any language that you understand. How, then, does Rebbi explain the word "hear"? He requires the word "hear" for the lesson: Let your ear hear what your mouth utters; that is, say it audibly.

In conversation the expression has come to mean, Listen to what you are saying.

HASID SHOTEH (חסיד שוטה). "A foolish pietist" (Sot. 20a). The Talmud (Sot. 21b) describes a foolish pietist as one who sees a woman drowning in the

river, and he says, "It is improper for me to look upon her and rescue her." That is, he refuses to perform a humane act for religious reasons. R. Joshua remarks that such a person brings destruction upon the world.

HATORAH HASAH AL MAMONAM SHEL YISRAEL (התורה חסה על ממונם של ישראל). "The Torah wished to spare Israel unnecessary expense" (R.H. 27a). A silver *shofar* was used on fast days and a gold one on Rosh Hashanah. The use of gold on holidays was to pay respect to the holiday, but on fast days the Torah had mercy on the money of Israel and spared them needless expense—thus the use of a silver *shofar*.

This expression can be applied whenever public Jewish money is spent needlessly.

HATZAD HASHAVEH SHEBAHEN (הצד השוה שבהן). "The feature common to them all," or "the common ground" (*Mishnah*, B.K. 1:1). For example, the *Mishnah* mentions four principle categories of damage, each having its own characteristic. The feature common to them all is that they are in the habit of doing damage and they have to be under control so that whenever any one of them does damage, the offender is liable for indemnity with the full value of his estate.

HAVAH AMINA (הוה אמינא). An Aramaic phrase meaning "I would have said" (Pes. 77a). A rebbe might ask a student, "What is your *havah amina*?" ("What would you say?"; "What is your interpretation?").

HAVERKHA KERAYIKH HAMRA UKAFA LEGABAYKH MOSH (חברך קרייך חמרא אוכפא לגביך מוש). "If thy neighbor calls thee an ass, put a saddle on your back" (B.K. 91b). In Yiddish, a corresponding expression is AZ DI VELT ZUHGT ZUHL MEN GLEYBN ("If the world says it, it should be believed").

HAVRAKH HAVRA IT LAYH, VEHAVRA DEHAVRAKH HAVRA IT LAYH (חברך חברא אית ליה, וחברא דחברך חברא אית ליה). "Your friend has a friend, and the friend of your friend has a friend" (Ket. 109b). The expression teaches that if you know of a matter, your friend and his friend will know of it and if it is known to one, it will be known to all. Therefore, do not tell even your friend.

HAVRU AL—KETARNEGOLIM (חברו על—כתרנגלים). An expression saying, "They joined as one against . . ." (Yeb. 84a). The Talmud relates that when Rabbi went to learn Torah at the school of R. Eleazar b. Shammu'a, his disciples combined against him like the cocks of Bet Bukya (a place in Upper Galilee noted for its fierce cocks who do not allow the intrusion of a strange cock among them), and they did not let him learn more than one simple thing in the *Mishnah*.

HAYEKHA KODMIN LEHAYAY HAVAYRKHA (חייך קודמין לחיי חבירך). See VEHAY AHIKHA IMAKH.

HAYKHI TIMATZAY (TIMTZA) LOMAR (היכי תמצא לומר). See IM TIMATZAY (TIMTZO LOMAR).

HAYN VELAV VERAFYA BEYADAYH (הן ולאו ורפיא בידיה). See HAYN SHELKHA TZEDEK, VELAV SHELKHA TZEDEK.

HAYOM KAN UMAHAR BAKEVER (היום כאן ומחר בקבר). "Here today and tomorrow in the grave" (Ber. 28b). Rabban Johanan ben Zakkai, before dying, uttered this phrase and compared a human king, who is ephemeral, to the King of Kings, the Holy One, blessed be He, Who lives and endures for ever and ever. A similar expression is HAYOM ODENU UMAHAR AYNENU ("Today here and tomorrow nothing") (Jer. Tal., San., end of *Perek vav*; *Targum Yonatan*, Isa. 2:22).

HAYOM ODENU UMAHAR AY-NENU (היום עודנו ומחר איננו). See HAYOM KAN UMAHAR BEKEVER.

HAZAK UVARUKH (חזק וברוך). "Be strong and blessed"; an expression similar to YISHAR KO'AH, uttered by *Ashkenazim* to a person who was honored by being called up to the Torah, to the *Kohanim* after *Birkat Kohanim*; or to the *Sheli'ah Tzibbur* or *Tokaya* after completing their tasks. Extending this greeting is based on the Talmud (Ber. 32b), which states that four need strengthening: the Torah, good deeds, prayer, and worldly occupation, as it is written, HAZAK VE'EMATZ, "Be strong in Torah, and courageous in good deeds." Moreover, since TORAH MATESHET KOHO SHEL ADAM ("Torah weakens the strength of man [through constant study]"), it is thus proper to say to him, *Hazak uvarukh.*

Although the *Kohanim* are obligated, according to the Torah, to bless the people, in any event, since they can cancel their obligation by stepping out of the synagogue, it is thus fitting to encourage them for the good (cf. Rabbi Yitzhak Yosef, *Sefer Yalkut Yosef*, vol. 1 [Jerusalem] 338:25).

HERESH SHOTEH VEKATAN PEGI'ATAN RA'AH (חרש שוטה וקטן פגיעתן רעה). "A deaf man, a fool, and a child are bad to meet" (B.K. 87a), because whoever harms them is liable for the damage done, while no compensation is recoverable from them for any damage done by them.

HESAH HADA'AT (היסח הדעת). "When the mind is diverted." It is written in the Talmud (San. 97a), "Three things happen when the mind is diverted [behesah hada'at]: the coming of the Messiah, a lost article that has been found, and a scorpion."

HEVAY PIKAYAH USHTOK (הוי פקח ושתוק). "Be clever and keep quiet"

(Yom. 7a). The Talmud discusses the case in which a priest was standing and offering up the sheaf of the *omer* and it became unclean in his hand; let him tell and another one will be brought in its place. If there is no other one available, one would say to him, "Be clever and keep quiet" (for the priest's frontplate procures forgiveness for such mishap). Scripture uses the expression, *Evil maharish hakham yayhashayv* ("He that shuts his lips is esteemed a man of understanding") (Prov. 17:28).

HEVAY ZAHIR MIN HAYO'-ETZKHA LEFI DARKO (הוי זהיר מן היועצך לפי דרכו). R. Kahana said, on R. Akiba's authority: "Beware of one who counsels you for his own benefit" (San. 76b).

HEVLAY MASHI'AH (HEVLO SHEL MASHI'AH) (חבלי משיח) חבלו של משיח). "Birth pangs [prior to the coming] of the Messiah." The advent of the Messiah is pictured as being preceded by years of great distress (cf. Shab. 118a; San. 98b). These tribulations preceding the birth of a new era have given rise to the Yiddish expression MASHI'AH'S TZAYTN ("Messiah's time").

HEZEK RE'IYAH SHEMAYH HEZEK (היזק ראייה שמיה היזק). "Damage by seeing is called damage" (B.B. 2b); that is, to be screened while in one's house or courtyard from the view of one's neighbors is a legal right. This legal maxim expresses the right of a householder to privacy.

HI NAYMA UDIKULA SHAPIL (היא ניימא ודיקולא שפיל). "When she [a woman] slumbers, the basket [upon her head] drops" (San. 7a); that is, laziness begets ruin. Scriptural verses conveying the same idea are *Ba'atzaltayim yimokh hamekareh uveshiflut yadayim yidlof habayit* ("By slothfulness the rafters sink in; and through idleness of the hands the house leaketh") (Eccl. 10:18) and *Shomayr ru'ah lo yizra vero'eh ve'avim lo yiktzor* ("He that observeth the wind shall not sow; and he that regardeth the clouds shall not reap") (ibid., 11:4). This means that if a farmer thinks of the possibility that winds will blow away the seed he sows, it will lead him to inaction. Similarly, if he gazes at the clouds during harvest time, thinking of the possibility of rain that will spoil the crops, he will stop doing his work and the corn will be left in the field uncut.

A Yiddish expression based on the same idea is *Az me'iz foyl huht men nisht in moyl* ("If you are lazy, you will not have sustenance").

HIDUR MITZVAH (הידור מצוה). "Honoring or adorning the *mitzvah*." R. Zera said: "For [performing a commandment in] an exemplary manner, one should go up to a third of [the ordinary expense involved in] the observance thereof" (B.K. 9b; cf. also *Orah Hayyim* 656). Concerning the verse "This is my God and I will adorn Him" (Ex. 15:2), it was taught: Adorn thyself before Him in the fulfillment of precepts; make a beautiful *sukkah* in His honor, a beautiful *lulav*, a beautiful *shofar*, beautiful fringes, and a beautiful Scroll of the Law, and write it with fine ink, a fine reed-pen, and a skilled penman, and wrap it about with beautiful silks (Shab. 133b).

HILLUL HA-SHEM (חלול השם). A term meaning "desecration of the Divine Name"; the antithetical term is KIDDUSH HA-SHEM. *Hillul Ha-Shem* means any unworthy act that may reflect or discredit Judaism, thereby defaming the Name of God, as Scripture states, "And ye shall not profane My Holy Name" (Lev. 22:24). The Talmud asks, "What constitutes *Hillul Ha-Shem*?" Rab said, "If, for example, I take meat from the butcher and do not pay him at once" (Yom. 86a). What is meant is that the butcher might learn from Rab's example and therefore delay or intentionally ignore his payment of debts.

Throughout Jewish history, both *Kiddush Ha-Shem* and *Hillul Ha-Shem* embody the highest standards of Jewish ethics, which were transmitted from generation to generation.

HILLUL SHABBAT (חלול שבת). "Desecration of the Sabbath" (Shab. 33a). Scripture states, "Happy is the man . . . that keepeth the Sabbath from profaning it" (Isa. 56:2).

HINI'AH MA'OTAV AL KEREN HATZVI (הניח מעותיו על קרן הצבי). A metaphor denoting, He lost his money; that is, he is as "one who put his money on a stag's horn" (Ket. 107b). It is a sure thing that his money will be lost because the stag will run away with it to distant places.

The *Mishnah* relates the instance in which a man went to a country beyond the sea and someone came forward and maintained his wife on his own free will. When the husband returned, he was not obligated in any way to pay anything to this man. Neither was he instructed to advance the money nor promised a refund. The person who maintained the man's wife lost his money and it was as though he put his money on a stag's horn.

HIZAHARU BAHAVURAH (הזהרו בחבורה). "Take good care [to study] in company" (Ned. 81a). The *Ran* comments that when studying in a group, each student sharpens the mind of the others, as well as that of the teacher.

HOMETZ BEN YAYIN (חמץ בן יין). Literally, "vinegar, son of wine"; referring to a wicked or degenerate son of a righteous father (B.M. 83b).

Diametrical difference in position or nature is the meaning of YAYIN BEN HOMETZ ("wine from vinegar"), referring to a righteous son of a wicked father. A good son of a good father is YAYIN BEN YAYIN.

HOVAYSH BAYT HAMIDRASH (חובש בית המדרש). "One who is bound to the schoolhouse" (Hag. 14a); a nickname for one who occupies all his days with study.

HOZARNI HALILAH (חוזרני חלילה). R. Eliezer and R. Joshua argued whether a sacrifice is valid if slaughtered under a different designation. After lengthy debate, R. Joshua said to R. Eliezer, "I am moving in a circle" (Zeb. 10b); that is, this way of arguing will lead to no conclusion.

HU NOTAYN ETZBA BAYN SHINE-HAH (הוא נותן אצבע בין שיניה). "He who puts his finger between her teeth" (Ket. 52a); an expression used in an abstract or obstruse manner to infer responsibility for wrongdoing or failure.

HUKHA VE'ITLULA (חוכא ואטלולא). "Derision and jest" (Erub. 68b).

I EFSHAR LEBAYT HAMIDRASH BELO HIDUSH (אי אפשר לבית המדרש בלא חידוש). The Talmud (Hag. 3a) relates that R. Johanan b. Beroka and R. Eleazar Hisma went to pay their respects to R. Joshua at Peki'in. Said he to them: "What new teaching was there at the *bayt midrash* today?" They replied: "We are the disciples and thy waters do we drink." Said he to them: "Even so, it is impossible for a *bayt-midrash* session to pass without some moral teaching [*I efshar lebayt midrash belo hidush*]."

I SAYAFA LO SAFRA, VE'I SAFRA LO SAYAFA (אי סייפא לא ספרא ואי ספרא לא סייפא). "If one is a warrior [robber], he is no scholar; and if one is a scholar, he is no warrior" (A.Z. 17b). This is what R. Eleazar b. Perata answered the dignitaries of Rome when he was brought up on trial and they asked him, "Why

have you been stealing and why have you been studying the Torah?"

The intention behind the expression is that a person cannot indulge in Torah and be a warrior at the same time. This applies to any two opposing and unrelated endeavors that a person pursues.

ILMALAY MESHAMRIN YISRAEL SHETAY SHABBATOT KEHILKHA-TAN MIYAD NIGALIN (אלמלי משמרין ישראל שתי שבתות כהלכתן מיד נגאלין). "[R. Johanan said, in the name of R. Simeon b. Yohai]: If Israel were to keep two Sabbaths according to the laws thereof, they would be redeemed immediately" (Shab. 118b). It is said, "Thus saith the Lord of the eunuchs that keep my Sabbaths" (Isa. 56:4), which is followed by, "even them will I bring to my holy mountain . . ." (ibid., 7).

IM ANI KAN HAKOL KAN (אם אני כאן הכל כאן). "If I am here, everyone is here" (Sukk. 53a). This statement was made by Hillel the Elder at the 'Rejoicing at the place of Water-Drawing.' According to *Rashi*, Hillel uses "I" to refer to the Holy One, blessed be He. According to the *Yerushalmi*, it seems that "I" refers to Israel (see *Tos.*, s.v. *Im Ani Kan*, ad loc.).

IM AYN DAYAH—HAVDALAH MI-NAYIN (אם אין דעה—הבדלה מנין). "If there is no knowledge or understanding, how can one make a distinction?" (Jer. Tal., Ber. 5:2). This is one of the reasons for reciting *Attah Honantanu* ("Thou hast favored us") as part of the fourth blessing of the weekday *Amidah* (the Blessing of Knowledge) at the conclusion of the Sabbath and festivals.

The expression is used to infer that if one has no understanding, he cannot differentiate between things.

IM KAYN AYN LEDAVAR SOF (אם כן אין לדבר סוף). "If so, the matter is endless." The *Mishnah* (Pes. 1:2) states that after a room has been searched and cleared of *hamaytz*, there is no fear that a weasel may have dragged it from one room to another or from one spot to another. For if so, we must also fear from courtyard to courtyard and from town to town, and the matter is endless. (See also B.M. 28b).

IM TA'AZVAYNI (TA'AZVENAH) YOM, YOMAYIM TA'AZVEKA (אם תעזבני (תעזבנה) יום, ימים תעזבך). "If you forsake it for one day, it will forsake you for two days" (Jer. Tal., end of *Berakhot*; *Rashi*, Deut. 11:13; *Sifri Aykev* 11:22). In other words, "Never stop studying."

IM TALMID HAKHAM NOKAYM VENOTAYR KENAHASH HU, HAGRAYHU AL MOTNEKHA (אם תלמיד חכם נוקם ונוטר כנחש הוא, חגריהו על מתניך). "[R. Abba (also) said, in the name of R. Simeon b. Lakish]: [Even] if a scholar is vengeful and vindictive like a snake, bind him around your waist" (Shab. 63a). *Rashi* explains, Cleave to him, for you will eventually derive benefit from his scholarship. Another interpretation is, Be not afraid of him.

IM TIMATZAY (TIMTZA) LOMAR (אם תמצא לומר). "If you can say"; "if you accept that"; "granted that" (Git. 82b). HAYKHI TIMATZAY LOMAR? would mean "How can you imagine that?"

INSHAY DE'ALMA (אינשי דעלמא). "Common people" (Kidd. 80b), as opposed to scholars. See ALMA DEKUSHTA (DESHIKRA); KULAY ALMA LO PELIGI; ASMAKHTA BE'ALMA; and MILAY DE'ALMA.

INVAY HAGEFEN BE'INVAY HAGEFEN DAVAR NA'EH UMITKABAYL (ענבי הגפן בענבי הגפן דבר נאה ומתקבל). The Talmud teaches that a man should sell all he has and marry the daughter of a scholar, and marry his daughter to a scholar. This may be compared to "[the grafting of] grapes of a vine with grapes of a vine, [which is] a seemly and acceptable thing" (Pes. 49a). In other words, "Like should marry like."

IPKHA MISTABRA (איפכא מסתברא). Literally, "the reverse stands to reason" or "the logic is the reverse" (Kidd. 53b; B.M. 28a). Sometimes the word ADERABA(H) is appended prior to *ipkha mistabra*, meaning "On the contrary, the reverse stands to reason." The word *aderaba(h)* is used as a dialectic term and implies "to turn to the stronger side." The word *aderaba(h)* is also often used in the Yiddish language.

The term *Ipkha mistabra* may be applied to a person who opposes others and says the opposite of what they say.

IR HANIDAHAT (עיר הנדחת). "An apostate city" or "a town condemned for idolatry" (San. 71a). When a city becomes desolate or the people in the city do not observe the Torah laws, the city is referred to as an *Ir hanidahat*.

ISTERA BELAGAYNA KISH-KISH KORYA (איסתרא בלגינא קיש-קיש קריא). "One stone in a pitcher cries out 'rattle-rattle'" (B.M. 85b); it makes a clapping sound (*kish-kish*). But if the pitcher is filled with stones, there is no room for rattling. That is how R. Ulla applied this saying to the verse in Proverbs 14:33: "Wisdom resteth in the heart of him that hath understanding"—this refers to a scholar, the son of a scholar; "but that which is in the midst of fools is made known"—refers to a scholar, the son of an AM HA'ARETZ. One scholar in a family of fools achieves fame, while a whole family of scholars is taken for granted.

In Yiddish, the expression is *Fun leydige feser iz der geshray greser* ("The clamor is greater from empty barrels," or "Empty vessels make the greatest sound").

KA MASHMA LAN (קא משמע לן (קמ"ל)). "It/he informs us"; "he teaches us"; "he tells us this new point" (Shab. 98a). See MAI KAMASHMA LAN.

KAFTZAH ALAV ZIKNAH (קפצה עליו זקנה). R. Nahman asked R. Isaac: What is the meaning of the verse, "And it came to pass when Samuel was old" (1 Sam. 8:1); he lived for only fifty-two years. Thus said R. Johanan: "Old age came prematurely upon him [*Kaftzah alav ziknah*]" (Ta'an. 5b).

KAKH HAYAH MA'ASEH (כך היה מעשה). "So it happened" or "this was the fact" (Ber. 34b; Yom. 78a). The Talmud (Ber., ibid.) tells us that once the son of R. Gamaliel fell ill and he sent two scholars to R. Hanina b. Dosa to ask him to pray for him. After praying, he said to them that they could leave because the fever had gone down. The two scholars asked if he was a prophet and he replied that "If the prayer is fluent in my mouth, I know it is accepted, but if not, I know that it is rejected." When they came to R. Gamaliel, he said to them: "By the Temple service! You have not been a moment too soon or too late, but so it happened (*Kakh hayah ma'aseh*]: at that very moment the fever left him and he asked for water to drink."

LO KAKH HAMA'ASEH is another expression in the same vein, which follows in the form of a question, such as: "Did it not happen" that R. Johanan said to Resh Lakish that R. Joshua went to R. Johanan b. Nuri to study Torah . . . (Erub. 11b).

KAKH ONSHO SHEL BADAI SHE'AFILU AMAR EMET AYN SHOM'IN LO (כך עונשו של בדאי שאפילו אמר אמת אין שומעין לו). "Such is the punishment of a liar, that even should he tell the truth, he is not listened to" (San. 89b).

KAL VAHOMER (קל וחמר). See AL AHAT KAMAH VEKHAMAH.

KALU KOL HAKITZIN VE'AYN HADAVAR TALUI ELA BITESHU-VAH UMA'ASIM TOVIM (כלו כל הקיצין ואין הדבר תלוי אלא בתשובה ומעשים טובים). "[Rab said]: All the predestined dates [for redemption] have passed, and the matter [now] depends only on repentance and good deeds" (San. 97b).

KAM LAYH BIDERABAH MINAYH (קם ליה בדרבה מיניה). The Talmud (Git. 52b) states: "With regard to the expression *menasaykh* ("makes a libation"), Rab says that it means literally making a libation [to a heathen diety] while Samuel says it means only *me'arayv* ['mixing Jewish with heathen wine']." The Talmud asks: "Why did the one who says it means mixing not accept the view that it means making a libation?" And answers: "[Menasaykh] *kam layh biderabah minayh* ['the offense involves a heavier penalty']"—that is, the death penalty. The rule is, whoever has committed two offenses simultaneously shall be held answerable only for the worse one.

KAMAY DESHATAY HAMRA-HAMRA; KAMAY RAFOKA—GERIDA DEYAVLAY (קמי דשתי חמרא-חמרא; קמי רפוקא—גרידא דיבלי). "[R. Papa said:] Before the wine-drinker, [set] wine; before the ploughman, a basket of roots" (Sot. 10a). That is, everyone should get the food to which he is accustomed.

KAME'A (קמיע). "An amulet." Talmudic literature (cf. *Mishnah* in Shab. 60a, 61a, b) discusses various aspects of the *kame'a*. According to *Rashi* (Shab. 61a), it is possible that the word comes from the root word that means "to bend"(*lashon kesher*). Another opinion is that it derives from an Arabic root word, meaning "to hang." In both instances, it is evident that it is either bound or hung on the person (cf. Kohut, *Arukh* 7:123). It was a piece of paper, parchment, or a metal disc on which various formulas were written, and a person wore it for curative powers or protection from troubles.

In the Middle Ages, there were pros and cons for wearing the amulet. Opposing its use were Maimonides, who followed the precedent of Sherira Gaon and his son Hai (Guide, 1:61; *Yad, Tefillin* 5:4). In favor of permitting its use were Solomon b. Abraham Adret and Nahmanides.

A variety of formulas and instructions for the preparation of amulets can be found in mystical works such as *Sefer Yetzirah* and the *Sefer Razi'el*. As for laws regarding amulets, see *Orah Hayyim* 301:24–27, 305:17, 334:14; and *Yoreh Dayah* 179:12.

KARKAFTA DELA MANAH TEFIL-LIN (קרקפתא דלא מנח תפלין). The Talmud (R.H. 17a) asks: "What is meant by wrongdoers of Israel who sin with their body?" Rab said: "This refers to the head that does not put on phylactery."

KARKUSHTA VESHUNRA AVDAY HILULA MITARBA DEVISH GADA (כרכושתא ושונרא עבדי הלולא מתרבא דביש גדא). "The weasel and the cat [when at peace with each other] had a feast on the fat of the luckless" (San. 105a). This was R. Papa's observation regarding Midian and Moab.

The saying is applied to two enemies who make peace with each other in order to harm a third party.

KARYANA DE'IGARTA IHU LE-HEVAY PARVANKA (קריינא דאיגרתא איהו ליהוי פרוונקא). A proverbial expression, meaning "Let him who dictates the letter be the carrier" (San. 83b); that is, let him who gives the advice be its executor.

KASHEH (KASHIN) LEZVOGAM KE-KERI'AT YAM SUF (קשה (קשין) לזווגם כקריעת ים סוף). See KERI'AT YAM SUF.

KASHIN MEZONOTAV SHEL ADAM KE-KERI'AT YAM SUF (קשין מזונותיו של אדם כקריעת ים סוף). See KERI'AT YAM SUF.

KAV VENAKI (קב ונקי). "Little and good" (Git. 67a). Issi b. Judah used to specify the distinctive merits of the various Sages. Among them, he would say, "The *Mishnah* of R. Eliezer b. Jacob [the Elder] was little and good"; that is, the *halakhah* follows him wherever he gives an opinion.

KAVYAKHOL (כביכול). Literally, "As if it were possible." The word is used in speaking of God to avoid offensive anthropomorphism, as in *Kavyakhol af Hu ba'amidah* ("The Holy One, blessed be He, also was standing") (Meg. 21a). See BA'AL YEKHOLET: KOL YAKHOL.

KAVATA ITIM LATORAH? (קבעת עתים לתורה?). Raba said that when man is led into the next world for judgment, among other questions he will be asked, "Did you fix regular times for learning Torah?" (Shab. 31a).

To set or fix a time generally, the Yiddish expression is *kovaya zayn.*

KAYRAYAH MIKAN UMIKAN (קרח מכאן ומכאן). Literally, "bald from here and from there" ("bald on both sides") (B.K. 60b); that is to say, "a loser in either case."

The Talmud (B.K. ibid.) relates the following: "When R. Ammi and R. Assi were sitting before R. Isaac, the smith, one of them asked him: 'Will the master please tell us some legal points?' while the other asked, 'Will the master please give us some homiletical instruction?' When he commenced a homiletical discourse, he was prevented by the one; and when he commenced a legal discourse, he was prevented by the other. He therefore said to them, 'I will tell you a parable: To what is this like? To a man who has two wives, one young and one old. The young one used to pluck out his white hair, whereas the old one used to pluck out his black hair. He thus finally became bald on both sides [*Kayrayah mikan umikan*]."

KAYVAN DEDASH DASH (כיון דדש דש). Literally, "since it trod, it trod." The Talmud (Git. 56b) cites numerous times that Titus blasphemed and insulted Heaven. Finally, a voice went forth from Heaven, saying: "Sinner, son of a sinner, descendent of Esau the sinner. I have a tiny creature in My world called a gnat." The gnat entered Titus's nose, and knocked against his brain for seven years. It was because of the noise of a blacksmith's hammer that the noise of the gnat stopped. Every day hence, a blacksmith was brought and he hammered before Titus. This went on for thirty days, but, being used to the hammer, the gnat did not heed it (*Kayvan dedash dash*).

The phrase *kayvan dedash dash* is used when something becomes habitual or common practice.

KAYVAN SHEHIGID, SHUV AYNO HOZAYR UMAGID (כיון שהגיד שוב אינו חוזר ומגיד). A witness is not acceptable if he testifies before the *Bet Din*, either in money matters or in capital cases, and then returns and says that he wants to change his testimony (San. 44b).

The expression may be applied to any person who, after he has made a statement, wants to renege on his words.

KEFUI TOVAH (כפוי טובה). "Ungrateful"; one who does not remember the good done for him. Moses said to the Israelites, *Kefui tovah benay kefui tovah* ("You are ungrateful people, the offspring of an ungrateful ancestor") (A.Z. 5a).

KEHUT HASA'ARAH (כחוט השערה). Literally, "like a hair thread" (Sukk. 52a; Yeb. 70a, 121b). R. Judah expounded that in the Messianic Age, the Holy One, blessed be He, will bring the evil inclina-

tion (*yaytzer hara*) and slay it in the presence of the righteous and the wicked. To the righteous it will have the appearance of a towering hill, and to the wicked it will have the appearance of a hair thread (*kehut hasa'arah*). Both the former and the latter will weep; the righteous will weep, saying, "How were we able to overcome such a towering hill!" The wicked also will weep, saying, "How is it that we were unable to conquer this hair thread!"

The expression became associated with one who is exact in every little detail, sometimes more than necessary. Of this person, it is said that he or she is *medakdayk kehut hasa'arah* ("is scrupulous up to the smallest detail"). See HAKADOSH BARUKH HU MEDAKDAYK IM SEVIVAV KEHUT HASA'ARAH.

KEROVIM HAPSULIM LEHA'AYD (קרובים הפסולים להעיד). See PASUL LE'AYDUT.

KESEF METAHAYR MAMZAYRIM (כסף מטהר ממזרים). R. Joshua b. Levi said: "Money purifies *mamzayrim*" (Kidd. 71a). The word *mamzayr* is usually translated as "bastard." It is a child born from a union prohibited under penalty of death or *karayt* (Divine punishment of premature or sudden death).

Money purifies *mamzayrim* (pl. for *mamzayr*) because, by means of their wealth, they intermarry and become assimilated among Israelites (cf. *Rashi*, ad loc.).

KESHAYM SHEMITZVAH AL ADAM LOMAR DAVAR HANISHMA, KAKH MITZVAH AL ADAM SHELO LO-MAR DAVAR SHE'AYNO NISHMA (כשם שמצוה על אדם לומר דבר הנשמע, כך מצוה על אדם שלא לומר דבר שאינו נשמע). R. Ile'a stated, in the name of R. Eleazar, son of Simeon: "As one is commanded to say that which will be obeyed, so is one commanded not to say that which will not be obeyed" (Yeb. 65b). Scripture states, "Thou shalt surely rebuke thy neighbor" (*hokhayah tokhi'ah*); the rep-

etition of the verb implies rebuke only when rebuke will be effective. If, however, a person is sure that if he reproves someone, he will ignore it, it is better not to rebuke at all.

KESHOT ATZMEKHA VE'AHAR KAKH KESHOT AHAYRIM (קשוט עצמך ואחר כך קשוט אחרים). An adage meaning, "First adorn yourself and then adorn others" (B.M. 107b). First be yourself, before demanding it of others! A similar saying is "Physician, heal thyself!"

KESHURAH (כשורה). A word meaning "as it should be," "properly," or "according to order," as in ra'ita she'ayno nohayg keshurah ("If you see [a man] who does not behave in a seemly fashion") (B.M. 73b); or nohagin keshurah ("conduct themselves in a proper manner") (B.B. 133b). See LIFNIM MISHURAT HADIN; SHURAT HADIN.

KESUMA BA'ARUBAH (כסומא באארובה). "Like a blind man groping his way through a window" (B.B. 12b). This was said concerning a great man who made a statement and then it was found that the same rule was a halakhah communicated to Moses on Mount Sinai. It was not by chance that his agreement was with Moses, but it was attributed to the spirit of prophecy.

KIDRA DEVAY SHUTFAY LA HA-MIMA VELA KERIRA (קדרא דבי שותפי לא חמימא ולא קרירא). "A pot belonging to two partners [cooks] is neither hot nor cold" (Erub. 3a). The English equivalent is "Too many cooks spoil the broth."

KILE'AHAR YAD (כלאחר יד). An expression connoting "doing anything in an unusual way." The Talmud (Shab. 153b) cites R. Adda b. Ahabah, saying: "If one's bundle is lying on his shoulder [as Friday is ending and Shabbat begins], he must run with it until he arrives home." After much pondering, the Talmud asks, "But

when he arrives at his house, it is impossible that he shall not stop for a moment, and so he carries it from public [reshut harabim] to private ground [reshut hayahid]?" The answer given is that "He throws it in a 'back-handed' [unusual] manner" (cf. Pes. 66b).

The phrase also took on the meaning of "offhand," "incidentally," or "unintentionally."

KINAT SOFRIM TARBEH HOKH-MAH (קנאת סופרים תרבה חכמה). "Competition among scholars increases wisdom" (B.B. 21a); rivalry is a blessing to man. The Talmud gives the following example: Raba said, If a teacher teaches his children and there is another who is a better teacher, the first is not replaced by the second, for fear that the second, when appointed, will become indolent, not having any competition. R. Dimi from Nehardia, however, held that he would exert himself still more if appointed because Kinat sofrim tarbeh hokhmah; that is, the jealousy of the one who has been replaced will be a stimulus to the other not to disgrace himself.

KOFAYR BA'IKAR (כופר בעיקר). "To deny God" (B.B. 16b). According to R. Johanan, the wicked Esau committed five sins; among them was the sin of denying God. The Talmud (ibid.) states, "We know that he denied God because it is written here, 'What benefit is this to me?' (Gen. 25:32) and it is written in another place, 'This is my God, and I will glorify Him'" (Ex. 15:2). Esau's remark "What benefit is this to me?" refers to his asking what profit shall the birthright be for me? His behavior was inconsistent with that expected from one who was to serve the supreme God. The redeemed Israelites at the Red Sea, on the other hand, had a unique realization of the help of God; they sang, "This is my God and I will glorify Him" (ibid.)

In the Haggadah, too, the wicked son says, "What does this service mean to you?" (Ex. 12:26). To you, but not to him. Since he excludes himself from the community, he rejects the basic foundations of the faith (kofayr ba'ikar).

KOFIN OTO AD SHEYOMAR ROTZEH ANI (כופין אותו עד שיאמר רוצה אני). "Subject him to pressure until he says, 'I am willing'" (R.H. 6a; Kidd. 50a); "force consent upon him."

KOL ADAM SHE'AYN BO DAYAH ASUR LERAHAYM ALAV (כל אדם שאין בו דעה אסור לרחם עליו). R. Eleazar said: "Whosoever lacks knowledge, one may have no mercy upon him (San. 92a), as it is written, 'For it is a people of no understanding, therefore He that made them will not have mercy upon them, and He that formed them will show them no favor'" (Isa. 27:11).

KOL ADAM SHEYAYSH BO YIRAT SHAMAYIM DEVARAV NISHMA'IN (כל אדם שיש בו יראת שמים דבריו נשמעין). See DEVARIM HAYOTZE'IM MIN HA-LAYV NIKHNASIM EL HALAYV.

KOL BE'ISHAH ERVAH (קול באשה ערוה). "A woman's voice is a sexual incitement" (Ber. 24a; Kidd. 70a), as it says, "For sweet is thy voice and thy countenance is comely" (S.O.S. 2:14). See the Shulkhan Arukh, Orah Hayyim 75:3, regarding the prohibition of female voices. As for mixed voices in day schools and at Zemirot, see R. Hayyim Hezekiah Medini, Seday Hemed, Ma'arekhet "Kuf," number 42; and Rabbi Yechiel Y. Weinberg, responsa in Seriday Aysh, vol. 2, numbers 8 and 14.

KOL DE'ALIM GAVAYR (כל דאלים גבר). "Whichever is stronger can take possession" (B.B. 34b). The Talmud (ibid.) speaks of two claimants to a property, and one says, "It belongs to my father," while the other says, "to my father" (without either bringing evidence).

R. Nahman says that whoever is stronger can take possession.

Colloquially, the expression took on the meaning "might makes right."

KOL EMET EMET TAFSAYH LEHAI (כל אמת אמת תפסיה להיא). "The whole of truth got hold of this man" (Ber. 14b). The Talmud discusses whether, after concluding the Shema with the word emet ("true"), a person has to repeat the word, which is really the beginning of the next paragraph in the prayers. A related incident is described in which a certain man, who acted as the reader before Rabbah, said the word "truth" twice, whereupon Rabbah remarked: "The whole of truth has got hold of this man."

This remark may be used to reveal a person who speaks too much in the name of truth and thus arouses suspicion.

KOL GAL VEGAL SHEBA ALAI NI-NATI LO ROSHI (כל גל וגל שבא עלי נענעתי לו ראשי). R. Gamliel related that once when he was traveling onboard a ship, he observed a shipwreck and was grieved because on it was R. Akiba. Later, when R. Gamliel landed, R. Akiba came and sat down beside him and discussed matters of halakhah. R. Gamliel asked R. Akiba how he was rescued and he answered that it was a plank of the ship; "to every wave that approached me I dipped my head under" (to let the wave pass over me) (Yeb. 121a).

A Yiddish saying expressing the same concept is Az meken nisht ariber, muz men arunter ("If you cannot go above, you must go below").

KOL HAKODAYM (BAHEN) ZA-KHAH (כל הקודם (בהן) זכה). The Mishnah (B.K. 3:3) relates the case of Kol hakodaym (bahen) zakhah ("Whoever seizes them first acquires title to them"): "If a man removes his straw and stubble into the public ground to be formed into manure, and damage results to some other person, there is liability for the damage, and whoever seizes them first acquires title to them."

The expression is used in many instances and implies "first come, first served" or "The early bird catches the worm." (Cf. also Ket. 80b, 84a.)

KOL HAMEHAZAYR AL HAGEDU-LAH, GEDULAH BORAHAT MI-MENU VEKHOL HABORAYAH MIN HAGEDULAH, GEDULAH ME-HAZERET AHARAV (על המחזר כל הגדולה, גדולה בורחת ממנו וכל הבורח ממן הגדולה, גדולה מחזרת אחריו). See KOL HARODAYF AHAR HAKAVOD, HAKAVOD BORAYAH MIMENU.

KOL HAMEKAYAYM NEFESH AHAT MIYISRAEL KE'ILU KAYAYM OLAM MALAY (כל המקיים נפש אחת מישראל כאילו קיים עולם מלא). The Talmud (B.B. 11a) relates an incident in which a woman came to Binyamin the Righteous in a year of scarcity and asked him to assist her. He told her that he had no money in the charity fund. She then said that if he would not help her, she and her seven children would perish. He obliged by giving her money out of his own pocket. Later, Binyamin became dangerously ill. The angels addressed the Holy One, blessed be He, saying; "Thou hast said that he who preserves one soul of Israel is considered as if he had preserved the whole world." Shall, then, Binyamin the Righteous, who has preserved a woman and her seven children, die at so early an age? Binyamin's sentence was torn up and twenty-two years were added to his life.

KOL HAMELAMAYD BITO TORAH KE'ILU LIMDAH TIFLUT (כל המלמד בתו תורה כאילו לימדה תפלות) "Whoever teaches his daughter Torah teaches her obscenity" (Sot. 20a). The Talmud adds, "Read, rather: as though he had taught her obscenity" (Sot. 21b). Another reference to this thought is "And ye shall teach them [to] your sons" (Deut. 11:19)—but not your daughters" (Kidd.

29b). This undoubtedly refers only to advanced talmudic education, to the Oral Law. However, there is no prohibition about teaching the Written Law (cf. *Rambam, Hilkhot Talmud Torah*, Chaps. 1, 13). According to the Hafetz Hayyim, the stringency only applied in previous generations. However, in these days, it is a great *mitzvah* to teach women *Tanakh* and other studies such as *Avot*, and so forth (cf. R. Yitzhak Yosef, *Sefer Otzar Dinim le-Ishah Ulebat* 32 [Jerusalem, 1989] footnote 3).

Women were always instructed in the elements of Judaism and, in Hezekiah's reign, women were fully educated. The Talmud (San. 94b) states: "Search was made from Dan unto Beer Sheba, and no ignoramus was found, from Gabbath unto Antipris, and no boy or girl, man or woman was found who was not thoroughly versed in the laws of cleanliness and uncleanliness." (See Tos. to Sot. 21a, s.v. *Ben Azai* and *Torah Temimah, Aykev* 11:48. See also the *Pentateuch and Haftorahs*, Dr. J.H. Hertz, ed. [London: Soncino Press, 1973], pp. 925–926.)

KOL HAMESHALAYM AYNO LO-KAH (כל המשלם אינו לוקה). "Who pays is not flogged" (*Mishnah*, Mak. 4a); that is, wherever the law orders compensation paid for an unlawful act, and the payment is made, punishment by whipping may not be inflicted.

KOL HAMITZTA'AYR ATZMO IM HATZIBBUR, ZOKHEH VERO'EH BENAHAMOT TZIBBUR (כל המצטער עצמו עם הציבור, זוכה ורואה בנחמות ציבור). "He who shares the distress of the community will merit to see its consolation" (Ta'an. 11a).

KOL HANEGA'IM ADAM RO'EH HUTZ MINIGAY ATZMO (כל הנגעים אדם רואה חוץ מנגעי עצמו). Literally, "A man may examine all leprosy signs except his own" (Neg. 2:5). Colloquially, a different meaning has been given

for this *mishnaic* statement: "A person sees the deficiencies of others, not his own." See KOL HAPOSAYL PASUL—BEMUMO POSAYL.

KOL HA'OMAYR DAVAR BESHAYM OMRO MAYVI GE'ULAH LA'OLAM (כל האומר דבר בשם אומרו מביא גאולה לעולם). "[R. Eleazar said, in the name of R. Hanina:] Whoever repeats a saying in the name of its originator brings deliverance to the world (Meg. 15a), as it says, 'And Esther told the king, in the name of Mordecai'" (Esth. 2:22). The miracle of Purim is due to the mention of Mordecai's name (Esth. 6:2). (See also *Avot* 6:6.)

KOL HA'OMAYR DEVAR HOKH-MAH AFILU BE'UMOT HA'OLAM NIKRA HAKHAM (כל האומר דבר חכמה אפילו באומות העולם נקרא חכם). "[R. Johanan said:] Whoever says a wise thing, even if he is non-Jew, is called wise" (Meg. 17a).

KOL HAPOSAYL PASUL—BEMU-MO POSAYL (כל הפוסל פסול—במומו פוסל). "He who [continually] declares [others] unfit is [himself] unfit—With his own blemish he stigmatizes [others] as unfit" (Kidd. 70a). A similar Yiddish expression is: *Bay yenem zet men a pintele, bay zikh zet men nit kayn balkn* ("By others one sees a dot, on himself he does not see a beam"). Or, *Vuhs eyner huht in zikh varft er fun zikh* ("What one has in himself, he discards"), intimating that he taints others. See KOL HANEGA'IM ADAM RO'EH HUTZ MINIGAY ATZMO.

KOL HARODAYF AHAR HAKA-VOD, HAKAVOD BORAYAH MI-MENU (כל הרודף אחר הכבוד, הכבוד בורח ממנו). A folk saying meaning "Whoever chases after honor, honor will flee from him." The *Mishnah* (*Avot* 4:28) states that seeking glory (*kavod*) is one of three things that "remove a man from the world."

The expression has its origin in the saying KOL HAMEHAZAYR AL HAGEDULAH, GEDULAH BORAHAT MIMENU, VEKHOL HABO-RAYAH MIN HAGEDULAH, GEDULAH MEHAZERET AHARAV ("From him who seeks greatness, greatness flees, but him who flees from greatness, greatness follows") (Erub. 13b). Similar expressions are: *Kol mi sherodayf ahar serarah, serarah borahat mimenu* ("He who runs after rulership [office], rulership flees from him") (*Tanhumah, Vayikra* 3); *Barahti min hakavod veradfuni hakavod* ("Honor follows him who flees it") (*Sefer Hasidim, Mekitzay Nirdamim* 9:11).

KOL MAH DE'AVID RAHAMANA, LETAV AVID (כל מה דעביד רחמנה, לטב עביד). "[R. Huna said, in the name of Rab, citing R. Meir, and so it was taught, in the name of R. Akiba], A man should always accustom himself to say, 'Whatever the All-Merciful does is for good'" (Ber. 60b). This is borne out by the following incident. R. Akiba was on the road and was looking for lodging but was refused everywhere. He said, "Whatever the All-Merciful does is for the good," and he spent the night in an open field. With him he had a cock, an ass, and a lamp. A wind came and blew out the lamp, a weasel ate the cock, and a lion ate the ass. He said, "Whatever the All-Merciful does is for the good." That night some brigands came and carried off the inhabitants of the town. Later, he said (either to the inhabitants of the town or to his disciples who were with him), "Did I not say to you, 'Whatever the All-Merciful does is for the good?'" See GAM ZU LETOVAH.

KOL MAH SHEYOMAR LEKHA BA'AL HABAYIT ASAYH (HUTZ MITZAY) (כל מה שיאמר לך בעה"ב (חוץ מצא)). "Whatever your host tells you, do (except depart)" (Pes. 86b). The Talmud places the words *hutz mitzay* in parenthesis. Rabbi Dr. H. Freedman comments, "The text reads better without this addition, but if it is retained it was probably meant humorously—a guest should not outstay his welcome lest he is told to go!" (cf. *Pesahim*, vol. 2 [London:

The Soncino Press, 1938], p. 456). The *Orah Hayyim* (170:5) deletes the phrase *hutz mitzay*. The *Magayn Avraham* (ibid., 10) copied this phrase and gives two different interpretations as to its meaning. According to the *Bach*, it means that if the host asks him to go into the marketplace to engage in some business or trade, he is not obligated to do so, since it is not fitting for him to go to marketplaces where he is not known. According to the *Matteh Moshe*, the explanation is that if the host asks him to leave his hotel, he must not go, unless he has packed his utensils. The same applies to improvised quarters. Another explanation is that a phrase in Isaiah 30:22 reads, *Tzay tomar lo* ("Get thee hence"). The *Radak* interprets the phrase to mean that you should tell the idol to leave; the word *tzay* is similar to *tzo'ah* ("filth," "excrement")—remove it! Thus, if your host says *hutz mitzay* and he does not want you to heed the *tzay tomar lo* in Isaiah (so that you indulge in idolatry and ugliness), do not listen to him.

KOL MAKOM SHENE'EMAR "VAYEHI" AYNO ELA LASHON TZA'AR (כל מקום שנאמר "ויהי" אינו אלא לשון צער). The Talmud (Meg. 10b) states, "[R. Levi, or some say R. Jonathan, said: The following remark is a tradition handed down to us from the Men of the Great Assembly]: Wherever in Scripture we find the term *veyehi* ('and it was' or 'and it came to pass'), it indicates that woe and sorrow will follow" (*vayehi* is read as *vai, hi*; "woe and sorrow"). The Talmud follows with several verses as examples. In several instances, however, the Talmud asks, Is joy expressed when using the word *vayehi*, as in "And it came to pass on the eighth day" (Lev. 9:1; the setting up of the Tabernacle), or "And there was [*vayehi*] one day" (Gen. 1:5)? R. Ashi replied that sometimes it does represent grief and sorrow and sometimes it does not, but the expression "and it came to pass in the days of" always indicates trouble. He lists five such instances, such

as *vayehi bimay* Ahasuerus ("And it came to pass in the days of Ahasuerus").

KOL MITZVAH SHEHAZEMAN GERAMA (כל מצוה שהזמן גרמא). See MITZVAT ASAYH SHEHAZEMAN GERAMA NASHIM PETUROT.

KOL OF LEMINO YISHKON, UVEN ADAM LEDOMEH LO (כל עוף למינו ישכון. ובן אדם לדומה לו). "Every fowl dwells near its kind, and man near his equal" (cf. B.K. 92b). The English equivalent is "like is attracted to like." See MATZA MIN ET MINO.

KOL YETER KENITUL DAMI (כל יתר כנטול דמי). "Every addition is deemed equal to the loss" (Hul. 58b). This principle is given in the case of an animal in whose body a limb is found to be wanting or too many.

The talmudic rule has given rise to the Yiddish expression *Vuhs tzu, iz iberik* ("Whatever is excessive is unnecessary").

KOL YISRAEL ARAYVIM ZEH BA-ZEH (כל ישראל ערבין זה בזה). Scripture states, "And they shall stumble one upon another" (Lev. 26:37). The Talmud (Shebu. 39a) comments, One because of the iniquity of the other; this teaches us that "*Kol Yisrael* [all Israel] are sureties one for another."

Rabbi Isaac Luria asked, "Why was the confession [prayer], *Al Hayt*, arranged in the plural, so that we say, 'We are guilt-laden,' instead of 'I am guilt-laden'? Because all Israel is one body, and every individual Israelite a member of that body"; all Israelites are responsible for one another.

KOL ZEMAN SHE'ADAM HAI YAYSH LO TIKVAH (כל זמן שאדם חי יש לו תקוה). "So long as the person is alive, there is hope" (Jer. Tal., Ber. 40:1).

KOTZO (KOTZAH) SHEL YUD (קוצו (קוצה) של יוד). "The hook of the

letter *yud*." It is written in the Talmud (Men. 29a), "The law has to be taught in respect of the tittle of the letter *yud* [*kotzah shel yud*]; that is, if even the lower [according to *Tos.*, the upper] stroke of the letter *yud* was missing, it is invalid" (as in a *Mezuzah*).

The phrase took on the meaning "a mere nothing," "trifle," or "iota." Therefore, when doing something precisely or exactly, the expression *kotzo shel yud* is used, implying that not one iota is missing.

Because of the minuteness of the letter *yud*, which resembles a dot, and because the letter *yud* is similar in sound to Yid (Jew), the expression PINTELE YID came into being. Although the Jew has sometimes strayed from his religion, he still maintains that spark and thus the term *Pintele Yid* is often applied.

KUDESHA BERIKH HU (קודשא בריך הוא) קב"ה (abbr. קב"ה). "The Holiness, blessed be He," referring to God (Ber. 7a). The Talmud (ibid.) asks if anger is a mood of the Holiness, and answers: Yes, for it has been taught: "A God that hath indignation every day" (Ps. 7:12). The Talmud then asks, How long does this indignation last? and concludes, one fifty-eight thousand, eight hundred and eighty-eighth part of an hour (cf. also Ket. 77b). See KUDESHA BERIKH HU, ORAITA VEYISRAEL HAD.

KULAY ALMA LO PELIGI (כולי עלמא לא פליגי). "Agreement in accordance to all authorities" (Ber. 36b). A similar expression is *aliba dekulay alma* ("With everyone's [unanimous] consent").

The word *alma* may also mean "in a general way" or "merely"—thus, *diburim be'alma* ("mere words" or "vain talk"). It may also mean "eternity," such as in the expression *Bayt almin* ("cemetery"), the house of eternity, a euphemism for the house of death or "burial grounds." See ALMA DEKUSHTA (DESHIKRA); ASMAKHTA BE'ALMA; INSHAY DE'ALMA; MILAY DE'ALMA.

KUPAT HAROKHLIM; KUPAH SHEL BESAMIM (קפת הרוכלים, קפה של בשמים). A description of scholars. The Talmud (Git. 67a) describes several types of scholars, among them R. Johanan b. Nuri as a "basket of fancy goods" (*kupat harokhlim*) and R. Eleazar b. Azariah as a "basket of spices" (*kupah shel besamim*). R. Johanan b. Nuria's scholarship has been thus depicted because, while his knowledge was well-arranged, it was not unified and correlated, as was that of R. Akiba, whose learning was classified under various headings—Scripture, *halakhah*, *aggadah*, and so forth. R. Eleazar b. Azariah's learning has been depicted as being of lesser quantity than R. Johanan's—only a basket of spices, which is a smaller amount than a basket of fancy goods.

LAMAI NAFKA MINAH? (למאי לפקא מינה?). Literally, "What is the practical bearing of this?" Or, "In regard to what practice, is there a difference?" (B.M. 103b). The Talmud employs the phrase in the following manner: "R. Joseph said: In Babylon it is the practice not to give [a share of the] straw to the *aris* [a tenant farmer who pays a fixed percentage of the crops in rent]." The Talmud asks, "*Lamai nafka minah?*" And answers, "That if there is a person who does give it, it is his generosity, and he creates no precedent." The Aramaic phrase is used in both the Hebrew and the Yiddish languages. See NAFKA MINAH.

LAMAYD LESHONKHA LOMAR AYNI YODAYA, SHEMA TITBA-DAYH (למד לשונך לומר איני יודע, שמא תתבדה). Both Moses and David knew exactly when it was midnight. The Talmud (Ber. 4a) asks: Why did David need the harp? And answers: That he might wake from his sleep. Moses also knew when it was midnight; why did he say "about midnight"? Because he thought that the astrologers of Pharaoh might make a mistake, and then they would say

that Moses was a liar. For this reason, a master said: "Let thy tongue acquire the habit of saying, 'I know not,' lest thou be led to falsehoods [lying]."

LAMED-VAV TZADIKIM (ל"ו צדיקים)

(צדיקים). A name applied to the thirty-six righteous men on whose merit the world exists. They are extremely modest and upright and earn their livelihood by the sweat of their brow. Their origin dates back to talmudic times, when it was handed down in the name of the *amora* Abaye: "The world must contain not less than thirty-six righteous men in each generation who are vouchsafed [the sight of] the Divine Presence, for it is written, 'Happy are all they that wait for Him' [*ashray kol hokhay Lo*]" (San. 97b; Sukk. 45b). The numerical value of the word *Lo* is thirty-six (*lamed* = 30 + *vav* = 6). It is said in folklore that a person who conceals his righteousness is a *lamedvavnik*.

LASHON TELITAI KATIL TELITAI (לשון תליתאי קטיל תליתאי)

(לשון תליתאי קטיל תליתאי). "The talk about third [persons] kills three persons": he who speaks [the slander], he who accepts it, and he of whom it is spoken (Ar. 15b). See AVAK LESHON HARA; LO TAYLAYKH RAKHIL BE'AMEKHA.

LAV BA'AL DEVARIM DIDI AT (לאו בעל דברים דידי את)

(בעל דברים דידי את). "You are not the party I have to deal with" (Ket. 94a). It is written in the Talmud that R. Huna stated: "If two brothers or two partners had a lawsuit against a third party and one of them went with that person to law [and lost his case], the other [brother or partner] cannot say to him [the third party] *lav ba'al devarim didi at* ("You are not my party") and thus demand a new trial on his share because [the one who went to law] acted on his behalf also."

Colloquially, the expression may be used whenever a person voices an opinion without being asked.

LAV DAVKA (לאו דוקא)

(לאו דוקא). Literally, "not exactly," "not quite," "not necessarily," or "loosely." The Talmud (Git. 44a) states: "R. Joshua b. Levi said: If a man sells his slave to a heathen, he can be penalized [by having to ransom him for] as much as a hundred times his value. Is this expression 'a hundred' here used exactly [*davka*] or loosely [*lav davka*]?"

LAYT DIN BAR INISH (NASH) (לית דין בר אינש (נש))

(דין בר אינש (נש)). Concerning R. Johanan, Hezekiah remarked, "This [scholar] is no [ordinary] man." His genius is supernatural. Others say, "Such [a scholar] is [the true type of] man" (Erub. 24a; A.Z. 10b; Shab. 112b).

LEHAYYIM (לחיים)

(לחיים). A toast, meaning "to life," uttered when drinking an alcoholic beverage during a festive meal or occasion. The custom of saying *Lehayyim* is rooted in the Talmud (Shab. 67b): *Hama vehayay lefum rabbanan* ("Wine and health to the mouth of our teachers"). The talmudic account for uttering *Lehayyim* when drinking is: "When one is led out to execution, he is given a goblet of wine containing a grain of frankincense, in order to benumb his senses" (San. 43a). When drinking alcoholic beverages nowadays, the term is used for "life" and not for "death," and all present answer *Lehayyim*! (*Iyyun Tefillah* in *Siddur Otzar Hatefillot*, vol. 1, s.v. *Kiddush Layl Shabbat*). This custom is currently practiced among *Sephardim* at *Kiddush*. Another explanation for this expression is found in the *Midrash* (*Tanhuma, Pekuday*). The question was asked: "Gentlemen, what is your opinion?" That is, is it safe to drink this wine? The answer was *Lehayyim*, which later became a drinking toast.

The response made by those present is LEHAYYIM TOVIM ULESHALOM ("For good life and for peace"). The reason for this (response) blessing is that the first time that drinking wine was mentioned in Scripture, shame and evil befell Noah, who was

considered righteous and blameless before God. The Torah relates, "And he
drank of the wine, and was drunken; and
he was uncovered within the tent" (Gen.
9:21). *Rashi* comments that, "Noah made
himself profane"; he degraded himself.
Therefore, this blessing signifies that the
wine should be for a good life. It is
reputed that the Maggid of Mezritch
would respond with *Lehayyim velivrakhah*
("For life and blessing") (*Hayom Yom—
"From Day to Day,"* compiled and arranged by R. Menachem Mendel
Schneerson, [Brooklyn, New York: Otzar
Hachassidim Lubavitch, 1988]).

LEHAYYIM TOVIM ULESHALOM
(לחיים טובים ולשלום). See LEHAYYIM.

**LEMI ATEM KORIN REBI,REBI?—
AL YIRBU KEMOTO BEYISRAEL**
(למי אתם קורין רבי,רבי?—אל ירבו
כמותו בישראל). See LE'OLAM YEHAY ADAM
RAKH KAKANEH VE'AL YEHI KASHEH KE'EREZ.

**LE'OLAM AL YAVI ADAM ATZMO
LIDAY NISAYON** (לעולם אל יביא
אדם עצמו לידי נסיון). Rab Judah said, in
Rab's name: "One should never intentionally bring himself to the test" (San. 107a).
It may not be possible to carry it out and
he will stumble (fail).

**LE'OLAM HALAKHAH KEDIVRAY
BET HILLEL** (לעולם הלכה כדברי בית
הלל). "As a general principle, the *halakhah* follows Bet Hillel" (R.H. 14b). Bet
Hillel and Bet Shammai were two schools
of *tannaim* during the first century C.E.,
which differed in their decisions on more
than three hundred legal interpretations.
The doctrines of the School of Hillel
gained the ascendancy (first and second
century), whereupon the *halakhah* was
laid down according to Bet Hillel. A BAT
KOL went forth at Yavneh, telling of a
proclamation to this effect (cf. Jer. Tal.,
Ber. 1:7, 3b). See LE'OLAM YEHAY ADAM
INVETAN KEHILLEL, VE'AL YEHAY KAPDAN KE-
SHAMMAI.

**LE'OLAM TEHAY DATO SHEL
ADAM ME'UREVET IM HABERI-
YOT** (לעולם תהא דעתו של אדם
מעורבת עם הבריות). See ME'OREV
(ME'URAV) BEDA'AT IM HABERIYOT.

**LE'OLAM YA'ASOK BETORAH
UVEMITZVOT AF AL PI SHELO
LISHMAH** (לעולם יעסוק בתורה
ובמצות אעפ"י שלא לשמה). See TORAH
LISHMAH and MITOKH SHELO LISHMAH BA
LISHMAH.

**LE'OLAM YEHAY ADAM INVETAN
KEHILLEL, VE'AL YEHAY KAP-
DAN KESHAMMAI** (לעולם יהא אדם
ענוותן כהלל. ואל יהא קפדן כשמאי). "A
man should always be gentle like Hillel,
and not impatient like Shammai" (Shab.
30b). The Talmud (Shab. 30b, 31a) relates
various incidents in which Hillel is proven
to be patient under provocation, whereas
Shammai is pedantic and has scolded and
repulsed in anger the person asking questions. See AL REGEL AHAT; LE'OLAM HALA-
KHAH KEDIVRAY BET HILLEL.

**LE'OLAM YEHAY ADAM RAKH
KAKANEH VE'AL YEHI KASHEH
KE'EREZ** (לעולם יהא אדם רך כקנה
ואל יהי קשה כארז). "A man should
always be gentle as the reed and never
unyielding as the cedar" (Taan. 20b). R.
Eleazar, son of R. Simeon, was once
greeted by an exceedingly ugly man and
did not return his salutation, but said to
him, "*Raykah* ('empty one' or 'good for
nothing'). Are all your fellow citizens as
ugly as you are?" The man replied, "I do
not know, but go and tell the Craftsman
who made me." R. Eleazar tried to ask for
forgiveness, but to no avail. R. Eleazar
walked behind him until he reached his
native city, where all came out to greet
him with the words, "Peace be upon you,
O Teacher, O Master." The man ex-
claimed, "Whom are you addressing as
teacher? If this is a teacher, may there not
be any more like him in Israel" (LEMI ATEM

KORIN REBI, REBI?—AL YIRBU KEMOTO BE-
YISRAEL). After the people begged that he
be forgiven, the man said, "For your sakes
I will forgive him, but only on condition
that he does not act in this manner in the
future." R. Eleazar entered the *Bet Midrash*
and expounded thus, "A man should
always be gentle as the reed and let him
never be unyielding as the cedar." And for
this reason, the reed merited that it should
be made into a pen for writing the Law,
the Phylacteries, and the *Mezuzot*.

LE'OLAM YEHAY ADAM ZAHIR
BIKHVOD ISHTO (לעולם יהא אדם
זהיר בכבוד אשתו). R. Helbo said: "One
must always observe the honor due his
wife." Raba said to the townspeople of
Mahuza, "Honor your wives, that ye may
be enriched," because blessings rest on a
man's home only on account of his wife
(B.M. 59a). See AYN BERAKHAH METZUYAH
BETOKH BAYTO SHEL ADAM ELA BISHVIL ISHTO.

LE'OLAM YESHANEH ADAM LE-
TALMIDO DEREKH KETZARAH
(לעולם ישנה אדם לתלמידו דרך קצרה).
R. Huna said, in Rab's name, and others
say, R. Huna said, in Rab's name, on R.
Meir's authority: "One should always
teach his pupil in concise terms" (Pes.
3b)—that is, in the shortest way.

LESHON BENAY ADAM (לשון בני
אדם). See DIBRAH TORAH KELASHON BENAY
ADAM. See also LESHON HAKHAMIM.

LESHON HAKHAMIM (לשון חכמים).
A phrase meaning "the language of the
Sages" (Ket. 103a). The Talmud (Hul.
137b) states, "The Torah uses its own
language and the Sages their own." That is
to say, *Leshon Hakhamim* is distinct from
that used in the Bible. See DIBRAH TORAH
KELASHON BENAY ADAM.

LETEKUNAY SHADARTIKH VELO
LE'IVUTI (לתקוני שדרתיך ולא לעוותי).
"I deputed you to improve my position,
not to make it worse" (Ket. 85a; Kidd.

42b; B.M. 108a). The expression denotes
that the messenger or agent is responsible
for his mission.

LIFNIM MISHURAT HADIN (לפנים
משורת הדין). Literally, "stop short of the
limit of strict justice" (Ber. 7a). In other
words, "beyond the line of strict justice";
"mercifully." R. Zutra b. Tobi said, in the
name of Rab, that God prays, "May it be
My will that My mercy may suppress My
anger, and that My mercy may prevail
over My [other] attributes, so that I may
deal with My children in the attribute of
mercy and, on their behalf, stop short of
the limit of strict justice" (cf. also *Rashi*,
Deut. 6:18).

Lifnim mishurat hadin is often said by
one when dealing leniently, or not according to the strict letter of the law, with
another person. The opposite would be
SHURAT HADIN ("in strict justice") (Git.
40b). See KESHURAH.

LIKA MIDAY DELA REMIZI BE'-
ORAITA (ליכא מידי דלא רמיזי
באורייתא). "There is nothing to which
allusion cannot be found in the Torah."
This saying is based on "Is there anything
written in the Hagiographa to which allusion cannot be found in the Torah?"
(Ta'an. 9a).

LIKHORAH (לכאורה). "At first sight";
the two Hebrew letters *lamed* and *kaf* are
prefixed to the noun *orah*, meaning
"light." This word is generally translated
as "apparently" or "evidently." The word
signifies that according to the first ap-
proach, it seems that it is so, as in *Likhorah
ke-Shmuel rahita* ("At first sight, it might
appear to run parallel to the principle of
Samuel") (Ket. 54a).

LIMUD MAYVI LIDAY MA'ASEH
(לימוד מביא לידי מעשה). "Study leads to
action" (Kidd. 40b). This is the final
decision to a question raised between R.
Tarfon and the Elders and R. Akiba. The
question was, Is study greater, or practice?

R. Tarfon said that practice was greater and R. Akiba said study is greater. At the conclusion, they all answered, "Study is greater, for it leads to action."

LO AMAR KLUM (לא אמר כלום). "He said nothing" or "what he said is disregarded." The *Mishnah* (B.B. 8:5) states that if anyone said before his death that his firstborn son should not receive a double portion, or that one of his sons should not be heirs with his brothers, "his instructions are disregarded." The reason is that one has no right to give instructions that are contrary to the law of the Torah.

The Talmud (Git. 85b) uses the expression LO AMAR VELO KLUM ("his words are of no effect"). This is the case when a man says to his wife, Behold, you are hereby a free woman.

LO AMAR VELO KLUM (לא אמר ולא כלום). See LO AMAR KLUM.

LO HAKHAM VELO TIPAYSH (לא חכם ולא טיפש). "Neither over-clever nor stupid" (Ber. 31b). Scripture states, "But wilt thou give unto thy handmaid a man-child" (1 Sam. 1:11). The Talmud (ibid.) asks, What is meant by "a man-child"? R. Dimi explained this to mean: Neither too tall nor too short, neither too thin nor too corpulent, neither too pale nor too red, neither over-clever nor stupid.

LO HAVAH PSIK PUMYAH MIGIR-SAYH (לא הוה פסיק פומיה מגירסיה). On the day that David was to die, the Angel of Death stood before him but could not prevail against him because "learning did not cease from his mouth" (Shab. 30b).

LO KOL HA'ADAM, VELO KOL HA-MAKOM, VELO KOL HASHA'OT SHAVIN (לא כל האדם, ולא כל המקום, ולא כל השעות שוין). R. Judah b. Bava said: "Neither all men, nor all places, nor all seasons are alike" (Yeb. 120a). The *Mishnah* (ibid.) discusses the evidence of

identity with respect to a dead man. Evidence of identification may be tendered by those who saw the corpse within three days after death. After this period, the decay of the corpse would hinder identification. R. Judah b. Bava differs and says that the three days must be varied according to physical and climatic conditions. That is, there is a person who changes immediately after death, as, for example, a fat man. There is a place where the deceased changes more quickly, as, for example, in a warm place. There is a season in which the deceased changes more quickly, as, for example, in the afternoon of a summer day. Thus, it is impossible to fix, from the beginning, one trait that will fit all persons, or one place, or one time. One must relate to each incident on its own.

LO MATZA YADAV VERAGLAV (לא מצא ידיו ורגליו). "He would not have found his hands and feet" (Yeb. 77b); that is, he would not have had a leg to stand on. This refers to R. Judah, whose position would have been untenable without his declaration that females (of Ammon and Moab) were also forbidden to enter the assembly of the Lord (Deut. 23:4ff).

Colloquially, the expression took on the meaning "one who is perturbed or confused." The Yiddish expression *Er veys nit fun zayn hent un fis* ("He doesn't know from his hands or feet").

LO MATZINU SHU'AL SHEMAYT BA'AFAR PIR (לא מצינו שועל שמת בעפר פיר). "It does not occur that a fox dies in the dust of its own rubble" (Ned. 81b). That is, a person does not stumble on a thing that is recognizable to him.

LO YEHAY DIBUREKHA SHEL SHABBAT KEDIBUREKHA SHEL HOL (לא יהא דבורך של שבת כדבורך של חול). "Thy speech [conversation] on the Sabbath should not be like thy speech on weekdays" (Shab. 113b). For example, conversation about business is forbidden (cf. *Rashi*, ad loc.).

LO YEHAY MALBUSHKHA SHEL SHABBAT KEMALBUSHKHA SHEL HOL (לא יהא מלבושך של שבת כמלבושך של חול).

"Thy Sabbath garments should not be like thy weekday garments" (Shab. 113a). R. Johanan called his garments, "My honorers." *Rashi* (ad loc.) comments that "the garments dignify the person."

LO YEHAY TAFAL HAMUR MIN HA'IKAR (לא יהא טפל חמור מן העיקר).

"The accessory cannot be more important than the principal" (Men. 8b). The Talmud gives the case, "If a peace-offering was slaughtered in the Temple, it is valid, for it is written, 'And he shall slaughter it at the door of the tent of meeting' (Lev. 3:2), and surely the accessory [the door of the tent] cannot be more important than the principal" (the Temple).

Colloquially, the expression is used regarding any situation in which an adjunct or accompaniment should not become greater than the highest or chief principal.

LO YISHTEH ADAM MIN HAKOS VEYITNENU LEHAVAYRO (לא ישתה אדם מן הכוס ויתננו לחבירו).

"A man should not drink from a cup and give it to his disciple" (Tam. 27b), without pouring some out so as to cleanse the rim. This rule was instituted, says the Talmud, because it happened once that a man drank some water and, without pouring it out, gave the cup to his disciple. The disciple was squeamish and did not like to drink, and he died of thirst.

LO YIZROK BERAKHAH MIPIV (לא יזרוק ברכה מפיו).

"One should not hurl the blessing, as it were, out of his mouth" (Ber. 47a); that is, he shall not utter it inarticulately, with rapid sounds in the manner of fowl.

LO'AYG LARASH (לעג לרש).

"Ridiculing the poor," as in the verse *Lo'ayg larash hayrayf osayhu* ("One who mocks the poor, insults his Maker") (Prov. 17:5). Rabbi David b. Samuel ha-Levi ruled, in the name of the *Rokeach*, that a mourner during *shiva* surely does not recite *Hallel*, since it would be as though ridiculing the poor (*ke-lo'ayg larash*) when uttering the phrase *Lo hamaytim yehallelu Yah* ("The dead cannot praise the Lord") (verse 17 in *Hashem Zekharanu*, cf. *Orah Hayyim, Taz* 422).

The Talmud (Men. 41a) gives another instance of *lo'ayg larash*. R. Tobi b. Kisma said, in the name of Samuel, that garments put away in a chest are subject to *tzitzit*. Samuel admits that if an old man made it for his shroud, it is exempt. Nevertheless, when the time comes for its use as a shroud, *tzitzit* should be attached on account of the injunction, "One who mocks the poor, insults his Maker." There is none so poor as the dead, and the *tzitzit* are inserted in the shroud so that no indignity be shown to the dead.

LO DUBIM VELO YA'AR (לא דבים ולא יער).

Literally, "[there were] no bears nor [was there] a forest"; used in conversation to imply a complete fabrication (Sot. 47a says *Lo ya'ar velo dubim havu*).

After Eliyahu went up into Heaven in a storm of wind (2 Kings 2:11), Elisha was jeered by some small boys. They said to him, "Go up, bald head; go up, bald head." And he turned back, and looked at them, and cursed them in the Name of the Lord. And two she-bears (*dubim*) came out of the wood (*haya'ar*) and tore forty-two of the children" (ibid., 24–25). "Rab and Samuel [differ in their interpretation]; one said it was a miracle, while the other said it was a miracle within a miracle." He who said it was a miracle did so because there was a forest but there were no bears (*ya'ar havah dubim lo havu*); he who said it was a miracle within a miracle did so because there was no forest nor were there any bears (*lo ya'ar havah velo dubim havu*). See LO HAYAH VELO NIVRA; DAVAR SHELO BA LE'OLAM.

LO HAYAH VELO NIVRA (לא היה ולא נברא). An expression literally meaning "never was and never existed." The phrase appears in the Talmud (B.B. 15a) in conjunction with Job's time and place in history. Among the various views is that Job never existed (*lo hayah velo nivrah*), and that the story is merely an allegory (*ela mashal hi*).

A similar expression in the Talmud (Erub. 40a) used in daily conversation is LO HAYU DEVARIM MAYOLAM ("that, in fact, it never happened" and is absolutely untrue). See DAVAR SHELO BA LE'OLAM and LO DUBIM VELO YA'AR.

LO HAYU DEVARIM MAYOLAM (לא היו דברים מעולם). See LO HAYAH VELO NIVRA.

LO MA'ALIN VELO MORIDIN (לא מעלין ולא מורידין). Literally, "neither ascends nor descends"; or "it neither enhances nor subtracts"; that is, "to add nothing or subtract nothing."

The Talmud (Git. 52a) cites R. Meir as saying, "Dreams are of no effect either one way or the other" (cf. also A.Z. 13b). See AYNO MA'ALEH VE'AYNO MORID in *Hullin* 45b.

LO RA'INU AYNAH RA'AYAH (לא ראינו אינה ראיה). The Sages say, "'We saw not' is no proof" (Eduy. 2:2). This statement refers to R. Hanina, chief of the Priests, who said: "All my days I never saw a hide taken out to the place of burning." Perhaps this may not have occurred in R. Hanina's time, or it may have occurred and he failed to notice it.

Therefore, this idiom is used when one claims, "I never saw it," "I never heard of it." A similar expression is AYN LO RA'INU RA'AYAH ("'I have never seen' is not proof") (Zeb. 103b).

LO RE'I ZEH KIRE'I ZEH (לא ראי זה כראי זה). "The character of one is not that of the other, and vice versa" (Ber. 35a; Shab. 28a, etc.). That is, there is no comparison between the two; the two things are not analogous. Usually, after this reasoning, the Talmud continues *Hatzad hashaveh shebahen* . . . ("the feature common to both is . . .").

MA'AMINIM BENAY MA'AMINIM (מאמינים בני מאמינים). See HAHOSHAYD BIKSHAYRIM LOKAH BEGUFO.

MA'ASAY AVOT SIMAN LEBANIM (מעשה (מעשי) אבות סימן לבנים). "The deeds and occurrences of the fathers are symbolic of what will take place with their descendents." While the Israelites were still in Jordan, Joshua said to them, "Take up every man of you a stone upon his shoulder, according to the number of the tribes of the children of Israel" (Josh. 4:5): that this may be a sign among you, that when your children ask their fathers in time to come, saying, What mean ye by these stones?" (ibid., 6). The Talmud (Sot. 34a) comments, "It was to be a sign for the children [*siman lebanim*] that their fathers had crossed the Jordan [*she'avru avot et hayardayn*]."

MA'ASAY YADAI TOVIM BAYAM, VE'ATEM OMRIM SHIRAH? (מעשי ידי טובעים בים, ואתם אומרים שירה?). "The work of My hands [My creatures] is being drowned in the sea, and shall you chant hymns?" This is the remark made to the ministering angels by the Holy One, blessed be He, when the Egyptians drowned in the Red Sea (cf. Meg. 10b; San. 39b).

MA'ASEH SHEHAYAH KAKH HAYAH (מעשה שהיה כך היה). "The case just happened to be of such a nature" (Erub. 65b). This expression may be used generally when describing any occurrence.

In Yiddish, one also uses the expression KAKH HAVAH ("and so it was," or "and sure enough").

MA'ASEKHA YEKARVUKHA UMA'-ASEKHA YERAHAKUKHA (מעשיך יקרבוך ומעשיך ירחקוך). Akabia said to his son Jose, "Your own deeds will cause you to be near and your own deeds will cause you to be far" (Eduy. 5:7); that is, your own conduct will win you friends or alienate them.

Similar expressions in Yiddish are: *Tust guts—tustu far zikh, tust shlekhts—tustu oykh far zikh* ("If you do good things, you do them for yourself; if you do bad things, you also do them for yourself"); *Guts getuhn zikh getuhn, shlekhts getuhn—zikh getuhn* ("Doing something good, you do it for yourself; doing something bad—you do it for youself").

MA'AVIR AL MIDOTAV (מעביר על מדותיו). "One who keeps silent concerning the injustices done to him" (Ta'an. 25b), a trait praised in the Talmud. The Talmud cites that R. Eliezer and R. Akiba were praying for rain and R. Akiba's prayer was answered "because he is ever forbearing and the other is not."

Similarly, the Talmud (Yom. 23a) praises "those who are insulted but do not insult others [in revenge] and who hear themselves reproached, without replying."

MADRAYGAH ELYONAH (TAHTONAH) (מדרגה עליונה (תחתונה)). A phrase meaning "highest degree" (or "lowest degree"). The *Tanna Devei Eliyahu* (9) has the expression *Yardu Yisrael mimadraygah elyonah lemadraygah tahtonah* ("The Israelites descended from the highest degree to the lowest"). The Talmud (San. 39b) states that R. Hanina b. Papa said: "In that hour the wicked of Israel descended to the lowest depths" (*Yardu rishayhen shel Yisrael lemadraygah hatahtonah*).

MAH LI HAKHA, MAH LI HATAM (מה לי הכא, מה לי התם). "What difference does one place or another make" (B.M. 36b); or, "it makes no difference to me."

MAH (MIMAH) NAFSHAKH (מה (ממה) נפשך). An expression literally meaning "what" or "which," thus inferring "whatever be your opinion" or "whichever side you take at all events." The Talmud (Shab. 35b) rules, *hayav hatat mima nafshakh* ("must bring a sin offering at all events," whether you consider twilight a part of the day or a part of the night).

The expression *mima nafshakh* is also used in the Yiddish language and has similarly come to mean "either/or," "one or the other," or "make up your mind."

MAH TIVO SHEL UBAR ZEH (מה טיבו של עובר זה). The Talmud (Ket. 12b) discusses the case of an unmarried woman who was pregnant and was asked, *Mah tivo shel ubar zeh* ("What is the nature of this embryo?")—that is, who is the father of this child? And she answers, "It is from the man so-and-so, and he is a priest." Rabban Gamliel and R. Eliezer say that she is to be believed.

Mah tivo shel ubar zeh is used in a jocular vein; when there is doubt about a person's lineage, his credibility, or his outlook on life, the expression took on the meaning, "Who is this person? Is there any substance to him?"

MAH YA'ASEH ADAM VEYAHKAYM? YARBEH BIYESHIVAH VEYAMIT BISHORAH—YEVAKAYSH RAHAMIM (מה יעשה אדם ויחכם? ירבה בישיבה וימעיט בסחורה—יבקש רחמים). The Alexandrians asked R. Joshua b. Hananiah twelve questions. One of the twelve questions concerned matters of conduct in worldly affairs. They asked, "What must a man do that he may become wise?" (He replied), "Let him engage much in study [in the *Yeshivah*] and little

in business—and seek mercy" (Nid. 70b) from Him to Whom is the wisdom, for it is said, "For the Lord giveth wisdom, out of His mouth cometh knowledge and discernment" (Prov. 2:6).

MAH YOM MIYOMAYIM (מה יום מיומים). "Wherein does this day differ from any other?" (San. 65b). This question was asked by Tineius Rufus, a Roman Governor of Judea, of R. Akiba, regarding the Sabbath day. R. Akiba replied: "Wherein does one man differ from another? [That is, why is one a noble and one a commoner?—referring to the high office that Rufus held.] Because my lord [the emperor] wishes it. The Sabbath, too," R. Akiba said, "is distinguished because the Lord wishes so."

Regarding the Manna, Scripture states, "And it came to pass that on the sixth day they gathered twice as much bread, two *omers* for each one; and all the rulers of the congregation came and told Moses" (Ex. 16:22). *Rashi* (ad loc.) comments, They asked him, "Why is today different from other days" (*Mah hayom yomayim?*).

The expression became a colloquialism when asking why any day stands apart because it is unlike another (See also B.M. 59b).

MAHASHAVAH TOVA HAKADOSH BARUKH HU METZARPAH LEMA'- ASEH (מחשבה טובה הקב"ה מצרפה למעשה). "Good intention is combined with deed" (Kidd. 40a); that is, both are rewarded. For it is said: "Then they that feared the Lord spoke one with another; and the Lord hearkened, and heard, and a book of remembrance was written before Him, for them that feared the Lord, and that thought upon His Name" (Mal. 3:16). Thus, good intention (*mahashavah tova*) was rewarded as good deed.

MAI BAYN KAKH UVAYN KAKH (מאי בין כך ובין כך). See BAYN KAKH UVAYN KAKH.

MAI DAHAVAH HAVAH (מאי דהוה הוה). The Talmud (Pes. 108a) discusses whether reclining during the *Seder* should take place for the first two cups of wine or for the last two cups. According to one explanation, the last two cups come after the meal, by which time the entire narrative of Israel's liberation has been completed. Hence, there is no need then to emphasize the theme of freedom; *Mai dahavah havah* ("What has been has been"). Colloquially, the phrase has come to mean "Let bygones be bygones." The Yiddish equivalent is *Vuhs iz geven iz geven.*

MAI DEKAMA (מאי דקמא). Literally, "What is this before [me]?" (Ket. 67b); that is, "What does this mean?" (cf. Marcus Jastrow, *A Dictionary,* vol. 2 [New York: Title Publishing Company, 1943], p. 1383).

MAI HAZIT DIDMA DIDAKH SU-MAK TEFAY, DILMA DEMA DE-HAHU GAVRA SUMAK TEFAY? (מאי חזית דדמא דידך סומק טפי, דילמא דמא דההוא גברא סומק טפי?). "What [reason] do you see [for thinking] that your blood is redder; perhaps that man's blood is redder?" (Pes. 25b). One came before Raba and said to him, "The governor of my town has ordered me to kill so-and-so; if not, he will kill me." Raba answered him, "Let him kill you rather than that you should commit murder. His life is no less valuable than your own; thus, you have no right to murder him to save yourself."

The expression is used to infer "What makes you think that you are more important than another person?"

MAI KA MASHMA LAN (מאי קא משמע לן). Literally, "What does he/it let us hear?"; meaning, What is there new in his words? or, What does he want to teach us? (Shab. 98a). See KA MASHMA LAN.

MAI KASHYAH LAKH (מאי קשיה לך). "What is your difficulty?" (Pes. 34a). The Talmud relates that Abaye b. Abin and R. Hanina studied the laws of *terumah* at Rabbah's academy. Rabbah b. Mattenah met them and asked them about the discussion they had concerning *terumah*. They then said to him, *Mai kashyah lakh?*

MAI NAFKA MINAH (מאי נפקא מינה). "What difference does it make?" (Bez. 6b).

MAI TAKANTAYH (מאי תקנתיה). "What is the remedy?" or "What shall he do?" (Yom. 84a).

MAI TIKKUN GADOL (מאי תיקון גדול). "What was the great improvement?" The *Mishnah* (Sukk. 5:2) states: "At the conclusion of the first festival day of Sukkot, they [the *Kohanim* and *Levi'im*] descended to the court of the women where they had made a great correction." The Talmud (Sukk. 51b) asks, *Mai tikkun gadol*? And answers, "It was enacted that the women should sit above [on the gallery] and the men below."

MAKAT MEDINAH (מכת מדינה). "A widespread epidemic" (B.M. 105b). The *Mishnah* and Talmud discuss the case in which a man leases a field from his neighbor and it (the crop) is eaten by grasshoppers or blasted by the tempest. If it was a widespread epidemic, he can deduct the loss from the rental; if it was not a widespread epidemic, he may not deduct the loss from the rental. The lender can say to him, It is on account of your bad luck.

Makat medinah became a colloquial expression for all widespread ills.

MAKHOR SA'AR HAROSH (מכר שער הראש). "To sell the hair of your head" (Ned. 65b); an expression uttered by R. Akiba, intimating "Even if you sell everything," you must pay her her *ketu-*

bah. The *Mishnah* (Pes. 48b) uses the phrase AMDU SA'AROTAV for "a man whose hair is standing on end" from fear.

MAKOM SHEBA'ALAY TESHUVAH OMDIN TZADIKIM GEMURIM AYNAM OMDIN (מקום שבעלי תשובה עומדין צדיקים גמורים אינם עומדין). It is written in the Talmud, "The place occupied by repentant sinners cannot be attained even by the completely righteous" (Ber. 34b; San. 99a). That is, a higher rank is assigned to the repentant sinner than to the completely righteous. For it is written, "Peace, peace, to him that is far off, and to him that is near" (Isa. 57:19); thus, first he that is "far off," then he that is "near." See BA'AL TESHUVAH.

MALAKH HAMAVET MAH LO HA-KHA MAH LO HATAM? (מלאך המות מה לו הכא מה לו התם?). Literally, "What difference does this place or another place make to the Angel of Death?" (B.M. 36b). The expression infers that death finds the person anywhere and one cannot hide or run away from it.

A Yiddish expression signifying that death is impending is *Der malakh hamavet kukt nisht in lu'ah* ("The Angel of Death does not look at a calendar"). (See A.Z. 5a, 20b).

MALAKHAY HABALAH (מלאכי חבלה). A phrase meaning "destroying angels." The Talmud relates that when Israel sinned through the Golden Calf one million, two hundred thousand destroying angels (*malakhay habalah*) descended and removed them (Shab. 88a). *Rashi* (Gen. 3:24) gives *malakhay habalah* as a description for the Cherubim that kept Adam away from the tree of life. *Rashi* (Yom. 67b) also tells of the two *malakhay habalah*, Uza and Azaayl, who descended to the ground in the day of Na'amah, the sister of Tubal-Cain.

The phrase *malakhay habalah* colloquially came to mean "saboteurs," "mischief-makers," or "damage-doers."

MALAY KERIMON (מלא כרמון).
"Crammed [with seeds] like a pomegranate." The Talmud (Ber. 57a) states, If one sees pomegranates in a dream and he is not learned, he may hope to perform precepts, "for even the illiterate among thee are full of precepts like a pomegranate [*Melayim mitzvot kerimon*]."

The phrase *malay kerimon* is sometimes applied to a person who is an erudite Torah scholar.

MALAY VEGADUSH (מלא וגדוש).
"Filled to overflowing" or "heaped." God tells Moses, "Take thee Joshua, the son of Nun, a man in whom is spirit, and lay thy hand upon him" (Numb. 27:18). *Rashi* (ibid., 27:23) comments that Moses did it with his two hands and made him like a vessel filled to overflowing (*malay vegadush*). The phrase is also used concerning the offering of the incense (*ketoret*), "and the small dish was in the middle of it, heaped with incense" (Tam. 5:4).

The expression *malay vegadush* is sometimes applied to a great scholar.

MAN DEKHAR SHEMAYH (מאן דכר שמיה). "Who mentioned his [its] name?"; that is, what has this to do here? (Shab. 57a).

MAN DEYAHAYV HAYAY YAHAYV MEZONAY (מאן דיהב חיי יהב מזוני). "Who gives life will also give sustenance." This is a paraphrase of R. Samuel b. Nahmani's statement *Dekhi yahayv Rahamana sova lehayay Hu deyahayv* ("When the All-Merciful gives plenty, He gives it for the living") (Taan. 8b). The saying implies, God will not forsake one in distress. One should trust in God.

MANHIG ATZMO BERABBANUT (מנהיג עצמו ברבנות). "To assume airs of authority" (Ber. 55a). Among the things that shorten a man's days is assuming airs of authority, "as R. Hama b. Hanina said, 'Why did Joseph die before his brethren?'"

(cf. Ex. 1:6). Because he assumed airs of authority.

The *Maharsha* comments that the expression *hamanhig atzmo berabbanut* (a self-made leader), rather than *hanohayg rabbanut* (leader of authority), was the reason for shortening his days. He was not appointed but, rather, his authority was forced.

MAR BAR RAV ASHI (מר בר רב אשי). "A particular name used as an attributed epithet for a revered and pedigreed person." Undoubtedly, using the name of the Babylonian *Amora* (died c. 468) can be attributed to the fact that he possessed great authority and is extensively quoted in the Babylonian Talmud. Known also by the name of Tavyomi (B.B. 12b), the *halakhah* follows him except in two cases (*Rashi*, Hul. 76b). This was due to Mar, who saw the completion of the Talmud after his father had served as editor in the previous generation.

MARIT AYIN (מראית עין). Literally, "appearance." The rule is: Wherever the Sages have forbidden anything because of appearances, it is forbidden even in the strictest privacy (Bez. 9a). If it is forbidden on public grounds because of appearances, it should also be forbidden on private ground. See HASHAD; AYN NIKHNASIM LEHURVAH MIPNAY HAHASHAD; HAHOSHAYD BIKSHAYRIM LOKAH BEGUFO.

MARGALIT TOVAH HAYETAH BE-YEDKHEM UVIKASHTEM LE'ABDAH MIMENI (מרגלית טובה היתה בידכם ובקשתם לאבדה ממני). "There was a fair jewel in your hand, and you sought to deprive me of it" (Hag. 3a).

This expression is used when a person will not reveal a new Torah interpretation or some good news.

MASA UMATAN (משא ומתן). "Dealings," "business," or "transaction." The *Mishnah* (Ta'an. 1:6) states: "If these [additional] fast days passed and there was still no answer to their prayers, then business is restricted [*mema'atin bemasa umatan*]."

Colloquially, the expression is used when one refuses to have dealings with another person and remarks, "I refuse to have *masa umatan* with you."

MASHI'AH'S TZAYTN (משיח'ס ציי'טן). See HEVLAY MASHI'AH (HEVLO SHEL MASHI'AH).

MATZA MIN ET MINO (מצא מין את מינו). "The like has found its like" (Erub. 9a); that is, "Birds of a feather flock together." See KOL OF LEMINO YISHKON; KOL ORAYV LEMINO.

MATZA O MOTZA (מצא או מוצא).
The Talmud (Ber. 8a) relates: "In the west they used to ask a man who married a wife thus: *Matza* or *Motza*? *Matza*, for it is written: 'Whoso findeth [*matza*] a wife findeth a great good' (Prov. 18:22). *Motza*, for it is written: 'And I find [*motza*] more bitter than death the woman'" (Eccl. 7:26). In the Bible the word *matza* is used in connection with a good wife and the word *motza* is used in connection with a bad wife.

The question is still humorously asked when a person marries or is married for a short time.

MAY-ALEF VE'AD TAV (מאלף ועד תיו). The first and last letters in the Hebrew alphabet, as "from A to Z" or "from *Alpha* to *Omega*," indicating from beginning to end. The Talmud (Shab. 55a) utilizes the expression for denoting those people who fulfill the precepts of the Torah from *alef* to *tav*. The same expression is used for those who transgressed (*shehatu*) *may-alef ve'ad tav* ("They sinned from *alef* to *tav*") (*Ekhah Rabbati* 1:23). The Talmud (San. 104a) states that the verses in the book of *Ekhah* begin with the twenty-two letters of the *Alef-bet*, in order to recall the fury that God unleashed upon the Israelites because "they

transgressed the Torah, which was given to them with the twenty-two letters."

When speaking of a complete ignoramus or one who is illiterate, the Yiddish expression is ER KEN NIT KAYN TZURAT ALEF (lit., "He does not recognize the form of an *alef*").

MAYAHORAY HAPARGOD (מאחורי הפרגוד). Literally, "behind the curtain"; a phrase used to signify what is going on behind the scenes.

The phrase is utilized several times in the Talmud (Ber. 18b; Hag. 15a, 16a; San. 89b) and in the *Midrash*. Regarding the martyrdom of the ten scholars at the hands of the Romans, after the Bar-Kokhba revolt, Gabriel said to his son Ishmael, "I swear by your life that I heard behind the partition [*mayahoray hapargod*] that the ten scholars of Israel will perish at the hands of the wicked government." Ishmael asked, "Why?" Gabriel said, "To expiate the guilt of the sons of Jacob, who sold their brother Joseph" (*Midrash*). In Yiddish, the expression would be *Ikh huhb es gehert mayahoray hapargod* ("I have heard it rumored").

MAYHAYKHA TAYTAY (מהיכא תיתי). Literally, "Whence does it come!" or "Let it come whence it may" (Hor. 10a). The phrase has also taken on the meaning "well and good," "granted," "all right," and "with pleasure." In Yiddish, an unassuming person is labeled *mayhaykha-taysinik*.

MAYHAYKHAN YEREK ZEH HAI (מהיכן ירק זה חי). The *Mishnah* (B.M. 10:6) discusses the case whereby two gardens are situated one above the other and vegetables grow in between them; to whom do the vegetables belong? R. Meir says: "Since both can prevent one another [from having vegetables at all], we consider whence the vegetables draw their sustenance [*mayhaykhan yerek zeh hai*]" and this determines their ownership.

The expression has given rise to the jesting utterance "How does this green-horn ["raw, inexperienced person"] live?"

MAYIGARA RAM LEVAYRA AMI-KATA (מאיגרא רם לבירא עמיקתא).
"From a roof so high to a pit as deep!" (Hag. 5b). This is what Rabbi said when he was holding the Book of Lamentations and reading the verse "He hath cast down from heaven unto the earth" (Lam. 2:1), and the book fell from his hands.

Colloquially the talmudic saying became associated with the expression "Hasty climbers have sudden falls."

A parallel Yiddish expression is *Az men flit tzu hoykh falt men tzu niderik* ("If you fly too high, you fall to the lowest").

MAYSI'AH LEFI TUMO (מסיח לפי תומו).
Literally, "to talk in one's simplicity" or "talking innocently without ulterior motive." It also implies "making a statement in ignorance of its legal bearing." For example, "when the gentile makes an incidental statement [not a formal testimony]" (Yeb. 121b) or, "whenever a gentile makes an informal statement, we believe him" (act on it as evidence) (Git. 28b).

MAYVIN DAVAR MITOKH DAVAR (מבין דבר מתוך דבר).
"One who understands one thing from another" (Hag. 14a); that is, he is able to draw conclusions on the basis of the knowledge imparted to him. This is the meaning of the phrase in the verse "and the skillful" (Isa. 3:3).

ME'AILIN PILA BEKUPA DE-MAHTA (מעיילין פילא בקופא דמחטא).
(Aram.) HAKHNAYS PIL BEKOF SHEL MAHAT (הכנס פיל בקוף של מחט). (Heb.) "To draw an elephant through the eye of a needle" (B.M. 38b); an expression signifying impossibility or exaggeration.

MEHADRIN MIN HAMEHADRIN (מהדרין מן המהדרין).
"The extremely zealous" (Shab. 21b). The expression is used in the Talmud regarding lighting the *Hanukkah* candles. It has also become associated with kosher food products; *mehadrin min hamehadrin* often appears on a product that is carefully supervised.

MEHARAYF UMEGADAYF (מחרף ומגדף).
"A blasphemer and a libeler." The Talmud (Kidd. 49a) states that R. Judah said that if one adds to a verse in the Torah, he is a *meharayf umegadayf*. Likewise, the Talmud (Shab. 118b) stated, "He who reads *Hallel* every day blasphemes and libels, because recital was set for special events only and by reading it every day, it becomes merely a song."

MELAMAYD ZEKHUT (מלמד זכות).
See ZEKHUTO YAGAYN ALAYNU.

MESAHAYK BEKUVYA (משחק בקוביא).
"A gambler with dice" (*Mishnah*, San. 3:3); a term indiscriminately applied by the Rabbis to any form of gambling. The *Mishnah* states, "And these are ineligible [to be witnesses or judges]: a gambler with dice, a usurer, a pigeon-trainer, and traders [in the produce] of the Sabbatical year." A reason given for the disqualification of the gambler is that wasting time and money on gambling, instead of engaging in studies or in a trade or profession, amounts to ignoring the general welfare of the world (*yishuv shel olam*) and that person is therefore not reliable (San. 24b, 25a; *Yad, Gezaylah Va'avaydah* 6:10–11).

MESANA DERAV MIKARAI LO BA'AYNA (מסאנא דרב מכרעאי לא בעינא).
"I do not want a shoe too large for my foot" (Kidd. 49a). If a man says to a woman, "Be thou betrothed unto me on condition that I am a Levite," and he is found to be a *Kohen*, she is not betrothed. Even though she merits someone of a

higher class, she does not want someone whose pedigree is too high for her, for he might be too haughty; and thus she prefers to marry a Levite and not a *Kohen*.

The Hebrew equivalent is *Ayni rotzeh bena'al gedolah mayragli*.

MESHANEH MAKOM MESHANEH MAZAL (משנה מקום משנה מזל).

"Who changes his place changes his luck." The Talmud (R.H. 16b) states, "Four things cancel the doom of a man, namely: charity, supplication, change of name, and change of conduct. Some say the change of place [*shinui makom*], as it is written, 'Now the Lord said unto Abram, Get thee out of thy country,' and its proceeds, 'and I will make thee a great nation'" (Gen. 12:1–2).

MESHUFRAY (DE)SHUFRAY (משופרי (ד)שופרי).

"The very best portion"; when giving *terumah* (the priestly dues from produce) to the *Kohen*, "of the very best therof" (*mikol shufrayh*) (cf. *Targum Onkelos*, Numb. 18:29) shall you set apart (see also *Targum* to verses 30 and 32). The Talmud (Pes. 3b) tells of a non-Jew who partook in the Passover sacrifice in Jerusalem and boasted that he ate of the very best pieces, the finest of the fine (*mishufray deshufray*) of the Passover lamb, even though it is written, "there shall no alien eat thereof . . . no uncircumcised person shall eat thereof" (Ex. 12:43, 48).

MESIRAT NEFESH (מסירת נפש).

"Self-sacrificing"; denoting one who is fully devoted to a cause, sometimes to the extent of taking his or her life in hand. The Talmud (Ber. 32a) states: "And Moses besaught [*vayehal*] the Lord his God" (Ex. 32:11). Samuel says, It teaches that he risked his life for them (*shemasar atzmo lemitah alayhem*; compare the word *vayehal* with *halal*, meaning "slain"), as it says, "And if not, blot me, I pray Thee, out of Thy book which Thou hast written" (Ex. 32:32).

MEZAKEH ET HARABIM (מזכה את הרבים).

"Whosoever causes a community to do good" (Yom. 87a). It is written in the Talmud, "Whoever causes the people to do good, no sin will occur through him" (cf. also *Avot* 5:18). God blesses him with a reward to keep him away from sin (*Rambam*).

MI SHE'AYNO KO'AYS HAKADOSH BARUKH HU OHAVO (מי שאינו כועס הקב"ה אוהבו).

"He who does not display temper is beloved by the Holy One, blessed be He" (Pes. 113b). The Talmud mentions two others who are in this category. They are: a person who does not become intoxicated and a person who does not insist on his full rights— that is, in the sense that he does not retaliate.

MI SHELO RA'AH SIMHAT BAYT HASHO'AYVAH LO RA'AH SIMHAH MIYAMAV (מי שלא ראה שמחת בית השואבה לא ראה שמחה מימיו).

"He who has not seen the rejoicing at the place of the Water-Drawing has never seen rejoicing in his life" (*Mishnah*, Sukk. 5:1). This proverbial saying refers to the ceremony in the Temple, which began on the second evening of the festival of Sukkot and lasted for six nights. Music and dance played an important role in the festivities. A great feature during the day was the procession that accompanied the priest who drew water for the libation ceremony from the pool of Siloam in Jerusalem. The water was poured upon the altar, along with a libation of wine. Pouring the water upon the altar marked the beginning of the rainy season in *Eretz Yisrael*.

After the destruction of the Temple, the ceremony ceased. It is commemorated today by reciting various psalms and poems. Singing and dancing and refreshments are part of the festivities. (For a description of how the occasion is celebrated in modern times, see *Arugat Ha-*

bosem in *Siddur Otzar Hatefillot*, vol. 2, p. 1172, s.v. *Hilkhot Hag Hasukkot*.)

MI SHETARAH BE'EREV SHABBAT YOKHAL BESHABBAT (מי שטרח בערב שבת יאכל בשבת). "He who took trouble [to prepare] on the eve of the Sabbath will eat on the Sabbath" (A.Z. 3a). The phrase became a colloquial expression when intimating that in order to achieve any goal, one must work for it.

Similar expressions in Yiddish are: *Ver es greyt nit uhn erev Shabbos huht nisht oyf Shabbos* ("He who does not prepare before the Sabbath, will not have for the Sabbath"); *Greyt dir uhn in der yugnt, vestu huhbn oyf dere elter* ("Prepare when you are young, you will have in later years").

MIBINTA DEROSHI VE'AD TUFRA DEKHARI (מבינתא דראשי ועד טופרא דכרעי). "From the hair of my head down to my toe nails" (Shab. 140a). This is the cooling sensation R. Joseph experienced in his body when he drank a cup of wine called *Aluntit* (a mixture of old wine, clear water, and balsam), which is prepared as a cooling draught in the baths.

MIDAH KENEGED MIDAH (מדה כנגד מדה). In talmudic-midrashic literature one finds the concept of "measure for measure" or "retaliation." The Talmud cites R. Hiyya b. Abba, who said in R. Johanan's name, "He who is disinclined to act and lament a Sage will not prolong his days, [this being] measure for measure" (Shab. 105b). Another example of *Midah keneged midah* is when the Egyptians ordered that the Jewish children should be drowned and, in turn, *they* were drowned in the sea (Sot. 11a). The Talmud also states, "In all the measures [of punishment or reward] taken by the Holy One, blessed be He, the Divine act befits the [human] deed" (San. 90a).

Expressions used in informal conversation are "tit for tat" or "the punishment fits the crime." In the Talmud (Sot. 8b) a similar expression is attributed to R. Meir,

BEMIDAH SHE'ADAM MODAYD BAH MODEDIN LO ("As a man deals, he will be dealt with)."

MIDAT HASIDUT (מדת חסידות). "Pious behavior" (B.M. 52b). For example, if one acquires a coin that is valued by weight and, after having been in use for some time, it depreciates, until what time is he (the defrauded party) permitted to retract (that is, cancel)? Said R. Hisda, Although he (the seller) is not legally bound to take it back, as a measure of piety (*Midat hasidut*) he should do so.

MIDE'ORAITA   (DE'ORAITA) (מדאורייתא (דאורייתא)). "From the Torah"; referring to a biblical precept (*mitzvah*) or decree (*hok*) that is directly prescribed in the Torah or is derived from a verse in the Torah. A distinction is made between pentateuchal origin (*De'oraita*) and rabbinic origin (MIDERABBANAN; DERABBANAN), those precepts enacted or ordained by the Rabbis (cf. Sukk. 44a).

MIDERABBANAN (DERABBANAN) (מדרבנן (דרבנן)). See MIDE'ORAITA (DE'ORAITA).

MIGDAL HAPORAYAH BA'AVIR (מגדל הפורח באויר). "A tower flying in the air" (San. 106b), an expression signifying something that is nonexistent, something not attainable. The Talmud (Shab. 29a) gives a situation in which a person swore concerning a thing that was impossible, as in GAMAL HAPORAYAH BA'AVIR ("I swear I have seen a camel flying in the air").

MIKAN VA'AYLEKH (מכאן ואילך). Literally, "thereafter" or "after that." When a son is reporting something he heard from the deceased (his father), he should say, "Thus said my father, my teacher, for whose resting place I may be an atonement." But that is only within twelve months (of his death). Thereafter (*Mikan Va'aylekh*) he should say, "His memory be

for a blessing, for the life of the World to Come" (Kidd. 31b).

MIKARNAY RE'AYMIN AD BAYTZAY KINIM (מקרני ראמים עד ביצי כנים).
Literally, "from the horned buffalo to the brood of vermin"; a phrase used in the Talmud (A.Z. 3b; Shab. 107b), describing God's act of feeding the world during the third quarter of the day.

The phrase constitutes a whole, as God gives sustenance to the largest and smallest animal. Therefore, the expression *Mikarnay re'aymin ad baytzay kinim* may be used to express the aspect of completeness.

MIKTZAT SHEVAHO SHEL ADAM OMRIM BEFANAV, VEKHULO SHELO BEFANAV (מקצת שבחו של אדם אומרים בפניו, וכולו שלא בפניו).
R. Jeremiah b. Eleazar said: "Only a part of a man's praise may be said in his presence, but all of it in his absence" (Erub. 18b). The Talmud elucidates that "only a part of a man's praise . . . in his presence," for it is written in Scripture, "For thee have I seen righteous before Me in this generation" (Gen. 7:1); (when God speaks to Noah he is described as righteous only) "but all of it in his absence," for it is written in Scripture, "Noah was in his generation a man righteous and wholehearted" (Gen. 6:9) (in his absence he is described as both righteous and wholehearted).

MILAH BESELA UMASHTOKA BITRIN (מלה בסלע ומשתוקא בתרין).
"A word is worth a *sela* [a coin], silence two *sela*'s" (Meg. 18a), a statement made by R. Dimi, who gave this interpretation for the phrase LEKHA DUMIYAH TEHILAH ("For you silence is praise"; Ps. 65:2). A similar saying is *Seyag lahokhmah shetikah* ("A protective fence for wisdom is silence") (Avot 3:17). By restricting speech, sin and controversy are avoided and thus wisdom can be increased by Torah study.

An English equivalent is "Speech is silver, silence is golden."

MILAY DE'ALMA (מלי דעלמא).
"Secular discourses," as opposed to Torah study (Shab. 82a).

MILHEMTAH SHEL TORAH (מלחמתה של תורה).
A verse in Isaiah 28:5 that reads "In that day shall the Lord of Hosts be for a crown of glory . . . and for strength to them that turn back the battles to the gate" (ibid., 28:6). The Talmud (San. 111b) comments on the phrase "that turn back the battle," that is, to those who engage in the battle of the Torah (*milhemtah shel Torah*). See TALMIDAY HAKHAMIM MARBIM SHALOM BA'OLAM.

MILTA DEBEDIHUTA (מילתא דבדיחותא).
"Something humorous" (Shab. 30b). The Talmud relates that before Rabbah commenced his discourse for the scholars, he used to say something humorous and the scholars were cheered; after that, he sat in awe and began the discourse.

MILTA DELA SHKHIHA (מלתא דלא שכיחא).
"Unusual or common occurrence [thing]" (Erub. 63b; B.M. 46b).

MIMAYLA (ממילא).
"Of itself," "as a matter of course," "automatically," or "perforce," as is written in the Talmud (B.M. 16a), *Yerushah mimayla hi* ("An inheritance comes of itself"), without any effort on the part of the recipient.

MIMERAY RASHVATAKH PARAY IFRA (ממרי רשוותך פארי אפרע).
"From a debtor of thine accept [even] bran in payment" (B.K. 46b); that is, take anything from him.

The Yiddish equivalent is *Fun a hazir a hor* ("From a swine [even] a hair").

MIN HASHAMAYIM YERAHAMU (מן השמים ירחמו).
See HASHEM YERAHAYM.

MINHAG AVOTAYHEM BEYADAY-HEM (מנהג אבותיהם בידיהם). See MIN-HAG MEVATAYL HALAKHAH.

MINHAG AVOTAYKHEM BEYAD-KHEM (מנהג אבותיכם בידכם). See MIN-HAG MEVATAYL HALAKHAH.

MINHAG AVOYTAYNU (YISRAEL) TORAH HI (מנהג אבותינו (ישראל) תורה היא). See MINHAG MEVATAYL HALA-KHAH.

MINHAG MEVATAYL HALAKHAH (מנהג מבטל הלכה). "Custom overrides the Law" (Jer. Tal., Yeb. 12:1, 12c). Similarly, MINHAG OKAYR HALAKHAH (DIN) ("Custom undoes law") (Sof. 14:18).

By custom is meant a practice not based on a particular scriptural passage, which has, through long observance, been handed down from generation to generation and has become binding by proper authorities. Thus, there are such proverbial sayings as MINHAG AVOTAYHEM BEYA-DAYHEM ("They retain their fathers' practice") (Shab. 35b), or MINHAG AVOTAYKHEM BEYADKHEM ("Give heed to the customs of your ancestors") (Bez. 4b). Another expression that came down through the ages is MINHAG AVOTAYNU (YISRAEL) TORAH HI ("The customs of our fathers [of Israel] are binding as the laws of the Torah") (Shulhan Arukh, Yoreh Dayah 376:4; Mat. Eph. 510:11). The Talmud (Pes. 119b) states that when coming into a city, one must guide oneself according to the customs of that vicinity—HAKOL KEMINHAG HAMEDINAH ("It all depends on local custom"). In this respect, the Maharil (cf. Moses Isserles, Orah Hayyim 619) ruled AL YESHANEH ADAM MIMINHAG HA'IR AFILU BENIGGUNIM ("Local custom and universal Jewish traditional melodies should not be changed").

In the course of time, superstitions became part of Jewish usages and rabbinical authorities such as the Rambam and

Rabbaynu Tam vigorously decried the multiplicity of customs that were being added. Rabbaynu Tam even commented that Minhag (mem, nun, hay, gimmel), when inverted, spells Gehinnom (gimmel, hay, nun, mem) [purgatory] and that if fools are accustomed to do certain things, it does not follow that the wise should do likewise. Thus arose the expression MINHAG SHTUT ("customs of fools"). See AL YESH-ANEH ADAM MIN HAMINHAG.

MINHAG OKAYR HALAKHAH (מנהג עוקר הלכה). See MINHAG MEVATAYL HALAKHAH.

MINHAG SHTUT (מנהג שטות). See MINHAG MEVATAYL HALAKHAH.

MIPI HASHEMU'AH (מפי השמועה). "On the basis of tradition" (San. 88a). The Talmud states, Hu omayr mipi hashemu'ah ("He says, I gave my decision on the basis of tradition").

MIPNAY DARKAY SHALOM (מפני דרכי שלום). "In the interests of peace" (Git. 59a). The Talmud (ibid., 59b) states, "The whole Torah exists only for the purpose of promoting peace." Hillel the elder taught, "Be among the disciples of Aaron, loving peace and pursuing peace" (Avot 1:12). Aaron, in talmudic literature, is described as the peacemaker par excellence; he used any means to make peace among husband and wife, as well as between feuding Jews.

For the sake of peace, R. Ile'a, in the name of R. Eleazar, son of R. Simeon, stated, MUTAR LO LE'ADAM LESHANOT BIDVAR HASHALOM ("One may modify a statement in the interest of peace") (Yeb. 65b), for Sripture states, "Thy father did command . . . so shall ye say unto Joseph: Forgive, I pray thee now . . ." (Gen. 50:16–17). According to Rashi (ad loc.), there is no record of this command attributed to Jacob; the brothers ascribed the request to Jacob, with the purpose of preserving the peace between themselves and Joseph.

In biblical days, as well as in later times, it was customary to greet one another with the word SHALOM, as the phrase appears in Genesis 43:23, *Shalom lakhem* ("Peace be to you") (see also Git. 61a). The *Mishnah* (*Avot* 4:20) says, "to meet every person with a friendly greeting." According to the Talmud (Ber. 6b), he who does not return a greeting is called a robber. The phrase ALAV HASHALOM ("May he [rest] in peace") is an expression of honor used when mentioning an important person, as for example, "when the day of death came for Moses our teacher, *alav hashalom*, to leave the world" (*Otzar Hamidrashim* 362, *Petirat Moshe Rabbaynu*).

A Yiddish expression underscoring the importance of peace is *A shlekhter shalom iz beser vi a guter krig* ("A bad peace is better than a good quarrel"). See HAS VESHALOM: IM AYN SHALOM AYN KELUM.

MISHENIKHNAS ADAR MARBIN BESIMHAH (משנכנס אדר מרבין בשמחה). "With the beginning of [the month of] *Adar*, rejoicing is increased" (Taan. 29a). *Rashi* (ad loc.) gives as the reason that this month is in anticipation of Purim and Pesah which represent *ge'ulah* (redemption). See MISHENIKHNAS AV MEMA'ATIN BESIMHAH.

MISHENIKHNAS AV MEMA'ATIN BESIMHAH (משנכנס אב ממעטין בשמחה). "With the beginning of [the month of] *Ab*, rejoicing is curtailed." The *Mishnah* (Ta'an. 26b) cites five misfortunes that befell our fathers on the seventeenth of *Tammuz* and five on the Ninth of *Ab*) (cf. also Ta'an. 28b, 29a, b). See MISHENIKHNAS ADAR MARBIN BESIMHAH.

MITAT NESHIKAH (מיתת נשיקה). Literally, "dying by a kiss"; that is, "an easy and dignified death" (M.K. 28a). The Talmud states, "If one has attained the 'age of strength' [eighty], a sudden death is dying by the kiss."

MITZVAH HABA'AH BA'AVAYRAH (מצוה הבאה בעבירה). Using a stolen palm-branch is forbidden because "it would be a precept fulfilled through a transgression" (Sukk. 30a; Ber. 47b). This would be making use of an illegitimately obtained object for a religious ceremony and it is deemed unlawful. This is derived from the verse "And ye have brought that which is stolen, and the lame and the sick" (Mal. 1:13). The stolen is thus compared with the lame. Just as the lame can never be rectified (to become a valid offering), so that which is stolen can never be rectified, (that is) irrespective of whether the stolen is used before abandonment (of hope of recovery by the owner) or after abandonment.

MITZVAH MIN HAMUVHAR (מצווה מן המובחר). "For a religious ceremony we require the best" (Ber. 50b). A dispute arose in the Talmud with regard to the proper blessing to be uttered on wine that was not mixed with water. *Rashi* comments that if water is not added, it is like fruit juice and thus it can be used for washing the hands. The outcome was that in the matter of the cup of wine used for Grace, a blessing should not be said over it until water has been added. R. Oshaiah gives the reason that "For religious ceremony we require the very best." Undiluted wine is suitable in mixing for medicinal purposes.

The saying *Mitzvah min hamuvhar* has become associated with all religious ceremonies.

MITZVAT ASAYH SHEHAZEMAN GERAMA NASHIM PETUROT (מצות עשה שהזמן גרמא נשים פטורות). "A positive commandment, the observance of which depends on a certain time of day or season of the year; women are exempt" (Kidd. 29a; Ber. 20b). For example, putting on *tefillin* (worn only during the day on weekdays) or *tzitzit* (worn only during the day), and so forth.

MI'UTA DEMI'UTA (מיעוטא דמיעוטא). "A minority of a minority" (Yeb. 119b). According to R. Meir, a minority is not taken into consideration; it has no value or influence.

MODEH BEMIKTZAT HATA'ANAH (מודה במקצת הטענה). "He who admits part of a claim" (B.K. 107a). The law is that he pays for the part that he admits and swears for the part that he denies.

MOSIFIN MIHOL AL HAKODESH (מוסיפין מחול על הקודש). "We add from the profane to the holy"; that is, we add a little from the ordinary weekday on to the holy day (R.H. 9a). This is derived from a scriptural verse in Exodus 34:21 (according to R. Akiba). R. Ishmael derives this rule from "And ye shall afflict your souls on the ninth day" (Lev. 23:32). The Talmud continues, "I might think [literally] on the ninth day. It therefore says, 'In the evening' (ibid.). If in the evening, I might think 'after dark?' It therefore says 'on the ninth day.' What, then, am I to understand? That we begin fasting while it is yet day, which shows that we add from the profane on to the holy." According to R. Akiba, the verse "And ye shall afflict your souls on the ninth day" is as if he fasted on both the ninth and the tenth days. This is because the eating and drinking on the ninth day is called in the text 'fasting.' There is a special *mitzvah* of eating and drinking on the ninth day, in that it serves as a preparation for the coming day's *inui* ("affliction"). The *Rosh* (*Yoma*, chap. 8:22) expresses the idea as follows: "Prepare yourself on the ninth of the month, strengthening yourselves through eating and drinking so that you will be able to afflict yourselves the next day. . . ."

Some authorities hold that one is required to add some part of the weekday to *Shabbat* (cf. *Orah Hayyim* 261:2; *Mishnah Berurah* 261:19 and 20).

MOTZI LA'AZ (מוציא לעז). It is written in Scripture, "And while the children were in the wilderness, they found a man gathering sticks upon the Sabbath day" (Numb. 15:32). According to R. Akiba, the gatherer was Zelophehad. R. Judah b. Bathyra said to him, "Akiba! In either case you will have to give an account [for your statement]: If you are right, the Torah shielded him, while you reveal him; and if not, you cast suspicion upon a righteous man [*motzi la'az al oto tzadik*]" (Shab. 96b). Proverbs (10:18) reads, "*Motzi dibah hu khsil* ("He that utters a slander is a fool").

MOTZI SHAYM RA (מוציא שם רע). "One who tells lies to dishonor another person" (Ket. 55a). For example, Scripture states that a husband who falsely accuses his wife of unchastity during betrothal is to be rebuked and fined, and loses the right to ever divorce her (cf. Deut. 22:13–21).

MUKTZEH MAHAMAT MI'US (מוקצה מחמת מיאוס). By *muktzeh* is meant "set apart" or "separated"; a term used for objects that are forbidden to be handled on Sabbath and festivals, though their use does not constitute actual labor (Shab. 44a; 124a). There are various types of *muktzeh* and one of them is *muktzeh mahamat mi'us* ("*muktzeh* on account of repulsiveness"). For example, a tree on which fish are hung to dry, a candelabra that was not used for the Sabbath and is repulsive, or something arousing aversion or disgust by itself, such as a dead mouse or a pot used for secretion or excrements.

The expression *Muktzeh mahamat mi'us* is used colloquially to express the idea "I would not touch it with a ten-foot pole; it is something contemptible."

MUM SHEBEKHA AL TOMAR LE-HAVAYREKHA (מום שבך אל תאמר לחברך). R. Nathan said: "Do not taunt your neighbor with the blemish you yourself have" (B.M. 59b). This refers to taunting a proselyte with being a stranger to the Jewish people, as the verse reads, "And a stranger shalt thou not wrong, neither shalt thou oppress him; for ye were strangers in the land of Egypt" (Ex. 22:20).

The expression may be applied to ridiculing any person for a flaw that you yourself have.

MUSHLAM BEKHOL HAMA'ALOT
(מושלם בכל המעלות). "To be complete in all manners" (Kallah Rabbati 3).

MUTAR LO LE'ADAM LESHANOT BIDVAR HASHALOM (מותר לו לאדם לשנות בדבר השלום). See MIPNAY DARKAY SHALOM.

NAFAL TORA HADAD LESAKINA
(נפל תורא חדד לסכינא). "When the ox is down, sharpen the knife" (Shab. 32a). When the ox has fallen, it is easier to slaughter than when it is standing. The same applies to human beings. When a person is down, advantage can be taken of him.

NAFKA MINAH (נפקא מינה). See MAI NAFKA MINAH.

NAHARA NAHARA UFASHTAYH
(נהרא נהרא ופשטה). "Every river has its own course" (Hul. 18b); that is, every place has its own ways or usages. A similar saying is "When in Rome, do as the Romans do."

NAHAT RU'AH (נחת רוח). "Delight" or "pleasure," as in keday la'asot nahat ru'ah lenashim ("for the sake of gratifying the women") (Hag. 16b).

Nahat ru'ah is also caused by sweet words that reflect the spirit or anything that gives a person a high degree of mental or physical gratification.

NASHIM RAHAMANIYOT HAYN
(נשים רחמניות הן). "Women are tender-hearted" (Meg. 14b).

NATON (NATATA) TORAT KOL EHAD VE'EHAD BEYADO? (נתון (נתת) תורת כל אחד ואחד בידו?). "Are you placing the law in the hands of each man?" (Sheb. 2:1). The Mishnah asks, Until when may a grain field be ploughed in the sixth year? And answers, Until moisture has dried up in the soil; or, as long as men still plough in order to plant cucumbers and gourds. R. Simeon said, "In this case, are you placing the law in the hands of each man?" That is, each person will interpret the halakhah for himself, according to his needs.

NAVON ZEH HAMAYVIN DAVAR MITOKH DAVAR (נבון זה המבין דבר מתוך דבר). See MAH BAYN HAKHAM LENAVON? NAVON DOMEH LESHULHANI TAGAR.

NAYR LE'EHAD NAYR LEMAYAH
(נר לאחד נר למאה). See BIRKAT HABAYIT BERUBAH.

NEFISHAY GAMLAY SAVAY DETE'INAY MASHKHAY DEHOGNAY
(נפישי גמלי סבי דטעיני משכי דהוגני). "Many an old camel is laden with the hides of younger ones" (San. 52a), meaning, many an old man survive the young.

This proverb, according to R. Papa, was prompted by the incident when Moses and Aaron were walking along with Nadab and Abihu behind them, and all Israel was following in the rear. Nadab said to Abihu, "O that these old men might die, so that you and I should be the leaders of our generation." But the Holy One, blessed be He, said unto them, "We shall see who will bury whom."

NIBUL PEH (נבל פה). One who speaks obscenities and wickedness. The Talmud (Shab. 13a) states: "Rabbah b. Shila said, in R. Hisda's name: He who speaks lewdly,

Gehenna [hell] is made deep for him, as it is said, "A deep pit is for the mouth [that speaketh] perversity" (Prov. 22:14). R. Nahman b. Isaac said, Also for one who hears and is silent, for it is said, "he that is abhorred of the Lord shall fall therein" (Prov. 22:14).

In the Yiddish language, one who speaks obscenities is called a *Nibul penik.* The Talmud (Pes. 3a) cites the teaching of the school of R. Ishmael: LE'OLAM YESAPAYR BELASHON NEKIYAH ("One should always discourse in decent language").

NIFTAR (NISTALAYK) (נפטר (נסתלק)). A person who has departed, as in *niftar beshaym tov min ha'olam* ("departed the world with a good name") (Ber. 17a). This is the usual expression uttered by kabbalists and *hasidim* upon the death of a rabbi or a great scholar.

Another word meaning "to die" is NIS-TALAYK, as in *Shemot Rabbah*:52, *Besha'at silukan shel tzadikim* ("When the righteous were about to die"). In Yiddish, the expression is *Iz nistalayk gevuhrn* ("[A saintly person] has died").

NIKAR HU ZEH SHELO AVAR AL PITHAH SHEL TORAH (נכר הוא זה שלא עבר על פתחה של תורה). "It is obvious that this person never learned anything" (Jer. Tal., Shab. 9:3).

NIKHNAS YAYIN YATZA SOD (נכנס יין יצא סוד). "When wine goes in counsel, [truth] departs" (Erub. 65a). YaYiN (*yud,* 10 + *yud,* 10 + *nun,* 50 = 70) and SOD (*samah,* 60 + *vav,* 6 + *daled,* 4 = 70) have the same numerical value. R. Hiyya observed, He who retains a clear mind under the influence of wine possesses the characteristics of the seventy elders.

In Yiddish, a similar expression is *Vuhs bay a nikhtern oyf dem lung, iz bay a shikurn oyf dem tzung* ("What a sober person has on his lung, a drunkard has on his tongue"). In English, one would say, "What sobriety conceals, drunkenness reveals."

NOGAYA BEDAVAR (נוגע בדבר). One who has a connection to, or a partial interest in, the matter. The Talmud (B.B. 43a) asks: "Why are they admitted to testify? Are they not interested witnesses?" (*Amai nogin be'aydutan hayn?*)—that is, are they not in contact with their evidence?

A person connected by some tie, as by blood, marriage, friendship, and so forth, is said to be a *nogaya bedavar.*

NOKAYM VENOTAYR (נוקם ונוטר). "Avenges and retains anger" (Yom. 23a). R. Johanan said, in the name of R. Simeon b. Jehozadak, "Any scholar who does not avenge himself and retain anger like a serpent is no real scholar." By this is meant that the scholar, to whom great wrong is done, should retaliate moderately, just as the serpent retaliates by bruising only the heel, a nonvital part of the human body. This saying may have come about as a reaction to the humble scholar who encourages others' outrageous behavior because of his extreme forbearance (cf. *Maharsha*).

O HAVRUTA O MITUTA (או חברותא או מיתותא). "Either companionship or death" (Taan. 23a); a saying that Raba used concerning Honi, the Circle-Drawer, who had slept for seventy years and, when he returned home, was not recognized or given the honor due him. This hurt him greatly and he prayed for death and died. Thus, it is inferred that if a person remains alone, without companionship, his life is not considered to be really living.

OKAYR HARIM (עוקר הרים). The Talmud (Ber. 64a) calls Rabbah an *okayr harim* (lit., "an uprooter of mountains"). Rabbah was exceptionally skillful in dialectic.

The phrase is currently applied to one who is a brilliant scholar and/or a powerful debater.

OLAM HAFUKH (עולם הפוך). Literally, "a topsy-turvy world." The Talmud (Pes. 50a) records that after R. Joseph, the son of R. Joshua b. Levi, recovered from becoming ill and falling into a trance, his father asked him, "What did you see?" He answered, *Olam hafukh ra'iti: elyonim lematah vehatahtonim lema'alah* ("I saw a topsy-turvy world: the upper [class] underneath and the lower on top").

OLAM HAZEH-OLAM HABA (עולם הזה-עולם הבא). The former is "this world" ("the living world"); the latter is "the World to Come" ("the world after death"). R. Aha b. Hanina said: "This world [*olam hazeh*] is not like the future world [*olam haba*]") (Pes. 5a). In this world, for good tidings one says, "He is good, and He doeth good," while for evil tidings one says, "Blessed be the true judge"; whereas in the future world it shall be only, "He is good and He doeth good."

In the Yiddish language, the term *olam-hazenik* means one who delights in enjoyment of luxury and pleasure, and in food and drink.

OMAYR VE'OSEH (אומר ועושה). A colloquial expression meaning "to fulfill one's promise immediately"; that is, "No sooner said than done." In Yiddish, the expression is *gezuhgt un getuhn.*

The Talmud (Ber. 57b) states that when one sees the ruins of the city of Babylon from which earth was taken for building elsewhere, one says, *Barukh omayr ve'oseh gozayr umekayaym* ("Blessed be He Who says and does, Who decrees and carries out").

The two words *omayr ve'oseh* appear in *Barukh She'amar*, the benediction in the second division of the *Shaharit* service, as an introduction to *Pesukay Dezimrah* and in the first blessing following the *Haftarah*.

OMDIN BERUMO SHEL OLAM (עומדין ברומו של עולם). "Of the most exalted position" (lit., "height of the world") (Meg. 14a). R. Hanin said that *Ramatayim-tzofim* in 1 Samuel 1:1 means "A man who came from ancestors of the most exalted position."

When speaking of very important matters or extremely weighty affairs, the expression used is *Devarim ha'omdim berumo shel olam.*

ORAYAH-PORAYAH (sing.), [pl. **ORHAY-PORHAY**] (אורחא-פורחא) [אורחי-פורחי]). An expression that became associated with a "wanderer," "vagabond," or "fly-by-night." The two words are used in the Talmud (Ket. 61a, 64b) and are translated as "guests and occasional visitors." *Rashi* (ad loc.) translates *orhay* as guests who spend a week or a month, and *porhay* (from *porha*, "flying") as visitors who pay only a short visit— that is, transient visitors. The rhyming sound of the two words may have given them their popular meaning.

OSAYK BEMITZVAH PATUR MIN HAMITZVAH (עוסק במצוה פטור מן המצוה). "He who is engaged in one religious duty is free from any other" (Sukk. 25a). The *Mishnah* (ibid.) states, "Those who are engaged in a religious errand [they go to study Torah or to redeem a captive] are free from the obligation of *Sukkah.* (For a further elucidation, see the discussion that follows in the Talmud.)

OTIYOT PORHOT (אותיות פורחות). The Talmud (A.Z. 17b, 18a) tells us that R. Hananiah (Hanina) b. Teradion, the second-century teacher and martyr, violated the Roman edict against teaching the Torah publicly. His punishment of death was horrible. Wrapped in the Torah scroll, he was placed on a pyre of green brush; fire was set to it, and wet wool was placed on his chest to prolong the agonies of death. His heartbroken disciples asked him, "Master, what seest thou?" He answered, "I see the parchment burning while the letters of the law soar upward" (*otiyot porhot*). This expression underscores the thought throughout generations that scrolls of the Torah may be destroyed, but its spirit is immortal and indestructible.

The meaning of the word *porhot* is not only "flying off," but also "blossoming" or "flourishing." Both meanings are from the same root, *porayah*; thus, even though the Torah is being burnt, the letters making up the words of the Torah will continue to flourish. They will remain and bear fruit.

OTIYOT SHEL EMET MEROHA-KIN ZEH MIZEH VESHEL SHEKER MEKORVIN (אותיות של אמת מרוחקין זה מזה ושל שקר מקורבין). See SHEKER AYN LO RAGLAYIM.

OTO HA'ISH (אותו האיש). Literally, "that person," referring to Yeshu Hanotzri. The *Mishnah* (Yeb. 4:13) uses the expression *Ish Peloni* ("that anonymous one") which seems to be an earlier appellation (cf. *The Jewish Encyclopedia*, vol. 7, p. 170; cf. also *The Babylonian Talmud, Sanhedrin* [London: The Soncino Press, 1935], pp. 456, 457, footnote 5).

In hasidic circles, the appellation *oto ha'ish* was used for a person who had strange religious thoughts. It served as a substitute for his real name, which they preferred not to use.

OY LAH LERABBANUT SHEMEKA-VERET ET BE'ALEHAH (אוי לה לרבנות שמקברת את בעליה). "[R. Johanan said:] Woe to lordship which buries [slays] its possessor, for there is not a single prophet who did not outlive four kings (Pes. 87b), as it is said, 'The vision of Isaiah, the son of Amoz, which he saw concerning Judah and Jerusalem, in the days of Uzziah, Jotham, Ahaz, and Hezekiah, kings of Judah'" (Isa. 1:1).

OY LAHEM LABRIYOT SHERO'OT VE'AYNAN YODOT MAH HAYN RO'OT (אוי להם לבריות שרואות ואינן יודעות מה הן רואות). "[R. Jose says:] Alas for people that they see but know not what they see" (Hag. 12b).

OY LERASHA OY LISHKHAYNO (אוי לרשע אוי לשכנו). If leprosy is found in a house, Scripture describes the method of cleansing the house (Lev. 14:40–42). From those verses, the Talmud (Neg. 12:6) infers, "Woe to the wicked [leprosy is a punishment for the sin of slander], woe to his neighbor [the owner of the leprous house and his neighbor on the other side of the wall]."

It is also implied that the wicked person influences his neighbors. See LO TAYLAKH RAKHIL BE'AMEKHA.

OY LI IM OMAYR, OY LI IM LO OMAYR (אוי לי אם אומר, אוי לי אם לא אומר). "Woe to me if I should speak [of them]; woe to me if I should not speak" (Kel. 17:16; B:B. 89b). This remark was made by R. Johanan b. Zakkai, concerning the objects mentioned in the *Mishnah*, which are susceptible to uncleanness and the sharp practices of traders. The Talmud (ibid.) states, "Should I speak of them," tricky deceitful people might learn them; and "should I not speak," the tricky deceitful persons might say, "The scholars are unacquainted with our practice," and will deceive us still more.

The English equivalent is "Damned if I do, damned if I don't."

PAMALYA SHEL MALAH (פמליא של מעלה). R. Safra, on concluding his morning prayers, would add a special prayer. Among other pleas, he requested of God to establish peace among the celestial family (*pamalya shel malah*—that is, the Guardian Angels of the various nations) and among the earthly family (*pamalya* *shel matah*—the assembly of the wise men) (Ber. 17a).

PANIM HADASHOT (פנים חדשות).
Literally, "new faces," referring to new guests participating in a joyous meal. The Talmud states, "Our rabbis taught, The blessing of the bridegrooms is said in the presence of ten persons all the seven days." Rab Judah said, "And that is only if new guests [*panim hadashot*] come" (Ket. 7b). *Tosafot* adds that a new guest is considered to be one who increases the joy for the bride and groom.

PARHESYA (BEFARHESYA) (פרהסיא (בפרהסיא)). Literally, "publicly" or "openly," in contradistinction to *betzinah* ("hidden") (Sukk. 49b). The Talmud (San. 74a, b) records that if a Jew is forced to transgress a religious law in public—even a minor law—he must surrender his life. And the presence of how many is required to call it a public act? A public is no less than ten persons.

PASHAT LO ET HAREGEL (פשט לו את הרגל). A phrase meaning, literally, "stretched out the leg towards him" (Ket. 108b), inferring "to default." It is as if to say, "Take the dust off my foot" or "Hang me by the leg, I have nothing to give you" (cf. *Rashi*, ad loc.). The instance cited in the *Mishnah* is the case in which a man promised a sum of money to his prospective son-in-law and then defaulted (*Pashat lo et haregel*).

PASUL LE'AYDUT (פסול לעדות).
"Disqualified as witnesses." Although the expression applies to different categories of people who are disqualified as witnesses, it is popularly used with the expressions HAMESAHAYK BEKUVYA and KEROVIM HAPESULIM LEHA'AYD. The former is the "habitual dice-player or gambler" (*Mishnah*, San. 3:3) and the latter is the "disqualification of relatives" (*Mishnah*, San. 3:4). Witnesses who are related to one another are incompetent to attest or

testify together (Mak. 6a). As relatives are incompetent to testify for or against the party to whom they are related, a fortiori, the party himself is incompetent to testify for or against himself, for "a man is related to himself" (San. 9b). See ADAM KAROV AYTZEL ATZMO; AYN ADAM MAYSIM ATZMO RASHA.

PATAH BEKHAD VESIYAYM BE-HAVIT (פתח בכד וסיים בחבית). "To commence with pitcher [*kad*] and conclude with barrel [*havit*]" (B.K. 27a). The *Mishnah* (ibid.) states a particular case and uses these two different terms within the same situation. The Talmud explains that it depends on the locality; although the majority of people refer to *kad* by the term *kad* and to *havit* by the term *havit*, there are some who refer to *havit* by the term *kad* and *kad* by the term *havit*.

Colloquially, the expression *Patah bekhad vesiyaym behavit* conveys the idea that the person concludes his words with a different intent or subject matter than the one with which he began.

PE'AMIM SHE'ADAM SHOTAYK UMEKABAYL SAKHAR AL SHETI-KATO, UFE'AMIM SHE'ADAM MEDABAYR UMEKABAYL SAKHAR AL DIBURO (פעמים שאדם שותק ומקבל שכר על שתיקתו, ופעמים שאדם מדבר ומקבל שכר על דבורו). "Sometimes a man is silent and is rewarded for his silence; at other times, a man speaks and is rewarded for his speaking" (Zeb. 115b). This is what was meant when Solomon said, "[There is . . .] a time to keep silence and a time to speak" (Eccl. 3:7).

PEH MAYFIK MARGALIYOT (פה מפיק מרגליות). Literally, "a mouth that utters gems" (Kidd. 39b)—that is, an eloquent speaker, with every word a pearl. This phrase often appears on a flyer or in a newspaper to publicize an orator-rabbi who will address a congregation or an audience.

PERUTAH UFERUTAH MITZTAREFET LEHESHBON GADOL

(פרוטה ופרוטה מצטרפת לחשבון גדול). "Every perutah [a small coin] reckons together into a large sum" (Sot. 8b). This example is used to infer adding up every minor offense that is reckoned toward punishment for the Sotah, as the verse reads, "adding one thing to another, [lit., 'one to one'] to find out the account" (Eccl. 7:27).

The expression is used colloquially for saving money and infers that every penny counts (cf. also B.B. 9b).

PIDYON SHEVUYIM MITZVAH RABBAH HI (פדיון שבויים מצוה רבה היא). "The redemption of captives is a religious duty of great importance" (B.B. 8b). In Jewish law it is placed above the important duty of feeding and clothing the poor. In the tannaitic period, however, it was ruled that a high ransom for Jewish captives was forbidden because kidnapping might become a lucrative trade. The Mishnah (Git. 4:6) states, "Captives should not be ransomed for more than their value [yotayr mikhday demayhem], as a precaution for the general good."

The Talmud (Git. 58a; Hul. 7a) is replete with incidents relating to luminaries involved in pidyon shevuyim. A society for redeeming captives, called Hevrat Pidyon Shevuyim, was organized in Venice in the seventeenth century. The Baal Shem Tov (c. 1700–1760), the father of Hasidism, would gather monies from the rich in order to redeem poor captives.

PILPUL (פילפול). A word derived from the Hebrew palpal, meaning "pepper." The term is employed in connection with talmudic studies in which logical disputation or debate takes place. Using this word suggests that the argument is as keen as strong pepper. The Talmud (Ned. 38a) discusses the giving of the Torah to Moses and his seed and concludes that "Only the Scripture dialects [pilpula

be'alma] were given to Moses alone" and in his generosity he gave it to Israel. (For other talmudic sources using the word pilpul, see B.B. 145b; B.M. 85b; Avot 6:6; Jer. Tal., Hor. 48:3.)

Aiming to clarify a talmudic subject by reasoning about matters of opinion, the pilpul at times became hair-splitting, especially in yeshivot in Poland during the sixteenth century. There were those (e.g., the Maharal, Isaiah Horowitz, Ephraim Lunctschitz, and Jair Hayyim Bacharach) who severely criticized the twisting of the plain truth by these sharp-witted arguments and felt that the pilpul should serve as a means of solving disputable problems and not serve as an end in itself. Toward the end of the eighteenth century, a change in the methods of the pilpul took place under the aegis of the Gaon of Vilna.

PINKAS (פנקס). A word derived from the Greek, meaning "account-book," "ledger," or "booklet," as in henvani al pinkaso ("the shopkeeper with his account-book") (Shab. 44b).

The Jewish community used to have a pinkas in which important occurrences and ordinances would be recorded.

PIRTZAH KORAH LAGANAV (פרצה קוראה לגנב). "A breach invites a thief" (Sukk. 26a). The Talmud states that "Keepers of gardens and orchards are free [from sitting in a sukkah] both by day and by night." The Talmud asks, Why should they not make a sukkah there and sit in it? Abaye said, "Ye shall dwell" (Lev. 23:42), which implies just as you normally dwell. Raba said, "A breach invites a thief." The thief will get his opportunity, knowing the watchman is within the sukkah. Thus, the expression Pirtzah korah laganav may have given rise to the English equivalent, "Opportunity makes a thief" (cf. also Rashi, Deut. 22:23).

PUK HAZI MAI AMA DAVAR (פוק חזי מאי עמא דבר). "Go forth and see how the public is accustomed to act" (Ber.

45a). If in doubt on a matter, go and see how the community practices. A similar advice in the Jer. Talmud (Pe'ah 7:5) is: *Kol halakhah shehi rofefet bebet din, ve'ayn attah yodaya mah tivah, tzay ure'ayh haykh hatzibbur nohayg venahog* ("All law that is wavering with *Bet Din* and you are not knowledgeable of its nature, go forth and observe the custom of the community and practice it").

PUNKT DRAYTZN (פונקט דרייצן). Literally, "just thirteen." This expression is spoken about anything that is not accurate or precise. The Talmud (Hul. 95b) relates that Samuel wrote and sent R. Johanan thirteen camel-loads of questions concerning doubtful cases of *trayfa* (*Telaysar gemalay safkay trayfata*). *Rashi* (s.v. *Traysar* [*Telaysar*] comments that this number is *lav dafka* (not necessarily). Similarly, the Talmud (Ber. 20a) states, "I see difficulties of Rab and Samuel here, and we have thirteen versions of *Uktzin* [stalks]." *Tosafot* (s.v. *Telaysar*) comments, *Utelaysar lav davka ela lashon hergil* ("It does not necessarily mean thirteen, but is used as a common wording").

Thus, when one hears an out-of-the-way figure one may say, *punkt draytzn.*

RA'AYV KEKELEV (רעב ככלב). "Hungry as a dog" (Git. 56a). During the Roman siege of Jerusalem, Ben Kalba Savu'a (first century C.E.) and his two wealthy friends, Nakdimon b. Guryon and Ben Zizit ha-Kassat, provided food and other necessities for the inhabitants of Jerusalem. The Talmud (ibid.) states, "Ben Kalba Savu'a was so-called because one would go into his house hungry as a dog [*ra'ayv kekelev*] and come out full [*savaya*]." He was well-known for his generosity and for feeding anyone who came to his home.

RABBI LO SHENA'AH (SHANAH), R. HIYA MINAYIN LO? רבי לא שנאה רב חייא מנין לו?)). "If Rabbi has not taught it, how would R. Hiyya know it?"

(Yeb. 43a; Erub. 92a). The Talmud discusses what the *halakhah* would be if a dispute was in the *Mishnah* and an anonymous statement in the *Baraita* appeared on the same subject matter and yet there was no dispute. The reply was: If Rabbi (the redactor of the *Mishnah*) had not taught it (as an anonymous ruling that was to represent the established *halakhah* and he didn't know how to settle the dispute), how would R. Hiyya (Rabbi's disciple and compiler of *Baraitot* and author of the *Tosefta*) know it? He surely would not know how to settle this dispute!

RABBI MEKHABAYD ASHIRIM (רבי מכבד עשירים). "Rabbi [and R. Akiba] showed respect to a rich man" (Erub. 86a). This is based on an exposition made by Raba b. Mari, "May he be enthroned before God forever! Appoint mercy and truth, that they may preserve him" (Ps. 61:8). When "may he be enthroned before God forever?" When he "appoint mercy and truth that they may preserve him." A person who is wealthy is able to exercise acts of mercy and truth and thus deserves respect and honor.

RAGZAN LO ALTAH BEYADAYH ELA RAGZANUTA (רגזן לא עלתה בידיה אלא רגזנותא). "[Bar Kappara lectured:] A bad-tempered man gains nothing but [the ill effect of] his temper" (Kidd. 41a). *Rashi* (ad loc.) comments that bad temper affects the health; the body becomes lean, but achieves nothing else.

RAHAMANA (HAKADOSH BARUKH HU) LIBA BA'AY (רחמנא (הקב"ה) ליבא בעי). "The All-Merciful One (the Holy One, blessed be He) requires the heart" (San. 106b); as it is written, "But the Lord looketh on the heart" (1 Sam. 16:7; cf. *Rashi*, ibid.).

RAHAMANA LITZLAN (NITZLAN) (רחמנא ליצלן (ניצלן). "The All-Merciful save us" (Shab. 84b); an expression uttered when saying something incorrect or to prevent a misfortune from occurring. The Talmud (B.K. 65b) has the word *nitzlan* instead of *litzlan*.

R. Elai and R. Hanina argued: R. Elai said to R. Hanina, "May the All-Merciful save me from accepting this view!" Then R. Hanina retorted to R. Elai, "May the All-Merciful save me from accepting your view."

RAHAMANIM BENAY RAHAMA-NIM (רחמנים בני רחמנים). "Merciful children of merciful ancestors"; a proverbial saying about the Children of Israel. The Talmud (Ket. 8b) records that Judah, the son of Nahmani, used the expression "bestowers of lovingkindness, sons of bestowers of lovingkindness, who held fast to the covenant of Abraham our father." Concerning the Israelites, it is said (Yeb. 79a) that the members of this nation are distinguished by three characteristics: They are merciful, bashful, and benevolent. "Merciful," for it is written, "And show thee mercy, and have compassion upon thee, and multiply thee" (Deut. 13:18); "Bashful," for it is written, "That His fear may be before you" (Ex. 20:17); "Benevolent," for it is written, "That he may command his children and his household . . ." (Gen. 18:19).

RATZAH HAKADOSH BARUKH HU LEZAKOT ET YISRAEL, LEFI-KHAKH HIRBAH LAHEM TORAH UMITZVOT (רצה הקד"ה לזכות את ישראל, לפיכך הרבה להם תורה ומצות). See YAGDIL TORAH VEYADIR.

REHAYLA BATAR REHAYLA AZLA, KE'UVDAY IMAH KAKH UVDAY BERATA (רחילא בתר רחילא אזלא, כעובדי אמה כך עובדי ברתא). "Ewe follows ewe; a daughter's acts are like those of her mother" (Ket. 63a). This proverb was said in conjunction with the daughter of R. Akiba, who acted in a similar way toward Ben Azzai as her mother had toward R. Akiba. Just as her mother had permitted R. Akiba to learn for twenty-four years, so did her daughter allow Ben Azzai to study for twenty-four years. Before this, Ezekiel had the epigram "Like mother, like daughter" (*ke'imah bitah*) (Ezek. 16:44)—that is, the mother was naturally the girl's primary teacher and model.

The Yiddish saying is *Duhs eple falt nisht vayt fun dem beymle* ("The apple does not fall far from the tree"). See BERA KARAYH DE'ABUHA.

RE'UYAN LE'OTAH ITZTALA (ראויין לאותה אצטלא). "[All Israel] are worthy of that robe" (Shab. 128a).

Colloquially, the phrase signifies "fit to wear the mantle suited to the post," or "worthy of the office."

RIBBON HA'OLAMIM (רבון העולמים). See RIBBONO SHEL OLAM.

RIBBONO SHEL OLAM (רבונו של עולם). "Sovereign of the Universe" (Taan. 23a); a name of God used by Honi ha-Me'aggel in a prayer for rain. In prayers it is usually used as an introduction to supplication. A similar expression with the same meaning is RIBBON HA'OLAMIM (Ber. 17a, 19a).

RO'EH VE'AYNO NIREH (רואה ואינו נראה). Literally, "sees but is not itself seen" (Ber. 10a). The Talmud asks, To whom did David refer when he said, "Bless the Lord, O my soul? And answers, He was alluding only to the Holy One, blessed be He, and to the soul. Among the five qualities of each, the Talmud states, "Just as the Holy One, blessed be He, sees, but is not seen, so the soul sees but is not seen."

Colloquially, the expression took on the connotation "He sees but doesn't take note of anything." Another interpretation is "He sees others but does not see himself."

ROSH HAMEDABRIM BEKHOL MAKOM (ראש המדברים בכל מקום).
"The chief spokesman on all occasions," a title given to the mid-second century C.E. *tanna*, Judah Bar Ilai. He was given this designation by the Roman government because he praised them, saying, "How fine are the works of this people! They have made streets, they have built bridges, they have erected public baths" (Shab. 33b). The Talmud (San. 20a) also describes the scholars of his generation as "the generation of Judah b. Ilai."

Rosh hamedabrin is sometimes applied to a principal speaker at any given occasion.

ROSHKHA VEHAR (RAYSHAYKH VEHAR) (ראשך והר (רישיך והר).
An expression meaning "strike your head against the mountain [or wall] (Hul. 39b). R. Aha, the son of R. Awia, asked R. Ashi the following: According to R. Eliezer's view, what would the law be if a heathen gave a *zuz* (a coin) to a Jewish butcher for that amount from the animal that was to be slaughtered by a Jew? His reply was that he must consider the case; if the idolator is an influential person whom the Israelite cannot put off by returning his *zuz*, then the animal is forbidden. But if he is not an influential person, the Israelite would be able to say to him, Hit your head against the mountain—that is, either take back your *zuz* or do without it.

Rashi comments on *Roshkha vehar: Haray roshkha veharay har, hakayh zeh al zeh* ("This is your head and this is a mountain, strike this on this").

The Yiddish expression *Klap zach kuhp in vant* ("Hit your head against the wall") is undoubtedly derived from this talmudic saying.

ROV GANVAY YISRAEL NINHU (רוב גנבי ישראל נינהו).
"The majority of thieves [in Pumbeditha] are Israelites" (A.Z. 70a). The Talmud states, "Some thieves came up to Pumbeditha and

opened many casks. Raba said, 'The wine is permitted' [and is not considered *yayin nesekh*]. What is the reason? Because the majority of thieves [in that part of the country] are Israelites."

Pumbeditha was known for its thieves and robbers. R. Giddal b. Torta said: "If a Pumbedithan joins you [on the road], change your inn [lest he rob you]" (Hul. 127a). See LO SIGNOV; SOF GANAV LITLIYAH.

RU'AH HAKODESH (רוח הקודש).
"Holy spirit." According to the Talmud (Yom. 9b; San. 11a), "With the passing of the last prophets, Haggai, Zechariah, and Malachai, the Holy Spirit [of prophetic inspiration] departed from Israel." The Talmud (A.Z. 20b) cites various progressions of saintliness, according to R. Phineas b. Jair. Among them is the degree that *Hasidut mayvi'ah liday ru'ah hakodesh* ("saintliness leads to the [possession of] the Holy Spirit"). Thus, when a saintly person has intuition concerning a certain matter, it is said of him that he has *ru'ah hakodesh*.

When speaking of spirituality, the term *ruhaniyut (ruhniyot)* is used, in contradistinction to *gashmiyut* ("corporeality" or "materiality").

SABA BEVAYTA PAHA BEVAYTA, SAVTA BEVAYTA SIMA BEVAYTA (סבא ביתא פאחא בביתא, סבתא בביתא סימא ביתא).
(R. Hezekiah said: People say), "an old man in the house is a burden in the house, and old woman in the house is a treasure in the house" (Ar. 19a). In popular opinion, a woman is never too old to be useful, whereas an old man may be a burden, in that he does nothing.

SADNA DE'ARA HAD HU (סדנא דארעא חד הוא).
"The land [although consisting of disconnected fields] is one block" (Kidd. 27b). By taking symbolical possession of one field, one takes possession of the whole complex contracted for. Conversely, if a person delivered ten cows tied to one cord and said to someone,

"Acquire this one," that person would not acquire all of them. The reason one would acquire all the fields is because all land is regarded as ultimately connected.

This expression has been paraphrased as "all customs of people are similar in every place."

SAKANOT NEFASHOT (סכנת נפשות).

"Danger of life." The Mishnah (Hul. 3:5) rules, "If [an animal] ate poison or was bitten by a snake, it is not forbidden as trefah, but it is forbidden as a danger to life."

The phrase sakanot nefashot is used in any instance in which any evil, harm, or injury is possible. The Talmud (Bez. 22a) states, Sakanot nefashot doheh Shabbat ("When danger of life is involved [e.g., extinguishing a conflagration] is permitted even on the Sabbath").

SATAN MEKATRAYG (שטן מקטרג).

"Satan, the accuser," whose main functions are temptation, accusation, and punishment. Although the word "Satan" is used in Numbers 22:22 and 32 as an angel trying to save Balaam from rushing to his own destruction, the Satan, as a particular angel who opposes with false accusations, first appears in Zechariah (3). In the Book of Job (1–2), he questions Job's integrity and suggests to the Lord that it be tested. In 1 Chron. 21:1, Satan is said to have provoked David to take a census of Israel and, as a result, seventy thousand Israelites perished.

The Talmud (B.B. 16b) states, "Resh Lakish said Satan, the evil impulse [yaytzer hara], and Angel of Death [Malakh Hamavet] are all one." Satan is identified with the evil impulse, who opposes and obstructs, and with the Angel of Death, who leads man astray, brings accusations against him, and eventually slays him. R. Jose warned, "A man should never speak in such a way as to give an opening to Satan" (AL YIFTAH ADAM PIV LASATAN). Only one day of the year, on Yom Kippur, is Satan silenced before the Throne of Glory

and he even becomes a defender of Israel; Satan has no permission to act as an accuser then. The Talmud (Yom. 20a) asks, "Whence [is that derived]?—Rama b. Hama said: HaSaTaN ("The Satan"), in numerical value, is three hundred and sixty-four. That means, on three hundred and sixty-four days he has permission to act as an accuser, but on Yom Kippur he has no permission to act as an accuser."

In time of danger, Satan accuses (Satan mekatrayg) against man (cf. Rashi, Gen. 42:4; Deut. 23:10). Several prayer recitals during the yearly cycle plead with God to drive Satan away. In the evening prayer Hashkivaynu, the text reads, "Remove from us the enemy, pestilence . . . and Satan." In the morning prayer Yehi Ratzon . . . shetatzilaynu, we ask to be spared from "the corruption of Satan." In the Hineni prayer on the High Holy Days, the Sheli'ah Tzibbur requests, "and rebuke the Satan that he accuse me not." On Rosh Hashanah, six biblical verses are uttered prior to blowing the shofar (beginning with Koli shamata, the initial letters of which form the acrostic Kera Satan— "tear Satan"). The Talmud (R.H. 16b) states that we sound a teki'ah and teru'ah when sitting, as well as when standing, so as "to confuse the accuser" (le'arvayv Ha-Satan). Rashi (ad loc.) comments that the Jews' devotion to the precepts nullifies Satan's accusations against them.

In order to mark a halt between the optional and obligatory blowing of the shofar, that is to say, between the blasts during Elul, which are a custom, and the blasts on Rosh Hashanah, which are Torah-commanded, the shofar is not blown on the day before Rosh Hashanah (S. Ganzfried, Kitzur Shulhan Arukh 128:2). This is done, according to R. Moses b. Abraham of Przemsyl (Premsla), to confuse Satan, to keep him ignorant of the coming of Rosh Hashanah when he brings charges against man, and to have him believe that the Day of Judgment has already passed (Matteh Moshe, reprint,

Rabbi M. Knoblowicz [England, 1958] sec. 5, 778).

SAYATA DISHMAYA (SAYATA HU MIN SHEMAYA) (סייעתא דשמיא (סייעתא הוא מן שמיא)). See YAGATI VELO MATZATI AL TA'AMAYN.

SE'UDAT MITZVAH (סעודת מצוה).
"A feast connected with a religious deed" (Pes. 49a). It is written in the Talmud (ibid.), "It was taught," R. Simeon said, "Every feast which is not in connection with a religious deed, a scholar must derive no enjoyment"—for example, the feast at the betrothal of the daughter of a priest to an Israelite. It was considered a blemish upon her family to marry beneath her. Another example is a marriage of a daughter of a scholar to an ignoramus.

SEVARA (סברא).
"A logical deduction" or "a conclusion by reasoning." The Talmud (Shab. 107b) states, *asvara li*, that is, Bar Hamdurie "explained it to me." Colloquially, one says *al pi sevara* ("according to reason").

SHAGUR BEFIV (שגור בפיו).
A phrase meaning "fluent." R. Hanina b. Dosa used to pray for the sick and say, "This one will die, this one will live." He was asked how he was able to determine this. He replied, "If my prayer comes out fluently [*im shegurah tefillati befi*], I know that he is accepted, but if not, then I know that he is rejected" (*Mish*. Ber. 5:5); that is, the prayer is rejected.

SHAKLA VETARYA (שקלא וטריא).
Literally, "to take up and throw back," that is, "to argue" or "negotiate" in matters such as *halakhah* or in a similar situation. The Talmud has *delo shakil vetari behadayh* ("with whom he was not accustomed to deal") (B.M. 64a), or *had shakil vetari* ("one engages in discussion") (Hag. 11b). In Yiddish, one may say *huhbn a shakla vetarya*, meaning "to deliberate carefully."

SHALOM BAYIT (שלום בית).
"Peace of the home" (Shab. 23b). Raba said, "If one must choose between the house light [for *Shabbat*] and the Hanukkah light or wine for *Kiddush*, the house light is preferable, on account of the peace of the home."

R. Abbahu said that the verse in Lamentations 3:17, "And thou hast removed my soul from peace," refers to the kindling of the light on the Sabbath. The loss of light brings loss of peace because one may stumble in the dark (cf. *Rashi*, Shab. 25b, s.v. *Hadlakat nayr be-Shabbat*).

SHAYM HAVAYA (שם הויה).
The transformed name of God used instead of the Divine Name (YHVH). The reason for the rearrangement of the letters is so that the Tetragrammaton should not be pronounced. The high priest pronounced it ten times in Temple times in the course of the Yom Kippur service (Yom. 39b). He uttered it inaudibly, so as to keep it concealed from the people.

The Divine Name, variously referred to as *Shaym Hameforash* ("Distinctive Name") *Shaym Hayihud* ("Unique Name"), and *Shaym ben Arba Otiyot* ("Quadriliteral Name") is not pronounced because Scripture states, "This my My Name forever" (*le'olam*) (Ex. 3:15). The word *le'olam*, written defectively without a *vav*, can be read *le'alaym* ("to conceal"). Thus, the Tetragrammaton is read *aleph dalet nun yud* (A-do-nai, meaning "Lord") (cf. Kidd. 71a). According to the *Mishnah* (San. 10:1), he who pronounces the Divine Name according to its letters loses his share in the future world.

SHAYV VE'AL TA'ASEH (שב ואל תעשה).
Literally, "sit and do not act" (Erub. 100a). If, in order to observe a *mitzvah*, one must sin, we say to this person, Abstain from doing the *mitzvah* and do not sin. The principle is that by abstaining from a *mitzvah* with *Shayv ve'al ta'aseh*, it is less stringent than committing a transgression with one's own hands.

SHE'AT HAKOSHER (שעת הכשר). "A period of fitness" (Shab. 136a; Pes. 83a); a propitious time.

SHEKER AYN LO RAGLAYIM (שקר אין לו רגלים). "A falsehood has no leg to stand on," because, in the final end, falsehood is revealed (cf. *Rashi*, Prov. 12:19). The Talmud (Shab. 104a) asks, "And why does falsehood [stand] on one foot, whilst truth has a bricklike foundation? (Each of the letters in the Hebrew word *SHeKeR* is insecurely poised on one leg—both the *kuf* and *raysh* stand on one leg. In ancient days the bottom of the *shin* also protruded a single leg, whereas the letters in *EMeT* are firmly set; both the letters on the ends and the *mem* in the middle are resting on a horizontal bar). The answer given is "Truth stands firm, falsehood does not" (*Kushta Ka'ay Shikra lo Ka'ay*; the basis for the expression *Sheker ayn lo raglayim*).

The Talmud also asks, Why are the letters of *SHeKeR* close together whilst those of *EMeT* are far apart? (*kuf, raysh,* and *shin* follow each other in the alphabet, whereas the three letters in *EMeT* are far apart: *aleph* at the beginning, *mem* in the middle, and *tav* as the final letter of the alphabet). The Talmud answers, "Falsehood is frequent, truth is rare."

A Yiddish saying, emphasizing the fact that the *sheker* (falsehood) is rampant, is: *Sheker ayn lo raglayim- der sheker huht nisht kayn fis, uhber der emet huht yuh fis; iz fuhrt der sheker in a karete un der emet geyt tzu fis.* (*Sheker ayn lo raglayim—sheker* has no feet; but *emet* [truth] has feet. Therefore, *sheker* rides in a chariot and *emet* goes on foot.) In a similar vein, the accent of the word *sheker* is *mile'ayl* (a penultimate accent; thus the accent is on *she*) and the Hebrew word *le'ayl* means "above," whereas the accent in the word *emet* is *milera* (an ultimate accent; thus the accent is on *met*) and the Hebrew word *lera* means "down" or "below." Here again, the *sheker* reigns over *emet*.

Another Yiddish saying concerning *Sheker ayn lo raglayim* is: *Der sheker huht kayn fis nit, iz er duh geblibn; der emet huht fis, iz er antluhfn* ("Falsehood has no leg to stand on, he remains here; truth has feet, it ran away"). Concerning truth (*emet*), a Yiddish saying is *Der emet iz in Siddur* ("The truth is in the prayerbook"), intimating that the truth doesn't exist. See SHEKER ASUR LEDABAYR, AVAL ET HA'EMET LO TAMID HOVAH LESAPAYR.

SHEKULAH TZEDAKAH KENEGED KOL HAMITZVOT (שקולה צדקה כנגד כל המצות). R. Assi said, "Charity is equivalent to all other religious precepts combined" (B.B. 9a).

SHA'ARAY DIMAH LO NINALU (שערי דמעה לא ננעלו). "The gates of weeping are not closed" (Ber. 32b), as it says, "Hear my prayer, O Lord, and give ear unto my cry, keep not silence at my tears" (Ps. 39:13). This verse shows that although R. Eleazar said that from the day on which the Temple was destroyed, the gates of prayer have been closed, the gates of tears remain open (see also B.M. 32a).

SHA'AT HADHAK SHANI (שעת הדחק שאני). "A time of emergency is different" (Shab. 45a). Rab was asked if it is permitted to move a Hanukkah lamp on the *Shabbat* after it has been extinguished on account of the Parsees? The Parsees, who were fire-worshipers, forbade the Jews to have fire in their homes during their (the Parsees') festivities. And since the Hanukkah lamp was lit near the street, it would have to be hidden. The answer was that in time of emergency, it was different and thus permitted.

The saying *besha'at hadhak* applies to any emergency, during which time the law is lenient.

SHELKHA KODEM LEKHOL ADAM (שלך קודם לכל אדם). The dictum, "Save that there shall be no poor among you" (Deut. 15:4) is an exhortation against bringing oneself to poverty; thus, "Thine takes precedence over all others" (B.M. 30b). It is as though to say ADAM KAROV AYTZEL ATZMO.

SHELO MATZINU SHU'AL SHE-MAYT BA'AFAR PIR (שלא מצינו שועל שמת בעפר פיר). "We do not find that a fox should die of the dust of his den" (Ket. 71b). Just as the fox does not die from the dust of his den because he is used to it, so one is not injured by an element to which one is accustomed.

SHELOSHAH DEVARIM MEVATLIN GEZAYRAH KASHAN: TEFILLAH, TZEDAKAH, UTESHUVAH (שלשה דברים מבטלין גזירה קשה: תפלה, צדקה, ותשובה). "Three things cancel evil decrees: prayer, alms, and repentence. Some say change of name, change of conduct, and change of place" (Jer. Tal., Ta'an. 2:1). See Bab. Tal., R.H. 16b.

SHEMOR ATZMEKHA SHELO TE-HETA (שמור עצמך שלא תחטא). R. Samuel b. Nahmani said, in the name of R. Jonathan, "Guard thyself so that thou shouldst not sin" (Ber. 23a). This is the meaning given to the verse, "Guard thy foot when thou goest to the house of God" (Eccl. 4:17).

SHEMOR LI VE'ESHMOR LAKH (שמור לי ואשמור לך). "[If a man said to another] keep this article for me and I will keep another for you" (Mishnah, B.M. 6:6), he ranks as a paid bailee, and if it is stolen, he is held responsible. Colloquially, the wording in the Mishnah took on a meaning as if to say, "If you do me a favor, I will return the favor" or "If you support me, I will support you." The English equivalent is "You scratch my back and I'll scratch yours." In Yiddish, Eyn hant vasht di tzveyte ("One hand washes the other").

SHENAYIM OHAZIM BETALIT (שנים אוחזים בטלית). The Mishnah (B.M. 1:1) discusses two who hold a garment,

each claiming that it is his. The expression is applied when there are rival claimants to ownership in business or domestic circles.

SHETIKAH KEHODA'AH DAMYA (שתיקה כהודאה דמיא). "Silence is tantamount to admission" (Yeb. 87b; B.M. 37b); that is, when a person listens and keeps quiet, it is as though he admits and agrees with or he accepts what is being said. See SHETIKUTEKHA YAFAH MIDIBUREKHA; MI SHELO YISHTOK MAYATZMO, YASHTIKUHU AHAYRIM.

SHETIKUTEKHA YAFAH MIDIBU-REKHA (שתיקותיך יפה מדיבוריך). "Your silence is better than your speech" (Git. 46b). The Mishnah states, If a man divorces his wife because he finds her to be incapable of bearing children and she remarries and has children from the second husband and then demands her ketubah settlement from the first, R. Judah says that he can say to her, The less you say the better. Rashi (ad loc.) explains that he can say, If I would have known in the end that I would have to give you a ketubah settlement, I would not have divorced you. See MI SHELO YISHTOK MAYATZMO, YASHTIKUHU AHAYRIM; SHETIKAH KEHODA'AH DAMYA.

SHFIKHUT DAMIM (שפיכות דמים). "Shedding of blood" (Ar. 15b); actually killing a person. The Talmud states that "Whosoever speaks slander increases his sins even up to [the degree of] the three [cardinal] sins: idolatry, incest, and the shedding of blood." Cain said to God, "My punishment is greater than I can bear" (Gen. 4:13). The Hebrew word translated as "than I can bear" may also be rendered as "to be forgiven." Putting another to shame in public is one of the gravest crimes. The Talmud states, "Shaming a fellow-man in public is like shedding blood" (B.M. 58b), since the blood is drained from the victim's face, which is equivalent to shedding his blood. "Let a

man throw himself into a blazing furnace rather than shame a fellow-man in public" (Ber. 43b).

SH'HI PH'I (שה"י פה"י). An abbreviation for *Shabbat Hayyom* ("Today is Sabbath"), *Pesah Hayyom* ("Today is Passover") (Meg. 13b). Haman, giving false accusations, told Ahasuerus that "neither do they [the Jews] keep the king's laws; they evade taxes the whole year by their loitering and sauntering [*sh'hi ph'i*]. They give empty excuses by saying it is Sabbath today or Pesah today and are unable to work for the king" (cf. *Rashi*, ad loc.). The expression among Jews became associated with "giving various pretexts" or "all sorts of excuses."

SHILHAY DEKAITA KASHYA MI-KAITA (שלהי דקייטא קשיא מקייטא). "The expiration of the summer is more trying than the summer itself" (Yom. 29a). By the conclusion of the summer, the atmosphere is so hot that any additional hot weather makes it relatively intolerable.

SHINUI HASHAYM (שנוי השם). "Change of name" (R.H. 16b). R. Isaac said: "Four things cancel the doom of a man": among them is change of name, as it is written, "As for Sarai thy wife, thou shalt not call her name Sarai, but Sarah shall be her name" (Gen. 23:15). *Rashi* (ad loc.) comments that the name "Sarai" denotes "My princess, for Me but not for others"; "Sarah" denotes "a princess for all."

Usually, when one is gravely ill, a name is changed or added. This practice dates back to the Middle Ages, when R. Yehudah he-Hasid wrote, "His name should be changed to reverse the decree" (*Sefer Hasidim*, no. 255). Adding such names as Hayyim or among *Sephardim*, Hai ("life"), Raphael ("may God heal"), Hezekiah ("may God give strength") for a male and Hayyah for females is desirable (cf. Macy Nulman, *The Encyclopedia of Jewish Prayer*

[Northvale, NJ: Jason Aronson Inc., 1993], pp. 302, 303).

SHIVAH MEDORAY GEHINNOM (שבעה מדורי גיהנום). In Scripture (Josh. 15:8; Jer. 32:35, ff.), Gay Ben-Hinam is mentioned as being a valley southwest of Jerusalem. Children were sacrificed there to Moloch and the name *Gehinnom* (*Gehenna*) became synonymous with hell—the place to which the wicked are condemned after death. The Talmud (Erub. 19a) tells of the various gates of *Gehenna*, as well as mentioning seven other appellations, the *shivah medoray gehinnom* ("The seven divisions of Gehinnim") (Sot. 10b). According to legend, there are "The Seven Departments of Hell" through which sinners must pass, with a different punishment in each (cf. *Rayshit Hokhmah; Shayvet Musar*).

When a person experiences much trouble and suffering, the phrase *Shivah medoray gehinnom* is often used.

SHOR HABAR (שור הבר). The *Shor-Habar* ("wild bull"), like the Leviathon ("great fish"), is reserved for the banquet arranged for the righteous in the days of Messiah and, according to others, in the World to Come. In the *Mishnah* (Kil. 8:6), the "*Shor-Habar* belongs to the category of *behaymah* [a domestic animal], but R. Jose said to the category of *hayyah* [a wild animal]."

The *Shor-Habar*, as well as the Leviathon, are part of a cumulative song in Yiddish, called *Vuhs vet zayn az Mashiah vet kumen* (cf. A.Z. Idelsohn, *The Folk Song of the East European Jews* [1932], vol. IX p. 6, no. 16). In Hebrew the song begins with the words *Mah nokhal bise'udah hazo?* (cf. *Oneg Shabbat*, R. Betzallel, ed. [Jerusalem, Israel], pp. 112, 113).

Colloquially, the term *Shor-Habar* has come to mean a "very strong man."

SHOTEH AYN LO TAKANAH (שוטה אין לו תקנה). "An imbecile has no remedy" (Nid. 13b). The Talmud discusses the case of a priest who is an imbecile and who can be fed with the *terumah* (the heave-offering). See AYN SHOTEH NIFGA.

SHRAGA BETIHARA MAI AHANI?
(שרגא בטיהרא מאי אהני). The moon cried out to the Sovereign of the Universe, "Of what use is a lamp in broad daylight?" (Hul. 60b). If something is untimely, of what use is it? (For the argument that the moon had with the Almighty for making it smaller than the sun, see the Talmud [ibid.].)

SIHAT HULIN (שיחת חולין). "Secular conversation," not involving Torah or wisdom. R. Eliezer said, "All my life did I ever utter secular speech" (*Miyamai lo sahti sihat hulin* (Sukk. 28a). The same is said of R. Johanan b. Zakkai (ibid.).

R. Aha b. Adda, in the name of Rab (some ascribe it to R. Aha b. Abba, in the name of R. Hamnuna, in the name of Rab), said, "Even the ordinary talk of scholars needs studying" (AFILU SIHAT HU-LIN SHEL TALMIDAY HAKHAMIM TZRIKHAH TAL-MUD) (A.Z. 19b), for it is said, "And whose leaf doth not wither, and whatsoever he doest shall prosper" (Ps. 1:3). The table-talk of the learned is likened to the leaves, the least useful produce of the tree (see also Sukk. 21b). See SIHATAN SHEL YISRAEL TORAH HI.

SIMAN YAFEH (סמן יפה). "A good sign" that the future will be good (Ber. 24b). R. Zera said, according to the school of R. Hamnuna, "If one sneezes in his prayer, it is a good sign for him, that as they give him relief below [on earth] so they give him relief above [in Heaven]."

SOF ADAM LAMUT VESOF BE-HAYMAH LISHHITAH (סוף אדם למות וסוף בהמה לשחיטה). When R. Johanan (another version reads, R. Johanan said it was R. Meir) finished the Book of Job, he said the following, "The end of man is to die, and the end of a beast is to be slaughtered" (Ber. 17b).

SOFO MOKHI'AH AL TEHILATO
(סופו מוכיח על תחלתו). "[A person's] final words reveal what his intent was in the beginning" (Ned. 48a).

STIRADIK (סתירהדיק). A Yiddish word derived from the Hebrew *satar*, meaning "to contradict" or "invalidate." It is written in the Talmud, *Lo dayikh shede-varekha sotrim divray David avikha ela shedevarekha sotrim zeh et zeh* ("Not only do thy words contradict those of David, thy father, but they contradict one another") (Shab. 30a).

TAFASTA MERUBAH LO TAFASTA, TAFASTA MU'AT TAFASTA (תפסת מרובה לא תפסת (תפסת), תפסת מועט תפסת (תפסת)). A prover-bial saying, "If you grasp a lot, you cannot hold it; if you grasp a little, you can hold it." Another way of phrasing it is "If you take hold of the larger thing, you may lose your hold; if of the smaller, you will hold it" (R.H. 4b; Sukk. 5b). Similar expressions in the English language are: "A bird in the hand is worth two in the bush," or "Grasp all, lose all," or "To overreach is to undergain." See MISTAPAYK BEMU'AT.

TALMID HAKHAM (pl. TALMIDAY HAKHAMIM) (תלמיד חכם (תלמידי חכמים). See MAH BAYN HAKHAM LENAVON? NAVON DOMEH LESHULHANI TAGAR.

TALMID HAHAM TZARIKH SHE-YEHAY VO EHAD MISHMONAH BISHMINIT (GA'AVAH) (תלמיד חכם צריך שיהא בו אחד משמונה בשמינית (גאוה). "A disciple of the Sages should possess an eighth [of pride]" in order to maintain his self-respect (Sot. 5a). A hint about this number is the eighth verse in the eighth *Sidrah* in *Bereishit: Katonti mikol hahasadim* ("I am not worthy of all the mercies") (Gen. 32:11).

TALMIDAY HAKHAMIM AYN LA-HEM MENUHAH (תלמידי חכמים אין להם מנוחה). ["R. Hiyya b.

Ashi said, in the name of Rab]: The learned men [scholars] have no rest either in this world or in the World to Come (Ber. 64a). It is written, 'They go from strength to strength; each one will appear before God in Zion'" (Ps. 84:8). As they achieve knowledge and scholarship, they do this by progressing slowly. Each obstacle overcome in study makes the *talmid hakham* stronger in realizing his spiritual strivings, until he reaches his objectives and appears before God.

TALMIDAY HAKHAMIM MARBIM SHALOM BA'OLAM (תלמידי חכמים מרבים שלום בעולם). "Disciples of the

wise [that is, scholars] increase peace in the world." This pronouncement is of talmudic origin and it appears in tractates Berakhot (64a in greater detail), Nazir, Yevamot, and Keritot. A mnemonic device to remember these tractates is the word *BaNaYiKH* ("your children"), as in the verse that follows in the detailed portion: "And all your children [*banayikh*] will be students of *Hashem*" (Isa. 54:13). It seems that this saying, by R. Eliezer, on behalf of R. Hanina, was deliberately placed at the end of these tractates so that a person, after studying them, would not think that the scholars were quarrelsome persons, constantly arguing with each other. On the contrary, scholars increase peace. Their objective in the controversial discussions and disputes during study is to clarify the *halakhah* and their mission is called MILHEMTAH SHEL TORAH ("to engage in the battle of the Torah"). As a result, AYLU VE'AYLU DIVRAY ELOHIM HAYYIM ("the utterance of both are words of the living God").

The Torah is known as *shirah* ("song"), as is written, "Now, therefore, write ye this song for you, and teach thou it the children of Israel" (Deut. 31:19). These talmudic disputations have been compared to *shirah*—specifically, choral singing. Choral singing can be of a polyphonic texture (two or more voice parts, each having individual melodic significance), atonal (disregarding any key relationship at all), one singing in a higher register and one singing in a lower register, or one having a lighter voice while the other a heavier voice, and it may sound like confusion and disorder—but, in truth, it is not. From these dissonances come beautiful melodies, sweet to the ears. So, too, when engaging in SHAKLA VETARYA ("discussion," "deliberation"), all the contradictions and altercations become rightful and beloved before the Almighty (cf. R. Barukh Halevi Epstein, *Barukh She'amar* [Tel Aviv: Am Olam Ltd. Publishing Co., 1968], p. 277).

TALMUD TORAH KENEGED KULAM (תלמוד תורה כנגד כלם). The

Mishnah (*Pe'a* 1:1) enumerates the good deeds for which man is rewarded in his life and concludes with the declaration that "study of the Torah is equal to them all." This selection from the *Mishnah*, as well as the talmudic selection *Aylu devarim she'adam* (Shab. 127a), are part of the Preliminary Section of the daily liturgy.

TARTAY DESATRAY (תרתי דסתרי).

"Two statements or things contradicting each other"—that is, discrepancies. The Talmud (B.K. 21a) gives the ruling for payment regarding two different types of rentals: the one ordering payment to Simeon deals with premises that were for hire; whereas the ruling in which payment of rent is not necessary refers to the absence of an agreement and the fact that the premises were not for hire. The Talmud asks, "Do not the two statements contradict each other?" *Rashi* (ad loc., s.v. *Tarti*) comments, *Tarti mili kamar desatrin ahadadi* ("The two situations contradict each other").

TARTAY KALAY MAYHAD GAVRA LO MISHTAMA'AY (תרתי קלי מחד) (גברא לא משתמעי). "Two utterances proceeding from one man cannot be distinguished" (R.H. 27a). The Talmud discusses a case of blowing the *shofar* into a pit or a cistern or a barrel and an echo accompanies the sound of the *shofar*. Has one performed one's duty? The Talmud states that one has not and then asks, "Why should this be? Cannot he have performed his duty [by hearing] the beginning of the blast before the sound is confused [with the echo]?" And answers, "The truth is that two utterances proceeding from one man cannot be distinguished."

This answer has come to be used for a person talking out of "both sides of his mouth." See TRAY KALAY LO MISHTAMA'AY.

TaRYaG MITZVOT (תרי"ג מצות). The total number of biblical precepts is referred to as *TaRYaG Mitzvot* (six hundred and thirteen commandments: *tav* = 400, *raysh* = 200, *yud* = 10, *gimmel* = 3). "R. Simlai, when preaching, said, Six hundred and thirteen precepts were communicated to Moses: three hundred and sixty-five negative precepts [*SHaSaH Mitzvot Lo Ta'aseh*], corresponding to the number of solar days [in the year], and two hundred and forty-eight positive precepts [*RaMaH Mitzvot Asayh*], corresponding to the number of members of man's body" (Mak. 23b). (See *Encyclopedia Judaica*, vol. 5, [Jerusalem: Keter Publishing House Ltd., 1973], pp. 763–782, for a complete listing. See also MINYAN OTIYOT SHEL ASERET HADIBROT HAYM TaRYaG.)

TAVO ALAV BERAKHAH (תבא עליו ברכה). A phrase appearing in numerous tractates (Erub. 29b; Pes. 32a, 92b; Yeb. 90a; Git. 54a; Ket. 19a; A.Z. 63b), meaning "May he be blessed," in that he acts rightly. Colloquially, the expression is used to say "good for him" for doing a

kind act or doing something LIFNIM MISHURAT HADIN.

TaYKU (TIKU) (תיקו). In talmudic discussions, when no answer is obtainable despite all attempts, the word TAYKU (TIKU) is used (B.B. 62b; B.K. 96a; Hul. 46a). It is composed of the initial letters of four words: *Tishbi Yetaraytz Kushyot Ve'abayot* ("Elijah the Tishbite will solve all difficulties and inquiries"), and is based on the tradition that Elijah, the forerunner of the Messiah, will settle all doubtful questions (c. *Tosafot Yom Tov*, Eduy., chap 8, *Mishnah* 7). According to others, it means "Let it stand"—that is, the question remains undecided (cf. Marcus Jastrow, *Dictionary*, vol. 2 [New York: Title Publishing Company, 1943], p. 1331). Another opinion is that it is derived from the word *tik* (meaning "briefcase" or "portfolio"). Just as one does not know its contents, so one does not know the answer (cf. *Arukh*, s.v. *Tak*).

One may even utter the word TAYKU (TIKU) in general parlance when a difficult problem arises and there is no solution.

TAYN LI YAVNEH VEHAKHAMEHAH (תן לי יבנה וחכמיה). "Give me Yavneh and its wise men" (Git. 56b). After the destruction of the Second Temple, R. Johanan b. Zakkai left besieged Jerusalem and arrived at the Roman camp. It was here that he requested of the emperor a special favor to spare Yavneh and its scholars. In Yavneh he assembled a group of scholars and re-established the Sanhedrin (R.H. 31a).

Between 70 and 132 C.E., Yavneh was the great city, the city of Jewish scholarship. Yavneh took the place of Jerusalem and became the religious and national center of Jewry.

TE'ANO HITIM VEHODAH LO BISE'ORIM (טענו חטים והודה לו בשעורים). Literally, "[the plaintiff] claims wheat while [the defendant] admits barley" (B.K. 35b). This talmudic saying means "to dodge the question" or "to

evade an issue." In Yiddish, the saying is Ikh zuhg im kluhtz, er entfert mir boydem ("I tell him 'beam' and he answers 'attic'").

TEFILLOT KENEGED TEMIDIN TIKNOM (תפלות כנגד תמידין תקנום). "The tefillot ['prayers'] were instituted [by the Men of the Great Assembly] to correspond to the daily sacrifices" (Ber. 26b).

TEVEN ATTAH MAKHNIS LA'AFARAYIM? (תבן אתה מכניס לעפריים?). "Wouldst thou carry straw to Hafarayim?" (Men. 85a). Hafarayim was a place where the supply of straw was plentiful. The expression implies, "Are you bringing something to a place that has an abundance of this type of product?" The English equivalent is "Like carrying coal to Newcastle."

TEVI'UT AYIN (טביעות עין). Literally, "an impression of the eye." The Talmud (Shab. 114a) records in the name of R. Johanan, "Who is a scholar to whom a lost article is returned on his recognition thereof (bitvi'ut ayin)?" (Generally, the ordinary person must give identification when claiming a lost article; the scholar, however, is believed simply if he states that he recognizes it; B.M. 23b.) The Talmud answers "That [scholar] who is particular to turn his shirt," (It seems that the scholar turned the seams and rough edges to be on the inside, demonstrating his meticulous character, a trait not popular with all the people).

TINOK SHENISHBAH (תינוק שנשבה). "A child who was taken captive among gentiles" (Shab. 68b). He or she is not to blame for committing any violation on the Sabbath because the laws of the Sabbath were never known to the child.

TITBAREKHU MIN HASHAMAYIM (תתברכו מן השמים). When the High Priest is consoled upon a death in his family, the people say to him, "May we be thy atonement." His answer to them is "Be

ye blessed of Heaven" (Titbarekhu min Hashamayim) (Mishnah, San. 2:1).

TOKH KEDAY DIBUR (תוך כדי דבור). "Within the time of an utterance" (B.K. 73b; Shebu. 32a). The blessing of Hashkivaynu on Friday evening concludes with Haporays sukkat shalom alaynu . . . ("Who spreads the shelter of peace upon us . . ."), instead of Shomayr amo Yisrael la'ad ("Who protects His people Israel forever"), as it would on a weekday. If one forgets and says, Shomayr amo Yisrael la'ad, instead of Haporays sukkat shalom alaynu, and he becomes aware of his error within the time period known as keday dibur (the amount of time needed to say the words Shalom alekha rabbi umori ("Peace be upon you, my rabbi and teacher"), he should immediately say, after the word la'ad, the words Haporays, and so forth. If he waited longer than keday dibur after completing the word la'ad, he need not say Haporays, nor must he repeat the blessing (Mishnah Berurah 267:9).

TOLEH BEDA'AT AHAYRIM (תולה בדעת אחרים). "Leaves the choice to others" (Git. 25a), as opposed to toleh beda'at atzmo (retaining it in one's own hand)— for example, if a person is married to two women whose names are the same and then he writes a get specifying that it should become valid for the wife who walks out of his door first. This is considered toleh beda'at ahayrim.

TORAH LISHMAH (תורה לשמה). "Torah study for its own sake." R. Alexandri said, "He who studies the Torah for its own sake makes peace in the Upper Family [i.e., the angels] and the Lower Family [man]." Rab said, "It is as though he built the heavenly and the earthly Temples." R. Johanan said, "He also shields the whole world [from consequences of its sins]." Levi said, "He also hastens the redemption" (San. 99b). R. Banna'ah said, "Whosoever occupies himself with the Torah for its own sake, his learning becomes an elixir of life to him. But, whosoever occupies himself with the Torah not for its own sake, it becomes to him a deadly poison" (Taan. 7a). The Talmud states in another tractate (Pes. 50b), Rab Judah said, in Rab's name, "A man should always occupy himself with Torah and good deeds, though it is not for their own sake, for out of [doing good] with an ulterior motive there comes [doing good] for its own sake" (MITOKH SHELO LISHMAH BA LISHMAH). (See also *Avot* 6:1.)

TORAH MATESHET KOHO SHEL ADAM (תורה מתשת כחו של אדם).
"Torah weakens [*mateshet*] the strength of man," through constant study. A verse in Isaiah 28:29 reads, "He is wonderful in counsel and excellent in wisdom [*tushiyah*]"—that is, referring to the Torah. "R. Hanina said, Why is the Torah called *tushiyah*? Because it weakens the strength of man" (San. 26b); *tushiyah* is linked with *mateshet*, "to weaken."

TORAH MEHAZERET AL AKHSANYA SHELAH (תורה מחזרת על אכסניא שלה).
"The Torah seeks its home" (B.M. 85a)—that is, it becomes hereditary in the family after three generations.

TORAH SHE'AYN LA BAYT AV AYNAH TORAH (תורה שאין לה בית אב אינה תורה).
"Torah [or halakhah] that is not inherited from ancestors [and has no foundation] is not Torah" (Jer. Tal., Shab. 17:1).

TORAH UGEDULAH BEMAKOM EHAD (תורה וגדולה במקום אחד).
"Torah and greatness in one place" (Git. 59a). The Talmud cites this remark when "Rabbah, the son of Raba, or, as some say, R. Hillel, the son of Wallas, said, Between Moses and Rabbi we do not find one who was supreme both in Torah and worldly affairs."

This became a colloquial expression, as did its Yiddish equivalent, TZU GOTT UN TZU LAYT ("To God and people"), signifying

that the person is both knowledgeable and well-rounded and is a delight for the community.

TORAKH HATZIBBUR (TIRKHA DETZIBBURA) (טרחא דציבורא) (טרחא דציבורא) (הציבור טורח).
The Talmud (Ber. 31a) records that when R. Akiba prayed with the congregation, he used to cut it short and finish, in order not to inconvenience the congregation (*torakh hatzibbur*). He did this so that he would not detain them, since the congregation would not resume the service until R. Akiba had concluded his *tefillah*. However, when he prayed by himself, a man would leave him in one corner and find him later in another, on account of his many genuflections and prostrations.

The idea of inconveniencing the congregation is found throughout rabbinic literature. For example, in the *Sheli'ah Tzibbur's* prayer *Hineni*, recited on the High Holy Days, it is recommended that he not prolong this prayer because of *torakh hatzibbur* (cf. Ephraim Zalman Margoliot, *Matteh Ephraim* [Zolkiev, 1835], 590:38).

TOV LASHAMAYIM VELABRIYUT ZEHU TZADIK TOV (טוב לשמים ולבריות זהו צדיק טוב).
"He who is good to Heaven and good to man, he is a righteous man" (Kidd. 40a).

TOV SHEBAROFIM LAGAYHINOM (טוב שברופאים לגיהנום).
"The best of doctors deserve *Gehinnom* ("Hell")" (Kidd. 82a). *Rashi* (ad loc.) explains that since doctors do not fear sickness, they are haughty before the Almighty. At times their treatment is fatal, and if they do not treat the poor, they may indirectly cause their death. Rabbi Samuel Eliezer Edels (known as MaHaRSHA—*Moraynu HaRav Shemu'el Edels*, 1555–1631) also writes that the doctor is self-confident and believes that there is none like him. Through a wrong diagnosis, he may cause death to a patient. It is thus suggested that

in a case in which there is deadly danger, he consult with other doctors.

Another interpretation is that the word *tov*, which has the numerical value of seventeen (*tet* = 9, *vav* = 6, *bet* = 2 = 17) is applied to those doctors who believe only in the seventeen blessings of the *Amidah* and omit the blessing of *Refa'aynu* ("Heal us"). See ASYA DEMAGAN BEMAGAN, MAGAN SHAVYAH.

TOVAYL VESHERETZ BEYADO

(טובל ושרץ בידו). "Immerses himself in water and grasps a reptile in his hand." This is a source of defilement, making him ritually unclean. This maxim is based on a talmudic writing, "One who has sinned and confesses his sin but does not repent may be compared to a man holding a dead reptile in his hand, for although he may immerse himself in all the waters of the world, his immersion is of no avail unto him" (Ta'an. 16a). An example of this type of action is when a robber repents after committing a robbery but does not return the object he holds in his hand. Or, after admitting he sinned, he thinks nothing of repeating the same transgression.

The expression is hurled at a person who is a religious hypocrite or a pious fraud.

TOVIYAH HATAH VEZIGUD MIN-GAD (טוביה חטא וזיגוד מנגד). "Tobias sinned and Zigud is punished" (Pes. 113b). The Talmud states that the Holy One, blessed be He, hates one who sees something in his neighbor and testifies against him. It happened once that Tobias sinned and Zigud came and testified against him before R. Papa, whereupon Zigud was punished.

The expression is applied to a situation in which one sins and another is punished in his place.

TRAY KALAY LO MISHTAMA'AY

(תרי קלי לא מישתמעי). It is written in the Talmud (Meg. 21b), "As regards the Torah, one reads and one translates [from

the Aramaic *Targum*], and in no case must one read and two translate [together]." *Rashi* comments, "All the more so, two cannot read [the Torah] because "two voices cannot be heard together [*shtay kalay lo mishtma'ay*]." The attention of the listener is diminished.

This reasoning is applied in daily conversation when two persons talk at the same time. A third person might say, "I cannot hear two people talking together; one at a time should talk." See TARTAY KALAY MAYHAD GAVRA LO MISHTAMA'AY.

TUL KISAYM MIBAYN SHINEKHA, TUL KORAH MIBAYN AYNEKHA

(טול קסם מבין שניך, טול קורה מבין עיניך). "[If the judge said to a man] 'Take the splinter from between your teeth,' [he would retort] 'Take the beam from between your eyes'" (B.B. 15b). That is to say, "Don't drop on me morals; your sins are greater and worse than mine." R. Johanan said that this is what is meant by "And it came to pass in the days of the judging of the judges" (Ruth 1:1). It was a generation that judged its judges.

TZA'AR GIDUL BANIM (צער גידול בנים). "The pains of rearing children" (San. 19b; Erub. 100b; Shab. 128b). A verse in Isaiah 29:22 reads: "Therefore, thus saith the Lord unto the house of Jacob, who redeemed Abraham." The Talmud (San. 19b) asks, "But where do we find that Jacob redeemed Abraham?" Rab Judah answered, "It means that he redeemed him from the pains of rearing children." It should have been Abraham's duty to rear the children since he was promised multiplication, but it fell upon Jacob.

The Yiddish language has the popular wish regarding raising children, *Ir zuhlt zokheh zayn zey megadayl tzu zayn* ("You shall merit to raise them").

TZADIKIM OMRIM ME'AT VE'OSIN HARBAYH (צדיקים אומרים מעט ועושין הרבה). "Righteous men promise little and

perform much" (B.M. 87a). Concerning the visit of the angels to Abraham, it is written, "And I [Abraham] will fetch a morsel of bread" (Gen. 18:5). Later, it is written that he served much more than he had offered, "And Abraham ran unto the herd" (ibid., 18:7). This teaches, said R. Eleazar, that righteous men say little and do much.

TZAPAYH LESHULHAN AHAYRIM
(צפה לשלחן אחרים). An expression dating from talmudic days and attributed to R. Nathan b. Abba, who said it in the name of Rab, meaning "He who is dependent on another's table, the world is dark to him" (Bez. 32b). This is derived from the verse in Job 15:23, "He wanders abroad for bread, saying, Where is it? He knows that the day of darkness is ready at his hand." R. Hisda added, "Also, his life is no life."

TZO'AKIN VE'AYNAM NE'ENIN
(צועקין ואינם נענין)."They cry out and are not answered" (B.M. 75B). The Talmud (ibid.) cites three who vent their grievances at law and receive no retaliatory action: he who has money and lends it without witnesses, he who accepts a master for himself, and a henpecked husband. By "he who acquires a master for himself" is meant, he who attributes his wealth to a gentile (and the latter demands its return), or he who transfers his property to his children in his lifetime, or he who is badly off in one town and does not go elsewhere to seek his fortune.

Generally, those bemoaning the past cry out and are not answered. Rashi (ad loc.) writes that they brought it upon themselves.

TZORVA MAYRABBANAN (צורבא מרבנן). Literally, "one that has caught fire by associating with rabbis," especially a young person, a student-scholar of rabbinical lore. R. Aha, the son of Raba, asked R. Ashi, "If a man has occasion to call another out of the synagogue, what is

he to do?" He replied, "If he is a rabbinical student [I tzorva rabbanan hu], let him say some halakhah" (Meg. 28b).

TZU GOTT UN TZU LAYT (צו גאט און צו לייט). See TORAH UGEDULAH BEMAKOM EHAD.

UMOT HA'OLAM (אומות העולם). Literally, "the nations of the world"; all nations except Jews are referred to as umot ha'olam. The Talmud (Sukk. 55b) states that the seventy sacrifices offered on Tabernacles are to atone for the seventy gentile nations. The phrase Tzadikay umot ha'olam ("The righteous nations of the world") is used to mean their virtue upon which the world continues to exist (Hul. 92a). The Rambam wrote that "The righteous among the nations [Hasiday umot ha'olam] have a portion in the World to Come."

Other appellations for non-Jews are goy (pl., goyim), nokhri, kuti, and akum. The latter is composed of the initials of the words Ovday Kokhavim Umazalot ("worshipers of stars and constellations") and refers to ancient idolaters.

YADO AL HA'ELYONAH (AL HATAHTONAH) (ידו על העליונה (על התחתונה). Literally, "his hand is uppermost"; that is, his hand has the advantage (B.M. 44a).

By Yado al hatahtonah is meant "to be at a disadvantage" (B.M. 76a).

YAFAH SHETIKAH LAHAKHAMIM, KAL VAHOMER LETIPSHIM (יפה שתיקה לחכמים. קל וחומר לטפשים). The Sages said, "Silence is better for the wise, and how much more so for fools" (Pes. 99a), as it is said, "Even a fool, when he holdeth his peace, is counted wise" (Prov. 17:28).

YAGATA UFATAHTA YEGA USETOM (יגעת ופתחת יגע וסתום). "As you have taken the trouble to open them, so you must take the trouble to close them"

(B.B. 59b). This refers to the instance in which a certain man made windows opening onto a courtyard that he shared with others. At first, no objection was made, but eventually he was summoned before R. Hiyya, who gave him the above order. In other words, "You damaged it, you fix it."

YAGATI VELO MATZATI AL TA'AMAYN (יגעתי ולא מצאתי אל תאמן). R. Isaac said, "If a man says to you, I have labored and not found, do not believe him" (Meg. 6b). The Talmud (ibid.) continues, "If he says, I have not labored but still have found, do not believe him." If he says, "I have labored and found, you may believe him." This is true of words of the Torah, but in business, all depends on the assistance of Heaven (SAYATA HU MIN SHEMAYA). And even for words of Torah, this is true only of penetrating to the meaning, but for remembering what one has learned, all depends on the assistance of Heaven (*Sayata min Shemaya hi*).

YAGO'A BE'ESER ETZBA'OT (יגוע בעשר אצבעות). "I labored with my ten fingers" (Ket. 104a). When Rabbi was about to die, he raised his ten fingers toward Heaven and said, "Sovereign of the Universe, you know that I have labored in the study of Torah with my ten fingers [*Sheyagati be'eser etzbe'otai ba-Torah*] . . . I did not enjoy any worldly benefits even with my little finger. May it be Thy will that there be peace in my last resting place." And it was thus granted.

The phrase *Yago'a be'eser etzba'ot* has been applied to any exertion of strength that strives to accomplish something. A person might say, "I labored with all my ten fingers."

YaKNeHaZ (יקנה"ז). An acrostic for the order of *Kiddush-Havdalah*, recited when the Sabbath is immediately followed by a festival. The order is as follows: Y = *Yayin* ("wine"), K = *Kiddush* ("sanctification"), N

= *Nayr* ("candle"), H = *Havdalah* ("separation") Z = *Zeman* ("season" = *Sheheheyanu*). (See Pes. 102b, 103a.)

YASHAYN KAN VERO'EH HALOM BE'ASPAMYAH (ישן כאן ורואה חלום באספמיה). "A person sleeping here [in Babylon] might see a dream in Spain" (Nid. 30b). This is what is said about an embryo in its mother's womb that is able to see from one end of the world to the other.

The expression took on the meaning "You are here and you're telling me what's going on there!"

YATUSH KADAMKHA BEMA'A-SAYH BEREISHIT (יתוש קדמך במעשה בראשית). "Our rabbis taught, Adam was created [last of all beings] on the eve of the Sabbath. And why? Lest the Sadducees say, The Holy One, blessed be He, had a partner [viz., Adam] in His work of creation. Another answer is, In order that, if a man's mind becomes [too] proud, he may be reminded that the gnats preceded him in the order of creation [*Yatush kadamkha bema'asayh Bereishit*]" (San. 38a).

YATZA ISH PELONI NAKI MIN-KHASAV (יצא איש פלוני נקי מנכסיו). "So-and-so has gone out clear from his property" (B.K. 41a; Kidd. 56b); that is, he lost all his wealth and has nothing left. The Talmud discusses the case in which an ox killed a person and the ox was stoned; one may neither eat it nor have any benefits from it. This is derived from the verse "And if an ox gore a man or a woman, that they die, the ox shall surely be stoned, and its flesh shall not be eaten; but the owner of the ox shall be quit" (Ex. 21:28). And the expression "but the owner of the ox shall be quit" is explained to mean that a person may say to his friend, *Yatza ish peloni naki minkhasav*, and he has no benefits whatsoever from it.

YATZO BESHAYN VA'AYIN (יצא בשן ועין). "He [the heathen slave] goes out [free] through [the loss of] his tooth or eye" (Kidd. 24a; cf. also Ex. 21:26–27), which was caused by his master.

The expression is applied to one who suffers serious losses.

YAVO HANAYS MIKOL MAKOM (יבא הנס מכל מקום). "Let the miracle be performed, no matter how" (Me'il. 17b); that is, let the miracle come in any shape or form, as long as it comes. This was said by R. Simeon.

YAYIN BEN HOMETZ (יין בן חמץ). See HOMETZ BEN YAYIN.

YAYIN BEN YAYIN (יין בן יין). See HOMETZ BEN YAYIN.

YAYIN HAMESHUMAR (יין המשומר). See YAYIN YESAMAH LEVAV ENOSH.

YEHAY HAVIV ALEKHA DIN PE-RUTAH KEDIN SHEL MAYAH MANEH (יהא חביב עליך דין פרוטה כדין של מאה מנה). It is written in Scripture, "Ye shall hear the small and the great alike" (Deut. 1:17). Resh Lakish says, "This verse indicates that a lawsuit involving a mere perutah [the smallest of coins] must be regarded as [being] of the same importance as one involving a hundred maneh [a weight in gold or silver, equal to one hundred common or fifty sacred shekels]" (San. 8a). For what practical purpose is this given? Is it not self evident? The Talmud answers, "Rather, it is to give the case due priority, if it should be first in order."

YEMAY HARA'AH – AYLU YEMAY HAZIKNAH (ימי הרעה – אלו ימי הזקנה). A verse in Ecclesiastes 12:1 reads, "Remember also thy Creator in the days of thy youth, before the evil days [yemay hara'ah] come." The Talmud (Shab. 151b) states that yemay hara'ah refer to the days

of old age (yemay haziknah). Rashi contrasts the happy days of life's prime, when man is full of vitality, to the days of old age and feebleness.

YESURIN SHEL AHAVAH (יסורין של אהבה). "Pain [accepted] with love" (Ber. 5a). The Holy One, blessed be He, brings suffering upon the righteous in this world so that they may inherit the future world (Kidd. 40b). The Talmud (Ber., ibid.) differentiates between general pain and pain accepted by the pious with love. Traditionally, the best way to relate to suffering is by silence (Ber. 62a). The Mishnah (Avot 6:2) specifies kabbalat hayesurim ("acceptance of suffering") among the forty-eight qualities by which the Torah is acquired. Praise is even given those who rejoice in suffering (Shab. 88b).

A Hebrew expression for great suffering is Yesuray Iyob or Iyobi ("like Job"). Job was stricken by poverty, loss of children, and painful disease, yet he declared God's acts to be just (Job 1:6–22).

YIHUS (יחוס יחוש). A term meaning "geneology," "pedigree," or "lineage." R. Simeon b. Azzai said, "I found a roll of geneological records [Megillat Yuhasin] in Jerusalem" (Mishnah, Yeb. 4:13). In the days of Ezra and Nehemiah, we read the verse "These sought their register, that is, the geneology, but it was not found; therefore, they were excluded from the priesthood as unfit" (Ez. 2:62; Neh. 7:64). In 1 Chronicles we read that all Israel were reckoned by geneologies.

Great importance was attached to yihus when R. Hama b. R. Hanina stated that "When the Holy One, blessed be He, causes His Divine Presence to rest, it is only upon families of pure birth [mishpahot meyuhasot] in Israel" (Kidd. 70b). In later days, too, yihus played an important role in marriage. The Talmud states that on the fifteenth of Ab and on Yom Kippur when the daughters of Jerusalem came out in their white garments, eligible for marriage, those who came of noble families [meyuhasot shebahen] called out, "Look for a good family, for woman has been created to bring up a family" (Ta'an. 31a).

A person who is distinguished by birth or who is of a good family is called a meyuhas. To be a meyuhas is advantageous. If a person has all the qualifications on his own (self-made), his pedigree is known as Yihus atzmo. In the Yiddish language, a privileged person is called a yahsan. In an argumentative tone, one may say Ikh bin a glaykher yahsan mit aykh ("I am as good as you"), or, Vuhs iz der yihus mit dir? ("What are you proud of?"), Mir zaynen glaykhe yahsanim ("We are of equal pedigree"); or In yihus veln mir zikh oysglaykhn ("We can match your pedigree").

YISHME'U OZNEKHA MAH SHE-PIKHA MEDABAYR (ישמעו אזניך מה שפיך מדבר). "Let your ears hear what your mouth talks!" (Jer. Tal., Ber. 2:4).

YISRAEL SAVA (ישראל סבא). This phrase refers to Jacob the patriarch, whose name was also Yisrael, as stated in Genesis 32:29, "Thy name shall be called no more Jacob, but Israel."

The Jewish people have often been called Yisrael sava, as the Talmud (Taan. 5b) interprets the verse "Therefore fear thou not, O my servant Jacob, says the Lord; neither be dismayed, O Israel; for lo, I will save thee from afar, and thy seed from the land of their captivity" (Jer. 30:10). The verse likens him (Jacob) to his seed (Israel); as his seed will then be alive, so he, too, will be alive (cf. Rashi, ad loc., s.v. Af Hu Lehayyim).

YOM NIKHNAS VEYOM YAYTZAY, SHABBAT NIKHNAS . . . HO-DESH . . . SHANAH. . . . (יום נכנס ויום יצא, שבת נכנס וכו', חודש וכו' שנה וכו'). "A day enters and a day departs, a week enters . . . a month . . . a year . . ." (Jer. Tal., Ber. 1:1). Every

moment, every day that passes is not just a day but a life's concern. Time must be watched over and guarded.

YOM PETIRAH (יום פטירה). The "death anniversary" or YAHRTZEIT. The Talmud (Tem. 16a) uses the expression besha'ah sheniftar Moshe Rabbaynu Legan Ayden ("When Moses departed [this world] for the Garden of Eden").

In Yiddish, it is customary to say niftar gevuhrn or nistalayk gevuhrn when a person dies. The former (niftar) is used in the Talmud and the latter (nistalayk) appears in Shemot Rabbah 52. The deceased person is called a niftar. See ALIYAT NESHAMAH; NIFTAR (NISTALAYK).

YOTZAY DOFEN (יוצא דפן). "A fetus extracted by means of the caesarean section"; that is, one who is brought out from the side (of his mother) (Bek. 47b).

The expression took on the meaning of "exceptional," "irregular," "unusual," or "extraordinary." The Yiddish term yotzay-dofnik has come to mean "queer."

ZAKHIN LE'ADAM SHELO BEFA-NAV (זכין לאדם שלא בפניו). "One may act for a person in his absence" (Ket. 11a). The Talmud discusses a case in which a proselyte (a minor) has no father to act for him and, therefore, the court can authorize his ritual immersion. In this case, the minor proselyte is immersed by the direction of the court, since one may act for a person in his absence to his advantage (to be received into the Jewish faith), but one cannot act for another person in his absence to his disadvantage (Ayn havin le'adam shelo befanav).

ZAROK EVEN LEMERCULIS (זרוק אבן למרקוליס). "To throw a stone at a Merculis" (an idolater) (Hul. 133a). Worship consisted of two stones beside each other and one above them, and sometimes simply in throwing stones at the figure. Just as this form of worship does not make sense, teaching a disciple who is unworthy or doing good for someone who does not appreciate it, is also meaningless, for it is written, "As a small stone in a heap of stones, so is he that giveth honor to a fool" (Prov. 26:8).

ZAYKHER TZADIK LIVRAKHAH (זכר צדיק לברכה).

"Blessed be the memory of the righteous" (Prov. 10:7); an expression uttered after mentioning the name of the deceased righteous person. The phrase, found originally in Scripture, is also used in *Rashi* and in the Talmud. *Rashi* (Gen. 6:9) is bothered, if it is written, "These are the generations of Noah," the names of Shem, Ham, and Japheth should have followed immediately; so, then, why should the phrase "Noah was a man righteous and wholehearted" follow? *Rashi* thus comments, "Since it [Scripture] mentions him, it relates his praise, as it is said (Prov. 10:7), Blessed be the memory of the righteous." "Hananyah, the son of of the brother of R. Joshua said [commenting on], 'Blessed be the memory of the righteous': The prophet said to Israel, When I make reference to the Righteous One of all the worlds, say a blessing!" (Yom. 37a).

Another expression of honor that is said after mentioning a deceased person's name is ZIKHRONO LIVRAKHAH ("His memory be for a blessing"). The Talmud (Kidd. 31b) states that twelve months after one's father's death, one must say, when repeating one of his statements, "His memory be for a blessing for the life of the World to Come."

ZEH NEHENEH VEZEH LO HASAYR (זה נהנה וזה לא חסר).

The Talmud (B.K. 20a, b) relates various instances in which the defendant gains and the plaintiff does not lose. In daily conversation, the expression is used as if to say, "It is no skin off your back," or "It doesn't harm you in any way—financially, morally, or physically."

ZEHIRUT MAYVI'AH LIDAY ZERIZUT (זהירות מביאה לידי זריזות).

R. Phineas b. Jair said, "Caution leads to zeal" (A.Z. 20b). *Rashi* (ad loc.) gives the example in which R. Huna b. Sehora was once standing before R. Hamnuna; he put some meat into R. Hamnuna's mouth, which he then ate. Said R. Huna, If you were not R. Hamnuna, I would not have fed you. The Talmud queries, "Now what was the reason for the exception in R. Hamnuna's case? Was it not because he was very careful [*zahir*] not to touch [the food]? No, it was because he was most scrupulous [*zariz*] and had certainly washed his hands previously" (Hul. 107b). *Rashi* expounds that *zariz* ("zeal") is better than *zahir* ("being careful"). When a person is *zahir*, he is careful at the moment that he shall not transgress, but when a person is *zariz*, he sees the future and improves himself so that he should not come to any misdeed—thus, the expression *zehirut mayvi'ah liday zerizut*.

ZEMAN TEFILLAH LEHUD UZEMAN TORAH LEHUD (זמן תפלה לחוד וזמן תורה לחוד).

"The time for prayer and Torah are distinct from each other" (Shab. 10a). This is what R. Hamnuna maintained when he was confronted by Raba. Raba saw R. Hamnuna prolonging his prayers and he said, "They forsake eternal life and occupy themselves with temporal life" (prayer is referred to as temporal since one petitions for health, sustenance, etc.). The Torah is eternal life (*hayay olam*).

ZIKHRONO LIVRAKHAH (זכרונו לברכה).

See ZAYKHER TZADIK LIVRAKHAH.

ZIL BATAR SHETIKUTA (זיל בתר שתיקותא).

"Follow the rule of silence" (Kidd. 71b). This was the suggestion of Ulla to Rab Judah of Pumbeditha, about whom his son R. Isaac should marry. He advised him to take someone from a peaceful family because those who are quarrelsome are probably unfit. He also gave him the test of the Palestinians: When two people quarrel, they see which one becomes silent first and say, This one is of superior birth.

ZO LO SHAMATI, KAYOTZAY BAH SHAMATI (זו לא שמעתי, כיוצא בה שמעתי). "This I have not heard, but something similar to this I have heard" (B.K. 107b). This expression appears in various tractates of the Talmud (e.g., Shab. 108b, 114a; Pes. 34b; Meg. 22a) concerning talmudic discourse. When a Sage was asked what the law was in a particular incident, he answered that he did not hear definitely what the law was but he heard something similar, and from that he was able to deduce what the law in question was.

ZU TORAH VEZU SEKHARAH? (זו תורה וזו שכרה?). "Such Torah, and such a reward?" (Ber. 61b). This is the question the ministering angels asked the Holy

One, blessed be He, regarding the execution of R. Akiba, who publicly brought gatherings together to study Torah in spite of the decree of the Roman government that forbade the Jews to study and practice the Torah. The Talmud concludes, "A BAT KOL went forth and proclaimed, Happy art thou, R. Akiba, that thou art destined for the life of the World to Come."

The expression is sometimes applied to someone who occupies himself with Torah and experiences much suffering.

ZUZA LE'ALALA LO SHKHIHA LITELITA SHKHIHA (זוזא לעללא לא שכיחא, לתליתא שכיחא). "For [purchasing] provision a zuz [a coin] is not on hand, but for [saving from] hanging it is" (Hag. 5a); that is, charity often waits for the most extreme distress.

In Yiddish, one says, *Far dem tayvl gefint zikh shoyn* ("For the devil one finds means").

LITURGY

תפלה

גדולה תפלה שבזכותה הקב"ה מוחל עוונותיהם
של ישראל—ישראל ניצולים מיד אויביהם

*Great is Prayer, in its merit the Holy One, blessed
be He, forgives the iniquities of Israel—Israel
is saved from the hand of its enemies. (Otzar
Midrashim)*

The Yiddish-Hebrew sayings in this section are interspersed with phrases from the liturgy and have their roots in the environs of the synagogue. Yiddish was the language that Jews assimilated into their culture from their foreign environment. It served as a spoken language to a majority of the Jewish people. Incorporating a large number of Hebrew words into their everyday conversation reinforced their Jewishness. Moreover, words of the *Siddur* and *Mahzor*, interwoven with the Yiddish, helped the commonfolk keep the Hebrew language alive in the Diaspora. This bilingualism contributed inestimably to the renaissance of spoken Hebrew in the twentieth century.

Perhaps the origin of the humorous and satirical quality underlying many of the sayings is the Jews' ceaseless struggle for survival in an anti-Jewish society; the laughter is often through tears. While the expressions carry a note of trenchant wit, irony, or sarcasm, they also provide a means of consolation by minimizing troubles and hoping for a brighter future.

The *Rambam* wrote, "The obligation of the *mitzvah* of prayer is that a person should plead and pray each day and recite the praises of the Holy One, blessed be he. After that, he should ask for things he needs, requesting and pleading, and afterwards he should offer praise and thanks to the Lord for the good which he gave him" (*Yad Hahazakah, Hilkhot Tefillah* 1:2). It is in this manner that man has been reaching out and communicating with God from antiquity. His prayers range over themes of adoration, thanksgiving, confession of sins, supplications and petitions, and God's unity and rulership. To attest to this fact is the prayerbook, which, in addition to uniting the dispersed people of Israel over the centuries, instilled in them the idea that prayer is Jacob's ladder, which joins earth to Heaven.

Liturgy
תפלה

Weekday Service / שחרית לחול   209

Grace After Meals / ברכת המזון   219

Minhah and Maariv / מנחה–מעריב   220

Friday Evening Service / קבלת שבת   221

Zemirot / זמירות   223

Shaharit and Musaf for Shabbat /
שחרית–מוסף לשבת   224

Blessing of the New Month /
ברכת החודש   225

Sabbath Minhah and
Motza'ay Shabbat /
מנחה לשבת–מוצאי שבת   226

Torah and Haftarah / תורה–הפטרה   229

Shalosh Regalim / שלש רגלים   231

Haggadah / הגדה   234

Elul and Selihot / אלול–סליחות   237

Rosh Hashanah / ראש השנה   238

Yom Kippur / יום כפור   243

Hanukkah / חנוכה   248

Purim / פורים   249

Fasts / תעניות   252

WEEKDAY SERVICE
(שחרית לחול)

A HOYKHE KEDUSHAH (א הויכע קדושה). "A loud *Kedushah*." Six of ten men who make up the *minyan* must be individuals who are obligated to recite their prayers. If there are less than six, there is no repetition of the entire *Amidah*. In this case, the *Sheli'ah Tzibbur* first recites the *Amidah* aloud only through the third blessing, thus enabling everyone present to join in saying the *Kedushah* aloud. The *Sheli'ah Tzibbur* continues to say the remainder of the *Amidah* quietly and the worshipers do likewise, but they start from the beginning.

A TAYERER KADDISH (א טײערער קדיש). See ER HUHT GEBOYRN A KADDISH.

AHARAY KIKHLOT HAKOL (אחרי ככלות הכל). "After all has ceased to be." This phrase is a quotation from *Adon Olam*, a hymn recited in the early morning service and after the evening service on Sabbaths and holidays. It was incorporated into the Yiddish language and means "finally" or "when all is said and done."

AMEN ZUHGER (אמן זאגער). See ENTFERN AMEN.

ARAYNKHAPN A KEDUSHAH (BAREKHU) (אריינכאפן א קדושה (ברכו)). See ARAYNKHAPN A MINHAH.

ASHER YATZAR PAPIR (אשר יצר פאפיר). "Toilet tissue." The blessing *asher yatzar* ("Who fashioned") is quoted in the Talmud (Ber. 60b) and is recited after washing the hands immediately following an act of responding to the call of nature, or as part of the *Shaharit* service (*Mishnah Berurah* 4:4 and 6:9).

ASHRAY YOSHVAY VAYTEKHA IZ DER BESTE HANDL (אשרי יושבי ביתך איז דער בעסטע האנדל). "'Happy are they who dwell in Thy house' is the best dealing." The opening three words of this phrase are from a prayer recited thrice daily and refer to those who spend their lives in God's service. Dwelling in the house of the Lord, one feels safe from all difficulties or troubles encountered in mercantile pursuits or transactions.

AZ BA(A)GALA IZ A VUHGN IZ UVIZMAN KARIV A SHLITN (אז בעגלא איז א וואגן איז ובזמן קריב א שליטן). An AM-HA'ARETZ translated the phrase *ba(a)gala uvizman kariv* in *Kaddish* as follows: "If *ba(a)gala* is a wagon, *uvizman kariv* is a sleigh." He mistook the word *ba'agala*, meaning "speedily," for the similar Hebrew word used in the Yiddish language, *ba'al agalah*, meaning "wagon" or "coachman." Since he translated *ba'agala* as "wagon," he then translated *uvizman kariv*, the next two words, as a "sleigh."

AZ MEN IZ IN KA'AS OYFN CHAZEN SHPRINGT MEN NIT KAYN KEDUSHAH? (אז מען איז אין כעס אויפן חזן שפרינגט מען ניט קיין קדושה?). "If you are angry at the cantor, you don't raise yourself at *Kedushah*?" At the words *Kadosh-Kadosh-Kadosh, Barukh*, and *Yimlokh*, it is customary to raise oneself slightly on one's toes to symbolize the movement of the angels described in Isaiah, "And with two wings, they fluttered about." It also symbolizes an uplifting of the spirit.
One responds to *Kedushah* in spite of any anger toward the cantor or other synagogue official and this expression even applies to any person who manifests animosity at anyone in the synagogue.

AZ MEN IZ IN KA'AS OYFN CHAZEN ZUHGT (ENTFERT) MEN NIT KEYN AMEN? (אז מען איז אין כעס אויפן חזן זאגט (ענטפערט) מען ניט קיין אמן?). See ENTFERN AMEN.

BESER UHNKUMEN TZU ALAYNU EYDER TZUM BESTN MENTCHN

(בעסער אנקומען צו עלינו איידער צום בעסטן מענטשן). "It is better to arrive at *Alaynu* than to rely on the best person." The Yiddish word *uhnkumen* can mean either "to come" or "depend." Therefore, it is a play on the word *uhnkumen*, meaning "I'd rather come late to *Alaynu* [recited toward the end of every prayer service] than depend upon the best person." See ER KUMT TZUM OYSHPAYEN.

DER OYLAM IZ SHOYN DU (דער

עולם איז שוין דו). It often occurs that while waiting for a quorum (*minyan*) in order to start the synagogue service, someone will direct the *Sheli'ah Tzibbur* to begin because "the congregation is here" or "the tenth person has arrived." Possibly, the expression came into existence because of the custom of counting the people by saying the ten-word verse *Hoshi'ah et amekha uvaraykh et nahalatekha uraym venase'aym ad ha'olam* ("Save Your nation, and bless Your inheritance; tend them and lift them forever") (Ps. 28:9).

Care must be taken not to count the people in a direct manner, in order to ascertain if there is a quorum for praying or for the purpose of performing a religious act, as it is written, "And Saul summoned the people, and numbered them with lambs" (1 Sam. 15:4; cf. R. Solomon Ganzfried, *Kitzur Shulhan Arukh* 15:3).

The word *olam* may refer either to "duration" or "world." Thus, *oylam* (another dialect), referring to the tenth word in the verse and the tenth man of the congregation (has arrived) is appropriate.

Calling the multitude *olam* may have come about because every Israelite is considered an *olam katan* (microcosm, an epithet of man) and it is from one man that the world (*olam*) was created (Isaac b. Mordecai Lipiec, *Sefer Matamim Hehadash*, [Warsaw, 1894]).

DUHS IZ MAYN KADDISH (דאס

איז מיין קדיש). See ER HUHT GEBOYRN A KADDISH.

DUHS LEBN IZ VI SHEMONEH-ESRAYH; MEN SHTEYT, MEN SHTEYT, BIZ MEN GEYT OYS (דאס

לעבן איז ווי שמונה-עשרה; מען שטייט, מען שטייט, ביז מען גייט אויס). "Life is like *Shemoneh-esrayh*, one stands and stands until expiring." The *Shemoneh esrayh* prayer, also known as the *Amidah* ("standing prayer"), is lengthy. It consists of nineteen blessings (originally eighteen, thus *Shemoneh-esrayh*) and takes quite some time to recite. At its conclusion, one takes three steps backward to indicate its conclusion (Yiddish, *oysgang* or *oysgeyn*).

This humorous expression bemoans a person's life, comparing it sarcastically to the prayer and intimating that a person hangs around until his death.

ENTFERN AMEN (ענטפערן אמן). "To

answer *Amen.*" *Amen* is an affirmation or an agreement following a blessing or statement; it means "so be it" or "so it shall be." So important is the responsorial *Amen* that it is considered to be paramount to the benediction that occasioned the response.

Yiddish expressions that are used in conjunction with *Amen* are: AMEN ZUHGER (a "yes man"), one who agrees with and approves of everything; FAR AMEN KUMT KEYN PATCH NIT ("for *Amen*, one does not deserve a slap"). This is another way of saying that if a person is agreeable, he or she does not deserve a rebuff; AZ MEN IZ IN KA'AS OYFN CHAZEN ZUHGT (ENTFERT) MEN NIT KEYN AMEN? ("If you are angry at the cantor, don't you say [answer] *Amen*?"). This retort is used when someone is slighted and you wish to indicate to this person that he or she should ignore it.

ER HUHT DEM KADDISH TZU HOYKH UHNGEHOYBN (ער האט

דעם קדיש צו הויך אנגעהויבן). "He began the *Kaddish* in too high a pitch"; a derisive and cynical expression about one who engages in a project or business in high gear and soon experiences failure.

ER HUHT GEBOYRN A KADDISH

(ער האט געבוירן א קדיש). "He gave birth to a *Kaddish*." The *Kaddish* prayer recited by sons is popularly thought to be a "prayer for the dead," to the extent that the firstborn son is often called "a *Kaddish*." If there are no sons to say *Kaddish*, the expression used is ER IZ GESHTORBN UHN A KADDISH ("He died without leaving a son"). A son may be introduced with DUHS IZ MAYN KADDISH ("This is my son, who will say *Kaddish* for me"), and, sarcastically, one may say, A TAYERER KADDISH ("a fine fellow").

ER HUHT UHPGEKLAPT DEM MIZMOR IN A REGA (ער האט

אפגעקלאפט דעם מזמור אין א רגע). See ES GEYT VI A MIZMOR.

ER IZ GESHTORBN UHN A KADDISH (ער איז געשטארבן אן א קדיש).

See ER HUHT GEBOYRN A KADDISH.

ER KUMT TZUM OYSHPAYEN (ער

קומט צום אויסשפייען). "He comes to 'spitting out'"; a variant is *Az men kumt uhn nukh Alaynu, shpayt men oys un men geyt aheym* ("If you arrive after *Alaynu*, you 'spit out' and go home"). Both expression are directed at a person who comes late to the services. The unbecoming practice of spitting while reciting the *Alaynu* prayer came into being from the phrase *shehaym mishtahavim lehevel umitpallelim el ayl lo yoshi'a* ("for they bow down to vanity and emptiness and pray to a god that cannot save") and directly from the double meaning of the word *varik* (*rik*, "emptiness," and *rok*, "spittle" or "saliva"). The censors ordered this phrase to be deleted from the prayerbook and prohibited it from being said. They claimed that it was intended to slur Christianity and that spitting was an additional insult. The Rabbis refuted both attacks by pointing

out that the phrase was uttered by Isaiah and its composition was pre-Christian. Furthermore, the practice of spitting was directed toward the idol-worshipers during the days of Joshua, who first uttered the prayer, and it was Isaiah who later said, "They pray to a god who cannot save." The censors remained adamant and constantly renewed their attacks. The indecorous practice of spitting while reciting the prayer was finally denounced and discouraged by the kabbalist R. Isaiah Horowitz and other leading authorities. See BESER UHNKUMEN TZU ALAYNU EYDER TZUM BESTN MENTCHN.

ER SHTEYT A LANGE SHE-MONEH ESRAYH (ער שטייט א לאנגע

שמונה עשרה). "He stands a long *Shemoneh Esrayh*." The eighteen benedictions recited on weekdays are called *Shemoneh Esrayh* (eighteen). Each word must be uttered slowly, with much concentration, while paying attention to the meaning of the words. In Jewish tradition, an early marriage is preferable—"eighteen for marriage" (*Avot* 5:21).

The word *Vehu*, in the phrase *Vehu hahatan yotzay mayhupato* ("Which is as a bridegroom coming out of his chamber") (Ps. 19:6), hints by way of numerology (*gematria*) at the number eighteen (*vav* = 6, *hay* = 5, *vav* = 6, *alef* = 1). The word *Vehu*, in *Vehu ishah vivtulehah yikah* ("And he shall take a wife in her virginity") (Lev. 21:13) also alludes to the number eighteen. Someone who stood for the recitation of the *Shemoneh Esrayh* for a long time prompted this facetious Yiddish expression that denotes one marrying way past one's prime.

A bachelor was once asked why he didn't get married, since our Sages say, "Eighteen for marriage." His answer was, "I am standing a long *Shemoneh Esrayh*." The retort to this was "If you will stand a long *Shemoneh Esrayh*, you will miss *Kedushah* [Sanctification]."

ER ZUHGT IVRE VI A VASER, NOR
DUHS VASER LOYFT UN ER
SHTEYT (ער זאגט עברי ווי א וואסער,
נאר דאס וואסער לאויפט און ער שטייט).
See HAMAKEH BE'EVRATO—GESHLUHGN OYF
DI IVRE.

ER ZUHGT NOR MAH-TOVU (ער
זאגט נאר מה–טובו). "He only says 'how
good' or 'what good.'" Mah-Tovu is a
prayer that is recited upon entering the
synagogue in the morning. Objections
were raised as to the inclusion of the verse
"How goodly are thy tents [ohalekha],
O Jacob, thy dwellings [mishkenotekha], O
Israel!" (Numb. 24:5), originally uttered
by the idolater, Balaam. According to
rabbinic interpretation, "tents" are synagogues and "dwellings" are houses of
Torah study (San. 105b). Balaam understood the secret of Israel's spiritual
strength and, therefore, his words were
introduced as the opening prayer of the
morning service to show that in the synagogue and house of Torah study lies our
hope; in their strength is our strength!
The Yiddish expression is a way of referring to a cruel or unsympathetic person
who does not offer help, but only says,
"How good!" or criticizes by saying,
"What good!"

ES GEYT VI A MIZMOR (עס גייט ווי
א מזמור). "It goes smoothly." The word
mizmor ("song," "hymn," or "psalm") is
mentioned fifty-seven times in the Book
of Psalms and several times in the weekday Shaharit service. Just as a song, hymn,
or psalm is usually uttered in an unin-
terrupted and flowing fashion, so any
undertaking that has no concealed or
unexpected obstacle is said to "proceed as
a mizmor." Reading the psalm quickly is
characterized as ER HUHT UHPGLEKLAPT DEM
MIZMOR IN A REGA ("He read off the psalm
in a jiffy").

EYNER HUHT HANA'AH FUN KEZ,
A TZVEYTER FUN "LANG VEHU
RAHUM", UN A DRITER FUN TIR
TZU DER GAS (איינער האט הנאה פון
קעז. א צווייטער פון "לאנג והוא רחום".
און א דריטער פון תיר צו דער גאס). "One
delights from cheese, another from the
'long Vehu Rahum,' and a third from the
door to the street." This expression personifies three simple tastes and characters
of people. The first person enjoys his
food, the second is naive and enjoys
reciting prayers such as Vehu Rahum (recited on Mondays and Thursdays), and
the third is an idler who enjoys running
around aimlessly.

FALN TAHANUN (פאלן תחנון). "Fall
Tahanun." After the weekday Amidah, the
worshipers recite Tahanun ("supplication"), assuming the posture of nefilat
apayim ("falling on one's face"). The reason for lowering the face onto the arm is
so that a neighbor cannot hear the con-
fessions made. Furthermore, expressions
of penitence demand intense concentration.

FANGT UHN BARUKH SHE'AMAR,
AN OYLEM VET SHOYN UHNKU-
MEN (פאנגט אן ברוך שאמר. אן עולם
וועט שוין אנקומען). "Begin Barukh
She'amar and the people will eventually
come." Barukh She'amar vehayah ha'olam
("Blessed is He Who spoke, and the world
came into being") are the initial words of
a hymn that introduces the biblical selections Pesukay Dezimrah ("Verses of Song")
in the daily morning service. Often the
preliminary part of the service is recited
by each individual and the worshipers
wait at Barukh She'amar for a minyan
("quorum") to be present. The word olam
can be translated as "world" or "crowd."
Thus, the sexton or another person may
say to the Sheli'ah Tzibbur, in jest, Begin
Barukh She'amar and the people (minyan)
will come along.

FAR AMEN KUMT KEYN PATCH NIT (פאר אמן קומט קיין פאטש ניט). See ENTFERN AMEN.

FAR LOYTER AHAVAH RABBAH KUMT ER NIT TZU SHEMA YIS-RAEL (פאר לויטער אהבה רבה קומט ער ניט צו שמע ישראל). "For pure love he does not come to Shema Yisrael." This expression may be applied to a *hatan* ("bridegroom") anticipating marriage, whose intentions are not always pure. The prayer *Ahavah Rabbah* ("with great love") precedes the prayer *Shema Yisrael* ("Hear, O Israel") in the *Shaharit* service. The first and last words in the *Ahavah Rabbah* prayer stress "love," which moves us by the unending love that God has shown us throughout Jewish history. If not for the prayers and blessings leading up to *Shema*, we would not be able to anticipate the main teachings of the *Shema* and understand and say *Ve'ahavta* ("You shall love God").

FUN BARUKH SHE'AMAR BIZ ADON OLAM (פון ברוך שאמר ביז אדון עולם). "From *Barukh She'amar* to *Adon Olam*"; an expression used to indicate "expanse" or "extension." *Barukh She'amar* is the beginning of the morning prayer service and *Adon Olam* is the prayer recited each night before retiring, in addition to being said in the preliminary part of the daily morning service. Similarly, the Hebrew expression *Mayarbah kanfot ha'aretz* ("from the four corners of the earth"), a phrase in the second benediction that precedes the *Shema*, is used to describe "prolonging."

FUN BARUKH SHE'AMAR BIZ BARUKH MESHALAYM IZ VAYT (פון ברוך שאמר ביז ברוך משלם איז ווייט). "It is a far distance from *Barukh She'amar* until *Barukh Meshalaym*." Both Hebrew phrases in the Yiddish expression are part of the same prayer recited in the daily *Shaharit* service. *Barukh She'amar*

("Blessed is He Who spoke"), the opening words of the prayer, are followed later on in the passage with the words *Barukh Meshalaym* ("Blessed is He who pays"). The Yiddish expression has no relation to the actual meaning of the words in the prayer and implies that there will be a long wait until payment is actually made, in spite of promises given to that effect.

FUN NEKI KHAPAYIM VERT MEN NIT RAYKH (פון נקי כפים ווערט מען ניט רייך). "From clean hands one does not become rich." The Hebrew words *neki khapayim* appear in Psalms 24:4 and are part of the psalm recited on the first day of the week. By clean hands is meant "unstained by violence or dishonesty." The Yiddish expression intimates that in order to be wealthy, sometimes a person's hands become "dirty" and can not be considered "clean."

HADAYSH YAMAYNU KEKEDEM-DER EYGENER SHLIMAZEL VUHS FRIER (חדש ימינו כקדם-דער אייגענער שלימזל וואס פריער). "Renew our days as of old—the same *shlimazel* as before." No matter what the *shlimazel* does, he reverts back to his unluckiness. The Hebrew opening is from Lamentations 5:21 and is said on weekdays and on Sabbath and holidays when the Torah is read. The word *shlimazel* is a combination of the German *schlim*, "unlucky," and the Hebrew word *mazal*, "constellation."

HELF MIR GOTTENYU, BIST DUHKH A AYL RAHUM VEHANUN (העלף מיר גאטעניו, ביסט דאך א אל רחום וחנון). "Help me, dear God, for You are a merciful and gracious God." A Jew in need of salvation often cried out this plea. The Hebrew is derived from the opening words of a paragraph in *Tahanun*, recited on Mondays and Thursdays. The three words (*Ayl rahum vehanun*) also appear in the prayer *Shelosh Esray Midot* (The Thirteen Attributes [Ex. 34:6–7]) which is recited on festivals, High Holy Days, and

during *Selihot.* They are the third, fourth, and fifth attributes in the prayer.

HUHZT MOYRE LAYEN KERI'AT SHEMA (האזט מורא לייען קריאת שמע).

"Do you have fear? Read *Keri'at Shema!*" Reading the *Shema* ("Hear O Israel, the Lord our God, the Lord is One") (Deut. 6:4) has been the Declaration of Faith of the Jews throughout the ages. It is the first prayer taught to a child as soon as he or she begins to speak and is the last prayer a Jew utters on the deathbed. The entire prayer actually consists of three paragraphs—Deuteronomy 6:4–9, Deuteronomy 11:13–21, and Numbers 15:37–41—and is the essential part of the liturgy. A person in danger or one crying out for help will often exclaim only the first two words *Shema Yisrael!* and this is known as SHRAYEN SHEMA YISRAEL ("crying *Shema Yisrael*"). Reciting *Shema* when fearful has its origin in the Talmud (Meg. 3a). "Rabina said . . . if a man is seized with fright though he sees nothing [the reason is that] his star [or "guardian angel" or "spirit"] sees. What is his remedy? He should recite the *Shema*."

When describing fear, a comparison used is VI A SHED FAR A MEZUZAH UHDER FAR SHEMA YISRAEL ("Like a demon for a *Mezuzah* or *Shema Yisrael*"). In talmudic times a protective power, especially to ward off evil spirits, was attributed to the *Mezuzah*, which contains the *Shema*.

IN DI KETORET IZ DUH HELBENAH UN IN DER FAYNSTER MISHPAHAH IZ FARANEN A MESHUMAD (אין די קטורת איז דא חלבנה) און אין דער פיינסטער משפחה איז פאראנען א משומד).

"In *ketoret* there is *helbenah* and in the finest family there is a *meshumad.*" *Ketoret* ("incense"), a section recited in the early morning service, has its origin in Exodus 30:34–38. It is said, according to the *Zohar,* "in order to remove impurity from the world prior to the prayers that take the place of *Korbanot* ['offerings']." Among the various spices

mentioned, *helbenah* ("galbanum"), a brownish gum resin of aromatic odor and unpleasant taste, is used in the incense mixture. Precisely as aromatic *helbenah,* with its foul taste, is included in the incense mixture, so the best of families may have the unpleasant situation of having an apostate among them.

IN VUHS FAR A SHUL MEN DAVENT, AZA KEDUSHAH ZUHGT MEN (SHPRINGT MEN) (אין וואס פאר א שול מען דאוענט, אזא קדושה זאגט מען (שפרינגט מען)).

See VI DI SHUL, AZOY SHPRINGT MEN KADOSH.

KENEN OYS(EN)VEYNIG VI A YID ASHRAY, VI A VASSER (קענען אויס(ען)ווייניג ווי א איד אשרי, ווי א וואסער).

See KLOR (IN _____) VI A YID IN ASHRAY.

KLEYN VI A TAL UMUHTORL (קלייין ווי א טל ומטר"ל).

"Small as a *Tal-umuhtorl*"; referring to minuteness and used to describe a petite person or a tiny object.

The phrase *vetayn tal umatar livrakhah* ("bestow dew and rain for a blessing") is inserted into the ninth blessing (*Baraykh Alaynu*) of the *Amidah* and is said only in the winter. In *Siddurim,* where the text is made up of a variety of type sizes, the phrase is usually printed in very small type. The little words appearing in the *Siddur* also gave rise to the expression TAL-UMATAR TUHG, signifying "a short day."

KLOR (IN——) VI A YID IN ASHRAY (קלאר (אין——) ווי א איד אשרי).

"Fully conversant [in _____] as a Jew in *Ashray*"; or, KENEN OYS(EN)VEYNIG VI A YID ASHRAY, VI A VASER ("to know [by heart] like a Jew is familiar with *Ashray,* as water flows"). *Ashray* is a psalm written in alphabetical acrostic form, probably as an aid to memory; it is recited daily, twice in the morning service and once in the afternoon service. By reciting the psalm three times a day, one is assured, according to the Talmud (Ber. 4b), of his share in the World to Come. Since it is uttered thrice daily, it becomes fluent in the mouth of the worshiper.

KOL ZEMAN SHEHANESHAMAH VEKIRBI (כל זמן שהנשמה בקרבי). "So long as the soul is within me"; a phrase of warmhearted agreement or approval used by a person who is about to close a deal or execute a task and who wants to assure the second party that he will fulfill his promise. The phrase is part of the prayer *Elokai Neshamah*.

Similar sayings are: *Kol zeman di oygn zaynen ofn* ("so long as my eyes are open"), *Kol zeman di fis truhgn* ("so long as my feet carry me"), and *Kol zeman meshteyt oyf di fis* ("so long as I can stand on my feet").

MAGID DEVARAV LEYA'A-KOV. . . . LO ASAH KHAYN; MAKHT RASHI: DER MAGGID SHTRUHFT KAHAL UN ALEYN TUT ER FARKERT (מגיד דבריו ליעקב. . . . לא עשה כן; מאכט רש"י: דער מגיד שטראפט קהל און אליין טוט ער פארקעט). "He relates His word to Jacob . . . He did not do so. *Rashi* expounds, The preacher lectures the community and he himself does the opposite." The Hebrew in this expression is from Psalms 147, verses 19 and 20, and is recited each morning in the *Shaharit* service. The expression *Makht Rashi* is used facetiously; parts of the text are omitted and taken out of context, in order to convey the humorous thought that "the preacher does not practice what he preaches."

MAKHN LELA'AG VAKELES (מאכן ללעג וקלס). "To expose to public scorn and derision"; from the prayer *Habayt Mishamayim*, recited in *Tahanun* on Mondays and Thursdays.

MEN DARF MIT IM KAYN ANAYNU NIT ZUHGN (מען דארף מיט אים קיין עניינו ניט זאגן). "With him, you need not say *Anaynu*." *Anaynu* is a

prayer recited on fast days. The expression alludes to a person who is well-off and does not know hunger; therefore, you need not worry about him.

MEN KEN SHOYN NUKH DEM ZUHGN A (RABBANAN) KADDISH (מען קען שוין נאך דעם זאגן א (רבנן) קדיש). "You might as well say a *Kaddish* after it." It implies that it might as well be considered lost, since *Kaddish* is popularly thought to be a "prayer for the dead."

There are four forms of *Kaddish*; the whole (or complete) *Kaddish*, the "half" *Kaddish*, the mourner's *Kaddish*, and *Kaddish de-Rabbanan* ("the scholar's *Kaddish*"). The *Kaddish de-Rabbanan* is recited by mourners in the synagogue after communal study, after the Preliminary *Shaharit* service, after *Bameh Madlikin*, and after *Ayn Kaylohaynu*. Of the four types, it is the only one that can be recited after Torah study any time during the day or night. Furthermore, *Kaddish de-Rabbanan* is not reserved for mourners and may even be recited by one whose parents are alive (*Piskay Teshuvah*, *Yoreh Dayah* 376:4). Thus, it is possible that the *Kaddish de-Rabbanan* is specified in the Yiddish expression to emphasize that it can be said any time by anyone.

MIT ALE ReMaH AYVARIM (מיט אלע רמ"ח אברים). "With all 248 limbs." The expression has its origin in *Keri'at Shema* and is directed at a person who puts his heart and soul into something he does or makes. In *Keri'at Shema* there are 245 words. With the three words *Adoshem Elohakhem Emet*, repeated by the *Sheli'ah Tzibbur*, the number is raised to 248, corresponding to the 248 parts of the human frame. When reciting *Keri'at Shema* without a *minyan*, this number is reached by adding *Ayl Melekh Ne'eman* before the *Shema* is begun. This is in order to teach that if we are careful in reciting the 248 words in *Keri'at Shema*, God will watch over the 248 parts of our body (*ReMaH ayvarim*).

OYFSHTEYN TEHIYAT HAMAY-
TIM (אויפשטיין תחיית המתים). "To rise
from the dead." Israel's Messianic redemption is connected with the doctrine of a
revival of the dead. This is expressed in
the second blessing of the Amidah, called
Gevurot ("Powers")—"Thou revivest the
dead."

An expression meant for one who is
deathly ill and recovers is Mehayay maytim
zayn ("to make from dead alive"). See
TEHIYAT HAMAYTIM.

OYSNEMENS (OYSHEYBENS) UN
AYNNEMENS   (אויסנעמענס
(אויסהייבענס) און איינעמענס)). "Taking
the Torah scroll from the Ark and returning it to the Ark." The Hebrew equivalent
is Hotza'ah and Hakhnasah. The two Hebrew words also mean "expense" and
"income" and the Yiddish expression uttered was UHN HOTZA'AH IS NITUH KAYN
HAKHNASAH ("Without outlay, there can be
no income").

SHPRING NIT KAYN KADOSH UN
BUK ZIKH NIT KAYN MODIM
(שפרינג ניט קיין קדוש און בוק זיך ניט
קיין מודים). "Don't leap at Kadosh and
don't bend at Modim." In the Amidah
prayer, it is a practice to raise oneself at
the words Kadosh-Kadosh-Kadosh and to
bow at Modim. This comment is jokingly
addressed to one who is either arrogant
or, vice versa, to one who shows too much
humility (neither being a desirable trait).
It may also mean "Don't be a hypocrite!" A
similar phrase indicating the latter meaning
is Modim biz drerd ("Modim to the ground").
The expression VUHS TIFER MEN BUKT
ZIKH MODIM, VUHS VAYTER GEYT MEN OSEH
SHALOM TZURIK ("The lower one bows at
Modim, the further does one go back at
oseh shalom") is also a sarcastic saying that
cautions against extremes.

SHRAYEN SHEMA YISRAEL (שרייען
שמע ישראל). See HUHZT MOYRE LAYEN
KERI'AT SHEMA.

SHTELN ZIKH (OYSGEYN) SHE-
MONEH ESRAYH (שטעלן זיך
(אויסגיין) שמונה עשרה). "Rising for [con-
cluding] Shemoneh Esray." There are various procedures to follow before, during,
and upon conclusion of Shemoneh Esrayh.
For example, when one is about to say the
Shemoneh Esrayh, one should rise and
prepare for the prayer by taking three
steps backward and then three steps forward, as if approaching a king. Upon
concluding (i.e., before oseh shalom) one
should bow and take three steps backward, beginning with the left foot, and
then turn the face to the left and say, oseh
shalom bimromav, then turn to the right
and say, hu ya'aseh shalom alaynu, and
again bow forward and conclude the
prayer.

Other expressions are: SHTILE SHEMONEH
ESRAYH ("the quiet Shemoneh Esrayh"), that
is, the one recited by each person in an
undertone; HOYKHE SHEMONEH ESRAYH ("the
loud Shemoneh Esrayh"), when the Sheli'ah
Tzibbur repeats the entire prayer aloud on
behalf of the congregation; VUHKHEDIGE
SHEMONEH ESRAYH ("weekday Shemoneh Esrayh"); and SHABBOSDIGE AND YOMTOVDIGE
SHEMONEH ESARAYH ("the Sabbath and festival Shemoneh Esrayh"). Originally, the
Shemoneh Esrayh (denoting eighteen) consisted of eighteen benedictions; in its
present form, however, there are nineteen.
On Sabbaths and festivals, only seven
benedictions are recited; thus, a more
accurate name for the prayer is Amidah
("standing") and it is sometimes used
instead for all occasions.

SHTILE (HOYKHE) SHEMONEH
ESRAYH (שטילע (הויכע) שמונה עשרה).
See SHTELN ZIKH (OYSGEYN) SHEMONEH ES-
RAYH.

SKUHTZL KUMT (סקאצל קומט).
"Welcome! How do you do?" A mere
greeting in an ejaculatory form of speech,
usually said to one upon entering. Its

origin stems from the fact that it was usually addressed to women, and was supposed that *skuhtzl* is a contraction of *Gott's vil* ("God's will")—an allusion to the blessing women say in the Preliminary Morning service; "Blessed _____ for having made me according to His will."

Another interpretation is that in early times a woman was referred to as *tzayl* ("shadow") because she followed her husband. Or, she was called *tzayla* ("rib") because she was created from Adam's rib (cf. Gen. 2:22, 23). Thus, when she came to a friend's house, her friend would say *Gott's tzayl* or *tzayla* and the expression eventually became *Skuhtzl kumt* (Isaac b. Mordecai Lipiec, *Sefer Matamim* [Warsaw, 1894], s.v. *Ish Ve'ishah*, p. 4).

TAL-UMATAR TUHG (טל ומטר טאג). See KLEYN VI A TAL UMUHTORL.

TZURIK GEYT MEN NOR BAY OSEH SHALOM (צוריק גייט מען נאר ביי עושה שלום). "You go back only at *oseh shalom*." Directed at someone who has a change of mind or who is regretful; this saying implies that only in the *Amidah* can one take three steps backward, and not in any other situation.

UHN HOTZA'AH IZ NITUH KAYN HAKHNASAH (אן הוצאה איז ניטא קיין הכנסה). See OYSNEMENS (OYSHEYBENS) UN AYNNEMENS.

UHNHEYBN FUN UHNHEYB (FUN ALEF-BET, FUN BEREISHIT, FUN MAH-TOVU, FUN BARUKH SHE'-AMAR) (פון אלף-, אנהייבן פון אנהייב בית, פון בראשית, פון מה-טובו, פון ברוך שאמר). "To begin from the beginning," or "let's start again." Each of the alternatives in the parenthesis represent a return to the starting point and may be used in lieu of the word *uhnheyb*. The *alef-bet* ("alphabet") is what the young child first learns to read; *Bereishit* is the

opening word of the Bible; *Mah-Tovu* is the first prayer recited upon entering the synagogue; and *Barukh She'amar* is the first prayer in *Pesukay Dezimrah*, recited by the reader and the congregation.

Additionally, the two Hebrew words *Rayshit Hokhmah* ("the beginning of wisdom"), forming part of the verse in Psalms 111:10, and recited after saying *Modeh Ani* upon arising, may also be used to indicate "start" or "opening." See LUHMIR UHNFANGEN (UHNHEYBN) FUN BEREISHIT.

UHPRIKHTN HATZOT (אפריכטן חצות). "To perform or celebrate midnight prayers." In Hebrew it is referred to as *Tikkun Hatzot* (the Hebrew *hatzot* is from *haytzi*, meaning "half," and refers to midnight), when pietists arise to recite psalms, lamentations for Zion (*Kinot*), and study the Torah. Instituted by Safed kabbalists of the sixteenth century, the observance has its origin in the statement made by David, "At midnight I will rise to give thanks unto Thee" (Ps. 119:62).

VAYOMER-DAVID-GLITSH (ויאמר-דוד-גליטש). "*Vayomer*-David-skating." *Tahanun* begins every day, except on Monday and Thursday, with *Vayomer David*. The procedure followed when reciting this prayer is to lower the head to rest on the forearm. Often, the eyes are covered when assuming this posture. Thus, youngsters used this expression when skating downhill with closed eyes. See FALN TAHANUN.

VE'AL KULAM (ועל כולם). "And for all these." The two Hebrew words are derived from the eighteenth benediction of the *Amidah* and refer to all the praises and laudations said before "Shall Thy Name be blessed and exalted," and so forth.

The borrowed phrase is used in Yiddish for "above all," "on top of all," "even more," or "additionally."

VETALMUD TORAH KENEGED KULAM; A BISL MAYHAYKHA-TAYSI IZ BILKHER FUN ALTZ (ותלמוד תורה כנגד כולם; א ביסל מהיכא-תיתי איז בילכר פון אלץ). "But the study of the Torah is equal to them all; a little pleasure is more important than everything." The first part of the expression appears in the talmudic selection *Aylu Devarim* (Pe'ah 1:1 and Shab. 127a) which enumerates the rewards for various commandments and concludes with the declaration that Torah study is equivalent to them all. The frivolous Yiddish comment appended to the Hebrew mirrors the life of the unassuming, downtrodden Jew who sometimes took a drink of whiskey for a little pleasure in his life. See MA-HAYKHA TAYTAY.

VI A SHED FAR A MEZUZAH UHDER FAR SHEMA YISRAEL (ווי א שד פאר א מזוזה אדער פאר שמע ישראל). See HUHZT MOYRE LAYEN KERI'AT SHEMA.

VI DI SHUL, AZOY SHPRINGT MEN KADOSH (ווי די שול, אזוי שפרינגט מען קדוש). "You raise your toes at *Kadosh*, according to the tradition of the synagogue." Similarly, IN VUHS FAR A SHUL MEN DAVENT, AZA KEDUSHAH ZUHGT MEN [SHPRINGT MEN] ("In whatever synagogue you pray, you recite the *Kedushah* [leap] according to their tradition"). This guide of conduct was given by the Ashkenazic authority Rabbi Jacob Molin (Maharil), who was notably responsible for unifying synagogue ritual and its music. His rule is that in addition to obedience to time-honored observances, local custom and universal Jewish traditional melodies should not be changed (*Orah Hayyim* 619).

VI KUMT AYSAV IN KERI'AT SHEMA ARAYN? (ווי קומט עשו אין קריאת שמע אריין?). "How does Esau become interlarded with the reading of *Shema*?" The Hebrew name "Aysav" (Esau) and the Hebrew word *aysev* ("grass") sound similar. "Aysav" is spelled with a *vav* at the end (in addition to having a *kametz* under the *sin*) and the word *aysev* is spelled with a *bet* at the end (with a *segol* under the *sin*). The Yiddish expression is directed at a person who makes a statement that is irrelevant.

VI KUMT HODU IN MIKVEH ARAYN (IN BUHD ARAYN)? (ווי קומט הודו אין מקוה אריין (אין באד אריין?). "How does *Hodu* come into the *mikveh* [or the bathhouse]?" *Hodu* is a prayer recited in the early morning *Sha-harit* service and a *mikveh* is a gathering of water used to purify oneself ritually. Just as *Hodu* and a *mikveh* have no connection, so the Yiddish expression is said when an irrelevant statement or remark is made that has no causal or logical relationship to the subject matter under discussion. Possibly, the prayer *Hodu* was adapted for this expression because the pious immerse themselves in a *mikveh* before the *Shaharit* service and, according to the hasidic Sephardic rite, *Hodu* is the first prayer recited congregationally right after the daily offerings (before Psalms 30 and *Barukh She'amar*).

VUHKHEDIGE, SHABBOSDIGE, YOMTOVDIGE SHEMONEH ES-RAYH (וואכעדיגע, שבת׳דיגע, יום-טובדיגע שמונה עשרה). See SHTELN ZIKH (OYSGEYN) SHEMONEH ESRAYH.

VUHS TIFER MEN BUKT ZIKH MODIM, VUHS VAYTER GEYT MEN OSEH SHALOM TZURIK (וואס טיפער מען בוקט זיך מודים וואס, ווייטער גייט מען עושה שלום צוריק). See SHPRING NIT KAYN KADOSH UN BUK ZIKH NIT KAYN MODIM.

YOTZAYR MESHARETIM VA'ASHER MESHARETAV-SHAF DIR MESHARTIM UN GEY DIR ALEYN (יוצר משרתים ואשר משרתיו- שאף דיר אין גיי דיר אליין משרתים).

"Bring into existence servants and do the chore yourself." The Hebrew in the phrase appears in the prayer *Titbarakh Tzuraynu*, of the *Shaharit* service. The first two words, *yotzayr mesharetim*, as they appear in the prayer, refer to God, "Who forms ministering angels" each day (cf. Hag. 14a). The common meaning of the word *mesharetim* is "servants." A person often engages a servant who proves to be incompetent, so the employer ends up doing the work himself.

ZIKH SHTELN KOMEMIYUT (זיך שטעלן קומעמיות).

"To rise up"; a phrase used when speaking of a person's erect posture. The word *komemiyut* appears in the prayer *Ahavah Rabbah*, in the phrase *vetolikhaynu komemiyut le'artzaynu* ("and lead us with upright pride to our land"). R. Chiya interprets the word *komemiyut*, "in an erect position, not fearing any living creature" (*Iyyun Tefillah* in *Otzer Hatefillot*, vol. 1).

GRACE AFTER MEALS (ברכת המזון)

BAKOL, MIKOL, KOL (בכל, מכל, כל).

A phrase meaning "in all, of all, all," uttered in *Birkat Hamazon*. The Talmud (B.B. 17a) comments that each word refers to the three patriarchs: Abraham, Isaac, and Jacob. "Abraham, because it is written of him, 'The Lord blessed Abraham in all [*bakol*] (Gen. 14:1); Isaac, because it is written, 'And I ate of all' [*mikol*] (Gen. 27:33); Jacob, because it is written, 'For I have all' [*kol*] (Gen. 33:11)." The phrase took on the meaning of "completeness" or "perfection."

In daily life, when one wishes to consummate a deal that includes many items,

one may facetiously say *bakol, mikol, kol* to indicate the total amount—or he may utter *hakol-pakol*.

ER KEN KAYN MOTZI NISHT MAKHN IBER A RETEKH (ער קען קיין מוציא נישט מאכן איבער א רעטעך).

When speaking of an ignoramus, an amusing expression used is "He does not know how to make a *motzi* [the blessing made for bread] for a radish." There is no connection between this saying and the blessing for these foods. The expression underscores a person's ignorance.

HAMOTZI LEHEM MIN HA'ARETZ-ES VI A PARITZ (המוציא לחם מן הארץ-עס ווי א פריץ).

The first part of the expression is the blessing made when eating bread, meaning "Blessed . . . Who bringest forth bread from the earth." The latter Yiddish part, which rhymes with part one, means "eat like an aristocrat." The saying signifies inviting a person "to make a *motzi* and eat to his heart's content."

SHELOSHAH SHE'AKHLU-ER EST FAR DRAYEN (שלשה שאכלו-ער עסט פאר דרייען).

The *Mishnah* (Ber. 7:1) states "Three who have eaten (*Sheloshah She'akhlu*) together are required to invite each other to join in reciting Grace together"; that is, the one invites the others by saying, "Let us bless [the Lord] Whose [food] we have eaten." The humorous saying is "Three who have eaten—[but] he eats for all three."

VE'AKHALTA VESAVATA UVAY-RAKHTA (ואכלת ושבעת וברכת).

"And thou shalt eat and be satisfied, and bless" (Deut. 8:10). From this verse, the Rabbis took it as a command that every meal must be followed by Grace. Rabbi Judah said, "Where do we find that Grace After Meals is ordained in the Torah?" Because it says, "And thou shalt eat and be satisfied, and bless" (Ber. 21a).

In a humorous manner the phrase, spelled differently, is often applied to a person who does not fulfill this precept: *Ve'akhalta* ("And thou shalt eat"); *vesavata* ("swear"). The root *shavo'a*, meaning "to swear," is the same as *savaya* ("satisfied"); both have the letters *shin*, (sin), *bet, ayin*; and *uvayrakhta* ("and run away"); this meaning is derived from spelling the word with a *het*, from *barah* ("to flee").

MINHAH and MA'ARIV
(מנחה–מעריב)

ARAYNKHAPN A MINHAH
(אריינכאפן א מנחה). "To grab in a *Minhah*," or VI A YID TZU KHAPN A MINHAH ("like a Jew rushing to *Minhah*"). The *Kitzur Shulkhan Arukh* writes, "A man should ever be careful in praying *Tefillat Minhah*" (69:1). The morning service (*Shaharit*) is fixed for morning, and he prays immediately upon rising, before he becomes absorbed in his daily affairs; likewise, the time is set for the evening prayer (*Ma'ariv*), when he comes home after he is free from his daily affairs; but *Tefillat Minhah* is to be prayed while the day is yet long, and a man is still absorbed in his affairs. A person must then think of it, stop all his business, and pray. Therefore, in order to fulfill the obligation of *Tefillat Minhah*, sometimes one must rush and grab in the *Minhah* service, especially in the winter months.

Similar expression are: ARAYNKHAPN A KEDUSHAH (BAREKHU). In these two instances, the time element is not an issue, but the aspect of being able to recite *Kedushah* and *Barekhu* with a quorum is the motive.

AZ MEN TZEYLT SEFIRAH KUMT OYF DI KLEZMER A PEGIRAH (אז
מען צייילט ספירה קומט אויף די כלי-זמר א פגירה). "When you count *Sefirah*, death comes to the instrumentalists." Since music is forbidden during *Sefirah*, depriving

the instrumentalists of their livelihood is tantamount to terminating any form of existence.

Sefirah is a period of sadness (see TZEYLN SEFIRAH). In the course of many years of exile, misfortune has frequently befallen the people of Israel in the *Sefirah* period. For example, the massacres of Jews in the days of the Crusades, the miseries that befell the Jews in Palestine in the days of Emperor Hadrian, and especially the great plague that raged among the disciples of Rabbi Akiba. Therefore, during this period, one abstains from festivities, rejoicing, and especially from listening to music.

ES HELFT NIT KI AYL SHOMRAYNU UMATZILAYNU-UVETZEYL!
(עס העלפט ניט כי אל שומרני ומצילנו–ובצל!). See GOTT ZUHL UNZ SHOMAYR UMATZIL ZAYN.

GOTT ZUHL UNZ SHOMAYR UMATZIL ZAYN (גאט זאל אונז שומר ומציל זיין). "Heaven protect us"; an expression said by someone who is troubled or provoked by worry. The two Hebrew words, *shomayr* and *umatzil*, have their source in the phrase in the evening prayer *Hashkivaynu*, *ki Ayl shomraynu umatzilaynu Attah* ("for, Almighty, You are our protector and rescuer").

The same Hebrew phrase is used in the witty expression ES HELFT NIT KI AYL SHOMRAYNU UMATZILAYNU—UVETZEYL! The additional word *uvetzayl*, in Hebrew, means "and in the shadow"; in Yiddish the word *tseyln* means "to count." The jocular expression is said by a lender to a borrower. "It will not help even if 'Almighty, You are our protector and rescuer,' *uvetzayl*—count up! or pay up!"

HAMAKEH BE'EVRATO—GESHLUHGN OYF DI IVRE (המכה
בעברתו–געשלאגן אויף די עברי). The two Hebrew words have nothing to do with the Yiddish that follows. *Hamakeh be'evrato* means "Who struck with His

wrath." The Yiddish means "to struggle with the Hebrew reading." Since the word be'evrato (from evrah, meaning "wrath," "rage," or "fury") is close to the Yiddish word ivre ("Hebrew reading"), the humorous expression became associated with a person whose ability to read Hebrew is poor or who is generally an ignoramus.

Other Yiddish expressions deriding those whose ability to read Hebrew is unsatisfactory are Er ken kayn ivre nit ("He cannot read Hebrew"); ER ZUHGT IVRE VI A VASER; NOR DUS VASER LOYFT UN ER SHTAYT ("He reads Hebrew like water; only the water runs and he stands").

MEM-TET SHA'ARAY TUMAH (מ״ט שערי טומאה). "Forty-nine degrees of spiritual uncleanliness" (Zohar Hadash, Parshat Yitro). When the Israelites were in Egypt, they became defiled and sank to the forty-ninth degree of impurity. When counting the Omer for forty-nine days, from the second night of Pesah until the festival of Shavu'ot, it reminds us that each day marks a step away from the defilement of Egypt and a step toward spiritual purity, thus making Israel worthy of receiving the Torah.

OYSLUHZN KOL HAMATO (אויסלאזן כל חמתו). "To wreak his anger," "to give vent to his wrath." The Hebrew words, borrowed from Psalms 78:38, are from the prayer Vehu Rahum, which is recited every weekday evening prior to Barekhu.

SEFIRAH TZAYT (ספירה צייט). See TZEYLN SEFIRAH (TZEYLN OMER).

TZEYLN SEFIRAH (TZEYLN OMER) (צײלן ספירה (צײלן עומר). The counting of seven weeks from Pesah until Shavu'ot, a period in which the omer offering of the new barley crop was brought to the Temple. The counting of each of the forty-nine days symbolizes and also commemorates the eagerness with which the Torah was received by

Israel. This period of time is known as SEFIRAH TZAYT.

VI A YID TZU KHAPN A MINHAH (ווי א איד צו כאפן א מנחה). See ARAYNKHAPN A MINHAH.

FRIDAY EVENING SERVICE (קבלת שבת)

A BAHUR MAKHT KIDDUSH IBER SHPENER (UN HAVDALAH IBER A KALTN FIERTUHP) (א בחור מאכט קידוש איבער שפענער (און הבדלה איבער א קאלטן פײערטאפ). "A bachelor makes Kiddush over chips or splinters (and Havdalah on a cold fire-pot)." This expression alludes to a bachelor not having any homelife. Marriage is an important institution in Jewish life, as these Hebrew and Yiddish sayings bear out: LO TOV HEYOT HA'ADAM LEVADO ("It is not good for man to be alone") and Aleyn zuhl zayn a shteyn ("Only a stone should be alone").

A HAZZAN A DRUNG (א חזן א דראנג). "A cantor, a 'log,' or a 'pole.'" In the vocabulary of cantors, this derogatory expression was applied to a cantor (or singer) whose voice had a wooden quality, or whose rendition was unmusical, or both. The following verse from the Friday evening service was often cited in jest with the appellation drung, "Then shall all the trees of the forest sing with joy" (Ps. 96:12).

The Yiddish expression A mazel fun a drung (fun a flukhn) ("the luck of a log [of a pole]") was used for someone who is inept but succeeds.

BAY BO'I VESHALOM SHTEYT DER UHREMAN OYBNUHN (בײ באי ושלום שטײט דער ארעמאן אויבנאן). "At Bo'i Veshalom the poor man stands at a place of honor—the head." At Bo'i Veshalom, the tenth stanza in Lekhah Dodi recited in the Friday evening service, the congregation turns to face the rear of the synagogue to welcome the Sabbath Queen as she makes her entrance. This ironic remark refers to the poor, who usually sat in the rear of the synagogue. Only when the worshipers turned to the rear did their location change, and they (the poor) were at the head.

DER BESTER MUHGN IZ DER MA-GAYN AVOT (דער בעסטער מאגן איז דער מגן אבות). "The best stomach is the *Magayn Avot*." *Magayn Avot* ("He was a shield to our ancestors") is a prayer recited after *Arvit* on Friday night and has no connection with the stomach. The Yiddish word *muhgn* and the Hebrew word *Magayn* are homonyms and the saying came into being among Eastern European Jews, who amused themselves in this manner as a pastime. Similar expressions are: *A guter muhgn ken fil fartruhgn* ("A good stomach can endure much"), or *A muhgn iz vi a vuhgn—vuhs men zol araynleygn muz er fartruhgn* ("A stomach is like a wagon—whatever you put in, must be carried away").

GUT SHABBOS (גוט שבת). See SHABBAT SHALOM UMEVORAKH.

MEKABL SHABBOS ZAYN (מקבל שבת זיין). "Welcoming the Sabbath." The Friday evening service consists of two parts: *Kabbalat Shabbat* ("Welcoming the Sabbath") and *Arvit* ("the evening service"). *Kabbalat Shabbat* was first introduced in the sixteenth century by the kabbalist Rabbi Moses Cordovero (1522–1570). Reciting Psalms 95–99, 29, and *Lekhah Dodi*, followed by Psalms 92 and 93, constitutes *Mekabl Shabbos Zayn*.

SHABBOS HUHT A YID A NESHA-MAH YETAYRAH (שבת האט אער ייד א נשמה יתירה). "On Sabbath a Jew has an additional soul." This denotes the extra measure of delight every Jew is given from the entrance of the Sabbath until its termination. It is written in the Talmud (Bez.

16a) that R. Simeon b. Lakish said, "On the eve of the Sabbath the Holy One, blessed be He, gives to man an enlarged soul and at the close of the Sabbath He withdraws it from him, for it says, 'He ceased from work and rested' [*vayinafash*] (Ex. 31:17); once it (the Sabbath) has ceased, woe that the additional soul is lost!" The word *vayinafash* is taken to mean *vai avdah nefesh* ("woe for the lost soul") or *vai aynah nefesh* ("the soul is no longer here").

The prayer *Nishmat*, recited on Sabbath morning, alludes to the *Neshamah Yetayrah* that a Jew has on the Sabbath, and its recital was instituted in its honor. Smelling the spices at the blessing *Boray minay besamim* ("Who creates species of fragrance") in *Havdalah* on Saturday night cheers the *Neshamah Yetayrah*, which is saddened at the departure of the Sabbath (*Abudraham*).

SHABBAT SHALOM UMEVORAKH (שבת שלום ומבורך). Rabbi Yaakov Emden quotes this greeting of the Ari in his *Siddur*, which means "Peaceful and blessed Sabbath." It is to be uttered in a loud voice when entering the home on Friday night after services (see also *Siddur Vilna*, [Mesores, Jerusalem] p. 289). It expresses the idea that "Sabbath, you are good, you are peaceful and blessed and are being accepted graciously and with great joy." Even if no other person is present in the home, it is proper to utter either this phrase or GUT SHABBOS. It also became customary to say it after the prayer service in the synagogue (Yitzhak b. Mordecai Lipiec, *Sefer Matamim Hehadash*, [Warsaw, 1894], p. 118).

The reason *gut abend* ("Good evening") is not said on Friday night, as it is on weekdays, is that Adam was created on the sixth day, and on both the sixth day and the evening of the seventh day it was light (*Otzer Shalaym Leminhagay Yisrael* 71:15).

SOF MA'ASEH—BEMAHASHAVAH TEHILAH (סוף מעשה—במחשבה תחילה).

"Last in creation, [but] first in (God's) thought"; a phrase in the Lekhah Dodi poem based on the midrashic idea of the architect who prepares the plans for the entire structure before beginning the construction. This is analagous to the Sabbath being the end-purpose of God's creation.

The phrase evokes several connotations in daily life: "First think, then act"; "Look before you leap"; and "Think twice before you speak once."

UHNGEHOYBN MIT KIDDUSH UN GE'ENDIKT MIT KADDISH (אנגעהויבן מיט קידוש און גיענדיקט מיט קדיש).

"Began with Kiddush and ended with Kaddish." Although Kiddush and Kaddish are translated as "sanctification," they are worlds apart in meaning. Kiddush is recited over wine, a symbol of joy, as is written, "wine that cheers men's heart" (Ps. 104:15), and Kaddish became a prayer to be recited for the departed (Mahzor Vitri). Each has its place in Jewish life. An irrelevant remark made without any connection to the subject under discussion or basis in fact would evoke this Yiddish expression.

Similar expression are: VUHS HUHT A PATCH TZUTUHN MIT YEKUM PURKAN? ("What connection is there between a slap and the prayer Yekum Purkan?"), or VI KUMT A PATCH TZU GUT SHABBOS? ("How does a slap come to Gut Shabbos?").

VI KUMT A PATCH TZU GUT SHABBOS? (ווי קומט א פאטש צו גוט שבת?).

See SHABBAT SHALOM UMEVORAKH.

ZAKHOR VESHAMOR—ZIKH TZU HALTN BEDIBUR EHAD (זכור ושמור—זיך צו האלטן בדיבור אחד).

"Remember and observe—to abide by one utterance." "Remember the Sabbath" (Ex. 20:8) and "Keep the Sabbath" (Deut. 5:12) are two phrases that appear in the

First and Second Tablets. In the popular hymn Lekhah Dodi, Shamor Vezakhor ("Keep and remember") appears in the first stanza. The Talmud remarks that they were both pronounced in one utterance (Shebu. 20b). The Yiddish expression connotes "warning"; that is, "Remember—keep your word!"

ZEMIROT (זמירות)

ASAKH ZEMIROT UN VEYNIG LUHKSHN (אסאך זמירות און וייניג לאקשן).

"A great deal of Zemirot but little noodles." This is to say that there is much spirituality but little essence.

AYSHET HAYIL MI YIMTZA, UHBER A VAYB A SHLIMAZEL IZ BENIMTZA (אשת חיל מי ימצא, אבער א ווייב א שלימזל איז בנמצא).

"A woman of valor, who can find? But a wife a shlimazel can be found." A bachelor may retort with this expression when asked, "When are you getting married?" An ideal, clever wife has always been described in Jewish life as an ayshet hayil. These are the opening words of the Zemirot recited on Friday evening, prior to the Sabbath meal. This alphabetical acrostic poem describes the ideal Jewish wife (Prov. 31:10–331). The faulty wife, of whom the latter part of the expression speaks, is called a shlimazel (from the German schlimm, "bad," and the Hebrew mazel, "luck"); in other words, an inept, ne'er-do-well person.

BARUKH HASHEM YOM YOM—OYF (FAR) MORGN ZUHL (VET) GOTT ZORGN (ברוך השם יום יום—אויף (פאר) מארגן זאל (וועט) גאט זארגן).

"Blessed be the Lord day by day—let God worry about tomorrow." The expression opens with the first words of the Sabbath table hymn, written by Shimon Bar Yitzhak. The poem gives praise to God for taking us out of Egypt and saving us from our enemies. With the Jew, there was daily concern for the morrow and for withstanding the vicissitudes of life. Therefore, the Jew said or thought to himself, "True, we bless God every single day, but we have faith in God that He will keep us alive tomorrow." See also the phrase *Barukh Hashem yom yom* in the prayer *Uva letziyon*.

DER UHREMAN HUHT BASOR VEDAGIM IN DI ZEMIROT (דער אָרעמאַן האָט בשר ודגים אין די זמירות). "The poor man has meat and fish in the *Zemirot*." The Sabbath hymn *Yom Zeh Mehubad* ("This day is most precious of all days") includes a stanza, "Eat rich foods, drink sweet drinks, for the Almighty will give to all who cling to Him garments to wear, bread as needed, meat and fish and all delicacies." Thus, the Yiddish expression alludes to the poor man who only sings of meat and fish but, in reality, does not have it on his table.

DER YID ENTFERT TAMID FAR-KERT: ZUHGT MEN IM SHALOM ALAYKHEM, ENTFERT ER ALAY-KHEM SHALOM (דער ייד ענטפערט תמיד פאַרקערט:זאָגט מען אים שלום עליכם ענטפערט ער עליכם שלום). "The Jew always answers the opposite; when saying to him *Shalom alykhem*, he answers *Alaykhem shalom*." The phrase *Shalom alykhem* (lit., "peace be upon you") is the usual manner in which greetings are extended; it is the opening of a Sabbath table hymn, and the greeting exchanged between three different people during *Kiddush Levanah* ("Sanctification of the Moon"). The word *shalom* has a wider meaning than "peace." It is a name of God (Judg. 6:24) and, consequently, one is not permitted to greet another person with the word *shalom* in unholy places (Shab. 10b). It also signifies welfare of every kind. Hence, the plural word *alaykhem* is used because it includes both body and soul. The inverted order *alaykhem shalom*, in response to the greeting *Shalom alykhem*, is derived from the Talmud, "It was also laid down that greeting should be

given in (God's) Name, in the same way as it says, and behold Boaz came from Bethlehem and said unto the reapers, *Hashem imakhem* ('the Lord be with you'), and they answered him, *Yevarekhekha Hashem* ('the Lord bless thee')" (Ber. 54a). Therefore, the same format is employed; that is, when one extends greetings one may say *Shalom* (God's Name) before *alaykhem*, but the person who answers inverts the order and says God's Name at the end (Yitzhak Lipiec, *Sefer Matamim* [Warsaw, 1894], p. 107). See TEKI'AT KAF.

MAH-YAFIT YID (MAYAFISNIK) (מה-יפית (מה-יפיתניק)). *Mah-Yafit*, meaning "How beautiful art thou," is a table hymn attributed to Mordecai b. Yitzhak Kimchi (c. 1290), sung on Friday evening. In the seventeenth, eighteenth, and nineteenth centuries, Polish land-owners urged their Jewish tenants to sing *Majufes* (Judeo-Polish pronunciation) at their wild orgies, accompanied by dances and comical gestures. A servile Jew who flattered his Polish landlord and condescended to sing the *Mah-Yafit* tune was called a *Mayafisnik*, an appellation eventually given to those who did not maintain their dignity and self-respect as Jews.

SHAHARIT and MUSAF for SHABBAT שחרית—מוסף (לשבת)

ER KEN MIKH UHPZUHGN DEM HAKOL YODUKHA (ער קען מיך אָפּזאָגן דעם הכל יודוך). "He can say to me *Hakol Yodukha*." *Hakol Yodukha* ("All shall thank Thee") is a prayer recited in the Sabbath *Shaharit* service. The prayer continues, "and all shall praise Thee, and all shall say there is none holy like the Lord." The Yiddish expression is turned around and directed at a person who is provoked to anger. However much the other party lauds him, his anger does not subside and he is not won over.

FARBAYTN DI YOTZROT (פֿאַרבײטן
די יוצרות). "To mix up the *Yotzrot.*"
Yotzrot (sing., *Yotzayr*) are the *Piyyutim*
("poems") inserted in the benedictions of
Shema in *Shaharit* on special Sabbaths and
holidays. Its name is derived from the first
benediction preceding the *Shema*, "Who
formest [*Yotzayr*] lights." Although there
are different categories of *Piyyut* (e.g.,
Ma'aravot, Kerovot) the appellation *Yotzrot*
is popularly applied to all *Piyyutim*. Often,
on a two-day holiday, the *Piyyutim* are
interchanged when one of the days occurs
on the Sabbath. This procedure occasionally results in confusion in the prayer
service and thus the Yiddish expression is
also used when one confuses several
things or compounds one thing with another.

The language of the *Piyyutim* is sometimes difficult to understand because it is
composed of exegetical and homiletical
allusions containing mystery or parables
(according to Abraham ibn Ezra, in his
commentary on Ecclesiastes 5:1). Thus,
the saying KELBERNE (*kalb*, the singular,
meaning "calf"; *kelber*, pl.). YOTZROT came
into existence and is directed at one who
recites the *Piyyutim* in a nonsensical, bab-
bling manner, as a calf babbles. The word
kelberne is also used in conjunction with
kelberne hitpa'alut ("foolish enthusiasm").

FARFALN,   LE'OLAM   VA'ED
(פֿאַרפֿאַלן, לעולם ועד). "Lost forever and
ever." The Hebrew words *le'olam va'ed*
appear in the *Shaharit Kedushah*, as well as
in other prayer recitals. The Yiddish expression is used when one has not paid
back a debt over a long period of time and
it is thus considered lost.

**HAZZAN ZET NIT VI KAHAL
HINTER LAKHT** (חזן זעט ניט ווי קהל
הינטער לאַכט). "The cantor does not see
how the congregation is laughing in back
of him." Many prayers in the liturgy, such
as *Anim Zemirot*, are recited in a respon-
sive form. Directions are given on each

line, which are marked either *Hazzan*
("cantor") or *Vekahal* ("and congregation"). Each of the letters in the Hebrew
are the first letters of the Yiddish expression: *HaZZaN (Hazzan zet nit) VeKaHaL*
(*Vi Kahal Hinter Lakht*). Some cantors
took themselves too seriously and displayed vanity. The Jew, who, throughout
the ages, had little to laugh about, developed a sense of humor that helped him
through many dark periods. In the synagogue, it manifested as laughing-up-one's-
sleeve; that is, he laughed privately or
secretly at the *Hazzan*, while appearing
grave or serious.

In some *Siddurim* and *Mahzorim*, the
direction given was HAZZAN ZUHGT FOR UN
DER KAHAL ENTFERT ("The cantor recites
and the congregation answers").

**HAZZAN ZUHGT FOR UN DER
KAHAL ENTFERT** (חזן זאָגט פֿאַר און
דער קהל ענטפֿערט). See HAZZAN ZET NIT
VI KAHAL HINTER LAKHT.

KELBERNE YOTZROT (קעלבערנע
יוצרות). See FARBAYTN DI YOTZROT.

VI A FLOY IN YEKUM PURKAN (ווי
אַ פֿלוי אין יקום פּורקן). "Like a flea in
Yekum Purkan." The expression is used in
a derogatory way in an imaginative comparison. Just as the idler has a disinclina-
tion to work, so the flea has no
relationship to *Yekum Purkan* (a prayer).

**VUHS HUHT A PATCH TZUTUHN
MIT YEKUM PURKAN?** (וואָס האָט
אַ פּאַטש צוטאָן מיט יקום פּורקן?). See
UHNGEHOYBN MIT KIDDUSH UN GE'ENDIKT MIT
KADDISH.

BLESSING OF THE NEW
MONTH (ברכת החודש)

ER KUMT UHP MIT YEHI RATZON
(ער קומט אָפ מיט יהי רצון). "He justifies
himself with 'May it be Thy will.'" *Yehi*

Ratzon are the opening words of a prayer that the talmudic Sage Rav recited (Ber. 16b). It serves as a prayer said at ROSH HODESH BENTCHN. The sarcastic Yiddish expression is directed at a person who can well afford to give charity but does not. He always says, "May it be Thy will," but lacks the conviction necessary to effect his own decision to give.

HAVAYRIM KOL YISRAEL (חברים כל ישראל). "United in friendship is all of Israel." This popular phrase is part of a prayer, *Mi She'asa Nisim* ("He Who performed miracles"), recited during the Blessing of the New Month on the Sabbath prior to *Rosh Hodesh*. The proclamation of the new month in ancient times was the supreme function of the *Sanhedrin* at Jerusalem. They decided the exact time of the new moon by actual observation. The current custom of proclaiming in the synagogue on the Sabbath the day(s) on which the coming month is to begin, is in remembrance of the ancient function of the *Sanhedrin*. When Israel will be redeemed, once again the new moon will be decided upon by actual observation. But how can this happen? Only when all of Israel will be united in friendship as one (*Sheviley Haleket*).

HAYNTIGER HODESH IZ HASAYR (היינטיגער חודש איז חסר). "This month is a defective one." The Jewish months are either *malay* ("full") or *hasayr* ("short"). The months *Nisan, Sivan, Ab, Tishre, Shevat,* and *Adar I* are always full months, that is, having thirty days. *Iyar, Tammuz, Elul, Tevet, Adar* (in an ordinary year, or *Adar II* in a leap year) are always short months—that is, having twenty-nine days. *Heshvan* and *Kislev* are sometimes full and sometimes short.

OYSRUFN DEM MOLAD (אויסרופן דעם מולד). "To call out the *Molad*." When the Blessing of the New Month takes place in the synagogue on Sabbath morning, the

Molad ("birth," from the root *yalad*) is announced by an officiant. He specifies the precise time (that is, the hour, the minute, and the portion of a minute or seconds) at which the new moon will become visible in Jerusalem.

ROSH HODESH BENTCHN (ראש חודש בענטשן). "Blessing of the New Month." This takes place on *Shabbat* morning, when most of the people are in the synagogue. The objectives are to pray that the month be good for the people of Israel and to inform them of the day(s) on which *Rosh Hodesh* occurs.

SABBATH *MINHAH* and *MOTZA'AY SHABBAT* (מנחה לשבת—מוצאי שבת)

A YIDENE UHN A TZE'ENAH URE'ENAH IZ VI A SHEYGETZ UHN A FIFL (א יידענע אן א צאינה וראינה איז ווי א שייגעטץ אן א פייפל). "A woman without a *Tze'enah Ure'enah* is like a gentile boy without a whistle." *Tze'enah Ure'enah* is a book with an exegetical rendering in Yiddish of the Pentateuch, *Haftarot*, and the Five Scrolls read by women on the Sabbath (afternoon). Attributed to Jacob Ashkenazi (1550–1621) of Janow, Poland, its title has been "Yiddishsized" to *Tzenerene* and it has become known as *Teitch Humash* (a translation of the Bible). Almost all women of Eastern Europe owned a *Tzenerene*, just as a gentile boy possessed a whistle to call his dog or cattle.

Often, a women read for other women who were illiterate. In the synagogue she read prayers in the women's section for other women to repeat. This woman was known as a *Zuhgerke*. She usually read from a *Korban Minhah Siddur* (title of a prayerbook) and also read *Vaybershe Tehinot* ("women's supplications").

AD KAN OMRIM BESHABBOS HAGADOL (עד כאן אומרים בשבת הגדול). "Until here it is said on Shabbos Hagadol." It is customary to recite from Avadim Hayinu until Lekhapayr al kol avonotaynu (part of the Haggadah) on Shabbos Hagadol after Minhah, since the miracles of the redemption began on the Sabbath prior to the Exodus. This expression is directed at a person to stop him from saying or doing something extraneous.

ES IZ LEHAVDIL BAYN KODESH LEHOL (עס איז להבדיל בין קודש לחול). "It is comparing sacred to secular." The Hebrew, borrowed from Havdalah ("distinction"), is the fourth benediction marking the end of the Sabbath. The distinction used in the expression is to underscore "difference" or "not-the-same," as in the English expression, "How do apples come to oranges?" Similar Yiddish expressions are Es iz lehavdil bayn tumah letaharah (comparing impurity to purity) and ES IZ LEHAVDIL ELEF HAVDALOT ("It is a thousand differences"). The closing benediction is also found in these rhyming Yiddish expressions:

Hamavdil bayn kodesh lehol (Heb.) Who maketh a distinction between holy and secular.
Az es geruht iz take voyl (Yidd.). If it meets with success, it is good.
Hamavdil bayn kodesh lehol (Heb.) Who maketh a distinction between holy and secular.
Ver es huht gelt (in keshene) dem iz voyl (Yidd.). He who has money (in his pocket), it is good for him.

Faced with abject poverty and the plight of barely managing to eke out a living in the coming working days, the Jew expressed his desires in his hour of need.

GOTT FUN AVRAHAM (גאט פון אברהם). "God of Abraham"; a meditation in Yiddish, marking the end of the Sabbath, recited by women at dusk in a poignant chant style. It is attributed to Reb Levi Yitzhak of Berdichev (1740–1809) and prescribed by him to be said three times by men, women, and children. The prayer is customarily said by women, since they did not recite Ma'ariv. They were able to follow this prayer by Barukh hamavdil bayn kodesh lehol ("Blessed is He Who separates between holy and secular"), instead of Attah honantanu ("You have graced us"), which is part of the Ma'ariv Amidah prayer on Saturday night. Rabbi Levi Yitzhak of Berdichev intoned the meditation after the third Sabbath meal (Shalosh Se'udot).

The meditation that occurs in several textual variants asks for a successful week, for good health, for wealth and honor, and for children, life, and sustenance. It originated in Eastern Europe when the prevailing language was Yiddish.

GUT VUKH (SHAVU'A TOV) (גוט וואך) (שבוע טוב). Both the Yiddish Gut vukh and Hebrew Shavu'a Tov mean "good week." It is the form of greeting used at the conclusion of the Sabbath. Asking for a good week in which tidings of joy and gladness are found is mirrored in different liturgical recitals (GOTT FUN AVRAHAM, Veyiten lekha, and Ribbon Ha'olamim).

HADAS (HUHDES) (הדס). "Spice box" (Yidd., Besamim-biksl); a perforated container for spices used in the Havdalah service. The name Hadas is derived from placing a myrtle-branch (hadas) into a special utensil designed to diffuse aromas (cf. R. Yisrael Meir Ha-Cohen, Mishnah Berurah 297:10).

In medieval Europe, herbs such as myrtle (hadas) were generally used. But when spices were substituted for herbs, the spice box retained the name Hadas. The earliest person to mention a special box is the tosafist and payyetan, Rabbi Ephraim of Regensburg (1110–1175). He made the blessing not over a myrtle branch but over spices contained in a special glass receptacle.

MAKHN BORAY ME'ORAY HA'AYSH

(מאכן בורא מאורי האש). Literally, to make the blessing of 'He Who creates the light of fire.'" At the departure of the Sabbath and holidays, one recites *Havdalah* and, among the four blessings, *Boray me'oray ha'aysh* is said while holding the fingers up to the flame to see the reflected light upon the nails. This is in keeping with Adam's first Sabbath on earth, when fear befell him as he saw that it was getting dark. Not only was he fearful of the dark and of not being able to see, but also of being excluded from the Garden of Eden.

The Yiddish phrase is ludicrously used to signify incendiarism or for one who commits arson.

MEHADAYSH ZAYN DI LEVANAH

(מחדש זיין די לבנה). "Blessing the moon's reappearance." Jewish tradition believes that by the moon's total disappearance from view at the very end of a month and its reappearance at the beginning of the month, there is a continuity in the process of creation. The moon is also seen as a symbol of the capacity of the Jewish people to regenerate themselves. Just as the moon is reborn after a period of decline and total disappearance, so, too, will Israel's decline cease and its light shine to its fullness. The blessing made is "Blessed art Thou, O Lord, Who renews the months" (San. 42a).

Due to the appearance and shape of the half-moon, SHRAYBN IN HALBE LEVANOT ("to write in half-moons") is the saying for "to write in parenthesis." In Hebrew, *hatzay levanah* is used.

MIT KIDDUSH LEVANAH KEN MEN ZIKH NIT UHPFASTN (מיט

קידוש לבנה קען מען זיך ניט אפפאסטן). "With *Kiddush Levanah* one cannot break a

fast." Tradition has it that *Kiddush Levanah* takes place after two important fasts: at the conclusion of *Tishah b'Ab* and after Yom Kippur. It is believed that at the conclusion of *Tishah b'Ab* the Messiah will be born. It is thus a proper time for *Kiddush Levanah*, when we proclaim the good tidings that Israel and the moon will renew themselves as of yore (*Ari*; cf. also *Be'er Haytayv* 551:25). On Yom Kippur night a particularly festive and joyous mood prevails; thus, it is a most appropriate time for this ceremony. Undoubtedly, the Yiddish expression was uttered on both occasions, when Jews fast all day and *Kiddush Levanah* obviously cannot satisfy the desire for food.

SHRAYBN IN HALBE LEVANOT

(שרייבן אין האלבע לבנות). See MEHADAYSH ZAYN DI LEVANAH.

SHRAYBN MIT KIDDUSH LEVANAH OSIYOT (שרייבן מיט קידוש

לבנה אותיות). "To write with *Kiddush Levanah* lettering." The typesetting for the prayers recited at *Kiddush Levanah* are usually very large in many *Siddurim*. This is done intentionally so that the worshipers are able to read the prayers at night out-of-doors. This expression denotes one who writes with headline lettering, or is used when one's writing is emphatic and attracts attention.

VETZIDKOSKHA BETZEDEK—ROSHAY TAYVOT: BIZ TZU DER KESHENE (וצדקתך בצדק—ראשי

תיבות: ביז צו דער קעשענע). The letters of the word *BeTZeDeK* form the initial letters of the words *Biz Tzu Der Keshene* ("up to the pocket"). In other words, this person acts holier-than-thou but when it comes to *tzedakah* ("charity"), he or she is miserly. See ZAY A TZADIK UHBER NIT KAYN VETZIDKOSKHA.

VEYITEN LEKHA-KAYN GELT IZ NITUH, MITAL HASHAMAYIM-NITUH VU TZU LAYEN, MISH-MANAY HA'ARETZ-DUHS GELT IZ BAYM PARITZ (ויתן לך-קײן געלט איז ניטא. מטל השמים-ניטא וואו צו לייען, (משמני הארץ-דאס געלט איז בײם פריץ). The Yiddish is not a translation of the Hebrew, but the words rhyme.

Veyiten lekha (Heb.)	May God give thee
kayn gelt iz nituh (Yidd.)	there is no money
mital hashamayim (Heb.)	of the dew of Heaven
nituh vu tzu layen (Yidd.)	there's nowhere to borrow
mishmanay ha'aretz (Heb.)	from the fat of the land
duhs gelt iz baym paritz (Yidd.)	the landowner has the money.

Veyiten Lekha, a collection of scriptural passages, is recited after the Ma'ariv service in the synagogue on Saturday night or in the house after Havdalah. In the week to come, the Jew would be faced with abject poverty and trying to eke out a living for his family. Veyiten Lekha represents a collection of blessing, beginning with that given to Isaac and Jacob. By reciting them at the beginning of the new week, we invoke God's blessing on the labor of the coming work days; thus, the expressions spoken in Yiddish explain one's thoughts in this hour of need.

ZAY A TZADIK UHBER NIT KAYN VETZIDKOSKHA (זײ א צדיק אבער נישט קײן וצדקתך). "Be righteous but not holier-than-thou." Tzidkatkha tzedek le'olam ("Your righteousness is an everlasting righteousness") is a prayer recited at Minhah on Sabbath afternoon. Adding the letter vav in the Hebrew language refers to something additional as ve-Adar, the month following Adar Rishon ("the first Adar"). The expression is thus directed to someone who pretends to be other and

better than he is, a holier-than-thou person. A person who manifests such sentiments or ideas by a gesture or a look is said to have a Vetzidkhoskha panim ("a holier-than-thou face").

TORAH and HAFTARAH (תורה-הפטרה)

A NUHMEN FUN DER HAFTARAH
(א נאמען פון דער הפטרה). "A name from the Haftarah." This alludes to a fictitious or rare name. For example, on Parashat Beshalakh the Haftarah read is from the Book of Judges. A name that appears in this Haftarah is Shamgar, the son of Anath (Judg. 5:6), which sounds fictitious. Thus, when someone's name sounds strange, the expression A nuhmen fun der Haftarah is used.

A TRUKENER MI SHEBAYRAKH HELFT VI A TOYTN BANKES (א טרוקענער מי שברך העלפט ווי א טױטן באנקעס). See A TRUKENER MI SHE-BAYRAKH HELFT VI TRUKENE BANKES.

A TRUKENER MI SHEBAYRAKH HELFT VI TRUKENE BANKES (א טרוקענער מי שברך העלפט ווי טרוקענע באנקעס). "A dry Mi Shebayrakh is useless, like dry bankes." Usually, when a Mi Shebayrakh is made, one donates to an important cause or gives a Kiddush to the congregation. Bankes ("cupping glasses") was a method to bring down a fever, by drawing blood to the skin. The rims of small glass cups were moistened and then applied with pressure to the chest and back. The humorous saying alludes to the fact that just as dry bankes will not stick, so a dry Mi Shebayrakh, without the act of giving, will not be effective. Similar is the adage A TRUKENER MI SHEBAYRAKH HELFT VI A TOYTN BANKES ("A dry Mi Shebayrakh helps like applying bankes to a dead person").

AYNER HUHT LIB ZOYERMILKH, DER TZVEYTER MAFTIR (איינער האט ליב זויערמילך. דער צווייטער מפטיר). Literally, "One likes sour milk, while another likes *Maftir*." A parallel Hebrew expression is *Al ta'am varayah ayn lehitvakayah* ("about taste and smell, you cannot argue"). Tastes differ.

BARUKH SHEPETARANI (ברוך שפטרני). "Blessed _____ who has freed me _____." After the *Bar Mitzvah* is called up to the Torah for his *Aliyah*, the father recites this blessing, signifying that now he is no longer responsible for his child's behavior. The two words became a jocular expression, used when getting rid of someone or something. A witticism expressed when marrying off a daughter would be BAY A YINGL MAKHT MEN BARUKH SHEPETARANI TZU BAR-MITZVAH, BAY A MEDYL-TZU DER HASUNAH ("For a young boy, *Barukh Shepetarani* is made at his *Bar-Mitzvah*; for a girl, at the wedding").

BAY A YINGL MAKHT MEN BA-RUKH SHEPETARANI TZU BAR-MITZVAH, BAY A MEYDL—TZU DER HASUNAH (ביי א יינגל מאכט מען ברוך שפטרני צו בר-מצוה, ביי א מיידל—צו דער חתונה). See BARUKH SHE-PETARANI.

BENTCHN GOMAYL (בענטשן גומל). A blessing said after escaping from a great danger during land or sea journeys, after recovery from a major illness, and after release from captivity. Offering this blessing is derived from Psalms 107, in which similar thanksgiving is offered on occasions such as these. (See also Ber. 54b.)

ER HUHT IM GEGEBN A MI SHE-BAYRAKH (ער האט אים געגעבן א מי שברך). "He gave him a *Mi Shebayrakh*." The prayer *Mi Shebayrakh* ("He Who blessed") is generally recited on Sabbath and festivals for one called up to the Torah for an *Aliyah*. The prayer asks

for the Almighty to bestow on the individual and his family good health, well-being, and prosperity. In daily parlance, the two Hebrew words are used as a euphemism. After the person finishes giving "a *Mi Shebayrakh*" ("reprimand"), the receiver then really needs good luck and a special prayer for good health, and so forth.

HASHKAVAH (ASHKAVAH) (השכבה (אשכבה)). A prayer for remembering the dead; as in *ashkavtayh de-Rabbi* ("the death of Rabbi") (Ket. 103b). The term is used among *Sephardim*.

HAZAK HAZAK VENITHAZAK (חזק חזק ונתחזק). "Be strong, be strong, and let us strengthen one another." This is a phrase uttered at the completion of each of the Five Books of Moses when they are read publicly in the synagogue (Isserles to *Shulhan Arukh, Orah Hayyim* 139:11). The congregation stands and exclaims it first and then it is uttered by the *Ba'al Keri'ah*. The response is reminiscent of the expression *Hazak venithazak be'ad amaynu* ("Be strong and let us be of good courage for our people") in 2 Samuel 10:12 and 1 Chronicles 19:13. This is understood to mean "Let us be strong and gather courage to carry out the teaching contained in the Book just completed, as well as in the other Books of the Torah." See HAZAK VE'EMATZ and HAZAK UVARUKH.

KRIGN (ZAYN) SHISHI (קריגן (זיין) שישי). "To get [to be] the sixth *Aliyah* at the Sabbath reading of the Torah." The same expression may be used for any of the other *Aliyot*. According to the Talmud (cf. Git. 59a) and other sources (cf. Rabbi G. Felder, *Sefer Yesoday Yeshurun*, vol. 4 [New York, 1962], pp. 383, 384), it is considered an honor to receive the highly valued third (*shlishi*) and sixth (*shishi*) *Aliyot*. It is customary to allot them to men of special learning or piety.

When one does something ordinary and does not merit any praise, a sarcastic remark made is *Kumt im shlishi [shishi]* (He deserves *shlishi [shishi]*).

MA'AVIR SIDRAH ZAYN (מעביר סדרה זיין). "To review the weekly portion of the Pentateuch." The *Sidrah* to be read publicly in the synagogue on Sabbath morning is reviewed either Friday afternoon or early Sabbath morning. The individual does this by cantillating the verse twice, according to the *Te'amim*, and then chanting the *Targum* in cantillatory style. In Hebrew this is referred to as *Shenayim mikra ve'ehad Targum*. The Talmud (Ber. 8a, b) comments, ". . . for if one completes his *Parashot [Sidrah* and *Parashah* are used interchangeably] together with the congregation, his days and years are prolonged." See LE'OLAM YASHLIM ADAM PARASHIYOTAV IM HATZIBBUR SHENAYIM MIKRA VE'EHAD TARGUM.

ZITZN AL HATORAH VE'AL HA'AVODAH (ויצן על התורה ועל העבודה). "To sit immersed in study of Torah and prayer." The Hebrew is derived from the final blessing after the *Haftarah* read on the Sabbath, in which we thank God for the Torah reading, for the prayer service, for the reading from the Prophets, and for the Sabbath day. The Yiddish saying reflects admiration and respect for the person who devotes his entire life and energy to the study of Torah and the recitation of prayers. (see also *Pirkay Avot* 1:2.)

SHALOSH REGALIM
(שלש רגלים)

A GUTN MO'AYD (א. גוטן מועד). See MO'ADIM LESIMHAH—HAGIM UZEMANIM LESASON.

AGIL VE'ESMAH—KAYLEKHDIK UN SHPITZEDIK (אגיל ואשמח— קיילעכדיק און שפיטצעדיק). "'I will exult and rejoice'—well rounded and sharp." The poem *Agil ve'esmah*, which

expresses joy over the Torah, is recited on *Simhat Torah* just before returning the Torah scroll to the Ark. The Yiddish part of the saying describes the well-rounded and sharp characteristics of a person, and much delight is derived from these attributes. The expression may also allude to a situation that is glowing and beautiful, just as the sun is round and gives off its rays at its peak (*shpitzik*), causing joyfulness.

ATTAH HARAYTA LADA'AT-NITUH KAYN BRUHNFN, TRINKT MEN KVASS (אתה הראת לדעת-ניטא קיין בראהנפן טרינקט מען קוואס). "'You have been shown to know'—if there's no whiskey you drink *kvass*." There is no relationship between the Hebrew and the Yiddish in this saying. *Attah Harayta* is a prayer recited on *Simhat Torah* and, since it is the most joyful time of the year, when singing, dancing, drinking, and prancing take place in the synagogue, it undoubtedly prompted this amusing expression. Also, the word *lada'at* in Hebrew rhymes with the Yiddish *kvass* (a fermented beverage generally drunk in Russia).

ATTAH VEHARTANU MIKOL HA'-AMIM; UN FARN SHEYGETZ HUHST DU MORE! (אתה בחרתנו מכל העמים; און פארן שייגעטץ האסט דו מורא!). See ATTAH VEHARTA(NU) NISM.

ATTAH VEHARTA (NU) NISM (אתה בחרת (נו) ניזם). *Attah Vehartanu* ("Thou hast chosen us") are the opening words of a prayer recited in the *Amidah* on the Three Pilgrimage Festivals. The special choosing is for Israel to teach mankind about God and the brotherhood of all men. It also imposes an extra responsibility upon Israel to live in accordance with moral law. The designation is used as a doctrine of the Jew's religious system, his theory, and practice.

To a person who is affected by fear and has to be reassured that no harm will befall him, the expression ATTAH VEHARTANU MIKOL HA'AMIM; UN FARN SHEYGETZ

HUHST DU MORE ("Thou hast chosen us from all the nations; and you fear the gentile boy!") was often used.

AYNAYIM LAHEM VELO YIRU (עינים להם ולא יראו). "They have eyes, but cannot see" (Jer. 5:21; Ps. 115:5). The phrase connotes idols, made by man, of silver and gold. The children of Israel trust in God alone.

"They have eyes, but cannot see" is sometimes directed at a person who has peripheral vision but does not discern.

DUKHENEN (דוכענען). "The Priestly Blessing." The Yiddish term is derived from the special platform, *dukhan*, on which the *Kohanim* ascended every morning and evening at the *Tamid* offering to bless the people with uplifted hands. This is known as NESI'AT KAPAYIM ("raising of the hands").

The Yiddish expression GEBN A YASHER KO'AH is used to express thanks to the *Kohanim* after *Dukhenen. Yasher Ko'ah* is found in the Talmud, which tells us that God approved and thanked Moshe when he broke the first tablets. "And how do we know the Holy One, blessed be He, gave His approval? Because it is said, 'which thou breakest' [*asher shibarta*] (Ex. 34:1) and Resh Lakish interpreted this, 'All strength to thee that thou breakest it' [*Yishar kohakha sheshibarta*]" (Shab. 87a).

ER IZ SHOYN A HALAKH LE'-OLAMO (ער איז שוין א הלך לעולמו). "He is already dead." The phrase *halakh le'olamo* ("went on to his world") is borrowed from *Ayl Malay Rahamim*, a prayer recited for the deceased. To recite this prayer for the dead is known as MAKHN AYL MALAY RAHAMIM ("to make an *Ayl Malay Rahamim*") and to read prayers for the repose of the soul is MAKHN HAZKARAT NESHAMOT ("to make the Memorial Service").

GEBN A YASHER-KO'AH (געבן א יישר-כח). See DUKHENEN.

GUT YOM TOV (גוט יום טוב). See MO'ADIM LESIMHAH—HAGIM UZEMANIM LESASON.

IKH HUHB NIT (ENTFER); LO LANU SHTEYT IN HALLEL (איך האב ניט (ענטפער); לא לנו שטייט אין הלל). "I don't have [answer]; 'Not unto us' is a phrase in *Hallel*." This is a dialogue between a borrower and a lender. The borrower says, "I don't have it." The lender, applying a phrase in *hallel* (Ps. 115:1), retorts, "'Not unto us' [that is, not having] is a phrase used [only] in *Hallel*."

IR ZUHLT ZIKH OYSBETEN A GUT YOR (A GUT KVITL) (איר זאלט זיך אויסבעטן א גוט יאר (א גוט קוויטל). "You should obtain a good year [a good verdict]." Beginning with the month of *Elul* until the end of Sukkot holiday, Jews exchange this wish and/or greeting with each other. According to kabbalistic tradition, a written final verdict (*kvitl*) is issued on *Hoshana Rabbah*, sealing the fate of every Jew for the year to come. See KVITL.

KOL HA'ADAM KOZAYV-ITLEKHER HUHT ZIKH ZAYNE MAKOS (כל האדם כזב-איטלעכער האט זיך זיינע מכות). "'All mankind is deceitful'—each has its blows." The Hebrew (Ps. 116:11) is a painful remark made by King David when his hiding place was revealed to King Saul by the people of Zif (cf. 1 Sam. 23:19–29). According to the Abarbanel, it refers to the bleak, dismal exile of the Jewish people, who, because of the exile, began to believe that the prophet's promises concerning the redemption were deceitful. The Yiddish expression takes off on this perfidy and applies it to an individual who undergoes hardships and calamities in life, which cause suffering or loss.

LANG VI A LULAV (לאנג ווי א לולב). "Long like a palm branch." The *lulav*, held during the blessing of *al netilat lulav* on

Sukkot, is the tallest of the Four Species and is considered "king" over all the fruit trees. Thus, when making a comparison, the Yiddish expression is utilized to signify extraordinary length or height.

A humorous description of a family might be Er vi a lulav, zi vi an etrog, un kinderlakh vi sekhakh (grine), ("He as a lulav, she as an etrog, and children like sekhakh [green]").

LO AMUT KI EHYEH-AZ S'IZ NIT BASHERT TZU SHTARBN SHTARBT MEN NIT (לא אמות כי אחיה-אז ס'איז ניט באשערט צו שטארבן שטארבט מען ניט). "'I shall not die, but I shall live'—if it is not destined that one should die, one does not die." The Hebrew phrase is derived from Psalms 118, which is part of Hallel. The psalmist declares, "I shall not die, but I shall live," that is, Israel speaks as a nation that has escaped from the annihilation that the exile threatened. The Yiddish saying is a simple and personal approach to death and asserts that a person does not die before his time is up.

MAKHN AYL MALAY RAHAMIM (מאכן אל מלא רחמים). See ER IZ SHOYN A HALAKH LE'OLAMO.

MAKHN HAZKARAT NESHAMOT (מאכן הזכרת נשמות). See ER IZ SHOYN A HALAKH LE'OLAMO.

MEKIMI MAYAFAR DAL—AZ GOTT HELFT DEM UHREMAN; MAYASHPOT YARIM EVYON—IZ IM GORNIT TZU DERKENEN (מקימי מעפר דל—אז גאט העלפט דעם אורעמאן; מאשפת ירים אביון—איז אים גארניט צו דערקענען). "'He raises the needy from the dust' (when God helps the poor man); 'from the trash heaps He lifts the destitute' (you cannot recognize him)." The Yiddish is basically a translation of two Hebrew phrases recited in Hallel (Ps. 113:7). However, the Yiddish adds a new dimension; that is, once God raises the poor out of the dust and the

needy out of the dunghill, the poor man is no longer the same.

MO'ADIM LESIMHAH—HAGIM UZEMANIM LESASON (מועדים לשמחה—חגים וזמנים לששון). A greeting spoken by Sephardic Jewry on festivals. One says, Mo'adim lesimhah ("Festivals of gladness") and the reply is Hagim uzemanim lesason ("Festivals and times for joy"). This greeting is culled from the Amidah text that is recited on festivals. Ashkenazic Jewry say, GUT YOM TOV ("Good Yom Tov").

During the Intermediary Days of Pesah and Sukkot, the greeting is A GUTN MO'AYD ("A good Mo'ayd"). One may say sarcastically, Gut Yom Tov, er iz duh ("All at once he is here!"). In other words, "Who needs him here now?" To indicate that someone is making a big thing out of nothing, the expression is Er makht a gantzn Yontif.

NUHKH AMOL ODEKHA (נאך אמאל אודך). "Once again Odekha." The verse in Hallel (Ps. 118) beginning with Odekha ("I thank You"), as well as verses that follow (up to Yehalelukha), are repeated. Up to this verse, each idea is repeated in the next verse or two, according the usual parallelism of Hebrew poetry. Since at Odekha (verse 21) the repetition ceases, it is customary to repeat the next four verses in this paragraph during the recitation as part of the hallel. Tedious repetition of any kind prompted this Yiddish remark.

SHLUHGN HOSHANOT (שלאגן הושענות). "Beating the bunch of willow twigs." To demonstrate rejoicing in accordance with biblical command, "Rejoice in your festival" (Deut. 16:14) and to symbolize our desire to drive the forces of stern judgment into the ground, never to rise again, the willows are beaten on Hoshana Rabbah.

Other expressions used in conjunction with Hoshanot are: Di grine Hoshana iz mayne, di uhpgeshluhgene iz dayne ("The green willow twig is mine, the frayed one is yours"); *Pasula Hoshana* ("unfit *Hoshana*"), referring to willows not meeting rabbinic requirements (cf. *Kitzur Shulhan Arukh*, chap. 136); UHPGESHLUHGENE HOSHANA ("frayed or shabby *Hoshana*"), denoting a person shorn of his glory.

UHPGESHLUHGENE HOSHANA
(אפגעשלאגענע הושענא). See SHLUHGN HOSHANOT.

VI A YAVAN IN SUKKAH (ווי א יון אין סוכה). "Ill-timed"; literally, "like a Greek (a 'Russian soldier' or a 'Russian boor') in a *sukkah*." The expression is applied to a person who shows up uninvited; it is possibly derived from the Talmud (A.Z. 3a). "The nations plead, 'Offer us the Torah anew and we shall obey it.' But the Holy One, blessed be He, will say to them, 'I have an easy command which is called *sukkah*; go and carry it out' [to test their self-exertion for the sake of a *mitzvah*] . . . but the Holy One, blessed be He, will cause the sun to blaze forth over them as at the summer solstice [the cycle of *Tammuz*] and every one of them will trample down his booth and go away." Thus, when someone comes uninvited, he is compared to the non-Jew, who rejected the *sukkah* and, therefore, "Who needs him here now?"

VI KUMT ATTAH HARAYTA TZU DER ARENDA? (ווי קומט אתה הראת צו דער ארענדע). "How does *Attah Harayta* come to the farm?" *Attah Harayta* and an *arenda* have no relationship; *Attah Harayta* is a prayer. The saying is directed at someone whose remark or statement is irrelevant and is not applicable or pertinent.

HAGGADAH (הגדה)

A HAKHAM FUN MAH NISH-TANAH (א חכם פון מה נשתנה). "A wise man of the Pesah questions"; actually, a euphemism for "a fool"). The four ques-

tions are usually asked by the youngest child at the *Seder*. When an adult asks irrelevant questions or makes wanting remarks, it is considered childish or foolish. In fact, the true *hakham*, who is referred to later in the *Haggadah*, seeks to know the entire situation. The child's questions asked earlier are answered with *Avadim hayinu*. The *hakham* now inquires, "What are the testimonies, statutes, and laws that the Lord our God commanded you?" And we are told, ". . . instruct him in the laws of Pesah, that one may not eat anything after eating the Pesah sacrifice." The *hakham* wants to know the laws to the last detail and is not satisfied with a partial explanation. Hence, a person making comments or observations, when ignorant of the facts or circumstances, is a fool, since he pursues a course contrary to the dictates of wisdom.

A RASHA FUN DER HAGGADAH
(א רשע פון דער הגדה). "A wicked person from the *Haggadah*"; a statement generally directed at a cruel, malicious person.

AFILU IN DER HAGGADAH GEFINT MEN DEM DAVAR AHAYR
(אפילו אין דער הגדה געפינט מען דעם דבר אחר). "Even in the *Haggadah*, you find the 'scoundrel' or 'detestable' person." The appellation *ahayr*—literally, "the other"—was applied to Elisha ben Abuya, who became a heretic and flourished in Palestine at the end of the first century and the beginning of the second. The Rabbis wanted to refrain from pronouncing his name and referred to him in terms used to designate some vile object, *davar ahayr* ("another thing"). In the *Haggadah*, however, the phrase means "another explanation" of the preceding sentence. This Yiddish remark is only made to be witty.

ARAYNGEZETZT IN HAD GADYA
(אריינגעזעצט אין חד גדיא). "To sit in the clink or jail." *Had Gadya* illustrates how the people of Israel were oppressed and

persecuted for centuries by all the nations of antiquity. The oppressors all perished, one by one, and Israel, the oppressed, survived. The conclusion of the poem tells how the *shohet* ("ritual slaughterer") was killed by the Angel of Death, who, in punishment, was destroyed by God. The Yiddish expression similarly alludes to a person who commits dishonest or villainous acts during his lifetime and eventually is punished (by going to jail).

BAY IM IZ KOL DIKHFIN YAYTAY VEYAYKHOL (ביי אים איז כל דכפין ייתי ויכול). "With him, it is 'whoever is hungry, let him come and eat.'" The Aramaic in this expression is recited at the outset of the *Seder*. The Yiddish expression intimates one who has a kind disposition and is goodhearted to all.

DREY MIR NIT KEYN KUHP MIT DAYNE HAD GADYA'S (דריי מיר ניט קיין קאפ מיט דיינע חד גדיא'ס). See HAD GADYA SHTEYT TAMID OYF AYN MEKAH.

DUHS BESTE FUN DI ESER MAKOT ZAYNEN DI KNEYDLAKH MIT YOYKH (דאס בעסטע פון די עשר מכות זיינען די קניידלאך מיט יויך). "The best of the Ten Plagues are the *matzah* balls with soup." A similar amusing expression is ER (IZ NIT OYSN) MEYNT NIT DI HAGGADAH NUHR DI KNEYDLAKH ("his purpose is not [saying] the *Haggadah* but [eating] the *matzah* balls").

ER HALT SHOYN BAY KOS REVI'I (ער האלט שוין ביי כוס רביעי). "He is already up to the fourth cup." The *Arba Kosot* ("the four cups of wine") are an integral part of the Passover *Seder* and correspond to the four ways God told the people of Israel that He will redeem them, "I will free you, deliver you, redeem you, and take you to be My people" (Ex. 6:6–7). The Yiddish expression is spoken in jest and is directed at a person who drinks to excess. Similarly, another expression used is *Fun harbah kosot kumt kayn guts nit aroys*

("No good comes from too much drinking")—a pun on the word *arba*, meaning "four" and *harba*, meaning "many."

ER (IZ NIT OYSN) MEYNT NIT DI HAGGADAH NUHR DI KNEYD-LAKH (ער (איז ניט אויסן) מיינט ניט די הגדה נאר די קניידלאך). See DUHS BESTE FUN DI ESER MAKOT ZAYNEN DI KNEYD-LAKH MIT YOYKH.

FREGN DI FIR KASHES (פרעגן די פיר קשיות). "To ask the four questions." The four questions refer to *Mah Nishtanah* ("Why is this night different?"), which a child asks at the *Seder* on Passover. Children introduce *Mah Nishtanah* with the Yiddish *Tate, ikh vel dir fregn fir kashes* ("Father, I will ask you four questions").

GOTT ZUHL OYF IM SHIKN FUN DI TZEN MAKOT DI BESTE (PA-ROH'S MAKOT) (גאט זאל אויף אים שיקן פון די צען מכית די בעסטע (פרעה'ס מכות). "God should send him the best of the Ten Plagues [Pharaoh's plagues]." Similar utterances or evil wishes are: *Ikh vintsh dir di drite makah fun Mitzrayim* ("I wish you the third plague of Egypt") and *Er zuhl huhbn Paroh's makot bashutn mit Iyob's kretz* ("He should have Pharaoh's plagues covered with Job's disease").

HAD GADYA SHTEYT TAMID OYF EYN MEKAH (חד גדיא שטייט תמיד אויף איין מקח). "Had Gadya always remains one price." The Aramaic poem that concludes the *Seder* on Passover allegorically tells of a goat that was bought with two *zuzim* ("two coins") by the father. The goat was devoured by a cat, the cat was bitten to death by a dog, the dog was slain by a stick, and so forth, until finally the Angel of Death was killed by God. Each of the ten verses reiterate buying the goat for two *zuzim*. Thus, a shopkeeper may say to the customer who tries to chisel down the price, "Don't bargain! *Had Gadya* has only one price!"

Because of the cumulative rhymes in the poem, an expression used is DREY MIR NIT KEYN KUHP MIT DAYNE HAD GADYA'S ("Don't turn my head with your nonsense").

MIDAYA VIFIL (מי-יודע וויפיל). "Who knows how much or how many." The Yiddish word *midaya* is a contraction of two Hebrew words, *mi yodaya* ("who knows?"). *Mi yodaya* is a phrase from the Song of Numbers sung at the Passover *Seder*, in which the numbers, from one to thirteen, are given religious meaning. The song begins with *Ehad Mi Yodaya* ("Who knows one?").

OYSLUHZN (OYSGISN) DEM TZUHRN (DEM KA'AS KOL HA-MOTO, DEM GANTZN SHEFOKH-HAMATKHA) OYF _____ (אויסלאזן (אויסגיסן) דעם צארן (דעם כעס כל חמתו, דעם גאנצן שפוך חמתך) אויף _____). "To leave out [vent] the fury [the anger—all his wrath, the entire 'Pour forth your wrath'] on _____ ." The Yiddish expression reiterates the aspect of wreaking one's anger when aroused by wrong or injury. Actually, it is an excess of rage, verging on madness. "Pour forth your wrath" is the opening of a passage recited at the *Seder*.

PATUR VERN FUN A HAMAYTZ (פטור ווערן פון א חמץ). "To get rid of something undesirable." The Torah explicitly states, "Seven days shall there be no *hamaytz* [leaven] found in your houses" (Ex. 12:19). In *Kabbalah, hamaytz* is regarded as a symbol of corruption and impurity. The Yiddish expression denotes the act of ridding or freeing oneself of a person or an object that is undesirable.

Another Yiddish expression for cleaning out the leavened bread is *Meva'ayr hamaytz zayn*.

SHE'AR YERAKOT (שאר ירקות). "All kinds of vegetables." This phrase is part of *Mah Nishtanah*. It is used disparagingly as

a general phrase to include people or wares of all sorts.

SHE'AYNO YODAYA LISHOL (שאינו יודע לשאול). One of the four sons of the *Haggadah* who "does not know to ask"; an appellation given to a "know-nothing" or "ignoramus."

S'IZ NUKH VAYT TZU KOL HAMIRA (ס'איז נאך ווייט צו כל חמירא). "There's still a long way to *Kol Hamira*." On the evening preceding the *Seder*, a search for *hamaytz* is conducted. At the end of the search and in the morning when the *hamaytz* is burned, a short paragraph, *Kol hamira* ("any *hamaytz* or leaven that is in my possession") is said. A great deal of cleaning to remove all *hamaytz* takes place prior to the Passover holiday. Just as one may utter the Yiddish expression to indicate the length of time needed to remove all *hamaytz*, so it can allude to someone who ventures or risks a great deal until his goal is realized.

TUHMER IZ BAY ZEY YUH AMUHL A SEDER FREGN ZEY: MAH NISH-TANAH (טאמער איז ביי זיי יא אמאל א סדר פרעגן זיי: מה נשתנה). "If they already do have a *Seder* [order], they ask: Why is this night different?" This remark relates to the Jewish people, who make a *Seder* on Passover with such methodical procedure and yet, in the midst of this, ask questions.

TZU DI ESER MAKOT NEMT MEN KAYN HATAN NIT TZU GAST (צו די עשר מכות נעמט מען קיין חתן ניט צו גאסט). "To the Ten Plagues you do not invite a bridegroom as a guest"; an expression said in jest, concerning inviting a bridegroom at an inopportune time.

UHPRIKHTN DEM SEDER (אפריכטן דעם סדר). "To perform the Passover *Seder*." The *Seder* is a home ceremony containing fifteen steps (*Kaddaysh-*

Urehatz, Karpas-Yahatz etc.), each of which stands for a specific element of the ritual. Each of the rituals observed are intended to remind the Jewish people that God redeemed them from bondage and made them a free people, dedicated to serve Him only.

VEKHOL HAMARBEH LESAPAYR HARAY ZEH MESHUBAH (וכל המרבה לספר הרי זה משובח). "And whoever tells at length is praiseworthy"; a phrase in the *Haggadah* of Passover, meaning that the more one talks about the Exodus from Egypt, the more he or she helps bring to the fore the universal recognition of God and ultimate redemption.

The root of the word *lesapayr* is *sipayr*, having two meanings: "to tell" or "to count." In jest, the Hebrew expression is directed at one who is told "to count and pay up!—then you will be praiseworthy."

ELUL and SELIHOT (אלול–סליחות)

AL TASHLIKHAYNU LE'AYT ZIK-NAH (אל תשליכנו לעת זקנה). "Do not cast us off in the time of old age"; a phrase in *Shema Kolaynu*, recited at the *Selihot* service. The letters in the word *ZiKNaH* have jestingly been construed to signify distinctive characteristics of the elderly: *Zayin* = *ziftzn* ("to sigh"); *Kaf* = *krekhtzn* ("to groan"); *Nun* = *nisn* ("to sneeze"); and *Hay* = *hustn* ("to cough"). See AL TASH-LIKHAYNI LE'AYT ZIKNAH.

IN HODESH ELUL TZITERN AFILU DI FISH IN VASER (אין חודש אלול ציטערן אפילו די פיש אין וואסער). "In the month of *Elul*, even the fish in the water tremble." The first day of *Elul* marks the beginning of a forty-day period of penitence that culminates with Yom Kippur. Designated as *Yemay Ratzon* ("days of favor"), special prayer recitals and blow-

ing the *shofar* are means by which the Jew is stirred to repentance and becomes fearful of the *Yom Hadin* ("the Day of Judgment"). Thus man, who is a living creature, is compared in this month to fish that also quiver involuntarily, as if in fear. A similar Yiddish expression is used when presenting a comparison: TZITERN VI A FRUMER YID IN DI ASERET YEMAY TESHUVAH ("to tremble like a pious Jew in the Ten Days of Penitence").

SELIHOT TEG (סליחות טעג). "*Selihot* days"; days on which *Selihot* ("penitential prayers") are said.

SHTEYT OYF (KINDER) LE'AVO-DAT HABORAY (שטייט אויף (קינדער) לעבודת הבורא). See SHTEYT OYF TZU SELI-HOT.

SHTEYT OYF TZU SELIHOT (שטייט אויף צו סליחות). "Wake up for the *Selihot* service"; an exhortation chanted by the beadle—*schulklopfer*—summoning the congregants to awaken for the *Selihot* service. Other such announcements were SHTEYT OYF [KINDER] LE'AVODAT HABORAY ("Wake up [children] for the service of the Creator"). At the crack of dawn the beadle made the rounds of the entire town, knocked three times on every door, and, in a drone, recited these phrases. He would sometimes extend the phrase and chant, "Israel, O holy folk, awake, arouse yourselves, and rise to the service of the Creator." This custom disappeared from Eastern European communities by the early 1900s.

When something is rattling or knocking, the comparison *Klapn vi tzu Selihot* ("knocking like at *Selihot*") is made.

TZITERN VI A FRUMER YID IN DI ASERET YEMAY TESHUVAH (ציטערן ווי א פרומער ייד אין די עשרת ימי תשובה). See IN HODESH ELUL TZITERN AFILU DI FISH IN VASER.

ZIBN VUHKHN TZEYLT MEN, DRAY VUHKHN VEYNT MEN, FIR VUHKHN BLUHZT MEN (זיבן וואכן ציילט מען. דריי וואכן וויינט מען. פיר וואכן בלאזט מען).

The summer passes by: "Seven weeks of counting [Sefirah], three weeks of mourning [between Shivah Asar b'Tammuz and Tishah b'Ab], and four weeks of blowing [the shofar in the month of Elul]." This witty saying, prevalent in Eastern European countries, signifies the Jews marking time in their religious, yet doleful, lives.

ZUHGN SELIHOT (זאגן סליחות).

"To say Selihot." The word zuhgn ("to say"), and not daven, is used in conjunction with the Selihot service. It is possible that the term is derived from the verse Vayomer Hashem salahti kidvarekha ("The Lord said, I have pardoned according to thy word") (Numb. 14:20).

ROSH HASHANAH (ראש השנה)

A MASHAL KEHERES HANISH-BAR (א משל כחרס הנשבר).

"A comparison to a broken shard." The Hebrew in this expression appears in the High Holy Day prayer Ki Keshimkha and signifies, among other things, man's weakness. The saying used in the Yiddish parlance is directed at someone whose remark is irrelevant and is not applicable. A similar expression indicating irrelevance is A MASHAL: IBER DEM BLUHZT MEN HAMAN UN MEN KLAPT SHOFAR ("a likeness: because of this you blow Haman and you beat the shofar"). The statement should be made the other way around, but it is purposely said this way to show the illogical or inapplicable comparison.

A PRUHSTER HAI VEKAYAM (א פראסטער חי וקיים).

"A simple or unconventional person." This saying probably has its origin in the prayer Vekhol ma'aminim. In Vekhol ma'aminim the text reads, "All believe that He lives eternally" (shehu hai vekayam), referring to God. As in the prayer Melekh Elyon ("The Supreme King"), we contrast it to man's utter limitations by saying melekh evyon ("the destitute king") so, too, in this Yiddish expression God, Who is a source of life, stands out in opposition to man, who is apportioned life by His power.

The Yiddish saying is sometimes used in a derogatory manner for one who is "a nonconformist," "a street person."

ADAM YESODO MAYAFAR VE-SOFO LE'AFAR—BAYNO LEVAY-NO IZ GUT A TRUNK BRUHNFN (BAYNOTAYIM KHAPT MEN A BLINTCHICK) (אדם יסודו מעפר וסופו לעפר—בינו לבינו איז גוט א טרונק בראנפן (בינותים כאפט) מען א בלינטשוק).

" 'A man's origin is from dust and his destiny is dust'—between them, it is good to take a drink of whiskey [between them, or meanwhile, you grab a blintze]." This is a philosophical comment on man's mortality. Man comes from dust and returns to dust; even so, you either take a drink or you eat something in between.

AKHILAH IZ DI BESTE TEFILLAH (אכילה איז די בעסטע תפילה).

See MIT AKHILAH HEYBT ZIKH UHN ZAYN TEFILLAH.

AL KOL PESHA'IM TEKHASEH BE'AHAVAH (על כל פשעים תכסה באהבה).

"Love draws a veil over wrongdoing"; a phrase similar in wording to a phrase in Hineni, pleading with God to pardon with His love, no matter how much we have sinned. The Yiddish usage is adapted to a man–woman situation, "that love covers all wrongdoing."

ASERET YEMAY TESHUVAH (עשרת ימי תשובה).

See BAYN KESEH LE'ASOR.

AZ DER BA'AL TOKAYA KEN NIT BLUHZN LEYGT ZIKH DER SATAN IN SHOFAR (אז דער בעל תוקע קען ניט בלאזן לייגט זיך דער שטן אין שופר). When the *Ba'al Tokayah* can not blow, (he gives the excuse) that Satan is blocking the *shofar*. This expression is applied to someone who does not have the skill required to blow the *shofar*.

BAYN KESEH LE'ASOR (בין כסה לעשור). This is another name for the ASERET YEMAY TESHUVAH ("The Ten Days of Penitence"). Referring to the prophetic admonition "See ye the Lord while He may be found (Isa. 55:6), the Talmud (R.H. 18a) concludes that the ten days between Rosh Hashanah and Yom Kippur are a period of special grace. The seven days between Rosh Hashanah and Yom Kippur are especially given these names since these days constitute the larger part of the total ten-day period set apart for repentance; the remaining three days are Rosh Hashanah (two days) and Yom Kippur (one day).

The name *Bayn Keseh Le'asor* ("between *keseh* and *asor*") is derived from the word *keseh* ("to conceal") and *asor* ("ten"). The word *keseh* is part of the verse "Blow the *shofar* at the new moon, at the covered time [*keseh*] for our festive day" (Ps. 81:4). The Talmud asks, "Which is the feast on which the new moon is covered over [*mitkhaseh*]? You must say that this is Rosh Hashanah" (R.H. 18a, b). Rosh Hashanah falls on the first day of the month, when the new moon may not yet have appeared; unlike other festival days that fall either when the moon is full or nearly full (that is, approximately at mid-month). On Sabbaths and festivals, the Israelites are symbolically compared to the moon that is radiant. On Rosh Hashanah the People of Israel diminish themselves and conceal their greatness in awe of the Day of Judgment. Furthermore, God, too, conceals His people's sins and forgives them. The word *asor* (ten) refers to Yom Kippur,

as is written, "Howbeit on the tenth [*asor*] day of this seventh month is the day of Atonement? [*Yom ha-Kippurim*]" (Lev. 23:27; cf. Eliyahu Kitov, *Sefer Hatoda'ah*, vol. 1 [Jerusalem: Machon Lehozoat Sefarim and Merkaz Lehazlfrut Chareidit, 1958], pp. 31, 32).

Bayn keseh le'asor is part of a refrain that appears in two *Pizmonim: Horayta derekh teshuvah* by Binyamin and *Bayn keseh le'asor* by Eliezer, son of R. Shlomo. See YAMIM NORA'IM.

BLUHZEN SHOFAR (בלאזן שופר). "To blow the ram's horn."

DERLEBN TZU HERN DEM SHOFAR SHEL MASHIAH (דערלעבן צו הערן דעם שופר של משיח). "To live to hear the *shofar* of the Messiah"; a wish that has its origin in the verse uttered in *Shofarot*, "And it will be on that day that a great *shofar* will be blown" (Isa. 27:13). The expression is also rooted in the weekday *Amidah*, "Sound the great *shofar* for our freedom" (Isa. 11:12).

ER KEN MIKH (UHN) KLUHGN (LUHDN) TZUM UNETANEH-TOKEF (ער קען מיך (אן) קלאגן (אן) לאדן) צום ונתנה-תוקף). "He can bring me up on charges [summon me] to *Unetaneh Tokef.*" The Yiddish expression is used by a person upon whom a claim is being made and who retorts as if to say, "I am faultless, go do me something." The prayer *Unetaneh-Tokef* ("Let us tell how utterly holy this day is") was selected since the text reads, "True it is that thou art judge and arbiter, discerner and witness." This person is so sure that he is innocent that he dismisses the claim by intimating, "Report me to the Heavenly Court; you can't touch me!"

EYN YEHI RATZON (איין יהי רצון). "One *Yehi Ratzon*." The two Hebrew words, *Yehi Ratzon* ("May it be Thy will"), are the opening of many poignant prayers uttered during the High Holy Days and

during the year. The Yiddish saying is used to signify things that are identical.

GEY SHRAY HAI VEKAYAM (גיי שריי חי וקים). "Go yell, 'He lives forever.'" The phrase *hai vekayam* appears in the liturgy of the High Holy Days, as well in the liturgy of the Three Pilgrimage Festivals and the Four Special Sabbaths. It was customary that when the *Sheli'ah Tzibbur* reached these words of praise, the congregation would repeat them in fortissimo. In older *Mahzorim*, the entire sentence is printed in bold lettering. The Yiddish saying is used to signify protesting in vain; that is, it is as if to say, "you can scream as loud as you want, but it will not help you."

GEYN TZU TASHLIKH (גיין צו תשליך). "To go to *Tashlikh*." On the first day of Rosh Hashanah, after *Minhah*, it is customary to go to a body of water "to throw the sins into the water"—*vetashlikh bimtzulot yam kol hatotam* ("and cast into the depths of the sea all their sins") (Micah 7:19). *Geyn tzu Tashlikh* includes the ritual of "throwing sins into water" (*Uhptreyslen di avayrot*) by shaking the pockets of one's garments over the water, as a symbol of washing away the sins, and reciting various verses from Scripture.

HA'OHAYZ BEYAD IZ DI BESTE TEFILLAH (האוחז ביד איז די בעסטע תפילה). "'Who grasps in hand' is the best prayer." The two Hebrew words, *Ha'ohayz beyad*, refer in this prayer to God grasping judgment to prevent it from overwhelming man. In jest, the Hebrew words in the Yiddish expression mean to say, "Whoever is holding the bag has the upper hand." A similar expression is HA'OHAYZ BEYAD SHTEYT GROYS GESHRIBN ("*hao'hayz beyad* is written in bold lettering"). In older *Mahzorim* these two Hebrew words were written in large lettering, as the opening of the prayer. Another expression is HA'OHAYZ BEYAD—SHALOM BEKESHENE ("Who grasps in hand—peace in his pocket"). This

alludes to the fact that by holding the object, one has tranquility and it will not cost him. Yet another expression is HA'OHAYZ BEYAD—VEKHOL MA'AMINIM SHEHU ("Who grasps in hand—all believe he is [it]").

HA'OHAYZ BEYAD—SHALOM BEKESHENE (האוחז ביד—שלום בקעשענע). See HA'OHAYZ BEYAD IZ DI BESTE TEFILLAH.

HA'OHAYZ BEYAD SHTEYT GROYS GESHRIBN (האוחז ביד שטייט גרויס געשריבן). See HA'OHAYZ BEYAD IZ DI BESTE TEFILLAH.

HA'OHAYZ BEYAD—VEKHOL MA'AMINIM SHEHU (האוחז ביד—וכל מאמינים שהוא). See HA'OHAYZ BEYAD IZ DI BESTE TEFILLAH.

KAHALOM YA'UF (כחלום יעוף). "A fleeting dream"; a phrase from the *Ki Keshimkha* prayer, adapted into the Yiddish language to describe lack of reality or a fleeting moment.

KOL HAMINIM, KOL MA'AMINIM (כל המינים, כל מאמינים). "All sorts, all believe." The two words, *haminim* and *ma'aminim*, sound alike; in jest, when one wishes to describe all kinds, the word *ma'aminim* is used.

KOL YAKHOL (כל יכול). "[He] can do everything," referring to God, as appearing in the prayer *Vekhol Ma'aminim* ("All believe that He can do everything").

The phrase has been applied to a person who is a jack-of-all trades (a person who can do passable work at various trades, or a handyman). See BA'AL YEKHOLET; KAVYAKHOL.

LE'AYLA LE'AYLA (לעלא לעלא). The word *le'ayla*, meaning "higher" or "above", appears in *Kaddish*. During the Ten Days of Penitence (ASERET YEMAY TESHUVAH), Ashkenazic Jewry double the word in

every *kaddish*, because, in this period, God's exalted place is far above and beyond all hymns and blessings uttered in the world. When doubling *le'ayla*, the contracted form, *mikol*, which follows, is used instead of *min kol* in order to keep the number at twenty-eight.

In popular parlance, the phrase *le'ayla le'ayla* is used to describe a situation or something that is of the highest degree or exceptional. Its tonal inflection is usually said with forceful utterance or strong feeling.

LESHANAH TOVAH TIKATAYVU (VETAYHATAYMU) לשנה טובה תכתבו (ותחתמו). "May a good year be inscribed [and sealed] for you"; a wish exchanged by Jews before and during the High Holy Days. In Ashkenazic *Mahzorim* and *Siddurim*, the formula for this wish on the first night of Rosh Hashanah is *Leshanah tovah tikatayv vetayhataym* (masc., sing.) *tikatayvi vetayhataymi* (fem., sing.) *le'altar lehayyim tovim uleshalom* ("May you be inscribed and sealed immediately for a good life and for peace"). According to the *Gra*, only *Leshanah tovah tikatayv* is said.

In the Sephardic rite, the formula for the wish varies. According to the *Lu'ah Shanah Beshanah* (Heichal Shlomo, Jerusalem) the formula is *Tizkeh leshanim rabot uleshanah tova tikatayv vetayhataym* ("May you merit long life and may you be inscribed for a good year"). The Moroccan wish is *Tikatayv (vetayhataym) lehayyim tovim uleshalom* ("May you be inscribed and sealed for peace"). Spanish-Portuguese Jews have the formula *Leshanah tovah tikatayv, tizke leshanim rabot ne'imot vetovot*, to which the response is *Tizke vetihye veta'arikh yamim*, often abbreviated to *Tizke vetihye* (cf. Rabbi H.C. Dobrinsky, *The Sephardic Laws and Customs* [New York: Ktav Publishing House, Inc. and Yeshiva University Press, 1986], pp. 321, 329).

The Yiddish equivalent is *A gut (gebentsht) yuhr* ("a good [blessed] year"). To augment the blessing, one may add *A gantz yuhr, a gantz geye(n)dik [kaylekh-(d)ik] yuhr* ("The entire year, all year round"). The saying *A Yid fun a gantz yuhr* is used to describe "an everyday man," "an ordinary person."

MAKHN A HILUF ANSIKHAH OYF AHALLELAH (מאכן א חילוף אנסיכה אויף אהללה). "To make an exchange [from saying] *Ansikhah* instead of *Ahallelah*." These two utterances are the initial words of the two poetical insertions recited in the *Malkhuyot* unit of *Musaf* on Rosh Hashanah. The former is said on the first day and latter on the second day. If the first day of Rosh Hashanah is a Sabbath, the two poems are interchanged. The reason for the exchange is that *Ansikhah* mentions the *shofar* and the *shofar* is not blown on the Sabbath. *Ahallelah*, however, mentions the *work kol* ("the sound") (cf. *Maharil*, *Levush*). Both poems describe the various occurrences that the people of Israel experienced in their long history and laud God, their King. The Yiddish remark is as if to say, "Why bother making the change when both are the same?"

ME'OREV (ME'URAV) BEDA'AT IM HABERIYOT (מעורב (מעורב) בדעת עם הבריות). A phrase appearing in the *Hineni* prayer, recited by the *Sheli'ah Tzibbur* on Rosh Hashanah and Yom Kippur, pleading with the Almighty to accept his prayers as if he were "well-pleasing [congenial] with other people."

The Talmud (Ket. 17a) states, LE'OLAM TEHAYH DATO SHEL ADAM ME'UREVET IM HABERIYOT ("Always should the disposition of man be pleasant with people"). *Rashi* (ad loc.) comments that a human being should be agreeable or compatible with every person. This is deduced from a discussion between Bet Hillel and Bet Shammai. Bet Hillel asked Bet Shammai, "If one has made a bad purchase in the market, should one praise it [the item purchased] in his eyes or deprecate it? Surely, one should praise it in his eyes." The expression is used in general conversation to depict one who is a "good mixer," or "one who is sociable" or "companionable."

MI VAHEREV UMI VARA'AV—VER ZUHL NIKHSHAL VERN DURKH DER SHVERD UN VER DURKHN RAV (מי בחרב ומי ברעב—ווער זאל נכשל ווערן דורך דער שווערד און ווער דורכן רב). "'Who by sword, who by famine'—who would be made to stumble by the sword and who by the rabbi." The Hebrew part of this saying is from Berosh Hashanah, referring to who should die and be killed by sword and who would die of famine. When not enunciating the word ra'av ("famine") with the ayin between the raysh and bet, it becomes rav, meaning "rabbi." Thus, in jest, the Hebrew intent is completely altered and alludes to a situation in which the rabbi's decision is incorrect and can lead to wrongdoing.

MIT AKHILAH HEYBT ZIKH UHN ZAYN YOTZAYR (מיט אכילה הייבט זיך אן זיין יוצר). "Food is foremost, his main desire." Yotzayr concerns itself with poetical insertions in the benediction of Shema. Its name is derived from the first benediction in Shaharit. All poetical insertions throughout the prayer service were often called yotzrot (pl.). Ohilah is the first word of a plea uttered by the Sheli'ah Tzibbur in the Musaf service on Rosh Hashanah and Yom Kippur, in which various poetical insertions are introduced. The word akhilah ("eating," "consumption"), with the letter khaf, has the same sound as ohilah ("I shall put my hope"), with the letter het. The word akhilah, instead of ohilah, has been emphasized in this jocular expression that signifies a person who lives to eat, rather than eats to live. A similar saying is AKHILAH IZ DI BESTE TEFILLAH ("Eating is the choicest prayer").

UM ROSH HASHANAH HUHT DER GRESTER KABTZN A TRUHPELE HUHNIK (אום ראש השנה האט דער גרעסטער קבצן א טראפעלע האניק). "On Rosh Hashanah the poorest person has a drop of honey." A poor person usually has a severe time eking out a livelihood. On Rosh Hashanah, when he dips the apple in honey and recites a blessing followed by "May it be Thy will," he, too, acquires a taste of sweetness.

VEST NUHKH A FULE DARFN ZUHGN AVINU MALKAYNU [BIZ DU VEST OYS-VEYNEN DEM KEREN] (וועסט נאך א פולע דארפן זאגן אבינו מלכינו [ביז דו וועסט אויסוויינען דעם קרן]). "You will have to say Avinu Malkaynu many more times [until you will cry out enough to regain the principal."] Avinu Malkaynu ("Our Father Our King") is a series of prayer sentences, each beginning with those two words, recited during the Ten Days of Penitence and on fast days. In the ritual, there are forty-four verses and, since it exceeds most other recitals in which requests are made of God, it was selected as part of the expression to mean that "You will have to sweat a great deal until you realize your investment."

VI DER ROSH HASHANAHDIKER MUSAF (ווי דער ראש השנה'דיקער מוסף). "Like the Rosh Hashanah Musaf prayer." The Musaf prayer service on Rosh Hashanah is the longest of all services in the yearly cycle. Thus, when mentioning something that is lengthy, the Musaf service is used as a comparison.

YAMIM NORA'IM (ימים נוראים). "Days of Awe," referring to the period beginning with Rosh Hashanah and concluding with Yom Kippur. Other names for this period are ASERET YEMAY TESHUVAH and BAYN KESEH LE'ASOR.

The term Yamim Nora'im is first used according to Haim Tchernowitz (Toldot ha-Poskim [New York, 1947], p. 257), in

Sefer Maharil, by Jacob ben Moses ha-Levi Moelin of Mainz (printed in Sabionetta, 1556).

YEDERER VEYNT OYF MI YIHYEH

(יעדערער וויינט אויף מי יחיה). "Each one cries at 'who will live'"; a phrase extracted from *Berosh Hashanah*, questioning how he will derive nourishment. The Yiddish expression may suggest that the need for sustenance is a universal cry. Similar expressions are *Men veynt oyf mi yihyeh vi oyf mi yamut* ("One cries at 'who will live' as [when saying] 'who will die'"), or *Men veynt nit oyf dem mi yamut, nuhr oyf dem mi yihyeh* ("One does not cry [when saying] 'who will die' but [when saying] 'who will live'").

YOM KIPPUR (יום כפור)

A SHEYNE REYNE KAPPARAH (א

שיינע ריינע כפרה). "A nice clean *kapparah*." In this Yiddish expression, as well as in those that follow, the word *kapparah* may refer to a regretted waste, vain effort, or financial or material loss. Other such sayings are *Af Kapparot darfst es huhbn* ("It's a total loss"); *Es toyg af kapparot* ("It's a vain effort"); and *Darfst es huhbn oyf nayn un nayntzig kapparot* ("You need it for ninety-nine *kapparot*")—that is, it has no value and there is no need for it. Other expressions are: *Toygn oyf kapparot* ("to be good for nothing"); *Ikh darf es huhbn oyf kapparot* ("I have no need for it"); *Tzarot toygn oyf kapparot* ("Troubles are not needed"); and *shlugn mit imetzin kapparot* ("to dismiss, desert, or abandon someone").

ALTZ NEMT AN EK, AFILU DER KI HINAYH KAHOMER (אלץ נעמט

אן עק. אפילו דער כי הנה כחמר). "All comes to an end, even [the prayer] *Ki hinayh Kahomer*." In the poem *Ki hinayh Kahomer* ("Like the clay"), recited on *Kol Nidre* night, we are likened, in the hands of God, to various raw materials or tools in the hands of those who mold them, such as clay in the hand of the potter, stone in the hand of the cutter, the ax in the hand of the blacksmith, the anchor in the hand of the sailor, glass in the hand of the blower, and the curtain in the hand of the embroiderer. These materials or tools are listed, ad infinitum, in the poem. This expression intimates that whatever is being said or done should be terminated, in the same fashion that the poem comes to a close. The phrase in the poem KAHOMER BEYAD HAYOTZAYR signifies elasticity or flexibility.

AZ MEN KEN NIT UN MEN VEYS NIT NEMT MEN ZIKH NIT UNTER

(אז מען קען נים און מען וויים נים נעמט) מען זיך נים אונטער). "One does not assume a task unless one is knowledgeable." This witty folksaying has often been associated with the *Kaddish* of *Ne'ilah*. The story is that the "so-called-cantor" was unable to remember the tune for the *Ne'ilah Kaddish*. His wife, sitting in the gallery and observing his hesitation in the beginning of the *Ne'ilah* service, began to chant this saying to the melody of the opening words of *Kaddish*. The cantor, hearing the theme, then remembered the tune and began the *Kaddish*.

BESER PESAH EYN MALKAH EYDER YOM KIPPUR FERTZIG MALKOT (בעסער פסח איין מלכה

איידער יום כפור פערציג מלקות). "One *malkah* ['queen'] on Pesah is preferable to forty *malkot* ['lashes'] on Yom Kippur." On Pesah all Jews, because of their freedom, are considered *Benay Melakhim* ("children of kings"). The woman of the house is regarded as a *malkah* ("a queen"). Prior to the *Kol Nidre* service, after *Minhah*, some congregations inflict lashes ("*malkot*") upon one another as a means of "mortifying the flesh." *Malkah* is spelled with a *kaf* and *malkot* with a *kuf*, and since both words have a similar sound, this witty Yiddish expression came into being.

DER MENTCH ZINDIKT UN DI HUHN VERT DI KAPPARAH (דער מענטש זינדיקט און האן די ווערט די כפרה). "The person sins and the hen becomes the *kapparah*"; this is as if to say, "Why should one suffer for another's sins."

DER YID IZ A KAPPARAH HUHN (דער ייד איז א כפרה האן). "The Jew is a victim or scapegoat." The word *kapparah* is used here to connote something that is sacrificed. Other expressions in this category are: *A kapparah a yahid far a rabim* ("The individual becomes a scapegoat for a majority"); that is, when he is outnumbered. Likewise, *Geyn a kapparah far imetzins zind* ("to suffer for somebody's sins") or *Zayn di kapparah far . . .* ("to be the scapegoat for . . ."). Also, *Zi vert di kapparah far im* ("She is mad about him"); that is she sacrifices herself for him.

DI NESHAMAH LIKHT (די נשמה ליכט). "The soul-light"; a long candle that burns from the evening of Yom Kippur until after dark the next day to commemorate the souls of the departed. When saying the *Havdalah* on the conclusion of Atonement Day, it is requisite to say the benediction only upon a light that was kindled before Atonement Day, and not upon a light that is now produced by means of a match and the like (cf. R. Solomon Ganzfried, *Kitzur Shulhan Arukh* 133:28). See NAYRO YA'IR.

ER HUHT ZIKH AYNGEKOYFT MAFTIR YONAH (ער האט זיך אייגעקויפט מפטיר יונה). "He bought for himself *Maftir Yonah*." The Book of Jonah is the *Haftarah* read at *Minhah* on Yom Kippur. Usually, this honor is given to the highest bidder. This Yiddish expression seems to be critical of the practice of buying this *Aliyah*. But since it receives such a high bid, the saying implies that a person will have to pay heavily for his course of action."

ER KLAPT ZIKH ASHAMNU MITN LINKN FUS IN DER REKHTER ZAYT ARAYN (ער קלאפט זיך אשמנו מיטן לינקן פוס אין דער רעכטער זייט אריין). "He beats himself [at] *Ashamnu* with his left foot on the right side." When saying *Ashamnu*, it is customary to strike the left side of the chest with the right fist as a further indication of repentance. This humorous expression is directed at someone who claims remorse but is not sincere about it. A similar saying alluding to a person's insincerity is ER SHLUHGT ZIKH AL-HAYT UN BALEKT ZIKH DERBAY ("He beats [his chest] at *Al-hayt* and is lapping it up at the same time").

ER KUKT VI A HUHN IN BENAY ADAM (ער קוקט ווי א האן אין בני אדם). ("He directs his eye like a cock [looks] into [the prayer] *Benay adam*"). *Benay adam* ("Children of man") are the initial words of a paragraph recited three times before revolving the cock around the head during the *Kapparot* ritual (see SHLUGN KAPPAROT). The Yiddish expression compares an ignorant, unlettered person to the cock who just gazes at the prayerbook during the *Kapparot* ceremony.

ER SHLUGT ZIKH AL-HAYT UN BALEKT ZIKH DERBAY (ער שלאגט זיך על-הטא אין באלעקט זיך דערביי). See ER KLAPT ZIKH ASHAMNU MITN LINKN FUS IN DER REKHTER ZAYT ARAYN.

ES IZ ENKAT MESALDEKHA (עס עיז אנקת מסלדיך). "It is 'the outcry of those who praise You.'" The two Hebrew words, *Enkat mesaldekha*, are the opening words of a prayer from the *Ne'ilah* service. The Yiddish expression depicts the many hardships and tragedies experienced by the Eastern European Jew.

FALN KORE'IM (פאלן קורעים). "To kneel." When saying *Alaynu* and *Vehakohanim* during the *Musaf* service on the High Holy Days, the congregation and

Sheli'ah Tzibbur fall to their knees. This Yiddish phrase is sometimes used to signify submission or humbleness.

FUN AL-HAYT VERT MEN NIT FET (פון על-חטא ווערט מען ניט פעט).
"From [saying] *Al-hayt*, one does not become obese." *Al-hayt* is said on Yom Kippur, when fasting, and surely one does not gain weight when abstaining from food. To regret or repent, the Yiddish phrase SHLUGN ZIKH AL-HAYT ("to beat [the breast] at *Al-hayt*") is used.

FUN VEKHAKH HAYAH OMAYR BIZ VEKHAKH HAYAH MONEH IZ A LANGE VAYLE [IZ A GROYSER UNTERSHEYD; FALT MEN ZIBN MUHL KORE'IM; IZ GUHR AN ANDER NIGGUN] (פון וכך היה אומר ביז וכך היה מונה איז א לאנגע ווײלע (איז א גרויסער אונטערשייד; פאלט מען זיבן מאל כורעים; איז גאר אן אנדער ניגון). "From *Vekhakh hayah omayr* to *Vekhakh hayah moneh*, it is a long while [it is a great difference; prostration takes place seven times; it is a different tune]." Both prayers are part of the *Avodah* service. *Vekhakh hayah omayr* ("And so would he say") is followed by *Vekhakh hayah moneh* ("And so would he count"). The Yiddish saying is irrelevant to the meaning and intent of the words in the prayer. It simply implies that there will be a long wait until money is counted out and paid, in spite of what he is saying and promising to that effect. In other words, "Just try to collect."

IMRU LAYLOHIM (אמרו לאלהים).
"Say unto God"; a *Piyyut* said in *Shaharit* and *Musaf* on Yom Kippur, derived from Psalms 66:3, "Say unto God, how awesome are Your works." This stinging expression is used in dialogue to mean the opposite; that is, to signify "wasted speech." In other words, "Don't talk to me, talk to God." A similar Yiddish saying with the same meaning would be *Red tzu der vant* ("Talk to the wall") or *Red tzum luhmp* ("Talk to the lamp").

KAKHOMER BEYAD HAYOTZAYR (כחמר ביד היוצר).
"As the clay is in the potter's hand" (Jer. 18:6). Jeremiah heard the word of the Lord to go down to the potter's house. He found that the vessel that the potter was making of clay was spoiled, so he made it again into another vessel. The voice of the Lord came to Jeremiah, saying, "O house of Israel, cannot I do with you as the potter?. . . . Behold, as the clay is in the potter's hand, so are you in My hand. . . ."

KOL NIDRE NAKHT (כל נדרי נאכט).
"*Kol Nidre* night"; the name given the eve of Yom Kippur because the prayer service begins with *Kol Nidre*.

KOL TEKI'AH VEKOL TERU'AH— UN ES KUMT NUKH ALTZ NIT DI YESHU'AH (קול תקיעה וקול תרועה— און עס קומט נאך אלץ ניט די ישועה).
"The sound of the *teki'ah* and the sound of the *teru'ah*—and still salvation does not come." At the close of the *Ne'ilah* service, the *shofar* is sounded to commemorate the blowing of the *shofar* in the Jubilee year in Temple days, which signaled the emancipation of slaves. The Yiddish saying bemoans the Jew's plight that although he hears the *shofar* sounds, he has still not achieved redemption and considers himself enslaved.

LIGN IN DER ADAMAH, IN SHE'OL TAHTIYAH (ליגן אין דער אדמה, אין שאול תחתיה).
"To be buried in the ground, in the nethermost depth." The latter two words are from the *Ezkerah* prayer in the *Ne'ilah* service. The Yiddish expression is directed at a person's low state or condition, just as, in the prayer, Jerusalem is spoken of as God's own city being degraded to the nethermost depth" (cf. Jer. 30:18).

MAH ANU MEH HAYAYNU? (מה אנו מה חיינו). "What are we, what is our life?"; a phrase bemoaning one's life situation, uttered in the *Ne'ilah* service in the prayer *Attah notayn yad laposhim* ("You reach out a hand to willful sinners").

MERUBIM TZORKHAY AMEKHA (מרובים צרכי עמך). "The needs of Your people are many." This phrase, in addition to being part of the *Ne'ilah* service, was on the lips of Eastern European Jewry who lived through many difficulties and tragedies.

MIMITZRAYIM VE'AD HAYNAH (ממצרים ועד הנה). "From Egypt to this point"; a biblical phrase (Numb. 14:19) uttered on Yom Kippur eve and during *Selihot*, which connotes the extent of expansion.

NAYRO YA'IR (נרו יאיר). It is customary, when writing to a person or about a person who is alive, to add the two Hebrew letters *nun* and *yud* after his name. These are the initial letters for the two Hebrew words *Nayro Ya'ir* ("May his candle shed light").

The origin of this practice is derived from the candle lit in the synagogue *erev* Yom Kippur. Each person would bring to the synagogue two candles: one was called *Nayr ha-hayyim* ("candle of life") and the other *Nayr Neshamot* ("candle of souls"). The former was lit for a good year and the latter for deceased parents.

Lighting the *Nayr ha-Hayyim* is symbolic; in case one is deservant of one of the four death-penalties, *serayfah* ("burning") the lit candle and its wax takes the place of the punishment. If the candle was extinguished during the day, it appeared to be a bad omen. It became a practice in many communities for the *shamash* (sexton) to supervise the lighting of the candles, so that the individual did not know which candle was his. Furthermore, it prevented the individual from becoming disheartened if his candle was blown out by a wind or an abundance of heat, or for any other reason (J.D. Singer, *Sefer Ziv Haminhagim*, Givath Shmuel, Israel: 1955], pp. 187, 188).

The phrase *Nayro Ya'ir* even became a wish that Jews would bid each other on Yom Kippur. Eventually, the two words—especially its abbreviation—crept into the daily parlance of Jews (Rabbi Yitzhak Hayyim Avigdor, "*Nayro Ya'ir—Zuhl Zayn Likhtel Laykhtn*," in *Algemeiner Journal* [September 13–16, 1994]). See DI NE-SHAMAH LIKHT.

SHLUHGN KAPPAROT (שלאגן כפרות). "To arrive at atonement." *Kapparot* is the plural of *kapparah*, meaning "expiation." On the eve of Yom Kippur, it is customary to recite a formula and various biblical passages and pass a fowl (or money) three times around the head of a person. While the fowl (or money) is overhead, the formula said is, "This is my exchange, this is my substitute, this is my atonement. This rooster (for a man), hen (for a woman) will go to its death (this money will go to charity), while I will enter and proceed to a good long life, and to peace." The money, known as *Kapparah gelt*, is distributed among the needy. The letters in the word *kesef* ("money") spelled *KaF, SaMaKH, FeH* are the numerical equivalent of the word *KaPaRaH* (305; cf. *Orah Hayyim* 605).

The Yiddish word *Shluhgn* (lit. "to hit" or "strike") may be derived from the fact that the symbolic act of waving the rooster or hen around the person's head is in place of *skilah* ("stoning"), one of the *arba mitot bet din* ("four death penalties of the human court"). In ancient days, *skilah* was carried out in the following manner. Instead of having all the people kill the convicted person by pelting him with stones, a "stoning place" was designed from which he was to be pushed down to his death on the stones (San. 6:4). The *shohet*, who slaughters the fowl by cutting its neck, symbolizes *hereg* ("beheading") *henek* ("strangling") and *serayfa* ("burning, which is eventually done to the chicken"), the additional three death penalties in exchange for the life of the individual (cf. *Be'ayr Haytayv, Hilkhot Yom Hakippurim* 605:1).

Other expressions used for this ceremony are *Koylen Kapparot* ("to slaughter the fowl") and *Kapparah huhn* or *Kapparah hendel* ("the hen that is slaughtered").

SHLUHGN ZIKH AL-HAYT (שלאגן זיך על-חטא). See FUN AL-HAYT VERT MEN NIT FET.

TZU GOTT'S NUHMEN (צו גאטס נאמען). "In the Name of God." This is the name applied to the day following Yom Kippur. It is derived from the prayer, when during the *Aseret Yemay Teshuvah* (Ten Days of Penitence) in the third blessing in the *Amidah*, instead of ending with "the Holy God," "the Holy King" is said. Thus, on the day after Yom Kippur, when we revert to "the Holy God," the day is called *Tzu Gott's Nuhmen* (cf. S.J. Sperling *Sefer Ta'amay Haminhagim, Inyanay Yom Kippur*, [Lwow, 1928], par. 780).

UHNMAKHN A YA'ALEH (אנמאכן א יעלה). "To create a turmoil or tumult." The prayer *ya'aleh* ("May our plea ascend") is recited on the eve of Yom Kippur. The use of such words in the poem as *shavataynu* ("our cry"), *kolaynu* ("our voice"), *na'akataynu* ("our wailing"), *dafkaynu* ("our knock"), and *enkataynu* ("our outcry") gave rise to the Yiddish expression that signifies "making a hubbub" or "disturbance."

UHPTZEYLN (OYSTZEYLN) AHAT VE'AHAT (AHAT USHTAYIM) (אפצייל (אויסצייל) אחת ואחת (אחת) ושתים). "To pay up [to count up] one plus one [one plus two]." *Ahat ve'ahat* is a prayer in the *Avodah* section describing the *Kohen Gadol's* counting aloud in order

not to skip or duplicate any "sprinkling." (The *Kohen Gadol* took the blood of the bull into the Holy of Holies, where he "sprinkled" it toward the Ark cover.) The Yiddish expression has no resemblance to the prayer and describes a person saying to another who owes him money that he will have to pay up to the last penny or double.

YOM KIPPUR TRUHPNS (יום כפור טראפנס). "Hartshorn drops"; also called *halashot*—*truhpns* ("fainting drops"); an aqueous solution of ammonia used to stimulate or revive a fainting person on Yom Kippur. Since it is a day of fasting, it is customary to pass around a smelling-bottle filled with this solution in case someone becomes weak. See YOM KIPPUR-DIG.

YOM KIPPUR ZUHGT MEN HATATI, UHBER MEN ZUHGT NIT LO EHTE (יום כפור זאגט מען חטאתי, אבער מען זאגט ניט לא אטחא). "Yom Kippur, one says I sinned but one does not say I will not sin." The word *Hatati* appears in *Vekhakh Hayah Omayr* ("And so would he say"), which describes the confession of the *Kohen Gadol* ("High Priest"). This Yiddish remark is critical of those who have remorse for their transgressions but do not say, "I will not sin any more."

YOM KIPPURDIG (יום כפורדיג). "Of the Day of Atonement"; an expression used to describe a mood similar to the one that prevails on the day of Yom Kippur.

In Scripture (Lev. 23:27), as well as in the liturgy (*Kol Nidre* and *Ya'aleh veyavo*), the holiday is known as *Yom Hakippurim* (the plural form of Yom Kippur). Rabbi Menahaym Mendel Auerbach (1620–1689) writes in his *Ateret Zekaynim*, in the name of Rabbi Ya'akov Weil, that the reason the word for the holiday is in the plural form is that it is a day of atonement both for the living and the dead.

HANUKKAH (חנוכה)

BENTCHN HANUKKAH LIKHT

(בענטשן חנוכה ליכט). "To make the blessings when kindling the candles on Hanukkah." The lamp that holds the candles (or oil) is called Hanukkah luhmp.

HANUKKAH UN PURIM VERN DI UHREME LAYT ASHIRIM (חנוכה

און פורים ווערן די אַרימע לייט עשירים). "On Hanukkah and Purim, the poor become wealthy." This Yiddish saying is the consequence of the poor receiving Hanukkah gelt (i.e., a few coins) on Hanukkah and on Purim; they are recipients of matanot le'evyonim ("gifts for the poor"). Thus, a pauper may say PURIM IZ NOR EYN TUHG UN A KABTZN IZ MEN A GANTZ YOR ("Purim is only one day, but an alms-receiver the entire year").

MA'OZ TZUR IZ GUT TZU FARBAYSN MIT HANUKKAH KEZ (מעוז

צור איז גוט צו פאַרבייסן מיט חנוכה קעז). "When [singing] Ma'oz Tzur, it is good to snack with Hanukkah cheese." Ma'oz Tzur is the popular hymn sung when lighting the Hanukkah candles. The practice of eating cheese products on Hanukkah originated when Judith, the daughter of Johanan (a leader of the Hasmoneans), was taken to the home of the Syrian Satrap to satisfy his lust. On that occasion she served him cheese, which he washed down with wine. He became drunk, fell into a deep slumber, and Judith thereupon decapitated him. Since cheese was one of the factors in the military victory, it became customary to serve dairy products on Hanukkah. This jovial remark is made by one who is not content with only singing the hymn, but wants gastronomical pleasures as well.

MA'OZ TZUR YESHUATI—OY GOTTENYU, GIB ZHE PARNASAH

מעוז צור ישועתי—אוי גאָטעניו, גיב) (זשע פרנסה). "'Stronghold, Rock of my deliverance'—O God, then give sustenance." The word ma'oz with a zayin, meaning "stronghold," and the word ma'os (Ashkenazic pronunciation) with a tav, meaning "coins," are interchanged. The Jew in his dire need pleads to God to give him support for life.

NAYS GADOL HAYAH SHAM (נס

גדול) היה שם). "A great miracle happened there." The initial letters of each of the four words are inscribed on each side of the dreydle (trendle), the top that became a children's game played during the eight days of Hanukkah. The game, which came upon the Jewish scene in the early Middle Ages, is a sort of "put and take" when playing with coins and signifies a gain or a loss or an even break. The dreydle is spun and each of the letters represents this aspect of "put and take" when the dreydle comes to rest on its side. Nun means nem ("to take"), or, according to others, nichts ("take nothing and give nothing"). Gimml means gib ("give"); others say it means gantz ("everything"— i.e., "take everything"). Hay stands for halb ("half," i.e., "take half"), and shin implies shtel ("put in more") or shtey ("do nothing").

In Israel the last word, sham ("there"), was changed to po ("here") so as to read "a great miracle happened here."

VEGN A BISL BOYML MAKHT MEN AZA GROYSN YOM-TOV

(ווען א ביסל בוימל מאַכט מען אַזא) (גרויסן יום-טוב). "Because of a little oil, one makes such a great holiday." Celebrating Hanukkah for eight days has its origin in the discovery of one remaining jar of pure oil marked with the Kohen Gadol's ("High Priest") seal, which lasted for eight days, the required time for the production of new oil. This Yiddish utterance was undoubtedly said in jest.

PURIM (פורים)

A MASHAL: IBER DEM BLUHZT MEN HAMAN UN MEN KLAPT SHOFAR (א משל: איבער דעם בלאזט מען המן און מען קלאפט שופר). See A MASHAL KEHERES HANISHBAR.

AD DELO YADA BAYN ARUR HAMAN LEBARUKH MORDECAI (עד דלא ידע בין ארור המן לברוך מרדכי).

Rabba said that it is the duty of man to revel on Purim (with wine) "until he cannot tell the difference between cursed be Haman [arur Haman] and blessed be Mordecai [barukh Mordecai]"; (Meg. 7b). Incidentally, both Hebrew phrases have the same numerical value, 502.

Drinking wine on Purim stems from the fact that the miracle of Purim occurred through wine. Esther replaced Vashti when she was removed from her throne because of a wine feast and Haman's downfall was brought about through wine feasting, which Esther held.

A person unable to drink much wine (until intoxication) because of health, or anxiety about forgetting the required blessings, or fear of coming to levity, may drink a little more than usual and thus become drowsy, whereupon he would not know the difference between a curse and a blessing. According to the Rambam, "one drinks wine on that day to the verge of inebriety so that one falls asleep while in one's cups." Rabbi Jacob Emden relates that his father was in the habit of observing ad delo yada.

In Israel, Adloyada became an occasion to be celebrated with carnival processions of decorated floats, parading through the main streets, accompanied by bands of music. The first Adloyada was held in Tel Aviv in 1912 and spread to other communities in Israel.

ALE SHIKURIM ZAYNEN NIKHTER PURIM (אלע שיכורים זיינען ניכטער פורים). "All drunkards are sober on Pu-

rim." On Purim a person may drink AD DELO YADA BAYN ARUR HAMAN LEBARUKH MORDECAI, that is, until he is approaching the point when he can no longer distinguish between Mordecai and Haman, but not up to and beyond it (Tur, Orah Hayyim, Bet Yosef; see also Arukh Hashulhan 695). The Yiddish expression infers that the drunkard who drinks daily may seem sober in comparison to the person who drinks on Purim only.

AMRI LAH LESHEVAH VE'AMRI LAH LIGNAI (אמרי לה לשבח ואמרי לה לגנאי). See YAYSH DORSHIN LESHEVAH VEYAYSH DORSHIN LIGNAI.

ASAKH HAMANS UN EYN PURIM (אסאך המנס און איין פורים). "Many Hamans and only one Purim." Throughout history the Jew has been a victim of many persecutions. Someone making this remark bemoans his destiny. A similar expression is Azoy fil Hamans un nor eyn Purim ("So many Hamans and only one Purim").

ATZ KOTZAYTZ, BEN KOTZAYTZ, KETZUTZAI LEKATZAYTZ, BEDIBUR MEFOTZAYTZ (אץ קוצץ, בן קוצץ, קצוצי לקצץ, בדבור מפוצץ). A Piyyut recited in the Kerovah section of Shaharit on Parashat Zakhor (the Sabbath prior to Purim), meaning "The thorn, son of a thorn [Amalek], hurried on to cut in pieces the circumcised nation, and to crush the bruised ones with his shattering speech." The Piyyut, by Eleazar birebi Kallir, became particularly popular because of its first two stanzas written in alliteration. Children, as well as adults, would often quote the first few phrases of the poem that describe the abominable villainy of Haman.

AZ ES KUMT PURIM FARGEST MEN IN ALE YESURIM (אז עס קומט פורים פארגעסט מען אין אלע יסורים). "When Purim arrives, you forget all suffering." The dramatic story of Purim

stands as a symbol of all the struggles of the Jewish people among the nations. The Talmud (Meg. 7b) comments that on Purim, "One must cheer oneself up with wine," and so forth. The many celebrations connected with this holiday resulted in this Yiddish remark.

DI GANTZE MEGILLAH (די גאנצע מגילה). The Megillah, meaning "scroll," is one of the five books (Song of Songs, Ruth, Ecclesiastes, Lamentations, and Esther) read in the synagogue on the festival of Purim. Known as Megillat Esther ("the Book of Esther"), it is an especially lengthy scroll, and thus Di Gantze Megillah (lit., "the entire Megillah") is the extension of any endlessly detailed and tedious account or story told with over-embroidered detail.

GAM HARVONAH (HARVONA) ZAKHUR LATOV (גם חרבונה זכור לטוב)(חרבונא). A phrase appearing toward the end of the liturgical Purim poem Shoshanat Ya'akov ("The rose of Jacob"), meaning "Let Harvonah, too, be remembered for good." Just as Harvonah's intentions were not a mark or token of favor, so the phrase is said of a person who does a good deed without meaning to.

Harvonah was the third of seven chamberlains who served King Ahasuerus (Esth. 1:10) and who suggested that Haman be hung on his own gallows (Esth 7:9). Originally, Harvonah had been in league with Haman and was among the conspirators to hang Mordecai (Meg. 16a). However, seeing that his plot had failed and that Haman was in disfavor, he became Haman's enemy and advised the king to hang him. It was also said (Esther Rabbah 10) that it was actually the prophet Elijah who appeared before Ahasuerus in the guise of Harvonah, and thus Harvonah should be remembered for good (see also Jer. Talmud, Meg. 3:7).

GANTZ YOR SHIKUR, PURIM NIKHTER (גאנץ יאר שיכור, פורים ניכטער). "All year drunk, on Purim sober"; a remark spoken of a person who is always doing things out of season.

HEDYOT KOFAYTZ BEROSH (הדיוט קופץ בראש). The Talmud (Meg. 12b) states, "And Memucan said" (Esth. 1:16). A tanna taught, Memucan is the same as Haman, and why was he called Memucan? Because he was destined (mukan) for punishment. R. Kahana said, "From here, we see that an ordinary man always pushes [jumps] himself in front [Hedyot kofaytz berosh]." Rashi [ad loc.] comments that the verse (ibid.) mentions Memucan last of the seven princes (yet it was he who spoke first), although he was inferior. The saying underscores the idea that a fool always hurries to the fore.

KA'ASHER AVADETI AVADETI (כאשר אבדתי אבדתי). "If I perish, I perish" (Esth. 4:16). Esther said she would go to the king in violation of the law. In other words, If I do not go, I will be killed together with my people. In any case, I will perish.

The expression is used colloquially to signify, "What will be, will be, and I will do whatever." "I am ready to carry it through and suffer the consequences."

KEYAD HAMELEKH (כיד המלך). An expression signifying "a large measure that only a king can give"; "with a wide hand", or "abundance," as in veyayn malkhut rav keyad hamelekh ("and royal wine in abundance according to the bounty of the king") (Esth. 1:7).

LO MIPNAY SHE'OHAVIM ET MORDECAI, ELA MIPNAY SHE-SONIN ET HAMAN (לא מפני שאוהבים את מרדכי, אלא מפני ששונאין את המן). The Book of Esther (chap. 6) relates that on that night, King Ahasuerus could not sleep. He ordered that the Book of Chronicles be brought and read for him. There it was found recorded that Mordecai had denounced Bigsona and Teresh, two of the king's chamberlains, of those that keep the door, who had plotted to lay hands on King Ahasuerus. The king said, "What honor and dignity has been done to Mordecai for this?" The king's servants answered, "There was nothing done for him." The Talmud (Meg. 16a) comments, on this latter phrase, that Raba said they answered him thus, "not because they loved Mordecai but because they hated Haman."

This adage was later applied to a situation in which one is extended a good word or favor, not out of love for his person, but out of hate for another person—doing a favor to one person to spite another.

NIT ALE PURIM TREFT ZIKH A NES (ניט אלע פורים טרעפט זיך א נס).
"A miracle does not occur every Purim." This infers that not every day does a miracle occur.

PURIM DANKT MEN NIT (פורים דאנקט מען ניט). "On Purim one does not say thanks." Two special features on Purim are *mishlo'ah manot ish lerayayhu* ("sending food gifts to friends") and *matanot le'evyonim* ("gifts for the poor"). Since these two actions are obligatory, the person receiving these gifts need not express gratitude.

PURIM IZ NIT KAYN YOM-TOV UN KADAHAT IZ NIT KAYN KREYNK (פורים איז ניט קיין יום-טוב און קדחת איז ניט קיין קריינק). "Purim is no holiday and fever is no malady." This jovial expression originated in the fact that on Purim, although it is a festival, Jews are not prohibited from doing work (cf. Meg. 5b).

PURIM IZ NOR EYN TUHG UN A KABTZN IZ MEN A GANTZ YOR (פורים איז נאר איין טאג און א קבצן איז מען א גאנץ יאר). See HANUKKAH UN PURIM VERN DI UHREMELAYT ASHIRIM.

PURIM KATAN DARF (MEG) MEN ZIKH UHNSHIKURN UHBER YOM KIPPUR KATAN DARF MEN NIT FASTN (פורים קטן דארף (מעג) מען זיך אנשיכורן אבער יום כפור קטן דארף מען ניט פאסטן). "On Purim Katan one must [may] get drunk but on Yom Kippur Katan one need not fast." *Purim Katan* is observed in a leap year in *Adar-rishon* ("the first *Adar*"). *Yom Kippur Katan* is observed by pietists on the day preceding Rosh Hodesh. Purim and Yom Kippur resemble each other since both are observed by *tzom* ("fast"), *kol* ("voice"), and *mamon* ("money"); *Yom Kippurim* is "like Purim"—*ke-Purim*. Both occasions utilize the term *katan* ("minor") and the saying jestingly expresses the idea of the positive versus the negative.

VEN MASHIAH VET KUMEN VELN ALE YAMIM TOVIM BATL VERN, NOR PURIM VET BLAYBN (ווען משיח וועט קומען וועלן אלע ימים טובים בטל ווערן, נאר פורים וועט בלייבן). "When the Messiah will come, all festivals will become void but Purim will remain." While the Sabbath was sanctified by God, the festivals were consecrated by Israel. In the future when the Messiah comes, the world will be completely redeemed and all its days will be like *Shabbat*. What purpose will there be, at that time, to add the light of Yom-Tov to the penetrating light of *Shabbat*? Moreover, the light of Purim was unfolded entirely by Divine Providence from above, rather than from the actions of Israel below. Thus, when Purim is celebrated in the future, the Jew will really learn to appreciate what God has done and His holiness will continue to shed light even

in the Messianic period (cf. *Yalkut Mishlay*, 94; see also *Maimonides, Yad,* end of *Hilkhot Megillah; Levush* 559:1).

FASTS (תעניות)

FASTN HAFSAKOT (פאסטן הפסקות). See PRAVEN TANEYSIM (TA'ANIYOT).

GOZER TANIS (TA'ANIT) ZAYN (גוזר תענית זיין). See PRAVEN TANEYSIM (TA'ANIYOT).

IN SHTUB IZ GEVEN TISHAH b'AB (אין שטוב איז געווען תשעה באב). See UHNMAKHN A TISHAH b'AB.

KLUHGN OYFN HURBAN (קלאגן אויפן חורבן). "To cry over the destruction." The word *hurban* refers to the *hurban Bayt Hamikdash* ("the destruction of the Temple"). The First Temple was destroyed by Nebuchadnezzar (586 B.C.E.) and the Second Temple by Titus (70 C.E.). The phrase *Veynen vi oyf hurban Bayt Hamikdash* ("to cry like for the Temple") is used as a comparison.

MEN TOR NIT ESN TISHAH b'AB, VAYL MEN LEYGT TEFILLIN TZU MINHAH (מען טאר ניט עסן תשעה באב, ווייל מען לייגט תפילין צו מנחה). "One may not eat on *Tishah b'Ab*, because *tefillin* are worn at *Minhah*." Wearing *tefillin* on *Tishah b'Ab* is delayed until the afternoon *Minhah* service because the *tefillin* are considered ornaments and the morning hours, when *tefillin* are worn daily, are moments when the grief is most intense. This jocular expression arose due to the fact that one does not eat prior to donning *tefillin*.

PRAVEN TANEYSIM (TA'ANIYOT) (פראווען תעניתים (תעניות)). "To carry-out fasts." Besides fasting on Yom Kippur and the four fasts— *Tzom Gedalia* ("Fast of Gedalia"), *Asarah be-Tevet* ("the Tenth

of *Tevet*"), *Shivah-asar be-Tamuz* (the Seventeenth day of *Tammuz*"), and *Tishah b'Ab* ("the Ninth of *Ab*")—there are those who fast on *Ta'anit BeHaB* (a cycle of Monday, Thursday, and Monday, kept after the festive seasons of Passover and Tabernacles), on a *Ta'anit Tzibbur* ("public fasts"), *Ta'anit Yahid* ("private fast"), *Ta'anit Bekhorim* (the fast of the firstborn on the eve of Passover), *Ta'anit Halom* (after having an evil dream), *Ta'anit Hatan Vekallah* (the fast of the bride and groom), *Ta'anit Yahrtzeit* (fast on the anniversary of the death of a parent), and other fasts recorded in the Talmud (Ta'an. 11a) and in rabbinic literature (*Soferim,* 17; *Kol Bo* 63; *Orah Hayyim* 580).

To ordain a fast is spoken of as GOZAYR TANIS ZAYN, and, when fasting at intervals, the expression FASTN HAFSAKOT is used. Jews had the practice of fasting on Mondays and Thursdays, since those days are known as *yemay ratzon* ("days of favor") (*Tos.* to B.K. 82A, s.v. *Keday*). This practice gave rise to the Yiddish saying YEDER MUHNTIK UN DUHNERSHTIK ("every Monday and Thursday"), meaning frequently.

UHNMAKHN A HURBAN (אנמאכן א חורבן). See UHNMAKHN A TISHAH b'AB.

UHNMAKHN A TISHAH b'AB (אנמאכן א תשעה באב). "To cause a *Tishah b'Ab*." The Yiddish expression generally signifies creating a mood of great sorrow. Similar expressions are IN SHTUB IZ GEVEN TISHAH b'AB ("The home was plunged into mourning"); UHNMAKHN A HURBAN ("to play havoc" or "to cause tremendous damage"). When one is hard hit, he or she may say A *hurban iz mir* ("I am destroyed"). To express even stronger emphasis on destruction, the two Hebrew words *harov venehrav* are used. In Yiddish, the word *harovdik* may express the idea of not feeling well.

YEDER MUHNTIK UN DUHNERSHTIK (יעדער מאנטיק און דאנערשטיק). See PRAVEN TANEYSIM (TA'ANIYOT).

RABBINIC
AND FOLK SAYINGS
מאמרי חכמים ודברי עם

מים עמוקים דבר פי איש, נחל נובע מקור חכמה

"The words of a man's mouth are as deep waters, a flowing brook, a fountain of wisdom" (Proverbs 18:4)

The Jewish people are known as AM HASEFER, the "People of the Book." Their ideal of learning led to the creation of the vast and varied literature that includes law, theology, ethics, philosophy, poetry, and grammar. The significant characteristic of this literature is that the greater part of it is directly or indirectly the outgrowth of the Bible.

The sayings in this section are from rabbinic and folk sources. They represent a wide range of subject matter culled from all periods, from many lands and diverse countries and different writers. Never has there been a generation that did not produce important books and sayings. These books and expressions served to inspire Jewry throughout the ages. Their content and style are not only a source of study and enjoyment to the Jew but an inspiration to all humanity.

AD SHETAVO HANEHAMAH, TAYTZAY HAS VEHALILAH HANESHAMAH (עד שתבוא הנחמה, תצא ח"ו הנשמה). "Until consolation comes, the soul, God forbid, may depart" (Folk Saying).

ADAM DO'AYG AL IBUD DAMAV VE'AYNO DO'AYG AL IBUD YAMAV (אדם דואג על אבוד דמיו ואינו דואג על אבוד ימיו). "Man worries about the loss of his money but does not worry about the loss of his time" (Sefer Hahayyim 10:1). A similar expression is AYN AVAYDA KE'AVAYDAT HAZMAN ("There is no greater loss than the loss of time") (R. Samuel b. Isaac Uzedah [Uceda], Midrash Shmuel 5:23).

ADMOR [pl., ADMORIM] (אדמו"ר (אדמו"רים)). The title bestowed upon hasidic rabbis. The term is an abbreviation of the three Hebrew words Adonaynu ("our master"), Moraynu ("our teacher"), and ve-Rabbaynu ("and our rabbi").

AHARAY DARGA (YAVO) TEVIR (אחרי דרגא (יבוא) תביר). Darga (meaning "step") and tevir (meaning "broken") are names of two accent marks below the words that follow each other in the printed Bible.

This wise remark infers that after darga, "he who climbs high," tevir, "falls heavily." This play on the words intimates that pride goes before a fall (cf. Tahkemoni, Sha'ar 3; SHeLaH, Derekh Hayyim 243).

AHARAY MA'ARIKH (YAVO) TARHA (אחרי מאריך (יבוא) טרחא). "After ma'arikh [comes] tarha" (R. Yitzhak b. Joseph Caro, Toldot Yitzhak [Constantinople, 1518]). Ma'arikh ("lengthener") and tarha ("trouble," "brother") are Sephardic names for two te'amim that follow each other in biblical cantillation. Ashkenazim call them, respectively, mayrkha tipha. A play on the words infers that after a longer period of time, when all is

quiet and uneventful, problems that may lurk beneath the surface rise up. This is similar to the expression "the calm before the storm."

AHARAY TARHA YAVO ETNAH (אחרי טרחא יבוא אתנח). Tarha and etnah are Sephardic names of two accent marks that follow each other in biblical cantillation. According to the Ashkenazim they are called, respectively, tipha and etnahta.

A play on the words gave rise to the saying, "After trouble (riot) comes rest (quiet)" (Isaiah b. Abraham Halevi Horowitz, SHeLaH, Derekh Hayyim [1649] 243).

AHARIT KOL KETATAH HARATAH (אחרית כל קטטה חרטה). "After every strife [comes] remorse" (Judah b. Samuel he-Hasid, Sefer Hasidim [Jerusalem: Lewin-Epstein: 1962], par. 88). Whoever sows hatred reaps remorse; thus, restrain yourself and you will not regret it.

AKAR MIN HASHORESH (עקר מן השרש). A phrase meaning to "uproot thoroughly" or "eradicate." In Yiddish, the expression is Akar-min-hashoresh zayn.

AL KOL PANIM (על כל פנים). "In any case," "at any rate," "at least," "be that as it may," "anyhow" (Folk Saying).

AL YEHI HAMASHAL HAZEH KAL BE'AYNEKHA, SHE'AL YEDAY HAMASHAL ADAM OMAYD AL DIVRAY TORAH (ADAM YAKHOL LA'AMOD BEDIVRAY TORAH) (אל יהי המשל הזה קל בעיניך, שעל ידי המשל אדם עומד על דברי תורה (אדם יכול לעמוד בדברי תורה). "Let not this parable be light in your eyes, for through it a man may gain a firm hold upon the Law (Shir Hashirim Rabbah 1:8). This is comparable to a king who had lost a piece of gold or a pearl, but by means of a wick, which was worth but a trifle, was able to find it again.

AL YESHANEH ADAM MIMINHAG HABERIYOT (אל ישנה אדם ממנהג הבריות). "A person should not change from the customs of the people" (*Derekh Eretz Zuta* 5).

ALAV HASHALOM (עליו השלום). See MIPNAY DARKAY SHALOM.

ALILAT DAM (עלילת דם). This term refers to the "blood accusations" that began against the Jews in the twelfth century and lasted until the early 1900s. The allegation that Jews used the blood of a murdered non-Jew in the preparation of *matzot* occurred in such cities as Fulda (1236), Prague (1305), Regensburg (1474), and Hungary (1882); and the last accusations happened before World War I in Kiev (1911). These allegations were hurled by perverted, bloodthirsty villains and were condemned, which eventually led to the Jews's acquittal.

Another name for this accusation is *Mamzayr-Bilbul* (Heb., "Illegitimate Perplexity") or *Blut Bilbulim* (Yidd., "Blood Confusion").

ALIYAT NESHAMAH (עלית נשמה). When righteous persons (*tzadikim*) pass away, their souls ascend to *Gan Eden* ("The Garden of Eden"). There is a belief that the soul of a great *tzadik* ascends to Heaven when he is alive and ordains or makes fit various aspects there and then returns. This, too, is referred to as *aliyat neshamah* ("spiritual elation" or "exultation"). The Zohar, as well as various hasidic volumes, speak of this event. There are even those who believe that when the Talmud (Sukk. 45b) mentions *Benay aliyah* ("the sons of Heaven"), it refers to this phenomenon. This, however, is not so; it means those who will see the Presence of God in the hereafter (cf. *Rashi*, ad loc.).

At a YAHRTZEIT it is customary to bring to the synagogue food and drink (TIKKUN). After the prayer service, the worshipers make blessings over the food and drink for the merit of the *neshamah* ("soul") of the deceased and wish that the *neshamah* will ascend (DI NESHAMAH ZUHL HUHBN AN ALIYAH).

ALMA DEKUSHTA (DIKSHOT) (DESHIKRA) (עלמא דקושטא (דקשוט) (דשקרא)). "The world of truth [falsehood]" (*Zohar, Vayayshev* 192b). See also Marcus Jastrow, *Dictionary*, vol. 2 (New York: Title Publishing Company, 1943), pp. 1084, 1085. See ASMAKHTA BE'ALMA, INSHAY DE'ALMA, KULAY ALMA LO PELIGI, MILAY DE'ALMA.

AM HASEFER (עם הספר). A phrase meaning "The People of the Book" (first mentioned in the Koran; cf. Reuben Alcaly, *The Complete Hebrew–English Dictionary* [Ramat-Gan, Jerusalem: Massada Publishing Company, 1970], referring to the Jews who gave the Bible to the world.

The expression took on a broader meaning because it is natural that many Jews collect materials of learning, since the idea of learning is so characteristically Jewish. According to tradition, each Israelite is to write a scroll of Law for himself, or, if he does not do so, he must have it written for him (cf. Deut. 31:19). The importance of books is also stressed in the Talmud (Ket. 50a); the Sages interpret the verse "Wealth and riches are in his house; and his merit endureth forever" (Ps. 112:3), as applying to a man who writes the Pentateuch, the Prophets, and the Hagiographa and lends them to others. By this is meant, the scrolls remain his, while his "merit endureth forever" for enabling others to study. Owning books is considered so meritorious that a person must not sell them except in order to marry, to study the Torah, or to redeem captives (*Shulhan Arukh, Yoreh De'ah* 270).

ANI HAKATAN (אני הקטן). An expression of modesty, meaning "I the insignificant," which is sometimes added to the signature of rabbis. It signifies placing a

moderate estimate on one's own merits. The phrase is rooted in Jacob's prayer, showing his humility and gratitude when he utters *Katonti mikol hahasadim* ("I am not worthy of all the mercies") (Gen. 32:11). The philosopher and *payyetan* Bahya (Bahye) b. Joseph ibn Paquda of Spain (second half of the eleventh century) is renowned for adding the expression *Katonti mikol hahasadim* to his writings. R. Yehudah Ha-Levi (c. 1075–1141), the Spanish Hebrew poet and philosopher, wrote a poem with the opening line *Ani katon me'od min hehasadim* ("I am too small for all the mercies") (cf. *Exile and Diaspora, Studies in the History of the Jewish People*, presented to Professor Haim Beinart on the occasion of his seventieth birthday [Jerusalem: Ben-Zvi Institute, Yad Izhak Ben Zvi and the Hebrew University of Jerusalem, 1988], pp. 149, 150).

In time, it became the vogue for scholars to append this unassuming description to their name. Once, this delineation was inappropriately used and a person who took notice of it sarcastically remarked in Yiddish, *Oykh mir a katan* ("Also a *katan*"); just take notice of who considers himself insignificant.

Hasidim believed that a person must be humble and avoid arrogance. To combat this, they preached that *ani* ("I") should be viewed as *ayn* ("nothing"). The letters in both words *ani* (*aleph, nun, yud*) and *ayn* (*aleph, yud, num*) are the same.

AV BEHOKHMAH VERAKH BE-SHANIM (אב בחכמה ורך בשנים). "Young in years and old in wisdom" (*Sifri*, Deut. 1); an old head on young shoulders.

AV EHAD YAKHOL LEFARNAYS ASARAH BANIM, VE'ASARAH BANIM AYNAM YEKHOLIM LE-FARNAYS AV EHAD (אב אחד יכול לפרנס עשרה בנים, ועשרה בנים אינם יכולים לפרנס אב אחד). "One father can sustain ten sons, and ten sons cannot sustain one father." This may be likened to two different talmudic incidents (Sot.

49a): R. Huna found a juicy date, which he took and wrapped in his mantle. His son, Rabbah, said to him, "I smell the fragrance of a juicy date." R. Huna gave it to him. Meanwhile, Rabbah's son, Abba, came. Rabbah took it and gave it to him. R. Huna said to Rabbah, "My son, thou hast gladdened my heart and blunted my teeth [he displayed more love for the son than for the father, by giving him the date]. The Talmud continues, That is what the popular proverb says, "A father's love is for his children; the children's love is for their own children." Another such incident was when R. Aha b. Jacob reared R. Jacob, his dauther's son. When he grew up, his grandfather said to him, "Give me some water to drink." He replied, "I am not your son." That is what the popular proverb says: "Rear me, rear me, I am thy daughter's son."

Rabbi Isaiah ha-Levi Horowitz writes that he heard it spoken in jest that when Jacob and his family came to Egypt to be fed at the table of his son Joseph, he said, "Now let me die, since I have seen thy face" (Gen. 46:30), meaning, "It is as difficult as death that I was forced to come to see you." This is like the common proverb, "One father can sustain ten children [with love and will] and ten children cannot support [with love and will] one father. No wise father should come to this point and cause himself harm (by giving away his wealth) unless it happens by the decree of God. Then he deserves it and God will help him" (*SHeLaH*, part 1, *Sha'ar Ha'otiyot*, p. 44 [87]).

AYN ADAM BA'OLAM BELO YESURIM (אין אדם בעולם בלא יסורים). "There is no person in the world without troubles" (*Yalkut, Aykev* 850).

AYN ASHAN BELI AYSH (אין עשן בלי אש). "Where there is smoke, there is fire"; based on the *Zohar* (1:70a; 3:137b) *Les tanena (tenana) belo isha-velo isha belo tanena* ("There is no smoke without fire and no fire without smoke"). The saying

Ayn ashan beli aysh implies that if people are talking, there must be some truth to it.

AYN AVAYDAH KE'AVAYDAT HAZEMAN (אֵין אֲבֵדָה כַּאֲבֵדַת הַזְמָן).

See ADAM DO'AYG AL IBUD DAMAV VE'AYNO DO'AYG AL IBUD YAMAV.

AYN BAH (BO) TA'AM VE'AYN BAH (BO) RAYAH (אֵין בָּהּ (בֹּו) טַעַם (וְאֵין בָּהּ (בֹּו) רֵיחַ).

"With neither savor nor flavor" (*Vayikra Rabbah* 30:11). The word *ta'am* may also mean "reason" or "meaning"—thus, "without rhyme or reason"—or can indicate "worthlessness."

A popular expression concerning *ta'am* ("taste") and *rayah* ("smell") is *Al ta'am verayah ayn lehitvakayah* ("About taste and smell, there is nothing to debate"), signifying that each person has his individual perception or sensation regarding taste and smell.

AYN HA'OR NIKAR ELA MITOKH HAHOSHEKH (אֵין הָאוֹר נִכָּר אֶלָּא מִתּוֹךְ הַחוֹשֶׁךְ).

"Light is not recognized except through darkness" (Abraham b. Samuel ha-Levi Hasdai; *Ben Hamelekh Vehanazir, sof sha'ar* 18 [Bologne, Italy, 1423]. Only the contrast between light and darkness lets the light be perceived. A similar saying is *Ilmalay hashaykha lo ishtamoda nehora* ("If not for darkness, light would not be able to be recognized") (*Zohar* 187; *Tazri'a* 47b). From this can be inferred ME'AT MIN HA'OR DOHEH HARBAYH MIN HAHOSHEKH ("A little light repels darkness") (*Tzaydah Laderekh* 12).

AYN HARASH AYTZIM BELO KARDOM (אֵין חָרָשׁ עֵצִים בְּלֹא קַרְדֹּם).

"There is no carpenter without a hatchet" (*Otzar Hamidrashim* 581). The phrase means that it is necessary for every artisan to have an instrument belonging to his profession.

AYN KISIM BATAKHRIKHIM (אֵין כִּיסִים בְּתַכְרִיכִים).

"Shrouds have no pockets." The word *takhrikhim* is derived

from *karakh*, meaning "to wrap"; a simple white linen cloth is used to wrap the dead body (M.K. 27b; cf. also the *Mishnah* in *Ma'asayr Shayni* 5:12). The *takhrikhim* are made differently for men and women; what they have in common is that both have no binding, seams, knots, or pockets.

This expression actually intimates that "You can't take it with you."

It was customary for people to prepare *takhrikhim* while still alive so that the shrouds would be a reminder of their day of death. Other reasons might have been so that they would not have to resort to *fremde takhrikhim* ("someone else's shrouds"), or they would not have to be prepared on a festival by a non-Jew if death occurred during the festival (cf. Y.D. Eisenstein, *Ozar Yisrael*, vol 10, [New York: Pardes Publishing House, Inc., 1952], p. 259).

AYN KOL VE'AYN ONEH (אֵין קוֹל וְאֵין עוֹנֶה).

"There is neither voice nor answer." Simply speaking there was "no answer" or "no reply." Similar expressions in Scripture are *Kerativ velo anani* ("I beseeched Him but He did not answer") (S.O.S. 5:6), or *Yikra velo yayaneh* ("He will cry [himself], but shall not be heard") (Prov. 21:13).

AYN RA SHE'AYN BO TOV (אֵין רַע שֶׁאֵין בּוֹ טוֹב).

"No ill is without its good" (*Tzeror Hamor* 24:2). A similar saying in Hebrew is the riddle that Samson gave to the Philistines: MAYAZ YATZA MATOK ("Out of the strong came forth sweetness") (Judg. 14:14). By this is meant that Samson tore a lion bare-handedly and later saw the carcass of the lion filled with a swarm of bees and honey. The *Zohar* (1:240a) comments on this phrase, saying that from the Written Law (Torah *shebikhtav*) is derived the Oral Law (Torah *shebe'al peh*).

In the Yiddish language, similar expressions are: *Fun ale ra'ot kumen aroys tovot* ("From all ills come good turns"); *Es iz nituh kayn guts uhn a bisl shlekhtz un es iz nituh kayn shlekhtz uhn a bisl guts* ("There is nothing good without a little bad and there is nothing bad without a little good"); *Bay yedn umglik iz oykh faran glik* ("With every misfortune, there is also good fortune"); and *Nituh kayn royz uhn derner* ("There is no rose without thorns"). An English equivalent is "Every cloud has a silver lining."

AYN VADAI SHE'AYN BO SAFAYK

(אין ודאי שאין בו ספק). "There is no certainty without a doubt." See M. Subar, Mikhol Hama'amarim *Vehapitgamim*, vol. 1 (Jerusalem: Mosad Harav Kook, 1961), p. 93.

AYNO DOMEH SHEMI'AH LIRE'IAH

(אינו דומה שמיעה לראיה). "Hearing is not to be compared to seeing" (*Mekhilta*, *Yitro* 19:9).

BA'AL HAMAYAH HU BA'AL HA-DAYAH

(בעל המאה הוא בעל הדעה). A colloquial saying, meaning "The influential person is he who has money." In other words, "Pay has the say." In Yiddish, the expression is *Der vuhs huht di mayah huht di dayah* ("He who has money is influential"). A similar English expression is "Who pays the piper calls the tune."

BA'AL YEKHOLET

(בעל יכולת). A phrase referring to the Almighty, Who is "capable of doing everything." Scripture states, Lest (the Egyptians) will say *mibli yekholet Hashem lahavi'am el ha'aretz* ("because the Lord was not able to bring them into the land") (Deut. 9:28).

The phrase has also been applied to one who is "a man of means" or "generally capable." See KAVAYAKHOL; KOL YAKHOL.

BA'AVONOTAYNU HARABIM

(בעונותינו הרבים). "Because of our many sins"; an expression generally uttered after speaking words that, in nature, are morally reprehensible.

BALEMER (ALMEMAR)

(באלעמער (אלמימר)). A word equivalent to BIMAH, from the Greek *bema* (tribune from which speakers address the public); also known as *almemar* (corrupted from the Arabic *al-minbar*, "the chair," "the pulpit"). In the synagogue, it is the platform from which the Torah is read. *Rashi* (Sukk. 51b) explains the word *bimah* as "our *almembra*" (*ke'ayn almembra shelanu*; see also Mishnah, Sot. 7:8).

The Yiddish word *balemer* is derived from two Hebrew words, *bal emor* ("not to say"), meaning, as long as the *Sefer Torah* is on the *bimah* it is prohibited for one to speak. Another explanation for the word is *bah laymor* ("about her saying")—that is, the *bimah* was founded to say (*laymor*) and read the missing *Sefer Torah* on it (Isaac b. Mordecai Lipiec, *Sefer Matamim Hehadash* [printed first in Warsaw, 1885] [Jerusalem/New York: Makhon Hape'ayr, 1993], s.v. *Bayt Hakeneset*, par. 8 and 9).

BARUKH HASHEM

(ברוך ה'). "Blessed be God" or "Thank God"; an expression uttered when experiencing pleasant occurrences, based on a phrase in Zechariah 11:5, "and they that sell them say, Blessed is the Lord" (*Barukh Hashem*).

A similar greeting uttered when relating something that has occurred or will occur is BE'EZRAT HASHEM YITBARAKH ("With the help of God, blessed be His Name").

The above two phrases are used in the headings of letters or books. The former is abbreviated with the letters *bet-hay* and the latter with *bet, ayin, zayin, hay-yud*.

BE'EZRAT HASHEM YITBARAKH

(בעזרת ה' יתברך). See BARUKH HASHEM.

BENAY ADAM (sing. BEN ADAM) SHEL HEFKAYR

(בני אדם (בן אדם) של הפקר). "People [a person] who lack[s] ethical character" (*Bereishit Rabbah* 5, end). This can refer to those who are licentious, unbridled, irresponsible, or spendthrift. A Yiddish equivalent is HEFKER YUNG.

The world has sometimes been described as an *olam shel hefkayr* ("A world that is null and void"), a world lacking order or meaning.

BERAKHAH LEVATALAH (ברכה לבטלה). "A futile blessing." It is written in the Talmud (Ber. 33a), "Whoever says a blessing which is not necessary transgresses the command of 'Thou shalt not take the Name of the Lord thy God in vain'" (Ex. 20:7). The *Mishnah Berurah* (215:18) elucidates what is meant by "an unnecessary blessing"; for example, if a person makes a blessing during the meal over foodstuff from which he was already exempt by virtue of the *Hamotzi* blessing that he made over the bread, an additional blessing is completely unnecessary. The decisors further stated that even if a blessing is not a futile blessing (*berakhah levatalah*), it sometimes may also be classified as an unnecessary blessing—for example, when a person's table is laid in front of him and he intends to wash his hands and eat a bread meal, but takes articles that he indends to eat during the bread meal and makes a blessing over them before he washes his hands. This, too, is forbidden because, by eating these articles before the meal, he creates a situation in which a blessing must be made unnecessarily.

The expression *berakhah levatalah* is sarcastically uttered when inferring that this person, thing, or event is worthless (futile).

BESHA'AH TOVAH UMUTZLAHAT (בשעה טובה ומוצלחת). A good wish, meaning "Good luck," or "All the best, in a good hour." The *Tanhumah* (Toldot 8) utilizes the phrase *Hasha'ah mesaheket lo* or *Hasha'ah omedet lo* (Tanhumah, Vayehi 3), meaning "The hour is smiling for him" or "The hour is standing for him," implying "to be in good fortune" or "to be lucky." The Yiddish equivalent is *In a mazeldige sha'ah* ("In a lucky hour").

BIMAH (בימה). See BALEMER (ALMEMAR)

DABAYR EL HA'AYTZIM VE'EL HA'AVANIM (דבר אל העצים ואל האבנים). Literally, "speak to the trees and to the stones." The colloquial expression took on the meaning "To speak in vain" or "to talk to someone who is inattentive."

This expression is possibly rooted in the Talmud (Yeb. 64a). Any particular person who has not engaged in the propagation of the race, R. Abba Hanan said, in the name of R. Eliezer, deserves the penalty of death. Others say that he causes the Divine Presence to depart from Israel, for it is said, "To be a God unto thee and to thy seed after thee" (Gen. 17:7). Where there exists "seed after thee," the Divine Presence dwells (among them); but where no "seed after thee," exists, among whom shall it dwell? Among the trees or among the stones? See AL HA'AYTZIM VE'AL HA'AVANIM.

DAI LAHAKIMA BIRMIZA (די לחכימא ברמיזא). "A word to the wise is enough" (cf. *Midrash Shemuel* 22:22). A similar proverb is LAHAKIMA BIRMIZA ULESHATYA BEKURMAYZA ("To the wise man a hint, to the fool a fist") (*Midrash Mishle* 22:6).

DAVENEN (DAVNEN) (דאוון(ע)נען). A term meaning "to pray," utilized by Eastern European Jews. Reference is made to the leader in prayer, as in *Eyner vuhs davent farn amud* ("one who intones the prayers at the prayer desk"), while the worshipers respond in a musical monotone. Several etymologies are given for the derivation of the term: (1) from the Aramaic word *de'avinun* ("of our fathers"), since it is believed that the patriarchs Abraham, Isaac, and Jacob instituted the recitation of the three daily prayers; (2) from the Aramaic *da ba'inan* ("this is what we ask for"), since prayers are made up of supplications (*bakkashot* and *tehinot*); (3) from the Latin *divinus* (divine) or *devovere*

(to exercise devotion); (4) from the English "dawn," referring especially to the prayer of the early morning (cf. Solomon ibn-Gabirol's poetic plea, beginning with the words *Shahar avakeshkha* ["At dawn I seek Thee"], in S. Baer, *Siddur Avodath Israel* [Rödelheim, 1868]; (5) from the Arabic *da'a* ("to pray"), an altered form taken from the speech of Turkish Jews, *du'a* or *da'wa*; and (6) from the Arabic *diwan*, a collection of poems (in Arabic-speaking lands, the prayerbook is called a *diwan*). Jews of Germany utilize the term *oren* (from the Latin *ora*, meaning "pray") for reciting prayers. In Spanish and Portuguese communities, *rezar* (from the Latin *recitare*, meaning "to recite") means "to pray." Thus, the various prayerbooks used in the services are called *reza*-books. The act of praying is called "reading" (*rezar*) or "saying *tefilla*" (H.P. Salomon, "Sephardi Terminology," in *American Sephardi*, vol. 5 [Yeshiva University, 1971], pp. 63, 64).

DEREKH ERETZ KADMAH LETO-RAH (דרך ארץ קדמה לתורה). "Good manners or social conduct precede the Torah" (*Vayikra Rabbah* 9:3; *Tanna Debay Eliyahu Rabbah* 1). *Derekh eretz* (lit., "the way of the land") includes local custom, good behavior, courtesy, politeness, and etiquette. The value of *derekh eretz* is often equated with that of the Torah itself and is part of the natural order of things. R. Ishmael b. Nahman held that *derekh eretz* preceded the Torah by twenty-six generations—that is, the time between the creation of the world and the giving of the Torah (*Vayikra Rabbah* 9:3).

Two tractates, *Derekh Eretz Rabbah* and *Derekh Eretz Zuta*, consisting of ethical teachings and morals and customs, have been appended to the Babylonian Talmud.

Another meaning of *derekh eretz* is "worldly occupation." It is written in the *Mishnah* (*Avot* 2:2, 3:21), "It is appropriate to combine study of Torah with a trade [*derekh eretz*]." Another *Mishnah* (Kidd. 1:9) states, "He who is versed in Bible,

Mishnah, and secular pursuits [*derekh eretz*] will not easily sin, for it is said, 'And a threefold cord is not quickly broken'" (Eccl. 4:12).

DER ZEKHUT FUN DER MITZVAH IZ IM BAYGESHTANEN (דער זכות פון דער מצוה איז אים בייגשטאנען). See ZEKHUTO YAGAYN ALAYNU.

DER ZIVUG ZUHL OLEH YAFAH ZAYN (דער זיווג זאל עולה יפה זיין). See HAKADOSH BARUKH HU MEZAVAYG ZIVUGIM.

DEVARIM HAYOTZE'IM MIN HA-LAYV NIKHNASIM EL HALAYV (דברים היוצאים מן הלב נכנסים אל הלב). "Words spoken from the heart reach the heart" (Moses ibn Ezra, *Shirat Yisrael*, p. 156), meaning, when a person speaks with sincerity his words become heartfelt.

This colloquial expression possibly has its origin in the talmudic statement of R. Helbo, who said, in the name of R. Huna, "If one is filled with fear of God, his words are listened to" (KOL ADAM SHEYAYSH BO YIRAT SHAMAYIM DEVARAV NISHMA'IN) (Ber. 6b).

DI NESHAMAH ZUHL HUHBN AN ALIYAH (די נשמה זאל האבן אן עליה). See ALIYAT NESHAMAH.

DIBBUK (דבוק). See GILGUL HANEFESH.

EMOR BEROMA VEKATIL BESURYA (אמור ברומא וקטיל בסוריא). "What is spoken in Rome may kill in Syria" (*Genesis Rabbah* 98:23). This is the result of spreading malicious reports or rumors.

ES IZ LEHAVDIL ELEF HAVDA-LOT (עס איז להבדיל אלף הבדלות). See ES IZ LEHAVDIL BAYN KODESH LEHOL.

ES VET ZIKH VENDN VI DER HAMOR SHTAYT (עס וועט זיך וועָנדן ווי דער חמור שטייט). The word *hamor*

may have two meanings: "ass" (or "fool") and "wine." The Maharil (*Likutay Maharil* 30) distinguishes between *hamra* (the letter *mem* with a *sheva*), meaning "wine," as in *Onkelos*, Genesis 19:32, and *hamara* (the letter *mem* with a *kamatz*), meaning "ass" or "fool," as in *Onkeles*, Genesis 22:5.

This saying refers to either a remark or an expression, depending upon how it is interpreted.

FREG(T) MIKH BEHAYREM

(פרעג(ט) מיך בחרם). A phrase intimating "I don't have the slightest idea." In Scripture the word *hayrem* has several connotations: "a thing devoted," as in *Kol hayrem kodesh kadashim la-Shem* ("Every devoted [thing] is most holy to the Lord") (Lev. 27:28); "banned," as in *veta'ayv teta'avenu ki hayrem hu* ("and thou shalt abhor it, for it is banned") (Deut. 7:26); and "excommunication," as in *Yaharam kol rekhusho vehu yibadayl mikhol hagolah* ("All his substance should be forfeited, and himself separated from the congregation of the exiles") (Ez. 10:8). The latter expresses the idea of confiscation, in conjunction with the act of putting someone in *hayrem* ("excommunication"). The Talmud (A.Z. 16a) uses the word *maharimin* to exclude a person from the religious community, which, among Jews, meant a practical prohibition of all intercourse with society. This came about by formal warning, public humiliation, and a solemn announcement in the synagogue, either before the Ark or while holding the Torah scroll, accompanied by lighted candles being extinguished to the blast of the *shofar*. The person was anathematized and excommunicated, and several biblical curses (*kelalot* and *haramot*) were invoked upon him. Currently, *hayrem* is sometimes imposed by extreme Torah authorities.

The expression *freg(t) mikh behayrem* possibly took on the meaning "If I am in *hayrem* [that is, isolated and not in contact with the community or world], how can I have any idea what you are saying to me." In Yiddish, the expression for the act of

ostracizing or banning someone is *Araynleygn in hayrem* or *Aroyfleygn a hayrem oyf*.

GARTL

(גארטל). A special belt or sash (also known in Hebrew as *ayzor* or *avnayt*) worn by *hasidim* and others during prayer. The *Kohen Gadol* and the *Kohanim* wore an *avnayt* ("a belt") during their service in the *Bet Hamikdash* (cf. Ex. 28:4, 28:40). The Talmud (Shab. 10a) states that one must wear a belt during prayer, based on the verse HIKON LIKRAT ELOHEKHA YISRAEL ("Prepare to meet your God, O Israel") (Amos 4:12). The *Orah Hayyim* (91:2), however, ruled that "if he has a belt underneath his garment so that there is a separation between his heart and his private parts," it is not necessary to wear a *gartl*. *Tosafot* (ibid., s.v. *Terihuta*) also states that the purpose of the belt is so that there should be a separation, and so forth, but this applies only to the Babylonians, who wore no trousers and therefore needed a belt during prayer; but since we wear belts on our trousers, it is not necessary to put on a special belt. *Hasidim* found a hint for the need of two belts (cf. Menahem Mendl of Rimanov, *Menahem Tziyon, Ki Taytzay*) in the verse "And righteousness shall be the girdle of his loins, and faithfulness the girdle of his reins" (Isa. 11:5). It has also been suggested that the blessing in the *Shaharit* morning service, "Blessed . . . Who girds Israel with strength" (Ber. 60b), pertains to putting on a special belt (cf. I. Lipiec, *Sefer Matamim* [first printed in Warsaw, 1885] [Jerusalem/New York: Makhon Hape'ayr, 1993], p. 5, 11).

A *gartl*, made from a long strip of material, is also used to bind or fasten the Torah after it is read. See WIMPEL.

GEFINEN A ZEKHUT (OYF)

(געפינען א זכות (אויף)). See ZEKHUTO YAGAYN ALAYNU.

GELOYBT IZ GOTT (גלויבט איז גאט).

"Praised be the Lord; a saying uttered when a misfortune befalls a person, as is written, "For the rage of man will acknowledge You; You will restrain the remnant of anger" (Ps. 76:11). When a person thanks the Lord concerning His anger, He sweetens the judgment and restrains the rest of the anger that should, Heaven forbid, not come upon him anymore (Isaac b. Mordecai Lipiec, *Sefer Matamim Hedadash* [Warsaw, 1885]).

GEMILUT HASADIM (גמילות חסדים). See HESED.

GEZAYROT KASHOT VERA'OT (גזירות קשות ורעות). "Harsh and bad edicts" against Jews. The Talmud (San. 97b) contains the phrase *Melekh shegezayrotav kashot* ("A king whose decrees shall be cruel"). One of the most sinister oppressors of Jews of all ages was Bogdan Chmielnicki, who initiated the terrible 1648–49 massacres (*Gezayrot tah ve-tat*).

GILGUL HANEFESH (גלגול הנפש). "Transmigration of the soul"; a belief of Jews that the soul of a dead person may pass to a newborn babe in order to continue life and atone for sins committed in the previous incarnation. In the tenth century Rav Saadyah Gaon considered this belief absurd and wrote of this in his work on Jewish religious philosophy, which was called *Emunot Vedayot* ("Beliefs and Opinions"). Among those who upheld this mystical belief were the *Zohar, Rambam*, Rabbi Yitzhak Luria (*Ari*), and R. Hayyim Vital.

On account of the enormity of their sins, souls were not permitted to transmigrate. Such a soul, in *Kabbalah*, becomes a DIBBUK, "denuded spirit" and enters a person's body after he has committed a secret sin that opened the door for the *dibbuk*. To exorcise *dibbukim* by adjuration is a meritorious deed, and is redeemed by providing a *tikkun* ("restoration"), either by transmigration or by causing the *dibbuk* to enter hell.

In Jewish folklore and popular belief, a *dibbuk* is an evil spirit or devil that sup-posedly possesses a person. It enters into the person, cleaves to the soul, causes mental illness, talks through his mouth, and represents a separate and alien personality. Concerning the *dibbuk*-belief, one would say, in Yiddish, *Es iz arayn in im a ru'ah* ("A spirit has entered into him").

GILUI ROSH (גלוי ראש). Literally, "uncovered head." As a sign of piety (*midat hasidut*) and fear of God (*yirat shamayim*), Jewish tradition requires men to cover the head. The *Kitzur Shulhan Arukh* writes, "A man must not walk four cubits [about six feet] with uncovered head. The little ones, too, must be accustomed to have their heads covered in order that the fear of God may be upon them" (Solomon Ganzfried 3:6). The mother of the *amora* R. Nahman b. Isaac is reputed to have said to him, "Cover your head so that the fear of Heaven may be upon you" (Shab. 156b). R. Huna, son of R. Joshua, said, "May I be rewarded for never walking four cubits bareheaded" (Shab. 118b; Kidd. 31a). The Talmud records that Rabina was sitting before R. Jeremiah of Dift, when a certain man passed by without a head-covering. Rabina then said, "What an impudent boor it is!"

Maimonides laid down the rule that no student of Torah should go bareheaded. Moreover, bareheadedness is equated with unseemly lightmindedness and frivolity (*kallut rosh; Yad, Dayot* 5:6). The SHeLaH wrote that even while sleeping, one should wear a head-covering. According to the Sages, covering the head is something that glorifies a person in Israel, and thus the blessing "Blessed . . . Who crownest Israel with glory" was instituted to be said in the Preliminary Morning Service (cf. *Etz Yosef, Siddur Otzar Hatefillot*, vol. 1 [Vilna, 1914]).

To cover the head, a skull cap called YARMLKE (Yidd.) or *kappel* (from the Italian *cappelo*, for "hat"), or *kippah* (Heb.) is worn. According to Shalom Aleichem (Shalom Rabinovitz), the etymology of the word *yarmlke* is derived from two Hebrew words, *yaray may-Elo'ah* ("fear of God"). When pronouncing God's Name, *kah* is said at the end, instead of *ah*, and thus the word *yarmlke* (*Yidishes Folksblat*, 1884, no. 22). Others attribute the name to a Slavic derivation.

It is customary for the ultra pious to wear the *yarmlke* under the hat. This is done in case one has to remove one's hat in honor of an important high official and thereupon to avoid standing bareheaded. It is also worn under the hat because it is clumsy to put on the *tallit* over a larger hat; thus, wearing a *yarmlke* under the hat makes it easer to put on the *tallit* over the head, and it also avoids bareheadedness (Isaac Lipiec, *Sefer Matamim* [first published in Warsaw, 1885] [Jerusalem/New York: Makhon Hape'ayr, 1993], p. 104). As for the proper size and material to be used for the *yarmlke*, see R. Gersion Appel, *The Concise Code of Jewish Law*, vol. 1 (New York: Ktav Publishing House, Inc., Yeshiva University Press), New York: p. 35, nos. 4, 5.

GOLEM (גלם). A word meaning "unformed" or "imperfect," as in *Golmi ra'u aynekha* ("Your eyes saw my unshaped form") (Ps. 139:16) or *gulmay kelay matkhot* ("unfinished metal vessels") (*Mishnah*, Kel. 12:6). The *Mishnah*, in *Avot* 5:9, uses the word *golem* in the sense of someone being a clod; that is, he possesses moral and intellectual virtues, but lacks understanding and does not function properly and, therefore, he is considered unfinished.

The *golem*, appearing as an artificial man who is creative in fulfilling tasks imposed upon it, as well as in bringing about destruction and havoc, first appeared in connection with Rabbi Elijah of Chelm (d. 1583). The best known of those who created a *golem* was R. Judah Löw b. Bezalel of Prague (c. 1525–1609), known as Der Hohe Rabbi Löw or the *Maharal*. Legend has it that the *golem* served him well but when it began to run amok and endanger people's lives, he had

to destroy it (cf. Macy Nulman, *The Encyclopedia of Jewish Prayer* [Northvale, New Jersey/London: Jason Aronson Inc., 1993], pp. 250, 251).

The Yiddish expression *leymener golem* ("*golem* made of clay") is used for a clumsy person. Similarly, if a person does something with his or her hands and is unsuccessful, the Yiddish expression is *Er/Si huht leymene hent* ("He or she has hands of clay").

GUT BAUEN (גוט בויען). See WIE HABEN SIE GEBAUT?

HAHAZIR BESHA'AH SHEHU ROVAYTZ POSHAYT ET TELAFAV KE'OMAYR: RE'U SHE'ANI TAHOR (החזיר בשעה שהוא רובץ פושט את טלפיו כאומר: ראו שאני טהור). "When the pig lies down, he spreads out his hoofs as though to say, See, I am kosher," (*Bereishit Rabbah* 65:1). The same can be said of an evil person, who shows his good side only to make himself look good.

HAKADOSH BARUKH HU MEZA-VAYG ZIVUGIM (הקב״ה מזווג זיווגים). The *Midrash* (*Bereishit Rabbah* 68) states that "God pairs women and men." Regarding pairing male and female, various sayings recorded are: AYN MEZAVGIN LO LE'ADAM ISHAH ELA LEFI MA'ASAV ("A woman is paired with a man according to his deeds")—that is, only if his actions are righteous does he have a faithful wife. Rabbi b. Bar Hanah said, in the name of R. Johanan: KASHIN LEZVOGAM KE-KERI'AT YAM SUF ("It is [as] difficult to pair them as the division of the Red Sea"); see KERI'AT YAM SUF. R. Judah said, in the name of Rab, "Forty days before the creation of a child, a BAT KOL issues forth and proclaims, 'The daughter of A is for B'" (Sot. 2a).

When wishing the wedding party good luck, the Yiddish expression used is DER ZIVUG ZUHL OLEH YAFAH ZAYN ("The union shall be auspicious") (cf. Pes. 49a). When two are most suited for each other, the saying is VI A ZIVUG MIN HASHAMAYIM ("like a union from Heaven"). Sometimes, instead of saying "my wife" or "your wife," the expression *zugati* or *zugatkha* is uttered.

HAKHAM (חכם). see MAH BAYN HAKHAM LENAVON? NAVON DOMEH LESHULHANI TAGAR.

HAKHAM BALAILAH (חכם בלילה). See HAKHAM, ZEH TALMID HAMAHKIM ET RABOTAV.

HAKHAM BASHI (חכם בשי). See MAH BAYN HAKHAM LENAVON? NAVON DOMEH LE-SHULHANI TAGAR.

HAKOL TALUI BEMAZAL AFILU SEFER TORAH SHEBEHAYKHAL (הכל תלוי במזל אפילו ספר תורה שבהיכל). "All depends on fate; even a Torah scroll in the Ark (*Zohar* 3:134; *Targum Kohelet* 9:2). This is said when there are numerous scrolls in the Ark and only one is read. Thus, even a Torah scroll has to have luck to be read.

This expression is often used when a person who is deserving of good luck does not attain it. See AYN MAZAL BEYISRAEL (cf. Shab. 156a; *Tos.* to M.K. 28a, s.v. *Ela Bemazla*).

HALASHON HU KULMUS HALAYV (הלשון הוא קולמות הלב). "Speech is the pen of the heart" (Aharon b. Tzvi Hakohen, *Keter Shem Tov*, vol. 2, p. 16). When a person speaks, it reveals what is in his heart.

HAMAKOM YENAHAYM ETKHEM (YENAHEMKHEM) (YENA-HEMKHA) IM (BETOKH) SHE'AR AVAYLAY TZIYON VIRUSHA-LAYIM (המקום ינחם אתכם (ינחמכם) (ינחמך) עם (בתוך) שאר אבלי ציון וירושלים). "May the Almighty comfort you among the mourners of Zion and Jerusalem." Comforting the mourners with this saying has its early beginnings in *Sefer Maharil* (Hilkhot Semahot [Jerusalem

edition, 1960], p. 84), in which the compiler writes, "I asked my teacher, the *Maharil*, what should we say? And he answered that he heard his father say, 'May *Hashem* comfort you together with the other mourners of Zion.'"

This expression of consolation is used when visiting the mourner(s) during the week of *Shivah* and when the mourner(s) come to the synagogue during or after *Shivah*. If a mourner is met on *Shabbat*, the expression used is *Shabbat hi milenahaym, venehamah kerovah lavo, veshivtu bashalom* ("Sabbath is not for consoling, may consolation soon come, hold [Sabbath] in peace") (Solomon Ben Ephraim Blogg, *Sefer ha-Hayyim* [Hannover, 1856], p. 89; cf. *The Hirsch Siddur* [Jerusalem/New York: Feldheim Publishers, 1969], p. 385; cf. *Siddur Otzar Hatefillot*, vol. 1 [Vilna, 1914], after *Seder Tikkunay Shabbat*).

HA'OLAM LESULAM HU DOMEH— ZEH OLEH VEZEH YORAYD (העולם לסלם הוא דומה—זה עולה וזה יורד). "The world is compared to a ladder—one goes up and the other down" (based on a *Tanhuma, Matot* 6).

HASIDAY UMOT HA'OLAM YAYSH LAHEM HAYLEK LE'OLAM HABA (חסידי אומות העולם יש להם חלק לעולם הבא). "Righteous gentiles (non-Jews who treat Jews kindly) have a share in the World to Come" (*Tosefta*, San. 13; *Rambam, Teshuvah* 3:5).

HASHEM YISHMERAYHU VI-HAYAYHU (השם ישמרהו ויחיהו). "May the Lord preserve him and keep him alive." This is usually said after mentioning a living person's name. The Hebrew abbreviation is *Hay, Yud, Vav*.

HATAN DOMEH LEMELEKH (חתן דומה למלך). "A groom is comparable to a king" (*Pirkay De-Rabbi Eliezer* 16). As a king is praised by everyone, so is the bridegroom praised by all during the seven days of the wedding feast. Just as a king is dressed in garments of glory, so is the bridegroom attired in garments of glory. As a king rejoices with a daily feast, so does the bridegroom during the week of his marriage.

HAZAL (חז"ל). An abbreviation for *Ha-khamim Zikhronam Livrakha* ("Our Sages of blessed memory"), used for Sages of the *Mishnah* and *Talmud*. It is not used for Sages after the period of the *Mishnah* and *Talmud*.

HEFKER YUNG (הפקר יונג). See BENAY ADAM (BEN ADAM) SHEL HEFKAYR.

HERGAYL NA'ASEH TEVA (הרגיל נעשה טבע). "Habit becomes second nature" (Meir Aldabi, *Shevilay Emunah* [Riva di Trento, 1518], 4:5). The *Kitzur Shulhan Arukh* wrote, "The physicians said that food to which a man becomes accustomed is never harmful even it be bad, because habit becomes second nature [*hergayl na'aseh teva*], providing he does not eat to excess" (R. Solomon Ganzfried 32:8).

HESED (חסד). By *hesed* is meant "kindness," "goodness," "mercy," or "charity." Scripture contains the phrase *ve'asita na imadi hased* ("and show kindness, I pray thee, unto me") (Gen. 40:14). According to the *Mishnah* (*Pe'ah* 1:1), GEMILUT HASADIM ("practice of kindness") has no limit. *Gemilut hasadim*, according to Maimonides (*Mishnah Torah, Hilkhot Matnot Aniyim*), includes, among other acts, lending money to the needy. Thus, the expression *Gemilut hesed* signifies lending money without a percentage (interest). In cities and towns where Jews lived, there were always "*Gemilut Hasadim*" organizations that lent money to people without interest.

An act of true kindness, without expectation of reward, is known as HESED SHEL EMET (lit., "a true charity"). The *Midrash Tanhuma* points out that kindness shown to the dead is a true *hesed* since there is no prospect of repayment or gratitude. This

was manifested when Jacob asked Joseph to deal kindly and truly with him after death (Gen. 47:29).

Kindness or mercy by the grace of God, or Divine grace, is known as HESED ELYON, a higher type of kindness.

HESED SHEL EMET (חסד של אמת). See HESED.

HESHBON HANEFESH (חשבון הנפש). "Moral stock-taking" or "introspection." Every person should take stock of himself as to his accomplishments and purpose in this world. Bahya (second half of the eleventh century) wrote a chapter called *Heshbon Hanefesh* in his *Hovot ha-Levavot*. He quotes a phrase from the Book of Psalms, *hishavti derakhai* ("I considered my ways") (Ps. 119:59). Hasidism puts great stress on *Heshbon Hanefesh*.

HETAYR ISKA (התר עסקא). The Torah law is "You shall not demand interest from your brother on a loan of money or of food or of anything else on which interest is usually demanded" (Deut. 23:20–21). In time, legalization of interest was established by means of a *heter iska* by forming a partnership, an agreement between borrower and lender. For a detailed description of this transaction, see *Encyclopedia Judaica*, vol. 16 (Jerusalem, Israel: Keter Publishing House Ltd.), pp. 31, 32.

HIBUT HAKEVER (חבוט הקבר). "Beating the grave." According to an early *Aggadah* that was considered by the kabbalists, the Angel of Death called Duma (cf. Ber. 18b) punishes the deceased for his sins by striking him with a fiery chain immediately after burial. Exemptions are made for those buried in Israel, or, if outside, those who are buried on Friday afternoon before sunset. The angel opens up the burial with a knock and asks the deceased his name. To ward off *Hibut hakever*, the kabbalists strongly suggested acts of charity and fervent recitation of prayers. A special power in this regard is, according to the *SHeLaH*, to remember one's Hebrew name when asked by the Angel of Death. To help remember one's name, pious Jews, after concluding the recitation of the *Amidah* prayer, add a verse from Scripture that begins and ends with the first and last letters of one's name. It is inserted between *Elohai netzor* and *Yihyu leratzon* in every *Amidah* (cf. Seligman Baer, *Avodat Yisrael* [Roedelheim, 1868], pp. 106, 107).

During the twelve months of mourning for a parent or close relative and on a YAHRTZEIT, it is customary to study the twenty-fourth chapter of *Kelim* ("Vessels") and/or the seventh chapter in *Mikva'ot* ("Ritual Bath") for the ascension of the *neshamah* ("soul"). After this study, a prayer beginning with *Ana Hashem malay rahamim* ("Please, God, full of mercy") is recited, in which a phrase reads, "He (She) shall be protected from *Hibut Hakever*, from maggot and worm, and be forgiven and pardoned for all his (her) sins" (cf. *Siddur Tefillah Hashalaym*, Tel Aviv, Israel: [Bet Shmuel], p. 626).

HITATAYF BE'ITZTELA DERABBANAN (דרבנן באצטלא התעטף). The word *itztela* means "an important outer garment" (cf. B.M. 17a). The expression *Hitatayf be'itztela derabbanan* is spoken of a person who beautifies himself in the clothing of great people when, in reality, it is unbecoming to him.

HOK VELO YA'AVOR (יעבר ולא חוק). See HOK NATAN VELO YA'AVOR.

HOLLE KREISH (HOLLEKREISH) (קרייש חול). The term *Holle Kreish* is a combination of the Hebrew *hol*, meaning "profane" or "secular," and *kreischen*, "to shout," to "call out" (Moses ha-levi Minz, Responsa 19). It is a ceremony that has been observed in Germany since approximately the fourteenth century, with the purpose of giving a secular name to infants in the cradle, especially girls. The boy is named at circumcision; the girl is

usually given a Hebrew name on the first Sabbath when the mother of the child attends synagogue.

The ceremony of *Holle Kreish*, marking the bestowal of a secular name upon the child, has the following features. Usually children of a tender age are invited to the house for the occasion. They form a circle around the cradle in which the infant lies. While lifting the cradle into the air three times, they cry out, "*Holle! Holle!* What shall this child's name be?" Whereupon the child's common, or non-Hebrew, name is called out in a loud voice. The father then recites the first verse of Leviticus. In some vicinities the Book of Leviticus is laid in the cradle, under the child's head. The reason for selecting Leviticus or *Torat Kohanim* ("The Law of the Priests"), another name for the third biblical book, is based on the *Midrash* (*Vayikra Rabbah* 7:3), which asks: Why do children begin learning *Torat Kohanim* and not *Bereishit*? And answers, "The children are pure and the sacrifices are pure, let those who are pure engage in things that are pure" (Leviticus or *Torat Kohanim* describes the function of the Priesthood and the duties of the priestly nation, which are purity of life, action, and thought). See Rabbi Benjamin S. Hamburger, *Sharashay Minhag Ashkenaz, Makhon Moreshet Ashkenaz* (Benei-Brak, Israel, 1995), pp. 415–455.

It has been suggested that *Holle* was the demon-witch who attacked infants, and the above ceremony was a dance intended to drive off the demon *Holle*, as in the WACHNACT ceremony in which measures were taken to ward off attacks by Lilit.

HUHGUH (HUHGOT) (חגאות] חגא). A Yiddish word meaning "a non-Jewish holiday." The Talmud speaks of a traveling merchants' season (*hagta detai'a*) (A.Z. 11b), a holiday in which all the merchants of the city gather to eat and drink for idol worship. In Yiddish, it was stated, *Az es klingt iz a huhguh* ("If it rings, it is a holiday"), intimating that if the church

bells are ringing, it is a Christian religious feast day.

HULYA, HULYA (הולייא, הולייא). It was customary when dancing to shout *hulya, hulya.* The two words are derived from the *Midrash* (*Bereishit Rabbah* 70:17), which relates that when Laban brought Leah into Jacob's room, the invited guests were told to dance and shout *ha Leah, ha Leah* ("This is Leah, this is Leah"). It is possible that *hulya, hulya* is the corruption of *ha Leah, ha Leah* (cf. Isaac b. Mordecai Lipiec [first printed in Warsaw, 1885] [Jerusalem/New York: Makhon Hape'ayr, 1993], pp. 31, 41).

Perhaps the Yiddish word *hulyen* ("frolic," "revel," "carouse," or a *hulye tuhn* ("have a fling") is derived from the same source.

HUTZPA (HUTZPAH) (חוצפא, חוצפה, חוצפה). A word meaning "impudence," "impertinence," "boldness," or "nerve," as appearing in the Talmud: HUTZPA, AFILU KELAPAY SHEMAYA MAHANAY or BE'IKVOT MESHIHA HUTZPA YISGAY VEYOKER YA'AMIR.

Sometimes *hutzpa* is considered a virtue, as the *Midrash* comments that Jews are *hatzufim shebe'umot;* they are bold and have the character of tenaciousness or steadfastness among the nations (*Shemot Rabbah* 42).

An impudent man is called a *hatzuf* or, in Yiddish, *hutzpanik;* an impudent women, a *hatzufah.* The latter term is also used for a frivolous woman (cf. Jer. Tal., Ta'an. 4). To act in an impudent or cocky manner, *hutzpadik* (Yidd.) is used.

ILULAY SHERA'ITI BE'AYNAI LO HE'EMANTI (אלולי שראיתי בעיני לא האמנתי). "Would I have not seen it with my own eyes, I would not have believed it" (*Pesikta Rabbati* 32).

IM ATTAH OSEH DALET RAYSH-ATTAH MAHARIV ET HA'OLAM KULO (אם אתה עושה דלי"ת רי"ש—). (אתה מחריב את העולם כולו). "If you

change a *dalet* into a *raysh,* you destroy the entire world" (*Vayikra Rabbah* 19:2). In the English language a similar maxim is, One should mind one's P's and Q's.

IM AYN TALMIDIM AYN HAKHAMIM (אם אין תלמידים אין חכמים). "Without disciples, there can be no wise men" (*Bereishit Rabbah* 42:4).

IM LO TIKANAYS HAMILAH KULAH TIKANAYS HETZYAH (אם לא תכנס המלה כולה תכנס חציה). "If the entire word does not go into [one's ears], half will" (*Bereishit Rabbah* 56:5); that is, if one listens to slander and profanity, even if all that he hears he does not believe, nevertheless, part of it wil be gathered in his ears.

IM SHEMO ASHAYR GAM LAHMO KASHAYR (אם שמו אשר, גם לחמו כשר). "If his name is Ashayr, his bread must also be *kashayr*" (kosher) (cf. Rabbi M. Subar, *Mikhlol Hama'amarim, Vehapitgamim,* vol. 1 [Jerusalem: Mosad Harav Kook, 1961], p. 196). Similarly, in Yiddish one says, *Az zayn nuhmen iz Mendel meg men esn fun zayn fendl* ("If his name is Mendel, you can eat from his pot"). In both instances, the names rhyme with the objects.

Undoubtedly, there may be a question as to the *kashrut,* but since the persons have Jewish names, they are facetiously said to be kosher.

IM TIRTZU AYN ZU AGGADAH (אם תרצו אין זו אגדה). "If you will, it is no legend"; or, "Where there is a will there is a way" (Theodore Herzl, 1860–1904). This motto, published in his Zionist novel *Altneuland* (1902), was written when Herzl, the father of political Zionism, became convinced that the only solution for the Jews was to leave their native countries, infested by anti-Semitism, and settle in their own land.

IM YIRTZEH HASHEM (אם ירצה השם). Literally, "God willing"; an expression usually said when anticipating some action. This utterance is derived from the verse "Many are the thoughts in the heart of man, but it is the counsel of the Lord that endures" (va'atzat Hashem hi takum) (Prov. 19:21). The initial letters of the word hi (hay, yud, aleph) are shorthand and reversed for Im yirtzeh Hashem. That is to say, if the counsel is according to the will of the Almighty and the person trusts that without His will, nothing can be accomplished, then he is assured that the matter will be finalized (Isaac b. Mordecai Lipiec, Sefer Matamim Hehadash [Warsaw, 1885], s.v. Dibbur, p. 20).

IN MITN VAYOMER (VAYEDA-BAYR) (אין מיטן ויאמר (וידבר)). "In the middle of saying [or speaking]." The phrase is used when someone interrupts in the middle of a discussion or in the process of doing something.

The two Hebrew words, vayomer and vayedabayr, signify "saying" and are generally combined with Vayomer Hashem ("And the Lord said") (Gen. 6:3) or Vayedabayr Hashem ("And the Lord spoke") (Ex. 6:10).

INISH BE'INISH PAGA, TURA BETURA LO PAGA (איניש באיניש פגע, טורא בטורא לא פגע). See TURA BETURA LO PAGA, INISH BE'INISH PAGA.

INYANAY DEYOMA (עניני דיומא). "Topic of the day," "a current topic," or "current affairs." It is sometimes announced that a speaker will give a talk and his discussion will be mayinyana deyoma.

ISHAH BEGIMATRI'A DEVASH (אשה בגימטריא דבש). "The numerical value of the Hebrew word 'woman' (ISHaH; aleph = 1, shin = 300, hay = 5) equals honey (DeVaSH; dalet = 4, bet = 2,

shin = 300)" (Judah da Modena, also known as Leon da Modena, Ari Nohem [Fürst, Leipsic, 1840]).

IVRI (sing.), IVRIM (pl.) (עברי; עברים). A name used for the people of Israel. The first to be called Ivri was the patriarch Abraham, vayagayd le-Avram Ha'ivri ("and told Abram the Hebrew") (Gen. 14:13). Various origins are given for the word Ivri (Hebrew): (1) "one from the other side," as in "And I took your father Abraham from the other side of the river" (mayayver hanahar) (Josh. 24:3), that is, the Euphrates (Isaac b. Mordecai Lipiec, Sefer Matamim Hehadash [first printed in Warsaw, 1885] [Jerusalem/New York: Makhon Hape'ayr, 1993], 123:1); (2) "a descendant of Eber" (Gen. 10:21); (3) from Habiri, a nomad people mentioned in the Tell-el-Amarna Tablets (cf. The Pentateuch and Haftorahs, 2nd ed. Dr. J.H. Hertz, ed., [London: Soncino Press, 1973], p. 51, note 13).

In Scripture, when making a differentiation between Jew and non-Jew, Ivri is used. As, for example, when the wife of Potiphar tells her husband about Joseph, she says, ish Ivri letzahek banu ("a Hebrew unto us to mock us") (Gen. 39:14). The chief butler tells Pharaoh about Joseph Vesham itanu na'ar Ivri ("And there was with us a young man, a Hebrew") (Gen. 41:12). Of Moshe, it is told that he saw "ish Mitzri makeh ish Ivri ("an Egyptian smiting a Hebrew") (Ex. 2:11).

The word Ivrit, denoting the Hebrew language, appears in the Mishnah (Git. 9:8), "A divorce document [get] that was written in Hebrew [Ivrit] and the witnesses signed in Greek [Yevanit]."

In Yiddish, the word Ivri denotes that one can read Hebrew (lashon kodesh). One who cannot read Hebrew at all, of him it is said, Er ken nisht kayn ivre ("He cannot read Hebrew"). The Hebrew language in Yiddish is Hebreish and a devotee of the Hebrew language is Hebrei'er. The method of teaching Hebrew by actual speaking, without the intermediacy of another language, is called *Ivrit be-Ivrit*.

KABBALAT KINYAN (קבלת קנין). By *Kabbalat kinyan* is meant "an agreement or affirmation to a transaction." For example, when a marriage contract (*ketubah*) is written, it is necessary to make a symbolic agreement (*kinyan*) with the bridegroom (by having him hold a kerchief or some other article of clothing), in which he obligates himself to fulfill whatever is provided in the marriage contract (Maimonides, *Ishut* 10:7; *Maggid Mishnah*; *Eben ha-Ezer* 61:1). Similarly, when selling the *Hamaytz* before Passover, the seller holds a kerchief, signifying that the transaction being made is valid.

KABDAYHU VEHASHDAYHU (כבדהו וחשדהו). "Respect him and suspect him"; that is, give him respect but be wary of him (*Kallah Rabbati* 9).

KAKH HAVAH (כך הוה). See MA'ASEH SHEHAYAH KAKH HAYAH.

KASHAH HI HAPARNASAH KIFLAYIM KELAYDAH (קשה היא הפרנסה כפלים כלידה). "Earning a livelihood is twice as hard as giving birth" (*Bereishit Rabbah* 20:22).

KAYN YIRBU (כן ירבו). "So may they multiply"; a wish expressed for an additional or greater amount. *Rashi*, quoting the Talmud, writes, "You say 'Lest he will multiply' and I [The Holy Spirit] say, 'He will certainly multiply'" (*kayn yirbeh*) (Ex. 1:12; Sot. 11a).

Various customs, based upon the names of foods that signify multiplying, are eaten in different communities. For example, on Rosh Hashanah Jews of Ashkenazic descent eat carrots (or carrot *tzimmes*). Carrots are also cooked whole and then sliced into circles, resembling coins in color and shape; this alludes to a desire for a prosperous year. The Yiddish for carrot is *mern*, which also means "to increase."

When eating carrots in any shape or form on Rosh Hashanah eve, this prayer is uttered: "May it be Your will . . . that our merits increase" (*sheyirbu zekhuyotoynu*).

KENANAS AL GABAY ANAK (כננס על גבי ענק). "Like a dwarf on a giant" (Zedekiah b. Abraham Pietosi of Rome, *Shibbolay Haleket* [Venice, 1546]; an expression used when comparing one's lower degree or rank to a person who is superior.

KETARNEGOLIM HAMENAKRIM BE'ASHPAH (כתרנוגלים המנקרים באשפה). "Like chickens who gnaw at the dunghill." This expression is applied to one who does not eat at a fixed time, but eats all day long (*Yalkut Shimoni, Beshalah* 228).

KO'AH HAPO'AYL BENIFAL (כוח הפועל בנפעל). "The strength of a [master] worker is reflected in his work" (attributed to Baal Shem Tov, in *Sefer Otzar Hesed*, p. 86). The Besht was able to recognize a worker's intent when looking at his creations (*Haykhal Haberakhah, Mikaytz*), as well as the meaning a performer conveyed while playing his instrument (*Likkutay Meharan* 225; *Or Hama'ir, Parshat Ha'azinu*).

KOL HAMON KEKOL SHADAI (קול המון כקול שדי). "The voice of the people is the voice of God" (Samuel b. Isaac Uceda, *Midrash Shemuel* [Venice, 1579], 1:111).

Ezekiel, the prophet, tells of hearing various voices and among them the voice of God, "And when they [the likeness of four living creatures] moved, I heard the noise of their wings, like the noise of great waters, like the voice of the Almighty [*kekol Shadai*], the noise of a tumult, like the noise of a host" (Ezek. 1:24).

KOL HASANDLARIM HOLKHIM YEHAYFIM (הולכים הסנדלרים כל יחפים). "All cobblers go barefoot" (attributed to Hayyim Nahman Bialik); that is, although they fix shoes for many persons, for themselves they are neglectful and wear torn shoes. In Yiddish, the expression is "Ale shusters geyen buhrves."

The same expression is adaptable to any person who has a trade and neglects himself.

KOL MAH SHEYAYSH LO TIKHLAH YAYSH LO TEHILAH (לו שיש מה כל תחלה לו יש תכלה). A saying with a play on the words tikhlah and tehilah, meaning, "Everything that has an end [naturally] has a beginning [as well]" (Bahya ibn Paquda, Hovot Halevavot, Sha'ar Hayihud 5).

KUDESHA BERIKH HU, ORAITA VEYISRAEL HAD (הוא בריך קודשא חד וישראל ואורייתא). "The Holiness, blessed be He, the Torah, and Israel are one" (Zohar, Aharay Mot 73a). The Jewish people are identified with God and the Torah as one and the same, to the point expressed in this proverbial saying. The Zohar (Emor 93b) also uses the expression Kudesha berikh Hu ukeneset Yisrael ikri ehad ("The Holiness, blessed be He, and the Assembly of Israel are called one").

A tune to which this text, with variation, was adapted is YISRAEL VE'ORAITA HAD HU ("Israel and the Torah are one"). The tune ends with Torah orah. Halleluyah ("Torah is light. Halleluyah"). See KUDESHA BERIKH HU.

KUZU BEMUKHSAZ KUZU (כוז'ו כוז'ו במוכס"ז). A fourteen-letter name of God written on the bottom of the blank side of the Mezuzah. It also appears in the prayer recital Ayl melekh ne'eman, said by the Sheli'ah Tzibbur prior to the Musaf of Rosh Hashanah in the Ashkenazic rite. According to the aleph-bet gimmel-dalet formula (every letter standing for the pre-

ceding letter), it reads Hashem Elohaynu Hashem of the Shema, with which the text of the Mezuzah opens. The earliest reference to this is attributed to the Gaon Sherira (Sefer Asufot, fourteenth century manuscript) and the earliest literary occurrence of this name is in Eshkol Hakofer, by the mid-twelfth century Karaite, Judah Hadassi. See also Zohar 18b, 23a).

The fourteen-letter name possessed high protective virtues. Before leaving home on a business journey, it was customary to kiss the Mezuzah in order to invoke God by referring to the name Kuzu Bemukhsaz Kuzu, declaring that in His Name they are about to go forth and they petition Him for success. (Sefer Maharil 87b; Joshua Trachtenberg, Jewish Magic and Superstition [Meridian Books and Jewish Publication Society, 1961], p. 149). The Sheli'ah Tzibbur, too, by uttering this fourteen-letter name before the longest prayer service in the year cycle (Musaf) possibly invokes guardianship and watchfulness over his voice and general well-being.

KVITL (Heb., PITKAH) (קוויטל (פתקה)). A request written on a piece of paper for the hasidic rebbe to intercede on behalf of a person's needs. The request is accompanied by a pidyon (money). Asking for advice or words of comfort in times of trouble or despair can be traced back to 1 Samuel 9:6–8, as well as to talmudic days, when R. Phineas b. Hama gave the following exposition, "Whosoever has a sick person in his home should go to the scholar and saint who will invoke [heavenly] mercy for him" (B.B. 116a); as it is said, "The wrath of a king is as messengers of death; but a wise man will pacify it" (Prov. 16:14). See also Ber. 34b, where the son of Rabban Gamaliel became ill and he sent two Torah scholars to R. Hanina b. Dosa to ask for mercy for him (cf. also A.J. Sperling, Sefer Ta'amay Haminhagim, Inyanay Rosh Hashanah [Lvov, 1850], no. 694).

At the Western Wall (*Kotel Ma'aravi*) in Jerusalem, it is customary for people to pray. Some place a *kvitl* between the clefts of the stones on which is written a request of God or a praise to the Almighty for some beneficence.

On Wednesday, 28 *Iyyar* 5727 (June 7, 1967), when the Western Wall was liberated, both Moshe Dayan, Minister of Defense, and General Yitzhak Rabin placed *kvitlakh* into the crevices of the wall. General Rabin inscribed a verse that King David had used when he liberated Jerusalem: "This is the Lord's doing, it is wondrous in our eyes" (Ps. 118:23) (cf. Dov Rosen, *Shema Yisrael*, vol. 2, trans. by L. Oschry [Jerusalem, 1972], p. 402). See IR ZUHLT ZIKH OYSBETN A GUT YOR (A GUT KVITL).

LAHAKIMA BIRMIZA, ULESHATYA BEKURMAYZA (לחכימא ברמיזא, ולשטיא בכורמיזא). See DAI LAHAKIMA BIRMIZA.

LAYT DIN VELAYT DAYAN (לית דין ולית דיין). An expression intimating that restrictions are removed; actually, "lawlessness," or "anarchy." Everybody does what he likes and there is no justice in the world (*Vayikra Rabbah* 28:1). The Jer. Talmud (Kidd. 4:1) has a similar expression, *Ayn din ve'ayn dayan* ("no case and no judge [to sit upon it]").

LEFI ANIYUT DATI (LA'ANIYUT DATI) (לפי עניות דעתי (לעניות דעתי)). "According to my humble opinion"; an expression used in halakhic literature when a particular situation or problem is discussed. The decisor says, "According to my humble opinion," the decision or ruling shall be thus (cf. *Lu'ah Hayovayl shel Ezrat Torah, Le'inyan Neshikat Sefer Torah* [1935], p. 67).

LEKHOL HARUHOT (לכל הרוחות). The word *ru'ah* (Heb.) means "wind." It is also used to designate "spirit" or "inspira-

tion," as in *ru'ah hakodesh* ("Divine Spirit") or *ru'ah hayyim* ("living spirit"). The word *ru'ah* can also refer to man's soul, as in *Zivhay Elohim ru'ah nishbarah* ("The sacrifices of God are a broken spirit") (Ps. 51:19). *Ru'ah* or *ruhot* also indicates the souls of the dead that hover around the world, as is written concerning the pious man who passed the night in the cemetery and heard *shetay ruhot mesaprot zu lazu* ("two spirits conversing with one another") (Ber. 18b).

Just as the word *ru'ah* conveys the idea of holy spirits, so, too, the word is used to designate evil spirits or clinging demons. The Lord asks, "Who shall entice Ahav, that he may go up and fall at Ramot-Gilead? . . . And there came forth a spirit . . . I will be a lying spirit" (*ru'ah sheker*) (1 Kings 22:20–22). It is written in the Talmud (Erub. 18b) that R. Jeremiah b. Eleazer further stated, "In all those years during which Adam was under the ban, he begot ghosts and male demons" (*ruhin veshaydin*).

The latter idea gave rise to the expression *Lekhol haruhot*, meaning, "Damnation" or "To the devil with you (him)!" The Yiddish equivalent is *Tzu al(d)e shvartze ruhot* or *khapt im der ru'ah*.

LERNEN PASUK (לערנען פסוק). By *lernen pasuk* is meant the study of the Prophets and Hagiographa (*Nevi'im* and *Ketuvim*). Studying the Pentateuch is referred to as *lernen humash* (from *hamaysh*, meaning "five," denoting the Five Books of Moses). The usage of these expressions was mainly in Poland.

The word *pasuk*, from the Aramaic *pesak* ("to cut off"), is the smallest part of a paragraph known as a verse. Dividing the Pentateuch into verses is attributed to Moses (Meg. 22a).

The origin of the phrase *lernen pasuk*, when studying *Nevi'im* or *Ketuvim*, may be when R. Meir was reputed to have taken Aher to thirteen schoolhouses, in which he asked children, "Recite for me thy verse!" (*Pesok li pesukha!*) (Hag. 15a, b). Each of the children quoted verses in a similar vein from *Nevi'im* and *Ketuvim*. The Talmud (Git. 56a) also describes the time when the Emperor said to a certain boy, *Pesok li pesukha* ("Recite for me thy verse") and he replied with, "And I will lay my vengeance upon Edom by the hand of my people Israel" (Ezek. 25:14), a verse in *Nevi'im*. According to Wilhelm Bacher (1850–1913), medieval authors called the whole of Scripture *pasuk* ("Review Etudes Juives," 16, 278).

The Masorites placed the accent mark called *silluk* (lit., "cessation," "close," or "final") under the tone-syllable of the word in the printed Bible at the end of every verse. The mark of *sof pasuk* (lit., "end of a sentence," represented by two points), similar to the colon mark at the end of the sentence, is not considered one of the *Te'amim*. It was placed there only as an additional sign, separating the verses (Wolf Heidenheim, *Sefer Mishpetay ha-Te'amim* [1808], p. 6).

It is told of the founder of a hasidic dynasty in Poland, Rabbi David b. Solomon of Lelov (Lelow, 1746–1813), that he once overheard a man praying, who after every verse, said the Name of God. He did this because of the two dots, one above the other at the close of each sentence. He took each dot to be the small letter *yud* and since God's Name is sometimes abbreviated in the form of two *yuds*, he thought that what he saw at the end of every verse was the Name of God. Rabbi David remarked: "Whenever it looks to you as if one Jew (*Yud*) is standing above the other, they are not Jews (*Yuds*) and it is not the Name of God. Only when two Jews (*Yuds*) stand side-by-side is the Name of God present." It is reputed that Rabbi David's teachings stressed love of the Jewish people (*ahavat Yisrael*) and of man in general. He was revered by the prominent hasidic leaders of his day.

LERNEN TAMID UN KENEN MAKKOT (לערנען תמיד און קענען מכות). Literally, "to study *Tamid* and know *Makkot*." *Tamid* and *Makkot* are two tractates in the Talmud. The former contains all the regulations for the offering of the regular daily sacrifices and the latter deals mainly with judicial floggings.

The two words also have other intent: *tamid* means "always" and *makkot*, "plagues." Thus, the sarcastic connotation is "he is always learning and knows nothing."

Similarly, another expression in the same vein is *Shabbat lernt er, Makkot Ken er* ("He studies [tractate] Shabbat and knows [tractate] Makkot"—that is, he knows nought.

LETORAH, LEHUPAH, ULEMA'ASIM TOVIM (לתורה, לחופה, ולמעשים טובים). "[May he enter] into Torah, the marriage canopy, and good deeds" is part of the liturgy for the Circumcision Service. This wish is uttered by those present at a *Brit Milah*. It may also be a wish to any young lad embarking upon life.

The rationale for this sequence is that a person must first learn Torah and then marry. Even though he is obligated to perform *mitzvot* from the day he is *Bar Mitzvah*, "good deeds" come later because he is not punished for any transgressions until the age of twenty (*Aytz Yosef, Siddur Otzar Yisrael, Seder Brit Milah*). Moreover, it is when he gets married at eighteen that he merits "good deeds," for he is spared transgressing by marriage (Isaac b. Mordecai Lipiec, *Sefer Matamim Hehadash*, [First printed in Warsaw, 1885] [Jerusalem/New York: Makhon Hape'ayr, 1993], 90:63). See WIMPEL.

LO KHOL HAKAROV KAROV VELO KHOL HARAHOK RAHOK (לא כל הקרוב קרוב ולא כל הרחוק רחוק). "Not all that is near is close [in heart and mind] and not all that is distant is far [from heart and mind]," (*Bemidbar Rabbah* 3:2). The saying is taken to mean, a person may be close to a situation yet he or she is far from it; and vice versa, someone may be far away and yet close.

LO MIT AN ALEF (לא מיט אן אלף). "No; positively not!" *Lo* ("no"), written with an *alef*, is identical in pronunciation with *lo*, "to him," written with a *vav*. When one wants to emphasize the negative, the expression *Lo mit an alef* is uttered.

LO TA'AM VELO RAYAH (לא טעם ולא ריח). See AYN BAH TA'AM VE'AYN BAH RAYAH.

LO YEHAY ADAM NOTAYN KOL MAMONO BEZAVIT AHAT (לא יהא אדם נותן כל ממנו בזוית אחת). "A person should not put all his money in one corner [place]" (*Bereishit Rabbah* 76:3). The English equivalent is "Don't put all your eggs in one basket."

LO YIDAG ADAM LOMAR PELONI YEKAPAYAH PARNASATI (לא ידאג אדם לומר פלוני יקפח פרנסתי). "A person should not worry, saying that so and so will deprive me of my livelihood" (*Rashi*, *Yoma* 38a). The Talmud (ibid.) states, "By your name you will be called, to your place you will be restored, and from what belongs to you will be given [that is, what is predestined to your lawful source of income]. No man can touch what is prepared for his fellow. . . ."

LO YITZLAH (YUTZLAH) (לא יצלח). The *Lo Yitzlah* is one who is "a failure," "ne'er-do-well," or "luckless." He is the opposite of the fortunate person who is prosperous in all his undertakings. Scripture (Gen. 39:2) refers to Joseph as an *ish matzli'ah* ("a prosperous man"); the Lord was with him and all that he did in Egypt prospered.

MAH BAYN HASIDIM LEMITNAGDIM? HARISHONIM HOSHVIM SHEYAYSH LAHEM REBBI, VEHA'AHARONIM HOSHVIN SHE'AYN LAHEM TZOREKH BEREBBI (מה בין חסידים למתנגדים? הראשונים חושבים שיש להם רבי, והאחרונים חושבין שאין להם צורך ברבי). "What is the difference between *hasidim* and *mitnagdim*? The former think they have a rebbe and the latter think they do not need a rebbe (Yisrael Salanter, 1810–1883). That is, *hasidim* most likely have a rebbe but do not heed him. *Mitnagdim* don't think they need a rebbe because they feel they know the *halakhah*. As a result, neither has a rebbe.

MAH HAHEVDAYL BAYN MATANAH LINEDAVAH? MATANAH NOTNIM LE'ADAM KEDAY LEKARAYV OTO, UNEDAVAH-KEDAY LEHIPATAYR MIMENU (מה ההבדל בין מתנה לנדבה? נותנים לאדם כדי לקרב אותו, ונדבה- כדי להפטר ממנו). "What is the difference between a gift and a donation? A gift is given to a person in order to become closer to that person and a donation is given [to a person] to get rid of him" (Folk Saying).

MAH SHEY'ASEH HAZEMAN LO YA'ASEH HASAYKHEL (מה שיעשה הזמן לא יעשה השכל). "The mind cannot do what time can" (*Hut Hashayni* 112:2); "Time heals" or "Time is the best medicine."

MAKH AN ETNAHTA! (מאך אן אתנחתא!). *Etnahta* is an accent sign, meaning "to rest," placed below words in the printed text of Scripture. The second strongest Masoretic accent, it divides the verse into two parts and is similar to the colon or semicolon in the English language. Hence, when a person speaks without a stop or pause, he or she is told to *makh an etnahta* ("make a rest" or "a pause").

MAN DE'IHU RAGIL BESHIKRA ISHTADAYL TADIR BESHIKRA (מאן דאיהו רגיל בשקרא אשתדיל תדיר בשקרא). "A person who gets used to telling lies will always be enticed to falsehood" (*Zohar* 1:192b).

MA'OT ROSH HODESH (מעות ראש חודש). "*Rosh-Hodesh-money*." It was customary at one time for children to bring money to their teachers on *Rosh Hodesh*. This practice originated in the fact that on *Rosh Hodesh*, we utter in the *Musaf* service, *Zeman kaparah lekhol toldotam* ("a time of atonement for all their offspring") (cf. Isaac b. Mordecai Lipiec, *Sefer Matamim*, [Printed first in Warsaw, 1885] [Jerusalem/New York: Makhon Hape'ayr, 1993], 65:11). By offspring is meant children who are spared epidemics (cf. *Aytz Yosef, Siddur Otzar Hatefillot*).

MAYROV AYTZIM LO YIREH HAYA'AR (מרוב עצים לא יראה היער). "Because of the abundance of trees, one cannot see the forest." See M. Subar, *Mikhol Hama'amarim Vehapitgamim*, vol. 3 (Jerusalem: Mosad Harav Kook, 1961), p. 1377.

MAZAL-TOV (מזל-טוב). See AYN MAZAL LEYISRAEL.

ME'AT MIN HA'OR DOHEH HARBAYH MIN HAHOSHEKH (מעט מן האור דוחה הרבה מן החשך). See AYN HA'OR NIKAR ELA MITOKH HAHOSHEKH.

MI-MOSHE VE'AD MOSHE LO KAM KE-MOSHE (ממשה ועד משה לא קם כמשה). See LO KAM NAVI OD BEYISRAEL KEMOSHE.

MI SHELO YISHTOK MAYATZMO, YASHTIKUHU AHAYRIM (מי שלא ישתוק מעצמו, ישתיקוהו אחרים). "One who does not silence himself will be silenced by others" (*Tzemah Tzedek* 40:75). See SHETIKUTEKHA YAFAH MEDIBUREKHA; SHETIKAH KEHODA'AH DAMYA.

MI SHEMEVAKAYSH YOTAYR MITZORKHO, TORAD NAFSHO MITO'ALTO (מי שמבקש יותר מצרכו, תורד נפשו מתועלתו). "Whosoever seeks more than he needs, tires his soul for usefulness" (attributed to Moshe ibn Gabirol); that is, he reaches a point of no return.

MI SHE'OMAYR ALEF YOMAR GAM BET (מי שאומר אל"ף יאמר גם בי"ת). Literally, "One who utters [the letter] *alef* will also say [the letter] *bet*." Most likely if you begin something, you will conclude it, as in the saying, *Hamathil bemitzvah yehayh gomayr et kulah* ("If one begins a *mitzvah*, one will most likely conclude it") (*Tanhuma, Aykev* 6).

MI SHEYAYSH LO MANEH ROTZEH MATAYIM (מי שיש לו מנה רוצה מאתים). "He who has a *maneh* ['portion' or 'part'] wants two hundred" (*Kohelet Rabbah* 1:34). Similarly, TEN LO MANEH VIVAKAYSH MATAYIM ("Give him a finger [an inch] and he will take an ell [hand]"); also, the more you have the more you want.

MIN ha-TaNaKH YADEKHA AL TANAH (מן התנ"ך ידך אל תנח). Loosely speaking, the acronym *TaNaKH* (formed from *Torah, Nevi'im, Ketuvim*) and the word *tanah*, "to rest" are homonyms. The expression means "Let not your hand relinquish Torah, *Nevi'im* [Prophets], and *Ketuvim* [Hagiographa]." The holy Bible should always be part of your life study and practice.

MISHMAR (משמר). In Temple days, the *Kohanim* were divided into family divisions to do service in the Temple in Jerusalem. Each division was called *mishmar*, from *mishmarot lakohanim* ("duty watches for the priests") (Neh. 13:30).

The *Kinah, Ekhah yashvah havatzelet hasharon*, lists the twenty-four places in which the divisions were stationed.

It is customary that in *yeshivot* the students assemble at *mishmar* and are up part of the night (usually on Thursday) to study. In Yiddish, the expression is *Oyf zayn a mishmar* ("To be up for *mishmar*").

MISTAMA (מסתמא). An Aramaic word derived from *min hasetam* ("to leave vague"), meaning "probably," "possibly," "seemingly," or "apparently."

This word is used in the Yiddish language as well.

MISTAPAYK BEMU'AT (מסתפק במועט). Literally, "undemanding," "content with little," or "minimalist." An example is "One who is content with little [*mistapayk bemu'at*] and who does not run after greatness will reach his goal." See TAFASTA MERUBAH LO TAFASTA, TAFASTA MU'AT TAFASTA.

MITZVAH LARUTZ LEVAYT HAKENESET (מצוה לרוץ לביהכנ״ס). "It is a *mitzvah* to run to the synagogue" (*Rambam* 8:2), as is written in Hosea 6:3, "Let us know, let us run to know God." The *Tur* (*Orah Hayyim* 90) adds that it is also a *mitzvah* to run to perform other commandments. When leaving the synagogue, writes the *Rambam* (ibid.), "a person should not take long steps. Instead, he should proceed [slowly] step-by-step." Leaving the synagogue hurriedly suggests, according to *Rashi* (Ber. 6b), that one views the synagogue and the obligations one has there as a burden.

MIZRAH (מזרח). Literally, "sunrise"— namely, "the east" (Numb. 21:11; Ps. 50:1). Jews living west of *Eretz Yisrael* turn toward the east (Jerusalem) when praying (cf. Dan. 6:10).

It also became associated with the decorated plate, or inscribed card, hung on the eastern wall of the house, or in front of the reading desk in the syna-

gogue. The name *Mizrah* is also applied to the row of seats in the synagogue on either side of the Ark reserved for the rabbi and other dignitaries (*Mizrah Vant*). In Yiddish, this pew was called *shtuht* (pl. *shtet*). See SHIVITI HASHEM LENEGDI TAMID.

MORENU (מורנו). A title meaning "our teacher," used since the fourteenth century and conferred upon talmudic scholars. Instituted by R. Meir b. Baruk ha-Levi of Vienna (1360–1390), the purpose of the title was to match the degree of doctor granted by the universities (Isaac Abravanel, commentary on *Avot* 5:1). Others simply say that it added to rabbinical dignity.

Originally, the title of *morenu* was given to married men only. As time passed, the title *morenu* was appended to a person's name who was called to the Torah. In Yiddish, there is a saying, *Er iz a gantzer morenu*, intimating "He thinks he is very important."

MUTAV YEHUDI BELI ZAKAYN MAYASHER ZAKAYN BELI YEHUDI מוטב יהודי בלי זקן מאשר זקן בלי יהודי). "A Jew without a beard is better than a beard without a Jew" (attributed to Shalom Jacob Abramowitsch, known as Mendele Mokher Sefarim). According to the Talmud (B.M. 84a), "the adornment of a man's face is his beard." Although in rabbinic literature controversy exists as to the question of whether a man's beard should be shorn or not, shaving is permitted as long as it is done according to *halakhah*.

The biting remark undoubtedly came about as a reaction to those Jews who wore a beard and did not exemplify piety.

NASOG AHOR (נסוג אחור). Literally, "stepping back" or "turned back"; a term used in grammar to indicate where the penultimate accentuation (*mileayl*) may be due to recession, as in *kara* (accent is on *ka*) *lailah* (Gen. 1:5). When a non-pausal accent (*munah*, in *kara*), due on the ultimate (*milera*), precedes a pausal accent (*etnahta*), due on the penultimate (as in *lailah*), the non-pausal then recedes to the penultimate.

The term *nasog ahor* is a nickname for a person who does not progress in his viewpoint or way of life (cf. Yehudah Grasovski (Goor), *Millon ha-Safah ha-Ivrit* [Tel-Aviv: Dvir Company, Ltd., 1938], p. 682).

NISTALAYK (נסתלק).See NIFTAR (NISTA-LAYK).

NITL (ניטל). A Judeo-German word derived from old Latin, *Dies Natalis*, or medieval Latin, *Natale Domini*, the day on which Yeshu Hanotzri was born. The English word for *Nitl* is "Christmas" (cf. Uriel Weinreich, *Modern English-Yiddish; Yiddish-English Dictionary*, [New York: Schocken Books, 1977], p. 529).

It became customary among Jews not to partake in study on the eve of *Nitl*. Several reasons given are: (1) In the early days the townspeople lay in wait for Jews and beat them on that night. Therefore, the Sages decreed that teachers and students should remain at home and not wander around outdoors (*Likutay Pardes*); (2) Since Jews were prohibited from participating in this holiday, they indulged in levity, and in the Middle Ages they were permitted to play cards, and so did not study. There is an opinion, however, that playing cards was a survival of the old German custom of merrymaking on this festival (cf. *The Jewish Encyclopedia*, vol. 9 [New York and London: Funk and Wagnalls Company, 1905], p. 318).

NOD (SHEL) DEMA'OT (נאד (של) דמעות). "Tear duct" or "lachrymal sac," as in *simah dimati benodekha* ("Put thou my tears into thy bottle") (Ps. 56:9). There is a belief that the tears, shed by the Jews the world over, for the destruction of the Temple, as well as for their subsequent misfortunes, were gathered in one vessel.

When it becomes full, Israel will be redeemed.

NUSAH (Aram. pl., NUSHA'OT; Heb. pl., NUSAHIM) (נוסח (נוסחאות, נוסחים). A term signifying "to remove," "to transfer," or "to copy," as in *Bayt gayim yisah Hashem* ("The Lord will pluck up the house of the proud") (Prov. 15:25), *ve-yisahakha mayohel* ("and tear you from the tent") (Ps. 52:7), or *yitnesah a min baitayh* ("Let a beam of timber be pulled down from the house") (Ez. 6:11). When a text was removed or copied from one book to another, that text or copy became known as *nusah*. Hence, forms of texts in prayerbooks belonging to different rites and with different versions, styles, or formulas (e.g., *nusah Ashkenaz, nusah Sepharad nusah Ari*) are known as *nusah hatefillah*.

The term, in its musical connotation, became known about the mid-1800s. In Jewish music, it signifies a melodic pattern or prayer mode governing the traditional character of the prayer texts. *Nusah* is a vehicle of almost every prayer within the synagogue service. Its general characteristics are: the motives have no fixed rhythm or meter, the motives are subject to repetition and omission and may generally be altered and varied according to the preference of the reader, and it affords opportunity for improvisation.

OHEL (pl., OHALIM) (אוהל (אוהלים)). An edifice erected above the grave of a *tzadik*. People come there to pray at any time, to leave requests on small pieces of paper (*kvitlakh*), and especially to pray on the *tzadik*'s YAHRTZEIT. The *ohel* is named after the rebbe: for example, "the *ohel* of the Ba'al Shem Tov" or "the *ohel* of Rabbi Nahman of Bratslav."

OLAM LESULAM HU DOMEH: ZEH OLEH VEZEH YORAYD (עולם לסולם הוא דומה: זה עולה וזה יורד). "The world is likened to a ladder; some climb, others descend" (*Tanhuma Matot* 9).

OTIYOT MAHKIMOT (אותיות מחכימות). Literally, "letters make one wise" (Ibn Gaon, Shem Tov b. Abraham, *Migdal Oz*). That is to say, if a person reads books, he will become informed and be guided by wisdom. Another expression in the same vein is *Nitay sefer venehezayh* ("Let a book be brought and we will see").

OZNAYIM LAKOTEL (אזנים לכותל). "Walls have ears" (*Vayikra Rabbah* 32:2). Be careful what you say! Your secret will eventually become known even if there is no one to hear you, as the verse reads, "For a bird of the air shall carry the voice" (Eccl. 10:20). The English idiom is "A little bird told me."

PARDAYS (פרדס). A word appearing in Songs of Songs 4:13, Ecclesiastes 2:4, and Nehemiah 2:8, meaning "park." It is also translated as "garden," "orchard," "orange grove," or "paradise." The Talmud (Hag. 14b) quotes the *Baraitha* about four men entering *Pardays*, namely, Ben Azzai, Ben Zoma, Aher, and R. Akiba. The only one to depart was R. Akiba.

In the Middle Ages the word *PaRDayS* was used as a mneumonic for the fourfold method of biblical interpretation: P, *Peshat* ("literal meaning"); R, *Remez* ("allusion" or "hint"); D, *Derash* ("homily"); and S, *Sod* ("mystical"). However, the general rule is AYN MIKRA YOTZAY MIDAY PESHUTO ("A verse cannot depart from its plain meaning") (Shab. 63a); that is, it must be compatible with what is meant.

The Yiddish language has the word PSHETL, inferring a type of sophistry invoking hair-splitting argumentation. *Pshetlin zikh* is to "quibble" or "stretch the point." See PILPUL.

PAREV (פארעוו). "Neither dairy nor meat." Three times the Bible warns against eating meat and milk together, in any way or form whatsoever, "Thou shalt not seethe a kid in its mother's milk" (Ex. 23:19; 34:26; Deut. 14:21). The word

parev is derived from *parbar*. The Talmud (Zeb. 55b) states, "There was a small passageway behind the place of the *Kapporet* ("Mercy Seat"), in order to make the whole Temple court fit for the consumption of most holy sacrifices and the slaughter of minor sacrifices . . . and thus it is written, 'And two *le-par bar*' (1 Chron. 26:18). What does *le-par bar* mean? Said Rabbah, son of R. Shila, "'As one says, facing without or the exterior' [*ke-lappay le-bar*]"—thus signifying *lo basar velo halav*, not meat or milk, but *parev* (Isaac b. Mordecai Lipiec, *Sefer Matamim Hehadash* [Warsaw 1885]).

Humorously, the word *parev* became associated with neutrality—thus, "wishy-washy."

PASUK BIZMANO, KENAHAMA BISHAT RE'AVON (RE'AVA) (פסוק בזמנו, כנהמא בשעת רעבון (רעבא)). "A timely verse is as good as bread in famine" (*Kallah Rabbati* 1).

PINTELE YID (פינטעלע ייד). See KOTZO (KOTZAH) SHEL YUD.

PSHETL (פשטל). See PARDAYS.

RAGLAY KADMA VE'AZLA (רגלי קדמא ואזלא). *Kadma-ve'azla* are the names of two tropal signs used in the cantillation of Scripture. Their shape is similar to quotation marks surrounding a word or phrase. The shape refers to a person having curved or crooked legs (bandy-legs) or knock-knees.

RaSHKeBeHaG (רשכבה"ג). An abbreviation for *Rabban Shel Kol Benay Hagolah* ("Rabbi of all the Jews living outside of Palestine [Diaspora]"). This title is given to a scholar, leader, and possessor of great authority. It has its origin in the Talmud (Shab. 58a), where the *Rabbanan de-be resh galuta* (Ar.) or *rosh hagolah* (Heb.) ("scholars of the house of the exilarch"), who headed the Babylonian Jews, wore certain badges on their garments to indicate their position.

In the Ashkenazic rite, pronouncing the blessing upon these leaders (*resh galuta*) is part of the *Yekum Purkan* prayer recited on Sabbath morning (cf. Macy Nulman, *The Encyclopedia of Jewish Prayer* [Northvale, New Jersey: Jason Aronson Inc., 1993], p. 374). In modern times Rabbi Isaac Blaser (1837–1907), originally a Russian rabbi and educator who emigrated to Jerusalem, left in his will instructions that he not be eulogized. When he died, the rabbis of Jerusalem did not heed his request and eulogized him. The reason they gave was that he was a *Rabban Kol Benay Hagolah* (cf. A.Y. Greenberg, *Turay Torah* [Tel Aviv, Israel: "Yavneh" Publishing House, Ltd., 1990], p. 176; see also *Pethay Teshuvah, Yoreh Dayah* 344:1).

REBI, LEKHA SHARAY VELI ASUR?
(רבי, לך שרי ולי אסור?). "Rebbe, can it be permissible to you and forbidden to me?" (*Bereishit Rabbah* 55:3; *Kohelet Rabbah* 8:8); or "Practice what you preach!"

ReHaSH (רח״ש).
An acronym formed from the first letters of three Hebrew titles, *rav* (rabbi), *hazzan* (cantor), and *shamash* (sexton). The term was the technical designation used as early as the thirteenth century for the fees and gifts given to the three religious functionaries for their participation in wedding ceremonies (Isaac b. Moses, *Or Zaru'a* 1, no. 113). The expression may be hinted at in Psalms 45:2, *Rahash libi davar tov* ("My heart overflowed with goodly matter"). The psalm itself is known as a "royal marriage song" (cf. Abraham Eliezer Hirshowitz, *Otzar Shalaym Leminhagay Yisrael* [New York: Pardes Publishing House, Inc., 1963], p. 50).

RISHON LE-ZION (ראשון לציון).
See MAH BAYN HAKHAM LENAVON? NAVON DOMEH LESHULHANI TAGAR.

SHABBAT LE'ONEG NITAN VELO LETZA'AR (שבת לעונג ניתן ולא לצער).
The *Kitzur Shulhan Arukh* (72:7) writes that for *Shabbat*, one should prepare choice meat, fish, dessert, and good wines, in accordance with one's means. It is desirable to eat fish at every Sabbath meal, provided it is not harmful; but if it does not agree with the person, it should not be eaten, "for the Sabbath is given us for pleasure and not for sorrow."

SHABBOS-GOY (שבת-גוי).
A non-Jew engaged to perform domestic chores forbidden to a Jew on the Sabbath—for example, lighting the fire, and so forth. Another meaning may be that it is used as an appellation for a Jew not observing the Sabbath.

SHADKHAN (שדכן).
A word derived from the verb *shidaykh*, meaning to "make a match"; thus *shadkhan* ("a matchmaker") or *shadkhanut* ("match-making" or "match-maker's fee").

The *shadkhan*, as a marriage broker, did not appear in rabbinic literature until the twelfth or thirteenth centuries (cf. Isaac of Vienna, *Or Zarua*; *Mordekhai*, B.K., chap. 10). Both Rabbi Jacob Molin (*Maharil*) and Rabbi Jacob Margolis acted as go-betweens in the Middle Ages, when fathers were anxious to obtain learned and respectable sons-in-law. The profession was regarded as highly meritorious.

Marriages today are still brought about with the assistance of a *shadkhan*, who performs a useful function.

SHaTZ MaTZ (ש״ץ מ״ץ).
An abbreviation for *Sheli'ah Tzibbur* and *Moreh Tzedek*; a title bestowed upon a religious functionary who acted in both these capacities: as the person who recited the prayers aloud before the congregation and as a teacher or leader in Israel.

SHAYMOT (שמות).
By *Shaymot* ("Divine Names") is meant timeworn or tattered sacred writings with references to God that are preserved from profanation by being deposited in the synagogue. From there, they are taken, from time to time, to

be buried in the cemetery. The *Yoreh Dayah* (282:10) formulated the *halakhah* for an old or unfit Torah scroll as follows, "A *Sefer Torah* which has become old or unfit for use is to be laid in an earthen vessel and buried beside a scholar."

SHAYNAH BESHABBAT TA'ANUG (שינה בשבת תענוג).

An acronym for the word *SHaB(B)aT*, meaning "sleep on Sabbath is enjoyment." After the Sabbath noon repast, one often goes to sleep; it is considered a *mitzvah* of *oneg Shabbat* ("Sabbath delight") (cf. *Yalkut Re'uvayni, Va'ethanan*).

SHAYTL (שייטל).

A Judeo-German word meaning "women's wig"; the wig was worn as a sign of chastity and modesty, for a woman's hair is a sexual incitement (Ber. 24a). *Rashi* (Numb. 5:18) writes that when suspicion arose as to marital unfaithfulness, the woman's hair would be unloosed. From this it is derived, regarding the daughters of Israel, that uncovering the hair is a shameful thing for them. The Talmud (Ket. 72a) states that going with uncovered head is deemed to be a wife's transgression and is cause for divorce, as well as cause for forfeiting her dowry (cf. also *Rambam, Hilkhot Ishut,* 24:12; *Shulhan Arukh, Even Ha'ezer* 21:2).

In biblical times, women wore a veil or scarf. It was only toward the end of the eighteenth century that women began to wear a *shaytl*. The latter was opposed by Rabbi Moses Sofer and others (*Leb ha-Ibri* [Lemberg, 1973], pp. 129, 189).

Another name for *shaytl* is *peruk* (from Fr. *perruque*). In the Orient, the special hair-kerchief is called *yazme.*

SHEKER ASUR LEDABAYR, AVAL ET HA'EMET LO TAMID HOVAH LESAPAYR (שקר אסור לדבר, אבל את האמת לא תמיד חובה לספר).

"It is forbidden to tell a falsehood, but it is not always obligatory to tell the truth" (Folk Saying). See SHEKER AYN LO RAGLAYIM.

SHETIKAH YAFAH BESHA'AT HATEFILLAH (שתיקה יפה בשעת התפילה).

"Silence is good during prayer," a slogan that still appears on the walls in many synagogues. The *Orah Hayyim* (124:7) writes, "One should not [engage in] ordinary conversation while the *Sheli'ah Tzibbur* repeats the *Amidah* prayer. If one does [engage in] such conversation, he is a sinner. His iniquity is more than can be borne and he should be rebuked." The *Mishnah Berurah* (124:27) comments that the *Eliyahu Rabbah* writes, in the name of the *Kol Bo*, "Woe to those people who speak during the prayer service, for we have seen several synagogues destroyed as a result of this sin." The *Mishnah Berurah* adds that it is proper to appoint specified people to watch over this.

SHIRAYIM (שיריים).

The "left-over" food at the hasidic rebbe's *tish* ("table") served to his followers. The Yiddish expression *khapn shirayim* pertains to those individuals who rush to the rebbe's *tish* to catch a morsel of food that is on the rebbe's plate.

This practice of leaving over food conveys the idea that the rebbe is compared to the *Kohen* (Priest), who sacrifices the food as at the *Minhah*("Meal-offering") (cf. Lev. 2:2, et al.) (cf. Dr. Simhah Petrushka, *The Jewish Popular Encyclopedia*, vol. 2 [1949], p. 842). *Shirayim* are considered to be a remedy for earning a living and a cure for pain, as the verse in Exodus 23:25 states, "And ye shall serve the Lord your God, and He will bless thy bread and thy water; and I will take sickness away from the midst of thee" (cf. R. Aaron Wertheimer, *Law and Custom in Hasidism* [Hoboken, New Jersey: Ktav Publishing House, Inc., 1992], p. 253).

SHIVITI (שויתי).

See SHIVITI HASHEM LENEGDI TAMID.

SHLITA (שליט״א). A good wish, usually appearing after a rabbi's name. It is an abbreviation for *sheyiheyeh le'orekh yamim tovim arukhim* ("May he live to a good, long life").

SHTIBL (שטיבל). Name of a place meaning "small room," where *hasidim* pray. Sometimes it is called *hasidim-shtibl* or it is named after the rebbe's city—for example, *Gerer Shtibl*.

Another name of a small synagogue where Jews of Eastern European countries would pray and study is *kloiz* (from the Lat. *claustrum*, "an enclosed place"). If it is really small, the disparaging appellation *kleizl* is given. In Germany, a small prayer synagogue was called *klaus* (from Lat. *clausura*).

SHTREIML BIMKOM TEFILLIN (שטריימל במקום תפילין). A *shtreiml* is a fur-edged hat, worn by rabbis and hassidic Jews on the Sabbath and holidays. The expression *shtreiml bimkom tefillin* ("*shtreiml* in place of *tefillin*") is attributed, by some, to Reb Pinhas of Koretz (1726–1791). It is an acronym of the word *SHaBBat*, inferring that on *Shabbat* when *tefillin* are not worn, the *shtreiml* is worn instead (cf. R. Aaron Wertheim, *Law and Custom in Hasidism* [Hoboken, New Jersey: Ktav Publishing House, Inc., 1992], p. 296).

SIHATAN SHEL YISRAEL TORAH HI (שיחתן של ישראל תורה היא). "The conversation of Israel is study" (*Midrash Tehillim, Shoher Tov*, 5:5). See SIHAT HULIN; AFILU SIHAT HULIN SHEL TALMIDAY HAKHAMIM TZRIKHAH TALMUD.

SITRA AHRA (סטרא אחרא). An expression in *Kabbalah* meaning "the other side," referring to the evil side (way), the devil's or Satan's domain (often mentioned in the *Zohar*).

SOF GANAV LITLIYAH (סוף גנב לתליה). "A thief in the end [is sent] to the gallows"; he is caught and, thus, crime does not pay. This saying is not found in rabbinic literature. However, the Talmud (San. 7a) contains the saying, Do not be surprised if a thief goes unhanged for ATARTI TELAT GANVAY LO MIKTAL ("Two or three thefts; he will be caught in the end"). See LO SIGNOV; ROV GANVAY YISRAEL GANVAY NINHU.

STAM MAKSHAN AM-HA'ARETZ (סתם מקשן עם הארץ). "An indefinite [that is, not precise or certain] arguer, or one who raises general difficulties, is an ignoramus" (Jair Hayyim Bacharach, *Havat Ya'ir*, responsum 219 [Frankfort, 1699]). See AM-HA'ARETZ.

TAKHLIT HAYEDI'AH SHENAYDA SHELO NAYDA (תכלית הידיעה שנדע שלא נדע). "The result [end] of knowledge is know that you don't know" (*Bekhinat Olam* 13:55). The more you know, the more you realize that you do not know anything.

TALMID HAKHAM TZARIKH SHELO YEHAY BO DAVAR SHEL DOFI (תלמיד חכם צרים שלא יהא בו דבר של דפי). "A scholar should be without [ever] the least flaw" (*Shir Hashirim Rabbah* 4:22).

TA'UT LE'OLAM HOZAYR (HOZERET) (טעות לעולם חוזר (חוזרת)). "A mistake can always be retracted" (*Rambam, Hilkhot Mekhirah* 15:1). The Talmud (Shab. 63b) records that when R. Dimi went up to Nehardea, he sent word, *Devarim she'amarti lakhem ta'ut haym beyadi* ("The things that I told you were erroneous").

TEHIYAT HAMAYTIM (תחיית המתים). "Resuscitation of the dead"; the belief that the dead will rise again. This belief is manifested in the last principle of the

Thirteen Principles of Faith, "I believe with complete faith that there will be a resuscitation of the dead . . ." (formulated by Maimonides in his *Mishnah* commentary to San. 10:1). It is also uttered in the second benediction (*Gevurot*) of the *Amidah, Barukh . . . mehayayh hamaytim* ("Blessed . . . He Who revives the dead"), as well as in the Preliminary Service, *Barukh . . . hamahazir neshamot lifgarim maytim* ("Blessed . . . Who restores souls to dead bodies"), and it appears in the two poetic hymns, *Adon Olam* ("Eternal Lord") and *Yigdal* ("Magnified and praised be the living God").

Early references hinting at *Tehiyat hamaytim* are: "The Lord kills and gives life; He brings down to the grave and brings up" (1 Sam. 2:6); "The dead men of Thy people shall live, my dead body shall arise" (Isa. 26:19); "For You will not abandon my soul to the grave, You will not allow Your devout one to witness destruction" (Ps. 16:10); and "And many of those who sleep in the dust of the earth shall awake" (Dan. 12:2).

Job is noted for denying the validity of resuscitation of the dead (B.B. 16a), as it is written, "As the cloud is consumed and vanisheth away, so he that goeth down to the grave shall come up no more" (Job 7:9). The doctrine of resuscitation was also denied by the Sadducees and the Samaritans. The Talmud (San. 90a) cites various arguments between the *tanna'im* and nonbelievers concerning *Tehiyat hamaytim*. The *Mishnah* (ibid.) states emphatically, however, that he who maintains that resuscitation is not a biblical doctrine has no portion in the World to Come (cf. *Rashi*, ad loc.). See OYFSHTEYN TEHIYAT HAMAYTIM.

TEKI'AT KAF (תקיעת כף). "Handshake, as a guarantee for the fulfillment of a promise," as in Proverbs 6:1, *takata lazar kapekha* ("if thou hast put out thy palms to a stranger"). *Teki'at kaf*, according to law, is considered an oath (*Yoreh Dayah, Hilkhot Shevu'ot* 239:2).

Concerning one who does not pay up one's debt, the following expression is spoken, *Shalom alaykhem befeh malay; teki'at kaf bishtay yadayim; aval kesef af perutah ahat lo* ("Overflowing with handshakes; a handshake with two hands; but, as for money, not even a coin").

TEN LO MANEH VIVAKAYSH MATAYIM (תן לו מנה ויבקש מאתים). See MI SHEYAYSH LO MANEH ROTZEH MATAYIM.

TEVALEH UTEHADAYSH (תבלה ותחדש). R. Moses Isserles writes that it is customary to say to a person wearing a new garment, *Tevaleh utehadaysh* ("May you wear it out and renew it"); that is, congratulations on putting on your new garment. When wearing a new pair of shoes, however, this is not said. The reason given is that in order to acquire new shoes, a living creature would have to die, since the shoes are made of the skin of an animal, and it is written, "His mercies are on all His works" (Ps. 145:9 cf. *Orah Hayyim* 223:6).

The expression used currently for one who is wearing a new garment for the first time is *tithadaysh*, signifying "wear it well." When putting on new shoes, the wish expressed in Yiddish is *Tzerayst es gezunterheyt* ("Tear it in good health"). It is possible that a differentiation is made between the wish for wearing new clothes and that for new shoes because, with clothing, one need only to renew them (thus, *tithadaysh*), but shoes are eventually torn. Thus, the words *tzurays es gezunterheyt* is actually a blessing denoting that the person should be on his or her feet and grow out of them or wear them out, and be healthy to achieve all this.

TIKKUN (תיקון). Literally, "improvement," a term used in *Kabbalah* for "revision" or "correction" of the *neshamah* ("soul") that was stricken or spoiled. At a YAHRTZEIT, in hasidic circles, it is customary to serve liquor, as well as other delicacies, for the *neshamah* of the deceased and this is called *tikkun*. Learning *Mishnah* at a *Yahrtzeit* is also a *tikkun* for the *neshamah* because the word *Mishnah* has the same letters as *NeSHaMaH*.

Tikkun Layl Shavu'ot and *Tikkun Layl Hoshana Rabbah* are two anthologies containing biblical and post-biblical selections, recited respectively on the first night of *Shavu'ot* and on the night of *Hoshana Rabbah*. *Tikkun Hatzot* is when pietists arise at midnight to recite psalms and lamentations on Zion and study the Torah.

The name *tikkun* is also applied to the unvocalized copy of the Torah that is used in preparation for reading the Torah scroll.

TIZKEH LESHANIM RABOT (תזכה לשנים רבות). Literally, "Long life to you." Life to the Jew is very much cherished. Scripture states, "See, I have set before thee this day life [*hayyim*] and good, and death and evil—therefore choose life" (Deut. 30:15–19). The Decalogue gives Heaven's reward of long life for honoring parents, "Honor thy father and mother, that thy days may be long upon the land which the Lord thy God giveth thee" (Ex. 20:12). The prayer service also includes texts requesting long life, "Sanctify us with Your holiness in order that we be worthy of good and long lives" (cf. *Ribbono Shel Olam*, said when removing the Torah scrolls from the Ark on festivals). See AD MAYAH VE'ESRIM SHANAH.

TOV BEGIMATRI'A YUD ZAYIN (טוב בגימטריא י"ז). "The equivalency of the letters in the word *tov* ('good') adds up to seventeen" (*tet* = 9, *vav* = 6, and *bet* = 2) (*Tanhumah, Korah* 12; *Bemidbar Rabbah* 18:17).

A Yiddish expression beginning with seventeen and ending with 101, depicting various phases of life, is ZIBETZN IZ KEMINYAN TOV, AKHTZN IZ KEMINYAN HAI, HAI TZUM LEBN; HUNDERT UN HUNDERT UN EYNS IS ALTZ EYNS ("Seventeen is equal to the count of

[the word] *tov*; eighteen is equal to the count of *hai, hai* to "life"; one hundred and one hundred and one is all the same") (cf. also *Rashi*, Isa. 11:1, s.v. *venaytzer misharashav yifreh*).

TOV ME'AT BEKAVANAH MAYHARBOT SHELO BEKAVANAH (טוב מעט בכוונה מהרבות שלא בכוונה). "It is better [to say] a little with intentin, rather than [to say] much without intention" (*Tur, Orah Hayyim* 1). This applies to the prayers uttered during the night pertaining to the destruction of the Temple.

Yiddish equivalents with wider ramifications are *Beser a bisl un rekhts eyder a fule un shlekhts* ("Better a little and right rather than a lot and bad") or *Beser gut un a bisl eyder shlekhts un a fule shisl* ("Better good and little rather than bad and a full bowl").

TURA BETURA LO PAGA, INISH BE'INISH PAGA (טורא בטורא לא פגע, איניש באיניש פגע). "A mountain [with another] mountain do not meet, [but] a person with another person do meet" (*Nayrot Shabbat* 3, pp. 42, 66). In other words, it's a small world. See INISH BE'INISH PAGA, TURA BETURA LO POGA.

TUSHLABA (תושלב"ע). The initial letters of six words—*Tam Venishlam, Shevah La'ayl, Boray Olam*—meaning "Complete and ended, praise to God, the Creator of the World." It has been customary to express humble thanks to God for enabling the author of a book to complete it satisfactorily. The author's gratitude expressed in one word, TUSHLABA, is usually found on the last page of a work.

TZARAT RABIM HATZI NEHAMAH (צרת רבים חצי נחמה). "Woe of many is partial comfort"; or, "A sorrow shared is a sorrow halved." That is to say, "company in misery lightens it" (*Davarim Rabbah* 2:22).

TZARIKH IYUN (צריך עיון). A problematic or moot point that "requires further study"; an expression used in talmudic or halakhic discussion.

TZON KADASHIM (צאן קדשים). Literally, "holy sheep" or "flock of sacrifices"; an enigmatic nickname for the People of Israel, based on the verse in Ezekiel 36:38, "Like the flock of sacrifices [Ketzon kadashim], like the flock of Jerusalem in her appointed times; so shall the waste cities be filled with flocks of men, and they shall know that I am the Lord." *Rashi* (ad loc.), commenting on the phrase *Ketzon kadashim*, writes, "that their sins should not be recalled"; they should be vindicated of all sins and transgressions.

The phrase *Tzon kadashim* appears in R. Eleazar ha-Kallier's alphabetical poem, *Om Ani Homa* ("Nation [that declares], 'I am a wall'") recited on Sukkot and *Hoshana Rabbah* in the *Hoshanot* service.

WACHNACHT (וואכנאכט). Literally, "watch-night." This is the Judeo-German term for the night preceding the day of circumcision during which watch was maintained over the child while the adults were feasting, studying Torah, and reciting hymns and prayers. The object of the watch was to ward off either the evil spirit and/or Satan, who strove to harm the child and prevent it from undergoing the religious rite of circumcision. Hinting at this practice is the biblical phrase *ve'attah et briti tishmor* ("And thou shalt keep My covenant") (Gen. 17:9); the word *tishmor* (from *shamor*) means "to watch," thus inferring that during the circumcision festivities, there must be protection from Satan (cf. Isaac b. Mordecai Lipiec, *Sefer Matamim* [first printed in Warsaw, 1885] [Jerusalem/New York: Makhon Hape'ayr, 1993], 74:3). Another opinion is that this custom is intimated in the Talmud (San. 32b) "The noise of grindstones at Burni [announced] a circumcision [was being performed]; and the light of a candle [by day, and many candles by night] at Beror Hail, showed that a feast [was being celebrated] there" (cf. *Rashi*, ad loc.).

When the *Wachnacht* developed is difficult to ascertain. References to it go back to about the sixteenth century, but the name itself was used later. Both *Mahzor Vitri* (twelfth century) and the *Zohar* (*Parashat Lekh Lekha*) contain passages concerning this custom. The former calls it *Minhag Avotaynu* ("a custom of our ancestors"), while the latter states that Torah should be studied the entire night.

WIE HABEN SIE GEBAUT? (ווי האבן זי געבויט). A question asked among German Jewry, meaning "How did you build?" This question stems from the special hymn *Addir Hu* ("Mighty is He"), sung at the *Seder* on Passover. The hymn is sometimes referred to as *Bimhayrah* ("Speedily") or *Baugesang* ("song of the rebuilding of the Temple").

The refrain *Gott nun bau dein Tempel shire (schiere)*, imploring God to rebuild the Temple speedily, gave rise to the Jews of southern and western Germany calling the *Seder* night *Baunacht*, and celebrating the Passover *Seder* was called *bauen*, meaning "to build." Consequently, the expression GUT BAUEN ("building well") became a popular saying.

It is possible, too, that the aspect of building on Passover is rooted in the Talmud (R.H. 30a), which relates that the third *Bet Hamikdash* (Temple) will be built on the first night of Passover. According to *Rashi*, there will be no violation in building on the holiday since the future Temple will be wrought by the hands of Heaven.

WIMPEL (ווימפל). A word used for cloth or veil, derived from *bewimfen*, meaning "to cover up" or "conceal." In Germany, it became customary to fashion a Torah binder, called *wimpel*, from the piece of cloth used on the occasion of a boy's circumcision.

On the cloth was painted the child's Hebrew name, as well as biblical imagery and other motifs, with the prayerful wish LETORAH, LEHUPAH, ULEMA'ASIM TOVIM. The *wimpel* was presented to the synagogue on the child's first visit.

The earliest *wimpel* dates back to 1570 in Worms. See GARTL.

YAHRTZEIT (יארצייט). Literally, "year time," referring to the anniversary of a death observed for parents, close relatives, and outstanding individuals. The Hebrew and Sephardic equivalents are respectively *Yom Hapekidah* ("day of remembrance") or *Yom Hashanah* ("the day of the year") and *Nahalah* ("inheritance"). R. Joseph Hayyim b. Elijah Al-Hakam writes, in his *Sefer Ben Ish Hai (Hilkhot Shanah Rishonah, Parashat Vayehi)*, that even *Sephardim* use the Ashkenazic word *Yahrtzeit* in their books.

The first to use the name *Jahrtzeit* (Ger. spelling) was Isaac of Tyrnau of the fourteenth century (*Sefer Haminhagim, Dinay Kaddish Yatom*, first printed in 1566). Observing the anniversary of the dead is described in the Talmud (Ned. 12a; B.K. 16b; *Rashi*, Yeb. 122a). Various customs observed at the *Yahrtzeit* are: reciting the *Kaddish*, lighting a memorial candle (to burn for a full day), conducting the service (if possible), receiving an *Aliyah* on the same day if the Torah is read (if not, one is called up on the preceding Sabbath), receiving *Maftir* and leading the *Musaf* service on the Sabbath preceding the *Yahrtzeit*, leading in the *Ma'ariv* service on Saturday night prior to the *Yahrtzeit*, fasting as an act of piety (cf. *Shulhan Arukh, Orah Hayyim* 568), and giving TIKKUN after the service. See also ALIYAT NESHAMAH; YOM PETIRAH; NIFTAR (NISTALAYK).

YAKO (יאכו). When a garment was made for a small child, the garment was called *Yako*. The word, possibly dating back to the sixteenth century, is an abbreviation. It is derived from the first letters in the blessing that the Patriarch Jacob conferred upon his grandchildren and that Jewish parents gave to their children

throughout history: *Yesimkha (Yud) Elohim (Alef) Ke'ephrayim (Kaf) Vekhimnasheh (vav)* ("May God make you like Ephraim and Menashe") (Gen. 48:20; cf. Isaac b. Mordecai Lipiec, *Sefer Matamim Hehadash* [Warsaw, 1885], quoting from *Sefer Ma'avor Yabok* by Avraham Berachia b'reb Moshe Mimodinah [1626]).

YAM HATALMUD (ים התלמוד). "The ocean of the Talmud." The Talmud, meaning "teaching," is the name applied to each of the two compilations known as the Babylonian Talmud (*Talmud Bavli*) and the Jerusalem Talmud (*Talmud Yerushalmi*). Little is known about the history of the latter Talmud. It reached its present form in the beginning of the fifth century; many sections of it are lost. The former extended for about a hundred years, from 400 to 500 C.E. The text of the Jerusalem Talmud is in Hebrew and Western or Palestinian Aramaic, while the Babylonian Talmud is in Hebrew and Eastern Aramaic.

Since the mid-sixth century, the Babylonian Talmud has become the chief source of education for Jews in many lands. Because of its depth and expansion, covering the whole gamut of human life, it came to be known as a bottomless pit. The Babylonian Talmud alone has been estimated to contain some two and a half million words, and, because of its vastness, the expressive phrase *Yam Hatalmud* has been applied to it.

YARMLKE (יארמלקע). See GILUI ROSH.

YAYSH LO MANEH ROTZEH MATAYIM (יש לו מנה רוצה מאתים). See MI SHEYASH LO MANEH ROTZEH MATAYIM.

YEHUDI (sing.), YEHUDIM (pl.) (יהודי (יהודים)). The term "Yehudi" was originally applied to members of the tribe of Judah, the fourth son of the Patriarch Jacob. Later, it was used for all Israelites. This is based on the scriptural verse *Yehudah attah yodukha ahekha* ("Judah, thee shall thy brethren praise") (Gen. 49:8), implying that all of Israel will be called by your name. *Targum Onkelos* translates *lam-eyaldot ha'ivriyot* ("Hebrew midwives") in Exodus 1:15 as *lehayata Yehudayata* (cf. Isaac b. Mordecai Lipiec, *Sefer Matamim Hehadash* [first printed in Warsaw, 1885] [Jerusalem/New York: Makhon Hape'ayr, 1993], 123:2). The *Sefat Emet* writes that Judah's mother gave him this name, as she said, "I will praise [*odeh*] God" (Gen. 29:35). The common name "Yehudi," regardless of tribal origin, is thus a statement that Jews always praise God. Although Mordecai was from the tribe of Benjamin, he is called *ish Yehudi* ("a Jewish man") (Esth. 2:5; 5:13). *Rashi* (ad loc.) comments that this name was given by the gentiles to all those who were exiled along with the Kings of Judah, regardless of their original tribe. See IVRI, IVRIM.

YERUSHALAYIM de-LITA (ירושלים דליטא)

Beginning with the seventeenth century, Vilna (a city in Lithuania) became known as a center of talmudic scholars and learning. Among its leading scholars were Elijah b. Solomon Zalmon (known as the Gaon of Vilna), Rabbi Israel Salanter, Rabbi Samuel b. Joseph Strashun, and others. In Vilna, too, the edition of the Talmud (the Vilna *Shas*) was printed by the Romm family; it became the standard throughout the world. Vilna became not only a religious and spiritual center, but also influenced Jewry in the sphere of both *halakhah* and *Kabbalah* and was thus dubbed *Yerushalayim de-Lita*.

YESHU'AT HASHEM KEHEREF AYIN (ישועת הי כהרף עין)

"Salvation of God [comes] as the wink of the eye [instantly]." The Jew's trust in God is so strong that he believes his redemption can come as quickly as it takes the eye to wink (cf. Yehuda Leib Zlotnick [Avida], *Minhah-li-Yehudah* [1950], pp. 27, 28).

YIBADAYL LEHAYYIM ARUKHIM (יבדל לחיים ארוכים)

"May he be separated for a long life." This expression is used

when mentioning a deceased person and, immediately afterwards, a living person.

The latter two words, *hayyim arukhim*, are part of Rav's (third century) daily private prayer (Ber. 16b), adopted in the eighteenth century for the Blessing of the New Month. The Yiddish equivalent is *Tzu lange lebedike yohrn*.

Other expressions used to differentiate between the living and dead are *Lehavdil bayn hahayyim vehamaytim* ("To differentiate between the living and dead") and *Zuhl er zayn vayt uhbgesheyt* ("Let him be far removed").

YIMAH SHEMO (VEZIKHRO) (ימח שמו (וזכרו)

"May his name be wiped out [and forgotten]"; an expression in the form of a curse, uttered when mentioning an evil person's name. The saying has its origin in the biblical phrase *Mahoh emheh et zaykher Amalek* ("I will utterly blot out the remembrance of Amalek") (Ex. 17:14). In the *Piyyut Uvekhayn Zakhor* ("And so remember"), said in the *Kerovot* section of *Parashat Zakhor*, the *Sheli'ah Tzibbur* and the congregation responsively recite *Umah shemo vezikhro venimah zekhuro, milehazkiro [bezikhron kadosh]* ("Let his name and memory be blotted out, let remembrance of him be expunged so that he will no longer be mentioned [in the memory of the Holy One]").

YISRAEL VE'ORAITA HAD HU (ישראל ואורייתא חד הוא)

See KUDESHA BERIKH HU, ORAITA VEYISRAEL HAD.

YOM (יום)

The word *yom* means "day." It became part of different expressions, such as Yom Tov (Lit., "a good day"), referring to a holiday, or Yom Kippur (lit., "a day of forgiveness"), the holiest day of the year. The word *yom* is also used when denoting the specific psalm to be recited each day at the end of the service. To introduce the psalm, the formula *Hayom yom rishon be-Shabbat* ("Today is the first day of the Sabbath") is said. The same formula, with a different day, is used for each day.

By *Yom Tehillim* is meant the portion of the Book of Psalms designated to be said for each of the seven days of the week.

YOM ALEF (RISHON)—ORAYAH, YOM BET (SHAYNI)—TORAYAH, YOM GIMMEL (SHELISHI)—SORAYAH (יום א' (ראשון)—אורח, יום ב' (שני)—טורח, יום ג' (שלישי)—סורח).

See AYN ORAYAH MAKHNIS ORAYAH.

YOTAYR MISHEYISRAEL SHAMRU ET HASHABBAT, SHAMRAH HASHABBAT OTAM (יותר משישראל שמרו את השבת, שמרה השבת אותם).

"More than Israel has kept the Sabbath, the Sabbath has kept Israel" (Asher Hirsch Ginsberg, known as Ahad Ha-am, *Al Parashat Derakhim* 3:30). It is impossible to comprehend the existence of Israel without the Sabbath. If not for the Sabbath, which restores to the people their soul and renews their spirit each week, Israel could not exist. The Sabbath is summed up in the *Kiddush* recited on Friday evening, "Blessed art Thou . . . who hast sanctified us with Thy commandments and hast been pleased with us; Thou hast graciously given us Thy Holy Sabbath as a heritage, in remembrance of the creation."

ZEKHUT AVOT (זכות אבות). See ZEKHUTO YAGAYN ALAYNU.

ZEKHUTO YAGAYN ALAYNU (זכותו יגן עלינו). In hasidic circles when a deceased *tzadik's* name is mentioned, the expression *Zekhuto yagayn alaynu* ("his merit should protect us") is appended. Some substitute *tagayn* (feminine) instead of *yagayn* (masculine), since the word *zekhut* is feminine. However, the *Mishnah* (*Avot* 5:21) contains the phrase *zekhut harabim talui bo* ("the merit of the masses was to his credit"). The Talmud (Shab. 32a) states, *Megalgelim zekhut al yeday*

zakai vehovah al yeday hayav ("Reward [*zekhut*] is brought about through a person of merit [*zakai*], and punishment [*hovah*] through a person of guilt").

ZEKHUT AVOT ("merit of the fathers") is a concept that is expressive of the idea that individuals profit by the meritorious acts of their ancestors. When performing a *mitzvah*, a person attains a *zekhut* from Heaven—that is, a reward that can help the person when he or she is in trouble. This gave rise to the Yiddish expression DER ZEKHUT FUN DER MITZVAH IZ IM BAYGESH-TANEN ("The merit of the *mitzvah* was of help to him"). When expressing the idea of "finding something in favor [of]," the Yiddish expression GEFINEN A ZEKHUT (OYF) is used. The *Mishnah* (*Avot* 1:6), states, *Vehevay dan et kol ha'adam lekhaf zekhut* ("Judge everyone favorably"). Other expressions in combination with the word *zekhut* are *zekhut atzmo* ("One's own [accumulated] merits"), *zekhut hakiyum* ("right to existence" or "raison d'etre"), and MELAMAYD ZEKHUT ("one part is in his favor"). It is written in the Talmud (Shab. 32a) that man's advocates are repentance and good deeds. "And even if nine hundred and ninety-nine argue for his guilt [*melamayd hovah*], while one argues in his favor [*melamayd zekhut*], he is saved, for it is said, 'If there be with him an angel, an advocate, one among a thousand to show unto man what is right for him, then He is gracious unto Him, and saith, deliver him from going down to the pit. . . .'" (Job 33:23ff.).

ZIBETZN IZ KEMINYAN TOV, AKHTZN IZ KEMINYAN HAI, HAI TZUM LEBN; HUNDERT UN HUNDERT UN EYNS IZ ALTZ EYNS (זיבעצן איז כמנין טוב, אכצן איז כמנין חי, חי צום לעבן; הונדערט און הונדערט אונס איז אלץ איינס). See TOV BEGIMATRI'A YUD ZAYN.

TUSHLABA (תושלביי"ע)

BIBLIOGRAPHY

Alcalay, R. (in collaboration with M. Nurock) *Words of the Wise*. Jerusalem: Masada Press Ltd., 1970.

Ayalti, H.J. *Yiddish Proverbs*. New York: Schocken Books, 1949 and 1963.

Ben-Amotz, D. *Netivah Ben-Yehudah, Millon Olami le-Ivrit Meduberet*. Tel-Aviv: vol. 1, 1972; vol. 2, 1982.

Bernstein, I. *Yiddishe Shprikhverter un Redensarten*. Warsaw, 1908.

Cohen, I. *Zeh Le'umat Ze, Otzar Pitgamim Makbilim*. Tel-Aviv, 1954.

Davidson, I. *Otzar ha-Meshalim ve-ha-Pitgamim* (*Thesaurus of Proverbs and Parables from Medieval Jewish Literature*). Jerusalem: Mosad Harav Kook, 1957.

Edelmann, M.I. *Pitgamay ha-Talmud*. Lomza, 1912.

Even-Shoshan, A. *Millon Hadash Menukad u-Mezuyyar*. Jerusalem, 1966–1970.

Grasovski, (Goor), Y. *Million ha-Safah ha-Ivrit*. Tel-Aviv: Devir, 1938.

Grossman, R. (in collaboration with H. Sachs). *Millon Ivri-Angli Shalaym*. Tel-Aviv: 1938.

Guri, Y. *All's Well that Ends Well*. Jerusalem: Tarbut, 1993.

Harkavy, A. *Yiddish-English—English-Yiddish Dictionary*. New York: Hebrew Publishing Company, 1898.

Hurwitz, A. *Sefer Hapitgamim*. Jerusalem: 1961.

Kogos, F. *1001 Yiddish Proverbs*. New York: Citadel Press, Inc., 1970.

Kumove, S. *Words Like Arrows*. New York: Warner Books, 1986.

Lederman, D. *Peninay Hatalmud Vehamidrash*, vol. 1. Buenos Aires, 1946.

Nulman, Y.L. *Kohah Shel Milah-Der Koah Fun A Vort*. Jerusalem, 1995.

Petrushka, S. *Yiddishe Folks-Encyclopediya* (2 vols). New York/Montreal: The Gilead Press, 1949.

Rabin, C.M. *Otzar ha-Millim* (letters A-M with Z. Raday). Jerusalem, 1971.

Rackover, N. (assisted by R. Jacoby). *Nivay Talmud*. Jerusalem: Sifriyot Hamishpat Ha'ivri, 1990.

Rawnitzki, Y.H., and Bialik, H.N. *Sefer Hameshalim Vehapitgamim*. Tel-Aviv/Berlin: Dvir, 1924.

Samet, H.S. *Hashpa'ot Safrotaynu Ha'atikah Al Pitgamay Ha'am*, vol. 1. Warsaw.

Stutchkoff, N. *Der Oytser fun der Yiddisher Shprakh* (ed: by M. Weinreich), New York, Yiddish Scientific Institute—YIVO, 1950.

Subar, M. *Mikhlol Hama'amarim Vehapitgamim*, 3 vols. Ed. A. Darom. Jerusalem: Mosad Harav Kook, 1961.

Tendlau, A. *Shprichwörter und Redensarten.* Berlin: Schocken Verlag, 1934.

Toibish, L. *Talmudishe Elementen Inem Yiddishen Shprichvort.* Vienna, 1928.

Weinreich, U. *Modern English-Yiddish—Yiddish-English Dictionary.* New York: YIVO, Institute for Jewish Research, Schocken Books, 1977.

GLOSSARY

AB—The name of the fifth month of the Jewish calendar, corresponding approximately to July or August.

ADAR—The twelfth month of the Jewish calendar, corresponding approximately to February or March.

AGGADAH—(Lit., "tale" or "narration"); this is the name given to those sections of rabbinic literature that are nonlegal and that contain homiletic expositions of the Bible, stories, legends, folklore, anecdotes, or maxims.

AHARON—The last *aliyah* of the weekly Sabbath portion (*Sidrah*).

ALAYNU—A prayer borrowed from the Rosh Hashanah *Musaf* service, circa 1200–1300 C.E., which became the closing prayer of every synagogue service.

ALIYAH—Pl., *Aliyot* (lit., "ascending"); a term describing a person who is "called up" to the reading of the Torah.

AMIDAH—(Lit., "standing"); the eighteen benedictions (now nineteen) that are said daily while standing. On Sabbath and festivals seven benedictions are recited

and in *Musaf* of Rosh Hashanah nine are said.

AMORA—Pl., *amora'im* ("interpreter"); a name given to the teacher who explained at length, in popular style, the teachings contained in the *Mishnah*. Subsequent references to the *amora'im* meant the rabbinic authorities who were responsible for the Talmud.

ASHKENAZ—A name applied to Germany. Jews of German origin and those who came from Central and Eastern Europe are called *Ashkenazim*. The term is also applied to distinguish their rituals from those of the *Sephardim*.

AVODAH—"Divine worship"; the term may refer to: (1) the sacrifices in the Temple; (2) a section in the prayer service recited in the *Musaf* of Yom Kippur in memory of the High Priest's performance of his sacred duties on that day; (3) the name given the seventeenth benediction of the *Amidah*.

AVOT—"Fathers"; (1) the first benediction in the *Amidah*, naming the three patriarchs—Abraham, Isaac, and Jacob; (2) one of the sixty-three tractates of the *Mishnah*.

BA'AL KERI'AH—Also called *ba'al koray*; officiant who reads the Torah from the scroll in the synagogue with the proper accentuation and cantillation.

BA'AL TOKAYA—Person officially designated to blow the *shofar* in the synagogue during the services on Rosh Hashanah.

BAKKASHOT—Sing., *bakkashah*; supplicatory prayers recited either prior to the prayer service or within the service.

BARAITA—(Pl., *beraitot*); a word literally meaning "outside," referring to a tannaitic teaching that is not part of the *Mishnah*. It was later incorporated into a collection compiled by R. Hiyya and R. Oshaiah and is generally introduced by "Our rabbis taught" or "It has been taught."

BET DIN—Lit., "house of law or judgment"; a rabbinical court composed of three or more erudite men who act as a Jewish court of law.

BET HAMIDRASH—House of study; synagogue. Where persons studied, they also prayed; thus the synagogue became known as a *Bet ha-Midrash*.

BET HAMIKDASH—The Holy Temple of Jerusalem.

DUCHENEN—A Yiddish term applied to the Priestly Blessing. In the Temple it was pronounced by the Priests who stood on a special raised platform called *dukhan*.

ELUL—The sixth month of the Jewish calendar, corresponding approximately to August or September.

GET—A writ of release or divorce, given by a husband to a wife.

GEVUROT—Lit., "Powers"; name given to the second benediction of the *Amidah*.

GEZAYRAH SHAVAH—From the similarity of words or phrases occurring in two passages, it is inferred that what is expressed in the one applies also to the other.

HAFTARAH—Lit., "leave-taking"; a portion from the prophetical books read after the Torah portion on Sabbaths, festivals, and fast days.

HALAKHAH—(1) Sections of rabbinic literature that deal with legal matters, in contradistinction to the *Aggadah*; (2) the final, accepted law of the Rabbis.

HALLEL—Lit., "praise"; Pss. 113–118, recited on special occasions.

HAMAYTZ—Lit., "leavened"; during the eight days of Passover, all leavened food must be excluded from the Jewish home.

HAMOTZI—Lit., "Who brings forth"; the blessing made over bread.

HASHEM—"The Name"; used as a substitute for the Divine Name.

HASIDIM—A pietistic movement founded by the Baal Shem (1700–1760) of Podolia.

HAVDALAH—Lit., "separation"; the blessings recited over wine, light, and spices, by which the Sabbath and festivals are ushered out.

IYYAR—The second month of the Jewish calendar, corresponding approximately to April–May.

KADDISH—Lit., "sanctification"; the doxology recited to mark the end of the principal sections in the prayer service. It is also the name given to the prayer for the departed, including *Kaddish Derabbanan* (the rabbinical *Kaddish*), generally said by mourners after the study of rabbinic writings.

KASHRUT—From the word *kashayr*, meaning "fit" or "proper." This term is used to indicate that such food is permitted according to Jewish ritual law. The term also implies the broader concept of something that is fit and good, such as a *kosher etrog*, a *kosher sukkah*, or even a righteous Jew, a *kusherer Yid* (Yidd.).

KEDUSHAH—Lit., "sanctification"; during the service, the prayer of sanctification is recited at the repetition of the *Amidah* (second benediction), in the first blessing of "The Reading of Shema" (of the morning), and in the prayer *Uva Letziyon*.

KETUVIM—Hagiographa; the third of the three divisions of the Bible, comprising the word *TaNaKH*.

KIDDUSH—Lit., "sanctification"; the blessing (over wine) by which the Sabbath or a festival is ushered in.

KINAH—Pl., *kinot*; name given to a lamentation, elegy, or dirge chanted over the death of an individual, or a fallen city or land. Rabbinic literature applied the name *kinot* specifically to the Book of Lamentations.

KOHEN—Pl., *Kohanim*; a priest, a descendant of Aaron. Present-day Jewish ritual bestows certain privileges upon the *Kohen*, such as giving him precedence for an *Aliyah*, etc. *Kohanim* also pronounce the Priestly Blessing.

LESHON ha-KODESH—"The holy tongue," Hebrew. The name is used in Jewish literature to distinguish it from the Aramaic vernacular or other languages spoken by Jews.

LEVI—"Levite"; a member of the tribe of Levi. He assisted the *Kohanim* in the Temple. When reading the Torah, the second portion is assigned to a descendant of the tribe of Levi.

LULAV—Palm branch; one of the Four Species used during the festival of Sukkot.

MAFTIR—The portion of the Torah read on *Shabbat* for the person called upon to read the *Haftarah* from the Prophets.

MAGGID—An itinerant preacher, skilled as a narrator of stories, who generally adopted the midrashic method of explaining by parables.

MAHATZIT HASHEKEL—Lit., "half-shekel"; after the Exodus from Egypt, everyone included in the census had to pay a half-shekel (Ex. 30:14–15).

MAHZOR—Pl., *mahzorim* (lit., "cycle"); festival prayerbook.

MALKHUYOT—The proclamation of the Kingdom of God; one of the three central sections of the *Musaf Amidah* for Rosh Hashanah.

MASORAH—From the verb *masar* ("to hand down"); thus, "tradition."

MATZOT—Unleavened bread eaten during Passover.

MEGILLAH—Lit., "scroll"; name given to the biblical Book of Esther, one of the four scrolls.

MELAMED—Teacher; one who gave instruction in Hebrew and/or religion in a *hayder* ("room").

MENORAH—Lit., "candelabrum"; (1) oil lamp of seven branches used in the Tabernacle and Temple; (2) eight-branched candelabrum used on *Hanukkah*; (3) the six or eight branches are usually part of the Ark equipment.

MEZUZAH—Pl., "*Mezuzot*"; a small roll of parchment containing selected verses, placed in a container and affixed to the doorposts in Jewish homes.

MINHAH—The afternoon prayer service.

MISHNAH—Pl., *mishnayot*; earliest legal codification of the Oral Law, compiled by Rabbi Yehudah Ha-Nasi.

MITNAGDIM—Lit., "opponents" or "antagonists"; those who opposed *hasidim*.

MITZVAH—Pl., *mitzvot*; "precept" or "good deed."

MUSAF—The additional prayer service recited on *Shabbat*, festivals, *Rosh Hodesh*, and *Hol Hamo'ayd*, which corresponds to the additional sacrifices offered in the Temple.

NE'ILAH—Lit., "closing"; the fifth and final service of Yom Kippur.

NEVI'IM—Prophets; the second of the three divisions of the Bible, comprising the word *TaNaKH*.

NISAN—The first month of the Jewish calendar, corresponding approximately to March or April.

OMER—Lit., "sheaf"; the sheaf of barley offered as a sacrifice on the sixteenth of *Nisan*, before which time the new cereals of that year were forbidden to use (Lev. 23:10).

PARASHAH—Pl. *parashot*; a section of the Pentateuch, that is, the "portion of the week" read in the synagogue on the Sabbath. The term is used interchangeably with SIDRAH.

PESAH—Passover; first of the Pilgrimage Festivals.

PESUKAY DEZIMRAH—"Verses of Song"; name designated for a number of psalms read at the beginning of the morning service.

PIRKAY AVOT—Lit., "Chapters of the Fathers"; applied to the five chapters of the *Mishnah Avot*; a sixth was added later.

PURIM—Lit., "lots"; festival observed on the fourteenth of *Adar*, commemorating the deliverance of the Jews from the hands of Haman.

SANHEDRIN—A word derived from the Greek language, meaning "sitting together"; it represented the court of the Jews. The Great Sanhedrin sitting in Jerusalem consisted of seventy-one members.

SEDER—Lit., "order"; the home ceremony celebrated on the first night of Passover (in Israel) or on the first two nights of Passover (outside of Israel).

SEFER TORAH—Scroll of the Torah.

SELA—A coin.

SELIHOT—Penitential prayers recited before and during the High Holy Days and on fast days.

SEPHARD—(1) The ritual adapted by the Spanish and Portuguese Jews; (2) The hasidic movement that adapted *Nusah Sephard*, with various forms, as their arrangement of prayers.

SE'UDAT HAVRA'AH—A meal prepared by friends for a mourner returning from a funeral, as an expression of sympathy and consolation.

SHAHARIT—Lit., "dawn"; the first prayer service of the day, which takes place in the morning.

SHAMASH—Beadle or sexton in a synagogue. A *shamash* may also be a person who assists the hasidic rebbe.

SHEKEL—Coin or weight (see MAHATZIT HASHEKEL).

SHEKNINAH—Lit., "abiding [of God]," "Divine Presence"; the spirit of the Omnipresent as manifested on earth.

SHELI'AH TZIBBUR—An all-embracing name, meaning "messenger" or "emissary" of the congregation, applied to the person who recites the prayers aloud before the congregation.

SHEMA—Lit., "Hear"; the opening word of a keynote prayer in Judaism, proclaiming the existence and the unity of God— "Hear, O Israel the Lord is our God, the Lord is One."

SHEMONEH ESRAYH—The eighteen (now nineteen) blessings said by Jews in the three daily prayers.

SHIRAH MELODY—The special melody applied to *Az Yashir* ("Then sang Moses" [Ex. 15:1–18]), known as *Shirat Hayam* (the "Song of the Sea").

SHIVA–The seven days of mourning after the death of a relative.

SHOFAR—Lit., "ram's horn"; an instrument used during the prayer service, particularly during the High Holy Days.

SHOFAROT—The third of the three prayer-units recited in the Rosh Hashanah *Musaf* service, proclaiming God's revelation on Mount Sinai and the *shofar* in its messianic role.

SHOHET—Ritual slaughter of animals or fowl.

SHTIBL—A small hasidic house of prayer.

SIDDUR—Pl. *siddurim*; word meaning "order," which was given to the daily and Sabbath prayerbook.

SIDRAH—Section of the Pentateuch assigned for the week's reading (see PARASHAH).

SIYUM—The completion of the writing of a *Sefer Torah* (*Siyum Hasefer*) or of the study of a talmudic tractate or one of the six divisions of the *Mishnah*.

SOFER—A scribe, especially of Torah scrolls, phylacteries, and *mezuzot*.

SUKKAH—A tabernacle erected in celebration of the Sukkot holiday, in which meals are eaten and in which persons sleep.

TA'ANIT BeHaB—A custom of fasting on Monday (*Bet*) and Thursday (*Hay*), and Monday (*Bet*) in the months of *Heshvan* and *Iyyar*. This is done with the view of celebrating the joyous festivals of Sukkot and Pesah of the preceding months and in the event that some frivolity may have occurred, for which atonement should be made by fasting.

TAHANUN—A supplicatory prayer recited in the daily morning and afternoon services.

TAMMUZ—The fourth month in the Jewish calendar, corresponding to the month of June or July.

TANNA—Lit., "one who repeats" or "teaches"; either a rabbi quoted in the *Mishnah* or *Baraita* or a scholar, in the Amoraic period, who principally memorized and recited *Beraitot* in the presence of expounding teachers.

TARGUM—"Translation"; the name by which the Aramaic translations of the various books of the Bible are known. The most popular is *Targum Onkelos*.

TE'AMIM—Oldest term (from *ta'am*, meaning "sense," "meaning," or "taste") for biblical accentuation.

TEFILLAH—Pl., *tefillot*; prayer(s), whether private or public; specifically, the AMIDAH prayer.

TEFILLIN—Phylacteries; small cases containing passages from Scripture and affixed to the forehead and arm.

TEHINOT—Devotional literature in Yiddish, usually favored by women, first developed in the sixteenth century.

TISHAH b'AB—The Ninth of Ab, a day on which Jews fast and mourn for the destruction of the Temples in Jerusalem (586 B.C.E. and 70 C.E.).

TORAH—"Teaching," "doctrine," or "instruction"; referring both to the Written Torah (*Torah Shebikhtav*) and Oral Torah (*Torah Shebe'alpeh*), as well as to the entire body of Jewish religious literature.

TOSEFTA—Lit., "addition" or "supplement"; it is a work resembling the *Mishnah*, but which contains additional subject matter in greater detail.

TRAYFA—Lit., "torn" (forbidden); originally applied to the prohibition that forbade eating the meat of animals that had been torn by beasts. *Trayfa* is now applied to all food forbidden in Jewish Law.

TZADIK—"Righteous one"; an appellation used by *hasidim* for their leader, since he has Divine inspiration (*ru'ah hakodesh*).

TZIMMES—A vegetable or fruit stew.

TZITZIT—"Fringes"; worn by a male on the corners of a four-cornered garment, e.g., a *tallit*.

YAYIN NESEKH—"Wine of libation"; wine prepared or handled by an idolator from which a libation to a heathen god was made.

YOTZAYR—Pl., *Yotzrot*; prayer-poems inserted into the first benediction preceding *Shema* in the *Shaharit* service.

ZIMMUN—Summons to prayer; when three or more males above the age of thirteen conclude their meal together, it is customary to include this as an introductory formula (*Birkat Hazimmun*) to the Grace After Meals.

ZUZ—A coin the value of a *denarius*.

INDEX OF TRANSLITERATIONS

A Bahur Makht Kiddush Iber Shpener (Un Havdalah Iber a Kaltn Fiertuhp), 221
A Gutn Mo'ayd, 231
A Hakham Fun Mah Nishtanah, 234
A Hazzan A Drung, 221
A Hoykhe Kedushah, 209
A Kol Fun An Aysav, 16
A Mashal: Iber Dem Bluhzt Men Haman un Men Klapt Shofar, 249
A Mashal Keheres Hanishbar, 238
A Nuhmen Fun Der Haftarah, 229
A Pruhster Hai Vekayam, 238
A Rasha Fun Der Haggadah, 234
A Sheyne Reyne Kapparah, 243
A Tayerer Kaddish, 209
A Trukener Mi Shebayrakh Helft Vi A Toytn Bankes, 229
A Trukener Mi Shebayrakh Helft Vi Trukene Bankes, 229
A Yidene Uhn A Tze'enah Ure'enah Iz Vi A Sheygetz Uhn A Fifl, 226
A Yuhr Mit A Mitvuhkh, 114
A'aleh Et Yerushalayim Al Rosh Simhati, 83
Ad Delo Yada Bayn Arur Haman Lebarukh Mordecai, 249
Ad Kan Omrim Beshabbos Hagadol, 227
Ad Matai?, 83
Ad Matai Elohim Yeharef Tzar, Yena'aytz Oyayv Shimkha Lanetzah, 83
Ad Mayah Ve'esrim Shanah, 79
Ad She'ol Tahtit, 78
Ad Shetavo Hanehamah, Taytzay Has Vehalilah Haneshamah, 257
Adam Do'ayg Al Ibud Damav Ve'ayno Do'ayg Al Ibud Yamav, 257
Adam Karov Aytzel Atzmo, 114
Adam Lahevel Damah, Yamav Ketzayl Ovayr, 83
Adam Le'amal Yulad, 83
Adam Mekadaysh Atzmo Me'at Mekadshin Oto Harbayh, Milmatah-Mekadshin Oto Milmalah, Ba'olam Hazeh- Mekadshin Oto L'olam Habah, 41
Adam Mu'ad Le'olam, 114

Adam She'ayn Bo Dayah Asur Lerahaym Alav, 114
Adam Yesodo Mayafar Vesofo Le'afar- Bayno Levayno Iz Gut a Trunk Bruhnfn (Baynotayim Kahpt Men a Blintchick), 238
Adashim Ma'akhal Tzarah Ve'ayvel Hayn, 17
Adayin Lo Higi'ah Lahatzi Yofyah Shel Sarah, 114
Aderaba (h), 114
Admor (pl. Admorin), 257
Af Al Pi Khayn, 114
Af Al Pi Shehakham Gadol Attah, Ayno Domeh Lomayd Mayatzmo Lelomayd Mayrabo, 114
Af Al Pi Shehata, Yisrael Hu, 115
Af Al Pi Shehayniho Lo Avotav Le'adam Sefer Torah, Mitzvah Likhtov Mishelo, 78
Af Al Pi Shekol Hamo'adim Mitzvah Lismo'ah Bahem, Aval Behag Hasukkot Hayetah Bamikdash Simhah Yetayrah, 48
Af Attah Oseh Oznekha Ke'afarkeset, 115
Afilu Herev Hadah Munahat Lo Al Tzavaro Shel Adam, Al Yimna Atzmo Min Harahamim, 115
Afilu In Der Haggadah Gefint Men Dem Davar Ahayr, 234
Agav Urha, 115
Agil Ve'esmah- Kaylekhdik Un Shpitzedik, 231
Agmat Nefesh, 115
Aharay Darga (Yavo) Tevir, 257
Aharay Kikhlot Hakol, 209
Aharay Ma'arikh (Yavo) Tarha, 257
Aharay Mot-Kedoshim-Emor, 44
Aharay Rabim Lehatot, 31
Aharay Tarha Yavo Etnah, 257
Aharit Kol Ketatah Haratah, 257
Aharon Aharon Haviv, 19
Ahavah Mevatelet (Mekalkelet) Et Hashurah, Vesinah Mevatelet (Mekalkelet) Et Hashurah, 115
Ahaynu Benay Yisrael, 116
Ahor Vakedem Tzartani, 83
Ahoz Bekarnot Hamizbayah, 83
Akar Min Hashoresh, 257
Akaydat Yitzhak (Akaydah), 15
Akhilah Iz Di Beste Tefillah, 238
Akhol Veshato Ki Mahar Namut, 83

Al Ahat Kamah Vekhamah, 116
Al De'atayft Atefukh, Vesof Metayefayikh Yetufun, 116
Al Ha'aytzim Ve'al Ha'avanim, 116
Al Harishonim Anu Mitzta'arim Ve'attah Ba Lehosif Alayhem!, 29
Al Kol Panim, 257
Al Kol Pesha'im Tekhaseh Be'ahavah, 238
Al Regel Ahat, 116
Al Rishon Rishon Ve'al Aharon Aharon, 20
Al Tagidu Vegat, 83
Al Tashlikhayni Le'ayt Ziknah, 83
Al Tashlikhaynu Le'ayt Ziknah, 237
Al Tatzar Tzarat Mahar Ki Lo Tayda Mah Yulad Yom, 116
Al Tehi Birkat (Killelat) Hedyot Kalah Be'aynekha, 116
Al Tifrosh Min Hatzibbur, 116
Al Tishal Et Harofayh, She'al et Haholeh, 116
Al Tivtehu Vindivim, Beven Adam She'ayn Lo Teshu'ah, 84
Al Ya'amod Adam Bemakom Sakanah Lomar She'osin Li Nays, 117
Al Yalbin Penay Havayro Berabim, 117
Al Yatil Adam Aymah Yetayrah Betokh Bayto, 117
Al Yehi Hamashal Hazeh Kal Be'aynekha, She'al Yeday Hamashal Adam Omayd Al Divray Torah (Adam Yakhol La'amod Bedivray Torah), 257
Al Yeshaneh Adam Beno Bayn Habanim, 117
Al Yeshaneh Adam Miminhag Haberiyot, 258
Al Yeshaneh Adam Min Haminhag, 33
Al Yeshaneh Adam Miminhag Ha'ir Afilu Beniggunim, 117
Al Yiftah (Tiftah) Adam Piv (Peh) Lasatan, 117
Al Yithalayl Hagibor Bigvurato, 84
Al Yithalayl Hogayr Kimfatayah, 84
Al Yotzi Adam Et Atzmo Min Haklal, 117
Alai Ve'al Tzavari, 118
Alai Yahshevu Ra'ah Li, 84
Alav Hashalom, 258
Ale Shikurim Zaynen Nikhter Purim, 249
Alilat Dam, 258
Aliyat Neshamah, 258
Alma Dekushta (Dikshot) (Deshikra), 258
Alter Terah, 11
Altz Nemt An Ek, Afilu Der Ki Hinay Kahomer, 243
Am-Ha'aretz, 16
Am Hasefer, 258
Amdu Sa'arotav, 118
Amen Zuhger, 209
Amkha, 72
Amod Al Devarav, 118
Amrah Torah: Tehay Temayah Shivat Yamim Keday

Shetehay Havivah Al Ba'alah Keshe'at Kenisatah Lehupah, 43
Amri Lah Leshevah Ve'amri Lah Lignai, 249
Ani Hakatan, 258
Ani Hashuv Kemayt, 118
Ani Ledodi Vedodi Li, 84
Ani Mayvi Lakhem Re'ayah Min Hatorah, Ve'atem Mevi'in Li Re'ayah Min Hashotim!, 118
Ani Omayr Lekha Devarim Shel Ta'am Ve'attah Omayr Li Min Hashamayim Yerahamu, 118
Ani Shelomoh, 118
Ani Ve'afsi Od, 84
Ani Ve'evyon, 75
Aniyay Irkha Kodmim, 118
Aniyut Kemitah, 119
Anshay Bereishit, 9
Anshay Sedom, 13
Anus Rahamana Petarayh, 119
Apikoros (Epikuros, Epikiros), 119
Aray Miklat, 65
Arayl, 27
Araylah Oznam Velo Yukhlu Lehakshiv, 84
Arayngezetzt In Had Gadya, 234
Araynkhapn A Kedushah (Barekhu), 209
Araynkhapn A Minhah, 220
Arayot, 44
Arba (Dalet) Amot, 119
Arba'im Yom Kodem Yetzirat Havlad Bat Kol Yotzayt Ve'omeret: Bat Ploni Liploni, 119
Arbakh Arba Tzarikh, 120
Arzay Halevanon, 84
Asha Atzmo Ke'ilu Lo Yada, 25
Asakh Hamans Un Eyn Purim, 249
Asakh Zemirot Un Veynig Luhkshn, 223
Asarah Batlanim, 120
Asayh Imi Ot Letovah, 85
Aseret Yemay Teshuvah, 238
Asher Yatzar Papir, 209
Ashirim Mekamtzin, 120
Ashirut Shel Korah, 60
Ashray Hagoy Asher Hashem Elohav, 85
Ashray Kol Hosay Vo, 85
Ashray Nesui Pesha Kesui Hata'ah, 85
Ashray Yoshvay Vaytekha Iz Der Beste Handl, 209
Ashraykhem Shetizku Lihyot Shamashim Lamakom, 58
Asmakhta Be'alma, 120
Asur Le'adam Sheyitom Kelum Kodem Sheyevaraykh, 45
Asya Demagan Bemagan, Magan Shavyah, 120
Asya Rehika Ayna Avira, 121
Atarti Telat Ganvay Lo Miktal, 121
Atik Yomin, 121

Attah Ba Aylai Beherev Uvahanit Uvkhidon
  Ve'anokhi Va Aylekha Beshaym Hashem
  Tzeva'ot, 85
Attah Harayta Lada'at- Nituh Kayn Bruhnfn, Trinkt
  Men Kvass, 231
Attah Veharta (Nu) Nism, 231
Attah Vehartanu Mikol Ha'amim; Un Farn Sheygetz
  Huhst Du More!, 231
Atz Kotzaytz, Ben Kotzaytz, Ketzutzai Lekatzaytz,
  Bedibur Mefotzaytz, 249
Atzeret, 48
Av Behokhmah Verakh Beshanim, 259
Av Ehad Yakhol Lefarnays Asarah Banim, Ve'asarah
  Banim Aynam Yekholim Lefarnays Av Ehad,
  259
Avad Hasid Min Ha'aretz, 85
Avak Leshon Hara, 121
Avanim Shahaku Mayim, 85
Avar Zemano (Yomo) Batayl Korbano, 63
Avinu Shebashamayim, 121
Avira De'eretz Yisrael Mahkim, 121
Avodah Zu Tefillah, 121
Avodat Perekh, 25
Avot Akhlu Voser Veshinay Banim Tikhenah, 85
Aygel Hazahav, 34
Ayin Hara, 121
Ayin Lo Ra'atah, 85
Ayin Tahat Ayin, 31
Ayl Na Refa Na Lah, 58
Aylu Ve'aylu Divray Elohim Hayyim Hayn, 121
Aymat Mavet, 85
Ayn Adam Asher Lo Yeheta, 85
Ayn Adam Ba'olam Belo Yesurim, 259
Ayn Adam Makneh Davar Shelo Ba Le'olam, 122
Ayn Adam Maysim Atzmo Rasha, 122
Ayn Adam Mitkana Bivno Vetalmido, 63
Ayn Adam Nitpas Bishat Tza'aro, 122
Ayn Adam Ro'eh Hovah Le'atzmo, 122
Ayn Adam Ro'eh Nega'ay Atzmo. R. Meir Omayr: Af
  Lo Nega'ay Kerovav, 122
Ayn Adam Yodaya Mah Belibo Shel Havayro, 122
Ayn Ani Ela Bedayah, 122
Ayn Ashan Beli Aysh, 259
Ayn Avaydah Ke'avaydat Hazeman, 260
Ayn Bah (Bo) Ta'am Ve'ayn Bah (Bo) Rayah, 260
Ayn Berayrah, 122
Ayn Berakhah Metzuyah Betokh Bayto Shel Adam
  Ela Bishvil Ishto, 123
Ayn Divray Torah Mitkaimin Ela Bemi Shemaymit
  Atzmo Alehah, 61
Ayn Dohim Even Aharay Hanofayl, 123
Ayn Domah Tefillat Tzadik Ben Tzadik Litefillat
  Tzadik Ben Rasha, 17
Ayn Gedulah Befaltin (Befaltayrin) Shel Melekh, 41

Ayn Habor Mitmalay Mayhulyato, 123
Ayn Hakadosh Barukh Hu Mekapayah Sekhar Kol
  Beriyah, Afilu Sekhar Sihah Na'ah, 123
Ayn Hakadosh Barukh Hu Notayn Hokhmah Ela
  Lemi Sheyaysh Bo Hokhmah, 123
Ayn Hakhi Nami, 123
Ayn Hakometz Masbi'a Et Ha'ari, 123
Ayn Hanavi Resha'i Lehadaysh Davar Mayatah, 52
Ayn Ha'olam Mitkayaym Ela Beshvil Mi Shemaysim
  Atzmo Kemi She'ayno, 79
Ayn Ha'or Nikar Ela Mitokh Hahoshekh, 260
Ayn Harash Aytzim Belo Kardom, 260
Ayn Hashkhinah Shorah Mitokh Atzvut, 123
Ayn Hatorah Niknit Ela Behavurah, 76
Ayn Havush Matir Atzmo Mibayt Ha'asurim, 123
Ayn Hayahid Omayr Kedushah, 49
Ayn Karov Ro'eh Et Hanega'im, 124
Ayn Kataygor Na'aseh Sanaygor, 124
Ayn Ketoret Beli Helbenah, 34
Ayn Kiddush Ela Bemakom Se'udah, 124
Ayn Kisim Batakhrikhim, 260
Ayn Kol Ve'ayn Oneh, 260
Ayn Lo Mo'ah Bekadkedo, 124
Ayn Lo Ra'inu Ra'ayah, 124
Ayn Ma'amidin Parnays Al Hatzibbur Ela Im Kayn
  Namlikhin Betzibbur, 36
Ayn Mahzikin Bemahloket, 60
Ayn Mazal Leyisrael, 124
Ayn Me'arvin Simhah Besimhah, 124
Ayn Meratzin Lo Le'adam Besha'at Ka'aso, 34
Ayn Mesihin Bise'udah, 124
Ayn Meshivin Et Ha'ari Le'ahar Mitah, 124
Ayn Mevi'in Re'ayah Min Hashotim, 125
Ayn Midrash Belo Hidush, 125
Ayn Mikra Yotzay Miday Peshuto, 125
Ayn Mukdam Ume'uhar Batorah, 59
Ayn Nikhnasim Lehurvah Mipnay Hahashad, 125
Ayn Omer Ve'ayn Devarim, 85
Ayn Onshin Ela Im Kayn Mazhirin, 125
Ayn Orayah Makhnis Orayah, 125
Ayn Osin Sherarot Al Hatzibbur Pahot Mishnayim,
  33
Ayn Ra She'ayn Bo Tov, 260
Ayn Ribui Ahar Ribui Ela Lema'ayt, 125
Ayn Shenay Kolot Nikhnasim Be'ozen Ahat, 125
Ayn Shoteh Nifga (Margish), 125
Ayn Somkhin Al Hanays, 126
Ayn Tzibbur Ani (Aram. Layt Tzibbur Kulayh
  Meya'ani), 126
Ayn Vadai She'ayn Bo Safayk, 261
Ayn Zakayn Ela Hakham (Mi Shekanah Hokhmah),
  59
Aynai Velibi Sham Kol Hayamim, 85
Aynay Kol Yisrael Alekha, 86

Aynayim Lahem Velo Yiru, 232
Ayner Huht Lib Zoyermilkh, Der Tzveyter Maftir, 230
Ayni Yodaya Mah Attah Sah, 126
Ayno Domeh Lomayd Mayatzmo Lelomayd
　Mayrabo, 126
Ayno Domeh Mi Sheyaysh Lo Pat Besalo Lemi
　She'ayn Lo Pat Besalo, 126
Ayno Domeh Shemi'ah Lire'iah, 261
Ayno Domeh Shonah Pirko Mayah Pe'amim
　Leshonah Pirko Mayah Ve'ahat, 126
Ayno Ma'aleh Ve'ayno Morid, 126
Ayrev Rav, 27
Ayshet Hayil Mi Yimtza, Uhber A Vayb A Shlimazel
　Iz Benimtza, 223
Aytzah Tovah Ka Mashma Lan, 126
Ayver Min Hahai, 12
Ayzehu Ashir? Kol Sheyaysh Lo Nahat Ru'ah
　Be'oshro, 127
Ayzehu Hakham? Haro'eh Et Hanolad, 127
Ayzehu Talmid Hakham? Kol Shesho'alin Oto
　Halakhah Bekhol Makom Ve'omerah, 127
Ayzer Kenegdo, 9
Az Ba(a) gala Iz a Vuhgn Iz Uvizman Kariv a Shlitn,
　209
Az Der Ba'al Tokaya Ken Nit Bluhzn Leygt Zikh Der
　Satan In Shofar, 239
Az Di Velt Zuhgt Zuhl Men Gleybn, 127
Az Es Kumt Purim Fargest Men In Ale Yesurim, 249
As Men Iz In Ka'as Oyfn Chazen Shpringt Men Nit
　Kayn Kedushah?, 209
Az Men Iz In Ka'as Oyfn Chazen Zuhgt (Entfert)
　Men Nit Keyn Amen?, 209
Az Men Ken Nit Un Men Veys Nit Nemt Men Zikh
　Nit Unter, 243
Az Men Tzeylt Sefirah Kumt Oyf Di Klezmer A
　Pegirah, 220
Az S'geyt Di Sedrah Korah Kumen Oyf: Karshn,
　Retekh, Khreyn, 60
Az Vayakhayl Iz a Knish Iz Pekuday a Varenik, 36
Azut Panim, 127

Ba Letahayr Mesai'in Oto, 127
Ba Shabbat Ba'ah Menuhah, 9
Ba'al Davar, 127
Ba'al Hamayah Hu Ba'al Hadayah, 261
Ba'al Hanays Ayno Makir Beniso, 127
Ba'al Teshuvah, 127
Ba'al Yekholet, 261
Ba'avotaynu Harabim, 261
Ba'erev Yalin Bekhi Velaboker Rinah, 86
Bahaday Hutza Leki Karba, 128
Bahaday Kivshay Derahamana Lamah Lakh?, 128
Bakdayrah Shebishayl Bah Nitbashayl, 128
Baki Behadray Torah, 128
Baki Beheshbonot Hayah, 129

Baki Berefu'ot, 129
Baki Besitray Torah, 129
Baki Lidrosh Batorah, 129
Bakol, Mikol, Kol, 219
Bal Tashhit, 74
Balemer (Almemar), 261
Bameh Kohakha Gadol, 86
Banim Gidalti Veromamti Vehaym Pashu Vi, 86
Bar-Bay Rav Dehad Yoma, 129
Bar Da'at, 129
Bar Samkha, 129
Bar Uryan, 129
Bari Veshema Bari Adif, 129
Barukh Dayan Ha'emet, 129
Barukh Hagever Asher Yivtah Bashem, 86
Barukh Hashem, 261
Barukh Hashem Yom Yom, 86
Barukh Hashem Yom Yom- Oyf (Far) Morgn Zuhl
　(Vet) Gott Zorgn, 223
Barukh Shepetarani, 230
Bat Kol, 129
Bat Tehilah Siman Yafeh Lebanim, 130
Batar Anya Azla Anyuta, 130
Batay Kenaysiyot Ayn Nohagin Bahen Kalut Rosh,
　130
Batayl Beshishim, 130
Ba'u Mayim Ad Nafesh, 86
Bay A Yingl Makht Men Barukh Shepetarani Tzu
　Bar-Mitzvah, Bay A Meydl- Tzu Der Hasunah,
　230
Bay Bo'i Veshalom Shteyt Der Uhreman Oybnuhn,
　221
Bay Im Iz Kol Dikhfin Yaytay Veyaykhol, 235
Bayn Kahkh Uvayn Kakh, 130
Bayn Keseh Le'asor, 239
Bayn Porat Yosayf, 21
Bayn Sorayr Umoreh, 75
Bayra Deshatit Minayh Lo Tishday Bayh Kela, 130
Bayt Hakevarot (Kevarot), 86
Be'al Korho (Korhah), 131
Bederekh She'adam Rotzeh Laylaykh, Bah Molikhin
　Oto, 131
Be'ezrat Hashem Yitbarakh, 261
Befiv Shalom Et Rayayhu Yedabayr, Uvekirbo Yasim
　Arbo, 86
Befiv Uvisfatav Kibduni Velibo Rihak Mimeni, 87
Befiv Yevaraykhu Uvekirbam Yekalelu, 87
Begapo Yavo Begapo Yaytzay, 31
Bahadray Hadarim, 131
Behukotayhem Lo Taylaykhu, 44
Be'ikvot Meshiha Hutzpa Yisgay Veyoker Ya'amir,
　131
Bekhol Adam Mitkana Hutz Mibno Vetalmido, 63
Belashon Sagi Nahor, 131
Belayv Shalaym, 87

Belayv Valayv Yedabayru, 87
Beli Ayin Hara (Ra'ah), 131
Beli Neder, 64
Bemakli Avarti Et Hayardayn, 20
Bemayzid, 132
Bemidah She'adam Modayd Bah Modedin Lo, 132
Ben Noah, 12
Ben (Yeled) Zekunim, 21
Benay Adam (sing. Ben Adam) Shel Hefkayr, 261
Benay Korah Lo Maytu, 63
Bentchn Gomayl, 230
Bentchn Hanukkah Likht, 248
Bera Karayah De'abuha, 132
Berahayl Bitkha Haketanah, 18
Berakhah Levatalah, 262
Bereishit Bari, 9
Berikh Rahamana Dihavakh Nihalan Vela Yehavakh
    Le'afra, 132
Beser Pesah Eyn Malkah Eyder Yom Kippur Fertzig
    Malkot, 243
Beser Uhnkumen Tzu Alaynu Eyder Tzum Bestn
    Mentchn, 210
Besha'ah Tovah Umutzlahat, 262
Besha'at Hadhak, 132
Beshogayg, 132
Bet-Hakeneset Sheharav...Kedushatan Af
    Keshehayn Shomemin, 52
Betah Ba-Shem Va'asay Tov, 87
Beyad Hazakah Uvizro'a Netuyah- Emlokh
    Alaykhem, 87
Bezayat Apekha Tokhal Lehem, 9
Bigedulah Mathilin Min Hagadol, Uviklalah
    Mathilin Min Hakatan, 42
Bila Hamavet Lanetzah, Umahah Hashem Dimah,
    87
Bima, 262
Binaraynu Uvizkaynaynu Naylaykh, 27
Birkat Habayit Berubah, 132
Birkat Hamazon De'oraita, 72
Bishat Hedvata Hedvata, Bishat Evla Evla, 9
Bishivah Shel Malah, 132
Bishloshah Devarim Adam Mishtaneh Mayhavayro:
    Bekol, Bemareh Uveda'at, 132
Bishlosah Devarim Adam Nikar: Bekoso, Bekiso
    Uveka'aso, Veyaysh Omrim Af Besahako, 132
Bivrito Shel Avraham Avinu, 14
Bizkhut Nashim Tzidkaniyot Shehayu Be'oto Hador
    Nigalu Yisrael Mimitzrayim, 133
Bizman Sheyisrael Osin Retzono Shel Makom Ayn
    Kol Umah Velashon Sholtot Bahen, 133
Bluhzen Shofar, 239
Bor Karah Vayahperayhu, Vayipol Beshahat Yifal, 87

Da Lifnay Mi Attah Omayd, 133
Dabayr El Ha'aytzim Ve'el Ha'avanim, 262

Dabayr, Ki Shomaya Avdekha, 87
Dai Lahakima Birmiza, 262
Damim Tartay Mashma, 133
Dan Et Havayrkha Lekhaf Zekhut, 45
Dardakay Melamayd, 133
Darko Shel Ish Lahzor Al Ishah Ve'ayn Darkah Shel
    Ishah Lahzor Al Ish, 75
Davar Ahayr, 133
Davar Ehad Ledor Ve'ayn Shenay Devarin Ledor,
    134
Davar She'afilu Tinokot Shel Bayt Raban Yodin Oto,
    134
Davar Shelo Ba Le'olam, 134
Davar Velo Hatzi Davar, 134
Davenen (Davnen), 262
Dayah Letzarah Beshatah, 25
De'alakh Sani Lehaverkha Lo Ta'avid, 45
Der Bester Muhgn Iz Der Magayn Avot, 222
Der In Himl Zuhl Unz (Mir) Helfn, 134
Der Kohen Huht Zikh In Im Tzeshpilt, 134
Der Mentch Zindigt Un Di Huhn Vert Di Kapparah,
    244
Der Oylam Iz Shoyn Du, 210
Der Uhreman Huht Basor Vedagim In Di Zemirot,
    224
Der Yid Entfert Tamid Farkert: Zuhgt Men Im
    Shalom Alaykhem, Entfert Er Alaykhem
    Shalom,224
Der Yid Iz A Kapparah Huhn, 244
Der Zekhut Fun Der Mitzvah Iz Im Baygeshtanen,
    263
Der Zivug Zuhl Oleh Yafah Zayn, 263
Derekh Agav, 135
Derekh Arukhah Uketzarah, Derekh Ketzarah
    Va'arukhah, 135
Derekh Eretz Kadmah Letorah, 263
Derekh Resha'im Tovayd, 87
Derlebn Tzu Hern Dem Shofar Shel Mashiah, 239
Devarim Betaylim, 135
Devarim Hayotze'im Min Halayv Nikhnasim El
    Halayv, 263
Devarim Shel Ta'am, 135
Devash Vehalav Tahat Leshonaykh, 87
Devaykut, 135
Di Gantze Megillah, 250
Di Neshamah Likht, 244
Di Neshamah Zuhl Huhbn An Aliyah, 263
Dibbuk, 263
Dibrah Torah Kelashon Benay Adam, 44
Din Perutah Kedin Mayah, 135
Dina Demalkhuta Dina, 135
Dinen Tzum Aygel Hazahav (Tzum Guhldenem
    Kalb), 34
Dirah Na'ah Ve'ishah Na'ah Vekhaylim Na'im
    Marhivin Dato Shel Adam, 136

Divray Kibushim, 136
Dok Bekhakay Vetishkah Benigray, 136
Dor Haflagah, 12
Dor Hamabul, 12
Dor Hamidbar, 57
Dor Yatom, 136
Drey Mir Nit Keyn Kuhp Mit Dayne Had Gadya's, 235
Duhs Beste Fun Di Eser Makot Zaynen Di Kneydlakh Mit Yoykh, 235
Duhs Iz Mayn Kaddish, 210
Duhs Lebn Iz Vi Shemoneh-Esrayh; Men Shteyt, Men Shteyt, Biz Men Geyt Oys, 210
Dukhenen, 232

Efro'ah Shelo Nitpathu Aynav, 136
Ehad Bepeh Ve'ehad Belayv, 136
Ehad Hamarbeh Ve'ehad Hamamit Uvilvad Sheyekhavayn Libo Lashamayim, 136
Ela Mai, 136
Emet Mayeretz Titzmah, 87
Emor Beroma Vekatil Besurya, 263
Entfern Amen, 210
Er Boyt Pithom Ve-Raamses, 25
Er Halt Shoyn Bay Kos Revi'i, 235
Er Huht Avekgeganvet Dem Humash Mitn Lo Tignov, 29
Er Huht Dem Kaddish Tzu Hoykh Ungehoybn, 210
Er Huht Geboyrn a Kaddish, 211
Er Huht Gehat Kefitzat Haderekh, 18
Er Huht Im Gegebn A Mi Shebayrakh, 230
Er Huht Upgeklapt Dem Mizmor In a Rega, 211
Er Huht Zikh Ayngekoyft Maftir Yonah, 244
Er Iz Geshtorbn Uhn A Kaddish, 211
Er (Iz Nit Oysn) Meynt Nit Di Haggadah Nuhr Di Kneydlakh, 235
Er Iz Shoyn A Halakh Le'olamo, 232
Er Iz Tzum Barg Sinai Nit Dergangen, 29
Er Ken Kayn Motzi Nisht Makhn Iber A Retekh, 219
Er Ken Mikh (Uhn) Kluhgn (Luhdn) Tzum Unetaneh- Tokef, 239
Er Ken Mikh Uhpzuhgn Dem Hakol Yodukha, 224
Er Klapt Zikh Ashamnu Mitn Linkn Fus In Der Rekhter Zayt Arayn, 244
Er Kukt Vi A Huhn In Benay Adam, 244
Er Kumt Tzum Oyshpayen, 211
Er Kumt Uhp Mit Yehi Ratzon, 225
Er Shlugt Zikh Al-Hayt Un Balekt Zikh Derbay, 244
Er Shraybt Noah Mit Zibn Grayzn, 12
Er Shteyt A Lange Shemoneh Esrayh, 211
Er Zuhgt Ivre Vi A Vaser, Nor Duhs Vaser Loyft Un Er Shteyt, 212
Er Zuhgt Nor Mah-Tovu, 212

Eretz Zavat Halav Udevash, 25
Es Gayt Vi A Mizmor, 212
Es Helft Nit Ki Ayl Shomraynu Umatzilaynu- Uvetzeyl!, 220
Es Iz Enkat Mesaldekha, 244
Es Iz Lehavdil Bayn Kodesh Lehol, 227
Es Iz Lehavdil Elef Havdalot, 263
Es Iz Nit Ma'alah Un Nit Morid, 33
Es Vet Zikh Vendn Vi Der Hamor Shteyt, 263
Esa Aynai El Heharim, Mayayin Yavo Ezri? 88
Even Maskit Lo Titnu Be'artzekhem Lehishtahavot Aleha, 50
Eyn Muhl In A Yovel, 50
Eyn Yehi Ratzon, 239
Eyner Huht Hana'ah Fun Kez, A Tzveyter Fun "Lang Vehu Rahum", Un A Driter Fun Tir Tzu Der Gas, 212

Faln Kore'im, 244
Faln Tahanun, 212
Fangt Uhn Barukh She'amar, An Oylem Vet Shoyn Uhnkumen, 212
Far Amen Kumt Keyn Patch Nit, 213
Far Loyter Ahavah Rabbah Kumt Er Nit Tzu Shema Yisrael, 213
Farbaytn Di Yotzrot, 225
Farfaln, Le'olam Va'ed, 225
Fastn Hafsakot, 252
Fregn Di Fir Kashes, 235
Freg(t) Mikh Behayrem, 264
Fun Al-Hayt Vert Men Nit Fet, 245
Fun Barukh She'amar Biz Adon Olam, 213
Fun Barukh She'amar Biz Barukh Meshalaym Iz Vayt, 213
Fun Neki Khapayim Vert Men Nit Raykh, 213
Fun Vekhakh Hayah Omayr Biz Vekhakh Hayah Moneh Iz A Lange Vayle (Iz A Groyser Untersheyd; Falt Men Zibn Muhl Kore'im; Iz Guhr An Ander Niggun), 245

Gadol Hador, 136
Gadol Hame'aseh (Hama'aseh) Yotayr Min Ha'oseh, 136
Gadol Ha'oseh Mayahavah Yotayr Min Haoseh Mayirah, 70
Galgal Hu Shehozayr Ba'olam, 136
Gam Alayikh Ta'avar Kos, 88
Gam Ani Hakham Kamoka, 88
Gam Bosh Lo Yayvoshu Vehikalaym Lo Yada'u, 88
Gam Et Hatov Nekabayl- Ve'et Hara Lo Nekabayl?, 88
Gam Harvonah (Harvona) Zakhur Latov, 250
Gam Navi Gam Kohen Hanayfu, 88
Gam Zu Letovah, 137

Gamal Haporayah Ba'avir, 137
Gan Eden, 9
Ganov Da'at Haberiyot, 137
Gantz Yor Shikur, Purim Nikhter, 250
Gartl, 264
Gavo'ah Lo Yisa Gevohit, Shema Yaytzay Mayhen Toren, 137
Gavra Rabbah, 137
Gebn A Yasher-Ko'ah, 232
Gedolah Sinah Shesonim Amay Ha'aretz Letalmiday Hakhamim, 137
Gedolah Tefillah Yotayr Mima'asim Tovim, 70
Gedolim Tzadikim Bemitatam Yotayr Mibehayayhem, 137
Gefinen A Zekhut (Oyf), 264
Geloybt Iz Gott, 264
Gemara Gemiray Lah, 137
Gemara Gemirna Sevara La Yedana, 138
Gemilut Hasadim, 265
Genayvat Da'at, 138
Gey Shray Hai Vekayam, 240
Geyn Tzu Tashlikh, 240
Gezayrot Kashot Vera'ot, 265
Gilgul Hanefesh, 265
Gilui Rosh, 265
Girsa Deyankuta (La Mishtakha), 138
Golem, 266
Gott Fun Avraham, 227
Gott Zuhl Oyf Im Shikn Fun Di Tzen Makot Di Beste (Paroh's Makot), 235
Gott Zuhl Unz Shomayr Umatzil Zayn, 220
Gozer Tanis (Tan'anit) Zayn, 252
Gut Bauen, 266
Gut Shabbos, 222
Gut Vukh (Shavu'a Tov), 227
Gut Yom Tov, 232

Ha Beha Talya, 138
Haba Letahayr Mesai'in Oto, 138
Habatalah Mevi'ah Liday Shi'amum, 138
Had Bedara, 138
Had Gadya Shteyt Tamid Oyf Eyn Mekah, 235
Hadelet Haninelet Lo Bimhayrah Tipatayah, 138
Hadas (Huhdes), 227
Hadaysh Yamaynu Kekedem-Der Eygener Shlimazel Vuhs Frier, 213
Hadrat Panim Zakan, 138
Hafokh Hake'arah al Pihah, 138
Hahazir Besha'ah Shehu Rovaytz Poshayt Et Telafav Ke'omayr: Re'u She'ani Tahor, 266
Hahoshayd Bikshayrim Lokah Begufo, 139
Hai Alma (Kevay) Hilula Damya, 139
Hai Sha'ah, 139
Haita Dekatri Savart Vekibalt, 139

Hakadosh Barukh Hu Liba Ba'ay, 139
Hakadosh Barukh Hu Makdim Refu'ah Lemakah, 139
Hakadosh Barukh Hu Medakdayk Im Sevivav Kehut Hasa'arah, 140
Hakadosh Barukh Hu Mezavayg Zivugim, 266
Hakadosh Barukh Hu Natan Be'ishah Binah Yotayr Miba'ish, 140
Hakham, 267
Hakham Balailah, 267
Hakham Bashi, 267
Hakham, Zeh Talmid Hamahkim Et Rabotav, 140
Hakhayl, 78
Hakol Biday Shamayim Hutz Miyirat Shamayim, 72
Hakol Biday Shamayim Hutz Mitzinim Pahim, 140
Hakol Keminhag Hamedinah, 140
Hakol Kol Ya'akov Vehayadayim Yeday Aysav, 17
Hakol Talui Bemazal Afilu Sefer Torah Shebehaykhal, 267
Hakot Balashon, 88
Hakshivah Bekol Tahanunotai, 88
Hakshivah Tefilati, 88
Halakhah Lema'aseh, 140
Halakhah Lemoshe Misinai, 140
Halakhah Ve'ayn Morim Kayn, 141
Halashon Hu Kulmus Halayv, 267
Halom Halamti, 21
Halomayd Torah Ve'aynah Melamdah Zehu 'Devar Hashem Bazah', 60
Halomayd Ve'ayno Hozayr Domeh Lezoraya Ve'ayno Kotzayr, 141
Hama'akhal Mayvi Et Hashaynah, 141
Hama'akhal Yolid Hashaynah, 141
Hamagbi'ah Yado Al Havayro Af Al Pi Shelo Hikahu Nikra Rasha, 25
Hamakeh Be'evrato- Geshluhgn Oyf Di Ivre, 220
Hamakom Yerahaym Alekha Betokh She'ar Holay Yisrael, 141
Hamakom Yenahaym Etkem (Yenahemkhem) (Yenahemkha) Im (Betokh) She'ar Avaylay Tziyon Virushalayim, 267
Hamalbin Penay Havayro Barabim Ke'ilu Shofaykh Damim, 141
Hamathil Bemitzvah Omrim Lo Gemor, 141
Hamekabayl Tzedakah Ve'ayno Tzarikh Lekakh, Sofo Ayno Niftar Min Ha'olam Ad Sheyavo Liday Kakh, 141
Hamesahayk Bekuvya, 141
Hamevakayr Holeh Notayl Ehad Mishishim Betza'aro, 141
Hamevazeh Talmid Hakham, Apikoros Havay, 142
Hamotzi Lehem Min Ha'aretz-Es Vi A Paritz, 219
Hamotzi Mayhavayro Alav Harayah, 31
Hana'aseh Ayn Lehashiv, 142

Haniftar Min Hamayt Al Yomar Lo Laykh Leshalom Ela Laykh Beshalom, 142
Hanosay Ishah Tzarikh Sheyivdok Be'ahehah, 142
Hanukkah Un Purim Vern Di Uhreme Layt Ashirim, 248
Ha'ohayz Beyad Iz Di Beste Tefillah, 240
Ha'ohayz Beyad-Shalom Bekeshene, 240
Ha'ohayz Beyad Shteyt Groys Geshribn, 240
Ha'ohayz Beyad-Vekhol Ma'aminim Shehu, 240
Ha'okhayl Bashuk Domeh Lekelev, 142
Ha'olam Lesulam Hu Domeh-Zeh Oleh Vezeh Yorayd, 267
Ha'omayr Ayn Lo Ela Torah Afilu Torah Ayn Lo, 71
Harbayh Lamadeti Mayrabotai, Umayhavayrai Yotary Mayrabotai-Umitalmidai Yotayr Mikulam, 142
Hararim Heteluyim Besa'arah (Ve'ayn Lahem Al Mah Sheyismokhu), 142
Haray Shulhan, Haray Basar, Veharay Sakin Ve'ayn Lanu (Peh) Le'ekhol, 143
Harhev Pikha Va'amalayhu, 88
Haro'eh Etrog Bahalom, Hadar Hu Lifnay Kono, 49
Haro'eh Shemen Zayit Bahalom Yetzapeh Lema'or Torah, 33
Has Vehalilah, 15
Has Veshalom, 143
Hasagat Gevul, 74
Hasar Lehem, 89
Hasaykh Et Raglav, 89
Hash Berosho Ya'asok Batorah, 143
Hashad, 143
Hashakh Ha'olam Ba'ado, 143
Hashem Li Lo Ira, Mah Ya'aseh Li Adam, 89
Hashem Morish Uma'ashir, 89
Hashem Natan Vashem Lakakh, 89
Hashem Yerahaym, 143
Hashem Yishmerayhu Vihayayhu, 267
Hashkavah (Ashkavah), 230
Hashmaya Le'oznekha Mah She'attah Motzi Mipikha, 143
Hashmi'ini Et Kolaykh, 89
Hoshohad Ye'avayr Pikhim Visalayf Divray Tzadikim, 31
Hashomer Ahi Anokhi?, 10
Hasid Shoteh, 143
Hasiday Umot Ha'olam Yaysh Lahem Haylek Le'olam Haba, 267
Hata'ai Ani Mazkir Hayom, 21
Hatan Domeh Lemelekh, 267
Hatorah Hasah Al Mamonam Shel Yisrael, 144
Hatzad Hashaveh Shebahen, 144
Hatzilayni Na Miyad Ahi Aysav, 20
Havah Amina, 144
Havah Li Verakhah, 89
Haval Al De'avdin Velo Mishtakhin, 26

Haverkha Kerayikh Hamra Ukafa Legabaykh Mosh, 144
Havayrim Kol Yisrael, 226
Havivim Yisrael Lifnay Hakadosh Barukh Hu Yotayr Mimalakhay Hasharayt, 71
Havrakh Havra It Layh, Vehavra Dehavrakh Havra It Layh, 144
Havru Al-Ketarnegolim, 144
Hayah Hakinor Le'ayvel, 89
Hayav Adam Letahayr Et Atzmo Baregel, 42
Hayav Adam Levaraykh Mayah Berakhot Bekhol Yom, 72
Hayav Adam Lilmod Et Beno Lashut Al Hamayim, Ve'im Lo Lamdo Hayav Lilmod Et Atzmo, 77
Hayav Adam Lilmod Et Beno Umanut, Ve'im Lav Hayav Lilmod Et Atzmo, 77
Hayekha Kodmin Lehayay Havayrkha, 144
Hayeled Aynenu, 20
Haykhi Timatzay (Timtza) Lomar, 144
Hayitpa'ayr Hagarzen Al Hahotzayv Bo?, 89
Hayn Shelkha Tzedek, Velav Shelkha Tzedek, 45
Hayn Velav Verafya Beyadayh, 144
Hayntiger Hodesh Iz Hasayr, 226
Hayom Kan Umahar Bakever, 144
Hayom Odenu Umahar Aynenu, 145
Hazak Hazak Venithazak, 230
Hazak Uvarukh, 145
Hazak Ve'ematz, 78
HaZaL, 268
Hazore'im Bedimah Berinah Yiktzoru, 89
Hazzan Zet Nit Vi Kahal Hinter Lakht, 225
Hazzan Zuhgt For Un Der Kahal Entfert, 225
Hedyot Kofaytz Berosh, 250
Hefker Yung, 268
Hefraysh Bayn Mah She'adam Ro'eh Lemah She'ahayrim Mesihin Lo, 29
Helf Mir Gottenyu, Bist Duhkh A Ayl Rahum Vehanun, 213
Heresh Shoteh Vekatan Pegi'atan Ra'ah, 145
Hergayl Na'aseh Teva, 268
Hesah Hada'at, 145
Hesed, 268
Hesed Shel Emet, 268
Heshbon Hanefesh, 268
Hetayr Iska, 268
Hetzyo Lashem Vehetzyo Lakhem, 63
Hevay Pikayah Ushtok, 145
Hevay Zahir Min Hayo'etzkha Lefi Darko, 145
Hevlay Mashi'ah (Hevlo Shel Mashi'ah), 145
Hevu Amaylim Batorah, 52
Hezek Re'iyah Shemayh Hezek, 145
Hi Nayma Udikula Shapil, 145
Hibut Hakever, 268
Hidur Mitzvah, 146
Hikavayd Veshayv Bevaytekha, 89

Hikon Likrat Elohekha Yisrael, 90
Hillul Hashem, 49, 146
Hillul Shabbat, 146
Hini'ah Ma'otav Al Keren Hatzvi, 146
Hitatayf Be'itztela Derabbanan, 269
Hizaharu Bahavurah, 146
Hok Natan Velo Ya'avor, 88
Hok Velo Ya'avor, 269
Hokhayah Tokhi'ah Et Amitekha- Afilu Mayah
  Pe'amim-Talmid Lerav, 46
Holle Kreish (Hollekreish), 269
Hometz Ben Yayin, 146
Hoshi'ah Hashem Ki Gamar Hasid, 90
Hovaysh Bayt Hamidrash, 147
Hoy Ha'omrim Lara Tov Velatov Ra, 90
Hozarni Halilah, 147
Hu Notayn Etzba Bayn Shinehah, 147
Huhguh (Huhgot), 269
Huhzt Moyre Layen Keri'at Shema, 214
Hukat Hagoy, 44
Hukha Ve'itlula, 147
Hulya, Hulya, 270
Hutzpa, Afilu Kelapay Shemaya Mahanay, 61
Hutzpa (Hutzpah), 270

I Efshar Lebayt Hamidrash Belo Hidush, 147
I Sayafa Lo Safra Ve'i Safra Lo Sayafa, 147
Iberkern Vi Sedom Ve'amorah, 14
Ikar Shirah Min Hatorah, 58
Ikh Huhb Nit (Entfer); Lo Lanu Shteyt In Hallel,
  232
Ikh Vel Mit Im Lernen Balak, 62
Ikhlu Mashmanim Ushetu Mamtakim, 90
Ilmalay Meshamrin Yisrael Shetay Shabbatot
  Kehilkhatan Miyad Nigalin, 147
Ilulay Shera'iti Be'aynai Lo He'emanti, 270
Im Ani Kan Hakol Kan, 147
Im Attah Oseh Dalet Raysh-Attah Mahariv Et
  Ha'olam Kulo, 270
Im Ayn Dayah-Havdalah Minayin, 147
Im Ayn Shalom Ayn Klum, 53
Im Ayn Talmidim Ayn Hakhamim, 270
Im Eshkahaykh Yerushalayim Tishkah Yemini, 90
Im Kayn Ayn Ledavar Sof, 147
Im Lavan Garti, 20
Im Lo Akhshav Aymatai?, 15
Im Lo Ta'aminu Ki Lo Tayamaynu, 90
Im Ta'azvayni (Ta'azvenah) Yom, Yomayim
  Ta'azveka, 148
Im Lo Tikanays Hamilah Kulah Tikanays Hetzyah,
  270
Im Shemo Ashayr Gam Lahmo Kashayr, 270
Im Talmid Hakham Nokaym Venotayr Kenahash
  Hu, Hagrayhu Al Motnekha, 148
Im Timatzay (Timtza) Lomar, 148

Im Tirtzu Ayn Zu Aggadah, 270
Im Yirtzeh Hashem, 271
Imru Laylohim, 245
In Di Ketoret Iz Duh Helbenah Un In Der Faynster
  Mishpahah Iz Faranen A Meshumad, 214
In Hodesh Elul Tzitern Afilu Di Fish In Vaser, 237
In Mitn Vayomer (Vayedabayr), 271
In Shtub Iz Geven Tishah b'Ab, 252
In Vuhs Far A Shul Men Davent, Aza Kedushah
  Zuhgt Men (Shpringt Men), 214
Inish Be'inish Paga, Tura Betura Lo Paga, 271
Inshay De'alma, 148
Invay Hagefen Be'invay Hagefen Davar Na'eh
  Umitkabayl, 148
Inyanay Deyoma, 271
Ipkha Mistabra, 148
Ir Hanidahat, 148
Ir Zuhlt Zikh Oysbeten A Gur Yor (A Gut Kvitl),
  232
Ish Damim, 90
Ish Hayashar Be'aynav Ya'aseh, 90
Ish Sefatayim, 90
Ish Tahat Gafno Vetahat Te'aynato, 91
Ishah Begimatri'a Devash, 271
Istera Belagayna Kish-Kish Korya, 148
Ivri (sing.), Ivrim (pl.), 271

Jerobo'am Ben Nebat, 91

Ka Mashma Lan, 148
Ka'anavim Bamidbar, 91
Ka'asher Asetah Asu Lah, 91
Ka'asher Asita Yayaseh Lakh, 91
Ka'asher Asiti Kayn Shilam Li Elohim, 91
Ka'asher Asu Li Kayn Asiti Lahem, 91
Ka'asher Avadeti Avadeti, 250
Ka'asher Dimiti Kayn Hayatah, Vekha'asher Ya'atzti
  Hi Takum, 91
Ka'asher E'eseh Kayn Ta'asun, 92
Ka'asher Yahalom Hara'ayv Vehinayh Okhayl,
  Vehaykitz Veraykah Nafsho, 92
Ka'asher Yateh Haro'eh Et Bigdo, 92
Ka'eved Kadonay, 92
Kahalom Ya'uf, 240
Kabbalat Kinyan, 272
Kabdayhu Vehashdayhu, 272
Kafa Hakadosh Barukh Hu Alayhem Et Hahar
  Kegigit, 30
Kaftor Vaferah, 32
Kaftzah Alav Ziknah, 149
Kakh Havah, 272
Kakh Hayah Ma'aseh, 149
Kakh Onsho Shel Badai She'afilu Amar Emet Ayn
  Shom'in Lo, 149
Kakhomer Beyad Hayotzayr, 245

Kal Shebekalim, 18

Kal Vahomer, 149

Kalu Kol Hakitzin Ve'ayn Hadavar Talui Ela Biteshuvah Uma'asim Tovim, 149

Kam Layh Biderabah Minayh, 149

Kamay Deshatay Hamra-Hamra; Kamay Rafoka-Gerida Deyavlay, 149

Kame'a, 149

Karkafta Dela Manah Tefillin, 150

Karkushta Veshunra Avday Hilula Mitarba Devish Gada, 150

Karov Hashem Lenishberay Layv, 92

Karyana De'igarta Ihu Lehevay Parvanka, 150

Kashah Alai Peridatkhem, 49

Kashah Hi Haparnasah Kiflayim Kelaydah, 272

Kashah Khishol Kinah, 92

Kasheh (Kashin) Lezvogam Ke-Keri'at Yam Suf, 150

Kashin Mezonotav Shel Adam Ke-Keri'at Yam Suf, 150

Kaspam Uzehavam Lo Yukhal Lehatzilam, 92

Katon Vegadol Sham Hu, 92

Katzon Asher Ayn Lahem Ro'eh, 63

Kav Venaki, 150

Kavyakhol, 150

Kavata Itim Latorah?, 150

Kayn Benot Tzelafhad Dovrot, 64

Kayn Yirbu, 272

Kayrayah Mikan Umikan, 150

Kayvan Dedash Dash, 151

Kayvan Shehigid, Shuv Ayno Hozayr Umagid, 151

Kedabayr Ahat Henevalot Tedabayri, 92

Kefatish Yefotzaytz Sela, 92

Kefitzat Haderekh, 18

Kefui Tovah, 151

Kehut Hasa'arah, 151

Kelberne Yotzrot, 225

Keli Ayn Hayfetz Bo, 92

Kenanas Al Gabay Anak, 272

Kenen Oys(en)veynig Vi A Yid Ashray, Vi A Vasser, 214

Kerahaym Av Al Banim, 92

Keratem Deror Ba'aretz Lekhol Yoshveha, 50

Kerav Aylekha, 93

Kerav Legabay Dehina Ve'idahayn, 69

Kerem Hashem Tzeva'ot Bayt Yisrael, 93

Keri'at Yam Suf, 28

Kerovim Hapsulim Leha'ayd, 151

Kesef Metahayr Mamzayrim, 151

Keshay Oref, 73

Keshaym Shemitzvah Al Adam Lomar Davar Hanishma, Kakh Mitzvah Al Adam Shelo Lomar Davar She'ayno Nishma, 151

Keshaym Sheyetzirato Shel Adam Ahar Behaymah, Hayah Ve'of, Kakh Torato Ahar Behaymah,

Hayah Ve'of, 43

Keshoshanah Bayn Hahohim, 93

Keshot Atzmekha Ve'ahar Kakh Keshot Ahayrim, 152

Keshurah, 152

Kesuma Ba'arubah, 152

Ketarnegolim Hamenakrim Be'ashpah, 272

Ketzapihit Bidvash, 28

Ketzutzay Payah, 93

Kevad Ozen, 93

Keyad Hamelekh, 250

Ki Ve'apam Hargu Ish, 22

Kiddush Hashem, 49

Kidra Devay Shutfay La Hamima Vela Kerira, 152

Kilayim, 46

Kile'ahar Yad, 152

Kinat Sofrim Tarbeh Hokhmah, 152

Kinder Megadayl Tzu Zayn Muz Men Huhbn Korah's Ashirut Un Shimshon Hagibor's Gevurah, 60

Kirhok Mizrah Mima'arav, 93

Kishmo Kayn Hu, Nabal Shemo Unebalah Imo, 93

Kleyn Vi A Tal Umuhtorl, 214

Klor (In…) Vi A Yid In Ashray, 214

Kluhgn Oyfn Hurban, 252

Ko'ah Hapo'ayl Benifal, 272

Kofayr Be'ikar, 152

Kofin Oto Ad Sheyomar Rotzeh Ani, 153

Kohen Koray Rishon Ve'aharav Levi, 78

Kol Adam She'ayn Bo Dayah Asur Lerahaym Alav, 153

Kol Adam She'ayn Lo Ishah Sharui Belo Simhah, Belo Berakhah, Belo Tovah, 10

Kol Adam Sheko'ays, Im Hakham Hu Hokhmato Mistakelet Mimenu, 64

Kol Adam Sheyaysh Bo Gasos Haru'ah Ke'ilu Kofayr Ba'ikar, 73

Kol Adam Sheyaysh Bo Yirat Shamayim Devarav Nishma'in, 153

Kol Asher Bilvavekha Agid Lakh, 93

Kol Asher Ya'aseh Yatzli'ah, 93

Kil Asher Yedabayr Bo Yavo, 93

Kil Atzmotai Tomarnah, 93

Kol Be'ishah Ervah, 153

Kol De'alim Gavayr, 153

Kol Demamah Dakah, 93

Kol Devar Ma'akhal Karui Lehem, 19

Kol Devar Sheker She'ayn Omrim Bo Ketzat Emet Bithilato Ayn Mitkayaym Besofo, 60

Kol Emet Emet Tafsayh Lehai, 153

Kol Gal Vegal Sheba Alai Ninati Lo Roshi, 153

Kol Ha'adam Kozayv-Itlekher Huht Zikh Zayne Makos, 232

Kol Haholayk Al Rabo Keholayk Al Hashekhinah, 64

Kol Hakodaym (Bahen) Zakhah, 153
Kol Hame'anayg Et Hashabbat Nitzul Mishibud
    Malkhuyot, 79
Kol Hamehalayl Et Hamo'adot, Ma'alin Alav Ke'ilu
    Hilayl Et Hashabbatot, 50
Kol Hamehazayr Al Hegedulah, Gedulah Borahat
    Mimenu Vekhol Haborayah Min Hagedulah,
    Gedulah Mehazeret Aharav, 154
Kol Hamekabayl Penay Rabo, Ke'ilu Mekabayl
    Penay Shekhinah, 34
Kol Hemekayaym Nefesh Ahat Miyisrael Ke'ilu
    Kayaym Olam Malay, 154
Kol Hamelamayd (Ben) Beno Torah Ma'alah Alav
    Hakatuv Ke'ilu Kiblah Mayhar Horeb, 71
Kol Hamelamayd Bito Torah Ke'ilu Limdah Tiflut,
    154
Kol Hamelamayd Et Ben Havayro Torah, Ma'alah
    Alav Hakatuv Ke'ilu Yoldo, 57
Kol Hamerahaym Al Haberiyot Merahamin Alav
    Min Hashamayim, 73
Kol Hameshalaym Ayno Lokah, 154
Kol Haminim, Kol Ma'aminim, 240
Kol Hamitzta'ayr Atzmo Im Hatzibbur, Zokheh
    Vero'eh Benahamot Tzibbur, 154
Kol Hamon Kekol Shadai, 272
Kol Hamosif Goraya, 32
Kol Hanega'im Adam Ro'eh Huhtz Minigay Atzmo,
    154
Kol Ha'omayr Davar Beshaym Omro Mayvi Ge'ulah
    La'olam, 155
Kol Ha'omayr Devar Hokhmah Afilu Be'umot
    Ha'olam Nikra Hakham, 155
Kol Ha'osayk Batorah Ayno Tzarikh Lo Olah Velo
    Minhah Velo Hatat Velo Asham, 41
Kol Ha'osayk Batorah Nekhasav Matzlihin Lo, 77
Kol Haposayl Pasul-Bemumo Posayl, 155
Kol Harodayf Ahar Hakavod Hakavod Borayah
    Mimenu, 155
Kol Hasandlarim Holkhim Yehayfim, 273
Kol Hathalot Kashot, 30
Kol Koray Bamidbar, 94
Kol Mah De'avid Rahamana, Letav Avid, 155
Kol Mah Sheyomar Lekha Ba'al Habayit Asayh
    (Hutz Mitzay), 155
Kol Mah Sheyaysh Lo Tikhlah Yaysh Lo Tehilah,
    273
Kol Makom Shene'emar "Vayehi" Ayno Ela Lashon
    Tza'ar, 156
Kol Me'ahavayikh Shekhayhukh, 94
Kol Mitzvah Shehazeman Gerama, 156
Kol Nidre Nakht, 245
Kol Of Lemino Yishkon, Uven Adam Ledomeh Lo,
    156
Kol Orayv Lemino, 42

Kol Ram: Bekolo Shel Ram, 77
Kol Roz La Anays Lakh, 94
Kol She'ayno Bemishnah Ayno Bema'aseh, 50
Kol Tayvah Shetzerikhah Lamed Bithilatah Hitil Lah
    Hakatuv Hay Besofah, 65
Kol Teki'ah Vekol Teru'ah-Un Es Kumt Nukh Altz
    Nit Di Yeshu'ah, 245
Kol Yakhol, 240
Kol Yeter Kenitul Dami, 156
Kol Yisrael Arayvim Zeh Bazeh, 156
Kol Zeman She'adam Hai Yaysh Lo Tikvah, 156
Kol Zeman Shehaneshamah Vekirbi, 215
Kotzo (Kotzah) Shel Yud, 156
Krign (Zayn) Shishi, 230
Kudesha Berikh Hu, 157
Kudesha Berikh Hu, Oraita Veyisrael Had, 273
Kulay Alma Lo Peligi, 157
Kupat Harokhlim; Kupah Shel Besamim, 157
Kuzu Bemukhsaz Kuzu, 273
Kvitl (Hib. Pitkah), 273

La'azazayl, 45
Laboker Mishpat, 94
Lahakima Birmiza, Uleshatya Bekurmayza, 274
Lailah Lakhem Mayhazon 94
Lakelev Tashlikhun Oto, 31
Lamah Kakhah Rimitini, 94
Lamah Tiheyeh Ke'ish Nidham, 94
Lamah Yomru Hagoyim, 94
Lamai Nafka Minah?, 157
Lamayd Leshonkha Lomar Ayni Yodaya, Shema
    Titbadayh, 157
Lamed-Vav Tzadikim, 158
Lang Vi A Lulav, 232
Lashav Hirbayt Refu'ot Te'alah Ayn Lakh, 94
Lashav Tityapi, 94
Lashon Medaberet Gedolot, 94
Lashon Remiyah, 95
Lashon Telitai Katil Telitai, 158
Lav Ba'al Devarim Didi At, 158
Lav Davka, 158
Laykh Bekhohakha Zeh, 95
Layt Din Bar Inish (Nash), 158
Layt Din Velayt Dayan, 274
Le'ayla Le'ayla, 240
Le'evil Yaharag Ka'as, Ufoteh Tamit Kinah, 95
Lefi Aniyut Dati (La'aniyut Dati), 274
Lahavdil Bayn Hakodesh Lekhol, 95
Lehayyim, 158
Lehayyim Tovim Uleshalom, 159
Lehem Le'ekhol Uveged Lilbosh, 19
Lehem Tzar Umayim Lahatz, 95
Lekh Lekha Iz Beser Vi Shelah Lekha, 14
Lekha Dumiyah Tehilah, 95

Lekhol Haruhot, 274
Lekhu Venakayhu Balashon, 95
Lema'an Tziyon Lo Ehesheh Ulema'an Yerushalayim Lo Eshkot, 95
Lemi Atem Korin Rebi, Rebi?- Al Yirbu Kemoto Beyisrael, 159
Lemi Attah Ve'ay Mizeh Attah?, 95
Le'olam Al Yavi Adam Atzmo Liday Nisayon, 159
Le'olam Halakhah Kedivray Bet Hillel, 159
Le'olam Tehay Dato Shel Adam Me'urevet Im Haberiyot, 159
Le'olam Ya'asok Betorah Uvemitzvot Af Al Pi Shelo Lishmah, 159
Le'olam Yashlim Adam Parshiyotav Im Hatzibbur Shenayim Mikra Ve'ehad Targum, 64
Le'olam Yehay Adam Invetan Kehillel, Ve'al Yehay Kapdan Keshammai, 159
Le'olam Yehay Adam Rakh Kakaneh Ve'al Yehi Kasheh Ke'erez, 159
Le'olam Yehay Adam Zahir Bikhvod Ishto, 160
Le'olam Yehay Kaspo Shel Adam Matzui Beyado, 73
Le'olam Yesadayr Adam Shevakho Shel Makom Ve'ahar Kakh Yitpalayl, 71
Le'olam Yesapayr Adam belashon Nekiyah, 43
Le'olam Yeshalaysh Adam Shenotav: Shlish Bemikra, Shlish Bemishnah, Shlish Bigemara, 71
Le'olam Yeshaneh Adam Letalmido Derekh Ketzarah, 160
Le'olam Yevakaysh Adam Rahamim Shelo Yehaleh, 76
Le'olam Yidor Adam Be'eretz Yisrael Ve'afilu Ba'ir Sherubah Nokhrim, 51
Le'olam Yilmod Adam Torah Ve'ahar Kakh Yehgeh, 77
Lerik Yagati Letohu Vehevel Kohi Khilayti, 95
Lernen Pasuk, 274
Lernen Tamid Un Kenen Makot, 275
Leshanah Tovah Tikatayvu (Vetayhataymu), 241
Leshaym Velithilah Uletifaret, 95
Leshon Benay Adam, 160
Leshon Hakhamim, 160
Leshonam Herev Hadah, 96
Letekunay Shadartikh Velo Le'ivuti, 160
Letorah, Lehupah, Ulema'asim Tovim, 275
Li Hakesef Veli Hazahav Ne'um Hashem Tzeva'ot, 96
Libi Uvesari Yeranenu El Ayl Hai, 96
Lifnay Ivayr Lo Titayn Mikhshol, 46
Lifnim Mishurat Hadin, 160
Lign In Der Adamah, In She'ol Tahtiyah, 245
Lika Miday Dela Remiza Be'oraita, 160
Likhorah, 160
Limdu Leshonam Daber Sheker, 96

Limud Mayvi Liday Ma'aseh, 160
Lishmo'a El Harinah Ve'el Hatefillah, 96
Lo Al Halehem Levado Yihyeh Ha'adam, 73
Lo Alaykhem (Lo Alaynu), 96
Lo Alman Yisrael, 96
Lo Amar Klum, 161
Lo Amar Velo Klum, 161
Lo Amut Ki Ehyeh-Az S'iz Nit Bashert Tzu Shtarbn Shtarbt Men Nit, 233
Lo Ayt Atah Leha'arikh Bitefillah Sheyisrael Netunin Betzarah, 27
Lo Dibarti Velo Altah Al Libi, 96
Lo Domeh Shomaya Lero'eh, 30
Lo Dubim Velo Ya'ar, 162
Lo El Hinam Dibarti, 96
Lo Emna Mikem Davar, 97
Lo Hakham Velo Tipaysh, 161
Lo Havah Psik Pumyah Migirsayh, 161
Lo Hayah Velo Nivra, 163
Lo Hayu Devarim Mayolam, 163
Lo Ish Besorah Attah Hayom, 97
Lo Kam Kamohu, 97
Lo Kam Navi Od Beyisrael Kemoshe, 79
Lo Katayf Velo Natef, 46
Lo Kayamim Harishonim, 97
Lo Khol Hakarov Karov Velo Khol Harahok Rahok, 275
Lo Kol Ha'adam, Velo Kol Hamakom, Velo Kol Hasha'ot Shavin, 161
Lo Le'ayzer Velo Leho'il, 97
Lo Lefanav Hanayf, 97
Lo Lema'ankhem Ani Oseh, 97
Lo Ma'alin Velo Moridin, 163
Lo Mahshevotai Mahshevotaykhem Velo Darkaykhem Derakhai, 97
Lo Matza Yadav Veraglav, 161
Lo Matzinu Shu'al Shemayt Ba'afar Pir, 161
Lo Mekomo Shel Adam Mekhabdo Ela Adam Mekhabayd Et Mekomo, 58
Lo Miduvshaykh Velo Mayuktzaykh, 62
Lo Mipnay She'ohavim Et Mordecai, Ela Mipnay Shesonin Et Haman, 250
Lo Mit An Alef, 276
Lo Navi Anokhi Velo Ben-Navi Anokhi, 97
Lo Nofayl Anokhi Mikem, 97
Lo Ra'inu Aynah Ra'ayah, 163
Lo Re'i Zeh Kire'i Zeh, 163
Lo Shalavti Velo Shakateti Velo Nahti Vayavo Rogez, 98
Lo Ta'am Velo Rayah, 276
Lo Ta'aminu Ki Yesupar, 98
Lo Ta'amod Al Dam Rayekha, 46
Lo Takum Pa'amayim Tzarah, 98
Lo Takum Velo Tiheyeh, 98

Lo Tasig Gevul Rayakha, 74
Lo Taylaykh Rakhil Be'amekha, 46
Lo Te'uneh Aylekha Ra'ah, 98
Lo Tevashayl Gedi Bahalayv Imo, 32
Lo Tignov, 30
Lo Tikom Velo Titor, 47
Lo Titgodedu, Lo Ta'asu Agudot Agudot, 73
Lo Tokhlu Kodem Shetitpalelu Al Dimkhem, 47
Lo Tosayf Alav Velo Tifra Mimenu, 74
Lo Tosifu, 72
Lo Tov Heyot Ha'adam Levado, 10
Lo Vehayil Velo Veko'ah Ki Im Beruhi, 98
Lo Vemoto Yikah Hakol, Lo Yayrayd Aharav
  Kevodo, 98
Lo Yada Bayn Yemino Lismolo, 98
Lo Yaknit Ish Havayro, 51
Lo Yashavti Vesod Mesahakim, 99
Lo Yehay Adam Notayn Kol Mamono Bezavit Ahat,
  276
Lo Yehay Diburekha Shel Shabbat Kediburekha Shel
  Hol, 161
Lo Yehay Malbushkha Shel Shabbat Kemalbushkha
  Shel Hol, 162
Lo Yehay Tafal Hamur Min Ha'ikar, 162
Lo Yeheratz Kelev Leshono, 27
Lo Yidag Adam Lomar Peloni Yekapayah Parnasati,
  276
Lo Yigra Mitzadik Aynav, 99
Lo Yipalay Mimekha Kol Davar, 99
Lo Yiravu Velo Yitzma'u Velo Yakaym Sharav
  Vashamesh, 99
Lo Yishteh Adam Min Hakos Veyitnenu Lehavayro,
  162
Lo Yitayn Le'olam Mot Latzadik, 99
Lo Yitzlah (Yutzlah), 276
Lo Yitzlah Lakol, 99
Lo Yizrok Berakhah Mipiv, 162
Lo Yodaya Aval Boshet, 99
Lo Yomar Adam Davar Lehavayro Ela Im Kayn
  Korahu, 41
Lo Yosifu Leda'avah Od, 99
Lo Zeh Haderekh, 99
Lo'ayg Larash, 162
Loveh Rasha Velo Yeshalaym Vetzadik Honayn
  Venotayn, 99
Luhmir Uhnfangen (Uhnheybn) Fun Bereishit, 10

Ma'alin Bakodesh Ve'ayn Moridin, 37
Ma'alay Gayrah, 42
Ma'aminim Benay Ma'aminim, 163
Ma'asay Avot Siman Lebanim, 163
Ma'asay Yadai Tovim Bayam, Ve'atem Omrim
  Shirah?, 163
Ma'aseh Shehayah Kakh Hayah, 163

Ma'asekha Yekarvukha Uma'asekha Yerahakukha,
  164
Ma'avir Al Midotav, 164
Ma'avir Sidrah Zayn, 231
Madraygah Elyonah (Tahtonah), 164
Madu'a Derekh Resha'im Tzalayhah, 100
Maggid Devarav Leya'akov...Lo Asah Khayn; Makht
  Rashi: Der Maggid Shtruhft Kahal Un Aleyn
  Tut Er Farkert, 215
Mah Anu Meh Hayaynu?, 246
Mah Bayn Hakham Lenavon? Navon Domeh
  Leshulhani Tagar, 69
Mah Bayn Hasidim Lemitnagdim? Harishonim
  Hoshvim Sheyaysh Lahem Rebbi,
  Veha'aharonim Hoshvim She'ayn Lahem
  Tzorekh Berebbi, 276
Mah Haberiyot Omrot?, 22
Mah Hahevdayl Bayn Matanah Linedavah? Matanah
  Notnim Le'adam Keday Lekarayv Oto,
  Unedavah- Keday Lehipatayr Mimenu, 276
Mah Inyan Shemitah Aytzel Har Sinai, 51
Mah Li Hakha, Mah Li Hatam, 164
Mah Matok Midvash Umeh Az Mayari?, 100
Mah (Mimah) Nafshakh, 164
Mah Paratzta Alekha Paretz?, 21
Mah Sheya'aseh Hazeman Lo Ya'aseh Hasaykhel,
  276
Mah Tivo Shel Ubar Zeh, 164
Mah Tov Umah Na'im Shevet Ahim Gam Yahad,
  100
Mah Tovu Ohalekha Ya'akov Mishkenotekha Yisrael,
  62
Mah Ya'aseh Adam Veyahkaym? Yarbeh Biyeshivah
  Veyamit Bishorah-Yevakaysh Rahamim, 164
Mah Yadata Velo Nayda, 100
Mah-Yafit Yid (Mayafisnik), 224
Mah Yom Miyomayim, 165
Mahashavah Tova Hakadosh Barukh Hu Metzarpah
  Lema'aseh, 165
Mahatzit Hashekel, 34
Mai Bayn Kakh Uvayn Kakh, 165
Mai Dahavah Havah, 165
Mai Dekama, 165
Mai Hazit Didma Didakh Sumak Tefay, Dilma Dema
  Dehahu Gavra Sumak Tefay?, 165
Mai Ka Mashma Lan, 165
Mai Kashyah Lakh, 166
Mai Nafka Minah, 166
Mai Takantayh, 166
Mai Tikkun Gadol, 166
Makah Asher Lo Katuv, 77
Makat Medinah, 166
Makh An Etnahta!, 276
Makhn A Hiluf Ansikhah Oyf Ahallelah, 241

Makhn Ayl Malay Rahamim, 233
Makhn Boray Me'oray Ha'aysh, 228
Makhn Hazkarat Neshamot, 233
Makhn Lela'ag Vakeles, 215
Makhor Sa'ar Harosh, 166
Makom Sheba'alay Teshuvah Omdin Tzadikim
   Gemurim Aynam Omdin, 166
Malakh Hamavet Mah Li Hakha Mah Li Hatam?,
   166
Malakhay Habalah, 166
Malay Kerimon, 167
Malay Vegadush, 167
Man De'ihu Ragil Beshikra Ishtadayl Tadir Beshikra,
   277
Man Dekhar Shemayh, 167
Man Deyahayv Hayay Yahayv Mezonay, 167
Manhig Atzmo Berabbarnut, 167
Ma'ot Rosh Hodesh, 277
Ma'oa Tzur Iz Gut Tzu Farbaysn Mit Hanukkah
   Kez, 248
Ma'oz Tzur Yeshuati- Oy Gottenyu, Gib Zhe
   Parnasah, 248
Mar Bar Rav Ashi, 167
Mar Nefesh, 100
Margalit Tovah Hayetah Beyadkhem Uvikashtem
   Le'abdah Mimeni, 167
Marit Ayin, 167
Masa Umatan, 167
Masa'ot, 65
Mashgi'ah Min Hahalonot, 100
Mashi'ah's Tzaytn, 168
Mayaz Yatza Matok, 100
Matza Min Et Mino, 168
Matza O Motza, 168
May-Alef Ve'ad Tav, 168
Mayahoray Hapargod, 168
Mayeminim Umasmilim, 100
Mayhaykha Taytay, 168
Mayhaykhan Yerek Zeh Hai, 168
Mayhayil El Hayil, 100
Mayigara Ram Levayra Amikata, 169
Mayresha'im Yaytzay Resha, 101
Mayrov Aytzim Lo Yireh Haya'ar, 277
Maysi'ah Lefi Tumo, 169
Mayvin Davar Mitokh Davar, 169
Mazal-Tov, 277
Me'ailin Pila Bekupa Demahta (Aram); Hakhnays Pil
   Bekof Shel Mahat (Heb), 169
Me'at Min Ha'or Doheh Harbayh Min Hahoshekh,
   277
Megaleh Zayn Dem Kaytz, 22
Meh Kol Hehamon Hazeh?, 100
Mehadaysh Zayn Di Levanah, 228
Mahadrin Min Hamehadrin, 169

Heharayf Umegadayf, 169
Mekabl Shabbos Zayn, 222
Mekablin Korbanot Miposhay Yisrael Keday
   Sheyahzeru Bahen Biteshuvah, 41
Mekhabdai Akhabayd Uvozai Yaykalu, 101
Mekimi Mayafar Dal-Az Gott Helft Dem Uhreman;
   Mayashpot Yarim Evyon-Iz Im Gornit Tzu
   Derkenen, 233
Melamayd Zekhut, 169
Mem-Tet Sha'aray Tumah, 221
Men Darf Mit Im Kayn Anaynu Nit Zuhgn, 215
Men Ken Shoyn Nukh Dem Zuhgn A (Rabbanan)
   Kaddish, 215
Men Tor Nit Esn Tishah b'Ab, Vayl Men Leygt
   Tefillin Tzu Minhah, 252
Menay Menay Tekayl Ufarsin, 101
Me'orev (Me'urav) Beda'at Im Haberiyot, 241
Merubim Tzorkhay Amekha, 246
Mesahayk Bekuvya, 169
Mesana Derav Mikarai Lo Ba'ayna, 169
Meshaneh Makon Meshaneh Mazal, 170
Meshufray (De)Shufray, 170
Mesirat Nefesh, 170
Mesushelah's Yuhrn (Tzaytn), 10
Metzora-Motzi Shem Ra, 43
Mezakeh Et Harabim, 170
Mi Lashem Aylai, 35
Mi Shama Kazot, Mi Ra'ah Ka'ayleh?, 101
Mi She'ayno Ko'ays Hakadosh Barukh Hu Ohavo,
   170
Mi She'ayno Notayn Leya'akov Notayn Le'aysav, 18
Mi Shelo Ra'ah Simhat Bayt Hasho'ayvah Lo Ra'ah
   Simhah Miyamav, 170
Mi Shelo Yishtok Mayatzmo, Yashtikuhu Ahayrim,
   277
Mi Shemevakshim Mimenu Mehilah Lo Yehay
   Akhzari Milimhol, 61
Mi Shemevakaysh Yotayr Mitzorkho, Torad Nafsho
   Mito'alto, 277
Mi She'omayr Alef Yomar Gam Bet, 277
Mi Shetarah Be'erev Shabbat Yokhal Beshabbat, 171
Mi Sheyaysh Lo Maneh Rotzeh Matayim, 277
Mi Vaherev Umi Vara'av-Ver Zuhl Nikhshal Vern
   Durkh Der Shverd Un Ver Durkhn Rav, 242
Mi Vami Haholkhim, 27
Mibinta Deroshi Ve'ad Tufra Dekhari, 171
Midah Keneged Midah, 171
Midat Hadin, Midat Harahamim, 10
Midat Hasidut, 171
Midat Rahamim Shitaf Hakadosh Barukh Hu
   Lemidat Hadin, 11
Midat Sedom, 14
Midaya Vifil, 236
Midbar (Midbardik), 57

Mide'oraita (De'oraita), 171
Miderabbanan (Derabbanan), 171
Midvar Sheker Tirhak, 32
Migdal Haporayah Ba'avir, 171
Mihut Ve'ad Serokh-Na'al, 14
Mikaf Raglo Ve'ad Kadkado Lo Hayah Vo Mum, 101
Mikaf Regel Ve'ad Rosh Ayn Bo Metom, 101
Mikhlal Lav Attah Shomaya Hayn, 35
Mikan Va'aylekh, 171
Mikarnay Re'aymin Ad Baytzay Kinim, 172
Mikol Melamdai Hiskalti, 101
Miktzat Shevaho Shel Adam Omrim Befanav,
    Vekhulo Shelo Befanav, 172
Milah Besela Umashtoka Bitrin, 172
Milay De'alma, 172
Milaydah Umibeten Umayhayrayon, 102
Milhemtah Shel Torah, 172
Milta Debedihuta, 172
Milta Dela Shkhiha, 172
Mimayla, 172
Mimeray Rashvatakh Paray Ifra, 172
Mimitzrayim Ve'ad Haynah, 246
Mimoshe Ve'ad Moshe Lo Kam Ke-Moshe, 277
Min Hapahat El Hapah, 102
Min Hashamayim Yerahamu, 172
Min ha-TaNakH Yadekha Al Tanah, 277
Min Hayom Hahu Vahalah, 102
Minhag Avotayhem Beyadayhem, 173
Minhag Avotaykhem Beyadkhem, 173
Minhag Avotaynu (Yisrael) Torah Hi, 173
Minhag Mevatayl Halakhah, 173
Minhag Okayr Halakhah, 173
Minhag Shtut, 173
Minyan Otiyot Shel Aseret Hadibrot Haym TaRYaG,
    30
Mipi Hashemu'ah, 173
Mipi Olelim Veyonkim Yisadeta Oz, 102
Mipnay Darkay Shalom, 173
Mipnay Sayvah Takum Vehadarta Penay Zakayn, 47
Mishayshet Yemay Bereishit, 11
Mishenikhnas Adar Marbin Besimhah, 174
Mishenikhnas Av Mema'atin Besimhah, 174
Mishikhmo Vamalah Gavo'ah Mikol Ha'am, 102
Mishmar, 277
Mishneh Torah, 70
Mistama, 278
Mistapayk Bemu'at, 278
Mit Akhilah Heybt Zikh Uhn Zayn Yotzayr, 242
Mit Ale ReMaH Ayvarim, 215
Mit Kiddush Levanah Ken Men Zikh Nit Uhpfastn,
    228
Mitat Neshikah, 174
Mitokh Shelo Lishmah Ba Lishmah, 62
Mitzvah Haba'ah Ba'avayrah, 174

Mitzvah Larutz Levayt Hakeneset, 278
Mitzvah Min Hamuvhar, 174
Mitzvah Sheba'ah Leyadekha Al Tahamitzena, 28
Mitzvat Asayh Shehazeman Gerama Nashim
    Peturot, 174
Mi'uta Demi'uta, 175
Mizrah, 278
Mo'adim Lesimhah-Hagim Uzemanim Lesason, 233
Modeh Bemiktzat Hata'anah, 175
Morenu, 278
Moshayl Ba'adam Tzadik Moshayl Yirat Elohim, 102
Moshe Anav Me'od Mikol Ha'adam, Af Mayavot, 59
Mosifin Mihol Al Hakodesh, 175
Motza Sefatekha Tishmor, 76
Motzi La'az, 175
Motzi Shaym Ra, 175
Muktzeh Mahamat Mi'us, 175
Mum Shebeha Al Tomar Lehavayrekha, 175
Mushlam Bekhol Hama'alot, 176
Mutar Lo Le'adam Leshanot Bidvar Hashalom, 176
Mutav Yehudi Beli Zakayn Mayasher Zakayn Beli
    Yehudi, 278

Na'alamim, 102
Na'aseh Venishma, 32
Nafal Tora Hadad Lesakina, 176
Nafka Minah, 176
Naflah Ateret Roshaynu, 102
Nahara Nahara Ufashtayh, 176
Nahat Ru'ah, 176
Nashim Rahamaniyot Hayn, 176
Nashim Tomar Lahen Belashon Rakah, 30
Nasog Ahor, 278
Naton (Natata) Torat Kol Ehad Ve'ehad Beyado?,
    176
Navon Zeh Hamayvin Davar Mitokh Davar, 176
Nayr Le'ehad Nayr Lemayah, 176
Nayro Ya'ir, 246
Nays Gadol Hayah Sham, 248
Naytzah Yisrael Lo Yeshakayr, 102
Nefishay Gamlay Savay Dete'inay Mashkhay
    Dehognay, 176
Nehba El Hakaylim, 102
Neshamah Yetayrah Notayn Hakadosh Barukh Hu
    Be'adam Erev Shabbat, Ulemotza'ay Shabbat
    Kodesh Notlin Otah Mimenu, 35
Neshekh: Deka Nakhit Layh, Deka Shakil Minayh
    Midi Delo Yahiv, 52
Neshekh: Ribit Shehi Kineshikhat Nahash-Ve'ayno
    Margish, Ufitom Hu Mevatbayt Venofayah Ad
    Kadkado, 52
Nesi'at Kapayim, 58
Netzor Leshonkha Mayra, 102
Nibul Peh, 176

Niftar (Nistalayk), 177
Nikar Hu Zeh Shelo Avar Al Pithah Shel Torah, 177
Nikhnas Yayin Yatza Sod, 177
Nilayti Hinahaym, 103
Nilayti Khalkayl Velo Ukhal, 103
Nilayti Neso,103
Nimshal Kabehaymot Nidmu, 103
Nisharnu Me'at Mayharbeh, 103
Nistalayk, 279
Nit Ale Purim Treft Zikh A Nes, 251
Nitl, 279
Noah Hayah Tzadik Bedorotav, 12
Nod (Shel) Dema'ot, 279
Nogaya Bedavar, 177
Nokaym Venotayr, 177
Nuhkh Amol Odekha, 233
Nun Hafukhah, 59
Nusah (Aram. pl. Nusha'ot; Heb. pl. Nusahim), 279

O Havruta O Mituta, 177
Od Me'at Usekaluni, 29
Odkha Mahazik Betumatekha, 103
Ohel (pl. Ohalim), 279
Okayr Harim, 177
Olam Hafukh, 178
Olam Hazeh- Olam Haba, 178
Olam Lesulam Hu Domeh: Zeh Oleh Vezeh Yorayd, 279
Omayr Ve'oseh, 178
Omdin Berumo Shel Olam, 178
Ona'at Devarim, 47
Oneg Shabbat, 103
Orayah-Porayah (sing.), (pl. Orhay-Porhay), 178
Osayk Bemitzvah Patur Min Hamitzvah, 178
Otiyot Mahkimot, 280
Otiyot Porhot, 178
Otiyot Shel Emet Merohakin Zeh Mizeh Veshel Sheker Mekorvin, 179
Oto Ha'ish, 179
Oy, 103
Oy Lah Lerabbanut Shemekaveret Et Be'alehah, 179
Oy Lahem Labriyot Shero'ot Ve'aynam Yodot Mah Hayn Ro'ot, 179
Oy Lerasha Oy Lishkhayno, 179
Oy Li Omayr, Oy Li Im Lo Omayr, 179
Oy Li Miyotzri Oy Li Miyitzri, 11
Oyfshteyn Tehiyat Hamaytim, 216
Oysluhzn Kol Hamato, 221
Oysluhzn (Oysgisn) Dem Tzuhrn (Dem Ka'as Kol Hamoto, Dem Gantzn Shefokh-Hamatkha) Oyf..., 236
Oysnemens (Oysheybens) Un Aynnemens, 216
Oysrufn Dem Molad, 226
Oznayim Lakotel, 280

Pamalya Shel Malah, 179
Panim shel Ekhah, 104
Panim Hadashot, 180
Parashat Emor Shert Men Di Lemer, 50
Pardays, 280
Parev, 280
Parhesya (Befarhesya), 180
Pashat Lo Et Haregel, 180
Pasuk Bizmano, Kenahama Bishat Re'avon (Re'ava), 280
Pasul Le'aydut, 180
Patah Bekhad Vesiyaym Behavit, 180
Patur Belo Kelum I Efshar, 42
Patur Vern Fun A Hamaytz, 236
Pe'amim She'adam Shotayk Umekabayl Sakhar Al Shetikato, Ufe'amim She'adam Medabayr Umekabayl Sakhar Al Diburo, 180
Peh Ehad, 104
Peh Mayfik Margaliyot, 180
Pere Adam, 14
Perutah Uferutah Mitztarefet Leheshbon Gadol, 181
Peshuto Kemashma'o, 12
Pi Keherev Hadah, 104
Pi Tzadik Yehegeh Hokhmah, 104
Pidyon Shevuyim Mitzvah Rabbah Hi, 181
Piku'ah Nefesh Doheh Shabbat, 35
Pilay Fela'ot (Pilay Fela'im), 26
Pilpul, 181
Pinkas, 181
Pintele Yid, 280
Pirtzah Korah Laganav, 181
Pishon Peh, 41
Posayah Al Shtay Hase'ipim, 104
Praven Taneysim (Ta'aniyot), 252
Pshetl, 280
Puk Hazi Mai Ama Davar, 181
Punkt Draytzn, 182
Purim Dankt Men Nit, 251
Purim Iz Nit Kayn Yom-Tov Un Kadahat Iz Nit Kayn Kreynk, 251
Purim Iz Nor Eyn Tuhg Un A Kabtzn Iz Men A Gantz Yor, 251
Purim Katan Darf (Meg) Men Zikh Uhnshikurn Uhber Yom Kippur Katan Darf Men Nit Fastn, 251

Ra'ah Gayhinom Petuhah Mitahtav, 19
Ra'ayv Kekelev, 182
Rabbi Lo Shena'ah (Shanah), R. Hiya Minayin Lo?, 182
Rabbi Mekhabayd Ashirim, 182
Rabu Misa'arot Roshi Sonai Hinam, 104
Raglay Kadma Ve'azla, 280
Ragzan Lo Altah Beyadayh Ela Ragzanuta, 182

Rahamana (Hakadosh Barukh Hu) Liba Ba'ay, 182
Rahamana Litzlan (Nitzlan), 182
Rahamanim Benay Rahamanim, 183
Rahel Mevakah Al Banehah, 104
Rasha Lamah Takeh Rayekha, 26
RaShKeBeHaG, 280
Ratzah Hakadosh Barukh Hu Lezakot Et Yisrael,
    Lefikhakh Hirbah Lahem Torah Umitzvot, 183
Raykh Vi Korah, 61
Rayshit Hokhmah Yirat Hashem, 104
Rebi, Lekha Sharay Veli Asur?, 281
ReHaSH, 281
Rehayla Batar Rehayla Azla, Ke'uvday Imah Kakh
    Uvday Berata, 183
Re'iyah Mayvi'ah Liday Zekhirah, 60
Re'uyan Le'otah Itztala, 183
Ribbon Ha'olamim, 183
Ribbono Shel Olam, 183
Ribit, 52
Rishon Le-Zion, 281
Ro'eh Ve'ayno Nireh, 183
Rofay Elil Kulkhem, 104
Romemot Ayl Bigronam, Veherev Pifiyot Beyadam,
    104
Rosh Hamedabrim Bekhol Makom, 184
Rosh Hodesh Bentchn, 226
Roshkha Vehar (Rayshaykh Vehar), 184
Rov Ganvay Yisrael Ninhu, 184
Ru'ah Hakodesh, 184

Saba Bevayta Paha Bevayta, Savta Bevayta Sima
    Bevayta, 184
Sadna De'ara Had Hu, 184
Sakanot Nefashot, 185
Satan Mekatrayg, 185
Sayata Dishmaya (Sayata Hu Min Shemaya), 186
Sefirah Tzayt, 221
Seh Fezurah Yisrael, 104
Sekhar Mitzvah Behai Alma Leka, 72
Selihot Teg, 237
Semikhut-Haparashah, 32
Se'udat Mitzvah, 186
Sevara, 186
Sha'atnez, 48
Sha'aray Dimah Lo Ninalu, 187
Sha'at Hadhak Shani, 187
Shabbat Le'oneg Nitan Velo Letza'ar, 281
Shabbat Shalom Umevorakh, 222
Shabbos-Goy, 281
Shabbos Huht A Yid A Neshamah Yetayrah, 222
Shadkhan, 281
Shagur Befiv, 186
Shakaytz Teshaktzenu Veta'ayv Teta'avenu Ki
    Hayrem Hu, 73

Shakla Vetarya, 186
Shalom, 21
Shalom Bayit, 186
Shalosh Shel Puranut, 70
Sham Tehay Kevuratkhem, 30
Shamor Mahsom Lefeh, 105
SHaTZ MaTZ, 281
Shaym Havaya, 186
Shaymot, 281
Shaynah Beshabbat Ta'anug, 282
Shaytl, 282
Shayv Ve'al Ta'aseh, 186
She'ar Yerakot, 236
She'at Hakosher, 187
She'ayno Yodaya Lishol, 236
Sheker Asur Ledabayr, Aval Et Ha'emet Lo Tamid
    Hovah Lesapayr, 282
Sheker Ayn Lo Raglayim, 187
Shekulah Tzedakah Keneged Kol Hamitzvot, 187
Shelkha Kodem Lekhol Adam, 187
Shelo Matzinu Shu'al Shemayt Ba'afar Pir, 188
Shelosh Esray Midot, 35
Sheloshah Devarim Mevatlim Gezayrah Kashah:
    Tefillah, Tzedakah, Uteshuvah, 188
Sheloshah She'akhlu-Er Est Far Drayen, 219
Sheloshah She'akhlu Ke'ehad Hayavin Lezamayn,
    79
Sheluho Shel Adam Kemoto, 28
Shemini Shemonah Shanah Shemaynah, 42
Shemor Atzmekha Shelo Teheta, 188
Shemor Li Ve'eshmor Lakh, 188
Shenayim Ohazim Betalit, 188
Shetikah Kehoda'ah Damya, 188
Shetikah Yafah Besha'at Hatefillah, 282
Shetikutekha Yafah Midiburekha, 188
Sheva Denehemta, 70
Sheva Mitzvot Benay Noah, 13
Shfikhut Damim, 188
Sh'hi Ph'i, 189
Shkor Vi Lot, 15
Shikroto Shel Lot, 15
Shilhay Dekaita Kashya Mikaita, 189
Shimu Na Hamorim, 61
Shinui Hashaym, 189
Shirayim, 282
Shivah Medoray Gehinnom, 189
Shiviti, 282
Shiviti Hashem Lenegdi Tamid, 105
Shlita, 283
Shluhgn Hoshanot, 233
Shluhgn Kapparot, 246
Shluhgn Zikh Al-Hayt, 247
Sho'alin Vedorshin Behilkhot Hapesah Kodem
    Hapesah Sheloshim Yom, 59

Shokhayn (Yorayd) Afar, 105
Sholayf Herev, 105
Shomayr Petayim Hashem, 105
Shor Habar, 189
Shoteh Ayn Lo Takanah, 189
Shpring Nit Kayn Kadosh Un Buk Zikh Nit Kayn
    Modim, 216
Shraga Betihara Mai Ahani?, 190
Shraybn In Halbe Lavanot, 228
Shraybn Mit Kiddush Levanah Osiyot, 228
Shrayen Shema Yisrael, 216
Shtay Torot Nitnu Leyisrael, Ahat Biktav Ve'ahat
    Be'al Peh, 53
Shteln Zikh (Oysgeyn) Shemoneh Esrayh, 216
Shteyt Oyf (Kinder) Le'avodat Haboray, 237
Shteyt Oyf Tzu Selihot, 237
Shtibl, 283
Shtile (Hoykhe) Shemoneh Esrayh, 216
Shtreiml Bimkom Tefillin, 283
Sihat Hulin, 190
Sihatan Shel Yisrael Torah Hi, 283
S'iz Nuhkh Vayt Tzu Kol Hamira, 236
Siman Yafeh, 190
Simu Yad Al Peh, 105
Sinat Hinam, 48
Sitra Ahra, 283
Skuhtzl Kumt, 216
Sof Adam Lamut Vesof Behaymah Lishhitah, 190
Sof Ganav Litliyah, 283
Sof Ma'aseh-Bemahashavah Tehilah, 223
Sofo Mokhi'ah al Tehilato, 190
Somaykh Hashem Lekhol Hanoflim, 105
Stam Makshan Am-Ha'aretz, 283
Stiradik, 190

Ta'ala Ve'idanayh Segid Layh, 22
Tafasta Merubah Lo Tafasta, Tafasta Mu'at Tafasta,
    190
Tahat Ahavati Yistenuni, 105
Takhlit Hayedi'ah Shenayda Shelo Nayda, 283
Tal-Umatar Tuhg, 217
Talmid Hakham (pl. Talmiday Hakhamim), 190
Talmid Hakham Tzarikh Shelo Yehay Bo Davar Shel
    Dofi, 283
Talmid Hakham Tzarikh Sheyehay Vo Ehad
    Mishmonah Bishminit (Ga'avah), 190
Talmid Shelo Ra'ah Siman Yafeh Bemishnato
    Hamaysh Shanim, Shuv Ayno Ro'eh, 57
Talmidim Keruyim Banim, Veharav Karui Av, 72
Talmiday Hakhamim Ayn Lahem Menuhah, 191
Talmiday Hakhamim Marbim Shalom Ba'olam, 191
Talmud Mayvi Liday Yirah, Vehirah-Liday Shemirah,
    Ushemirah-Liday Ma'aseh, 74
Talmud Torah Keneged Kulam, 191

Tamot Nafshi Im Pelishtim, 105
Tartay Desatray, 191
Tartay Kalay Mayhad Gavra Lo Mishtama'ay, 192
TaRYaG Mizvot, 192
Ta'ut Le'olam Hozayr (Hozeret), 283
Tavo Alav Berakhah, 192
TaYKU (Tiku), 192
Tayn Aynekha Velibkha Al Devarekha, 35
Tayn Li Yavneh Vehakhamehah, 192
Tazri'a-Metzora Rayst Keri'ah Der Ba'al Keri'ah
    (Koray), 43
Te'ano Hitim Vehodah Lo Bise'orim, 192
Tefillot Keneged Temidin Tiknom, 193
Tehay Havivah Alekha Mitzvah Kalah Kemitzvah
    Hamurah, 74
Tehay Temayah Shivat Yamim, 44
Tehay Yetzi'atkha Min Ha'olam Kevi'atkha Le'olam-
    Belo Hayt, 77
Tehiyat Hamaytim, 283
Tehiyat Hamaytim Min Hatorah, 70
Teki'at Kaf, 284
Temotayt Rasha Ra'ah, 106
Ten Lo Maneh Vivakaysh Matayim, 284
Tevaleh Utehadaysh, 284
Teven Attah Makhnis La'afarayim?, 193
Tevi'ut Ayin, 193
Tikkun, 284
Tinok Shenishbah, 193
Tibtarekhu Min Hashamayim, 193
Tizkeh Leshanim Rabot, 285
Tohu Vavohu, 11
Tokh Keday Dibur, 193
Tokhahah, 53
Tokhho Kevaro, 33
Toleh Beda'at Ahayrim, 193
Torah Lishmah, 193
Torah Mateshet Koho Shel Adam, 194
Torah Mehazeret Al Akhsanya Shelah, 194
Torah She'ayn La Bayt Av Aynah Torah, 194
Torah Shebe'al Peh Halakhah Lemoshe Misinai, 18
Torah Ugedulah Bemakom Ehad, 194
Torakh Hatzibbur (Tirkha Detzibbura), 194
Torat Hashem Temimah, 106
Tov Begimatri'a Yud Zayin, 285
Tov Lashamayim Velabriyut Zehu Tzadik Tov, 194
Tov Latzadik Vetov Lishkhayno, 57
Tov Me'at Bekavanah Mayharbot Shelo Bekavanah,
    285
Tov Shebarofim Lagayhinom, 194
Tovayl Vesheretz Beyado, 195
Toviyah Hatah Vezigud Mingad, 195
Tray Kalay Lo Mishtama'ay, 195
Tuhmer Iz Bay Zey Yuh Amuhl A Seder Fregn Zey:
    Mah Nishtanah, 236

Tul Kisaym Mibayn Shinekha, Tul Korah Mibayn Aynekha, 195
Tura Betura Lo Paga, Inish Be'inish Paga, 285
TUSHLABA, 285
Tza'ar Ba'alay Hayyim, 76
Tza'ar Gidul Banim, 195
Tzadikim Omrim Me'at Ve'osin Harbayh, 195
Tzapayh Leshulhan Ahayrim, 196
Tzarah Korah Lehavertah, 106
Tzarat Rabim Hatzi Nehamah, 285
Tzarikh Iyun, 286
Tzaydah Laderekh, 21
Tzedek Tzedek Tirdof, 74
Tzeyln Sefirah (Tzeyln Omer), 221
Tzitern Vi A Frumer Yid In Di Aseret Yemay Teshuvah, 237
Tzo'akin Ve'aynam Ne'enin, 196
Tzon Kadashim, 286
Tzorva Mayrabbanan, 196
Tzu Di Eser Makot Nemt Men Kayn Hatan Nit Tzu Gast, 236
Tzu Gott Un Tzu Layt, 196
Tzu Gott's Nuhmen, 247
Tzurik Geyt Men Nor Bay Oseh Shalom, 217

Ugah Beli Hafukhah, 106
Uhn Hotza'ah Iz Nituh Kayn Hakhnasah, 217
Uhngehoybn Mit Kiddush Un Ge'endikt Mit Kaddish, 223
Uhnheybn Fun Uhneyb (Fun Alef-Bet, Fun Bereishit, Fun Mah-Tovu, Fun Barukh She'amar), 217
Uhnkumen Vi Keri'at Yam Suf, 29
Uhnmakhn A Hurban, 252
Uhnmakhn A Tisha b'Ab, 252
Uhnmakhn A Ya'aleh, 247
Uhpgeshluhgene Hoshana, 234
Uhprikhtn Dem Seder, 236
Uhprikhtn Hatzot, 217
Uhptzeyln (Oystzeyln) Ahat Ve'ahat (Ahat Ushtayim), 247
Um Rosh Hashanah Huht Der Grester Kabtzn A Truhpele Huhnik, 242
Umot Ha'olam, 196
Uvayom Hashmini Yimol, 43
Uvi'arta Hara Mikirbekha, 75

Va'ani Va'ar Velo Ayda, 106
Vahai Bahem Velo Sheyamut Bahem, 45
Vayakam Melekh Hadash, 26
Vayakhayl Moshe-Ukhenash Moshe, 36
Vayishman Yeshurun Vayivat, 79
Vayomer-David-Glitsh, 217
Ve'ahavta Lerayakha Kamokha, 48

Ve'akhalta Vesavata Uvayrakhta, 219
Ve'al Kulam, 217
Vegn A Bisl Boyml Makht Men Aza Groysn Yom-Tov, 248
Vehagita Bo Yomam Valaila, 106
Vehay Ahikha Imakh, 52
Vekhol Hamarbeh Lesapayr Haray Zeh Meshubah, 237
Velamah Titgareh Bera'ah, 106
Ven Mashiah Vet Kumen Veln Ale Yamin Tovim Batl Vern, Nor Purim Vet Blaybn, 251
Verosho La'av Yagi'a, 106
Vest Nuhkh A Fule Darfn Zuhgn Avinu Malkaynu (Biz Du Vest Oysveynen Dem Keren), 242
Vetalmud Torah Keneged Kulam; A Bisl Mayhaykha-Taysi Iz Bilkher Fun Altz, 218
Vetzidkatkha Betezedek-Roshay Tayvot: Biz Tzu Der Keshene, 228
Veyatayd Tihyeh Lekha Al Azaynekha, 76
Veyiten Lekha-Kayn Gelt Iz Nituh, Mital Hashamayim- Nituh Vu Tzu Layen, Mishmanay Ha'aretz-Duhs Gelt Iz Baym Paritz, 229
Vi A Floy In Yekum Purkan, 225
Vi A Shed Far A Mezuzah Uhder Far Shema Yisrael, 218
Vi A Yavan In Sukkah, 234
Vi A Yid Tzu Khapn A Minhah, 221
Vi Der Rosh Hashanadiker Musaf, 242
Vi Di Shul, Azoy Shpringt Men Kadosh, 218
Vi Kumt A Patch Tzu Gut Shabbos?, 223
Vi Kumt Attah Harayta Tzu Der Arenda?, 234
Vi Kumt Aysav In Keri'at Shema Arayn?, 218
Vi Kumt Hodu In Mikveh (In Buhd Arayn)?, 218
Vuhkhedige, Shabbosdige, Yomtovdige Shemoneh Esrayh, 218
Vuhs Far A Semikhut Haparshah Huht Duhs Tzutuhn Mit...?, 32
Vuhs Huht A Patch Tzutuhn Mit Yekum Purkan?, 225
Vuhs Tifer Men Bukt Zikh Modim, Vuhs Vayter Geyt Men Oseh Shalom Tzurik, 218

Wachnacht, 286
Wie Haben Sie Gebaut?, 286
Wimpel, 286

Yado Al Ha'elyonah (Al Hatahtonah), 196
Yado Vakol Veyad Kol Bo, 14
Yafah Shetikah Lahakhamim, Kal Vahomer Letipshim, 196
Yagata Ufatahta Yega Usetom, 196
Yagati Velo Matzati Al Ta'amayn, 197
Yagdil Torah Veyadir, 106

Yagi'ah Yardayn El Pihu, 107
Yago'a Be'eser Etzba'ot, 197
Yahayv Hokhmeta (Hokhmah) Lehakimin, 107
Yahrtzeit, 287
YaKNeHaZ, 197
Yako, 287
Yam Hatalmud, 287
Yamim Nora'im, 242
Yamin Yedabayru, 107
Yarmlke, 287
Yarshi'akha Fikha Velo Ani, Usefatekha Ya'anu Vakh,
    107
Yashayn Kan Vero'eh Halom Be'aspamyah, 197
Yashvu Ish Tahat Gafno Vetahat Te'ayno, 107
Yatush Kadamkha Bema'asayh Bereishit, 197
Yayin Nesekh, 107
Yayin Yesamah Levav Enosh, 107
Yatza Ish Peloni Naki Minkhasav, 197
Yatzo Beshayn Va'ayin, 198
Yavo Hanays Mikol Makom, 198
Yayin Ben Hometz, 198
Yayin Ben Yayin, 198
Yayin Hameshumar, 198
Yaysh Dorshin Leshevah Veyaysh Dorshin Lignai, 13
Yaysh Lo Maneh Rotzeh Matayim, 287
Yaytzer Layv Ha'adam Ra Mine'urav, 13
Yeder Muhntik Un Duhnershtik, 252
Yederer Veynt Oyf Mi Yihyeh, 243
Yefay-Fiyah, 108
Yegi'a Kapekha Ki Tokhayl, Ashrekha Vetov Lakh,
    108
Yehay Haviv Alekha Din Perutah Kedin Shel Mayah
    Maneh, 198
Yeherad Libi Veyitar Mimekomo, 108
Yehi Makiraykh Barukh, 108
Yehudi (sing.), Yehudim (pl.), 287
Yemay Hara'ah-Aylu Yemay Haziknah, 198
Yerushalayim de-Lita, 288
Yesharim Darkhay Hashem, Tzadikim Yaylkhu Vam
    Ufoshim Yikashlu Vam, 108
Yeshu'at Hashem Keheref Ayin, 288
Yesurin Shel Ahavah, 198
Yibadayl Lehayyim Arukhim, 288
Yiftah Bedoro Kishmuel Bedoro, 75
Yihus, 198
Yimah Shemo (Vezikhro), 288
Yirat Hashem Hi Hokhmah, Vesur Mayra Binah, 108
Yirat Shamayim, 72
Yishar Ko'ah (Yishar Kohekha), 36
Yishme'u Oznekha Mah Shepikha Medabayr, 199
Yisrael Sava, 199
Yisrael Ve'oraita Had Hu, 288
Yisro's Nemen, 31
Yodaya Sefer, 108

Yom, 288
Yom Alef (Rishon)-Orayah, Yom Bet (Shayni)-
    Torayah, Yom Gimmel (Shelishi)- Sorayah, 289
Yom Besorah Hu Va'anahnu Mahshim, 108
Yom Kippur Truhpns, 247
Yom Kippur Zuhgt Men Hatati, Uhber Men Zuhgt
    Nit Lo Ehteh, 247
Yom Kippurdig, 247
Yom Nikhnas Veyom Yaytzay, Shabbat Nikhnah etc.,
    Hodesh etc., Shanah etc., 199
Yom Petirah, 199
Yoshayv Ohel, 18
Yosif Al Hatato Fesha, 109
Yotayr Misheyisrael Shamru Et Hashabbat, Shamrah
    Hashabbat Otam, 289
Yotzay Dofen, 199
Yotzayr Mesharetim Va'asher Mesharetav- Shaf Dir
    Meshartim Un Gey Dir Aleyn, 219
Yovel, 52
Yud Gimmel Midot, 36

Zakharti Lakh Hesed Ne'urayikh Ahavat
    Kelulotayikh, 109
Zakhin Le'adam Shelo Befanav, 199
Zakhor Veshamor- Zikh Tzu Haltn Bedibur Ehad,
    223
Zarok Even Lemerculis, 199
Zay A Tzadik Uhber Nit Kayn Vetzidkoskha, 229
Zaykher Tzadik Livrakhah, 200
Zeh Bekhoh Vezeh Bekhoh, 109
Zeh Neheneh Vezeh Lo Hasayr, 200
Zehirah Mayv'iah Liday Zerizuf, 200
Zekhirah Mayv'iah Liday Ma'aseh, 60
Zekhut Avot, 289
Zekhuto Yagayn Alaynu, 289
Zeman Tefillah Lehud Uzeman Torah Lehud, 200
Zrizin Makdimin Lemitzvot, 16
Zerok Hutra Le'avirah A'ikarayh Ka'ay, 16
Zibetzn Iz Keminyan Tov, Akhtzn Iz Keminyan Hai,
    Hai Tzum Lebn; Hundert Un Hundert Un Eyns
    Iz Altz Eyns, 289
Zibn Vuhkn Tzeylt Men, Dray Vuhkhn Veynt Men,
    Fir Vuhkhn Bluhzt Men, 238
Zikh Shteln Komemiyut, 219
Zikhrono Livrakhah, 200
Zil Batar Shetikuta, 200
Zitzn Al Hatorah Ve'al Ha'avodah, 231
Zo Lo Shamati, Kayotzay Bah Shamati, 201
Zokheh Tzu Zayn Tzu Zen Benehamat Tziyon
    Virushalayim, 109
Zu Torah Veru Sekharah?, 201
Zuhgn Selihot, 238
Zuza Le'alala Lo Shkhiha Litelita Shkhiha, 201

Index of Hebrew, Yiddish, and Aramaic

א בחור מאכט קידוש איבער שפעגער (און הבדלה איבער א קאלטן פייערטאפ), 221

א גוטן מועד, 231

א הויכע קדושה, 209

א חזן א דראנג, 221

א חכם פון מה נשתנה, 234

א טייערער קדיש, 209

א טרוקענער מי שברך העלפט ווי א טויטן באנקעס, 229

א טרוקענער מי שברך העלפט ווי טרוקענע באנקעס, 229

א יאר מיט א מיטוואך, 114

א יידענע אן א צאינה וראינה איז ווי א שייגעטץ אן א פייפל, 226

א משל: איבער דעם בלאזט מען המן און מען קלאפט שופר, 249

א משל כחרס הנשבר, 238

א נאמען פון דער הפטרה, 229

א פראסטער חי וקים, 238

א קול פון אן עשר, 16

א רשע פון דער הגדה, 234

א שיינע ריינע כפרה, 243

אב אחד יכול לפרנס עשרה בנים, ועשרה בנים אינם יכולים לפרנס אב אחד, 259

אב בחכמה ורך בשנים, 259

אבד חסיד מן הארץ, 85

אבות אכלו בסר ושני בנים תקהינה, 85

אגב אורחא, 115

אבינו שבשמים, 121

אבן משכית לא תתנו בארצכם להשתחות עליה, 50

אבנים שחקו מים, 85

אבק לשון הרע, 121

אבר מן החי, 12

אגיל ואשמח-קיילעכדיק און שפיטצעדיק, 231

אדם דואג על אבוד דמיו ואינו דואג על אבוד ימיו, 257

אדם יסודו מעפר וסופו לעפר-בינו לבינו איז גוט א טרונק בראנפן (בינותים כאפט מען א בלינטשיק), 238

אדם להבל דמה, ימיו כצל עובר, 83

אדם לעמל יולד, 83

אדם מועד לעולם, 114

אדם מקדש עצמו מעט מקדשין אותו הרבה, מלמטה-

מקדשין אותו מלמעלה, בעוה"ז-מקדשין אותו לעוה"ב, 41

אדם קרוב אצל עצמו, 114

אדם שאין בו דעה אסור לרחם עליו, 114

אדמו"ר (אדמו"רים), 257

אדרבא (אדרבה), 114

אהבה מבטלת (מקלקלת) את השורה, ושנאה מבטלת (מקלקלת) את השורה, 115

או חברותא או מיתותא, 177

אוהל (אוהלים), 279

אוי, 103

אוי לה לרבנות שמקברת את בעליה, 179

אוי להם לבריות שרואות ואינן יודעות מה הן רואות, 179

אוי לי אם אומר, אוי לי אם לא אומר, 179

אוי לי מיוצרי אוי לי מיצרי, 11

אוי לרשע אוי לשכנו, 179

אויסלאזן (אויסגיסן) דעם צארן (דעם כעס כל חמתו, דעם גאנצן שפוך חמתך) אויף..., 236

אויסלאזן כל חמתו, 221

אויסנעמענס (אויסהייבענס) און איינעמענס, 216

אויסרופן דעם מולד, 226

אויפשטיין תחית המתים, 216

אוירא דארץ ישראל מחכים, 121

אום ראש השנה האט דער גרעסטער קבצן א טראפעלע האניק, 242

אומות העולם, 196

אומר ועושה, 178

אונאת דברים, 47

אורח-פורח (אורחי-פורחי), 178

אותו האיש, 179

אותיות מחכימות, 280

אותיות פורחות, 178

אותיות של אמת מרוחקין זה מזה ושל שקר מקורבין, 179

אז בעגלא איז א וואנן איז ובזמן קריב א שליטן, 209

אז די וועלט זאגט זאל מען גלייבן, 127

אז דער בעל תוקע קען ניט בלאזן לייגט זיך דער שטן אין שופר, 239

אז ויקהל איז א קניש איז פקודי א ווארעניק, 36

אז מען איז אין כעס אויפן חזן זאגט (ענטפערט) מען ניט קיין אמן? 209

אז מען איז אין כעס אויפן חזן שפרינגט מען ניט קיין קדושה? 209

אז מען צײלט ספירה קומט אויף די כלי-זמר א פגירה, 220

אז מען קען נאט ניט און מען ווייס ניט נעמט מען זיך ניט אונטער, 243

אז ס'גייט די סדרה קרח קומען אויף: קארשן, רעטעך, כריין (חריין), 60

אז עס קומט פורים פארגעסט מען אין אלע יסורים, 249

אזנים לכותל, 280

אחד בפה ואחד בלב, 136

אחד המרבה ואחד הממעיט ובלבד שיכוין לבו לשמים, 136

אחוז בקרנות המזבח, 83

אחור וקדם צרתני, 83

אחינו בני ישראל, 116

אחרי דרגא (יבוא) תביר, 257

אחרי טרחא יבוא אתנח, 257

אחרי ככלות הכל, 209

אחרי מאריך (יבוא) טרחא, 257

אחרי מות-קדושים-אמר, 44

אחרי רבים להטת, 31

אהרן אחרון חביב, 19

אחרית כל קטטה חרטה, 257

אי אפשר לבית המדרש בלא חידוש, 147

אי סייפא לא ספרא ואי ספרא לא סייפא, 147

איבערקריען ווי סדם ועמרה, 14

איזהו חכם? הרואה את הנולד, 127

איזהו עשיר? כל שיש לו נחת רוח בעשרו, 127

איזהו תלמיד חכם? כל ששואלין אותו הלכה בכל מקום ואומרה, 127

איין יהי רצון, 239

איין מאל אין א יובל, 50

איינער האט הנאה פון קעז, א צווייטער פון "לאנג והוא רחום" און א דריטער פון טיר צו דער גאס, 212

איינער האט ליב זויערמילך, דער צווייטער מפטיר, 230

איך האב ניט (ענטפער); לא לנו שטייט אין הלל, 232

איך וועל מיט אים לערנען בלק, 62

אימת מות, 85

אין אבדה כאבדת הזמן, 260

אין אדם אשר לא יחטא, 85

אין אדם בעולם בלא יסורים, 259

אין אדם יודע מה בלבו של חברו, 122

אין אדם מקנה דבר שלא בא לעולם, 122

אין אדם משים עצמו רשע, 122

אין אדם מתקנא בבנו ותלמידו, 63

אין אדם נתפש בשעת צערו, 122

אין אדם רואה חובה לעצמו, 122

אין אדם רואה נגעי עצמו. ר' מאיר אומר: אף לא נגעי קרוביו, 122

אין אומר ואין דברים, 85

אין ארח מכניס ארח, 125

אין בה (בו) טעם ואין בה (בו) ריח, 260

אין ברירה, 122

אין ברכה מצויה בתוך ביתו של אדם אלא בשביל אשתו, 123

אין גדולה בפלטין (בפלטרין) של מלך, 41

אין דברי תורה מתקיימין אלא במי שממית עצמו עליה, 61

אין דוחים אבן אחרי הנופל, 123

אינ דומה תפלת צדיק בן צדיק לתפלת צדיק בן רשע, 17

אין די קטורת איז דא חלבנה און אין דער פיינסטער משפחה איז פאראנען א משומד, 214

אין האור נכר אלא מתוך החושך, 260

אין הבור מתמלא מחוליתו, 123

אין היחיד אומר קדושה, 49

אין הכי נמי, 123

אין הנביא רשאי לחדש דבר מעתה, 52

אין העולם מתקיים אלא בשביל מי שמשים עצמו כמי שאינו, 79

אין הקב"ה מקפח שכר כל בריה, אפילו שכר שיחה נאה, 123

אין הקדוש ברוך הוא נותן חכמה אלא למי שיש בו חכמה, 123

אין הקומץ משביע את הארי, 123

אין השכינה שורה מתוך עצבות, 123

אין התורה נקנית אלא בחבורה, 76

אין ודאי שאין בו ספק, 261

אין וואס פאר א שול מען דאוונט, אזא קדושה זאגט מען (שפרינגט מען), 214

אין זקן אלא חכם (מי שקנה חכמה), 59

אין חבוש מתיר עצמו מבית האסורים, 123

אין חודש אלול ציטערן אפילו די פיש אין וואסער, 237

אין חרש עצים בלא קרדום, 260

אין כיסים בתכריכים, 260

אין לא ראינו ראיה, 124

אין לו מוח בקדקדו, 124

אין מביאין ראיה מן השוטים, 125

אין מדרש בלא חידוש, 125

אין מוקדם ומאוחר בתורה, 59

אין מזל לישראל, 124

אין מחזיקין במחלוקת, 60

אין מיטן ויאמר (וידבר), 271

אין מסיחין בסעודה, 124

אין מעמידין פרנס על הצבור אלא א"כ נמלכין בצבור, 36

אין מערבין שמחה בשמחה, 124

אין מקרא יוצא מידי פשוטו, 125

אין מרצין לו לאדם בשעת כעסו, 34

אין משיבין את הארי לאחר מיתה, 124

אין נכנסים לחורבה מפני החשד, 125

אין סומכין על הנס, 126

אין עונשין אלא אם כן מזהירין, 125

אין עושין שררות על הצבור פחות משנים, 33

אין עני אלא בדעה, 122

אין עשן בלי אש, 259

אין קול ואין עונה, 260

אין קטורת בלי חלבנה, 34

אין קטיגור נעשה סניגור, 124

אין קידוש אלא במקום סעודה, 124

אין קרוב רואה את הנגעים, 124

אין צבור עני (לית צבור כולי מיעני), 126

אין רבי אחר רבי רבוי אלא למעט, 125

אין רע שאין בו טוב, 260

אין שוטה נפגע (מרגיש), 125

אין שוטה איז גערוען תשעה באב, 252

אין שני קולות נכנסים באזן אחת, 125

אינו דומה לומד מעצמו ללומד מרבו, 126

אינו דומה מי שיש לו פת בסלו למי שאין לו פת בסלו,
126

אינו דומה שונה פרקו מאה פעמים לשונה פרקו מאה
ואחת, 126

אינו דומה שמיעה לראיה, 261

אינו מעלה ואינו מוריד, 126

איני יודע מה אתה שח, 126

איניש באיניש פגע, טורא בטורא לא פגע, 271

אינשי דעלמא, 148

איסתרא בלגינא קיש-קיש קריא, 148

איפכא מסתברא, 148

איר זאלט זיך אויסבעטן א גוט יאר (א גוט קוויטל), 232

איש דמים, 90

איש הישר בעיניו יעשה, 90

איש שפתים, 90

איש תחת גפנו ותחת תאנתו, 91

אכול ושתו כי מחר נמות, 83

אכלו משמנים ושתו ממתקים, 90

אכילה איז די בעסטע תפלה, 238

אל יהי המשל הזה קל בעיניך, שעל ידי המשל אדם עומד
על דברי תורה (אדם יכול לעמוד בדברי תורה), 257

אל יוציא אדם את עצמו מן הכלל, 117

אל יטיל אדם אימה יתרה בתוך ביתו, 117

אל ילבין פני חבירו ברבים, 117

אל יעמוד אדם במקום סכנה סבנה לומר שעושין לי נס, 117

אל יפתח (תפתח) אדם פיו (פה) לשטן, 117

אל ישנה אדם בנו בין הבנים, 117

אל ישנה אדם ממנהג הבריות, 258

אל ישנה אדם ממנהג העיר אפילו בניגונים, 117

אל ישנה אדם מן המנהג, 33

אל יתהלל הגבור בגבורתו, 84

אל יתהלל חגר כמפתח, 84

אל נא רפא לה לה, 58

אל תבטחו בנדיבים, בבן אדם שאין לו תשועה, 84

אל תגידו בגת, 83

אל תהי ברכת (קללת)הדיוט קלה בעיניך, 116

אל תפרוש מן הציבור, 116

אל תצר צרת מחר כי לא תדע מה ילד יום, 116

אל תשאל את הרופה, שאל את החולה, 116

אל תשליכני לעת זקנה, 237

אל תשליכני לעת זקנה, 38

אלא מאי, 136

אלו ואלו דברי אלהים חיים הן, 121

אלולי שראיתי בעני לא האמנתי, 270

אלטער תרח, 11

אלמלי משמרין ישראל שתי שבתות כהלכתן מיד נגאלין,
147

אלע שיכורים זיינען ניכטער פורים, 249

אלץ נעמט מן עק, אפילו דער כי הנה כחמר, 243

אם אין דעה-הבדלה מנין, 147

אים אין שלום אין כלום, 53

אם אין תלמידים אין חכמים, 270

אם אני כאן הכל כאן, 147

אם אשכחך ירושלים תשכח ימיני, 90

אם אתה עושה דלי"ת רי"ש-אתה מחריב את העולם כולו,
270

אם ירצה השם, 271

אם כן אין לדבר סוף, 147

אם לא עכשיו אימתי?, 15

אם לא תאמינו כי לא תאמנו, 90

אם לא תכנס האלה כלה תכנס חציה, 270

אם שמו אשר, גם לחמו כשר, 270

אם תלמיד חכם נוקם ונוטר כנחש הוא, חגריהו על מתניך,
148

אם תמצא לומר, 148

אם תעזבני (תעזובנה) יום, ימים תעזבך, 148

אם תרצו אין זו אגדה, 270

אמור ברומא וקטיל בסוריא, 263

אמן זאגער, 209

אמרה תורה: תהא טמאה שבעת ימים כדי שתהא חביבה
על בעלה כשעת כניסתה לחופה, 43

אמרו לאלהים, 245

אמרי לה לשבח ואמרי לה לגנאי, 249

אמת מארץ תצמח, 87

אן הוצאה איז ניטא קיין הכנסה, 217

אנגעהויבן מיט קידוש און ג׳ענדיקט מיט קדיש, 223
אנהייבן פון אנהייב (פון אלף-בית, פון בראשית, פון מה-
טובו, פון ברוך שאמר), 217
אנוס רחמנא פטרייה, 119
אני אומר לך דברים של טעם ואתה אומר לי מן השמים
ירחמו, 118
אני הקטן, 258
אני ואפסי עוד, 84
אני לדודי ודודי לי, 84
אני מביא לכם ראיה מן התורה, ואתם מביאין לי ראיה מן
השוטים, 118
אני שלמה, 118
אנמאכן א חורבן, 252
אנמאכן א יעלה, 247
אנמאכן א תשעה באב, 252
אנקומען ווי קריעת ים סוף, 29
אנשי בראשית, 9
אנשי סדום, 13
אסאך המן׳ס און איין פורים, 249
אסאך זמירות און וויניג לאקשן, 223
אסור לאדם שיטעום כלום קודם שיברך, 45
אסיא דמגן במגן, מגן שוויה, 120
אסיא רחיקא עינא עוירא, 121
אסמכתא בעלמא, 120
אעלה את ירושלים על ראש שמחתי, 83
אף אתה עושה אזנך כאפרכסת, 115
אף על פי כן, 114
אף על פי שהניחו לו אבותיו לאדם ס״ת, מצוה לכתוב
משלו, 78
אף על פי שחטא, ישראל הוא, 115
אף על פי שחכם גדול אתה, אינו דומה לומד מעצמו
ללומד מרבו, 114
אף על פי שכל המועדים מצוה לשמוח בהם, אבל בחג
הסכות היתה במקדש שמחה יתירה, 48
אפגעשלאגענע הושענא, 234
אפילו אין דער הגדה געפינט מען דעם דבר אחר, 234
אפילו חרב חדה מונחת לו על צווארו של אדם, אל ימנע
עצמו מן הרחמים, 115
אפיקורוס, 119
אפרח שלא נתפתחו עיניו, 136
אפריכטן דעם סדר, 236
אפריכטן חצות, 217
אפצעילין (אויסצעילין) אחת ואחת (אחת ושתים), 247
אץ קוצץ, בן קוצץ, קצוצי לקצץ, בדבור מפוצץ, 249
ארבע (ודלת) אמות, 119
ארבעים יום קודם יצירת הולד בת קול יוצאת ואומרת: בת
פלוני לפלוני, 119
ארזי הלבנון, 84
אריינגעזעצט אין חד גדיא, 234

אריינכאפן א מנחה, 220
אריינכאפן א קדושה (ברכו), 209
ארץ זבת הלב ודבש, 25
אשא עיני אל ההרים, מאין יבא עזרי? 88
אשה בגימטריא דבש, 271
אשר יצר פאפיר, 209
אשרי הגוי אשר ה׳ אלהיו, 85
אשרי יושבי ביתך איז דער בעסטע האנדל, 209
אשרי כל חוסי בו, 85
אשרי נשוי פשע כסוי חטאה, 85
אשריכם שתזכו להיות שמשים למקום, 58
אשת חיל מי ימצא, אבער א ווייב א שלימזל איז בנמצא,
223
אתה בא אלי בחרב ובחנית ובכידון ואנכי בא אליך בשם ה׳
צבאות, 85
אתה בחרתנו מכל העמים: און פארן שייגעטץ האסט דו
מורא! 231
אתה בחרתנו(ו) ניזם, 231
אתה הראת לדעת-ניטא קיין בראנפן טרינקט מען קוואס,
231
אתרתי תלת גנבי לא מיקטל, 121

בא לטהר מסייעין אותו, 127
בא שבת באה מנוחה, 9
באו מים עד נפש, 68
באלעמער (אלמימר), 261
בבריתו של אברהם אבינו, 14
בגדולה מתחילין מן הגדול, ובקללה מתחילין מן הקטן, 42
בגפו יבא ובגפו יצא, 31
בדרך שאדם רוצה לילך, בה מוליכין אותו, 131
בהדי הוצא לקי כרבא, 128
בהדי כבשי דרחמנא למה לך?, 128
בור כרה ויחפרהו, ויפל בשחת יפעל, 87
בזכות נשים צדקניות שהיו באותו הדור נגאלו ישראל
ממצרים, 133
בזמן שישראל עושין רצונו של מקום אין כל אומה ולשון
שולטות בהן, 133
בזעת אפיך תאכל לחם, 9
בחדרי חדרים, 131
בחקתיהם לא תלכו, 44
בטח בה׳ ועשה טוב, 87
בטל בששים, 130
ביד חזקה ובזרוע נטויה-אמלוך עליכם, 87
ביי א יינגל מאכט מען ברוך שפטרני צו בר-מצוה, ביי א
מיידל-צו דער חתונה, 230
ביי באי ושלום שטייט דער ארעמאן אויבנאן, 221
ביי אים איז כל דכפין ייתי ויכול, 235
בימה, 262
בין כך ובין כך, 130

בין כסה לעשור, 239
בירא דשתית מיניה לא תשדי ביה קלא, 130
בישיבה של מעלה, 132
בית הכנסת שחרב... קדושתן אף כשהן שוממין, 52
בית הקברות (קברות), 86
בכל אדם מתקנא חוץ מבנו ותלמידו, 63
בכל, מכל, כל, 219
בל תשחית, 74
בלאן שופר, 239
בלב ולב ידברו, 87
בלב שלם, 87
בלי נדר, 64
בלי עין הרע (רעה), 131
בלע המות לנצח, ומחה ה' דמעה, 87
בלשון סגי נהור, 131
במה כחך גדול, 86
במדה שהאדם מודד בה מודדין לו, 132
במזיד, 132
במקלי עברתי את הירדן, 20
בן סורר ומורה, 75
בן (ילד) זקונים, 21
בן נח, 12
בן פרת יוסף, 21
בני אדם (בן אדם) של הפקר, 261
בני קרח לא מתו, 63
בנים גדלתי ורוממתי והם פשעו בי, 86
בנערינו ובזקנינו נלך, 27
בעונותינו הרבים, 261
בעזרת ה' יתברך, 261
בעל דבר, 127
בעל המאה הוא בעל הדעה, 261
בעל הנס אינו מכיר בנסו, 127
באל יכולת, 261
בעל כרחו (כרחה), 131
בעל תשובה, 127
בענטשן גומל, 230
בענטשן חנוכה ליכט, 248
בעסער אנקומען צו עלינו איידער צום בעסטן מענטשן, 210
בעסער פסח אין מלכה איידער יום כפור פערציג מלקות, 243
בעקבות משיחא חוצפא יסגא וויוקר יאמיר, 131
בערב ילין בכי ולבוקר רנה, 86
בפיו ובשפתיו כבדוני ולבו רחק ממני, 87
בפיו יברכו ובקרבם יקללו, 87
בפיו שלום את רעהו ידבר, ובקרבו ישים ארב, 86
בקדרה שבשל בה נתבשל, 128
בקי בחדרי תורה, 128
בקי בחשבונות היה, 129

בקי בסתרי תורה, 129
בקי ברפואות, 129
בקי לדרוש תורה, 129
בר אורין, 129
בר-בי רב דחד יומא, 129
בר דעת, 129
בר סמכא, 129
ברא כרעיה דאבוה, 132
בראשית בריא, 9
ברוך דין האמת, 129
ברוך הגבר אשר יבטח בה', 86
ברוך ה', 261
ברוך ה' יום יום, 86
ברוך השם יום יום-אויף (פאר) מארגן זאל (וועט) גאט זארגן, 223
ברוך שפטרני, 230
ברחל בתך הקטנה, 18
ברי ושמא ברי עדיף, 129
בריך רחמנא דיהבך ניהלן ולא יהבך לעפרא, 132
ברכה לבטלה, 262
ברכת הבית ברובה, 132
ברכת המזון דאורייתא, 72
בשוגג, 132
בשלשה דברים אדם משתנה מחברו: בקול, במראה ובדעת, 132
בשלשה דברים אדם ניכר: בכוסו, בכיסו ובכעסו, ויש אומרים אף בשחקו, 132
בשעה טובה ומצלחת, 262
בשעת הדחק, 132
בשעת חדותא חדותא, בשעת אבלא אבלא, 9
בת קול, 129
בת תחלה סימן יפה לבנים, 130
בתי כנסיות אין נוהגין בהן קלות ראש, 130
בתר עניא אזלא עניותא, 130

גאט זאל אויף אים שיקן פון די צען מכות די בעסטע (פרעה'ס מכות), 235
גאט זאל אונז שומר ומציל זיין, 220
גאט פון אברהם, 227
גאנץ יאר שיכור, פורים ניכטער, 250
גארטל, 264
גבוה לא ישא גבוהית, שמא יצא מהן תורן, 137
גברא רבה, 137
גדול הדור, 136
גדול המעשה יותר מן העושה, 136
גדול העושה מאהבה יותר מן העושה מיראה, 70
גדולה שנאה ששונאים עמי הארץ לתלמידי הכמים, 137
גדולה תפלה יותר ממעשים טובים, 70
גדולים צדיקים במיתתם יותר מבחייהם, 137

גוזר תענית זיין, 252
גוט בריען, 266
גוט וואך (שבוע טוב), 227
גוט יום טוב, 232
גוט שבת, 222
גזירות קשות ורעות, 265
גיי שרַיי חי וקים, 240
גיין צו תשליך, 240
גלגול הנפש, 265
גלגל הוא שחוזר בעולם, 136
ג׳לויבט איז גאט, 264
גלוי ראש, 265
גלם, 266
גם אני חכם כמוך, 88
גם את הטוב נקבל-ואת הרע לא נקבל?, 88
גם בוש לא יבשו והכלם לא ידעו, 88
גם זו לטובה, 137
גם חרבונה (חרבונא) זכור לטוב, 250
גם נביא גם כהן חנפו, 88
גם עליך תעבר כוס, 88
גמילות חסדים, 265
גמל הפורח באויר, 137
גמרא גמירי לה, 137
גמרא גמירנא סברא לא ידענא, 138
גן עדן, 9
גונבת דעת, 138
גונב דעת הבריות, 137
געבן א יישר-כח, 232
געפֿינען א זכות (אויף), 264
גרסא דינקותא (לא משתכחא), 138

דאוו(ע)נען, 262
דאס איז מיין קדיש, 210
דאס בעסטע פון די עשר מכות זיינען די קניידלאך מיט יויך, 235
דאס לעבען איז ווי שמונה-עשרה; מען שטייט, מען שטייט, ביז מען גייט אויס, 210
דבוק, 263
דבקות, 135
דבר אחד לדור ואין שני דברין לדור, 134
דבר אחר, 133
דבר אל העצים ואל האבנים, 262
דבר ולא חצי דבר, 134
דבר, כי שמע עבדך, 87
דבר שאפילו תינוקות של בית רבן יודעין אותו, 134
דבר שלא בא לעולם, 134
דברה תורה כלשון בני אדם, 44
דברי כבושים, 136
דברים בטלים, 135

דברים היוצאים מן הלב נכנסים אל הלב, 263
דברים של טעם, 135
דבש וחלב תחת לשונך, 87
דוכענען, 232
דוק בככי ותשכח בניגרי, 136
דור המבול, 12
דור המדבר, 57
דור הפלגה, 12
דור יתום, 136
די גאנצע מגילה, 250
די לחכימא ברמיזא, 262
די נשמה זאל האבן אן עליה, 263
די נשמה ליכט, 244
דיה לצרה בשעתה, 25
דין פרוטה כדין מאה, 135
דינא דמלכותא דינא, 135
דינען צום עגל הזהב (צום גאלדענעם קאלב), 34
דירה נאה ואשה נאה וכלים נאים מרחיבין דעתו של אדם, 136
דמים תרתי משמע, 133
דן את חברך לכף זכות, 45
דע לפני מי אתה עומד, 133
דעלך סני לחברך לא תעביד, 45
דער אין היטל זאל אונז (מיר) העלפֿן, 134
דער ארעמאן האט בשר ודגים אין די זמירות, 224
דער בעסטער מאגן איז דער מגן אבות, 222
דער זיווג זאל עולה יפה זיין, 263
דער זכות פון דער מצוה איז אים בייגעשטאנען, 263
דער ייד איז א כפרה האן, 244
דער ייד ענטפֿערט תמיד פֿארקערט: זאגט מען אים שלום עליכם ענטפֿערט ער עליכם שלום, 224
דער כהן האט זיך אין אים צעשפֿילט, 134
דער מענטש זינדיקט און די האן ווערט די כפרה, 244
דער עולם איז שוין דו, 210
דרדקי מלמד, 133
דרײַ מיר נייט קיין קאפ מיט דיינע חד גדיא׳ס, 235
דרך אגב, 135
דרך ארוכה וקצרה, דרך קצרה וארוכה, 135
דרך ארץ קדמה לתורה, 263
דרך רשעים תאבד, 87
דרכו של איש לחזר על אשה ואין דרכה של אשה לחזר על איש, 75
דערלעבען צו הערן דעם שופר של משיח, 239

ה׳ לי לא אירא, מה יעשה לי אדם, 89
ה׳ מוריש ומעשיר, 89
ה׳ נתן וה׳ לקח, 89
הא בהא תליא, 138
האוחז ביד די בעסטע תפלה, 240

האוחז ביד-וכל מאמינים שהוא, 240
האוחז ביד-שלום בקעשינגע, 240
האוחז ביד שטייט גרויס געשריבן, 240
האט מורא לייען קריאת שמע, 214
האוכל בשוך דומה לכלב, 142
האומר אין לו אלא תורה אפילו תורה אין לו, 71
האי עלמא (כבי) הלולא דמיא, 139
הבא לטהר מסייעין אותו, 138
הבה לי ברכה, 89
הבטלה מביאה לידי שעמום, 138
הדיוט קופץ בראש, 250
הדלת הנגעלת לא במהרה תפתח, 138
הדס, 227
הדרת פנים זקן, 138
הוא נותן אצבעו בין שיניה, 147
הוה אמינא, 144
הוו עמלים בתורה, 52
הוי האומרים לרע טוב ולטוב רע, 90
הוי זהיר מן היועצך לפי דרכו, 145
הוי פקח ושתוק, 145
הוכח תוכיח את עמיתך-אפילו מאה פעמים-תלמיד לרב, 46
הולייא, הולייא, 270
הושיעה ה' כי גמר חסיד, 90
הזהרו בחבורה, 146
הזורעים בדמעה ברנה יקצורו, 89
החושד בכשרים לוקה בגופו, 139
החזיר בשעה שהוא רובץ פרשט את טלפיו כאומר: ראו שאני טהור, 266
היא ניימא ודיקולא שפיל, 145
הידור מצוה, 146
היה הכבור לאבל, 89
היום כאן ומחר בקבר, 144
היום עודנו ומחר איננו, 145
היזק ראייה שמיה היזק, 145
היינטיגער חודש איז חסר, 226
הילד איננו, 20
היכי תמצא לומר, 144
היסח הדעת, 145
היתפאר הגרזן על החוצב בו?, 89
הכבד ושב בביתך, 89
הכון לקראת אליהיך ישראל, 90
הכות בלשון, 88
הכל בידי שמים חוץ מיראת שמים, 72
הכל בידי שמים חוץ מצינים פחים, 140
הכל כמנהג המדינה, 140
הכל תלוי במזל אפילו ספר תורה שבהיכל, 267
הלומד ואינו חוזר דומה לזורע ואינו קוצר, 141
הלומד תורה ואינה מלמדה זהו 'דבר ה' בזה,' 60

הלכה ואין מורים כן, 141
הלכה למעשה, 140
הלכה למשה מסיני, 140
הלשון הוא קולמות הלב, 267
המאכל יוליד השינה, 141
המאכל מביא את השינה, 141
המבזה תלמיד חכם, אפיקורוס הוי, 142
המבקר חולה נוטל אחד משישים בצערו, 141
המגביה ידו על חבירו אע"פ שלא הכהו נקרא רשע, 25
המוציא לחם מן הארץ-עס ווי א פריץ, 219
המוציא מחבירו עליו הראיה, 31
המכה בעברתו-געשלאגן אויף די עברי, 220
המלבין פני חבירו ברבים כאלו שופך דמים, 141
המקבל צדקה ואינו צריך לכך, סופו אינו נפטר מן העולם עד שיבא לידי כך, 141
המקום ינחם אתכם (ינחמכם)(ינחמך) עם (בתוך) שאר אבלי ציון וירושלים, 267
המקום ירחם עליך בתוך שאר חולי ישראל, 141
המשחק בקוביא, 141
המתחיל במצוה אומרים לו גמור, 141
הן ולאו ורפיא בידיה, 144
הן שלך צדק ולאו שלך צדק, 45
הנושא אשה צריך שיבדוק באחיה, 142
הניח מעותיו על קרן הצבי, 146
הנעשה אין להשיב, 142
הנפטר מן המת אל יאמר לו לך לשלום אלא לך בשלום, 142
הסגת גבול, 74
הסך את רגליו, 89
העולם לסלם הוא דומה-זה עולה וזה יורד, 267
העלף מיר גאטעניו, ביזט דאך א אל רחום וחנון, 213
הפוך הקערה על פיה, 138
הפקר יונג, 268
הפרש בין מה שאדם רואה למה שאחרים משיחין לו, 29
הצד השוה שבהן, 144
הצילני נא מיד אחי מיד עשו, 20
הקב"ה לבא בעי, 139
הקב"ה מדקדק עם סביביו כחוט השערה, 140
הקב"ה מזווג זיווגים, 266
הקב"ה מקדים רפואה למכה, 139
הקב"ה נתן באשה בינה יותר מבאיש, 140
הקהל, 78
הקל קול יעקב והידים ידי עשר, 17
הקשיבה בקול תחנונותי, 88
הקשיבה תפלתי, 88
הרבה למדתי מרבותי, ומחברי יותר מרבותי ומתלמדי יותר מכלם, 142
הרגל נעשה טבע, 268

הרואה אתרג בחלום, הדר הוא לפני קונו, 49
הרואה שמן זית בחלום יצפה למאור תורה, 33
הרחב פיך ואמלאהו, 88
הרי שלחן, הרי בשר, והרי סכין ואין לנו (פה) לאכל, 143
הררים התלוים בשערה (ואין להם על מה שיסמכו), 142
השחד יעור פקחים ויסלף דברי צדיקים, 31
השכבה (אשכבה), 230
השם ירחם, 143
השם ישמרהו וחיהו, 267
השמיעיני את קולך, 89
השמע לאזניך מה שאתה מוציא מפיך, 143
השמר אחי אנכי?, 10
התורה חסה על ממונם של ישראל, 144
התעטף באצטלא דרבנן, 269
התר עסקא, 268

ואהבת לרעך כמוך, 48
ואכלת ושבעת וברכת, 219
ואני בער ולא אדע, 106
רביום השמיני ימול, 43
ובערת הרע מקרבך, 75
והגית בו יומם ולילה, 106
ואך נאכט, 286
וואכעדזיגע, שבת׳דיגע, יום-טובדיגע שמונה עשרה, 218
וואס האט א פאטש צוטאן מיט יקום פורקן?, 225
וואס טיפער מען בוקט זיך מודים וואס ווייטער גייט מען עושה שלום צוריק, 218
וואס פאר א סמיכות הפרשה האט דאס צוטאן מיט ... ?, 32
ווי א איד צו כאפן א מנחה, 221
ווי א יון אין סוכה, 234
ווי א פלוי אין יקום פורקן, 225
ווי א שד פאר א מזוזה אדער פאר שמע ישראל, 218
ווי די שול, אזוי שפרינגט מען קדוש, 218
ווי דער ראש השנה׳דיקער מוסף, 242
ווי האבן זי געבוייט, 286
ווי קומט א פאטש צו גוט שבת?, 223
ווי קומט אתה הראת צו דער ארענדע?, 234
ווי קומט הודו אין מקוה אריין (אין באד אריין)?, 218
ווי קומט עשו אין קריאת שמע אריין?, 218
ווימפל, 286
וועגן א ביסל בוימל מאכט מען אזא גרויסן יום-טוב, 248
ווען משיח וועט קומען וועלן אלע ימים טובים בטל ווערן, נאר פורים וועט בלייבן, 251
וועסט נאך א פולע דארפן זאגן אבינו מלכינו (ביז דו וועסט אויסוויינען דעם קרן), 242
וחי אחיך עמך, 52
וחי בהם ולא שימות בהם, 45
ויאמר-דוד-גליטש, 217
ויקהל משה-וכנס משה, 36

ויקם מלך חדש, 26
וישמן ישורון ויבעט, 79
ויתד תהיה לך על אזנך, 76
ויתן לך-קין געלט איז ניטא, מטל השמים-ניטא וואו צו ליינען, משמני הארץ-דאס געלט איז ביים פריץ, 229
וכל המרבה לספר הרי זה משבח, 237
ולמה תתגרה ברעה, 106
ועל כולם, 217
וצדקתך בצדק-ראשי תיבות; ביז צו דער קעשענע, 228
וראשו לעב יגיע, 106
ותלמוד תורה כנגד כולם; א ביסל מהיכא-תיתי איז בילכר פון אלץ, 218

זאגן סליחות, 238
זה בכה רזה בכה, 109
זה נהנה וזה לא חסר, 200
זהירות מביאה לידי זריזות, 200
זו לא שמעתי, כיוצא בא שמעתי, 201
זו תורה וזו שכרה?, 201
זוזא לעללא לא שכיחא, לתליתא שכיחא, 201
זוכה צו זיין צו זען בנחמות ציון וירושלים, 109
זיבן וואכן צײלט מען, דריי וואכן וויינט מען, פיר וואכן בלאזט מען, 238
זיבעצען איז כמנין טוב, אכצן איז כמנין חי, חי צום לעבן; הונדערט און הונדערט און איינס איז אלף איינס, 289
זיי א צדיק אבער ניט קיין רשע וצדקתך, 229
זיך שטעלן קוממיות, 219
זיל בתר שתיקותא, 200
זיצן על התורה ועל העבודה, 231
זכור ושמור-זיך צו האלטן בדיבור אחד, 223
זכות אבות, 289
זכותו יגן עלינו, 289
זכין לאדם שלא בפניו, 199
זכירה מביאה לידי מעשה, 60
זכר צדיק לברכה, 200
זכרנו לברכה, 200
זכרתי לך חסד נעוריך אהבת כלולתיך, 109
זמן תפלה לחוד וזמן תורה לחוד, 200
זרוק אבן למרקוליס, 199
זרוך חוטרא לאוירא אעיקריה קאי, 16
זריזין מקדימין למצות, 16

חבוט הקבר, 268
חביבין ישראל לפני הקב״ה יותר ממלאכי השרת, 71
חבל על דאבדין ולא משתכחין, 26
חבלי משיח (חבלו של משיח), 145
חברו על-כתרנגלים, 144
חברים כל ישראל, 226
חברך חברא אית ליה, וחברא דחברך חברא אית ליה, 144

חברך קרייך חמרא אוכפא לגביך מוש, 144

חגא (חגאות), 269

חד בדרא, 138

חד גדיא שטייט תמיד אויף איין מקח, 235

חדש ימינו כקדם-דער אייגענער שלימזל וואס פריער, 213

חובש בית המדרש, 147

חוזרני חלילה, 147

חוכא ואטלולא, 147

חול קרייש, 269

חוצפא (חצפה, חוצפה), 270

חוצפא, אפילו כלפי שמיא מהניא, 61

חז"ל, 268

חזן זעט ניט ווי קהל הינטער לאכט, 225

חזן זאגט פאר און דער קהל ענטפערט, 225

חזק ואמץ, 78

חזק וברוך, 145

חזק חזק ונתחזק, 230

חטאי אני מזכיר היום, 21

חיי שעה, 139

חייב אדם לברך מאה ברכות בכל יום, 72

חייב אדם לטהר את עצמו ברגל, 42

חייב אדם ללמד את בנו אומנות, ואם לאו חייב ללמד את עצמו, 77

חייב אדם ללמד את בנו לשוט על המים, ואם לא למדו חייב ללמד את עצמו, 77

חייך קודמין לחיי חבירך, 144

חייתא דקטרי סברת וקבלת, 139

חכם, 267

חכם בלילה, 267

חכם בשר, 267

חכם, זה תלמיד המחכים את רבותיו, 140

חלול השם, 49, 146

חלול שבת, 146

חלום חלמתי, 21

חמץ בן יין, 146

חנוכה און פורים ווערן די אריעמע לייט עשירים, 248

חס וחלילה, 51

חס ושלום, 143

חסד, 268

חסד של אמת, 268

חסיד שוטה, 143

חסידי אומות העולם יש להם חלק לעולם הבא, 267

חסר לחם, 89

חציו לה' וחציו לכם, 63

חק ולא יעבר, 269

חק נתן ולא יעבור, 88

חקת הגוי, 44

חרש שוטה וקטן פגיעתן רעה, 145

חש בראשו יעסוק בתורה, 143

חשבון הנפש, 268

חשד, 143

חשך העולם בעדו, 143

חתן דומה למלך, 267

טאמער איז ביי זיי יא אמאל א סדר פרעגן זיי; מה נשתנה, 236

טוב בגימטריא י"ז, 285

טוב לצדיק וטוב לשכנו, 57

טוב לשנים ולבריות זהו צדיק טוב, 194

טוב מעט בכוונה מהרבות שלא בכוונה, 285

טוב שברופאים לגיהנום, 194

טוביה חטא וזיגוד מנגד, 195

טביעות עין, 193

טובל ושרץ בידו, 195

טול קסם מבין שניך, טול קורה מבין עיניך, 195

טורא בטורא לא פגע, איניש באיניש פגע, 285

טורח הציבור (טרחא דציבורא), 194

טל ומטר טאג, 217

טעות לעולם חוזר (חוזרת), 283

טענו חטים והודה לו בשעורים, 192

יאכו, 287

יארמלקע, 287

יארצייט, 287

יבא הנס מכל מקום, 198

יבדל לחיים ארוכים, 288

י"ג מדות, 36

יגדיל תורה ויאדיר, 106

יגוע בעשר אצבעות, 197

יגיח ירדן אל פיהו, 107

יגיע כפיך כי תאכל, אשריך וטוב לך, 108

יגעת ופתחת יגע וסתום, 196

יגעתי ולא מצאתי אל תאמן, 197

ידו בכל ויד כל בו, 14

ידו על העליונה (על התחתונה), 196

יהא חביב עליך דין פרוטה כדין של מאה מנה, 198

יהב חכמתא (חכמה) לחכימין, 107

יהודי (יהודים), 287

יהי מכירך ברוך, 108

יובל, 52

יודע ספר, 108

יום, 288

יום א'(ראשון)-אורח, יום ב'(שני)-טורח, יום ג'(שלישי)-סורח, 289

יום בשרה הוא ואנחנו מחשים, 108

יום כפור זאגט מען חטאתי, אבער מען זאגט ניט לא אחטא, 247

יום כפור טראפנס, 247
יום כפורדיג, 247
יום נכנס ויום יצא, שבת נכנס כו', חודש כו',
שנה כו', 199
יום פטירה, 199
יוצא דפן, 199
יוצר משרתים ואשר משרתיו-שאף דיר משרתים און גיי
דיר אליין, 219
יושב אהל, 18
יותר מישישראל שמרו את השבת, שמרה השבת אותם,
289
יחוס (יחוש), 198
יחרד לבי ויתר ממקומר, 108
יין בן חמץ, 198
יין בן יין, 198
יין המשומר, 198
יין ישמח לבב אנוש, 107
יין נסך, 107
יישר כח (יישר כחך), 36
ים התלמוד, 287
ימח שמו (וזכרו), 288
ימי הרעה-אלו ימי הזקנה, 198
ימים ידברו, 107
ימים נוראים, 242
יסורין של אהבה, 198
יסיף על חטאתו פשע, 109
יעדער מאנטיק און דאנערשטיק, 252
יעדערער וויינט אויף מי יחיה, 243
יפה-פיה, 108
יפה שתיקה לחכמים, קל וחומר לטפשים, 196
יפתח בדורו כשמואל בדורו, 75
יצא איש פלוני נקי מנכסיו, 197
יצוא בשן ועין, 198
יצר לב האדם רע מנעריו, 13
יקנה"ז, 197
יראת ה' היא חכמה, וסור מרע בינה, 108
יראת שמים, 72
ירבעם בן נבט, 91
ירושלים דליטא, 288
ירשיעך פיך ולא אני, ושפתיך יענו בך, 107
יש דורשין לשבח ויש דורשין לגנאי, 13
יש לו מנה רוצה מאתים, 287
ישבו איש תחת גפנו ותחת תאנתו, 107
ישועת ה' כהרף עין, 288
ישמעו אזניך מה שפיך מדבר, 199
ישן באן וראה חלום באספמיה, 197
ישראל ואורייתא חד הוא, 288
ישראל סבא, 199
ישרים דרכי ה', צדיקים ילכו בם ופושעים יכשלו בם,
108

יתרוש קדמך במעשה בראשית, 197
יתרו'ס נעמען, 31

כאשר אבדתי אבדתי, 250
כאשר אעשה כן תעשון, 92
כאשר דמיתי כן היתה, וכאשר יעצתי היא תקום, 91
כאשר יחלום הרעב והנה אוכל, והקיץ ורקה נפשו, 92
כאשר יעטה הרועה את בגדו, 92
כאשר עשו לי כן עשיתי להם, 91
כאשר עשית יעשה לך, 91
כאשר עשיתי כן שלם לי אלהים, 91
כאשר עשתה עשו לה, 91
כבד אזן, 93
כבדהו וחשדהו, 272
כביכול, 150
כדבר אחת הנבלות תדברי, 92
כהן קורא ראשון ואחריו לוי, 78
כוז"ו במוכס"ז כוז"ו, 273
כולי עלמא לא פליגי, 157
כופין אותו עד שיאמר רוצה אני, 153
כופר בעיקר, 152
כח הפועל בנפעל, 272
כחוט השערה, 151
כחלום יעוף, 240
כחמר ביד היוצר, 245
כי באפם הרגו איש, 22
כיד המלך, 250
כיון דדש דש, 151
כיון שהגיד שוב אינו חוזר ומגיד, 151
כך הוה, 272
כך היה מעשה, 149
כך עונשו של בדאי שאפילו אומר אמת אין
שומעין לו, 149
כל אדם שאין בו דעה אסור לרחם עליו, 153
כל אדם שאין לו אישה שרוי בלא שמחה, בלא ברכה,
בלא טובה, 10
כל אדם שיש בו גסות הרוח כאלו כפר בעיקר, 73
כל אדם שיש בו יראת שמים דבריו נשמעין, 153
כל אדם שכרעס, אם חכם הוא חכמתו מסתלקת ממנו, 64
כל אמת אמת תפסיה להיא, 153
כל אשר בלבבך אגיד לך, 93
כל אשר ידבר בוא יבוא, 93
כל אשר יעשה יצליח, 93
כל גל וגל שבא עלי נענעתי לו ראשי, 153
כל דאלים גבר, 153
כל דבר מאכל קרוי לחם, 19
כל דבר שקר שאין אומרים בו קצת אמת בתחלתו אין
מתקיים בסופו, 60
כל האדם כזב-איטלעכער האט זיך זיינע מכות, 232
כל האומר דבר בשם אומרו מביא גאולה לעולם, 155

כל האומר דבר חכמה אפילו באומות העולם נקרא חכם, 155

כל החולק על רבו כחולק על השכינה, 64

כל המוסיף גורע, 32

כל המחזר על הגדולה, גדולה בורחת ממנו וכל הבורח מן הגדולה, גדולה מחזרת אחריו, 154

כל המחלל את המועדות, מעלין עליו כאילו חלל את השבתות, 50

כל המינים, כל מאמינים, 240

כל המלמד את (בן) בנו תורה מעלה עליו הכתוב כאילו קבלה מהר חורב, 71

כל המלמד את בן הבירו תורה, מעלה עליו הכתוב כאלו ילדו, 57

כל המלמד בתו תורה כאלו לימדה תפלות, 154

כל המענג את השבת נצול משעבוד מלכיות, 79

כל המצטער עצמו עם הציבור, זוכה ורואה בנחמות ציבור, 154

כל המקבל פני רבו, כאלו מקבל פני שכינה, 34

כל המקיים נפש אחת מישראל כאלו קיים עולם מלא, 154

כל המרחם על הבריות מרחמין עליו מן השמים, 73

כל המשלם אינו לוקה, 154

כל הנגעים אדם רואה חוץ מנגעי עצמו, 154

כל הסנדלרים הולכים יחפים, 273

כל העוסק בתורה אינו צריך לא עולה ולא מנחה ולא חטאת ולא אשם, 41

כל העוסק בתורה נכסיו מצליחין לו, 77

כל הפוסל פסול-בממו פוסל, 155

כל הקודם (בהן) זכה, 153

כל הרודף אחר הכבוד, הכבוד בורח ממנו, 155

כל התחלות קשות, 30

כל זמן שאדם חי יש לו תקוה, 156

כל זמן שהנשמה בקרבי, 215

כל יכול, 240

כל ישראל ערבין זה בזה, 156

כל יתר כנטול דמי, 156

כל מאהביך שכחוך, 94

כל מה דעביד רחמנה, לטב עביד, 155

כל מה שיאמר לך בעה"ב עשה (חוץ מצא), 155

כל מה שיש לו תכלה יש לו תחלה, 273

כל מצוה שהזמן גרמא, 156

כל מקום שנאמר "ויהי" אינו אלא לשון צער, 156

כל נדרי נאכט, 245

כל עוף למינו ישכון, ובן אדם לדומה לו, 156

כל עורב למינו, 42

כל עצמתי תאמרנה, 93

כל רז לא אנס לך, 94

כל שאינו במשנה אינו במעשה, 50

כל תיבה שצריכה למ"ד בתחילתה הטיל לה הכתוב ה' בסופה, 65

כלאחר יד, 152

כלאים, 46

כלו כל הקיצין ואין הדבר תלוי אלא בתשובה ומעשים טובים, 149

כלי אין חפץ בו, 92

כן בנות צלפחד דברת, 64

כן ירבו, 272

כנס על גבי ענק, 272

כסומא בארובה, 152

כסף מטהר ממזרים, 151

כספם וזהבם לא יוכל להצילם, 92

כעבד כאדניו, 92

כענבים במדבר, 91

כפה הקב"ה עליהם את ההר כגיגית, 30

כפוי טובה, 151

כפטיש יפוצץ סלע, 92

כפתור ופרח, 32

כצאן אשר אין להם רעה, 63

כצפיחת בדבש, 28

כרחם אב על בנים, 92

כרחק מזרח ממערב, 93

כרכושתא ושונרא עבדי הלולא מתרבא דביש גדא, 150

כרם ה' צבאות בית ישראל, 93

כשורה, 152

כשושנה בין החוחים, 93

כשם שיצירתו של אדם אחר בהמה חיה ועוף, כך תורתו אחר בהמה חיה ועוף, 43

כשם שמצוה על אדם לומר דבר הנשמע, כך מצוה על אדם שלא לומר דבר שאינו נשמע, 151

כשמו כן הוא, נבל שמו ונבלה עמו, 93

כתרנגלים המנקרים באשפה, 272

לא איש בשרה אתה היום, 97

לא אל חנם דברתי, 96

לא אליכם (עליכם) (לא עלינו), 96

לא אלמן ישראל, 96

לא אמות כי אחייה-ס'איז ניט באשערט צו שטארבן שטארבט מען ניט, 233

לא אמנע מכם דבר, 97

לא אמר ולא כלום, 161

לא אמר כלום, 161

לא בחיל ולא בכח כי אם ברוחי, 98

לא במותו יקח הכל, לא ירד אחריו כבודו, 98

לא דבים ולא יער, 162

לא דברתי ולא עלתה על לבי, 96

לא דומה שומע לרואה, 30

לא הוה פסיק פומיה מגירסיה, 161

לא היה ולא נברא, 163

לא היו דברים מעולם, 163

לא זה הדרך, 99
לא חכם ולא טיפש, 161
לא טוב היות האדם לבדו, 10
לא טעם ולא ריח, 276
לא יאמר אדם דבר לחבירו אלא אם כן קורהו, 41
לא יגרע מצדיק עיניו, 99
לא ידאג אדם לומר פלוני יקפח פרנסתי, 276
לא ידע בי ימינו לשמאלו, 98
לא יהא אדם נותן כל ממנו בזוית אחת, 276
לא יהא דבורך של שבת כדבורך של חול, 161
לא יהא טפל חמור מן העיקר, 162
לא יהא מלבושך של שבת כמלבושך של חול, 162
לא יודע עול בשת, 99
לא יוסיפו לדאבה עוד, 99
לא יזרוק ברכה מפיו, 162
לא יחרץ כלב לשונו, 27
לא יפלא ממך כל דבר, 99
לא יקניט איש חבירו, 57
לא ירעבו ולא יצמאו ולא יכם שרב ושמש, 99
לא יצלח, 276
לא יצלח לכל, 99
לא ישבתי בסוד משחקים, 99
לא ישתה אדם מן הכוס ויתננו לחבירו, 162
לא יתן לעולם מוט לצדיק, 99
לא כימים הראשונים, 97
לא כל האדם, ולא כל המקום, ולא כל השעות שוין, 161
לא כל הקרוב קרוב ולא כל הרחוק רחוק, 275
לא כתף ולא נטף, 46
לא למענכם אני עשה, 97
לא לעזר ולא להועיל, 97
לא לפניו חנף, 97
לא מדורבשך ולא מעוקצך, 62
לא מחשבותי מחשבותיכם לוא דרכיכם דרכי, 97
לא מיט אן אלף, 276
לא מעלין ולא מורידין, 163
לא מפני שאוהבים את מרדכי, אלא מפני ששונאין את המן, 250
לא מצא ידיו ורגליו, 161
לא מצינו שועל שמת בעפר פיר, 161
לא מקומו של אדם מכבדו אלא אדם מכבד את מקומו, 58
לא נביא אנכי ולא בן-נביא אנכי, 97
לא נופל אנכי מכם, 97
לא על הלחם לבדו יחיה האדם, 73
לא עת עתה להאריך בתפלה שישראל נתונים בצרה, 27
לא קם כמהו, 97
לא קם נביא עוד בישראל כמשה, 79
לא ראי זה כראי זה, 163
לא ראינו אינה ראיה, 163
לא שלוחי ולא שקטתי ולא נחתי ויבוא רוגז, 98

לא תאונה אליך רעה, 98
לא תאכלו קודם שתתפללו על דמכם, 47
לא תאמינו כי יספר. 98
לא תבשל גדי בחלב אמו, 32
לא תגנב, 30
לא תוסף עליו ולא תגרע ממנו, 74
לא תוסיפו, 72
לא תלך רכיל בעמיך, 46
לא תסיג גבול רעך, 74
לא תעמוד על דם רעך, 46
לא תקום ולא תהיה, 98
לא תקום ולא תטור, 47
לא תקום פעמים צרה, 98
לא תתגודדו, לא תעשו אגודות אגודות, 73
לאו בעל דברים דידי את, 158
לאו דוקא, 157
לאויל יהרג כעש, ופתה תמית קנאה, 95
לאמיר אנפאנגען (אנהייבן) פון בראשית, 10
לאנג ווי א לולב, 232
לבוקר משפט, 94
לבי ובשרי ירננו אל אל חי, 96
להבדיל בין הקדש לחל, 95
ל"ו צדיקים, 158
לוה רשע ולא משלם וצדיק חונן ונותן, 99
לחיים, 158
לחיים טובים ולשלום, 159
לחכימא ברמיזא, ולשטיא בכורמיזא, 274
לחם לאכל ובגד ללבש, 19
לחם צר ומים לחץ, 95
לי הכסף ולי הזהב נאום ה' צבאות, 96
ליגן אין דער אדמה, אין שאול תחתיה, 245
ליכא מידי דלא רמיזי באורייתא, 160
לילה לכם מחזון, 94
לימוד מביא לידי מעשה, 160
לית דין בר אינש(נש), 158
לית דין ולית דיין, 274
לך בכחך זה, 95
לך דמיה תהלה, 95
לך לך איז בעסער ווי שלך לך, 14
לכאורה, 160
לכו ונכבה בלשון, 95
לכל הרוחות, 274
לכלב תשליכון אותו, 31
למאי נפקא מינה?, 157
למד לשונך לומר איני יודע, שמא תתבדה, 157
למדו לשונם דבר שקר, 96
למה יאמרו הגוים, 94
למה ככה רמיתני, 94
למה תהיה כאיש נדהם, 94

למי אתה, ואי מזה אתה?, 95

למי אתם קורין רבי, רבי?—אל ירבו כמותו בישראל, 159

למען ציון לא אחשה ולמען ירושלים לא אשקוט, 95

לעג לרש, 162

לעולם אל יביא אדם עצמו לידי נסיון, 159

לעולם הלכה כדברי בית הלל, 159

לעולם יבקש אדם רחמים שלא יחלה, 76

לעולם ידור אדם בארץ ישראל ואפילו בעיר שרובה
נכרים, 51

לעולם יהא אדם זהיר בכבוד אשתו, 160

לעולם יהא אדם ענוותן כהלל, ואל יהא קפדן כשמאי, 159

לעולם יהא אדם רך כקנה ואל יהי קשה כארז, 159

לעולם יהא כספו של אדם מצוי בידו, 73

לעולם ילמוד אדם תורה ואחר כך יהגה, 77

לעולם יסדר שבחו של מקום ואח״כ יתפלל, 71

לעולם יספר אדם בלשון נקיה, 43

לעולם יעסוק בתורה ובמצות אעפ״י שלא לשמה, 159

לעולם ישלים אדם פרשיותיו עם הצבור שנים מקרא
ואחד תרגום, 64

לעולם ישלש אדם שנותיו: שליש במקרא, שליש
במשנה, שליש בגמרא, 71

לעולם ישנה אדם לתלמידו דרך קצרה, 160

לעולם תהא דעתו של אדם מעורבת עם הבריות, 159

לעזאזל, 45

לעלא לעלא, 240

לערנען פסוק, 274

לערנען תמיד און קענען מכות, 275

לפי עניות דעתי (לעניות דעתי), 274

לפני עור לא תתן מכשול, 46

לפנים משורת הדין, 160

לריק יגעתי לתהו והבל כחי כליתי, 95

לשוא הרבית רפאות, העלה אין לך, 94

לשוא תיפיי, 94

לשון בני אדם, 160

לשון חכמים, 160

לשון מדברת גדולות, 94

לשון רמיה, 95

לשון תליתאי קטיל תליתאי, 158

לשונם חרב חדה, 96

לשם ולתהלה ולתפארת, 95

לשמע אל הרנה ואל התפלה, 96

לשנה טובה תכתבו (ותחתמו), 241

לתורה, לחופה, ולמעשים טובים, 275

לתקוני שדרתיך ולא לעוותי, 160

מאחורי הפרגוד, 168

מאי בין כך ובין כך, 165

מאי דהוה הוה, 165

מאי דקמא, 165

מאי חזית דדמא דידך סומק טפי, דילמא דמא דההוא
גברא סומק טפי?, 165

מאי נפקא מינה, 166

מאי קא משמע לן, 165

מאי קשיה לך, 166

מאי תיקון גדול, 166

מאי תקנתיה, 166

מאיגרא רם לבירא עמיקתא, 169

מאך אן אתנחתא!, 276

מאכן א חילוף אנסיכה אויף אהללה, 241

מאכן אל מלא רחמים, 233

מאכן בורא מאורי האש, 228

מאכן הזכרת נשמות, 233

מאכן ללעג וקלס, 215

מאלף ועד תיו, 168

מאמינים בני מאמינים, 163

מאן דאיהו רגיל בשקרא אשתדל תדיר בשקרא, 277

מאן דיהב חיי יהב מזוני, 167

מאן דכר שמיה, 167

מבין דבר מתוך דבר, 169

מביינתא דראשי ועד טופרא דכרעיי, 171

מגדל הפורח באויר, 171

מגיד דברי דבריו ליעקב ... לא עשה כן; מאכט רש״י: דער מגיד
שטראפט קהל און אליין טוט ער פארקערט, 215

מגלה זיין דעם קץ, 22

מדאורייתא (דאורייתא), 171

מדבר (מדבריק), 57

מדבר שקר תרחק, 32

מדה כנגד מדה, 171

מדוע דרך רשעים צלחה, 100

מדרבנן (דרבנן), 171

מדרגה עליונה (תחתונה), 164

מדת הדין, מדת הרחמים, 10

מדת חסידות, 171

מדת סדום, 14

מדת רחמים שיתף הקב״ה למדת הדין, 11

מה אנו מה חיינו, 246

מה בין חכם לנבון? נבון דומה לשלחני תגר, 69

מה בין חסידים למתנגדים? הראשונים חושבים שיש להם
רבי, והאחרונים חושבין שאין להם צורך ברבי, 276

מה הבריות אומרות?, 22

מה ההבדל בין מתנה לנדבה? מתנה נותנים לאדם כדי
לקרב אותו, ונדבה-כדי להפטר ממנו, 276

מה טוב ומה נעים שבת אחים גם יחד, 100

מה טובו אהליך יעקב משכנתיך ישראל, 62

מה טיבו של עובר זה, 164

מה ידעת ולא נדע, 100

מה יום מיומים, 165
מה יעשה אדם ויחכם? ירבה בישיבה וימעיט בסחורה-יבקש רחמים, 164
מה-יפית (מה-יפיתניק), 224
מה לי הכה, מה לי התם, 164
מה (ממה) נפשך, 164
מה מתוק מדבש ומה עז מארי?, 100
מה ענין שמיטה אצל הר סיני, 51
מה פרצת עליך פרץ?, 21
מה קול המון הזה?, 100
מה שיעשה הזמן לא יעשה השכל, 276
מהדרין מן המהדרין, 169
מהיכא תיתי, 168
מהיכן ירק זה חי, 168
מודה במקצת הטענה, 175
מוטב יהודי בלי זקן מאשר זקן בלי יהודי, 278
מום שבך אל תאמר לחברך, 175
מוסיפין מחול על הקדש, 175
מועדים לשמחה-חגים וזמנים לששון, 233
מוציא לעז, 175
מוציא שם רע, 175
מוצא שפתיך תשמר, 76
מוקצה מחמת מיאוס, 175
מורנו, 278
מושל באדם צדיק מושל יראת אלהים, 102
מושלם בכל המעלות, 176
מותר לו לאדם לשנות בדבר השלום, 176
מזכה את הרבים, 170
מזל-טוב, 277
מזרח, 278
מחדש זיין די לבנה, 228
מחוט ועד שרוך-נעל, 14
מחיל אל חיל, 100
מחרף ומגדף, 169
מחצית השקל, 34
מחשבה טובה הקב"ה מצרפה למעשה, 165
מ"ט שערי טומאה, 221
מי בחרב ומי ברעב-וער זאל נכשל ווערן דורך דער שווערד און ווער דורכן רב, 242
מי ומי ההולכים, 27
מי-יודע וויפיל, 236
מי לה' אלי, 35
מי שאומר אל"ף יאמר גם בי"ת, 277
מי שאינו כועס הקב"ה אוהבו, 170
מי שאינו נותן ליעקב נותן לעשו, 18
מי שטרח בערב שבת יאכל בשבת, 171
מי שיש לו מנה רוצה מאתים, 277
מי שלא ישתוק מעצמו, ישתיקוהו אחרים, 277
מי שלא ראה שמחת בית השואבה לא ראה שמחה מימיו,
170

מי שמבקש יותר מצרכו, טורד נפשו מתועלתו, 277
מי שמבקשים ממנו מחילה לא יהא אכזרי מלמחול, 61
מי שמע כזאת, מי ראה כאלה?, 101
מיט אכילה הייבט זיך אן זיין יוצר, 242
מיט אלע רמ"ח אברים, 215
מיט קידוש לבנה קען מען זיך ניט אפפאסטן, 228
מילתא דבדיחותא, 172
מימינים ומשמאלים, 100
מיעוטא דמיעוטא, 175
מיתת נשיקה, 174
מכאן ואילך, 171
מכבדי אכבד ובזי יקלו, 101
מכה אשר לא כתוב, 77
מכל מלמדי השכלתי, 101
מכלל לאו אתה שומע הן, 35
מכף רגל ועד ראש אין בו מתם, 101
מכף רגלו ועד קדקדו לא היה בו מום, 101
מכר שער הראש, 166
מכת מדינה, 166
מלא וגדוש, 167
מלא כרמון, 167
מלאך המות מה לי הכא מה לי התם?, 166
מלאכי חבלה, 166
מלדה ומבטן ומהריון, 102
מלה בסלע ומשתוקא בתרין, 172
מלחמתה של תורה, 172
מלי דעלמא, 172
מלמד זכות, 169
מלתא דלא שכיחא, 172
ממילא, 172
ממצרים ועד הנה, 246
ממרי רשוותך פארי אפרע, 172
ממשה ועד משה לא קם כמשה, 277
מן היום ההוא והלאה, 102
מן הפחת אל הפח, 102
מן השמים ירחמו, 172
מן התנ"ך ידך אל תנח, 277
מנא מנא תקל ופרסין, 101
מנהג אבותיהם בידיהם, 173
מנהג אבותיכם בידכם, 173
מנהג אבותינו (ישראל) תורה היא, 173
מנהג מבטל הלכה, 173
מנהג עוקר הלכה, 173
מנהג שטות, 173
מנהיג עצמו ברבנות, 167
מנין אותיות של עשרת הדברות הם תרי"ג, 30
מסאנא דרב מכרעאי לא בעינא, 169
מסיח לפי תומו, 169
מסירת נפש, 170
מסעות, 65

מסתמא, 278

מסתפק במועט, 278

מעביר סדרה זיין, 231

מעביר על מדותיו, 164

מעוז צור איז גוט צו פארבייסן מיט חנוכה קעז, 248

מעוז צור ישועתי-אוי גאטעניו, גיב זשע פרנסה, 248

מעות ראש חודש, 277

מעז יצא מתוק, 100

מעט מן האור דוחה הרבה מן החשך, 277

מעיילין פילא בקופא דמחטא-הכנס פיל בקוף של מחט, 169

מעלה גרה, 42

מעלין בקודש ואין מורידין, 37

מען דארף מיט אים קיין ענינו ניט זאגן, 215

מען טאר ניט עסן תשעה באב, וווייל מען לייגט תפילין צו מנחה, 252

מען קען שוין נאך דעם זאגן א (רבנן) קדיש, 215

מערב (מערב) בדעת עם הבריות, 241

מעשה (מעשי) אבות סימן לבנים, 163

מעשה שהיה כך היה, 163

מעשי ידי טובעים בים, ואתם אומרים שירה?, 163

מעשיך יקרבוך ומעשיך ירחקוך, 164

מפי השמועה, 173

מפי עוללים וינקים יסדת עז, 102

מפני דרכי שלום, 173

מפני שיבה תקום והדרת פני זקן, 47

מצא או מוצא, 168

מצא מין את מינו, 168

מצוה הבאה בעבירה, 174

מצוה לרוץ לביהכנ"ס, 278

מצוה מן המובחר, 174

מצוה עשה שהזמן גרמא נשים פטורות, 174

מצוה שבאה לידך אל תחמיצנה, 28

מצורע-מוציא שם רע, 43

מקבל שבת זיין, 222

מקבלין קרבנות מפושעי ישראל כדי שיחזרו בהן בתשובה, 41

מקום שבעלי תשובה עומדין צדיקים גמורים אינם עומדין, 166

מקימי מעפר דל-אז גאט העלפט דעם ארעמאן: מאשפּת ירים אביון-איז אים גארניט צו דערקענען, 233

מקצת שבחו של אדם אומרים בפניו, וכולו שלא בפניו, 172

מקרני ראמים עד ביצי כנים, 172

מר בר רב אשי, 167

מר נפש, 100

מראית עין, 167

מרגלית טובה היתה בידכם ובקשתם לאבדה ממני, 167

מרוב עצים לא יראה היער, 277

מרובים צרכי עמך, 246

מרשעים יצא רשע, 101

משא ומתן, 167

משגיה מן החלונות, 100

משה עניו מאד מכל האדם, אף מאבות, 59

משופרי (ד)שופרי, 170

משחק בקוביא, 169

משיח'ס צייטן, 168

משכמו ומעלה גבה מכל העם, 102

משמר, 277

משנה מקום משנה מזל, 170

משנה תורה, 70

משנכנס אב ממעטין בשמחה, 174

משנכנס אדר מרבין בשמחה, 174

מששת ימי בראשית, 11

מתוך שלא לשמה בא לשמה, 62

מתושלח'ס יארן (צייטן), 10

נאד(של) דמעות, 279

נאך אמאל אודך, 233

נבון זה המבין דבר מתוך דבר, 176

נבל פה, 176

נהרא נהרא ופשטה, 176

נוגע בדבר, 177

נון הפוכה, 59

נוסח (נוסחאות, נוסחים), 279

נוקם ונוטר, 177

נח היה צדיק בדורותיו, 12

נחבא אל הכלים, 102

נחת רוח, 176

ניט אלע פורים טרעפט זיך א נס, 251

ניטל, 279

נכנס יין יצא סוד, 177

נכר הוא זה שלא עבר על פתחה של תורה, 177

נלאיתי הנחם, 103

נלאיתי כלכל ולא אוכל, 103

נלאיתי נשא, 103

נמשל כבהמות נדמו, 103

נס גדול היה שם, 248

נסוג אחור, 278

נסתלק, 279

נעלמים, 102

נעשה ונשמע, 32

נפטר (נסתלק), 177

נפישי גמלי סבי דטעיני משכי דהוגני, 176

נפל תורא חדד לסכינא, 176

נפלה עטרת ראשנו, 102

נפקא מינה, 176

נצח ישראל לא ישקר, 102

נצור לשונך מרע, 102

נר לאחד נר למאה, 176

נרו יאיר, 246

נשארנו מעט מהרבה, 103

נשיאת כפים, 58

נשים רחמניות הן, 176

נשים תאמר להן בלשון רכה, 30

נשך: דקא נכית ליה, דקא שקיל מיניה מידי דלא יהיב, 52

נשך: ריבית שהיא כנשיכת נחש-ואינו מרגיש, ופתאום הוא מבטבט ונופח עד קדקדו, 52

נשמה יתירה נותן הקב״ה באדם ערב שבת, ולמוצאי שבת קודש נוטלין אותה ממנו, 35

נתון (נתת) תורת כל אחד ואחד בידו?, 176

ס׳איז נאך ווייט צו כל חמירא, 236

סבא בביתא פאחא בביתא, סבתא בביתא סימא בביתא, 184

סברא, 186

סדנא דארעא חד הוא, 184

סומך ה׳ לכל הנפלים, 105

סוף אדם למות וסוף בהמה לשחיטה, 190

סוף גנב לתליה, 283

סוף מעשה-במחשבה תחלה, 223

סופו מוכיח על תחלתו, 190

סטרא אחרא, 283

סייעתא דשמיא (סייעתא הוא מן שמיא), 186

סכנת נפשות, 185

סליחות טעג, 237

סמיכות-הפרשה, 32

סימן יפה, 190

סעודת מצוה, 186

ספירה צייט, 221

סקאצל קומט, 216

סתירהדיק, 190

סתם מקשן עם הארץ, 283

עבודה זו תפלה, 121

עבודת פרך, 25

עבר זמנו (יומו) בטל קרבנו, 63

עברי; עברים, 271

עגה בלי הפוכה, 106

עגל הזהב, 34

עגמת נפש, 115

עד דלא ידע בין ארור המן לברוך מרדכי, 249

עד כאן אומרים בשבת הגדול, 227

עד מאה ועשרים שנה, 79

עד מתי?, 83

עד מתי אלהים יחרף צר, ינאץ אויב שמך לנצח, 83

עד שאול תחתית, 78

עד שתבוא הנחמה, תצא ח״ו הנשמה, 257

עדיין לא הגיעה לחצי יופיה של שרה, 114

עדשים מאכל צרה ואבל הן, 17

עוד מעט וסקלוני, 29

עודך מחזיק בתומתך, 103

עולם הזה-עולם הבא, 178

עולם הפוך, 178

עולם לסולם הוא דומה: זה עולה וזה יורד, 279

עומדין ברומו של עולם, 178

עוסק במצוה פטור מן המצוה, 178

עוקר הרים, 177

עזות פנים, 127

עזר כנגדו, 9

עין הרע, 121

עין לא ראתה, 85

עין תחת עין, 31

עיני ולבי שם כל הימים, 85

עיני כל ישראל עליך, 86

עינים להם ולא יראו, 232

עיקר שירה מן התורה, 58

עיר הנדחת, 148

על אחת כמה וכמה, 116

על דאטפת אטפוך, וסוף מטיפיך יטופון, 116

על העצים ועל האבנים, 116

על הראשונים אנו מצטערים ואתה בא להוסיף עליהם!, 29

על כל פנים, 257

על כל פשעים תכסה באהבה, 238

על ראשון ראשון ועל אחרון אחרון, 20

על רגל אחת, 116

עלי ועל צוארי, 118

עלי יחשבו רעה לי, 84

עליו השלום, 258

עלילת דם, 258

עלית נשמה, 258

עלמא דקרושטא (דקשוט)(דשקרא), 258

עם-הארץ, 16

עם הספר, 258

עם לבן גרתי, 20

עמדו שערותיו, 118

עמוד על דבריו, 118

עמך, 72

ענבי הגפן בענבי הגפן דבר נאה ומתקבל, 148

ענג שבת, 103

ענטפערן אמן, 210

עני ואביון, 75

עני חשוב כמת, 118

עניות כמיתה, 119

עניי עירך קודמים, 118

עניני דיומא, 271

עס איז אנקט מסלדיך, 244

עס איז להבדיל אלף הבדלות, 263

עס איז להבדיל בין קודש לחול, 227

עס איז ניט מעלה און ניט מוריד, 33

עס גייט ווי א מזמור, 212

עס העלפֿט ניט כי אל שומרנו ומצילנו-ובצלי, 220

עס ווערט זיך ווענדן ווי דער חמור שטייט, 263

עצה טובה קא משמט לן, 126

עצרת, 48

עקדת יצחק (עקידה), 15

עקר מן השרש, 257

ער איז געשטאָרבן אן א קדיש, 211

ער (איז ניט אויסן) מיינט ניט די הגדה נאר די קניידלאך, 235

ער איז צום בארג סיני ניט דערגאנגען, 29

ער איז שוין א הלך לעולמו, 232

ער בויט פּתם ורעמסס, 25

ער האט אוועקגעגנבעט דעם חומש מיטן לא תגנב, 29

ער האט אים געגעבן א מי שברך, 230

ער האט אפֿגעקלאפּט דעם מזמור אין א רגע, 211

ער האט געבוירן א קדיש, 211

ער האט געהאט קפיצת הדרך, 18

ער האט דעם קדיש צו הויך אנגעהויבן, 210

ער האט זיך איינגעקויפֿט מפֿטיר יונה, 244

ער האלט שוין ביי כוס רביעי, 235

ער זאגט נאר מה-טובו, 212

ער זאגט עברי ווי א וואסער, נאר דאס וואסער לאויפֿט אן ער שטייט, 212

ער קומט אף מיט יהי רצון, 225

ער קומט צום אורישפּיעל, 211

ער קוקט ווי א האן אין בני אדם, 244

ער קלאפֿט זיך אשמנו מיטן לינקן פֿוס אין דער רעכטער זייט אריין, 244

ער קען מיך (אן) קלאגן (לאדן) צום ונתנה-תוקף, 239

ער קען מיך אפֿזאגן דעם הכל יודך, 224

ער קען קיין מוציא נישטו מאכן איבער א רעטעך, 219

ער שטייט א לאנגע שמונה עשרה, 211

ער שלאגט זיך על-חטא און באלעקט זיך דערביי, 244

ער שרייבט נח מיט זיבן גרייזן, 12

ערב רב, 27

ערבך ערבא צריך, 120

ערי מקלט, 65

עריות, 44

ערל, 27

ערלה אזנם ולא יוכלו להקשיב, 84

עשה עמי אות לטובה, 85

עשה עצמו כאלו לא ידע, 25

עשירות של קרח, 60

עשירים מקמצין, 120

עשרה בטלנים, 120

עשרת ימי תשובה, 238

עתיק יומין, 121

פאלן כורעים, 244

פֿאלן תחנון, 212

פֿאנגט אן ברוך שאמר, אן עולם וועט שוין אנקומען, 212

פאסטן הפסקות, 252

פֿאר אמן קומט קיין פּאטש ניט, 213

פֿאר לויטער אהבה רבה קומט ער ניט צו שמע ישראל, 213

פֿארבייטן די יוצרות, 225

פֿאראוו, 280

פֿארפֿאלן, לעולם ועד, 225

פדיון שבויים מצוה רבה היא, 181

פה אחד, 104

פה מפיק מרגליות, 180

פֿון ברוך שאמר ביז אדון עולם, 213

פֿון ברוך שאמר ביז ברוך משלום איז ווייט, 213

פֿון וכך היה אומר ביז וכך היה מונה איז א לאנגע ווייַלע (איז א גרויסער אונטערשייד; פֿאלט מען זיבן מאל כורעים; איז גאר אן אנדער ניגון), 245

פֿון נקי כפים וערט מען ניט רייך, 213

פֿון על-חטא וערט מען ניט פעט, 245

פונקט דרייצן, 182

פּוסח על שתי הסעיפים, 104

פוק חזי מאי עמא דבר, 181

פורים איז נאר איין טאג און נאר א קבצן איז מען א גאנץ יאר, 251

פורים איז ניט קיין יום-טוב און קדחת איז ניט קיין קריינק, 251

פורים דאנקט מען ניט, 251

פורים קטן דארף (מעג) מען זיך אנשיכורן אבער יום כפור קטן דארף מען ניט פאסטן, 251

פטור בלא כלום אי אפשר, 42

פטור ווארן פון א חמץ, 236

פי כחרב חדה, 104

פי צדיק יהגה חכמה, 104

פילפול, 181

פינטעלע ייד, 280

פלאי פלאות (פלאי פלאים), 26

פמליא של מעלה, 179

פנים חדשות, 180

פנים של איכה, 104

פנקס, 181

פסול לעדות, 180

פסוק בזמנו, כנהמא בשעת רעבון (רעבא), 280

פעמים שאדם שותק ומקבל שכר על שתיקתו, ופעמים שאדם מדבר ומקבל שכר על דבורו, 180

פקוח נפש דוחה שבת, 35

פרא אדם, 14

פראוועץ תעניתים (תעניות), 252
פרדס, 280
פרהסיא (בפרהסיא), 180
פרוטה ופרוטה מצטרפת לחשבון גדול, 181
פרעגו(ט) מיך בחרם, 264
פרעגן די פיר קשיות, 235
פרצה קוראה לגנב, 181
פרשת אמר שערט מען די לעמער, 50
פשט לו את הרגל, 180
פשוטו כמשמעו, 12
פשטל, 280
פתח בחד וסיים בחויות, 180
פתחון פה, 41

צאן קדשים, 286
צדה לדרך, 21
צדיקים אומרים מעט ועושין הרבה, 195
צדק צדק תרדף, 74
צו גאט און צו לייט, 196
צו גאטס נאמען, 247
צו די עשר מכות נעמט מען קיין חתן ניט צו גאסט, 236
צועקין ואינם נענין, 196
צורבא מרבנן, 196
צוריק גייט מען נאר ביי עושה שלום, 217
ציטערן ווי א פרומער ייד אין די עשרת ימי תשובה, 237
צייל ספירה (צייל עומר), 221
צער בעלי חיים, 76
צער גידול בנים, 195
צפה לשלחן אחרים, 196
צרה קוראה לחברתה, 106
צריך עיון, 286
צרת רבים חצי נחמה, 285

קא משמע לן (קמ"ל), 148
קב ונקי, 150
קבלת קנין, 272
קבעת עתים לתורה?, 150
קדרא דבי שותפי לא חמימא ולא קרירא, 152
קודשא בריך הוא (קב"ה), 157
קודשא בריך הוא, אורייתא וישראל חד, 273
קוויטל (פתקה), 273
קול באשה ערוה, 153
קול דממה דקה, 93
קול המון כקול שדי, 272
קול קורא במדבר, 94
קול רם: בקולו של רם, 77
קול תקיעה וקול תרועה-און עס קומט נאך אלץ ניט די ישועה, 245
קוצו (קוצה) של יוד, 156

קטן וגדול שם הוא, 92
קידוש השם, 49
קינדער מגדל צו זיין מוז מען האבן קורח'ס עשירות און שמשון הגיבור'ס גבורה, 60
קל וחומר, 149
קל שבקלים, 18
קלאגן אויפן חורבן, 252
קלאר (אין ...) ווי א איד אין אשרי, 214
קליין ווי א טל ומטר"ל, 214
קם ליה בדרבה מיניה, 149
קמי דשתי חמרא-חמרא; קמי רפוקא-גרידא דיבלי, 149
קמיע, 149
קנאת סופרים תרבה חכמה, 152
קעלבערנע יוצרות, 225
קענען אויס(ען) וויינעג ווי א איד אשרי, ווי א וואסער, 214
קפיצת הדרך, 18
קפצה עליו זקנה, 149
קפת הרוכלים, קפה של בשמים, 157
קצוצי פאה, 93
קראתם דרור בארץ לכל ישביה, 50
קרב אליך, 93
קרב לגבי דהינא ואידהן, 69
קרוב ה' לנשברי לב, 92
קרובים הפסולים להעיד, 151
קרח מכאן ומכאן, 150
קריגן (זיין) ששי, 230
קריינא דאיגרתא איהו ליהוי פרוונקא, 150
קריעת ים סוף, 28
קרקפתא דלא מנח תפלין, 150
קשה היא הפרנסה כפלים כלידה, 272
קשה כשאול קנאה, 92
קשה (קשין) לזווגם כקריעת ים סוף, 150
קשה עלי פרידתכם, 49
קשה ערף, 73
קשוט עצמך ואחר כך קשוט אחרים, 152
קשין מזונותיו של אדם כקריעת ים סוף, 150

ראה גיהנם פתוחה מתחתיו, 19
ראויין לאותה אצטלא, 183
ראיה מביאה לידי זכירה, 60
ראש המדברים בכל מקום, 184
ראש חודש בענטשן, 226
ראשון לציון, 281
ראשית חכמה יראת ה', 104
ראשך והר (רישיך והר), 184
רבא משערות ראשי שנאי חנם, 104
רבון העולמים, 183
רבונו של עולם, 183

רבי לא שנאה (שנה) רב חייא מנין לו?, 182

רבי, לך שרי ולי אסור?, 281

רבי מכבד עשירים, 182

רגזן לא עלתה בידיה אלא רגזנותא, 182

רגלי קדמא ואזלא, 280

רואה ואינו נראה, 183

רוב גנבי ישראל נינהו, 184

רוח הקודש, 184

רוממות אל בגרונם, וחרב פיפיות בידם, 104

רחילא בתר רחילא אזלא, כעובדי אמה כך עובדי ברתא, 183

רחל מבכה על בניה, 104

רחמנא (הקב"ה) ליבא בעי, 182

רחמנא ליצלן (ניצלן), 182

רחמנים בני רחמנים, 183

רח"ש, 281

ריבית, 52

רייך ווי קרח, 61

רעב כבלב, 182

רפאי אלל כלכם, 104

רצה הקב"ה לזקות את ישראל, לפיכך הרבה להם תורה ומצות, 183

רשכבה"ג, 280

רשע למה תכה רעך, 26

שאינו יודע לשאול, 236

שאר ירקות, 236

שב ואל תעשה, 186

שבע דנחמתא, 70

שבע מצות בני נח, 13

שבעה מדורי גיהנום, 189

שבת-גוי, 281

שבת האט א יד א נשמה יתירה, 222

שבת לעונג ניתן ולא לצער, 281

שבת שלום ומבורך, 222

שגור בפיו, 186

שדכן, 281

שה פזורה ישראל, 104

שה"י פה"י, 189

שואלין ודורשין בהלכות הפסח קודם הפסח שלשים יום, 59

שוטה אין לו תקנה, 189

שויתי, 282

שויתי ה' לנגדי תמיד, 105

שוכן (יורד) עפר, 105

שולף חרב, 105

שומר פתאים ה', 105

שור הבר, 189

שטיבל, 283

שטייט אויף [קינדער] לעבודת הבורא, 237

שטייט אויף צו סליחות, 237

שטילע (הויכע) שמונה עשרה, 216

שטן מקטרג, 185

שטעלן זיך (אייסגיין) שמונה עשרה, 216

שטריימל במקום תפילין, 283

שיחת חולין, 190

שיחתן של ישראל תורה היא, 283

שייטל, 282

שימו יד על פה, 105

שינה בשבת תענוג, 282

שיריים, 282

שכור ווי לוט, 15

שכר מצוה בהי עלמא ליכא, 72

שכרותו של לוט, 15

שלא מצינו שועל שמת בעפר פיר, 188

שלאגן הושענות, 233

שלאגן זיך על-חטא, 247

שלאגן כפרות, 246

שלהי דקייטא קשיא מקייטא, 189

שלוחו של אדם כמותו, 28

שלום, 21

שלום בית, 186

שליט"א, 283

שלך קודם לכל אדם, 187

שלש עשרה מדות, 35

שלש של פרענות, 70

שלשה דברים מבטלין גזירה קשה: תפלה, צדקה, ותשובה, 188

שלשה שאכלו כאחד חייבין לזמן, 79

שלשה שאכלו-ער עסט פאר דרייען, 219

שם הויה, 186

שם תהא קבורתכם, 30

שמור לי ואשמור לך, 188

שמור מחסום לפה, 105

שמור עצמך שלא תחטא, 188

שמות, 281

שמיני שמונה שנה שמנה, 42

שמעו נא המורים, 61

שנאת חנם, 48

שנוי השם, 189

שנים אוחזים בטלית, 188

שעטנז, 48

שערי דמעה לא ננעלו, 187

שעת הדחק שאני, 187

שעת הכשר, 187

שפיכות דמים, 188

שפרינגט ניט קיין קיין קדוש און בוק זיך ניט קיין קיין מודים, 216

ש"ץ מ"ק, 281

שקולה צדקה כנגד כל המצות, 187

שקלא וטריא, 186

שקץ תשקצנו ותעב תתעבנו כי חרם הוא, 73

שקר אין לו רגלים, 187

שקר אסור לדבר, אבל את האמת לא תמיד חובה לספר, 282

שרגא בטיהרא מאי אהני?, 190

שרייבן אין האלבע לבנות, 228

שרייבן מיט קידוש לבנה אותיות, 228

שרייען שמע ישראל, 216

שתי תורות ניתנו לישראל אחת בכתב ואחת בע״פ, 53

שתיקה יפה בשעת התפילה, 282

שתיקה כהודאה דמיא, 188

שתיקותיך יפה מדיבוריך, 188

תבא עליו ברכה, 192

תבלה ותחדש, 284

תבן אתה מכניס לעפריים?, 193

תהא חביבה עליך מצוה קלה כמצוה חמורה, 74

תהא טמאה שבעת ימים, 44

תהא יציאתך מן העולם כביאתך לעולם-בלא חטא, 77

תוהו ובוהו, 11

תוך כדי דבור, 193

תוכו כברו, 33

תוכחה, 53

תולה בדעת אחרים, 193

תורה וגדולה במקום אהד, 194

תורה לשמה, 193

תורה מחזרת על אכסניא שלה, 194

תורה מתשת כחו של אדם, 194

תורה שאין לה בית אב אינה תורה, 194

תורה שבעל פה הלכה למשה מסיני, 18

תורת ה׳ תמימה, 106

תושלב״ע, 285

תזכה לשנים רבות, 285

תזריע-מצורע רייטט קרייה דער בעל-קריאה (קורא), 43

תחית המתים, 283

תחית המתים מן התורה, 70

תחת אהבתי ישטנוני, 105

תינוק שנשבה, 193

תיקו, 192

תיקון (תקון), 284

תכלית הידיעה שנדע שלא נדע, 283

תלמוד מביא לידי יראה, ויראה-לידי שמירה, ושמירה-
לידי מעשה, 74

תלמוד תורה כנגד כלם, 191

תלמיד חכם (תלמידי הכמים), 190

תלמיד חכם צריך שיהא בו אחד משמונה בשמינית
(גאוה), 190

תלמיד חכם צריך שלא יהא בו דבר של דפי, 283

תלמיד שלא ראה סימן יפה במשנתו חמש שנים, שוב אינו
רואה, 57

תלמידי חכמים אין להם מנוחה, 191

תלמידי חכמים מרבים שלום בעולם, 191

תלמידים קרויים בנים, והרב קריו אב, 72

תמותת רשע רעה, 106

תמת נפשי עם פלשתים, 105

תן לו מנה ויבקש מאתים, 284

תן לי יבנה וחכמיה, 192

תן עיניך ולבך על דבריך, 25

תעלא בעידניה סגיד ליה, 22

תפלות כנגד תמידין תקנום, 193

תפשת (תפסת) מרובה לא תפשת (תפסת), תפשת (תפסת)
מועט תפשת (תפסת), 190

תקיעת כף, 284

תרי קלי לא מישתמעי, 195

תרי״ג מצות, 192

תרתי דסתרי, 191

תרתי קלי מחד גברא לא משתמעי, 192

תתברכו מן השמים, 193

INDEX OF BIBLICAL, TALMUDIC, AND RABBINIC PASSAGES

BIBLE

Pentateuch

Genesis/Bereishit   בראשית

1:1	9, 10
1:1	11
1:2	11
1:5	156, 278
2:2	9
2:4	11
2:7	11
2:8	9
2:14	69
2:18	9, 10
2:19	11
2:22	140
2:22–23	217
3:19	9
4:9	10
4:13	188
5:26	10
5:28–32	12
6:3	271
6:8–22	12
6:9	12, 172, 200
6:11	12
7:1	172
7:8	12
8:7	12
8:21	13
9:4	12
9:19	12
9:21	159
10:21	271
11:9	12
11:27–31	15
11:31	11
12:1	14
12:1–2	170
13:13	13
14:1	219
14:13	271
14:21	14
14:23	14
15:6	139
15:15	142
16:12	14
16:16	14
17:7	116, 262
17:9	286
17:10	14
17:17–22	15
18:5	196
18:7	196
18:19	183
18:25	15
19:24–25	14
19:31	15
19:32–33	15
22:3	16, 115
22:1–19	15
22:20	176
23:12	16
23:15	189
25:19	17
25:21	17
25:27	16, 18
25:32	152
26:5	18
27:22	17
27:33	19, 219
27:40	16, 17
28:10	19
28:20	19
29:18	18
29:21	18
29:35	288
32:5	20
32:11	20, 190, 259
32:12	20
32:29	199
33:1–2	19
33:11	219
34:25–26	22

(continued)

37:30	21		12:48	27, 170
38:25	117		13:5	25
38:29	21		14:15	27
39:2	276		15:2	146, 152
39:14	271		16:31	28
40:14	268		16:35	57
41:9	21		16:26–36	29
41:12	271		17:3–4	29
41:15	21		17:14	288
42:5	49		18:2	29
42:25	21		18:11	128
43:23	174		19:3	30
44:20	21		19:5	30
45:21	21		19:11	29
46:30	259		19:17	30
47:28	22		20:1	115
47:29	268		20:7	262
47:31	22		20:8	223
49:6	22		20:12	285
49:8	288		20:13	30
49:22	22		20:17	183
50:16–17	173		21:2–3	31
50:21	22		21:24	31
			21:26–27	198
Exodus/Shemot		שמות	21:28	197
1:6	167		22:20	176
1:8	25, 26		22:24	118
1:11	25		22:30	31
1:12	272		23:2	31
1:13	25		23:8	31
1:15	288		23:19	32, 280
2:11	271		23:25	282
2:13	25		24:7	32
3:8	25		24:14	31
3:14	25		25:10	32
3:15	186		25:11	33
4:6	139		25:33	32
4:19, 20, 27	29		26:7	32
4:31	139		27:7	32
5:23	26		27:20	32, 33
6:6–7	235		28:4	264
6:9	26		28:5	33
6:10	271		28:40	264
6:23	142		29:27	33
9:22	26		30:11–16	34
10:8	28		30:14–15	34
10:9	27		30:17–21	35
11:7	27		30:34	34
12:6	28		30:34–38	214
12:17	28		31:6	123
12:19	236		31:13–14	35
12:26	153		31:17	35, 222
12:38	27		32:19	30
12:43	170		32:26	35

32:32	170		21:13	211
33:7	34		22:23	50
33:12	35		22:24	146
33:14	34		22:31	50
34:1	36, 232		22:32	49
34:6–7	35, 213		23:2	50
34:21	175		23:27	50, 239, 247
34:26	130, 280		23:32	175
34:28	34		23:40	48, 49
35:30	36		23:42	181
40:18	37		25:10	50
			25:13	52
Leviticus/Vayikra		ויקרא	25:36	52
1:1	41		25:38	51
1:2	41		25:48	123
1:9	41		26:1	50
2:2	282		25:4–5	53
3:2	162		26:31	52
6:3	41		26:37	156
7:37	41		27:28	264
9:1	156		37:34	52
9:17	46			
10:6	42		Numbers/Bemidbar	במדבר
10:12	42		3:1	57
11:3–4	42		3:2	57
11:8	42		4:3	57
11:15	42		4:23	57
11:44	42		5:2	58
11:46	42		8:15	57
13:2	124		8:24	57
14:2	43		10:35–36	59
14:40–42	179		11:16	59
15:19	43		11:18	29
16:4	124		12:13	58
16:7–8	45		13:2	14
16:23	124		13:27	25, 60
17:3	44		14:19	246
18:3	44		14:20	238
18:5	45		14:35	57
18:6–18	44		15:31	60
19:10	46		15:32	175
19:11	30		15:37–41	60, 214
19:14	46, 72		16:21	49
19:15	45		16:25	60
19:16	46, 47		18:29	170
19:17	48		19:14	61
19:18	47, 48, 116		20:4–5	57
19:19	46, 48		20:10	61
19:24	45		20:12	139
19:26	47		21:5	61
19:32	47		21:11	278
19:33	48		22:12	62
19:35–36	45		22:20	62
20:23	44		(continued)	

22:21	116
22:22	185
22:32	185
24:5	62, 212
26:9	64
26:11	63
27:7	64
27:17	63
27:18	167
27:23	63
29:35	63
30:3	64
31:14	64
31:21	64
32:3	64
33:47	65
35:9–15	65

Deuteronomy/Devarim   דברים

1:7	69
1:8	70
1:13	69
1:17	198
3:23	71
3:25	71
3:26	71
3:27	71
4:2	33
4:9–10	57
5:1	53, 71
5:12	223
5:16	72
5:17	30
6:4	71, 143, 214
6:4–9	214
6:6	143
6:7	71
6:13	72
7:26	73, 264
8:3	73
8:10	219
8:14	73
9:6	73
9:25	58
9:26	72
10:12	72, 73
11:1	33
11:13	121
11:13–21	214
11:19	154
13:1	33
13:5	135
13:18	73, 183
14:1	71, 73
14:21	32, 280

14:25	73
14:26	10
15:4	187
15:10	137
16:8	49, 63
16:14	233
16:20	74
17:2–7	75
17:7	75
17:19	74
19:3	65
19:14	74
19:15	134
20:19	74
21:18	75
22:8	76
22:9–11	46
22:11	48
22:13	75
22:13–21	175
22:26	119
23:4	161
23:8	130
23:14	75, 76
23:20–21	268
23:24	64, 76
24:1	75
24:14	75
25:4	76
27:9	76
27:14	77
27:17	74
28:6	77
28:61	77
29:8	77
30:2	127
30:15–19	285
30:19	77
31:7	78, 134
31:9	78
31:10	78
31:12	78
31:19	78, 191, 258
31:21	143
31:23	134
32:1–43	78
32:3	79
32:15	79
32:22	78
32:38	108
33:27	79
33:29	79
34:7	79
34:10	79

Rashi

Rashi on Genesis   רש״י בראשית
1:1	9, 10
2:2	9
3:24	166
6:6	9
6:9	13
21:21	16
23:1	114
25:30	17, 137
27:33	19, 219
28:17	19
29:21	18
31:54	19
32:19	20
33:1–2	19
42:4	185
47:28	22
47:31	22
48:7	104
50:21	22

Rashi on Exodus   רש״י שמות
1:8	25
1:13	25
3:14	25
6:9	26
9:22	26
12:6	28
12:17	28
14:15	27
16:22	165
18:1	31
18:2	29
20:19	29
21:1	32
22:24	52
33:12	35

Rashi on Leviticus   רש״י ויקרא
12:2	43
19:10	46
19:14	46, 72
19:16	46, 47
23:3	50
23:36	49
25:1	51
25:10	52
25:17	51
25:36	52
26:3	52
26:6	53
26:46	53

Rashi on Numbers   רש״י במדבר
3:38	58
5:18	282
8:6	58
9:1	59
13:27	25, 60
21:7	61
22:12	62
27:23	167
28:10	63
29:36	49

Rashi on Deuteronomy   רש״י דברים
1:13	69
6:18	160
11:13	148
12:28	74
14:1	71
19:17	75
22:23	181
23:10	185
31:10	78
31:12	78

Midrash Rabbah

Bereishit Rabbah   בראשית רבה
3	13
12	11
20:22	272
42:4	270
55:3	281
56:5	270
65:1	266
70:17	270
76:3	276
91:12	32
98:23	263

Shemot Rabbah   שמות רבה
42	270
52	177, 199

Vayikra Rabbah   ויקרא רבה
7:3	269
9:3	263
14:1	43
19:2	270
28:1	274
30:11	260
32:2	280
36:13	18

Bemidbar Rabbah	במדבר רבה	9:6	93
3:2	276	9:6–8	273
18:17	285	9:19	93
22:4	130	10:22	102
22:7	61	15:4	210
		15:29	102
Devarim Rabbah	דברים רבה	16:7	182
2:22	285	17:45	85
3:3	49	19:17	94
		22:2	100
Prophets	נביאים	23:19–29	232
		24:13	101
Early Prophets	נביאים ראשונים	25:5–11	93
		25:25	93
Joshua	יהושע	25:33	133
1:7	78	26:19	51
1:8	77	30:13	95
4:5–6	163		
9:2	104	Second Samuel	שמואל ב׳
15:8	189	1:20	83
24:2	11	3:29	89
24:3	271	10:12	230
		15:6	138
Judges	שופטים	18:20	97
1:7	91	23:3	102
1:8	106		
1:15	89	First Kings	מלכים א׳
3:24	89	1:4	114
5:6	229	1:20	86
6:14	95	1:51	83
6:24	224	3:4	62
7:17	92	5:11	57
8:10	105	8:28	96
8:25	92	8:46	85
9:13	107	9:3	86
14:14	260	11:26–40	91
14:18	100	13:1	91
15:11	91	13:18	88
16:6	86	14:9	47
16:30	105	15:30	91
17:6	90	18:21	46, 104
18:25	100	19:12	93
		20:11	84
First Samuel	שמואל א׳	22:20	109
1:1	178	22:20–22	274
1:11	161		
2:6	284	Second Kings	מלכים ב׳
2:7	89	2:3	71
2:30	101	2:11	162
3:10	87	2:12	72
4:7	103	4:33–35	137
4:14	100	6:19	99
8:1	149	7:9	109
9:2	102	11:9	63

13:21	137	54:13	191
14:10	89, 106	55:1	85
18:5	97	55:6	239
23:25	97	55:7	128
		55:8	97
Latter Prophets	נביאים אחרונים	56:2	146
		56:4	147
Isaiah	ישעיה	57:13	103
1:1	179	57:19	166
1:2	86	58:13–14	79
1:6	101	59:1	93
1:9	117	62:1	95
1:14	103	64:3	85
2:13	84	65:5	93
3:3	169	66:8	101
5:7	93		
5:20	90	Jeremiah	ירמיה
6:3	71	2:2	57, 109
7:7	98	4:30	94
7:9	90	5:21	232
10:15	89	6:10	84
11:5	264	9:4	96
11:12	239	9:7	86
14:8	84	9:22	84
14:24	91	9:25	93
19:22	139	11:19	19
22:13	83	12:1	100
23:18	121	13:7	99
24:2	92	13:11	96
24:18	102	14:9	94
25:8	87	15:6	103
26:19	105, 284	16:17	99
27:11	114, 153	17:7	86
27:13	239	18:6	245
28:5	172	18:18	88, 95
28:6	172	19:5	96
28:29	194	20:9	103
29:8	92	21:12	94
29:11	108	22:6	57
29:13	87	22:28	92
29:22	195	23:11	88
30:5	97	23:29	92
30:20	95	30:10	199
30:22	156	30:14	94
32:17	136	30:18	245
40:1	109	31:11	99
40:3	94	31:14	104
42:21	106	31:28	85
47:8	84	32:17	99
47:10	84	32:35	189
49:2	104	42:2	103
49:4	95	42:4	97
49:10	99	43:12	92
54:9	12	*(continued)*	

46:11	94
46:20	108
48:38	92
50:15	91
50:17	104
51:1	96
51:5	96

Ezekiel   יחזקאל
1:24	272
2:62	198
5:7	44
6:10	96
6:11	103, 279
7:19	92
11:12	44
16:44	183
16:63	41
18:2	85
20:33	87
25:14	275
29:21	41
33:19	128
36:22	97
36:38	286
39:22	102
42:20	95
44:30	10
46:17	51

Twelve Minor Prophets   תרי עשר

Hosea   הושע
4:4	135
7:1	139
7:8	106
8:5	83
9:10	91
9:11	102
14:10	108

Joel   יואל
| 2:3 | 10 |

Amos   עמוס
4:12	90, 264
5:21	49
7:14, 15	97

Obadiah   עובדיה
| 1:15 | 91 |

Jonah   יונה
| 4:11 | 98 |

Micah   מיכה
3:6	94
4:4	91, 107
7:1	103
7:2	85
7:18–19	85
7:19	240

Nahum   נחום
| 1:9 | 98 |

Habakkuk   חבקוק
| 1:5 | 98 |
| 2:5 | 107 |

Zephania   צפניה
| 1:18 | 92 |
| 3:5 | 99 |

Haggai   חגי
| 2:8 | 96 |
| 2:9 | 96 |

Zechariah   זכריה
4:6	98
8:11	97
11:5	261

Malachi   מלאכי
| 1:13 | 174 |
| 3:16 | 165 |

Hagiographa   כתובים

Psalms   תהלים
1:2–3	77
1:3	93, 190
1:6	87
2:12	85
5:7	90
7:12	157
7:16	87
8:3	102
12:2	90
12:3	87, 94
16:8	105
16:10	284
19:4	85
19:6	211
19:8	106
24:4	213
26:4	102
28:9	210
29:10	12

30:6	86		107:4	57
32:1	85		107:33–36	57
31:10	131		109:4	105
33:12	85		111:10	104, 217
34:14	102		112:3	258
34:19	92		113:7	233
34:22	106		115:1	232
35:10	93		115:5	232
37:2	87		116:6	105
37:3	103		116:11	232
37:21	99		118:6	89
37:30	104		118:23	274
39:2	105		119:59	268
39:13	187		119:99	101
41:8	84		120:3	95
45:3	139		120:5	103
49:13	103		121:1	88
49:18	98		126:5	89
50:1	278		127:3	138
50:5	57		128:2	108
51:19	274		133:1	100
52:7	279		136:13	28
55:5	85		136:25	28
55:23	99		137:5	90
56:9	279		137:6	83
57:5	96		139:5	83
61:2	88		139:16	266
61:8	182		144:4	83
62:5	87		145:9	284
65:2	95, 172		145:14	105
68:20	86		146:3	84
69:2	86		147:19–20	215
69:5	104		148:6	88
71:9	83		149:6	104
72:18	127			
73:22	106	Job		איוב
74:10	83	1:6–22	198
76:11	265	1:21	89
78:38	221	2:9	103
79:10	94	2:10	88, 92
81:4	239	3:18	92
81:6	50	3:25	98
81:11	88	5:2	95
84:3	96	5:7	83
84:8	100, 191	11:2	90
85:12	87	12:3	98
86:6	88	12:4	98
86:17	85	13:2	98
91:10	98	13:4	104
92:13	84	13:15	115
96:12	221	13:16	97
103:12	93	14:19	85
103:13	92	15:6	107
104:15	107, 223	(continued)	

15:9	100
15:23	196
20:6	106
21:5	105
28:28	72
30:31	89
32:7	107
33:23	289
34:10	15
34:35	122
34:37	109
36:7	99
37:1	108
40:23	107

Song of Songs   שיר השירים

2:2	93
2:9	100
2:14	89, 153
3:6	57
4:11	87
4:13	280
5:6	260
6:3	84
8:6	92

Ruth   רות

| 1:1 | 195 |
| 2:19 | 108 |

Lamentations   איכה

1:12	96
2:1	169
3:17	186
4:21	88
5:16	102
5:21	213

Ecclesiastes   קהלת

2:4	280
2:11	83
3:7	180
4:12	263
4:17	188
5:1	225
7:12	132
7:26	168
7:27	181
10:18	146
10:19	107
10:20	280
11:4	146
12:1	198

Esther   אסתר

1:1	13
1:10	250
2:22	155
6:2	155

Daniel   דניאל

1:8	108
2:21	107, 123
4:6	94
4:23	134
4:28	129
5:1	19
5:3	101
5:25	101
6:10	278
7:9	121
7:13	121
7:26	168
12:2	284
12:6	22

Ezra   עזרא

2:62	198
9:11	16
10:8	264

Nehemiah

2:3	86
2:8	280
5:8	116
7:64	198
8:10	90
10:31	16
13:30	277

First Chronicles   דברי הימים א'

12:2	100
19:13	230
21:1	185
22:13	78
26:18	280
29:9	87

Second Chronicles   דברי הימים ב'

7:9	49
7:16	86
29:11	72

Midrashim

Shir Hashirim Rabbah   שיר השירים רבה

| 1:8 | 257 |
| 3:6 | 57 |

4:11 87
4:22 283

Ekhah Rabbah איכה רבה
1:1 104

Kohelet Rabbah קהלת רבה
1:34 277
8:8 281

Esther Rabbah אסתר רבה
10 250

Mishnah משנה

Berakhot ברכות
3:5 119
5:5 186
7:1 219

Pe'ah פאה
1:1 191, 218, 268
2:6 140
7:4 46
7:5 181

Demai דמאי
1:3 16
2:3 16

Kilayim כלאים
8:6 189
9:1 48
9:8 48

Ma'asayr Shayni מעשר שני
5:12 260

Pesahim פסחים
1:2 147

Yoma יומא
1:4 141

Sukkah סוכה
3a,b 119
5:1 170
5:2 166

Rosh Hashanah ראש השנה
1:8 141

Ta'anit תענית
1:6 167
15a 136

Megillah מגילה
1:3 120
3:4 34
3:6 53

Hagigah חגיגה
1:8 142

Yebamot יבמות
4:13 179, 198

Sotah סוטה
7:6 78
7:8 261
9:15 121

Gittin גיטין
4:6 181
9:8 271

Kiddushin קידישין
1:9 263
4:1 115

Baba Kama בבא קמא
1:1 144
3:3 153

Baba Metzi'a בבא מציעא
1:1 188
6:6 188
10:6 168

Baba Batra בבא בתרא
2:4 119
8:5 161

Sanhedrin סנהדרין
1:6 120
2:1 193
3:3 169, 180
3:4 180
6:4 246
10:1 186, 284
10:3 57

Shebu'ot שבועות
2:1 176

Eduyyot עדיות
1:4 118
2:2 163
5:7 164

Avot   אבות
  1:2   231
  1:3   134
  1:6   289
  1:12   173
  1:14   15
  1:30   45
  2:2   263
  2:5   117
  2:6   116
  2:13–14   131
  3:15   14
  3:17   172
  3:21   263
  4:1   101, 127
  4:15   72
  4:20   174
  4:23   34
  4:28   155
  5:9   266
  5:11   49
  5:18   170
  5:21   211, 289
  6:1   194
  6:2   198
  6:6   155, 181

Hulin   חולין
  3:5   185

Tamid   תמיד
  5:4   167

Kelim   כלים
  12:6   266
  17:16   179

Oholot   אהלות
  11:7   130

Nega'im   נגעים
  2:5   122, 154
  12:6   179

TALMUD

Babylonian Talmud   תלמוד בבלי

Berakhot   ברכות
  3a   130, 143
  3b   123, 159
  4a   157
  4b   214
  5a   116, 198

  5b   123
  6a   96
  6b   174, 263, 278
  7a   34, 116, 157, 160
  8a,b   64, 119, 168
  9a   31
  9b   25
  10a   115, 183
  10b   47, 122, 128
  13a   143
  14b   153
  16b   72, 226, 288
  17a   16, 136, 177, 180, 183
  17b   190
  18a   119
  18b   168, 268, 274
  19a   117, 183
  20a   182
  20b   174
  21a   219
  21b   49, 57
  23a   188
  24a   140, 153, 282
  24b   190
  26b   193
  28a   33, 37
  28b   10, 133, 144
  31a   135, 194
  31b   44, 161
  32a   71, 170, 289
  32b   70, 78, 145, 187
  33a   262
  33b   72
  34a   58
  34b   28, 108, 149, 166
  35a   45, 163
  36b   157
  43b   117
  45a   79, 182
  47a   162
  47b   16, 174
  49b   117
  50a   88
  50b   174
  54a   129, 224
  54b   132, 138, 230
  55a   36, 123, 167
  55b   98
  56b   26
  57a   33, 49, 167
  57b   136, 178
  58a   131
  59a   124
  59b   129

60b	155, 209, 264
61a	11
61b	201
62a	198
63a	136
63b	61, 76, 114, 116
64a	100, 142, 177, 191

Shabbat	שבת
10a	139, 200, 264
10b	117, 224
12a,b	141
13a	176
13b	125
16b	33
21b	138, 169
23b	186
25b	127, 186
28a	163
29a	171
30a	190
30b	159, 161, 172
31a	48, 116, 123, 150, 159
32a	76, 117, 176
32b	48
33a	146
33b	184
35b	164, 173
39a	137
41a	119
44a	175
44b	181
45a	187
55a	168
57a	167
58a	280
60a	149
61a,b	42
63a	148
63b	283
67b	158
68b	193
82a	172
83b	61
84b	182
87a	36, 232
88a	31, 166
88b	198
89b	133
96b	175
97a	139
98a	149, 165
104a	42, 187
104b	125

105b	74, 171
107b	172, 186
108b	201
112b	158
113a	46, 162
113b	161
114a	127, 193, 201
115a	115
116a	59
118a	145
118b	79, 103, 147, 169, 265
119a	122
122a	132
124a	175
125b	130
127a	125, 191, 218
128a	183
128b	76, 195
129a	74
129b	105
132a	35
133b	146
135b	138
136a	187
138b	143
140a	171
140b	74
151a	73
151b	11, 137, 198
152a	136, 138
153b	152
156a	124, 267
156b	265

Erubin	עירובין
3a	152
9a	168
11b	149
13b	121, 155
18b	172, 274
19a	189
24a	158
29b	192
40a	163
48a	119
53b	135
54a	139, 143
63b	172
65a	15, 177
65b	133, 163
68b	147
69b	41
70b	132

(continued)

86a	182		33a	138
92a	182		37a	200
100a	186		38b	42
100b	195		39a	42
			39b	186
Pesahim	פסחים		49a	128
3a	43, 131, 177		67b	45, 166
3b	160, 170		72b	33
4a	16		75a	29
5a	178		78a	149
6a	59		83a	117
6b	59		84a	166
8b	118		85a,b	35
22b	72		86a	22, 49, 119, 146
23a	125		86b	127
25b	165		87a	170
32a	192			
34a	166		Sukkah	סוכה
34b	201		5b	190
42b	136		21b	190
48b	166		25a	178
49a	148, 186		26a	120, 181
49b	137		28a	190
50a	129, 178		30a	174
50b	62, 126, 194		44a	171
53b	132		45b	158, 258
54b	122		49b	180
64b	126		51b	166, 261
66b	64, 152		52a	151
68b	63		53a	116, 128, 147
77a	144		55b	196
83a	187			
86b	155		Bezah	ביצה
87b	179		4b	173
92b	192		6b	136, 166
99a	196		9a	167
101a	124		16a	35, 86, 222
102b	197		22a	185
103a	197		28b	141
108a	165		32b	73, 196
110a	118			
113b	136, 170, 195		Rosh Hashanah	ראש השנה
118a	28		4b	190
119a	61, 121		6a	76, 153
119b	140, 173		9a	175
			12a	20
Yoma	יומא		14b	159
4b	41		16b	42, 170, 185, 188, 189
7a	145		17a	150
9b	184		18a,b	239
18b	126		23a	60
20a	185		25b	75
23a	116, 164, 177		26a	124
29a	189		27a	144, 192

28b	33
29b	142
30a	286
31a	192
31b	79
35b	18

Ta'anit	תענית
2a	121
5b	124, 149, 199
7a	142, 194
7b	127
8b	167
9a	160
10b	30, 127
11a	117, 154, 252
15b	42
16a	128, 136, 195
20b	159
21a	137
21b	58
23a	177, 183
25b	164
26b	174
28b	174
29a	174
31a	199

Megillah	מגילה
3a	214
5a	120
5b	251
6b	28, 197
7b	250
10b	156, 163
11a	13
12b	250
13b	34, 139, 189
14a	178
14b	133, 176
15a	116, 155
16a	250, 251
17a	155
18a	172
21a	150
21b	195
22a	201, 274
23b	49
28a	52, 130
28b	196
29a	44
31a	44

Mo'ed Katan	מועד קטן
8b	124
17a	46
21b	116
22b	136
28a	174

Hagigah	חגיגה
3a	78, 125, 147, 167
3b	115, 136
5a	132, 201
5b	129, 169
9b	126
11b	186
12b	134, 179
14a	69, 140, 147, 169, 219
14b	280
15a	168
15a,b	275
16a	168
16b	176

Yebamot	יבמות
12b	105
13b	65
25b	122
43a	182
53a	132
62b	10
63b	116
64a	17, 116, 262
64b	129
65b	151, 173
70a	151
77b	161
79a	183
84a	144
87b	188
90a	192
109b	71
119b	175
120a	161
121a	153
121b	140, 151, 169

Ketubot	כתובות
2a	114
5a,b	76
7b	180
8b	11, 117, 183
11a	199
12b	129, 164
17a	138, 241

(continued)

18b	122
19a	192
30a	140
50a	258
52a	147
54a	160
55a	175
57a	114
58b	134
59b	138
61a	178
63a	183
64b	178
66b	133
67b	165
68a	141
71b	188
72a	282
77b	157
85a	160
93a	139
94a	158
96b	126
103a	132, 160
103b	230
104a	197
105a	31
107b	146
108b	180
109b	144
110b	51
111a	115, 126
111b	25

Nedarim — נדרים

7b	118, 119
10a	123
12a	287
27a	119
28a	136
30b	118
38a	59, 181
39b	141
41a	122
48a	190
64b	118
65b	166
81a	146
81b	161

Sotah — סוטה

2a	120, 266
2b	28
4b	73

5a	190
8b	171
9b	61
10a	149
10b	50
11a	25, 26, 128, 133, 171, 272
14a	135
20a	131, 143, 154
21b	143, 154
22a	16
22b	62
31a	70
34a	163
35a	60, 134
36b	131
47a	63, 162
49a	131, 259
49b	131

Gittin — גיטין

3a	127
6b	117, 129
7a	117
24b	122
25a	193
28b	169
31b	129
40b	160
44a	158
46b	188
52a	163
52b	149
54a	192
56a	182, 275
56b	151, 192
57b	17
58a	181
59a	78, 173, 194, 230
61a	174
67a	150, 157
68b	118
82b	148
83a	125
85b	161

Kiddushin — קידושין

2b	75
5a	124
6a	123
10b	128
20b	123
24a	198
27b	184
29a	174

29b	154
30a	71
31a	265
31b	172, 200
32b	47, 59
39b	72, 180
40a	165, 194
40b	142, 160, 198
41a	182
41b	28
42b	160
44a	129
46a	143
49a	169
50a	153
53b	148
56b	197
69a	115
70a	153
70b	127, 135, 198
71a	151, 155, 186
71b	200
80b	148
82a	194

Baba Kamma   בבא קמא

3b	114
9a	139
9b	146
16b	287
20a,b	200
21a	191
27a	180
35b	192
38b	123
41a	197
46b	31, 172
59a	137
60b	150
65b	183
70b	134
73b	193
80b	138
82a	120
85a	120
87a	145
91b	144
92a	128, 130
92b	130, 156
96a	192
107a	175
107b	201
118a	129

Baba Metzi'a   בבא מציעא

14b	139
16a	172
17a	269
23b	193
28a	148
28b	148
30b	188
31a	46
32a	187
32b	76
33b	76, 122, 133
36b	164, 166
37b	188
38b	169
42a	73
44a	196
46b	172
49a	45
52b	171
58b	48, 51, 141, 188
59a	31, 117, 123, 160
59b	165, 176
60b	52
61b	52
62a	52
64a	186
71a	118
73b	152
75b	196
76a	196
80b	129
83b	146
84a	278
85a	194
85b	148, 181
86b	34
87a	196
103b	157
105b	166
107a	77
107b	131, 152
108a	160
111b	75

Baba Batra   בבא בתרא

2b	145
8b	33, 181
9a	136, 187
9b	181
11a	154
12b	152, 167
15a	163

(continued)

15b	195
16a	138, 284
16b	17, 122, 152, 185
17a	219
21a	133, 152
34b	153
43a	177
59b	197
60b	107
62b	192
63a	134
89b	179
98b	125
108b	20
110a	60, 142
116a	273
133b	152
141a	130
145b	181
155b	131
158b	121
164b	121
165a	121

Sanhedrin	סנהדרין
7a	145, 283
8a	134, 135,198
9b	114, 122, 180
11a	184
19b	57, 195
20a	184
21b	78
22a	28, 143
24b	169
25a	169
26b	194
28b	137
29a	32
32b	74
38a	132, 197
39a	85
39b	114, 163, 164
42a	228
43a	158
44a	115
44b	151
46a	86
52a	176
56a	44
56b	13, 125
58b	25
63a	46
65b	165
71a	75, 148

74a,b	180
74b	50
76b	145
83b	150
86a	30
88a	173
89b	149, 168
90a	119, 171, 284
90b	70
91b	70
92a	114, 153
94b	154
95a,b	19
96b	158
97a	131, 145
97b	22, 149, 158, 265
98b	145
99a	60, 119, 141, 166
99b	57, 83, 193
101b	91
104a	168
104b	96
105a	62, 131, 150
105b	62, 63, 115, 212
106b	171, 182
107a	77, 159
109a,b	13
110a	61, 64
110b	57
111a	26
111b	172

Makkot	מכות
4a	154
10b	131
11a	65
23b	192

Shebu'ot	שבועות
20b	223
30a	45
32a	193
39a	156
47b	69
49b	126
104a	52

Abodah Zarah	עבודה זרה
2b	31
3a	171, 234
3b	140, 172
5a	151, 166
10b	158
11b	103, 269

13b	163
16a	264
17b	147, 178
18a	118, 135, 143, 178
18b	44
19b	77, 190
20b	166, 184, 200
30a	118
63b	192
69a	130
70a	184

Horayot   הוריות
| 10a | 168 |

Zebahim   זבחים
10b	147
55b	280
101b	124
102a	124
103b	163
108b	44
115b	180

Menahot   מנחות
8b	162
29a	157
41a	162
43b	60, 73
80b	124
85a	193
86a	120
92b	120
99a	37
99b	36, 76
109a	133
110a	16, 41, 136

Hullin   חולין
2b	19
5a	41
7a	181
7b	137
11a	31
18b	176
24a	57
27b	42
39b	184
45b	163
46a	120, 192
58b	156
59a	94
60b	190
76b	167

89a	79
91b	19
92a	196
94a	125, 138
95b	182
98a	130
102a	12
107b	200
115b	32
127a	184
133a	199
137b	160

Bekhorot   בכורות
6b	25
45b	137
47b	199

Arakin   ערכין
11a	58
15b	43, 158, 188
16b	48
19a	184

Temurah   תמורה
| 16a | 199 |

Me'ilah   מעילה
| 17b | 198 |

Tamid   תמיד
| 27b | 162 |
| 32a | 127 |

Niddah   נדה
9b	132
13b	189
30b	118, 197
31a	127
31b	43
45b	140
70b	165

Jerusalem Talmud   תלמוד ירושלמי

Berakhot   ברכות
1:1	199
2:4	199
5:2	147
6:1	45
7:3	49
40:1	156

Pe'ah   פאה
  1:1   47
  7:5   182

Shabbat   שבת
  9:3   177
  10:3   41
  17:1   194

Erubin   עירובין
  5:1   34

Yoma   יומא
  1:1   48
  1:5   125

Ta'anit   תענית
  2:1   188
  3:6   88
  4   270

Megillah   מגילה
  3:7   250
  4:1   125

Yebamot   יבמות
  12:1   173

Ketubot   כתובות
  5:4   128

Sotah   סוטה
  3.4   125
  7:2   77

Gittin   גיטין
  45:1   126

Kiddushin   קידושין
  1:7   77
  4:1   274

Baba Metzi'a   בבא מציעא
  2:8c   49

Sanhedrin   סנהדרין
  6:end   144
  40a   44

Horayot   הוריות
  48:3   181

RABBINIC WORKS–POST TALMUDIC

Shulhan Arukh Orah Hayyim
שלחן ערוך אורח חיים
  75:3   153
  91:2   264
  124:7   282
  131:8   50
  146:6   131
  170:5   156
  215:2   119
  223:6   284
  261:2   175
  301:24–27   150
  349   119
  422   162
  568   287
  580   252
  605   246
  619   173, 218
  656   146

Kitzur Shulhan Arukh
קצור שלחן ערוך
  3:6   265
  15:3   210
  32:8   268
  69:1   220
  72:7   281
  128:2   185
  133:28   244
  136   234
  221:1   9

About the Author

Macy Nulman is the former director of the Philip and Sarah Belz School of Jewish Music of The Rabbi Isaac Elchanan Theological Seminary at Yeshiva University and was an adjunct assistant professor at Brooklyn College. He is the author of *The Encyclopedia of Jewish Prayer*, a 1993 winner of the Association of Jewish Libraries Reference Book Award, published by Jason Aronson Inc. His other books are *Concise Encyclopedia of Jewish Music* (McGraw-Hill) and *Concepts of Jewish Music and Prayer* (C.C.A.). He is also the editor of the *Journal of Jewish Music and Liturgy*.